Taking Sides: Clashing Views
on Political Issues, 19/e

**by William Miller**

http://create.mcgraw-hill.com

ISBN-10: 1259215733    ISBN-13: 9781259215735

# Contents

# Preface

**A**s I write this, the federal government is recovering from the shutdown, the Tea Party is calling into question the future of the Republican Party, Barack Obama is rolling out the Affordable Care Act, the FDA is inspecting food I'll consume next week, my Homeowner's Association is measuring my grass, a parent is lamenting the loss of their child to gun violence, the FCC is monitoring the National Football League game on television, a college football player is being ejected for a clean hit in the name of safety, the Social Security bathtub is running dry, a young African female is being taught how to pull the detonating device on a suicide vest, the NSA is watching my text messages, my institution is screening my e-mails, and I am unable to kick the urge to pull the tag off of my mattress. In short, public policy is happening around me. And I cannot possibly imagine in all the ways it is doing so.

In the past three months, the world has seen how important political issues truly are. From a failed website rollout to a world leader utilizing chemical weapons against his own citizens, we have witnessed enough chasing of views on political issues to fill volumes, let alone a single reader. At the end of the day, we work to frame issues in macro-level terms when possible to assure applicability and continued relevancy, even after the initial moment of interest has passed. We strive to encourage dialogue on these ever important issues occurring around us in our daily lives. And we hope to hearten a more meaningful debate than the one Americans witness among talking heads every evening. Rather than simply observing two ships as they pass in the night, this volume aims to provide a groundwork that allows all readers to critically assess the political world around them.

If Americans are forced to rely on talking heads, they will likely fail to ever grasp the complexities of government and policy in the democratic context. Talking heads, after all, have both an audience and an agenda. Consequently, it is highly unlikely that they will provide the necessary context and clarity for a given issue so that the average viewer can formulate their own opinion. As debate continues, everyone involved will typically utilize vague, emotion-laden language and tend to speak past many viewers, in some cases intentionally. If the conversation gets too heated, they may rely on epithets or simply spewing party-based rhetoric meant to win over viewers with an impressive dose of partisanship. For example, when the discussion of affirmative action comes down to both sides accusing the other of "racism," or when the controversy over abortion degenerates into taunts and name-calling, then no one really listens and learns from the other side.

I still believe there is value in learning from an opponent. No matter how diametrically opposed two sides may be, there is knowledge to be gained from fully comprehending the arguments made against you. Your own case, after all, can be made significantly stronger if you account for your own potential weaknesses. Sometimes, after listening to others, we change our view entirely. But in most cases, we either incorporate some elements of the opposing view—thus making our own richer—or else learn how to answer the objections to our viewpoint. Either way, we gain from the experience. For these reasons, I believe that encouraging dialogue between opposed positions is the most certain way of enhancing public understanding.

The purpose of this 19th edition of *Taking Sides* is to continue to work toward the revival of political dialogue in America while encouraging the development of a sense of relevancy. As has occurred in the past 18 editions, I examine leading issues in American politics from the perspective of sharply opposed points of view. I have tried to select authors who argue their points vigorously but in such a way as to enhance comprehension of the issue. In short, I have aimed to include works that will stimulate interest and encourage understanding of multiple angles in any given issue.

I hope that readers who confront lively and thoughtful statements on vital issues will be stimulated to ask some of the critical questions about American politics. What are the highest priority issues with which government must deal today? What positions should be taken on these issues? What should be the attitude of Americans toward their government? I firmly believe that in order to be a truly great, stable democracy, citizens must be willing to consider such questions, even if they are unsure of where they stand. Acknowledging a need to become more informed will forever be favored as opposed to apathy, passivity, or misunderstood resentment.

**Book organization** The text is divided into four units, each addressing a different aspect of politics. At the beginning of each unit is a unit opener that briefly identifies the specific issues in the section. Next are the issues themselves, each of which starts with an introduction that sets the stage for the debate as it is argued in the YES and NO selections. The Exploring the Issue section follows the selections and provides some final observations and comments about the topic. The Exploring the Issue section contains critical thinking and reflection questions, the common ground between the two viewpoints, and print and Internet suggestions for further reading.

**Acknowledgments** I must start by giving my sincere appreciation and thanks to George McKenna and Stanley Feingold who have overseen this *Taking Sides* title since its inception. I am thrilled to be joining the team and moving this volume ahead long into the future. I thank Jill Meloy for her confidence in me and her never ending assistance throughout the process. At my own institution, I thank Alan Woolfolk for permitting me the time needed to complete this project while still undertaking my normal duties. I look forward to hearing from readers—instructors and especially students—about their thoughts on the issues and materials selected. Feel free to reach out at any time via email: wmiller@flagler.edu. It goes without saying that anything found to be incorrect throughout the book is of no one's fault but my own.

**William J. Miller**
*Flagler College*

## Editors of This Volume

**WILLIAM J. MILLER** is Director of Institutional Research and Effectiveness at Flagler College and teaches courses in both political science and public administration. He is the Editor of *Tea Party Effects on 2010 U.S. Senate Elections: Stuck in the Middle to Lose* (Lexington, 2012), *Taking Sides: Clashing Views on Public Administration & Policy* (McGraw-Hill, 2012), *The Election's Mine—I Draw the Line: The Political Battle over Congressional Redistricting at the State Level* (Lexington, 2013), *The Battle to Face Obama: The 2012 Republican Nomination and the Future of the Republican Party* (Lexington, 2013), *The Tea Party in 2012: The Party Rolls On* (Lexington, forthcoming), and *Handbook on Teaching and Learning in Political Science and International Relations* (Edward Elgar, forthcoming). His research appears in *Journal of Political Science Education, Journal of Political Marketing, Political Science Quarterly, Studies in Conflict & Terrorism, International Studies Quarterly, Nonproliferation Review, Afro-Americans in New York Life and History, Journal of South Asian and Middle Eastern Studies, American Behavioral Scientist, PS: Political Science and Politics,* and *Journal of Common Market Studies.*

**GEORGE MCKENNA** is Professor Emeritus and former Chair of the Department of Political Science, City College of New York. He has written or edited eight books on politics and society, including his latest, *The Partisan Origins of American Patriotism* (Yale, 2007). He is currently working on a biography of Booker T. Washington.

**STANLEY FEINGOLD,** recently retired, held the Carl and Lily Pforzheimer Foundation Distinguished Chair for Business and Public Policy at Westchester Community College of the State University of New York. He received his bachelor's degree from the City College of New York, where he taught courses in American politics and political theory for 30 years, after completing his graduate education at Columbia University. He spent four years as Visiting Professor of Politics at the University of Leeds in Great Britain, and he has also taught American politics at Columbia University in New York and the University of California, Los Angeles. He is a frequent contributor to the *National Law Journal* and *Congress Monthly,* among other publications.

## Academic Advisory Board Members

Members of the Academic Advisory Board are instrumental in the final selection of articles for *Takings Sides* books and ExpressBooks. Their review of the articles for content, level, and appropriateness provides critical direction to the editor(s) and staff. We think that you will find their careful consideration reflected in this book.

# Correlation Guide

The *Taking Sides* series presents current issues in a debate-style format designed to stimulate student interest and develop critical thinking skills. Each issue is thoughtfully framed with learning outcomes, an issue summary, an issue introduction, and an Exploring the Issue section. The pro and con essays—selected for their liveliness and substance—represent the arguments of leading scholars and commentators in their fields.

**Taking Sides: Clashing Views on Political Issues, 19/e** is an easy-to-use reader that presents issues on important topics such as *democracy and the American political process, the institutions of government, social change and public policy,* and *America and the world*. For more information on *Taking Sides* and other McGraw-Hill Create™ Contemporary Learning Series titles, visit www.mcgrawhillcreate.com.

This convenient guide matches the units in *Taking Sides: Political Issues, 19/e* with the corresponding chapters in three of our best-selling McGraw-Hill political science textbooks by Harrison et al., Patterson, and Losco/Baker.

| Taking Sides: Political Issues, 19/e | American Democracy Now, 3/e by Harrison et al. | The American Democracy, 11/e by Patterson | American Government 2012, 3/e by Losco/Baker |
|---|---|---|---|
| Should Americans Believe in a Unique American "Mission"? | **Chapter 1:** People, Politics, and Participation<br>**Chapter 6:** Political Socialization and Public Opinion | **Chapter 1:** Political Thinking and Political Culture: Becoming a Responsible Citizen<br>**Chapter 2:** Constitutional Democracy: Promoting Liberty and Self-Government<br>**Chapter 3:** Federalism: Forging a Nation<br>**Chapter 6:** Public Opinion and Political Socialization: Shaping the People's Voice | **Chapter 1:** Citizenship in Our Changing Democracy<br>**Chapter 3:** Federalism: Citizenship and the Dispersal of Power<br>**Chapter 4:** Civil Liberties: Expanding Citizens' Rights<br>**Chapter 6:** Public Opinion |
| Does the Tea Party Represent a Revival of America's Revolutionary Ideals? | **Chapter 1:** People, Politics, and Participation<br>**Chapter 6:** Political Socialization and Public Opinion<br>**Chapter 7:** Interest Groups<br>**Chapter 8:** Political Parties<br>**Chapter 9:** Elections, Campaigns, and Voting | **Chapter 1:** Political Thinking and Political Culture: Becoming a Responsible Citizen<br>**Chapter 6:** Public Opinion and Political Socialization: Shaping the People's Voice<br>**Chapter 7:** Political Participation: Activating the Popular Will<br>**Chapter 8:** Political Parties, Candidates, and Campaigns: Defining the Voter's Choice<br>**Chapter 9:** Interest Groups: Organizing for Influence | **Chapter 1:** Citizenship in Our Changing Democracy<br>**Chapter 6:** Public Opinion<br>**Chapter 7:** Political Participation: Equal Opportunities and Unequal Voices<br>**Chapter 9:** Parties and Political Campaigns: Citizens and the Electoral Process<br>**Chapter 11:** Congress: Doing the People's Business<br>**Chapter 13:** Bureaucracy: Citizens as Owners and Consumers |
| Is Bigger Government Better Government? | **Chapter 1:** People, Politics, and Participation<br>**Chapter 3:** Federalism<br>**Chapter 14:** The Bureaucracy<br>**Chapter 16:** Economic Policy | **Chapter 3:** Federalism: Forging a Nation<br>**Chapter 14:** The Federal Bureaucracy: Administering the Government<br>**Chapter 15:** Economic and Environmental Policy: Contributing to Prosperity | **Chapter 1:** Citizenship in Our Changing Democracy<br>**Chapter 3:** Federalism: Citizenship and the Dispersal of Power<br>**Chapter 13:** Bureaucracy: Citizens as Owners and Consumers<br>**Chapter 15:** Public Policy: Responding to Citizens |
| Is America Approaching Equality within Society? | **Chapter 1:** People, Politics, and Participation<br>**Chapter 5:** Civil Rights<br>**Chapter 16:** Economic Policy<br>**Chapter 17:** Domestic Policy | **Chapter 1:** Political Thinking and Political Culture: Becoming a Responsible Citizen<br>**Chapter 5:** Equal Rights: Struggling toward Fairness<br>**Chapter 15:** Economic and Environmental Policy: Contributing to Prosperity<br>**Chapter 16:** Welfare and Education Policy: Providing for Personal Security and Need | **Chapter 1:** Citizenship in Our Changing Democracy<br>**Chapter 5:** Civil Rights: Toward a More Equal Citizenry<br>**Chapter 15:** Public Policy: Responding to Citizens |
| Does the President Have Unilateral War Powers? | **Chapter 12:** Congress<br>**Chapter 13:** The Presidency<br>**Chapter 18:** Foreign Policy and National Security | **Chapter 11:** Congress: Balancing National Goals and Local Interests<br>**Chapter 12:** The Presidency: Leading the Nation<br>**Chapter 17:** Foreign Policy: Protecting the American Way | **Chapter 11:** Congress: Doing the People's Business<br>**Chapter 12:** The Presidency: Power and Paradox<br>**Chapter 16:** Foreign and Defense Policy: Protecting American Interests in the World |

| Taking Sides: Political Issues, 19/e | American Democracy Now, 3/e by Harrison et al. | The American Democracy, 11/e by Patterson | American Government 2012, 3/e by Losco/Baker |
|---|---|---|---|
| Should the Courts Seek the "Original Meaning" of the Constitution? | **Chapter 2:** The Constitution of the United States of America **Chapter 4:** Civil Liberties **Chapter 5:** Civil Rights **Chapter 15:** The Judiciary | **Chapter 2:** Constitutional Democracy: Promoting Liberty and Self-Government **Chapter 4:** Civil Liberties: Protecting Individual Rights **Chapter 5:** Equal Rights: Struggling toward Fairness **Chapter 14:** The Federal Judicial System: Applying the Law | **Chapter 2:** The Constitution: The Foundation of Citizen's Rights **Chapter 4:** Civil Liberties: Expanding Citizens' Rights **Chapter 5:** Civil Rights: Toward a More Equal Citizenry **Chapter 14:** The Courts: Judicial Power in a Democratic Setting |
| Is Congress a Dysfunctional Institution? | **Chapter 2:** The Constitution of the United States of America **Chapter 12:** Congress | **Chapter 2:** Constitutional Democracy: Promoting Liberty and Self-Government **Chapter 11:** Congress: Balancing National Goals and Local Interests | **Chapter 2:** The Constitution: The Foundation of Citizens' Rights **Chapter 11:** Congress: Doing the People's Business |
| Do Whistleblowers Help Government? | **Chapter 14:** The Bureaucracy | **Chapter 13:** The Federal Bureaucracy: Administering the Government | **Chapter 13:** Bureaucracy: Citizens as Owners and Consumers |
| Does Affirmative Action Advance Racial Equality? | **Chapter 4:** Civil Liberties **Chapter 5:** Civil Rights **Chapter 6:** Political Socialization and Public Opinion **Chapter 7:** Interest Groups **Chapter 15:** The Judiciary | **Chapter 4:** Civil Liberties: Protecting Individual Rights **Chapter 5:** Equal Rights: Struggling toward Fairness **Chapter 6:** Public Opinion and Political Socialization: Shaping the People's Voice **Chapter 9:** Interest Groups: Organizing for Influence **Chapter 14:** The Federal Judicial System: Applying the Law | **Chapter 2:** The Constitution: The Foundation of Citizens' Rights **Chapter 4:** Civil Liberties: Expanding Citizens' Rights **Chapter 5:** Civil Rights: Toward a More Equal Citizenry **Chapter 6:** Public Opinion **Chapter 8:** Interest Groups in America **Chapter 14:** The Courts: Judicial Power in a Democratic Setting |
| Should Abortion Be Restricted? | **Chapter 4:** Civil Liberties **Chapter 6:** Political Socialization and Public Opinion **Chapter 7:** Interest Groups **Chapter 15:** The Judiciary | **Chapter 4:** Civil Liberties: Protecting Individual Rights **Chapter 6:** Public Opinion and Political Socialization: Shaping the People's Voice **Chapter 9:** Interest Groups: Organizing for Influence **Chapter 14:** The Federal Judicial System: Applying the Law | **Chapter 2:** The Constitution: The Foundation of Citizens' Rights **Chapter 4:** Civil Liberties: Expanding Citizens' Rights **Chapter 6:** Public Opinion **Chapter 8:** Interest Groups in America **Chapter 14:** The Courts: Judicial Power in a Democratic Setting |
| Should the United States Be More Restrictive of Gun Ownership? | **Chapter 2:** The Constitution of the United States of America **Chapter 7:** Interest Groups **Chapter 15:** The Judiciary **Chapter 17:** Domestic Policy | **Chapter 2:** Constitutional Democracy: Promoting Liberty and Self-Government **Chapter 9:** Interest Groups: Organizing for Influence **Chapter 14:** The Federal Judicial System: Applying the Law | **Chapter 2:** The Constitution: The Foundation of Citizens' Rights **Chapter 8:** Interest Groups in America **Chapter 14:** The Courts: Judicial Power in a Democratic Setting **Chapter 15:** Public Policy: Responding to Citizens |
| Will the Affordable Care Act Successfully Transform the American Health Care System? | **Chapter 2:** The Constitution of the United States of America **Chapter 3:** Federalism **Chapter 12:** Congress **Chapter 13:** The Presidency **Chapter 14:** The Bureaucracy **Chapter 17:** Domestic Policy | **Chapter 2:** Constitutional Democracy: Promoting Liberty and Self-Government **Chapter 3:** Federalism: Forging a Nation **Chapter 11:** Congress: Balancing National Goals and Local Interests **Chapter 12:** The Presidency: Leading the Nation **Chapter 13:** The Federal Bureaucracy: Administering the Government | **Chapter 2:** The Constitution: The Foundation of Citizens' Rights **Chapter 3:** Federalism: Citizenship and the Dispersal of Power **Chapter 11:** Congress: Doing the People's Business **Chapter 12:** The Presidency: Power and Paradox **Chapter 13:** Bureaucracy: Citizens as Owners and Consumers **Chapter 15:** Public Policy: Responding to Citizens |
| Is Same-Sex Marriage Close to Being Legalized Across the United States? | **Chapter 2:** The Constitution of the United States of America **Chapter 3:** Federalism **Chapter 15:** The Judiciary **Chapter 17:** Domestic Policy | **Chapter 2:** Constitutional Democracy: Promoting Liberty and Self-Government **Chapter 3:** Federalism: Forging a Nation **Chapter 14:** The Federal Judicial System: Applying the Law **Chapter 18:** State and Local Politics: Maintaining Our Differences | **Chapter 2:** The Constitution: The Foundation of Citizens' Rights **Chapter 3:** Federalism: Citizenship and the Dispersal of Power **Chapter 14:** The Courts: Judicial Power in a Democratic Setting **Chapter 15:** Public Policy: Responding to Citizens |

| Taking Sides: Political Issues, 19/e | American Democracy Now, 3/e by Harrison et al. | The American Democracy, 11/e by Patterson | American Government 2012, 3/e by Losco/Baker |
|---|---|---|---|
| Do Corporations Have the Same Free Speech Rights as Persons? | **Chapter 1:** People, Politics, and Participation<br>**Chapter 2:** The Constitution of the United States of America<br>**Chapter 9:** Elections, Campaigns, and Voting<br>**Chapter 15:** The Judiciary | **Chapter 1:** Political Thinking and Political Culture: Becoming a Responsible Citizen<br>**Chapter 2:** Constitutional Democracy: Promoting Liberty and Self-Government<br>**Chapter 8:** Political Parties, Candidates, and Campaigns: Defining the Voter's Choice<br>**Chapter 14:** The Federal Judicial System: Applying the Law<br>**Chapter 18:** State and Local Politics: Maintaining Our Differences | **Chapter 1:** Citizenship in Our Changing Democracy<br>**Chapter 2:** The Constitution: The Foundation of Citizens' Rights<br>**Chapter 9:** Parties and Political Campaigns: Citizens and the Electoral Process<br>**Chapter 14:** The Courts: Judicial Power in a Democratic Setting |
| Should "Recreational" Drugs Be Legalized? | **Chapter 4:** Civil Liberties<br>**Chapter 5:** Civil Rights<br>**Chapter 15:** The Judiciary<br>**Chapter 17:** Domestic Policy | **Chapter 4:** Civil Liberties: Protecting Individual Rights<br>**Chapter 5:** Equal Rights: Struggling toward Fairness<br>**Chapter 14:** The Federal Judicial System: Applying the Law | **Chapter 4:** Civil Liberties: Expanding Citizen's Rights<br>**Chapter 5:** Civil Rights: Toward a More Equal Citizenry<br>**Chapter 6:** Public Opinion<br>**Chapter 14:** The Courts: Judicial Power in a Democratic Setting |
| Do We Need to Curb Global Warming? | **Chapter 1:** People, Politics, and Participation<br>**Chapter 7:** Interest Groups<br>**Chapter 10:** The Media | **Chapter 1:** Political Thinking: Becoming a Responsible Citizen<br>**Chapter 9:** Interest Groups: Organizing for Influence<br>**Chapter 10:** The News Media: Communicating Political Images<br>**Chapter 15:** Economic and Environmental Policy: Contributing to Prosperity | **Chapter 8:** Interest Groups in America<br>**Chapter 10:** Media<br>**Chapter 15:** Public Policy: Responding to Citizens |
| Should Homeland Security Focus More on Cyber Crime Moving Forward? | **Chapter 4:** Civil Liberties<br>**Chapter 13:** The Presidency<br>**Chapter 14:** The Bureaucracy<br>**Chapter 18:** Foreign Policy and National Security | **Chapter 4:** Civil Liberties: Protecting Individual Rights<br>**Chapter 12:** The Presidency: Leading the Nation<br>**Chapter 13:** The Federal Bureaucracy: Administering the Government<br>**Chapter 17:** Foreign Policy: Protecting the American Way | **Chapter 4:** Civil Liberties: Expanding Citizens' Rights<br>**Chapter 12:** The Presidency: Power and Paradox<br>**Chapter 13:** Bureaucracy: Citizens as Owners and Consumers<br>**Chapter 16:** Foreign and Defense Policy: Protecting American Interests in the World |
| Is Warrantless Wiretapping Ever Justified to Protect National Security? | **Chapter 4:** Civil Liberties<br>**Chapter 10:** The Media<br>**Chapter 12:** Congress<br>**Chapter 13:** The Presidency<br>**Chapter 15:** The Judiciary<br>**Chapter 18:** Foreign Policy and National Security | **Chapter 4:** Civil Liberties: Protecting Individual Rights<br>**Chapter 11:** Congress: Balancing National Goals and Local Interests<br>**Chapter 12:** The Presidency: Leading the Nation<br>**Chapter 14:** The Federal Judicial System: Applying the Law<br>**Chapter 17:** Foreign Policy: Protecting the American Way | **Chapter 2:** The Constitution: The Foundation of Citizens' Rights<br>**Chapter 4:** Civil Liberties: Expanding Citizens' Rights<br>**Chapter 12:** The Presidency: Power and Paradox<br>**Chapter 14:** The Courts: Judicial Power in a Democratic Setting<br>**Chapter 16:** Foreign and Defense Policy: Protecting American Interests in the World |
| Are Entitlement Programs Creating a Culture of Dependency? | **Chapter 16:** Economic Policy<br>**Chapter 17:** Domestic Policy | **Chapter 16:** Welfare and Education Policy: Providing for Personal Security and Need | **Chapter 13:** Bureaucracy: Citizens as Owners and Consumers<br>**Chapter 15:** Public Policy: Responding to Citizens |
| Should the United States Launch a Preemptive Strike Against Iran? | **Chapter 18:** Foreign Policy and National Security | **Chapter 17:** Foreign Policy: Protecting the American Way | **Chapter 16:** Foreign and Defense Policy: Protecting American Interests in the World |

# Topic Guide

This topic guide suggests how the selections in this book relate to the subjects covered in your course.

**All the issues that relate to each topic are listed below the bold-faced term.**

**Abortion**

Should Abortion Be Restricted?

**Affirmative Action**

Does Affirmative Action Advance Racial Equality?

**American Mission**

Should Americans Believe in a Unique American "Mission"?

**Bureaucracy**

Do Whistleblowers Help Government?

**Capitalism**

Do Corporations Have the Same Free Speech Rights as Persons?

**Congress**

Is Congress a Dysfunctional Institution?

**Corporations**

Do Corporations Have the Same Free Speech Rights as Persons?

**Discrimination**

Does Affirmative Action Advance Racial Equality?

**Drugs**

Should "Recreational" Drugs Be Legalized?

**Environment**

Do We Need to Curb Global Warming?

**Equality**

Does Affirmative Action Advance Racial Equality?
Is America Approaching Equality within Society?

**Ethics**

Do Whistleblowers Help Government?

**Free Speech**

Do Corporations Have the Same Free Speech Rights as Persons?

**Gays**

Is Same-Sex Marriage Close to Being Legalized Across the United States?

**Global Warming**

Do We Need to Curb Global Warming?

**Government**

Do Whistleblowers Help Government?
Is Bigger Government Better Government?

**Guns**

Should the United States Be More Restrictive of Gun Ownership?

**Health Insurance**

Will the Affordable Care Act Successfully Transform the American Health Care System?

**National Security**

Is Warrantless Wiretapping Ever Justified to Protect National Security?
Should Homeland Security Focus More on Cyber Crime Moving Forward?
Should the United States Launch a Preemptive Strike Against Iran?

**Nuclear Weapons**

Should the United States Launch a Preemptive Strike Against Iran?

**Presidency**

Does the President Have Unilateral War Powers?

**Same-Sex Marriage**

Is Same-Sex Marriage Close to Being Legalized Across the United States?

**Social Issues**

Is America Approaching Equality within Society?
Is Same-Sex Marriage Close to Being Legalized Across the United States?
Should Abortion Be Restricted?
Should "Recreational" Drugs Be Legalized?
Should the United States Be More Restrictive of Gun Ownership?
Will the Affordable Care Act Successfully Transform the American Healthcare System?

**Supreme Court**

Should the Courts Seek the "Original Meaning" of the Constitution?

**Tea Party**

Does the Tea Party Represent a Revival of America's Revolutionary Ideals?

**Terrorism**

Is Warrantless Wiretapping Ever Justified to Protect National Security?
Should Homeland Security Focus More on Cyber Crime Moving Forward?

**U.S. Constitution**

Do Corporations Have the Same Free Speech Rights as Persons?
Is Same-Sex Marriage Close to Being Legalized Across the United States?
Is Warrantless Wiretapping Ever Justified to Protect National Security?
Should Abortion Be Restricted?
Should the Courts Seek the "Original Meaning" of the Constitution?

**Welfare**

Are Entitlement Programs Creating a Culture of Dependency?
Is Bigger Government Better Government?

**Wiretapping**

Is Warrantless Wiretapping Ever Justified to Protect National Security?

# Introduction

## Labels and Alignments in American Politics

Only a little over a year has passed since Barack Obama was re-elected for a second term as president of the United States. Yet unlike in a first term, there is no honeymoon period. As quickly as the votes were calculated, criticism continued. Republicans—unhappy with chunks of Obama's first-term agenda and nervous about what would come from the next four years—accused the president of being out of touch with the average American and attempting to govern from the "far left." It appears as if the democratic bargain is little more than an afterthought. There was a time in our country's history where parties put candidates up for election and accepted the election results, win or lose. Yet today both Democrats and Republicans alike take electoral losses and throw them aside while determining ways to be obstructive. And few seem willing to mention that the country loses as a whole when this happens. We often talk about right and left, red and blue. But such simple dichotomies unfortunately oversimplify the political realities facing the United States today. All the while, talking heads continue to throw around ideological labels designed to help simplify our understanding and allow us to better categorize ourselves. Unfortunately, the opposite often occurs.

*Liberal, conservative, moderate, pluralist, radical, right wing, left wing, "classical" economics, "progressive"*—what do these terms mean? Or do they have any meaning? Some political analysts regard them as arbitrary labels slapped on by commentators seeking quick ways to sum up candidates (or in some cases to demonize them). The reaction against the ideological labels is understandable, not only because they are often used too loosely but, as we shall see, because the terms themselves can evolve over time. Nevertheless, we think there are some core meanings left, so if they are used carefully, they can help us locate positions on the political stage and the actors who occupy them. In this Introduction we shall try to spell out the meanings of these terms, at least as they are used in American politics.

### Liberals versus Conservatives: An Overview

Let us examine, very briefly, the historical evolution of the terms *liberalism* and *conservatism*. By examining the roots of these terms, we can see how these philosophies have adapted themselves to changing times. In that way, we can avoid using the terms rigidly, without reference to the particular contexts in which liberalism and conservatism have operated over the past two centuries.

### Classical Liberalism

The classical root of the term *liberalism* is the Latin word *libertas*, meaning "liberty" or "freedom." In the early nineteenth century, liberals dedicated themselves to freeing individuals from all unnecessary and oppressive obligations to authority—whether the authority came from the church or the state. They opposed the licensing and censorship of the press, the punishment of heresy, the establishment of religion, and any attempt to dictate orthodoxy in matters of opinion. In economics, liberals opposed state monopolies and other constraints upon competition between private businesses. At this point in its development, liberalism defined freedom primarily in terms of freedom *from*. It appropriated the French term *laissez-faire,* which literally means "leave to be." Leave people alone! That was the spirit of liberalism in its early days. It wanted government to stay out of people's lives and to play a modest role in general. Thomas Jefferson summed up this concept when he said, "I am no friend of energetic government. It is always oppressive."

Despite their suspicion of government, classical liberals invested high hopes in the political process. By and large, they were great believers in democracy. They believed in widening suffrage to include every white male, and some of them were prepared to enfranchise women and blacks as well. Although liberals occasionally worried about "the tyranny of the majority," they were more prepared to trust the masses than to trust a permanent, entrenched elite. Liberal social policy was dedicated to fulfilling human potential and was based on the assumption that this often-hidden potential is enormous. Human beings, liberals argued, were basically good and reasonable. Evil and irrationality were believed to be caused by "outside" influences; they were the result of a bad social environment.

A liberal commonwealth, therefore, was one that would remove the hindrances to the full flowering of the human personality. The basic vision of liberalism has not changed since the nineteenth century. What has changed is the way it is applied to modern society. In that respect, liberalism has changed dramatically. Today, instead of regarding government with suspicion, liberals welcome government as an instrument to serve the people. The change in philosophy began in the latter years of the nineteenth century, when businesses—once small, independent operations—began to grow into giant structures that overwhelmed individuals and sometimes even overshadowed the state in power and wealth. At that time, liberals began reconsidering their commitment to the *laissez-faire* philosophy. If the state can be an oppressor, asked liberals, can't big business also oppress people? By then, many were convinced that commercial and industrial monopolies were crushing the souls and bodies of the working classes. The state, formerly the villain, now was viewed by liberals as a potential savior. The concept of freedom was transformed into something more than a negative freedom *from;* the term began to take on a positive meaning. It meant "realizing one's full potential." Toward this end, liberals believed, the state could prove to be a valuable instrument. It could educate children, protect the health and safety of workers, help people through hard times, promote a healthy economy, and—when necessary—force business to act more humanely and responsibly. Thus was born the movement that culminated in New Deal liberalism.

## New Deal Liberalism

In the United States, the argument in favor of state intervention did not win an enduring majority constituency until after the Great Depression of the 1930s began to be felt deeply. The disastrous effects of a depression that left a quarter of the workforce unemployed opened the way to a new administration—and a promise. "I pledge you, I pledge myself," Franklin D. Roosevelt said when accepting the Democratic nomination in 1932, "to a new deal for the American people." Roosevelt's New Deal was an attempt to effect relief and recovery from the Depression; it employed a variety of means, including welfare programs, public works, and business regulation—most of which involved government intervention in the economy. The New Deal liberalism relied on government to liberate people from poverty, oppression, and economic exploitation. At the same time, the New Dealers claimed to be as zealous as the classical liberals in defending political and civil liberties.

The common element in *laissez-faire* liberalism and welfare-state liberalism is their dedication to the goal of realizing the full potential of each individual. Some still questioned whether this is best done by minimizing state involvement or whether it sometimes requires an activist state. The New Dealers took the latter view, although they prided themselves on being pragmatic and experimental about their activism. During the heyday of the New Deal, a wide variety of programs were tried and—if found wanting—abandoned. All decent means should be tried, they believed, even if it meant dilution of ideological purity. The Roosevelt administration, for example, denounced bankers and businessmen in campaign rhetoric but worked very closely with them while trying to extricate the nation from the Depression. This set a pattern of pragmatism that New Dealers from Harry Truman to Lyndon Johnson emulated.

## Progressive Liberalism

Progressive liberalism emerged in the late 1960s and early 1970s as a more militant and uncompromising movement than the New Deal had ever been. Its roots go back to the New Left student movement of the early 1960s. New Left students went to the South to participate in civil rights demonstrations, and many of them were bloodied in confrontations with southern police; by the mid-1960s they were confronting the authorities in the North over issues like poverty and the Vietnam War. By the end of the decade, the New Left had fragmented into a variety of factions and had lost much of its vitality, but a somewhat more respectable version of it appeared as the New Politics movement. Many New Politics crusaders were former New Leftists who had traded their jeans for coats and ties; they tried to work within the system instead of always confronting it.

Even so, they retained some of the spirit of the New Left. The civil rights slogan "Freedom Now" expressed the mood of the New Politics. The young university graduates who filled its ranks had come from an environment where "nonnegotiable" demands were issued to college deans by leaders of sit-in protests. There was more than youthful arrogance in the New Politics movement, however; there was a pervasive belief that America had lost, had compromised away, much of its idealism. The New Politics liberals sought to recover some of that spirit by linking up with an older tradition of militant reform, which went back to the time of the Revolution. These new liberals saw themselves as the authentic heirs of Thomas Paine and Henry David Thoreau, of the abolitionists, the radical populists, the suffragettes, and the great progressive reformers of the early twentieth century.

While New Deal liberals concentrated almost exclusively on bread-and-butter issues such as unemployment and poverty, the New Politics liberals introduced what came to be known as social issues into the political arena. These included the repeal of laws against abortion, the liberalization of laws against homosexuality and pornography, the establishment of affirmative action programs to ensure increased hiring of minorities and women, and the passage of the Equal Rights Amendment.

In foreign policy, too, New Politics liberals departed from the New Deal agenda. Because they had keener memories of the unpopular and (for them) unjustified war in Vietnam than of World War II, they became doves, in contrast to the general hawkishness of the New Dealers. They were skeptical of any claim that the United States must be the leader of the free world or, indeed, that it had any special mission in the world; some were convinced that America was already in decline and must learn to adjust accordingly. The real danger, they argued, came not from the Soviet Union but from the mad pace of America's arms race with the Soviets, which, as they saw it, could bankrupt the country, starve its social programs, and culminate in a nuclear Armageddon. New Politics liberals were heavily represented at the 1972 Democratic national convention, which nominated South Dakota senator George McGovern for president. By the 1980s the New Politics movement was no longer new, and many of its adherents preferred to be called progressives.

By this time their critics had another name for them: radicals. The critics saw their positions as inimical to the interests of the United States, destructive of the family, and fundamentally at odds with the views of most Americans. The adversaries of the progressives were not only conservatives but many New Deal liberals, who openly scorned the McGovernites. This split still exists within the Democratic Party, although it is now more skillfully managed by party leaders. In 1988 the Democrats paired Michael Dukakis, whose Massachusetts supporters were generally on the progressive side of the party, with New Dealer Lloyd Bentsen as the presidential and vice presidential candidates, respectively.

In 1992 the Democrats won the presidency with Arkansas governor Bill Clinton, whose record as governor seemed to put him in the moderate-to-conservative camp, and Tennessee senator Albert Gore, whose position on environmental issues could probably be considered quite liberal but whose general image was middle-of-the-road. Both candidates had moved toward liberal positions on the issues of gay rights and abortion. By 1994 Clinton was perceived by many Americans as being "too liberal," which some speculate may have been a factor in the defeat of Democrats in the congressional elections that year. Clinton immediately sought to shake off that perception, positioning himself as a "moderate" between extremes and casting the Republicans as an "extremist" party. (These two terms will be examined presently.)

President Obama comes from the progressive liberal wing of the Democratic Party, although in his campaign for office he attempted to appeal to moderates and even some conservatives by stressing his determination to regard the country not in terms of red (Republican) states and blue (Democratic) states but as a nation united. Once in office, however, his agenda, which included a $830-billion "stimulus" expenditure to jump-start the economy and an ambitious social insurance program, came from the playbook of progressive liberalism; by 2010 it faced unanimous resistance from the Republican minority in Congress. In the 2010 congressional races its unpopularity in so-called "swing" districts and states, that had swung Democrat in the 2008 election, cost many moderate Democrats their seats in Congress. Yet by 2012, the Democrats seemed to be recovering.

# Conservatism

Like liberalism, conservatism has undergone historical transformation in America. Just as early liberals (represented by Thomas Jefferson) espoused less government, early conservatives (whose earliest leaders were Alexander Hamilton and John Adams) urged government support of economic enterprise and government intervention on behalf of certain groups. But today, in reaction to the growth of the welfare state, conservatives argue strongly that more government means more unjustified interference in citizens' lives, more bureaucratic regulation of private conduct, more inhibiting control of economic enterprise, more material advantage for the less energetic and less able at the expense of those who are prepared to work harder and better, and, of course, more taxes—taxes that will be taken from those who have earned money and given to those who have not.

Contemporary conservatives are not always opposed to state intervention. They may support larger military expenditures in order to protect society against foreign enemies. They may also allow for some intrusion into private life in order to protect society against internal subversion and would pursue criminal prosecution zealously in order to protect society against domestic violence. The fact is that few conservatives, and perhaps fewer liberals, are absolute with respect to their views about the power of the state. Both are quite prepared to use the state in order to further *their* purposes. It is true that activist presidents such as Franklin Roosevelt and John Kennedy were likely to be classified as liberals. However, Richard Nixon was also an activist, and, although he does not easily fit into any classification, he was far closer to conservatism than to liberalism. It is too easy to identify liberalism with statism and conservatism with antistatism: it is important to remember that it was liberal Jefferson who counseled against "energetic government" and conservative Alexander Hamilton who designed bold powers for the new central government and wrote, "Energy in the executive is a leading character in the definition of good government."

# The Religious Right

The terms "right" and "left," as in "right wing of the Republican Party" and "leftist Democrats," came from an accident of seating in the French National Assembly during the Revolution of the early 1790s. It just happened that the liberals flocked to the left side of the assembly hall while conservatives went to the right. "Left" and "right," then, are almost synonyms for liberals and conservatives, the main difference being that they give a sense of continuum and degree—someone can be "center-left" or "center-right" instead of at the extremes.

Even so, the terms have a certain hard edge. To call someone a "leftist" or a "right-winger" is to give an impression that they are strident or excessively zealous. That impression is conveyed in the term "religious right," a term few of its adherents would use to describe themselves, preferring softer terms like "religious conservatives" or "cultural conservatives."

For better or worse, though, the term "religious right" has entered the media mainstream, so we shall use it here to designate observant Christians or Jews whose concerns are not so much high taxes and government spending as the decline of traditional Judeo-Christian morality, a decline they attribute in part to wrongheaded government policies and judicial decisions. They oppose many of the recent judicial decisions on socio-cultural issues such as abortion, school prayer, pornography, and gay rights, and they were outspoken critics of the Clinton administration, citing everything from President Clinton's views on gays in the military to his sexual behavior while in the White House.

Spokesmen for progressive liberalism and the religious right stand as polar opposites: The former regard abortion as a woman's right; the latter see it as legalized murder. The former tend to regard homosexuality as a lifestyle that needs protection against discrimination; the latter are more likely to see it as a perversion. The list of issues could go on. The religious right and the progressive liberals are like positive and negative photographs of America's moral landscape. Sociologist James Davison Hunter uses the term *culture wars* to characterize the struggles between these contrary visions of America. For all the differences between progressive liberalism and the religious right, however, their styles are very similar. They are heavily laced with moralistic prose; they tend to equate compromise with selling out; and they claim to represent the best, most authentic traditions of America.

This is not to denigrate either movement, for the kinds of issues they address are indeed moral issues, which do not generally admit much compromise. These issues cannot simply be finessed or ignored, despite the efforts of conventional politicians to do so.

## Neoconservatism

The term *neoconservatism* came into use in the early 1970s as a designation for former New Deal Democrats who had become alarmed by what they saw as the drift of their party's foreign policy toward appeasing Communists. When Senator George McGovern, the party's presidential nominee in 1972, stated that he would "crawl to Hanoi on my knees" to secure peace in Vietnam, he seemed to them to exemplify this new tendency. They were, then, "hawks" in foreign policy, which they insisted was the historic stance of their party; they regarded themselves as the true heirs of liberal presidents such as Truman and Kennedy and liberal senators such as Henry ("Scoop") Jackson of Washington State. On domestic policy, they were still largely liberal, except for their reactions to three new liberal planks added by the "progressives": gay rights, which neoconservatives tended to regard as a distortion of civil rights; abortion, which to some degree or another went against the grain of their moral sensibilities; and affirmative action, which some compared to the "quota system" once used to keep down the number of Jews admitted to elite universities. In fact, a number of prominent neoconservatives were Jews, including Norman Podhoretz, Midge Decter, Gertrude Himmelfarb, and Irving Kristol (although others, such as Michael Novak and Daniel Patrick Moynihan, were Roman Catholics, and one, Richard John Neuhaus, was a Lutheran pastor who later converted to Catholicism and became a priest).

The term *neoconservative* seemed headed for oblivion in the 1980s, when some leading neoconservatives dropped the "neo" part and classified themselves as conservatives, period. By the time the Soviet Union collapsed in 1991, it appeared that the term was no longer needed—the Cold War with "world Communism" was over. But the rise of Islamic terrorism in the 1990s, aimed at the West in general and the United States in particular, brought back alarms analogous to those of the Cold War period, with global terrorism now taking the place of world Communism. So, too, was the concern that liberal foreign policy might not be tough enough for the fight against these new, ruthless enemies of Western democracy. The concern was ratcheted up considerably after the events of 9/11, and now a new generation of neoconservatives was in the spotlight—some of its members literally the children of an earlier "neo" generation. They included Bill Kristol, John Podhoretz, Douglas Feith, Paul Wolfowitz, Richard Perle, David Brooks, and (although he was old enough to overlap with the previous generation) Bill Bennett.

## Radicals, Reactionaries, and Moderates

The label *reactionary* is almost an insult, and the label *radical* is worn with pride by only a few zealots on the banks of the political mainstream. A reactionary is not a conserver but a backward-mover, dedicated to turning the clock back to better times. Most people suspect that reactionaries would restore us to a time that never was, except in political myth. For most Americans, the repeal of industrialism or universal education (or the entire twentieth century itself) is not a practical, let alone desirable, political program.

Radicalism (literally meaning "from the roots" or "going to the foundation") implies a fundamental reconstruction of the social order. Taken in that sense, it is possible to speak of right-wing radicalism as well as left-wing radicalism—radicalism that would restore or inaugurate a new hierarchical society as well as radicalism that calls for nothing less than an egalitarian society. The term is sometimes used in both of these senses, but most often the word *radicalism* is reserved to characterize more liberal change. While the liberal would effect change through conventional democratic processes, the radical is likely to be skeptical about the ability of the established machinery to bring about the needed change and might be prepared to sacrifice "a little" liberty to bring about a great deal of more equality.

*Moderate* is a highly coveted label in America. Its meaning is not precise, but it carries the connotations of sensible, balanced, and practical. A moderate person is not without principles, but he or she does not allow principles to harden into dogma. The opposite of moderate is *extremist,* a label most American political leaders eschew. Yet there have been notable exceptions. When Arizona senator Barry Goldwater, a conservative Republican, was nominated for president in 1964, he declared, "Extremism in defense of liberty is no vice! . . . Moderation in the pursuit of justice is no virtue!" This open embrace of extremism did not help his electoral chances; Goldwater was overwhelmingly defeated. At about the same time, however, another American political leader also embraced a kind of extremism, and with better results. In a famous letter written from a jail cell in Birmingham, Alabama, the Reverend Martin Luther King, Jr., replied to the charge that he was an extremist not by denying it but by distinguishing between different kinds of extremists. The question, he wrote, "is not whether we will be extremist but what kind of extremist will we be. Will we be extremists for hate, or will we be extremists for love?" King aligned himself with the love extremists, in which category he also placed Jesus, St. Paul, and Thomas Jefferson, among others. It was an adroit use of a label that is usually anathema in America.

## Pluralism

The principle of pluralism espouses diversity in a society containing many interest groups and in a government containing competing units of power. This implies the widest expression of competing ideas, and in this way, pluralism is in sympathy with an important element of liberalism. However, as James Madison and Alexander Hamilton pointed out when they analyzed the sources of pluralism in their *Federalist* commentaries on the Constitution, this philosophy springs from a profoundly pessimistic view of human nature, and in this respect it more closely resembles conservatism. Madison, possibly the single most influential member of the convention that wrote the Constitution, hoped that in a large and varied nation, no single interest group could control the government. Even if there were a majority interest, it would be unlikely to capture all of the national agencies of government—the House of Representatives, the Senate, the presidency, and the federal judiciary—each of which was chosen in a different way by a different constituency for a different term of office. Moreover, to make certain that no one branch exercised excessive power, each was equipped with "checks and balances" that enabled any

agency of national government to curb the powers of the others. The clearest statement of Madison's, and the Constitution's, theory can be found in the 51st paper of the *Federalist:* It may be a reflection on human nature that such devices should be necessary to control the abuses of government. But what is government itself, but the greatest of all reflections on human nature? If men were angels, no government would be necessary.

This pluralist position may be analyzed from different perspectives. It is conservative insofar as it rejects simple majority rule; yet it is liberal insofar as it rejects rule by a single elite. It is conservative in its pessimistic appraisal of human nature; yet pluralism's pessimism is also a kind of egalitarianism, holding as it does that no one can be trusted with power and that majority interests no less than minority interests will use power for selfish ends. It is possible to suggest that in America pluralism represents an alternative to both liberalism and conservatism. Pluralism is anti-majoritarian and anti-elitist and combines some elements of both.

## Synthesis

Despite our effort to define the principal alignments in American politics, some policy decisions do not fit neatly into these categories. Suffice it to say that through the following pages, readers will be able to pull nuggets of the labels and alignments introduced above. Yet some will be far more obvious than others. Obviously one's position on the issues in this book will be directed by circumstances. However, we would like to think that the essays in this book are durable enough to last through several seasons of events and controversies. We can be certain that the issues will survive. The search for coherence and consistency in the use of political labels underlines the options open to us and reveals their consequences. The result must be more mature judgments about what is best for America. That, of course, is the ultimate aim of public debate and decision making, and it transcends all labels and categories.

# Unit 1

# UNIT

# Democracy and the American Political Process

*D*emocratic societies are known for allowing individuals to participate in the political process. Democracy is derived from two Greek words, demos and kratia, which mean, respectively, "people" and "rule." While there are clear differentiations between varying types of democracies, citizens have access and opportunities not present in other forms of government. For example, while a citizen in a representative democracy, such as the United States, may not get to individually vote on every issue that comes up for debate (like a citizen living in a direct democracy,) they do have substantially more influence than a citizen living under a totalitarian dictator.

Regardless of the type of democracy, questions still remain. Who are "the people," and how much "rule" should there be? Does the Tea Party accurately represent the opinions of the people? Do the people need more, or fewer, "rules"? Does "special interest" money in elections undermine the general interest? Some analysts of democracy believe that a viable democratic system requires widespread belief in their country's unique mission? But is that necessary?

**Selected, Edited, and with Issue Framing Material by:**
**William J. Miller,** *Flagler College*
**George McKenna,** *City College, City University of New York*
**and**
**Stanley Feingold,** *City College, City University of New York*

# ISSUE

## Should Americans Believe in a Unique American "Mission"?

**YES: Wilfred M. McClay,** from "The Founding of Nations," *First Things* (March 2006)

**NO: Howard Zinn,** from "The Power and the Glory: Myths of American Exceptionalism," *Boston Review* (Summer 2005)

---

### Learning Outcomes

**After reading this issue, you will be able to:**

- Explain the idea of American exceptionalism.
- Explain the idea of America's myth.
- Describe how America reminds itself of its past sins.
- Explain the significance of the term "city on a hill."
- Describe what makes America unique compared to other nations.

---

### ISSUE SUMMARY

**YES:** Humanities Professor Wilfred M. McClay argues that America's "myth," its founding narrative, helps to sustain and hold together a diverse people.

**NO:** Historian Howard Zinn is convinced that America's myth of "exceptionalism" has served as a justification for lawlessness, brutality, and imperialism.

Take a dollar from your wallet and look at the back of it. On the left side, above an unfinished pyramid with a detached eye on top, are the words "Annuit Coeptis," Latin for "He has favored our endeavors." The "He" is God.

Since the time of the Puritans, Americans have often thought of themselves collectively as a people whose endeavors are favored by God. "We shall be as a city upon a hill, the eyes of all people are upon us," said Puritan leader John Winthrop aboard the Arbella, the Puritans' flagship, as it left for the New World in 1630. Later in that century another Puritan, the Rev. Samuel Danforth, famously spoke of New England's divinely assigned "errand into the wilderness." By the eighteenth century, the role of New England had become the role of America: God had led his people to establish a new social order, a light to the nations. "Your forefathers," John Jay told New Yorkers in 1776, "came to America under the auspices of Divine Providence." For Patrick Henry, the American Revolution "was the grand operation, which seemed to be assigned by the Deity to the men of this age in our country." In his First Inaugural Address, George Washington saw an "invisible hand" directing the people of the United States. "Every step they have taken seems to have been distinguished by some token of providential agency." Even the most secular-minded founders thought of their nation in providential terms. Thomas Jefferson paid homage to the "Being . . . who led our fathers, as Israel of old, from their native land and planted them in a country flowing with all the necessaries and comforts of life; who has covered our infancy with His providence and our riper years with his wisdom and power." At the Constitutional Convention in Philadelphia, Benjamin Franklin declared that "God governs in the affairs of men," adding: "And if a sparrow cannot fall to the ground without his notice, is it probable that an empire cannot rise without his aid?"

Throughout the nineteenth and twentieth centuries, this notion of America as "a people set apart" was a perennial feature of American public discourse. Its most eloquent expression came in the speeches of Abraham Lincoln. Perhaps in deference to biblical literalists, Lincoln did not call Americans a "chosen people" (a name limited to the Jews in the Bible), but he came close: he said Americans were God's "almost chosen people." In other speeches, particularly in his Second Inaugural Address, he stressed the role of Divine Providence in directing the course of American history. Frederick Douglass, the black abolitionist leader, called the Second Inaugural "more like a sermon than a state paper."

So it has gone, down through the nation's history. Herbert Croly, the influential Progressive writer in the early twentieth century, called on Americans to realize "the promise of American life." In 1936 Franklin Roosevelt told a newer generation of Americans that they had a "rendezvous with destiny." John F. Kennedy proclaimed that "God's work must truly be our own." Martin Luther King, in his prophetic "I Have a Dream" speech identified his dream with the God-given promises of America. Ronald Reagan, paraphrasing John Winthrop's speech of 1630, saw America as a "shining city on a hill."

All of this sounds inspiring, and no doubt it did help inspire many worthy reforms, from the abolition of slavery in the 1860s to the landmark civil rights laws a century later. But is there a darker side to it? To its critics, American "exceptionalism" is a dangerous notion. They remind us that other nations, too, such as the ancient Romans, the Dutch, the Spanish, the British, and the Germans, have at various times boasted of themselves as an exceptional people, and that this has led them down the path to chauvinism, imperialism, and even genocide. To them, the invocation "God bless America" sounds like hubris, as if God is being asked to bless whatever it is that America decides to do. Such a spirit lay behind "Manifest Destiny," a slogan from the mid-nineteenth century that was used to justify American expansion into territory claimed by Mexico, and in the 1890s American imperialists justified American expansion into Cuba and the Philippines in nearly similar language. From Indian removal at home to imperial adventures abroad, there have been few dark episodes in American history that have not found defenders ready to put them in terms of American exceptionalism.

Yet America's perceived exceptionalism has not always been viewed positively across the globe. If we think back to the terrorist attacks of September 11, 2001, many of the reasons cited by Osama bin Laden for his desire to tear down the United States centered on perceived uniqueness. In bin Laden's letter to America (delivered two months after the collapse of the World Trade Center), he first cites American aggression toward Muslims in Palestine and Somalia before noting that America tells other nations to attack Muslims daily and continually causes economic hardship by exerting influence to lower oil prices. While most of the early argument centers on policy concerns, bin Laden then turns toward attacking American culture. He calls on Americans to stop their "oppression, lies, immorality, and debauchery" and to "reject the immoral acts of fornication, homosexuality, intoxicants, gambling,

and trading with interest." Perhaps most pointedly, bin Laden directly states how America's perceived uniqueness directly led to his targeting the country for attack: "Let us not forget one of your major characteristics: your duality in both manners and values; your hypocrisy in manners and principles. All manners, principles and values have two scales: one for you and one for the others." This duality is American uniqueness and exceptionalism and presents as a double-edged sword.

Even more recently, Russian President Vladimir Putin publicly lambasted American President Barack Obama for invoking exceptionalism as a justification for unilaterally striking against Syria when Assad was accused of using chemical weapons against his own citizens. American citizens responded negatively and rallied against Putin's perceived slight. Senate Foreign Relations Committee Chair Robert Menendez (D-NJ) went as far as to say that Putin made him want to vomit. Yet was Putin incorrect in his disapproval of America's view of itself? After all this is no longer World War II or the Cold War, in which the United States is fighting to protect a repressed group or save off nuclear war. Since that time, battles in various countries and alleged bullying in diplomatic relationships have tarnished the American image abroad. Much like the generation of trophy children who struggle to accept Cs in college after being given trophies for the most basic level of participation throughout life, the United States is now facing pushback on its own vision of itself for perhaps the first time in its existence.

By no means are Americans the first to view themselves as exceptional. The Greeks and Romans both held themselves as being unique from the rest of the world. At a time, British imperialism clearly demonstrated a tendency to inflate internal assessments. During the height of Marxist–Leninist ideology the Soviets spoke of becoming the new Rome. In all of these examples, exceptionalism relied on two things: ideology and myth. Yet each of these civilizations was ultimately forced to face the downside of perceived exceptionalism and uniqueness. And now, it appears Americans are being forced to do the same. While September 11 appeared to be a wake-up call for a short period among the American public, our political actions and public persona has not necessarily continued to recognize the fact that to many in the international community, the American mission reeks of unwarranted arrogance.

In the selections that follow, humanities professor Wilfred M. McClay looks at the brighter side of American providentialism, while historian Howard Zinn argues that what he calls "American exceptionalism" is a dangerous idea because it has served as a justification for lawlessness, brutality, and imperialism.

# YES

**Wilfred M. McClay**

## The Founding of Nations

**D**id the United States really have a beginning that can be called its "Founding"? Can any society, for that matter, be said to have a founding moment in its past that ought to be regarded as a source of guidance and support?

Much of the intellectual culture of our time stands resolutely opposed to the idea of a founding as a unique moment in secular time that has a certain magisterial authority over what comes after it. The cult of ancestors, in its many forms, is always one of the chief objects of modernity's deconstructive energies. Kant's famous command, *Sapere Aude*—"Dare to Reason," the battle cry of the Enlightenment—always ends up being deployed against arguments claiming traditional authority.

Foundings, in this view, are fairy tales that cannot be taken seriously—indeed, that it is dangerous to take seriously, since modern nation-states have used them as tools of cultural hegemony. One has a moral obligation to peek behind the curtain, and one ought to have a strong presupposition about what one will find there. There is a settled assumption in the West, particularly among the educated, that every founding was in reality a blood-soaked moment, involving the enslavement or exploitation of some for the benefit of others. Foundational myths are merely attempts to prettify this horror. Our ancestors were not the noble heroes of epic. They were the primal horde or the Oedipal usurpers, and their authority derived ultimately from their successful monopolization of violence—and then their subsequent monopolization of the way the story would be told.

The perfect expression of this view is Theodor Adorno's dictum, "There is no monument of civilization that is not at the same time a monument of barbarism." Every achievement of culture involves an elaborate concealment of the less-than-licit means that went into its making. Property is theft, in Proudhon's famous phrase, which means that legitimacy is nothing more than the preeminent force, and our systems of law are the ways that the stolen money is laundered and turned into Carnegie libraries and Vanderbilt universities and other carved Corinthian pillars of society. From this point of view, the credulous souls who speak of the American founding are merely trying to retell a heroic myth about the Founding Fathers, a group of youthful and idealistic patriarchs who somehow reached up into the heavens and pulled down a Constitution for all time.

Admittedly, American filiopietism about the Founding can get out of hand. On the ceiling of the rotunda of the United States Capitol building—the inside of the dome which, in its external aspect, is arguably the single most recognizable symbol of American democracy—there is painted a fresco called "The Apotheosis of George Washington." It is as if the Sistine Chapel were transposed into an American key. The first president sits in glory, flanked by the Goddess of Liberty and the winged figure Fame sounding a victorious trumpet and holding aloft a palm frond. The thirteen female figures in a semi-circle around Washington represent the thirteen original states. On the outer ring stand six allegorical groups representing classical images of agriculture, arts and sciences, commerce, war, mechanics, and seafaring. This figure of a deified Washington, painted significantly enough in the year 1865, reflects a vision that appealed powerfully to the American public. But it is actually a rather disturbing image, and it cries out for debunking.

Still, debunking is a blunt instrument of limited value, despite the modern prejudice in its favor. To the question "What is a man?" André Malraux once gave the quintessential modern debunking answer: "A miserable little pile of secrets." That answer is too true to dismiss—but not quite true enough to embrace. And it is, in its way, the exact opposite number to the saccharin image of a deified and perfected George Washington dwelling in the clouds atop the Capitol dome. Such a conflict between grand moral oversimplications impoverishes our thinking and sets us a false standard of greatness—one that is too easily debunked and leaves us too easily defrauded. . . .

When we speak of American national identity, one of the chief points at issue arises out of the tension between *creed* and *culture*. This is a tension between, on the one hand, the idea of the United States as a nation built on the foundation of self-evident, rational, and universally applicable propositions about human nature and human society; and, on the other hand, the idea of the United States as a very unusual, historically specific and contingent entity, underwritten by a long, intricately evolved, and very particular legacy of English law, language, and customs, Greco-Roman cultural antecedents, and Judeo-Christian sacred texts and theological and moral teachings, without whose presences the nation's flourishing would not be possible.

All this makes a profound tension, with much to be said for both sides. And the side one comes down on will say a lot about one's stance on an immense number of issues, such as immigration, education, citizenship,

From *First Things*, March 2006, pp. 33–39. Copyright © 2006 by Institute on Religion and Public Life. Reprinted by permission.

cultural assimilation, multiculturalism, pluralism, the role of religion in public life, the prospects for democratizing the Middle East, and on and on.

Yet any understanding of American identity that entirely excluded either creed or culture would be seriously deficient. Any view of American life that failed to acknowledge its powerful strains of universalism, idealism, and crusading zeal would be describing a different country from the America that happens to exist. And any view of America as simply a bundle of abstract normative ideas about freedom and democracy and self-government that can flourish just as easily in any cultural and historical soil, including a multilingual, post-religious, or post-national one, takes too much for granted and will be in for a rude awakening.

⋅⟨⊙⟩⋅

The antagonism of creed and culture is better understood not as a statement of alternatives but as an antinomy, one of those perpetual oppositions that can never be resolved. In fact, the two halves of the opposition often reinforce each other. The creed needs the support of the culture—and the culture, in turn, is imbued with respect for the creed. For the creed to be successful, it must be able to presume the presence of all kinds of cultural inducements—toward civility, restraint, deferred gratification, nonviolence, loyalty, procedural fairness, impersonal neutrality, compassion, respect for elders, and the like. These traits are not magically called into being by the mere invocation of the Declaration of Independence. Nor are they sustainable for long without the support of strong and deeply rooted social and cultural institutions that are devoted to the formation of character, most notably the traditional family and traditional religious institutions. But by the same token, the American culture is unimaginable apart from the influence of the American creed: from the sense of pride and moral responsibility Americans derive from being, as Walter Berns has argued, a carrier of universal values—a vanguard people.

⋅⟨⊙⟩⋅

Forcing a choice between creed and culture is not the way to resolve the problem of cultural restoration. Clearly both can plausibly claim a place in the American Founding. What seems more urgent is the repair of some background assumptions about our relation to the past. It is a natural enough impulse to look back in times of turbulence and uncertainty. And it is especially natural, even obligatory, for a republican form of government to do so, since republics come into being at particular moments in secular time, through self-conscious acts of public deliberation. Indeed, philosophers from Aristotle on have insisted that republics *must* periodically recur to their first principles, in order

to adjust and renew themselves through a fresh encounter with their initiating vision.

A constitutional republic like the United States is uniquely grounded in its foundational moment, its time of creation. And a founding is not merely the instant that the ball started rolling. Instead, it is a moment that presumes a certain authority over all the moments that will follow—and to speak of a founding is to presume that such moments in time are possible. It most closely resembles the moment that one takes an oath or makes a promise. One could even say that a constitutional founding is a kind of covenant, a meta-promise entered into with the understanding that it has a uniquely powerful claim on the future. It requires of us a willingness to be constantly looking back to our initiating promises and goals, in much the same way that we would chart progress or regress in our individual lives by reference to a master list of resolutions.

Republicanism means self-government, and so republican liberty does not mean living without restraint. It means, rather, living in accordance with a law that you have dictated to yourself. Hence the especially strong need of republics to recur to their founding principles and their founding narratives, is a never-ending process of self-adjustment. There should be a constant interplay between founding ideals and current realities, a tennis ball bouncing back and forth between the two.

And for that to happen, there needs to be two things in place. First, founding principles must be sufficiently fixed to give us genuine guidance, to *teach* us something. Of course, we celebrate the fact that our Constitution was created with a built-in openness to amendment. But the fact that such ideals are open to amendment is perhaps the least valuable thing about them. A founding, like a promise or a vow, means nothing if its chief glory is its adaptability. The analogy of a successful marriage, which is also, in a sense, *a res publica* that must periodically recur to first principles, and whose flourishing depends upon the ability to distinguish first principles from passing circumstances, is actually a fairly good guide to these things.

⋅⟨⊙⟩⋅

Second, there needs to be a sense of connection to the past, a reflex for looking backward, and cultivating that ought to be one of the chief uses of the formal study of history. Unfortunately, the fostering of a vital sense of connection to the past is not one of the goals of historical study as it is now taught and practiced in this country. The meticulous contextualization of past events and ideas, arising out of a sophisticated understanding of the past's particularities and discontinuities with the present, is one of the great achievements of modern historiography. But we need to recognize that this achievement comes at a high cost when it emphasizes the *pastness* of the past—when it makes the past completely unavailable to us, separated from us by an impassable chasm of contextual difference.

In the case of the American Founding, a century-long assault has taken place among historians, and the sense of connection is even more tenuous. The standard scholarly accounts insist this heated series of eighteenth-century debates—among flawed, unheroic, and self-interested white men—offers nothing to which we should grant any abiding authority. That was then, and this is now.

The insistence on the pastness of the past imprisons us in the present. It makes our present antiseptically cut off from anything that might really nourish, surprise, or challenge it. It erodes our sense of being part of a common enterprise with humankind. An emphasis on scholarly precision has dovetailed effortlessly with what might be called the debunking imperative, which generally aims to discredit any use of the past to justify or support something in the present, and is therefore one of the few gestures likely to win universal approbation among historians. It is professionally safest to be a critic and extremely dangerous to be too affirmative.

Scholarly responsibility thus seems to demand the deconstruction of the American Founding into its constituent elements, thereby divesting it of any claim to unity or any heroic or mythic dimensions, deserving of our admiration or reverence. There was no coherence to what they did, and looking backward to divine what they meant by what they were doing makes no sense.

The Founders and Framers, after all, fought among themselves. They produced a document that was a compromise, that waffled on important issues, that remains hopelessly bound to the eighteenth century and inadequate to our contemporary problems, etc. And so—in much the same manner as the source criticism of the Bible, which challenges the authority of Scripture by understanding the text as a compilation of haphazardly generated redactions—the Constitution is seen as a concatenation of disparate elements, a mere political deal meant to be superseded by other political deals, and withal an instrument of the powerful. The last thing in the world you would want to do is treat it as a document with any intrinsic moral authority. Every text is merely a pretext. This is the kind of explanation one has learned to expect from the historical guild.

⁂

In this connection, it is amusing to see the extent to which historians, who are pleased to regard the Constitution as a hopelessly outdated relic of a bygone era, are themselves still crude nineteenth-century positivists at heart. They still pride themselves on their ability to puncture myths, relying on a shallow positivistic understanding of a myth as a more or less organized form of falsehood, rather than seeing myth as a structure of meaning, a manner of giving a manageable shape to the cosmos, and to one's own experience of the world, a shape that expresses cultural ideals and shared sentiments, and that guides us through the darkness of life's many perils and unanswerable questions by providing us with what Plato called a "likely story."

To be sure, there are good things to be said of a critical approach to history, and there are myths aplenty that richly deserve to be punctured. I am glad, for example, that we know beyond a shadow of a doubt that Washington, D.C., in the Kennedy years had very little in common with the legendary Camelot, aside from the ubiquity of adulterous liaisons in both places. That kind of ground-clearing is important, and we are better off without that kind of propagandistic myth. We might even be better off without the Apotheosis of George Washington sitting atop the Capitol dome.

But ground-clearing by itself is not enough. And to think otherwise is to mistake an ancillary activity for the main thing itself—as if agriculture were nothing more than the application of insecticides and weedkillers. History as debunking is ultimately an empty and fruitless undertaking, which fails to address the reasons we humans try to narrate and understand our pasts. It fails to take into account the ways in which a nation's morale, cohesion, and strength derive from a sense of connection to its past. And it fails to acknowledge how much a healthy sense of the future—including the economic and cultural preconditions for a critical historiography to ply its trade—depends on a mythic sense of the nation. The human need to encompass life within the framework of myth is not merely a longing for pleasing illusion. Myths reflect a fundamental human need for a larger shape to our collective aspirations. And it is an illusion to think that we can so ignore that need, and so cauterize our souls, that we will never again be troubled by it.

Indeed, the debunking imperative operates on the basis of its own myth. It presumes the existence of a solid and orderly substratum, a rock-solid reality lying just beneath the illusory surfaces, waiting to be revealed in all its direct and unfeigned honesty when the facades and artifices and false divisions are all stripped away. There is a remarkable complacency and naiveté about such a view. The near-universal presumption that the demise of the nation-state and the rise of international governance would be very good things has everything, except a shred of evidence, to support it. And as for the debunking of bourgeois morality that still passes for sophistication in some quarters and has been the stock-in-trade of Western intellectuals for almost two centuries now—well, this has always been a form of moral free-riding, like the radical posturing of adolescents who always know they can call Mom when they get into trouble.

⁂

One residue of the debunking heritage is the curious assumption that narratives of foundings are mere fairy tales—prettified, antiseptic flights of fancy, or wish-fulfillment fantasies, telling of superlative heroes and maidens acting nobly and virtuously to bring forth the status quo or its antecedents. I think it's fair to say that foundational narratives, including creation myths, tend to be conservative in character, in the sense that they tend to provide historical and moral support for existing regimes and social arrangements. It's hard to imagine them being any other way. But the part about their being prettifying fairy tales is demonstrably wrong. In fact, one could say that the most amazing feature of the great foundational myths is their moral complexity.

One need not even consider the appalling creation myths of Greek antiquity, such as the story of Kronos, who castrated his father Ouranos with a sickle given him by his mother, and then, in order to protect himself against the same dismal fate, swallowed his own children until his youngest child, Zeus, also aided by his mother, was able to overthrow him and assume primacy among the gods.

Consider instead the great Biblical stories of the Pentateuch, foundational texts not only for the Jewish people but for the entire family of monotheistic Abrahamic religious faiths—which is to say, those faiths that have been most constitutive of Western civilization. These Biblical texts are anything but tracts of unrelieved patriotism. In fact, one would be justified in seeing them as an exercise in collective self-humiliation. They are replete with the disreputable deeds of their imperfect and dissembling patriarchs, who pawn off their wives as sisters, deceive their fathers, cheat their brothers, murder, and commit incest—together with tales of an incorrigibly feckless people, the people of Israel, sheep-like fools who manage to forget every theophany and divine favor shown them, and prove unable and unwilling to follow the law that has been given to them.

The narrative does not blink at those things. It is itself the harshest critic of the things it describes, and every one of its human heroes is presented as deeply flawed. But what holds all this together is not the greatness of the heroes but the enduring quality of God's successive covenants with them and with His people. The God of the Hebrew Bible makes promises and keeps them, operating through covenants and laws that superintend and take precedence over the force of passing events. In that sense, the complexity of the Biblical account registers, in a remarkably accurate way, the same set of moral directives regarding the authority of the past—and the elements of pain and suffering and shame in that past—that goes into the making of any durable founding. The Passover seder, which is also the template for the Christian gospel story, is not a story of heroic triumph but of deliverance from slavery by a promise-keeping Deity. . . .

Perhaps the most interesting question about these foundational stories is why they are so complex. And the answer is surely to be found in the complexity of the mythic dimension itself, the ways in which it can register and mirror and instruct a civilization, precisely by virtue of its being a rich and truthful narrative that is widely shared. This quality can be neglected in an overly politicized or rationalized age, which wants to see the play of tangible and measurable material interests or causes always at the bottom of things. And it certainly eludes a culture that has ceased to understand the human necessity of looking backward.

⁂

Human knowledge about human affairs always has a reflexive quality about it. It is never a matter of the tree falling unheard and unwitnessed in the forest. There is always someone listening and watching, always a feedback effect—and most prophecies tend to be either self-fulfilled or self-averted. The best social scientists understand this perfectly well (after all, they were the ones who gave us the term "self-fulfilling prophecy"), but they give us such knowledge in a vocabulary and form that are often all but self-subverting. Who, after all, wants to embrace a myth while *calling* it a myth?

But to do so may be preferable to the alternative of nineteenth-century positivism, so long as we are able to proceed with a capacious understanding of "myth," as something more than a mere tall tale, something that can be both life-giving and true. In this connection, there may be particular value in revisiting Ernest Renan's celebrated 1882 essay "What Is a Nation?", a rich evocation of the nation's mythic dimension. For Renan, a nation was fundamentally "a soul, a spiritual principle," constituted not only by "present-day consent" but also by the residuum of the past, "the possession in common of a rich legacy of memories" which form in the citizen "the will to perpetuate the value of the heritage that one has received in an undivided form." He declared:

> The nation, like the individual, is the culmination of a long past of endeavors, sacrifice, and devotion. Of all cults, that of the ancestors is the most legitimate, for the ancestors have made us what we are. A heroic past, great men, glory (by which I understand genuine glory), this is the social capital upon which one bases a national idea. To have common glories in the past and to have a common will in the present, to have performed great deeds together, to wish to perform still more—these are the essential conditions for being a people. . . . A nation is therefore a large-scale solidarity, constituted by the feeling of the sacrifices that one has made in the past and of those that one is prepared to make in the future.

Renan strongly opposed the then-fashionable view that nations should be understood as entities united by racial or linguistic or geographical or religious or material factors. None of those factors were sufficient to account for the emergence of this "spiritual principle." Active consent had to be a part of it. But it was insufficient without the presence of the past—the past in which that consent was embedded and through which it found meaning.

The ballast of the past, and our intimate connection to it, is similarly indispensable to the sense of American national identity. It forms a strain in our identity that is in some respects far less articulate (and less frequently articulated) than the universalistic principles that some writers have emphasized, precisely because it seems to conflict with American assertions of universalism, and its intellectual basis is less well-defined. But it is every bit as powerful, if not more so, and just as indispensable. And it is a very *particular* force. Our nation's particular triumphs, sacrifices, and sufferings—and our memories of those things—draw and hold us together, precisely because they are the sacrifices and sufferings, not of all humanity, but of us in particular.

No one has spoken of American national identity with greater mastery than Abraham Lincoln. In his 1838 speech on "The Perpetuation of Our Political Institutions," delivered to the Young Men's Lyceum of Springfield, Illinois, Lincoln responded to the then-raging violence directed at blacks and abolitionists in Southern and border states with an admonition that could have come from Toynbee: "If destruction be our lot, we must ourselves be its author and finisher. As a nation of free-men, we must live through all time, or die by suicide." The danger he most feared was that rampant lawlessness would dissolve the "attachment of the People" to their government. And the answer he provides to this danger is remarkable for the way it touches on the same themes that Renan recounts:

> Let every American, every lover of liberty, every well wisher to his posterity, swear by the blood of the Revolution, never to violate in the least particular, the laws of the country; and never to tolerate their violation by others. As the patriots of seventy-six did to the support of the Declaration of Independence, so to the support of the Constitution and Laws, let every American pledge his life, his property, and his sacred honor;—let every man remember that to violate the law, is to trample on the blood of his father, and to tear the character of his own, and his children's liberty. Let reverence for the laws, be breathed by every American mother, to the lisping babe, that prattles on her lap—let it be taught in schools, in seminaries, and in colleges;—let it be written in Primmers, spelling books, and in Almanacs;—let it be preached from the pulpit, proclaimed in legislative halls, and enforced in courts of justice. And, in short, let it become the political religion of the nation; and let the old and the young, the rich and the poor, the grave and the gay, of all sexes and tongues, and colors and conditions, sacrifice unceasingly upon its altars.

The excerpt shows Lincoln's remarkable ability to intertwine the past and the present, and evoke a sense of connection between them. The speech performs the classic republican move, back to the founding origins, connecting the public order explicitly with something so primal as a son's love of, and respect for, his father. Obedience to the law and reverence for the Constitution—these are directly connected with memory, the reverence owed to the sufferings of the patriot generation, and the blood of one's own father. Such words gesture toward his even more famous invocation of "the mystic chords of memory" in his First Inaugural Address, chords "stretching from every battlefield and patriot grave to every living heart and hearthstone all over this broad land," chords that provide the music of the Union. He performs a similar move of memorial linkage in the Gettysburg Address, beginning with the Founding Fathers and ending with a rededication and recommitment, drawn from knowledge of the "honored dead" who hallowed the ground with their sacrifice.

It is pointless to ask whether such a vision of the Union reflects an "objective" reality. The mythic reality on which such rhetoric depends, and which it helps to create and sustain, is powerful in its own right, too compelling to be dismissed or deconstructed into the language of "state formation" or "cultural hegemony." You could say that the antiseptic scholarly language offers insights that Lincoln cannot give us, and you would be right. But you could also say that Lincoln's reverent and hortatory language offers insights that the antiseptic scholars cannot provide, and you would be equally right. The real question is which language tells us more, and for what purposes.

A belief in the particularly instructive and sustaining qualities of the American Founding does not depend on a belief in the moral perfection of the Founders themselves, or the presumption that they were completely pure and disinterested regarding the measures they sought, or that they were invariably wise or prudent or far-sighted, or that they agreed in all important things, or that the Constitution they created is perfect in every way. The stories that we tell ourselves about ourselves, in order to remember who we are, should not neglect to tell us the ways we have fallen short and the ways we have suffered, both needfully and needlessly, by necessity or by chance.

We should not try to edit out those stories' strange moral complexity, because it is there for a reason. Indeed, it is precisely our encounter with the surprise of their strangeness that reminds us of how much we have yet to learn from them.

---

**Wilfred M. McClay** holds the SunTrust Chair of Humanities at the University of Tennessee at Chattanooga.

Howard Zinn

# The Power and the Glory: Myths of American Exceptionalism

The notion of American exceptionalism—that the United States alone has the right, whether by divine sanction or moral obligation, to bring civilization, or democracy, or liberty to the rest of the world, by violence if necessary—is not new. It started as early as 1630 in the Massachusetts Bay Colony when Governor John Winthrop uttered the words that centuries later would be quoted by Ronald Reagan. Winthrop called the Massachusetts Bay Colony a "city upon a hill." Reagan embellished a little, calling it a "shining city on a hill."

The idea of a city on a hill is heartwarming. It suggests what George Bush has spoken of: that the United States is a beacon of liberty and democracy. People can look to us and learn from and emulate us.

In reality, we have never been just a city on a hill. A few years after Governor Winthrop uttered his famous words, the people in the city on a hill moved out to massacre the Pequot Indians. Here's a description by William Bradford, an early settler, of Captain John Mason's attack on a Pequot village.

> Those that escaped the fire were slain with the sword, some hewed to pieces, others run through with their rapiers, so as they were quickly dispatched and very few escaped. It was conceived that they thus destroyed about 400 at this time. It was a fearful sight to see them thus frying in the fire and the streams of blood quenching the same, and horrible was the stink and scent thereof; but the victory seemed a sweet sacrifice, and they gave the praise thereof to God, who had wrought so wonderfully for them, thus to enclose their enemies in their hands and give them so speedy a victory over so proud and insulting an enemy.

The kind of massacre described by Bradford occurs again and again as Americans march west to the Pacific and south to the Gulf of Mexico. (In fact our celebrated war of liberation, the American Revolution, was disastrous for the Indians. Colonists had been restrained from encroaching on the Indian territory by the British and the boundary set up in their Proclamation of 1763. American independence wiped out that boundary.)

Expanding into another territory, occupying that territory, and dealing harshly with people who resist occupation has been a persistent fact of American history from the first settlements to the present day. And this was often accompanied from very early on with a particular form of American exceptionalism: the idea that American expansion is divinely ordained. On the eve of the war with Mexico in the middle of the 19th century, just after the United States annexed Texas, the editor and writer John O'Sullivan coined the famous phrase "manifest destiny." He said it was "the fulfillment of our manifest destiny to overspread the continent allotted by Providence for the free development of our yearly multiplying millions." At the beginning of the 20th century, when the United States invaded the Philippines, President McKinley said that the decision to take the Philippines came to him one night when he got down on his knees and prayed, and God told him to take the Philippines.

Invoking God has been a habit for American presidents throughout the nation's history, but George W. Bush has made a specialty of it. For an article in the Israeli newspaper *Ha'aretz*, the reporter talked with Palestinian leaders who had met with Bush. One of them reported that Bush told him, "God told me to strike at al Qaeda. And I struck them. And then he instructed me to strike at Saddam, which I did. And now I am determined to solve the problem in the Middle East." It's hard to know if the quote is authentic, especially because it is so literate. But it certainly is consistent with Bush's oft-expressed claims. A more credible story comes from a Bush supporter, Richard Lamb, the president of the Ethics and Religious Liberty Commission of the Southern Baptist Convention, who says that during the election campaign Bush told him, "I believe God wants me to be president. But if that doesn't happen, that's okay."

Divine ordination is a very dangerous idea, especially when combined with military power (the United States has 10,000 nuclear weapons, with military bases in a hundred different countries and warships on every sea). With God's approval, you need no human standard of morality. Anyone today who claims the support of God might be embarrassed to recall that the Nazi storm troopers had inscribed on their belts, "Gott mit uns" ("God with us").

Not every American leader claimed divine sanction, but the idea persisted that the United States was uniquely justified in using its power to expand throughout the world. In 1945, at the end of World War II, Henry Luce, the owner of a vast chain of media enterprises—*Time, Life, Fortune*—declared that this would be "the American Century," that victory in the war gave the United States the right "to exert upon the world the full impact of our influence, for such purposes as we see fit and by such means as we see fit."

This confident prophecy was acted out all through the rest of the 20th century. Almost immediately after World War II the United States penetrated the oil regions of the Middle East by special arrangement with Saudi Arabia. It established military bases in Japan, Korea, the Philippines, and a number of Pacific islands. In the next decades it orchestrated right-wing coups in Iran, Guatemala, and Chile, and gave military aid to various dictatorships in the Caribbean. In an attempt to establish a foothold in Southeast Asia it invaded Vietnam and bombed Laos and Cambodia.

The existence of the Soviet Union, even with its acquisition of nuclear weapons, did not block this expansion. In fact, the exaggerated threat of "world communism" gave the United States a powerful justification for expanding all over the globe, and soon it had military bases in a hundred countries. Presumably, only the United States stood in the way of the Soviet conquest of the world.

Can we believe that it was the existence of the Soviet Union that brought about the aggressive militarism of the United States? If so, how do we explain all the violent expansion before 1917? A hundred years before the Bolshevik Revolution, American armies were annihilating Indian tribes, clearing the great expanse of the West in an early example of what we now call "ethnic cleansing." And with the continent conquered, the nation began to look overseas.

On the eve of the 20th century, as American armies moved into Cuba and the Philippines, American exceptionalism did not always mean that the United States wanted to go it alone. The nation was willing—indeed, eager—to join the small group of Western imperial powers that it would one day supersede. Senator Henry Cabot Lodge wrote at the time, "The great nations are rapidly absorbing for their future expansion, and their present defense all the waste places of the earth. . . . As one of the great nations of the world the United States must not fall out of the line of march." Surely, the nationalistic spirit in other countries has often led them to see their expansion as uniquely moral, but this country has carried the claim farthest.

American exceptionalism was never more clearly expressed than by Secretary of War Elihu Root, who in 1899 declared, "The American soldier is different from all other soldiers of all other countries since the world began. He is the advance guard of liberty and justice, of law and order, and of peace and happiness." At the time he was saying this, American soldiers in the Philippines were starting a bloodbath which would take the lives of 600,000 Filipinos.

The idea that America is different because its military actions are for the benefit of others becomes particularly persuasive when it is put forth by leaders presumed to be liberals, or progressives. For instance, Woodrow Wilson, always high on the list of "liberal" presidents, labeled both by scholars and the popular culture as an "idealist," was ruthless in his use of military power against weaker nations. He sent the navy to bombard and occupy the Mexican port of Vera Cruz in 1914 because the Mexicans had arrested some American sailors. He sent the marines into Haiti in 1915, and when the Haitians resisted, thousands were killed.

The following year American marines occupied the Dominican Republic. The occupations of Haiti and the Dominican Republic lasted many years. And Wilson, who had been elected in 1916 saying, "There is such a thing as a nation being too proud to fight," soon sent young Americans into the slaughterhouse of the European war.

Theodore Roosevelt was considered a "progressive" and indeed ran for president on the Progressive Party ticket in 1912. But he was a lover of war and a supporter of the conquest of the Philippines—he had congratulated the general who wiped out a Filipino village of 600 people in 1906. He had promulgated the 1904 "Roosevelt Corollary" to the Monroe Doctrine, which justified the occupation of small countries in the Caribbean as bringing them "stability."

During the Cold War, many American "liberals" became caught up in a kind of hysteria about the Soviet expansion, which was certainly real in Eastern Europe but was greatly exaggerated as a threat to western Europe and the United States. During the period of McCarthyism the Senate's quintessential liberal, Hubert Humphrey, proposed detention camps for suspected subversives who in times of "national emergency" could be held without trial.

After the disintegration of the Soviet Union and the end of the Cold War, terrorism replaced communism as the justification for expansion. Terrorism was real, but its threat was magnified to the point of hysteria, permitting excessive military action abroad and the curtailment of civil liberties at home.

The idea of American exceptionalism persisted as the first President Bush declared, extending Henry Luce's prediction, that the nation was about to embark on a "new American Century." Though the Soviet Union was gone, the policy of military intervention abroad did not end. The elder Bush invaded Panama and then went to war against Iraq.

The terrible attacks of September 11 gave a new impetus to the idea that the United States was uniquely responsible for the security of the world, defending us all against terrorism as it once did against communism. President George W. Bush carried the idea of American exceptionalism to its limits by putting forth in his national-security strategy the principles of unilateral war.

This was a repudiation of the United Nations charter, which is based on the idea that security is a collective matter, and that war could only be justified in self-defense. We might note that the Bush doctrine also violates the principles laid out at Nuremberg, when Nazi leaders were convicted and hanged for aggressive war, preventive war, far from self-defense.

Bush's national-security strategy and its bold statement that the United States is uniquely responsible for peace and democracy in the world has been shocking to many Americans.

But it is not really a dramatic departure from the historical practice of the United States, which for a long time has acted as an aggressor, bombing and invading other countries (Vietnam, Cambodia, Laos, Grenada, Panama, Iraq) and insisting on maintaining nuclear and non-nuclear supremacy. Unilateral military action, under the guise of prevention, is a familiar part of American foreign policy.

Sometimes bombings and invasions have been cloaked as international action by bringing in the United Nations, as in Korea, or NATO, as in Serbia, but basically our wars have been American enterprises. It was Bill Clinton's secretary of state, Madeleine Albright, who said at one point, "If possible we will act in the world multilaterally, but if necessary, we will act unilaterally." Henry Kissinger, hearing this, responded with his customary solemnity that this principle "should not be universalized." Exceptionalism was never clearer.

Some liberals in this country, opposed to Bush, nevertheless are closer to his principles on foreign affairs than they want to acknowledge. It is clear that 9/11 had a powerful psychological effect on everybody in America, and for certain liberal intellectuals a kind of hysterical reaction has distorted their ability to think clearly about our nation's role in the world.

In a recent issue of the liberal magazine *The American Prospect,* the editors write, "Today Islamist terrorists with global reach pose the greatest immediate threat to our lives and liberties. . . . When facing a substantial, immediate, and provable threat, the United States has both the right and the obligation to strike preemptively and, if need be, unilaterally against terrorists or states that support them."

Preemptively and, if need be, unilaterally; and against "states that support" terrorists, not just terrorists themselves. Those are large steps in the direction of the Bush doctrine, though the editors do qualify their support for preemption by adding that the threat must be "substantial, immediate, and provable." But when intellectuals endorse abstract principles, even with qualifications, they need to keep in mind that the principles will be applied by the people who run the U.S. government. This is all the more important to keep in mind when the abstract principle is about the use of violence by the state—in fact, about preemptively initiating the use of violence.

There may be an acceptable case for initiating military action in the face of an immediate threat, but only if the action is limited and focused directly on the threatening party—just as we might accept the squelching of someone falsely shouting "fire" in a crowded theater if that really were the situation and not some guy distributing anti-war leaflets on the street. But accepting action not just against "terrorists" (can we identify them as we do the person shouting "fire"?) but against "states that support them" invites unfocused and indiscriminate violence, as in Afghanistan, where our government killed at least 3,000 civilians in a claimed pursuit of terrorists.

It seems that the idea of American exceptionalism is pervasive across the political spectrum.

The idea is not challenged because the history of American expansion in the world is not a history that is taught very much in our educational system. A couple of years ago Bush addressed the Philippine National Assembly and said, "America is proud of its part in the great story of the Filipino people. Together our soldiers liberated the Philippines from colonial rule." The president apparently never learned the story of the bloody conquest of the Philippines.

And when the Mexican ambassador to the UN said something undiplomatic about how the United States has been treating Mexico as its "backyard" he was immediately reprimanded by then–Secretary of State Colin Powell. Powell, denying the accusation, said, "We have too much of a history that we have gone through together." (Had he not learned about the Mexican War or the military forays into Mexico?) The ambassador was soon removed from his post.

The major newspapers, television news shows, and radio talk shows appear not to know history, or prefer to forget it. There was an outpouring of praise for Bush's second inaugural speech in the press, including the so-called liberal press (*The Washington Post, The New York Times*). The editorial writers eagerly embraced Bush's words about spreading liberty in the world, as if they were ignorant of the history of such claims, as if the past two years' worth of news from Iraq were meaningless.

Only a couple of days before Bush uttered those words about spreading liberty in the world, *The New York Times* published a photo of a crouching, bleeding Iraqi girl. She was screaming. Her parents, taking her somewhere in their car, had just been shot to death by nervous American soldiers.

One of the consequences of American exceptionalism is that the U.S. government considers itself exempt from legal and moral standards accepted by other nations in the world. There is a long list of such self-exemptions: the refusal to sign the Kyoto Treaty regulating the pollution of the environment, the refusal to strengthen the convention on biological weapons. The United States has failed to join the hundred-plus nations that have agreed to ban land mines, in spite of the appalling statistics about amputations performed on children mutilated by those mines. It refuses to ban the use of napalm and cluster bombs. It insists that it must not be subject, as are other countries, to the jurisdiction of the International Criminal Court.

What is the answer to the insistence on American exceptionalism? Those of us in the United States and in the world who do not accept it must declare forcibly that the ethical norms concerning peace and human rights should be observed. It should be understood that the children of Iraq, of China, and of Africa, children everywhere in the world, have the same right to life as American children.

These are fundamental moral principles. If our government doesn't uphold them, the citizenry must. At certain times in recent history, imperial powers—the British in India and East Africa, the Belgians in the Congo, the French in Algeria, the Dutch and French in Southeast Asia, the Portuguese in Angola—have reluctantly surrendered their possessions and swallowed their pride when they were forced to by massive resistance.

Fortunately, there are people all over the world who believe that human beings everywhere deserve the same rights to life and liberty. On February 15, 2003, on the eve of the invasion of Iraq, more than ten million people in more than 60 countries around the world demonstrated against that war.

There is a growing refusal to accept U.S. domination and the idea of American exceptionalism. Recently, when the State Department issued its annual report listing countries guilty of torture and other human-rights abuses, there were indignant responses from around the world commenting on the absence of the United States from that list. A Turkish newspaper said, "There's not even mention of the incidents in Abu Ghraib prison, no mention of Guantánamo." A newspaper in Sydney pointed out that the United States sends suspects—people who have not been tried or found guilty of anything—to prisons in Morocco, Egypt, Libya, and Uzbekistan, countries that the State Department itself says use torture.

Here in the United States, despite the media's failure to report it, there is a growing resistance to the war in Iraq. Public-opinion polls show that at least half the citizenry no longer believe in the war. Perhaps most significant is that among the armed forces, and families of those in the armed forces, there is more and more opposition to it.

After the horrors of the first World War, Albert Einstein said, "Wars will stop when men refuse to fight." We are now seeing the refusal of soldiers to fight, the refusal of families to let their loved ones go to war, the insistence of the parents of high-school kids that recruiters stay away from their schools. These incidents, occurring more and more frequently, may finally, as happened in the case of Vietnam, make it impossible for the government to continue the war, and it will come to an end.

The true heroes of our history are those Americans who refused to accept that we have a special claim to morality and the right to exert our force on the rest of the world. I think of William Lloyd Garrison, the abolitionist. On the masthead of his antislavery newspaper, *The Liberator,* were the words, "My country is the world. My countrymen are mankind."

**Howard Zinn,** Historian, Playwright, and Social Activist, is best known for his book *A People's History of the United States.* He Has taught at Spelman College and Boston University, and has been a Visiting Professor at the University of Paris and the University of Bologna.

# EXPLORING THE ISSUE

## Should Americans Believe in a Unique American "Mission"?

### Critical Thinking and Reflection

1. What does Wilfred McClay mean by America's "myth"? Does he mean it disparagingly, as in "falsehood," or does he use it approvingly?
2. What does Howard Zinn mean by American "exceptionalism"? What does he think is wrong with that concept?
3. Is it good for a nation to remind itself of its past sins? Can this collective contrition be pushed too far?
4. What does the term "city upon a hill" mean?
5. What makes the United States potentially unique when compared to other nations? How has this possible uniqueness shaped the country?

### Is There Common Ground?

It is important to remember that what one views as uniqueness another may see as cocky or off-putting. The United States does not operate in a bubble. Despite our relative geographic isolation, Americans operate in an increasingly global world. While it may be quite easy to pretend to not hear descending voices when they are located oceans away, negative attitudes toward the United States do matter. This is not to say that Americans should allow international opinions to drive policy decisions or actions, but an increased awareness and understanding of global views could help allow for Americans to maintain their uniqueness without it costing them capital abroad. In short, it is imperative that the United States take efforts to assure that perceived uniqueness does not imply a sense of excellence or superiority.

In the 1960s, the former Socialist candidate for president, Norman Thomas, admonished an angry crowd of antiwar demonstrators not to burn the flag but to wash it. Thomas was one of many critics of American policies who would insist that they love America more, not less, because they can acknowledge how far their country falls short of achieving its professed goals of "liberty and justice for all." That suggests that perhaps there is common ground between both sides, if each is able to say, "America is a country founded on great principles which

on memorable occasions it has put into effect, though on other occasions it has shamefully contradicted its ideals. May this nation always and forevermore live by its grand principles!" There is at least a chance that both Zinn and McClay might say "amen" to that.

### Create Central

www.mhhe.com/createcentral

### Additional Resources

Neil Baldwin, *The American Revelation: Ten Ideals That Shaped Our Country from the Puritans to the Cold War* (St. Martin's Griffin, 2006)

James A. Monroe, *Hellfire Nation* (Yale University Press, 2004)

Alexis de Tocqueville, *Democracy in America* (Knopf, 1951)

Stephen H. Webb, *American Providence: A Nation with a Mission* (Continuum, 2004)

Howard Zinn, *People's History of the United States: 1942 to Present* (Harper Perennial Modern Classics, 2005)

# *Internet References . . .*

**American Exceptionalism, American Freedom**

www.themontrealreview.com/2009/American
-Exceptionalism-American-Freedom.php

**How the World Sees America**

http://newsweek.washingtonpost.com/postglobal
/america/

**Obama and American Exceptionalism**

www.salon.com/2011/03/29/exceptionalism_4/

**The American Creed: Does It Matter? Should It Change?**

www.foreignaffairs.com/articles/51853/michael-lind
/the-american-creed-does-it-matter-should-it-change

**The Right to Be Different**

www.opendemocracy.net/democracy
-letterstoamericans/article_2032.jsp

Selected, Edited, and with Issue Framing Material by:
William J. Miller, *Flagler College*
George McKenna, *City College, City University of New York*
and
Stanley Feingold, *City College, City University of New York*

# ISSUE

# Does the Tea Party Represent a Revival of America's Revolutionary Ideals?

**YES: Dick Armey and Matt Kibbe,** from *Give Us Liberty: A Tea Party Manifesto* (HarperCollins, 2010)

**NO: Jill Lepore,** from *The Whites of Their Eyes: The Tea Party's Revolution and the Battle over American History* (Princeton University Press, 2010)

| Learning Outcomes |
| --- |
| **After reading this issue, you will be able to:** |
| • Describe the central principles of the Tea Party movement. |
| • Explain the concept of liberty and its importance to America today. |
| • Assess the successes and failures of the Tea Party movement. |
| • Describe how the Tea Party is impacting the Republican Party. |
| • Explain the potential long-term impact of the Tea Party on American politics. |

## ISSUE SUMMARY

**YES:** FreedomWorks Founder Dick Armey and FreedomWorks President Matt Kibbe believe that the Tea Party movement is a reawakening of the spirit of the American Revolution.

**NO:** Harvard University Professor of American history Jill Lepore believes that the modern Tea Party movement is antihistorical, anti-intellectual, and antipluralist.

**O**n the evening of December 16, 1773, American colonists boarded English ships in Boston harbor and tossed crates of British tea into the sea to protest the British government's new tax on tea. Their bold action was a seminal moment in inciting the revolution that ended with the independence of the American colonies and the creation of the United States of America. The contemporary Tea Party movement began early in 2008, gathered momentum during that year's election, and began to challenge the traditional leadership of the Republican Party in the congressional primaries and elections in 2010. For the Tea Partiers, there are clear parallels with the tyrannical exercise of power by the British government against the American colonies.

As the Boston Tea Party did then, the modern Tea Party movement sees an improper and illegal exercise of power by the national government. It believes that its success will lead to the restoration of individual liberty and constitutional government, which have been undermined by the present national government. The immediate incitement for the Tea Party movement was the economic decline of middle-class and working-class people in the

sharply diminished economy that followed the banking and housing crises. Many conservatives (as well as many liberals) resented the government's decision to bailout banks and financial institutions because they were "too big to fail," unlike the ordinary Americans who were too small to save.

The modern Tea Party movement is a loosely affiliated combination of a number of political groups, like Tea Party Nation, Tea Party Patriots, and Tea Party Express. Some add conservative social issues to their agenda, such as opposition of abortion rights, same-sex marriage, and illegal immigration, while other Tea Party supporters would confine their goals to economic ends. An intriguing element in the modern movement is that some Tea Partiers express support for libertarianism, a hostility to governmental interference in personal or social affairs except when absolutely necessary for a secure and stable society. Where traditional Republicans saw President George W. Bush as a true conservative, Tea Party speakers are often critical of Bush policies that increased the national debt. Where traditional Democrats see President Barack Obama as a moderate liberal, the Tea Party condemns him as a socialist. Still seeking a dominant role within the Republican Party, the Tea Party movement has started to convert its antitax, antigovernment stance into concrete political programs, seeking to cut taxes and federal programs.

The modern Tea Party is not (any more than the Boston Tea Party) a political party. Almost always, its impact upon the political process has been directed to influencing the Republican Party by securing the nomination of candidates who share its views, even if this means defeating Republican incumbents that do not adequately subscribe to Tea Party principles.

Critics of the Tea Party movement believe that there is no real parallel between the contemporary Tea Party movement and the protest movements preceding and accompanying the American Revolution. The Boston Tea Party was fundamentally inspired by colonial resentment of being unrepresented in the British government. By contrast, today's Tea Party movement freely seeks and has already won political representation.

Recent polls indicate that a majority of Democratic voters believe the Tea Party's opposition to President Obama surpasses simple political differences. Many see evidence of racial bias in widespread suspicion of the president's native citizenship despite the existence of his birth certificate, as well as a persisting conviction among his critics that Obama is a Muslim despite the evidence of his Christian adherence. Liberal opponents see something sinister in what they perceive as an intolerant coalition opposed not only to President Obama, but also to liberals, intellectuals, minorities, and the mainstream media.

In the aftermath of the government shutdown and near debt-default of October 2013, some mainstream Republicans criticized the brinksmanship of Tea Party legislators. Senate Minority Leader Mitch McConnell announced, "There won't be another government shutdown—you can count on that." When the President of the U.S. Chamber of Commerce was asked about Senator Ted Cruz of Texas, the seeming architect of the failed shutdown-default scheme, the representative of the business community offered strategic advice: "If you're going to rush the net all the time, you better have a lot of motion to the left and right. [Cruz] hasn't proved that to me yet." Back home, Cruz was unrepentant. Returning to address his fellow Texans, Cruz received an eight-minute standing ovation and then commenced lashing out at Washington politics and colleagues in the United States Senate.

The applause was coming from voters in a state where support for repeal of the Seventeenth Amendment—

that is, returning the selection of U.S. senators to state legislatures—had "become an article of faith among many on the right." To *Washington Post* blogger Jonathan Bernstein, the drive to repeal the amendment epitomized a bidding war inside the Republican Party: "[T]he key thing within the GOP isn't 'establishment' vs. 'tea party,' but a general, party-wide obsession with being a True Conservative in a party where pretty much every party actor agrees on matters of ideology and on specific issues of public policy." To Bernstein, Republicans were caught in a programmatic spiral, "[a] constant search among radicals for ideas that can separate them from everyone else (and thus prove the radicals to be the True Conservatives), along with rapid adoption of those idea by everyone else." Cruz was disappointed with some leaders in his party: "I think it was unfortunate that you saw multiple members of the Senate Republicans going on television attacking House conservatives, attacking the effort to defund Obamacare, saying it cannot win, it's a fool's errand, we will lose, this must fail. That is a recipe for losing the fight, and it's a shame."

There are limits to the bidding, as reactions from McConnell and business pragmatists attest, but differentiation from mainstream politics seems to be a core value of Tea Party activism. Some in the established GOP party structure may hope the activism will fade, but a close examination of the movement's historical development, its conception of constitutional liberty, and its strategic situation vis-à-vis mainstream Republicanism show ample opportunity for endurance. Indeed, the Tea Party's merger of conservative libertarianism and conservative traditionalism has deep roots in the party shaped by President Ronald Reagan in the 1960s, 1970s, and 1980s. Its ideological soul embraces a wide range of contemporary issues. When the movement's libertarian and traditional wings align against the mainstream of the GOP, they can be a powerful force. Like it or not, the Tea Party wields power.

Dick Armey and Matt Kibbe believe that this movement can "take the country back" from powerful government and privileged interests by a grassroots citizen rebellion, which they see is already well under way. Jill Lepore argues that today's Tea Partiers have a superficial and largely incorrect understanding of what the American Revolution was about and what the Constitution established, permitted, and denied. Whatever its future may be, the Tea Party movement clearly is an important element in determining how the national government moves in this decade.

# YES ↵

**Dick Armey and Matt Kibbe**

# Give Us Liberty: A Tea Party Manifesto

An on-air commentator for cable news network CNBC, Rick Santelli was a fixture at the Chicago Mercantile Exchange, where he offered news and commentary on corn futures, yield rates, and other market data. On the morning of February 19, 2009, news coverage was dominated by Obama's proposal for yet another housing bailout. CNBC studio analysts calmly reported the news, discussing vast sums of taxpayer money in a tone ordinarily reserved for reporting on weather patterns over the Midwest. Standing by for a floor report, Santelli heard the commentary on his earpiece and began to fume.

After reporting on the latest housing bailouts, an anchor tossed to Santelli for his usual update. Santelli unexpectedly unleashed an impassioned rant.

"The government is promoting bad behavior!" Santelli shouted. "This is America! How many people want to pay for your neighbor's mortgages that have an extra bathroom and can't pay their bills? Raise your hand! President Obama, are you listening? You know Cuba used to have mansions and a relatively decent economy. They moved from the individual to the collective. Now they're driving '54 Chevys. It's time for another Tea Party. What we are doing in this country will make Thomas Jefferson and Benjamin Franklin roll over in their graves. We're thinking of having a Chicago Tea Party in July, all you capitalists. I'm organizing."

As he spoke, a group of traders formed around him on the trading floor. Capitalists to a man, they cheered the outburst and drowned out the planned transition, extending the segment and creating an indelible TV moment. Within hours, Santelli's rant had gone viral, earning more than a million views on YouTube and countless water-cooler and dinner-table discussions across the country. The frustration that had been building, and which had begun to turn into street action, now had a name. The Tea Party was ready for the national stage.

## Conceived in Liberty

Across the nation, private citizens who had never protested, never agitated, never taken a public political stand were gathering and organizing to make a difference. United by common principles and outraged by the complacence and indifference of their elected leaders, these individuals were ready to do something. Early meetings were filled with entrepreneurs, retirees, school-teachers, civil rights leaders, lawyers, those who had prospered in recent years, and some who had fallen on hard times. All believed that the time to act had come, that their children and grandchildren deserved better and it was up to them to change the course of a nation.

But for all the excitement, the first wave of Tea Party activists faced significant challenges. They were poorly funded. They lacked national organization. They were greeted with skepticism by the political establishment. They included none of the political intelligentsia in their ranks, none of the gatekeepers and message experts and focus group gurus. How could they hope to influence a Congress of incumbent leaders with strong ties to interest groups and well-funded corporate backers? How could they challenge an administration that had swept into the White House with a landslide victory in the presidential campaign?

To many, the answer could be found in another group of unlikely activists who were overmatched and outgunned but fought anyway. Also comprised of ordinary citizens, this group had toppled an entrenched regime that seemed invincible. In fact, it had happened in 1773, right here in America.

. . . History teaches us that nothing could be more American than a protest. What made the opening salvos of the Tea Party movement so jarring to political, academic, and news media observers was its unlikely source—an irate group of citizens from across the political spectrum who were agitating and demanding change. For generations, guerrilla tactics had been a trademark of the Left, best demonstrated in ecoterrorism and virulent antiwar campaigns. Accustomed to Code Pink public disturbance stunts and blood-tossing animal rights' activists, students of political activism had come to understand public protest as left-leaning by definition and reserved for those who were willing to damage public property and disrupt legal activities. Now that middle-class Americans of all backgrounds were taking to the Internet, airwaves, and streets, conventional wisdom was turned on its head and the original Tea Party was seen in a new light. . . .

The spark that ignited the modern Tea Party movement was not just a question of bad economics—it cut to the core of basic American values of individual choice and individual accountability. Millions of Americans were still angry over the new culture of bailouts that had taken Washington by storm since the popping of the housing bubble in 2008 and they were just itching for a fight. They thought that candidate Obama would prove different, having run on a mantra of fiscal responsibility. Regardless of their limited choices at the ballot box, the American people were hungry for accountability, for the American way of doing things.

The entire founding enterprise, including America's Declaration of Independence from the British Crown in 1776 happened only because of the Tea Party ethos, the tradition of rising up against tyranny and taking to the streets in protest. Indeed, the period of American history leading up to the signing of the Declaration is the definitive case study in effective grassroots organization and the power of a committed, organized minority to defeat powerful, entrenched interests.

For any activist who fought in the trenches against Obama's hostile take-over of the health care system, the process that produced the Declaration will sound all too familiar: debate inside the Continental Congress was often dominated by lies, vote buying, and the influence of deep-pocketed business interests enjoying the favored treatment of the executive branch (King George III, that is). Does any of this ring a bell?

How did the advocates of liberty prevail over the entrenched interests and apathetic citizens that might have stifled the efforts of Thomas Jefferson and Benjamin Franklin? The answer, of course, is grassroots activism of citizens outside of the formal political process. The Declaration was radical in principle and revolutionary in practice—sweeping political change driven by a grassroots cadre of committed individuals armed only with their passion and their principles. Politics as usual did not stop them, and neither did lack of popular support. The political momentum for liberty was in large part created by the efforts of citizen patriots from Massachusetts, later joined by men in the other colonies. These so-called Sons of Liberty, led by a struggling entrepreneur named Samuel Adams—yes, the guy on the beer label—used targeted grassroots activism to undercut American support for British rule and create the political conditions that made ratification of the Declaration of Independence and the American Revolution possible.

Speaking truth to power was important, Adams knew, but nothing beat the power of grassroots activism. In the early 1750s Adams began recruiting activists to the cause of liberty, targeting men in taverns and workers in the shipyards and on the streets of Boston. His tactics often involved antitax protests under the Liberty Tree, a large elm across from Boylston Market. Tax collectors were hung in effigy and Crown-appointed governors mocked, belittled, and verbally abused. The Sons of Liberty organized boycotts of British goods and monopolistic practices that were de facto taxes on the colonists. Adams packed town hall meetings at Faneuil Hall, filling the room with patriots so that Tory voices were overwhelmed. Every oppressive new policy handed down by King George and the House of Commons was used to build the ranks of the Sons of Liberty. Taxes imposed by the Stamp Act of 1765,

trade duties created by the Townshend Acts—each was an excuse to rally new recruits to the cause of American independence.

The most famous act of Whig defiance against the Crown—the Boston Tea Party—is now viewed as a tipping point in the battle for American independence. It had a profound impact on public opinion among the uncommitted population. It was not a spontaneous looting by angry tea drinkers but an operation carefully choreographed by Samuel Adams and the Sons of Liberty. When a Parliament-granted monopoly to the East India Trading Company dramatically drove up the price of tea in the colonies, Adams saw an opportunity to channel outrage into action. The "Mohawks" who emptied British tea into Boston Harbor on December 16, 1773, were his activists disguised by Indian war paint to protect their identities from Tory spies. Because property was not destroyed (other than the tea) and the ships' crews not harmed, the Boston Tea Party gave the Sons of Liberty broader public acceptance in the colonies. . . .

. . . The Tea Party is the product of a perfect storm of (1) broken Republican commitments, (2) the aggressive left-wing agenda of a Democratic regime motivated by redistributionist values that are antithetical to the values of most Americans, and (3) technological innovations that allow people to find one another, organize, and get essential information in real time from competitive sources.

We call this complex and diverse movement "beautiful chaos." Or better yet, to borrow Nobel Prize–winning economist F. A. Hayek's weighty notion: "spontaneous order." By this we [refer to] what is now the dominant understanding in organizational management theory: decentralization of personal knowledge is the best way to maximize the contributions of people, their talents, and the total productivity of any enterprise, no matter how big. Let the "leaders" be the regional activists who have the best knowledge of the local personalities and issues. In the real world, this is common sense. In Washington, D.C., this is known as radical. Even dangerous. . . .

. . . When you think about it, a decentralized model for social change is most consistent with the values of independence self-reliance, and personal liberty that embody America. Those activists who gathered at Boston's Old South Meeting House in 1773 knew it. Thomas Jefferson understood this when he wrote, "I would rather be exposed to the inconveniences attending too much liberty than to those attending too small a degree of it."

The big government crowd, on the other hand, is naturally drawn to the compulsion demanded by a centralized authority. They can't imagine an undirected social order. *Someone needs to be in charge.* "We can't give people a choice or they might take it," said Senator Ted Kennedy during a closed-door House–Senate conference committee dealing with health savings accounts.

Big government is audacious. It is conceited. It knows better. Government is, by definition, the means by which you are compelled by force to do that which you would not do voluntarily. Like pay high taxes. Or "purchase," by federal mandate, a government-defined health insurance plan that you cannot afford, do not need, or simply do not want. For the Left, and for today's monolithically liberal Democratic Party, every solution to every perceived problem involves more government: top-down dictates from new laws enforced by new bureaucrats who are presumed to care more and, most important, know better what you need. "I'm from the government, and I'm going to help you whether you want it or not." . . .

Those liberals now in control of our government seem bent on apologizing for the United States, striving to, in the words of Barack Obama, "remake America." They want to remake us to look more like European social democracies. Liberals don't talk about democratic socialism anymore; they prattle on about "social justice." They misuse the phrase. Justice means treating every individual with respect and decency and exactly the same as anyone else is treated under the laws of the land. As best we can tell, "social justice" translates to really wise elected officials (you know, smarter than you) redistributing your hard-earned income to their favored social agendas, all dutifully administered by a well-intentioned bureaucrat. In Europe, this translates into bloated social welfare programs that punish work; massive tax burdens, particularly on the working class through hidden value-added taxes that crush economic expansion; and structural barriers to opportunity for younger generations of have-nots trying to enter the workforce.

The politics of greed is always wrapped in the language of love. When you hear someone go on about social justice, read between the lines. More government control of health care is not really about improving access to health care; it's about controlling your health care.

If you want to comprehend the energy and passion behind the citizen activists who are fighting this corrosive ideology of redistribution, understand this: we believe that America's founders got it right and that Europe got it wrong. America is different because we are all about the individual over the collective. . . .

It is time to take America back. We need to reclaim America from the advocates of big government in both political parties, from the rent-seeking corporations eager to use the power of government to enrich themselves at the expense of consumers and taxpayers, and from the web of left-wing special interests who feed at the public trough and consider it their right to do so.

The political potential of the broad grassroots movement against big government that we are witnessing today should not be underestimated. There is a small-"l" libertarian, commonsense fiscal conservatism out there that transcends partisan definitions. These are independent voters who are united around the idea that government is spending too much money it does not have, and that government is getting involved in things, like controlling health care and running car companies, that it cannot do effectively, and should not try to do at all.

These highly motivated concerns about fiscal issues now represent the very center of electoral opinion among Republicans, most independents, and a growing number of Democrats who have developed buyer's remorse. Today the liberals who control Congress make even Bill Clinton look conservative by comparison and they are scaring Americans with their fiscal lasciviousness. This overreach is the stage upon which to build a revolt. We can take America back from moneyed special interests, leftist advocacy groups, and arrogant politicians. We can stop the monumental legislative threats to our economic liberties. Most important, perhaps, we can do these things by building a national community of activists—organized on the ground and connected online—that will be able to hold the next generation of political leaders, whether they are Democrats or Republicans, accountable for their actions.

The Tea Party is different. Consider the comparable events that led to the political backlash in 1994. That was a voter uprising that too quickly waned when the imminent threat of one-party rule under the Democratic establishment seemed contained. The new activists who had risen up to throw the bums out of power eventually left the playing field again, leaving our political system in the hands of politicians. Left unattended, these politicians, as they all eventually will, returned to tending to their own self-indulgent needs. At best, they became inconvenience-minimizers, eager to compromise for the lesser of two evils. At worst, they grew their own power at the expense of the American people and the fiscal health of our economy. All of the corruptions that followed—the ballooning federal debt, the frenzied spending, the political favors, the bailouts, and the government takeovers—now confront our economy, our futures, and the American way of life built upon freedom, opportunity, and prosperity.

This political boom-and-bust cycle, not unlike the government-generated business cycle that caused the housing bubble and the massive mistakes that went with it, generates periods of accountability followed by years of neglect and an inevitable slip back to business as usual. The problem with this cycle, beyond the policy damage done, is the difficulty in reversing the trend toward more government spending and more government control over our lives. With each new government program, the baseline of total spending is raised, phony budget estimates become very real red ink, and the federal take grows as a percentage of the total private economy. When a constitutional barrier is breached, as happened with the extraordinary ceding of power to an unelected secretary of the treasury under TARP, there is permanent damage done to that constitutional wall that stands between free citizens and a tyrannical government. When informal constraints against hasty legislative actions are torn, as happened with the Democrats' decision to create a massive new health care entitlement through parliamentary chicanery, there is no going back to the way it was before. A future Congress will certainly try to use its new power to enact sweeping legislation with similar tactics, permanently end-running the "cooling off" function the authors of the Constitution envisioned in their design of a deliberative Congress.

The Tea Party movement is rising up because we know we cannot leave public policy to the politicians, or to the "experts," or to someone else with a parochial agenda, a concentrated benefit that comes first, before the public good, and at your expense. The broad community of patriotic citizens that have stood up to take their country back from an unholy alliance of government power and privileged interests are making a difference in ways that defy easy comparisons to the boom and bust of other recent shifts in the political winds. The Tea Party has evolved from political revolt to social movement. We the people are that force more powerful, a force that can save our great nation for future generations.

The establishment doesn't like it one bit. They will kick and scream and throw every possible roadblock in our path.

But we suspect George Washington would love it. He, after all, demanded as much of us. "The preservation of the sacred fire of liberty, and the destiny of the Republi-

can model of government are justly considered as deeply, perhaps as finally staked, on the experiment entrusted to the hands of the American people."

Or, as we like to say, freedom works.

---

**DICK ARMEY** served for 18 years as a Republican Member of the House of Representatives from Texas before becoming the leader of FreedomWorks, one of the earliest groups in the Tea Party movement.

**MATT KIBBE** is President and CEO of FreedomWorks. He has been with the organization for over 13 years. An economist by training, Kibbe is a well-respected national public policy expert, bestselling author, and political commentator. *Newsweek* has called him "one of the masterminds" of Tea Party politics, expertise which has led to frequent appearances on national news shows including FOX News, NBC, ABC News, CNN, MSNBC, FOX Business, PBS, and CSPAN.

**Jill Lepore**

# The Whites of Their Eyes: The Tea Party's Revolution and the Battle over American History

. . . On March 5, 2010, the 240th anniversary of the Boston Massacre, Glenn Beck issued a special Fox News report on "Indoctrination in America": "Tonight, America, I want you to sit down and talk to your kids and hold your kids close to you," he began. "Get the kids out of this indoctrination or our republic will be lost." He was talking about environmentalism and about a lot of other things, too: "Our kids are being brainwashed with the concept of—I've shown it to you before, earth worship. Earth worship. I pledge allegiance to the earth. Social justice. What is social justice? God is being eliminated from the equation entirely." He found occasion to reach back to the Revolution: "Let me give you the words of George Washington, 'It is impossible to rightly govern a nation without God and the Bible.'" Like Hannity, Beck had begun giving history lessons. He outfitted his studio with chalk and a blackboard and even old-fashioned oak school chairs and desks, as if from a one-room schoolhouse. What our children are learning, Beck warned, darkly, is nothing short of learn-to-hate-America lunacy.

. . . From the start, the Tea Party's chief political asset was its name: the echo of the Revolution conferred upon a scattered, diffuse, and confused movement a degree of legitimacy and the appearance, almost, of coherence. Aside from the name and the costume, the Tea Party offered an analogy: rejecting the bailout is like dumping the tea; health care reform is like the Tea Act; our struggle is like theirs. Americans have drawn Revolutionary analogies before. They have drawn them for a very long time. When in doubt, in American politics, left, right, or center, deploy the Founding Fathers. Relying on this sort of analogy, advocates of health care reform could have insisted that, since John Hancock once urged the Massachusetts legislature to raise funds for the erection of lighthouses, he would have supported state health care reform, because, like a lighthouse, health care coverage concerns public safety. That might sound strained, at best, but something quite like it has been tried. In 1798, John Adams signed an "Act for the relief of sick and disabled Seamen": state and later federal government officials collected taxes from shipmasters, which were used to build hospitals and provide medical care for merchant and naval seamen. In the 1940s, health care reformers used this precedent to bolster their case. Government-sponsored health care wasn't un-American, these reformers argued; Adams had thought of it.

That political tradition is long-standing. But the more I looked at the Tea Party, at Beck and Hannity as history teachers, and at the Texas School Board reforms, the more it struck me that the statement at the core of the far right's version of American history went just a bit further. It was more literal than an analogy. It wasn't "our struggle is like theirs." It was "we are there" or "they are here." The unanswered question of the Bicentennial was, "What ails the American spirit?" Antihistory has no patience for ambiguity, self-doubt, and introspection. The Tea Party had an answer: "We have forsaken the Founding Fathers." Political affiliates are, by nature, motley. But what the Tea Party, Beck and Hannity, and the Texas School Board shared was a set of assumptions about the relationship between the past and the present that was both broadly anti-intellectual and, quite specifically, anti-historical, not least because it defies chronology, the logic of time. To say that we are there, or the Founding Fathers are here, or that we have forsaken them and they're rolling over in their graves because of the latest, breaking political development—the election of the United States' first African American president, for instance—is to subscribe to a set of assumptions about the relationship between the past and the present stricter, even, than the strictest form of constitutional originalism, a set of assumptions that, conflating originalism, evangelicalism, and heritage tourism, amounts to a variety of fundamentalism.

Historical fundamentalism is marked by the belief that a particular and quite narrowly defined past—"the founding"—is ageless and sacred and to be worshipped; that certain historical texts—"the founding documents"—are to be read in the same spirit with which religious fundamentalists read, for instance, the Ten Commandments; that the Founding Fathers were divinely inspired; that the academic study of history (whose standards of evidence and methods of analysis are based on skepticism) is a conspiracy and, furthermore, blasphemy; and that political arguments grounded in appeals to the founding documents, as sacred texts, and to the Founding Fathers, as prophets, are therefore incontrovertible.

The past haunts us all. Just how is a subject of this book. But time moves forward, not backward. Chronology is like gravity. Nothing falls up. We cannot go back to the eighteenth century, and the Founding Fathers are not, in fact, here with us today. They weren't even called the Founding Fathers until Warren G. Harding coined that phrase in his keynote address at the Republican National Convention in 1916. Harding also invoked the Founding Fathers during his inauguration in 1921—"Standing in this presence, mindful of the solemnity of this occasion, feeling the emotions which no one may know until he senses the great weight of responsibility for himself, I must utter my belief in the divine inspiration of the founding fathers"—in what is quite possibly the worst inaugural address ever written. . . .

The Founding Fathers haven't been rolling over in their graves for very long, either. Not one was roused from his eternal slumber with any regularity until about the time that Harding called the founders our fathers (and, more particularly, his) and said they were divinely inspired (which had the curious effect of granting to his presidency something akin to the divine right of kings). . . .

On March 20, 2010, the day before the U.S. House of Representatives was scheduled to vote on the health care bill, the Boston Tea Party held an Anti-Obamacare rally in front of Faneuil Hall. A few dozen people turned up. Most carried signs: "The Constitution SPEAKS." Some waved flags of thirteen stars. Acolytes of Ayn Rand urged, "READ ATLAS SHRUGGED." Christen Varley told a woman who showed up with a Hitler sign to leave. The place was bustling with tourists on their way to shop at Quincy Market. Austin Hess, wearing his tricorn and a mock–Obama campaign T-shirt that read NOPE instead of HOPE, summed up his objectives for the Tea Party movement: "I want to replace the current political establishment, get all incumbents out and replace them with fiscal conservatives who will abide by the Constitution."

Hess had moved to Massachusetts from Virginia three years before. "We're trying to get back to what the founders had," he told me. "We're trying to bring people back to Boston's roots. Liberty above all." A nurse from Worcester who grew up in the Midwest and was registered as an Independent explained what getting back to those eighteenth-century roots meant to her: "I don't want the government giving money to people who don't want to work. Government is for the post office, and to defend our country, and maybe for the roads. That's all."

"The history of our revolution will be one continued lye from one end to the other," Johns Adams once predicted. He was right to worry. In every nation, as in every family, some stories are remembered, others are forgotten, and there are always some stories too painful to tell. Adams expected that the Revolution, a messy, sprawling, decades-long affair, would, over time, be shortened and simplified. In the national imagination, the Revolu-

tion is a fable. Much of what most people picture when they think about the Revolution comes from the world of juvenilia—*Johnny Tremain,* paper dolls, elementary school art projects, and family vacations—which isn't surprising, and wouldn't be a problem, except that every history of a nation's founding makes an argument about the nature of its government. . . .

On Sunday, March 21, 2010, the U.S. House of Representatives passed the health care bill, in a vote that fell along partisan lines. All but 34 Democrats voted for it, and all 178 Republicans voted against it. On Monday, eleven state attorneys general announced a plan to challenge the law as a violation of state sovereignty. Across the country, there followed scattered threats of violence against legislators who had voted in favor of the bill and against the president who signed it into law on Tuesday, by which time there had already been talk of nullification.

The next night, I met Austin Hess and Kat Malone at the Warren Tavern in Charlestown. The tavern, built in 1784, was named after Dr. Joseph Warren, who died in the Battle of Bunker Hill, and was just a cobbled street away from Monument Square, where a granite obelisk commemorated the patriots who died alongside him. We sat near the bar, beneath a dark ceiling of massive oak timbers. Tin lanterns hung from the wall. Hess took off his tricornered hat and set it down on the table between us. Malone was quiet. Hess was frustrated. "I have recently started a committee to elect the corpse of Calvin Coolidge," he said, "because anyone's better than Obama." He was dismayed by the vote, but he was also, as always, courteous and equable. "It's the law of the land now, so, it's up to us to blunt its impact and overturn it if we can." The vote, and House Speaker Nancy Pelosi's maneuvering around a potential filibuster made possible by Brown's election to the Senate, had deepened Hess's conviction about the aptness of his analogy. "One of the things people like to say about us is that they like to think that we don't know what we're talking about, that we don't know what the tea party was about. But to the people who say we have taxation with representation, I would just say that they should look to the bill that just passed. We sent Scott Brown to Washington to kill this bill, but the people in Washington did everything they could to thwart the will of the people, and especially the people of Massachusetts. How is my voice being represented?" . . .

"I really feel like this is a modern-day Intolerable Act," Austin Hess said, about the new health care law, when we met at the Warren Tavern. Every time Hess talked about the Intolerable Acts, I got to thinking about the limits of tolerance, tolerance of racial equality, of religious diversity, of same-sex marriage, of a global economy, of democracy, of pluralism, of change. Hess labored in a world of uneasy alliances. I asked him if he was troubled by Christen Varley's work with the Coalition for Marriage and the Family. "We do not discuss social issues and foreign policy issues," he said. He was frustrated that journalists kept getting the Tea Party wrong. Hess's girlfriend was black. He was tired of people calling the movement racist. "I will simply say this," he e-mailed me. "I know what is in my heart."

In 2010, nationwide polls reported that people who identified themselves as sympathetic with the Tea Party were overwhelmingly white, although estimates varied, and the Tea Party didn't appear to be much whiter than, say, the Republican Party. Whatever else had drawn people into the movement—the bailout, health care, taxes, Fox News, and, above all, the economy—some of it, for some people, was probably discomfort with the United States' first black president, because he was black. But it wasn't the whiteness of the Tea Party that I found most striking. It was the whiteness of their Revolution. The Founding Fathers were the whites of their eyes, a fantasy of an America before race, *without* race. There were very few black people in the Tea Party, but there were no black people at all in the Tea Party's eighteenth century. Nor, for that matter, were there any women, aside from Abigail Adams, and no slavery, poverty, ignorance, insanity, sickness, or misery. Nor was there any art, literature, sex, pleasure, or humor. There were only the Founding Fathers with their white wigs, wearing their three-cornered hats, in their Christian nation, revolting against taxes, and defending their right to bear arms. . . .

The scholarship academic historians have written since the 1960s, uncovering the lives of ordinary people and examining conflict among groups and especially races, sexes, classes, and nations, was not without substantial shortcomings. Critics, both within and outside the academy, had charged scholars of American history not only with an inability to write for general readers and an unwillingness to examine the relationship between the past and the present, but also with a failure to provide a narrative synthesis, to tell a big story instead of many little ones. Those criticisms were warranted. They were also criticisms academic historians had made of themselves. Scholars criticize and argue—and must, and can—because scholars share a common set of ideas about how to argue, and what counts as evidence. But the far right's American history—its antihistory—existed outside of argument and had no interest in evidence. It was much a fiction as the Lost Cause of the Confederacy, reductive, unitary, and, finally, dangerously antipluralist. It erased slavery from American history and compressed a quarter century of political contest into "the founding," as if ideas worked out, over decades of debate and fierce disagreement, were held by everyone, from the start. "Who's your favorite Founder?" Glenn Beck asked Sarah Palin. "Um, you know, well," she said. "All of them."

There was, though, something heartbreaking in all this. Behind the Tea Party's Revolution lay nostalgia for an imagined time—the 1950s, maybe, or the 1940s—less riven by strife, less troubled by conflict, less riddled with ambiguity, less divided by race. In that nostalgia was the remembrance of childhood, a yearning for a common past, bulwark against a divided present, comfort against

an uncertain future. "History is not a dry academic subject for us," as Hess put it. "It is our heritage." . . .

The National Center for Constitutional Studies was started in Utah in 1967, to promote originalism, the idea that the original intent of the framers is knowable and fixed and the final word. When the framers were still alive, people who wanted to know what they meant, by, say, a particular phrase, couldn't really ask them. Delegates to the Constitutional Convention pledged themselves to secrecy. And the more time passed, the remoter the Revolution, the more inscrutable the documents (even the meaning of the *words* changed), the greater the distance between now and then, the more demanding the act of interpretation. In 1816, when Jefferson was seventy-three, many of his Revolutionary generation having already died, he offered this answer, when asked what the framers would suggest about how to deal with this problem. "This they would say themselves, were they to rise from the dead": "laws and institutions must go hand in hand with the progress of the human mind." (To paraphrase the historian Carl Becker, the question the Enlightenment asked was not, "What would our forefathers do?" but "How can we make society better?") Jefferson put it this way: "Some men look at constitutions with sanctimonious reverence, and deem them like the ark of the covenant, too sacred to be touched. They ascribe to the men of the preceding age a wisdom more than human." In Federalist 14, Madison asked, "Is it not the glory of the people of America, that, whilst they have paid a decent regard to the opinions of former times and other nations, they have not suffered a blind veneration for antiquity, for custom, or for names, to overrule the suggestions of their own good sense, the knowledge of their own situation, and the lessons of their own experience?" The founders were not prophets. Nor did they hope to be worshipped. They believed that to defer without examination to what your forefathers believed is to become a slave to the tyranny of the past. . . .

Precisely what the founders believed about God, Jesus, sin, the Bible, churches, and hell is probably impossible to discover. They changed their minds and gave different accounts to different people: Franklin said one thing to his sister, Jane, and another thing to David Hume; Washington prayed with his troops, but, while he lay slowly dying, he declined to call for a preacher. This can make them look like hypocrites, but that's unfair, as are a great many attacks on these men. They approached religion more or less the same way they approached everything else that interested them: Franklin invented his own, Washington proved diplomatic, Adams grumbled about it (he hated Christianity, he once said, but he couldn't think of anything better, and he also regarded it as necessary), Jefferson could not stop tinkering with it, and Madison defended, as a natural right, the free exercise of it. That they wanted to preserve religious liberty by separating church and state does not mean they were irreligious. They wanted to protect religion from the state, as much as the other way around.

Nevertheless, if the founders had followed their fore-fathers, they would have written a Constitution establishing Christianity as the national religion. Nearly every British North American colony was settled with an established religion; Connecticut's 1639 charter explained that the whole purpose of government was "to mayntayne and presearve the liberty and purity of the gospel of our Lord Jesus." In the century and a half between the Connecticut charter and the 1787 meeting of the Constitutional Convention lies an entire revolution, not just a political revolution but also a religious revolution. Following the faith of their fathers is exactly what the framers did not do. At a time when all but two states required religious tests for office, the Constitution prohibited them. At a time when all but three states still had an official religion, the Bill of Rights forbade the federal government from establishing one.

Originalism in the courts is controversial, to say the least. Jurisprudence stands on precedent, on the stability of the laws, but originalism is hardly the only way to abide by the Constitution. Setting aside the question of whether it makes good law, it is, generally, lousy history. And it has long since reached well beyond the courts. Set loose in the culture, and tangled together with fanaticism, originalism looks like history, but it's not; it's historical fundamentalism, which is to history what astrology is to astronomy, what alchemy is to chemistry, what creationism is to evolution.

In eighteenth-century America, I wouldn't have been able to vote. I wouldn't have been able to own property, either. I'd very likely have been unable to write, and, if I survived childhood, chances are that I'd have died in childbirth. And, no matter how long or short my life, I'd almost certainly have died without having once ventured a political opinion preserved in any historical record, except that none of these factors has any meaning or bearing whatsoever on whether an imaginary eighteenth-century me would have supported the Obama administration's stimulus package or laws allowing the carrying of concealed weapons or the war in Iraq, because I did not live in eighteenth-century America, and no amount of thinking that I could, not even wearing petticoats, a linsey-woolsey calico smock, and a homespun mobcap, can make it so. Citizens and their elected officials have all sorts of reasons to support or oppose all sorts of legislation and government action, including constitutionality, precedence, and the weight of history. But it's possible to cherish the stability of the law and the durability of the Constitution, as amended over two and a half centuries of change and one civil war, and tested in the courts, without dragging the Founding Fathers from their graves. To point this out neither dishonors the past nor relieves anyone of the obligation to study it. To the contrary.

"What would the founders do?" is, from the point of view of historical analysis, an ill-considered and unanswerable question, and pointless, too. Jurists and legislators need to investigate what the framers meant, and some Christians make moral decisions by wondering what Jesus would do, but no NASA scientist decides what to do about the Hubble by asking what Isaac Newton would make of it. People who ask what the founders would do quite commonly declare that they know, they know, they just know what the founders would do and, mostly, it comes to this: if only they could see us now, they would be rolling over in their graves. They might even rise from the dead and walk among us. We have failed to obey their sacred texts, holy writ. They suffered for us, and we have forsaken them. Come the Day of Judgment, they will damn us.

That's not history. It's not civil religion, the faith in democracy that binds Americans together. It's not originalism or even constitutionalism. That's fundamentalism.

---

**JILL LEPORE** is a Professor of American History at Harvard University and a regular contributor to *The New Yorker*; and the author of *A Is for American*, a study of language and politics in America's first century.

# EXPLORING THE ISSUE

## Does the Tea Party Represent a Revival of America's Revolutionary Ideals?

### Critical Thinking and Reflection

1. What does the Tea Party movement stand for in American national politics?
2. Are parallels with the Boston Tea Party justified or unjustified?
3. Is the Tea Party more likely to win over independent voters than traditional Republican leadership?
4. What impact do you believe the Tea Party played in the governemnt shutdown in October 2013?
5. What do you believe will be the long-term impact of the Tea Party on American politics?

### Is There Common Ground?

There is no basis for common ground between those who are persuaded that there is one true meaning of the American constitutional system and those who maintain that the convictions of the Founding Fathers are open to differing interpretations. This has the potential to make the ideological opposition of the major parties more divisive, leaving little or no room for compromise. At the same time, there is a similar resentment of what is characterized as the "bailout of *Wall Street*" on the part of both much of the Tea Party movement and the radical sentiment that led to the Occupy Wall Street sit-ins. Whether this convergence of views can go further is doubtful in view of the basic distinction between the radical support for liberal government intervention in other areas and the adamant Tea Party opposition to taxation and any substantial government role in dealing with economic issues.

The more interesting common ground question will likely have to be answered within the Republican Party, where pragamtists, social conservatives, and libertarians will need to determine whether they are capable of collectivizing efforts behind a single candidate prior to the 2016 presidential election. As was made clear in 2012, a fractured Republican base leads to a long, drawn out primary process that ultimately leads the GOP nominee beating, battered, and vulnerable upon entering a general election. While all three legs of the party seem to agree on the fundamental sense of constitutional liberty, the next four years will determine whether the Mitch McConnells and Ted Cruzes of the Republican Party can get along well enough to move the interests of the party as a whole forward.

### Create Central

www.mhhe.com/createcentral

### Additional Resources

William J. Miller and Jeremy D. Walling, *Tea Party Effects on 2010 U.S. Senate Elections: Stuck in the Middle to Lose* (Lexington, 2011)

Christopher S. Parker and Matt A. Barreto, *Change They Can't Believe In: The Tea Party and Reactionary Politics in America* (Princeton University Press, 2013)

Scott Rasmussen and Doug Schoen, *Mad as Hell: How the Tea Party Movement Is Fundamentally Remaking Our Two-Party System* (Harper, 2010)

Theda Skocpol and Vanessa Williamson, *The Tea Party and the Remaking of American Conservatism* (Oxford University Press, 2012)

Kate Zernike, *Boiling Mad: Inside Tea Party America* (Times Book, 2010)

# *Internet References . . .*

**FreedomWorks**

www.freedomworks.org

**New York Times/CBS News Poll: National Survey of Tea Party Supporters**

http://documents.nytimes.com/new-york-timescbs
-news-poll-national-survey-of-tea-party-supporters

**Tea Party**

www.teaparty.org/

**Tea Party Express**

www.teapartyexpress.org/

**Tea Party Patriots**

www.teapartypatriots.org/

**Selected, Edited, and with Issue Framing Material by:**
William J. Miller, *Flagler College*
George McKenna, *City College, City University of New York*
**and**
Stanley Feingold, *City College, City University of New York*

# ISSUE

## Is Bigger Government Better Government?

**YES: Jeff Madrick,** from *The Case for Big Government* (Princeton University Press, 2008)

**NO: David Boaz,** from "The Return of Big Government," *Cato Policy Report* (January/February 2009)

---

### Learning Outcomes

**After reading this issue, you will be able to:**

- Discuss the benefits of government expansion.
- Assess the weaknesses of limited government.
- Describe the economic benefits of government.
- Discuss the role of libertarian ideals in American society.
- Analyze how the size of government has impacted the current economic crisis.

---

### ISSUE SUMMARY

**YES:** Humanities Professor Jeff Madrick surveys the numerous government interventions in the economy since the end of World War II and concludes that they have been essential to America's growth and well-being.

**NO:** Executive Vice President of the Cato Institue David Boaz traces America's libertarian traditions and reminds readers that there are times where government's best course of action is simply deciding to do nothing.

A continuing debate about government runs through the course of American history. The debate is between those who see government as an instrument for doing good versus those who see it as a potentially oppressive institution. Those who take the latter view usually concede that, yes, we do need government for strictly limited purposes—but, in the words of Thomas Paine, government "even in its best state, is but a necessary evil."

Paine wrote those words in 1776, when America was still governed by a foreign nation. Does the situation change when a nation becomes self-governed? Alexander Hamilton thought so. Hamilton fought fiercely against the imperial government of Great Britain, but once American independence was achieved he became a champion of what he called "energetic" government, a term that included the pursuit of public programs aimed at increasing the nation's prosperity. He helped create the first federally owned Bank of the United States, encouraged the government to subsidize domestic industries, and even experimented with government-owned mills in New Jersey. Opposing him was Secretary of State Thomas Jefferson. Jefferson wanted government to stay out of the domestic economy.

Despite the protestations of Jefferson and those who followed him, government became increasingly energetic during the nineteenth century. Though Andrew Jackson killed the rechartering of the Bank of the United States with his presidential veto, the federal government passed tariffs and financed the building of roads, canals, and railroads; during and after the Civil War federal power expanded into areas such as civil rights and higher education, areas once reserved to the states. By the close of the nineteenth century, government began tentatively moving into the areas of social welfare and business regulation—though not without resistance.

In the twentieth century, government growth expanded during World War I, contracted in the 1920s, and exploded during the years of President Franklin Roosevelt, 1933–1945. A host of "alphabet" bureaucracies (e.g., WPA, PWA, NLRB, NRA, and so on) were created, government spending increased to unprecedented levels, and new entitlement programs such as Social Security and Aid to the Families of Dependent Children (AFDC) were created. During this period the terms "liberal" and "conservative" crystallized into descriptions of the two sides in the debate: liberals were those who championed government activism and conservatives were those resisting it. Today, almost 70 years later, "liberal" and "conservative" still work reasonably well, at least in the economic sphere, as thumbnail labels for those who favor government and those who don't.

Liberals and conservatives have won some and lost some since the end of the 1940s. President Dwight Eisenhower was a moderate conservative, yet it was under his administration that the Federal-Aid Highway Act was passed, which put the federal government into the business of financing the construction of 41,000 miles of instate highways throughout the nation; Eisenhower also established a new cabinet department, Health, Education and Welfare (later renamed the Department of Health and Human Services).

During President Lyndon Johnson's term, 1964–1968, the largest expansion of the federal government since the Roosevelt administration took place. Johnson boldly declared an "unconditional war on poverty." He created a variety of new federal agencies to teach job skills, stimulate community action, and dispense welfare. He pushed Medicaid and Medicare through Congress, and led Congress in passing new civil rights laws.

During Ronald Reagan's administration there was a serious challenge in the White House to liberal economic programs. The number of pages added to the *Federal Register*, which records the rules and regulations issued by federal agencies, declined each year of Reagan's presidency, breaking a sharp increase since 1960. The centerpiece of his economic program was his tax cuts, enacted in 1981, which lowered the top personal tax bracket from 70 to 28 percent in seven years. Reagan failed, however, to lower government expenditures, and the deficit soared.

What many conservative Americans today seem to be clamoring for is right-sized government. This type of government performs all functions necessary to protect life, liberty, and property of citizens. The word necessary is the key. Only those things that individuals are incapable of doing themselves should government step in to perform. Government should be practicing concerted constraint

to not become an aggressor against its citizens or compel them to do things that they either would not choose to do or would prefer not to do.

Yet conservatives who strongly disagree with Barack Obama's alleged government expansion seem to not realize how many layers of government President George W. Bush brought to the federal government through the creation of the Department of Homeland Security. Going directly against the ideals of Reagan, Bush chose to increase spending and employment in the name of security. While everything was on the table in the aftermath of September 11, the new Cabinet-level department will continue to require significant federal investments for as long as it exists.

Today's conservatives have made Reagan's approach their model, while liberals seek to build on Franklin Roosevelt's legacy. The Obama administration's decision to mandate individuals to have health insurance, first proposed as a form of universal health care by President Harry Truman in 1945, rests on assumptions about government broadly shared by liberals since Roosevelt's time but whose philosophical roots can be traced to Alexander Hamilton. Yet again, whether one believes government is inherently good or bad seemingly follows Miles' Law. Those who see the benefit of government (or who personally benefit) will be the most likely to stand up and call for expansion. Perhaps this is the great irony of American politics today. The Tea Party movement has been shown to have a significant number of elderly support. The same folks who are clamoring for government to cease to exist would also like government to keep its hands off of their Medicare. Who ever said that citizens must be consistent?

Professor Jeff Madrick takes the liberal view that activist government has done much to enhance the quality of life and increase American prosperity. However, David Boaz, of the Cato Institute, traces America's libertarian traditions and reminds readers that there are times where government's best course of action is simply deciding to do nothing—no matter how difficult this can be to admit.

# YES ↵

**Jeff Madrick**

# The Case for Big Government

After World War II, almost all economists feared a reprise of the Depression. It was hard to imagine what could replace all the lost military demand. But the opposite occurred. After a pause in 1947, the economy grew as rapidly on average as it ever did before, and the incomes of most working Americans grew faster than ever before. The progressive turn of policy, despite a resurgence of antigovernment sensibility, did not deter growth. Nor did higher income tax rates, which were raised by Roosevelt during the Depression and were raised again to record levels during World War II, where they remained for more than a decade. The highest tax bracket reached approximately 90 percent, where it remained until 1964. To the contrary, bigger government seemed to go along with ever faster growth. Roosevelt had proposed a G.I. Bill of Rights in 1943, among other things, to provide aid for veterans to go to college and to buy a house. Congress raised objections, but in 1944 the G.I. Bill was passed. By the late 1950s, half of the returning sixteen million soldiers financed college or other training programs as a result. Millions of mortgages were guaranteed. The nation was thus directed in a particular way. The Marshall Plan under President Truman, and named after the secretary of state who strongly advocated it, provided billion of dollars of aid to rebuild Europe.

Dwight Eisenhower, as a former president, incurred the ire of the Republican right wing by proposing to expand Social Security coverage to another ten million workers—to include farm workers and professionals such as teachers, accountants, and dentists. He also increased benefits. Eisenhower said that it was simply clear that not all could save enough for retirement. Eisenhower also advocated the development and federal financing of a national highway system. He had strong support from the major auto companies, of course, and the bill passed in 1956. By the late 1950s, 90 percent of all homes in America were reachable by road, and often by highway. It was an explicit case of national government coordination and investment that deeply influenced the development of the nation into a new geography of suburbs, based on cheap gas, cheap property, and mostly free roads.

In these decades, the federal government financed and administered the antipolio vaccines. In the wake of the Soviet launch of the first space satellite, Sputnik, Congress passed the National Defense Education Act, providing billions of dollars of annual grants and loans to support higher education, technical training, and other educational programs. Young people were further spurred to go to college. The National Institutes of Health, as an extension of late nineteenth-century government investment in health research, were expanded dramatically after World War II, and accounted for a high proportion of medical breakthroughs. Research and development (R&D) was undertaken in many federal agencies, not least the Defense Department, where the Internet had its origins. The federal government accounted for most of America's R&D, in fact, through the 1960s, topping out at 67 percent of all such research in 1963. Many economists contend that such intense research efforts account for greater American economic superiority in these years than any other single factor. The Supreme Court under Eisenhower, led by Johnson's appointee as chief justice, Earl Warren, ordered that public schools be integrated.

In the 1960s, President Johnson passed Medicare and implemented his War on Poverty, including health care for the poor under Medicaid. Regulatory changes were significant, and included landmark civil rights legislation, which protected voting rights for blacks, ended Jim Crow laws once and for all, and forbade gender and racial discrimination in labor markets. Other regulatory reforms involved cigarettes, packaging, motor vehicle safety, consumer credit, and the expansion of the authority of the Food and Drug Administration.

Between 1948 and 1970, the share of spending in GDP by the federal, state, and local governments rose from 16.5 percent to 27.5 percent, nearly eleven percentage points. Most of this increase was in social expenditures. Yet productivity, wages, and overall GDP grew very rapidly, as noted. What is the complaint then in light of all this success? It is hard to escape the conclusion as noted earlier in this section that government did not hurt but significantly helped economies to grow.

## The Economic Benefits of Government

. . . Few economists disagree with the theory that some measure of public investment in infrastructure, education, and health care is necessary. Because public goods such as roads and schools benefit society overall more than any individual or business, such investment would not have been adequately undertaken by private firms. . . .

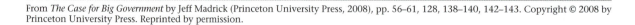

Government support is required for primary education, roads, and the poor.

Far less frequently discussed is the fact that government can be the focus of needed and useful coordination. When railroads used different size track (gauge), government was needed to standardize them. By organizing communities to use a single public water system, government creates economies of scale for such a public good. The highway system was an immense act of coordination that probably couldn't have been attained through a private network; there is no example of one in the world, in any case. The system of international trade and currency valuation is a government-led example of coordination.

Similarly, regulations can and often do make economies work better. They can make information about products and services more open. They can reduce corruption, monopolistic pricing, and anticompetitive policies regarding research, innovation, and new products. They can temper financial speculation, which distorts the flow of capital toward inefficient uses and can often lead to costly corrections and serious recessions, as occurred yet again in 2008.

Some regulations can be poorly administered and reduce economic efficiency. Others will outlive their usefullness; they should be pruned and streamlined over time. But other regulations will be a short-term cost to business that the nation chooses to bear for quality of life and even a better economy. Maintaining the safety of products that consumers cannot judge for themselves is an example; but the safety and effectiveness of products also makes consumers more confident buyers of products. Environmental regulations adopted in the early 1970s have probably been costly to all of us, but they are a cost we bear for cleaner air and water and the diminution of global warming. It is no cause for alarm that regulations have multiplied as the economy supplies so many more goods and services to the people. As economies change and grow more complex, it is only natural that more oversight is needed.

At the still more liberal end of the political spectrum, some economists will argue—though not the American mainstream—that programs that help raise and make wages more equal, such as laws that facilitate union organizing, minimum wages, and equal rights, may well aid economic growth, not undermine productivity, by creating demand for goods and services, and also reinforcing faith in workers that they will be fairly rewarded for their effort. . . .

One of the key benefits of the larger post–World War II government, if in some quarters still a controversial one, is also that it makes the economy more stable. Well before Keynes's work during the Depression there were calls for government spending to create jobs and support incomes. Massive public works projects that reignited economic growth, such as Baron Hausmann's rebuilding of Paris, are common in history. But in the post–World War II era, such activities gained new theoretical justification from Keynes's theories. Both Keynesian liberals and some

Friedmanite conservatives accepted, to one degree or another, that fiscal and monetary policy—deficit spending by the treasury or the adjustment of interest rates by the central bank—could help avoid or ameliorate recessions and thereby raise the rate of growth over time. A large government is itself, despite conservative arguments cited earlier, a bulwark against rapidly declining spending. Unemployment insurance, Social Security, and government employment itself are stabilizing factors.

If the size of government truly and directly caused the inflation of the 1970s and contributed demonstrably to slower economic growth, it would be reason for concern. But we have seen that it did not in the United States, and nations with far larger governments have produced neither more rapid inflation nor substandard levels of income for their citizens. The public goods and social programs of many countries—from Sweden and Norway to France and Germany—are significantly more generous than America's. . . .

In fact, enlightened regulation has been imperative for economic growth at least since Jefferson's policies for governing the distribution of land. When done well, regulation keeps competition honest and free, enables customers to know and understand the products they receive, and fosters new ideas. When neglected, abuse becomes easy, information in markets is suppressed, capital investment is channeled to wasteful and inefficient uses, and dangerous excesses occur. The open flow of products and services information is critical to a free-market economy. The conditions for healthy competition have simply not been maintained under a free-market ideology of minimal government that professes great faith in competition. Competition requires government oversight; the wool has been pulled over our eyes.

We now know the following. If federal, state, and local governments absorb roughly 35 percent of GDP in America, rather than the current roughly 30 percent, it will not inhibit growth and undermine entrepreneurial spirits, productivity, or prosperity if the spending is well-channeled. Government absorbs much more of national income in other nations whose prosperity is the equivalent of or perhaps superior to America's. In European nations, government spending absorbs approximately 40 percent of all spending, and standards of living are high. If government programs are managed well, they will on balance enhance productivity. A rise to 35 percent will raise approximately $700 billion a year to the federal, state, and local governments to provide protections to workers, finance social programs, maintain an adequate regulatory presence, and raise significantly the level of investment in transportation, energy, education, and health care. Part and perhaps all of this $700 billion can be paid for with higher taxes. . . .

. . . The most productive way to address rising global competition is not trade restrictions per se but for the government to invest in the nation. Consumer spending leaks to foreign imports and business investment leaks across borders. But potential returns to the economy from spending on transportation projects are at this point significant, partly due to years of neglect, and the jobs created to implement them largely stay at home. The proportion of the federal budget spent on investment in the nation—including transportation, science, technology, and energy—are well down from the levels of the 1970s. Federal spending on education as a proportion of GDP fell under Clinton but was raised under his successor, George Bush, and it remains slightly higher as a proportion of GDP than it was in the 1970s. Overall, public investment equaled nearly 3 percent of GDP in the 1970s, which would come to more than $400 billion today. Under Clinton it fell to half of that proportion, and under Bush it rose but remains at less than 2 percent of GDP. Merely raising it to 1970s levels would produce $140 billion more a year to spend. To reemphasize, such spending usually creates domestic jobs and builds future productivity at the same time.

To take one estimate, a House Transportation Committee report cites a Federal Highway Administration model that claims that a $75 billion investment will create more than 3.5 million jobs and $464 billion in additional nationwide sales. Every $1 billion, in other words, yields 47,500 jobs and an other $6 billion in sales. Spending has been so inadequate that such estimates can be accepted confidently. The Society of Civil Engineers suggest that much of America's infrastructure should get a grade of D. While these studies are hardly definitive, they are suggestive of the possibilities.

The most exciting potential returns are for high-quality pre-K education. A wide range of studies has been undertaken on several high-quality programs that have long been underway in the United States. The benefits of such programs include not only improving the ability of children to learn, but also long-term reduction in crime rates, reduced need for special education and repeating grades, and lower welfare enrollment rates. A conventional conservative economist such as James Heckman, a Nobel laureate who opposes college subsidies, nevertheless favors significant funding of preschool programs. Some estimate these programs create benefits that exceed costs by five to ten times. A highly sophisticated recent analysis by two economists estimates that if a high-quality program was

instituted nationwide, the federal moneys spent would be fully paid for in increased tax revenues due to improved incomes and would reduce welfare, crime, and special education expenses. In other words, it would pay for itself. . . .

As a consequence of neglect and change, an adequate agenda for America is a lengthy one, but it is not an antigrowth agenda. It favors growth. Growing personal income is more necessary to a full life than is recognized, in part because the cost of some key needs rise very fast, in part because a wealthy society can finance innovation, and in part because a wealthy populace will find it easier and more congenial to pay for communal needs through taxes. But for too long, mainstream economists have accepted the notion that more savings and technology will alone lead to faster growth. The agenda for government is therefore inappropriately limited; government spending, for example, will allegedly erode savings. America has been able to test this economic philosophy for a full generation and it has failed. Years of below-par productivity growth, low and stagnating wages, inattention to basic needs, persistent poverty, and the undermining of assets necessary to future growth, including education, health care, energy alternatives, and transportation infrastructure are the consequences.

The gap between a growing economy and falling wages is the major contemporary mystery. Global competition and off-shoring may explain part of the gap, but the trend began decades ago. Research shows that a gap in worker compensation and productivity began to open up slowly in the late 1980s: typical workers got less than their historical share, while capital (profits) and high-income workers got more. This gap widened explosively in the 2000s.

Furthermore, there was little explanation as to why male incomes in particular fared especially poorly over this long period we have described. A major reason is the withdrawal of government from its traditional purposes.

---

**JEFF MADRICK** is the editor of *Challenge* magazine, the author of *The End of Affluence* (1995) and other books, a frequent contributor to *The New York Review of Books*, and a Visiting Professor of Humanities at The Cooper Union in New York.

**David Boaz**  **NO**

# The Return of Big Government

It's been a long time since a U.S. election generated feelings of actual joy beyond the ranks of partisan activists. If Barack Obama hasn't yet ushered in a new "era of good feelings," all Americans can take pride in the demise of yet another glass ceiling in a nation conceived in liberty and dedicated to the proposition that all of us are created equal, entitled to the inalienable rights of life, liberty, and the pursuit of happiness.

Indeed, we can take some satisfaction in observing that something normal happened: A party that had given Americans a long war and an economic crisis, led by a strikingly unpopular president, was defeated. Republican government requires that failed parties be turned out of office. The American Founders believed firmly in the principle of rotation in office. They thought that even successful officeholders should go back home to live under the laws after a short period in office. No doubt more members of the 110th Congress would have been given that privilege were it not for the vast incumbent protection complex of laws and regulations and subsidies.

George W. Bush and the Republicans promised choice, freedom, reform, and a restrained federal government. As far back as the Contract with America in 1994, congressional Republicans pledged "the end of government that is too big, too intrusive, and too easy with the public's money." But over the past eight years they delivered massive overspending, the biggest expansion of entitlements in 40 years, centralization of education, a war that has lasted longer than World War II, an imperial presidency, civil liberties abuses, the intrusion of the federal government into social issues and personal freedoms, and finally a $700 billion bailout of Wall Street that just kept on growing in the last month of the campaign. Voters who believe in limited government had every reason to reject that record.

At the Cato Institute we stand firmly on the principles of the Declaration of Independence and the Constitution, and on the bedrock American values of individual liberty, limited government, free markets, and peace. And throughout our 32 years we have been willing to criticize officials of both parties when they sought to take the country in another direction. We published papers critical of President Clinton's abuse of executive authority, his administration's misguided antitrust policies, his nation-building experiments, and his unwillingness to take on corporate welfare. Our analysts were among the first to

point out the Bush administration's profligate spending, as well as the administration's policies on executive power, habeas corpus, privacy, expansion of entitlements, the federal marriage amendment, and the misbegotten war in Iraq.

But we have also been pleased to work with administrations of both parties when they seek to expand freedom or limit government—with the Clinton administration on free trade, welfare reform, and a few tentative steps toward Social Security reform; with the Bush administration on tax cuts, the initial response to the 9/11 attacks, health savings accounts, immigration reform, and Social Security accounts. We look forward to opportunities to work with the Obama administration when it moves to reverse the worst mistakes of the Bush years or otherwise to advance policies that would enhance peace, freedom, and prosperity.

## The Current Crisis

In the current economic crisis, our first task is to understand it and its causes. This was a crisis caused by regulation, subsidization, and intervention, and it won't be cured by more of the same. Christopher Hitchens had a point when he wrote, "There are many causes of the subprime and derivative horror show that has destroyed our trust in the idea of credit, but one way of defining it would be to say that everybody was promised everything, and almost everybody fell for the populist bait."

The backdrop is central banking and implicit federal guarantees for risky behavior. The Federal Reserve Board creates money and adjusts interest rates, so any notion that our financial system was an example of laissez-faire fails at the start. Meanwhile, Congress and regulators pushed Fannie Mae and Freddie Mac to become a vast duopoly in the mortgage finance industry. Their debt was implicitly backed by the U.S. Treasury, and they were able to expand their debt and engage in risky transactions. As Lawrence Summers wrote, "Little wonder with gains privatized and losses socialized that the enterprises have gambled their way into financial catastrophe."

There was substantial agreement in Washington that home ownership was a good thing and that more homeownership would be even better. Thus Congress and regulators encouraged Fannie, Freddie, and mortgage lenders to extend credit to underqualified borrowers. To generate more mortgage lending to low- and moderate-income people, the federal government loosened down-payment standards, pressured lenders to increase their percentages of "affordable" loans, and implicitly guaranteed Fannie and Freddie's dramatic expansion. All that hard work paid off: The share of mortgages classified as nonprime soared, and the quality of those loans declined. And Federal Reserve credit expansion helped to make all of this lending possible, as Lawrence H. White wrote in his Cato Briefing Paper, "How Did We Get into This Financial Mess?"

"Everybody was promised everything"—cheap money, easy lending, and rising home prices. All that money and all those buyers pushed housing prices up sharply. But all good things—at least all good things based on unsustainable policies—must come to an end. When housing prices started to fall, many borrowers ran into trouble. Financial companies threatened to fall like dominos, and an ever-expanding series of bailouts began issuing from the Treasury department. And instead of the usual response to businesses that make bad decisions—let them go into bankruptcy or reorganization and let their workers and assets go to more effective companies—the federal government stepped in to keep every existing enterprise operating.

At this point it is important that the recent emergency measures be recognized as just that: emergency—if not panic—measures and not long-term policy. Congress should turn its attention to extricating the government from financial firms and basing long-term policies on a clear diagnosis of what went wrong. Congress should repeal the Community Reinvestment Act and stop pressuring lenders to make loans to underqualified borrowers. The Treasury should use its authority as conservator to liquidate Fannie Mae and Freddie Mac. The federal government should refrain from using its equity investments in companies to exercise power over their operations and should move with all deliberate speed to withdraw from corporate ownership.

One lesson of the credit crisis is that politicians prefer to "promise everybody everything"—low interest rates, affordable mortgages, higher housing prices, lower gas prices, a chicken in every pot. That's why it's important to keep politics out of such matters.

## The End of Libertarianism—or a New Beginning?

Various pundits and public figures have claimed that the credit crisis means "the end of libertarianism" or even more dramatically "the end of American capitalism." As noted above, the crisis can hardly be considered a failure of laissez-faire, deregulation, libertarianism, or capitalism, since it was caused by multiple misguided government interventions into the workings of the financial system. It was and is precisely a failure of interventionism.

But could capitalism or libertarianism come to an end despite the facts? After all, the Great Depression was primarily caused by poor Federal Reserve policy and high

tariffs. But a false impression that it was somehow caused by laissez-faire led to New Deal policies (pursued first by Herbert Hoover and then by Franklin D. Roosevelt) that turned a contraction into the Great Depression. What policies? Restrictive banking regulations, increases in top marginal tax rates, interventions to keep wages and prices from adjusting, and government rhetoric and activism that created (in the words of historian Robert Higgs) "pervasive uncertainty among investors about the security of their property rights in their capital and its prospective returns." That set of policies lengthened the Great Depression by eight years or more and is uncomfortably similar to recent and proposed policy responses to the 2008 credit crisis.

In *Newsweek*, Jacob Weisberg declared that the financial crisis is "the end of libertarianism." But it was in fact "progressive" interventionism that caused the crisis—just the economic philosophy that Weisberg supports. So if one big failure can kill an ideology, then let's hear it for "the end of interventionism."

If this crisis leads us to question the "American-style capitalism" in which a central monetary authority manipulates money and credit, the central government taxes and redistributes $3 trillion a year, huge government-sponsored enterprises create a taxpayer-backed duopoly in the mortgage business, tax laws encourage excessive use of debt financing, and government pressures banks to make bad loans—well, it might be a good thing to reconsider that "American-style capitalism." Or indeed, as a *Washington Post* editorial put it in October, "Government sponsored, upside-only capitalism is the kind that's in crisis today, and we say: Good riddance."

Libertarianism calls for freedom and responsibility, free markets and civil liberties, a minimal government that stays out of both boardrooms and bedrooms. Obviously libertarianism wasn't in the driver's seat in either the Clinton or the Bush administration.

Even if there are misperceptions about the causes of the crisis, both the system of capitalism and the idea of libertarianism are going to have more staying power than pundits such as Weisberg would like. There was a time when half the world rejected capitalism, and leading intellectuals in the "free world" worried that the centrally planned economies would obviously out compete the capitalist countries and that "convergence" on some sort of half-capitalist, half-socialist model was the wave of the future. But after the world got a look at the results of the two systems in East and West Germany, North and South Korea, Hong Kong and Taiwan and China, the United States and the Soviet Union, it became clear that socialism is a clumsy, backward looking prescription for stagnation at best and tyranny at worst.

Meanwhile, the half-planned economies of the West—Great Britain, New Zealand, the United States, and more—developed a milder version of economic sclerosis. Starting in the 1970s many of those countries began eliminating price controls, removing restrictions on market competition, opening up the economy, cutting tax rates, and reducing trade barriers. It came to be widely recognized—eventually on both sides of the Iron Curtain—that private property and markets are indispensable in organizing a modern economy. A nearly simultaneous cultural revolution opened up society. Women, racial minorities, and gays and lesbians entered the mainstream of society throughout the Western world. Art, literature, and lifestyles became more diverse and more individualized. The Sixties and the Eighties both led us to what Brink Lindsey in *The Age of Abundance* called "the implicit libertarian synthesis" of the United States today.

Some people see a future of ever more powerful government. Others see a future of greater freedom. *Reason* editors Nick Gillespie and Matt Welch write: "We are in fact living at the cusp of what should be called the Libertarian Moment, the dawning of . . . a time of increasingly hyper-individualized, hyper-expanded choice over every aspect of our lives. . . . This is now a world where it's more possible than ever to live your life on your own terms; it's an early rough draft version of the libertarian philosopher Robert Nozick's 'utopia of utopias. . . . This new century of the individual, which makes the Me Decade look positively communitarian in comparison, will have far-reaching implications wherever individuals swarm together in commerce, culture, or politics."

Is it possible that Congress will choose to pursue policies—tax increases, yet higher spending, continued subsidies for risky decisions, intrusion into corporate decision making—that would slow down U.S. economic growth, perhaps make us more like France, with its supposedly kinder, gentler capitalism and its GDP per capita of about 75 percent of ours? Yes, it's possible, and clearly there are proposals for such policies. But if we want economic growth—which means better health care, scientific advance, better pharmaceuticals, more leisure opportunities, a cleaner environment, better technology; in short, more well being for more people—there is no alternative to market capitalism. And if we want more growth, for more people, with wider scope for personal choice and decision making, libertarian policy prescriptions are the roadmap.

## A Libertarian Agenda

Beyond the immediate financial crisis, there are many more issues confronting us. Fiscal reform, for instance. Federal spending increased by more than a trillion dollars during the Bush years, or more than 70 percent (even before the budget busting bailout and stimulus packages). The national debt rose even more sharply, from $5.727 trillion to more than $10.6 trillion, or an increase of more than 85 percent. The 2009 budget deficit may exceed $1 trillion. Trends like this are unsustainable, yet elected officials continue to promise more spending on everything from new weaponry to college tuitions. Congress and the administration must find a way to rein in this profligacy.

The current rates of spending don't yet reflect the acceleration of entitlement spending as the baby boomers start retiring. Entitlements are already about 40 percent of the federal budget. In 20 years they may double as a share of national income. The unfunded liability of Social Security and Medicare is now over $100 trillion, an unfathomably large number. Within barely a decade, the two programs will require more than 25 percent of income tax revenues, in addition to the payroll taxes that currently fund them. Congress needs to think seriously about this problem. Are members prepared to impose the tax burden necessary to fund such levels of transfer payments? Do we want that many Americans dependent on a check from the federal government? Eventually, the projected level of entitlements will not be feasible. It would be best to start now to make changes rationally rather than in a panic a few years from now.

Private property, free markets, and fiscal restraint are important foundations for liberty, and the party that claims to uphold those values has done a poor job of it lately. But there are restrictions on liberty beyond the realm of taxes and regulations. We hope that elected officials of both parties will recognize the dangers of censorship, drug prohibition, entanglement of church and state, warrantless wiretapping, indefinite detention, government interference with lifestyle and end-of-life choices, and other such policies. Americans declared in 1776 that life, liberty, and the pursuit of happiness are inalienable rights, and in 1787 they wrote a Constitution that empowers a limited government to protect those rights.

Fidelity to those founding principles of respect for civil liberties and limited government may be easy when times are easy. The true test of our faith in those principles comes when we are beset by diabolical assaults from without and economic turmoil within, when public anxiety may temporarily make it seem expedient to put those principles aside. The importance of paying scrupulous deference to the Constitution's limits on federal power, of respecting its careful system of checks and balances, is greatest precisely when the temptation to flout them is strongest.

For those who go into government to improve the lives of their fellow citizens, the hardest lesson to accept may be that Congress should often do nothing about a problem—such as education, crime, or the cost of prescription drugs. Critics will object, "Do you want the government to just stand there and do nothing while this problem continues?" Sometimes that is exactly what Congress should do. Remember the ancient wisdom imparted to physicians: First, do no harm. And have confidence that free people, left to their own devices, will address issues of concern to them more effectively outside a political environment.

**DAVID BOAZ** is the Executive Vice President of the Cato Institute and has played a key role in the development of the Cato Institute and the libertarian movement. He is a provocative commentator and a leading authority on domestic issues such as education choice, drug legalization, the growth of government, and the rise of libertarianism.

# EXPLORING THE ISSUE

## Is Bigger Government Better Government?

### Critical Thinking and Reflection

1. Madrick argues that the federal government's expansion since World War II has been good for the country. Why does he reach that conclusion? What sort of evidence does he cite?
2. Madrick often refers to the success of big government in Western Europe and cites it as a model for this country. Do you think the European model fits the United States? Why, or why not?
3. How does Boaz categorize libertarianism in the United States? Does it appear that libertarian ideals are gaining momentum today? Why or why not?
4. Why is it difficult for politicians to choose not to act on a problem facing society?
5. How do we assess whether government is working in the United States? Do different individuals utilize different metrics? Why does it matter?

### Is There Common Ground?

There might be common ground between Madrick and Boaz if the latter could convince the former to limit government to (a) protecting people from other people or countries that want to harm them and (b) guaranteeing that all citizens be treated equally and fairly. But it does not seem likely that Madrick would consent to these limited functions of government, unless of course terms like "fairness" and "equality" were given very expansive definitions—which is what Boaz and other conservatives seem to complain that liberals always do!

Ultimately, America will never find agreement on the size of government. Those who need government will likely always favor expanding its power and reach while those who do not need assistance will wonder why they are paying taxes. Unless citizens begin to look past their own self-interest and realize the larger societal goals of government, we will be faced with constant clamoring for government to both expand and condense. For elected officials and government workers, this means being stuck in a never ending tug-of-war in which nothing that is done is pleasing to half of Americans.

### Create Central

www.mhhe.com/createcentral

### Additional Resources

Timothy P. Carney, *The Big Ripoff: How Big Business and Big Government Steal Your Money* (Wiley, 2006)

Milton Friedman, *Capitalism and Freedom* (University of Chicago Press, 1962)

John K. Galbraith, *The Affluent Society* (Houghton Mifflin, 1960)

Max Neiman, *Defending Government: Why Big Government Works* (Prentice Hall, 2009)

Amity Shales, *The Forgotten Man* (Harper Perennial, 2007)

# *Internet References . . .*

**Brookings Institute**

www.brookings.edu

**Cato Institute**

www.cato.org

**Center for American Progress**

www.americanprogress.org

**Center for Small Government**

www.centerforsmallgovernment.org

**Foundation for Economic Education**

www.fee.org

**Selected, Edited, and with Issue Framing Material by:**
**William J. Miller,** *Flagler College*
**George McKenna,** *City College, City University of New York*
**and**
**Stanley Feingold,** *City College, City University of New York*

# ISSUE

# Is America Approaching Equality within Society?

**YES: Barack Obama,** from "Remarks at the 'Let Freedom Ring' Ceremony Commemorating the 50th Anniversary of the March on Washington for Jobs and Freedom," speech delivered at Lincoln Memorial in Washington, DC (August 28, 2013)

**NO: Joseph E. Stiglitz,** from "Of the 1%, by the 1%, for the 1%," *Vanity Fair* (May 2011)

---

## Learning Outcomes

**After reading this issue, you will be able to:**

- Describe what is meant by the term equality.
- Assess whether America has become more or less equal.
- Describe how American society is currently structured economically.
- Assess differences between racial, gender, and economic inequality.
- Explain historical and modern approaches to understanding equality.

---

### ISSUE SUMMARY

**YES:** U.S. President Barack Obama honors Martin Luther King, Jr. by discussing how King's dreams have begun to be realized and continue to fuel the actions and directions of many Americans.

**NO:** Nobel Prize winning economist Joseph Stiglitz examines growing economic discrepancies in the United States and how these disparities impact even the most fundamental aspects of American society.

There has always been a wide range in real income in the United States. In the first three decades after the end of World War II, family incomes doubled, income inequality narrowed slightly, and poverty rates declined. Prosperity declined in the mid-1970s, when back-to-back recessions produced falling average incomes, greater inequality, and higher poverty levels. Between the mid-1980s and the late 1990s, sustained economic recovery resulted in a modest average growth in income, but high poverty rates continued.

Defenders of the social system maintain that, over the long run, poverty has declined. Many improvements in social conditions benefit virtually all people and, thus, make us more equal. The increase in longevity (attributable in large measure to advances in medicine, nutrition, and sanitation) affects all social classes. In a significant sense, the U.S. economy is far fairer now than at any time in the past. In the preindustrial era, when land was the primary measure of wealth, those without land had no way to improve their circumstances. In the industrial era, when people of modest means needed physical strength

and stamina to engage in difficult and hazardous labor in mines, mills, and factories, those who were too weak, handicapped, or too old stood little chance of gaining or keeping reasonable jobs.

In the postindustrial era, many of the manufactured goods that were once "Made in U.S.A.," ranging from clothing to electronics, are now made by cheaper foreign labor. Despite this loss, America achieved virtually full employment in the 1990s, largely because of the enormous growth of the information and service industries. Intelligence, ambition, and hard work—qualities that cut across social classes—are likely to be the determinants of success.

In the view of the defenders of the American economic system, the sharp increase in the nation's gross domestic product has resulted in greater prosperity for most Americans. Although the number of superrich has grown, so has the number of prosperous small business owners, middle-level executives, engineers, computer programmers, lawyers, doctors, entertainers, sports stars, and others who have gained greatly from the longest sustained economic growth in American history. For example, successful young pioneers in the new technology and the entrepreneurs whose capital supported their ventures have prospered, and so have the technicians and other workers whom they hired. Any change that mandated more nearly equal income would greatly diminish the incentives for invention, discovery, and risk-taking enterprises. As a result, the standard of living would be much lower and rise much more slowly, and individual freedom would be curtailed by the degree of state interference in people's private lives.

None of these objections will satisfy those who deplore what they see as an increasing disparity in the distribution of income and wealth. In 2008 the first full year since the recession that began in 2007, the wealthiest 10 percent of Americans, those making more than $138,000 a year, earned 11.4 times the $12,000 earned by those living near or below the poverty line in 2008. Poverty jumped to 13.2 percent, an 11-year high. Nearly 10 million households used food stamps. There has been a long-term acceleration of a gap between rich and poor in the United States. Between 1979 and 2005 (the latest year for which the non-partisan Congressional Budget Office has complete statistics), the average after-tax income of the top 1 percent of households, after adjusting for inflation, increased by $745,000, or 228 percent; that of the 20 percent of Americans in the middle of the income spectrum grew an average of $8,700, or 21 percent; by contrast, that of the poorest 20 percent of Americans grew by $900, or 6 percent.

The financial wealth of the top 1 percent of households exceeds the combined household financial wealth of the bottom 98 percent. Contrary to popular cliché, a rising tide does not lift all boats; it does not lift leaky boats or those who have no boats. Advocates of more nearly equal income argue that this would produce less social conflict and crime as well as more and better social services. They maintain that more egalitarian nations (Scandinavia and Western Europe are often cited) offer more nearly equal access to education, medical treatment, and legal defense. Is democracy diminished if those who have much more also enjoy greater political power than those who have much less?

The rise of the Occupy Movement demonstrated that there is a significant amount of anger being leveled at capitalists in the United States. Consisting of younger Americans with college degrees unable to find jobs at which they can earn livable wages, the rallying cry of the 99 percent focused clearly on income inequality. While the movement fizzled out rather quickly, it nonetheless succeeded in raising awareness for the growing economic tensions in the United States today. And in his first apostolic exhortation, Pope Francis echoed many Occupy sentiments when railing against the negative impacts of capitalism on the ideals of equality, stating:

> In this context, some people continue to defend trickle-down theories which assume that economic growth, encouraged by a free market, will inevitably succeed in bringing about greater justice and inclusiveness in the world. This opinion, which has never been confirmed by the facts, expresses a crude and naïve trust in the goodness of those wielding economic power and in the sacralized workings of the prevailing economic system. Meanwhile, the excluded are still waiting. To sustain a lifestyle which excludes others, or to sustain enthusiasm for that selfish ideal, a globalization of indifference has developed. Almost without being aware of it, we end up being incapable of feeling compassion at the outcry of the poor, weeping for other people's pain, and feeling a need to help them, as though all this were someone else's responsibility and not our own. The culture of prosperity deadens us; we are thrilled if the market offers us something new to purchase; and in the meantime all those lives stunted for lack of opportunity seem a mere spectacle; they fail to move us.

What Francis makes clear is that capitalism fails at assuring the safety of all within a society. As long as a nation relies on trickle down impacts, there will always be someone left behind.

In the following selections, President Obama echoes the sentiments of Martin Luther King, Jr. in assessing how America has moved toward racial and economic equality since his assassination. While he does not believe we have accomplished everything King set out to do, he believes we are making steady progress. On the other hand, Joseph Stiglitz points to growing economic disparities and cautions against possible long-term impacts that these discrepancies could have on society as a whole.

# YES

**Barack Obama**

## Remarks at the "Let Freedom Ring" Ceremony Commemorating the 50th Anniversary of the March on Washington for Jobs and Freedom

To the King family, who have sacrificed and inspired so much; to President Clinton; President Carter; Vice President Biden, Jill; fellow Americans.

Five decades ago today, Americans came to this honored place to lay claim to a promise made at our founding: "We hold these truths to be self-evident, that all men are created equal, that they are endowed by their Creator with certain unalienable rights, that among these are life, liberty, and the pursuit of happiness."

In 1963, almost 200 years after those words were set to paper, a full century after a great war was fought and emancipation proclaimed, that promise—those truths— remained unmet. And so they came by the thousands from every corner of our country, men and women, young and old, Blacks who longed for freedom and Whites who could no longer accept freedom for themselves while witnessing the subjugation of others.

Across the land, congregations sent them off with food and with prayer. In the middle of the night, entire blocks of Harlem came out to wish them well. With the few dollars they scrimped from their labor, some bought tickets and boarded buses, even if they couldn't always sit where they wanted to sit. Those with less money hitch-hiked or walked. They were seamstresses and steelworkers, students and teachers, maids and Pullman porters. They shared simple meals and bunked together on floors. And then, on a hot summer day, they assembled here, in our Nation's Capital, under the shadow of the Great Emancipator, to offer testimony of injustice, to petition their Government for redress, and to awaken America's long-slumbering conscience.

We rightly and best remember Dr. King's soaring oratory that day, how he gave mighty voice to the quiet hopes of millions, how he offered a salvation path for oppressed and oppressors alike. His words belong to the ages, possessing a power and prophecy unmatched in our time.

But we would do well to recall that day itself also belonged to those ordinary people whose names never appeared in the history books, never got on TV. Many had gone to segregated schools and sat at segregated lunch counters. They lived in towns where they couldn't vote and cities where their votes didn't matter. They were couples in love who couldn't marry, soldiers who fought for freedom abroad that they found denied to them at home. They had seen loved ones beaten and children firehosed, and they had every reason to lash out in anger or resign themselves to a bitter fate.

And yet they chose a different path. In the face of hatred, they prayed for their tormentors. In the face of violence, they stood up and sat in with the moral force of nonviolence. Willingly, they went to jail to protest unjust laws, their cells swelling with the sound of freedom songs. A lifetime of indignities had taught them that no man can take away the dignity and grace that God grants us. They had learned through hard experience what Frederick Douglass once taught: that freedom is not given, it must be won through struggle and discipline, persistence and faith.

That was the spirit they brought here that day. That was the spirit young people like John Lewis brought to that day. That was the spirit that they carried with them, like a torch, back to their cities and their neighborhoods. That steady flame of conscience and courage that would sustain them through the campaigns to come: through boycotts and voter registration drives and smaller marches far from the spotlight; through the loss of four little girls in Birmingham and the carnage of the Edmund Pettus Bridge and the agony of Dallas and California and Memphis. Through setbacks and heartbreaks and gnawing doubt, that flame of justice flickered; it never died.

And because they kept marching, America changed. Because they marched, a civil rights law was passed. Because they marched, a voting rights law was signed. Because they marched, doors of opportunity and education swung open so their daughters and sons could finally imagine a life for themselves beyond washing somebody else's laundry or shining somebody else's shoes. Because they marched, city councils changed, and State legislatures changed, and Congress changed, and yes, eventually, the White House changed.

Because they marched, America became more free and more fair, not just for African Americans, but for

Obama, Barack. From speech delivered at Lincoln Memorial in Washington, DC, August 28, 2013.

women and Latinos, Asians and Native Americans; for Catholics, Jews, and Muslims; for gays; for Americans with disabilities. America changed for you and for me. And the entire world drew strength from that example, whether the young people who watched from the other side of an Iron Curtain and would eventually tear down that wall or the young people inside South Africa who would eventually end the scourge of apartheid.

Those are the victories they won with iron wills and hope in their hearts. That is the transformation that they wrought with each step of their well-worn shoes. That's the debt that I and millions of Americans owe those maids, those laborers, those porters, those secretaries—folks who could have run a company maybe if they had ever had a chance; those White students who put themselves in harm's way, even though they didn't have to; those Japanese Americans who recalled their own internment; those Jewish Americans who had survived the Holocaust; people who could have given up and given in, but kept on keeping on, knowing that "weeping may endure for a night, but joy cometh in the morning."

On the battlefield of justice, men and women without rank or wealth or title or fame would liberate us all in ways that our children now take for granted, as people of all colors and creeds live together and learn together and walk together and fight alongside one another and love one another and judge one another by the content of our character in this greatest nation on Earth.

To dismiss the magnitude of this progress—to suggest, as some sometimes do, that little has changed—that dishonors the courage and the sacrifice of those who paid the price to march in those years. Medgar Evers, James Chaney, Andrew Goodman, Michael Schwerner, Martin Luther King, Jr.—they did not die in vain. Their victory was great.

But we would dishonor those heroes as well to suggest that the work of this Nation is somehow complete. The arc of the moral universe may bend towards justice, but it doesn't bend on its own. To secure the gains that this country has made requires constant vigilance, not complacency. Whether by challenging those who erect new barriers to the vote or ensuring that the scales of justice work equally for all and the criminal justice system is not simply a pipeline from underfunded schools to overcrowded jails, it requires vigilance.

And we'll suffer the occasional setback. But we will win these fights. This country has changed too much. People of good will, regardless of party, are too plentiful for those with ill will to change history's currents.

In some ways, though, the securing of civil rights, voting rights, the eradication of legalized discrimination, the very significance of these victories may have obscured a second goal of the march. For the men and women who gathered 50 years ago were not there in search of some abstract ideal. They were there seeking jobs as well as justice, not just the absence of oppression, but the presence of economic opportunity.

For what does it profit a man, Dr. King would ask, to sit at an integrated lunch counter if he can't afford the meal? This idea—that one's liberty is linked to one's livelihood, that the pursuit of happiness requires the dignity of work, the skills to find work, decent pay, some measure of material security—this idea was not new. Lincoln himself understood the Declaration of Independence in such terms, as a promise that in due time, "the weights should be lifted from the shoulders of all men, and that all should have an equal chance."

And Dr. King explained that the goals of African Americans were identical to working people of all races: "Decent wages, fair working conditions, livable housing, old-age security, health and welfare measures, conditions in which families can grow, have education for their children, and respect in the community."

What King was describing has been the dream of every American. It's what's lured for centuries new arrivals to our shores. And it's along this second dimension—of economic opportunity, the chance through honest toil to advance one's station in life—where the goals of 50 years ago have fallen most short.

Yes, there have been examples of success within Black America that would have been unimaginable a half century ago. But as has already been noted: Black unemployment has remained almost twice as high as White employment, Latino unemployment close behind. The gap in wealth between races has not lessened, it's grown. And as President Clinton indicated, the position of all working Americans, regardless of color, has eroded, making the dream Dr. King described even more elusive.

For over a decade, working Americans of all races have seen their wages and incomes stagnate, even as corporate profits soar, even as the pay of a fortunate few explodes. Inequality has steadily risen over the decades. Upward mobility has become harder. In too many communities across this country, in cities and suburbs and rural hamlets, the shadow of poverty casts a pall over our youth, their lives a fortress of substandard schools and diminished prospects, inadequate health care and perennial violence.

And so as we mark this anniversary, we must remind ourselves that the measure of progress for those who marched 50 years ago was not merely how many Blacks could join the ranks of millionaires. It was whether this country would admit all people who are willing to work hard, regardless of race, into the ranks of a middle class life.

The test was not and never has been whether the doors of opportunity are cracked a bit wider for a few. It was whether our economic system provides a fair shot for the many: for the Black custodian and the White steelworker, the immigrant dishwasher and the Native American veteran. To win that battle, to answer that call—this remains our great unfinished business.

We shouldn't fool ourselves: The task will not be easy. Since 1963, the economy has changed. The twin forces of technology and global competition have subtracted those jobs that once provided a foothold into the middle class, reduced the bargaining power of American workers. And our politics has suffered. Entrenched interests, those who benefit from an unjust status quo, resisted any government efforts to give working families a fair deal, marshaling an army of lobbyists and opinion makers to argue that minimum wage increases or stronger labor laws or taxes on the wealthy who could afford it just to fund crumbling schools, that all these things violated sound economic principles. We'd be told that growing inequality was a price for a growing economy, a measure of this free market, that greed was good and compassion ineffective, and that those without jobs or health care had only themselves to blame.

And then, there were those elected officials who found it useful to practice the old politics of division, doing their best to convince middle class Americans of a great untruth: that government was somehow itself to blame for their growing economic insecurity; that distant bureaucrats were taking their hard-earned dollars to benefit the welfare cheat or the illegal immigrant.

And then, if we're honest with ourselves, we'll admit that during the course of 50 years, there were times when some of us claiming to push for change lost our way. The anguish of assassinations set off self-defeating riots. Legitimate grievances against police brutality tipped into excuse-making for criminal behavior. Racial politics could cut both ways, as the transformative message of unity and brotherhood was drowned out by the language of recrimination. And what had once been a call for equality of opportunity—the chance for all Americans to work hard and get ahead—was too often framed as a mere desire for government support, as if we had no agency in our own liberation, as if poverty was an excuse for not raising your child and the bigotry of others was reason to give up on yourself.

All of that history is how progress stalled. That's how hope was diverted. It's how our country remained divided. But the good news is, just as was true in 1963, we now have a choice. We can continue down our current path, in which the gears of this great democracy grind to a halt and our children accept a life of lower expectations; where politics is a zero-sum game; where a few do very well while struggling families of every race fight over a shrinking economic pie. That's one path. Or we can have the courage to change.

The March on Washington teaches us that we are not trapped by the mistakes of history, that we are masters of our fate. But it also teaches us that the promise of this Nation will only be kept when we work together. We'll have to reignite the embers of empathy and fellow feeling, the coalition of conscience that found expression in this place 50 years ago.

And I believe that spirit is there, that truth force inside each of us. I see it when a White mother recognizes her own daughter in the face of a poor Black child. I see it when the Black youth thinks of his own grandfather in the dignified steps of an elderly White man. It's there when the native born recognizes that striving spirit of the new immigrant, when the interracial couple connects the pain of a gay couple who are discriminated against and understands it as their own.

That's where courage comes from: when we turn not from each other or on each other, but towards one another, and we find that we do not walk alone. That's where courage comes from. And with that courage, we can stand together for good jobs and just wages. With that courage, we can stand together for the right to health care in the richest nation on Earth for every person. With that courage, we can stand together for the right of every child, from the corners of Anacostia to the hills of Appalachia, to get an education that stirs the mind and captures the spirit and prepares them for the world that awaits them. With that courage, we can feed the hungry and house the homeless and transform bleak wastelands of poverty into fields of commerce and promise.

America, I know the road will be long, but I know we can get there. Yes, we will stumble, but I know we'll get back up. That's how a movement happens. That's how history bends. That's how, when somebody is faint of heart, somebody else brings them along and says, come on, we're marching.

There's a reason why so many who marched that day, and in the days to come, were young. For the young are unconstrained by habits of fear, unconstrained by the conventions of what is. They dared to dream differently, to imagine something better. And I am convinced that same imagination, the same hunger of purpose stirs in this generation.

We might not face the same dangers of 1963, but the fierce urgency of now remains. We may never duplicate the swelling crowds and dazzling procession of that day so long ago—no one can match King's brilliance—but the same flame that lit the heart of all who are willing to take a first step for justice, I know that flame remains.

That tireless teacher who gets to class early and stays late and dips into her own pocket to buy supplies because she believes that every child is her charge, she's marching.

That successful businessman who doesn't have to, but pays his workers a fair wage and then offers a shot to a man, maybe an ex-con who is down on his luck, he's marching.

The mother who pours her love into her daughter so that she grows up with the confidence to walk through the same doors as anybody's son, she's marching.

The father who realizes the most important job he'll ever have is raising his boy right, even if he didn't have a father—especially if he didn't have a father at home—he's marching.

The battle-scarred veterans who devote themselves not only to helping their fellow warriors stand again and walk again and run again, but to keep serving their country when they come home, they are marching.

Everyone who realizes what those glorious patriots knew on that day, that change does not come from Washington, but to Washington; that change has always been built on our willingness, we the people, to take on the mantle of citizenship, you are marching.

And that's the lesson of our past. That's the promise of tomorrow: that in the face of impossible odds, people who love their country can change it. That when millions of Americans of every race and every region, every faith and every station can join together in a spirit of brotherhood, then those mountains will be made low and those rough places will be made plain and those crooked places, they straighten out towards grace, and we will vindicate the faith of those who sacrificed so much and live up to the true meaning of our creed, as one Nation, under God, indivisible, with liberty and justice for all.

---

**BARACK OBAMA** served as U.S. Senator for Illinois prior to defeating John McCain in the 2008 presidential election to become the 44th President of the United States. He is the first African American to hold the position. In 2012, President Obama defeated Republican challenger Mitt Romney to win a second term.

Joseph E. Stiglitz  **NO**

# Of the 1%, by the 1%, for the 1%

It's no use pretending that what has obviously happened has not in fact happened. The upper 1 percent of Americans are now taking in nearly a quarter of the nation's income every year. In terms of wealth rather than income, the top 1 percent control 40 percent. Their lot in life has improved considerably. Twenty-five years ago, the corresponding figures were 12 percent and 33 percent. One response might be to celebrate the ingenuity and drive that brought good fortune to these people, and to contend that a rising tide lifts all boats. That response would be misguided. While the top 1 percent have seen their incomes rise 18 percent over the past decade, those in the middle have actually seen their incomes fall. For men with only high-school degrees, the decline has been precipitous—12 percent in the last quarter-century alone. All the growth in recent decades—and more—has gone to those at the top. In terms of income equality, America lags behind any country in the old, ossified Europe that President George W. Bush used to deride. Among our closest counterparts are Russia with its oligarchs and Iran. While many of the old centers of inequality in Latin America, such as Brazil, have been striving in recent years, rather successfully, to improve the plight of the poor and reduce gaps in income, America has allowed inequality to grow.

Economists long ago tried to justify the vast inequalities that seemed so troubling in the mid-19th century—inequalities that are but a pale shadow of what we are seeing in America today. The justification they came up with was called "marginal-productivity theory." In a nutshell, this theory associated higher incomes with higher productivity and a greater contribution to society. It is a theory that has always been cherished by the rich. Evidence for its validity, however, remains thin. The corporate executives who helped bring on the recession of the past three years—whose contribution to our society, and to their own companies, has been massively negative—went on to receive large bonuses. In some cases, companies were so embarrassed about calling such rewards "performance bonuses" that they felt compelled to change the name to "retention bonuses" (even if the only thing being retained was bad performance). Those who have contributed great positive innovations to our society, from the pioneers of genetic understanding to the pioneers of the Information Age, have received a pittance compared with those responsible for the financial innovations that brought our global economy to the brink of ruin.

Some people look at income inequality and shrug their shoulders. So what if this person gains and that person loses? What matters, they argue, is not how the pie is divided but the size of the pie. That argument is fundamentally wrong. An economy in which *most* citizens are doing worse year after year—an economy like America's—is not likely to do well over the long haul. There are several reasons for this.

First, growing inequality is the flip side of something else: shrinking opportunity. Whenever we diminish equality of opportunity, it means that we are not using some of our most valuable assets—our people—in the most productive way possible. Second, many of the distortions that lead to inequality—such as those associated with monopoly power and preferential tax treatment for special interests—undermine the efficiency of the economy. This new inequality goes on to create new distortions, undermining efficiency even further. To give just one example, far too many of our most talented young people, seeing the astronomical rewards, have gone into finance rather than into fields that would lead to a more productive and healthy economy.

Third, and perhaps most important, a modern economy requires "collective action"—it needs government to invest in infrastructure, education, and technology. The United States and the world have benefited greatly from government-sponsored research that led to the Internet, to advances in public health, and so on. But America has long suffered from an under-investment in infrastructure (look at the condition of our highways and bridges, our railroads and airports), in basic research, and in education at all levels. Further cutbacks in these areas lie ahead.

None of this should come as a surprise—it is simply what happens when a society's wealth distribution becomes lopsided. The more divided a society becomes in terms of wealth, the more reluctant the wealthy become to spend money on common needs. The rich don't need to rely on government for parks or education or medical care or personal security—they can buy all these things for themselves. In the process, they become more distant from ordinary people, losing whatever empathy they may once have had. They also worry about strong government—one that could use its powers to adjust the balance, take some of their wealth, and invest it for the common good. The top 1 percent may complain about the kind of government we have in America, but in truth they like it just fine: too gridlocked to re-distribute, too divided to do anything but lower taxes.

Economists are not sure how to fully explain the growing inequality in America. The ordinary dynamics of supply and demand have certainly played a role: labor-saving technologies have reduced the demand for many "good" middle-class, blue-collar jobs. Globalization has created a worldwide marketplace, pitting expensive unskilled workers in America against cheap unskilled workers overseas. Social changes have also played a role—for instance, the decline of unions, which once represented a third of American workers and now represent about 12 percent.

But one big part of the reason we have so much inequality is that the top 1 percent want it that way. The most obvious example involves tax policy. Lowering tax rates on capital gains, which is how the rich receive a large portion of their income, has given the wealthiest Americans close to a free ride. Monopolies and near monopolies have always been a source of economic power—from John D. Rockefeller at the beginning of the last century to Bill Gates at the end. Lax enforcement of anti-trust laws, especially during Republican administrations, has been a godsend to the top 1 percent. Much of today's inequality is due to manipulation of the financial system, enabled by changes in the rules that have been bought and paid for by the financial industry itself—one of its best investments ever. The government lent money to financial institutions at close to 0 percent interest and provided generous bailouts on favorable terms when all else failed. Regulators turned a blind eye to a lack of transparency and to conflicts of interest.

When you look at the sheer volume of wealth controlled by the top 1 percent in this country, it's tempting to see our growing inequality as a quintessentially American achievement—we started way behind the pack, but now we're doing inequality on a world-class level. And it looks as if we'll be building on this achievement for years to come, because what made it possible is self-reinforcing. Wealth begets power, which begets more wealth. During the savings-and-loan scandal of the 1980s—a scandal whose dimensions, by today's standards, seem almost quaint—the banker Charles Keating was asked by a congressional committee whether the $1.5 million he had spread among a few key elected officials could actually buy influence. "I certainly hope so," he replied. The Supreme Court, in its recent *Citizens United* case, has enshrined the right of corporations to buy government, by removing limitations on campaign spending. The personal and the political are today in perfect alignment. Virtually all U.S. senators, and most of the representatives in the House, are members of the top 1 percent when they arrive, are kept in office by money from the top 1 percent, and know that if they serve the top 1 percent well they will be rewarded by the top 1 percent when they leave office. By and large, the key executive-branch policymakers on trade and economic policy also come from the top 1 percent. When pharmaceutical companies receive a trillion-dollar gift—through legislation prohibiting the government, the largest buyer of drugs, from bargaining over price—it should not come as cause for wonder. It should not make jaws drop that a tax bill cannot emerge from Congress unless big tax cuts are put in place for the wealthy. Given the power of the top 1 percent, this is the way you would *expect* the system to work.

America's inequality distorts our society in every conceivable way. There is, for one thing, a well-documented lifestyle effect—people outside the top 1 percent increasingly live beyond their means. Trickle-down economics may be a chimera, but trickle-down behaviorism is very real. Inequality massively distorts our foreign policy. The top 1 percent rarely serve in the military—the reality is that the "all-volunteer" army does not pay enough to attract their sons and daughters, and patriotism goes only so far. Plus, the wealthiest class feels no pinch from higher taxes when the nation goes to war: borrowed money will pay for all that. Foreign policy, by definition, is about the balancing of national interests and national resources. With the top 1 percent in charge, and paying no price, the notion of balance and restraint goes out the window. There is no limit to the adventures we can undertake; corporations and contractors stand only to gain. The rules of economic globalization are likewise designed to benefit the rich: they encourage competition among countries for *business,* which drives down taxes on corporations, weakens health and environmental protections, and undermines what used to be viewed as the "core" labor rights, which include the right to collective bargaining. Imagine what the world might look like if the rules were designed instead to encourage competition among countries for *workers.* Governments would compete in providing economic security, low taxes on ordinary wage earners, good education, and a clean environment—things workers care about. But the top 1 percent don't need to care.

---

**Joseph E. Stiglitz** is Professor of Economics at Columbia University. He is the former Senior Vice President and Chief Economist at the World Bank and is a former member and Chairman of the Council of Economic Advisors. He won the Nobel Prize in Economics in 2001.

# EXPLORING THE ISSUE

## Is America Approaching Equality within Society?

## Critical Thinking and Reflection

1. What factors contribute to increased inequality of income and wealth in the United States?
2. Is economic inequality in America increasing or decreasing? Why? Is the process reversible?
3. Is racial inequality in America increasing or decreasing? Why? Is the process reversible?
4. How are racial and economic inequality linked? Is there a way to make inroads on both simultaneously?
5. Do you believe Martin Luther King, Jr. would be satisfied with the progress made in the United States since his assassination? Why or why not?

## Is There Common Ground?

Both those who deplore increasing inequality and those who believe that Americans have achieved an impressive level of equality agree that equality of opportunity is critical. They disagree as to how much opportunity is necessary and whether American society has achieved it. Where Joseph Stiglitz and other critics of American inequality advocate much greater public investment in education, health, and other areas as the most effective means of equalizing opportunity, Barack Obama concludes that economic freedom has produced both the challenge of social ills and the development of social solutions. While he by no means would argue that our nation has become equal, he points to historical growth and reminds the country of how far it has come. The divide is between those who approach equal justice in public policies that reduce sharp areas of inequality and those who seek it in the social forces of a free society.

A study released October 27, 2011 by the Bertelsmann Stiftung Foundation in Germany comparing poverty rates, income inequality, pre-primary education, and health rating in 32 member countries of the Organisation for Economic Co-operation and Development ranked the United States 27 among 31 countries overall in what it characterized as social justice, with the United States among the bottom five in poverty prevention, overall poverty rate, child poverty rate, and income inequality; among the bottom 10 in senior citizen poverty rate,

pre-primary education and health rating, and in the bottom 15 in intergenerational justice, which includes family and pension policies, environmental policies, and assessment of political-economic being established for future generations. In none of the eight categories did the United States place in the top half of 31 nations.

## Create Central

www.mhhe.com/createcentral

## Additional Resources

Larry Bartels, *Unequal Democracy: The Political Economy of the New Gilded Age* (Princeton University Press, 2008)

James Lardner and David A. Smith, *The Growing Economic Divide in America with Its Poisonous Consequences* (The New Press, 2006)

Ron Paul, *The Revolution: A Manifesto* (Grand Central Publishing, 2009)

Richard Rothstein, *Class and Schools: Using Social, Economic, and Educational Reform to Close the Black-White Educational Gap* (The Economic Policy Institute and Teachers College Press, 2004)

Will Wilkinson, *Thinking Clearly About Economic Inequality* (Cato Institute, 2009)

# *Internet References . . .*

**Equality and the Fourteenth Amendment**

www.pbs.org/tpt/constitution-usa-peter-sagal/equality/

**How Economic Inequality Harms Societies**

www.ted.com/talks/richard_wilkinson.html

**International Society for Peace**

www.societyforpeace.com

**National Association for the Advancement of Colored People**

www.naacp.org

**The United States of Inequality**

http://billmoyers.com/segment/bill-moyers-essay-the-united-states-of-inequality/

# Unit 2

# UNIT

# The Institutions of Government

*T*he Constitution divides authority between the national government and the states, delegating certain powers to the national government and providing that those not thus delegated "are reserved to the states respectively, or to the people." The national government's powers are further divided between three branches, Congress, the president, and the federal judiciary, each of which can exercise checks on the others.

Americans are familiar with these bodies—some more than others. Most everyone is aware of who the president is, but they cannot necessarily determine whether he (or she) is doing a good job using appropriate metrics. They know their member of Congress (and overwhelmingly approve of his or her performance, in most cases), yet they rank the trustworthiness of the body as a whole to a degree comparable to lawyers and used cars salesmen. And most Americans know there is a Supreme Court that issues important decisions, but they are unaware of the rest of the federal judiciary, let alone the individuals who sit on the bench. As a result, these powerful institutions must regularly remember to show Americans how they are relevant and how they are fulfilling objectives for the betterment of society as a whole.

How vigorously and faithfully are these branches performing their respective functions? Do they remain true to the authentic meaning of the Constitution? What legitimate defenses does each branch possess against encroachment by the others? These issues have been debated since the earliest years of the Republic, and the debate continues today.

Selected, Edited, and with Issue Framing Material by:
**William J. Miller,** *Flagler College*
**George McKenna,** *City College, City University of New York*
**and**
**Stanley Feingold,** *City College, City University of New York*

# ISSUE

# Does the President Have Unilateral War Powers?

**YES: John C. Yoo,** from *The President's Constitutional Authority to Conduct Military Operations Against Terrorists and Nations Supporting Them: Memorandum Opinion for the Deputy Counsel to the President* (September 25, 2001)

**NO: Barack Obama,** from "The Future of Our Fight Against Terrorism," remarks of President Barack Obama— as prepared for delivery at National Defense University (May 23, 2013)

| Learning Outcomes |
| --- |
| **After reading this issue, you will be able to:** <br><br> • Explain how war is declared in the United States. <br> • Describe the legal precedents that allow the president to have unilateral war powers. <br> • Assess the arguments against the president having unilateral war powers. <br> • Discuss how Congress and the presidency work together during times of war. <br> • Identify when it may be prudent for the president to have unilateral war powers. |

## ISSUE SUMMARY

**YES:** John C. Yoo, a Law Professor at the University of California, Berkeley, argues that the language of the Constitution, long-accepted precedents, and the practical need for speedy action in emergencies all support broad executive power during war.

**NO:** American President Barack Obama examines how he has made concerted efforts during his time in the White House to expand consultations with Congress in order to provide the best opportunity for the United States to be successful in fighting terrorism.

Dramatic and bitter as they are, the current struggles between the White House and Congress over the president's unilateral authority to conduct military operations and foreign affairs are not without precedent. Episodically, they have been occurring since the administration of George Washington.

The language of the Constitution relating to war powers almost seems to invite struggles between the two branches. Congress is given the power to declare war and "to raise and support armies." The president is authorized to serve as commander-in-chief of the armed forces "when called into actual service of the United States." While the power to "declare" or authorize war rests squarely with the U.S. Congress, the Founders gave some leeway to the president when it came to war making. At the Constitutional Convention, some delegates wanted to give Congress the exclusive power to make war, not simply to declare it. That would have ruled out any presidential war making. But James Madison successfully argued the need for "leaving to the Executive the power to repel sudden attacks."

Down through the years, several presidents have interpreted very broadly these emergency war-making powers. In 1801, President Jefferson ordered his navy to seize the ships of Barbary pirates in the Mediterranean, and 45 years later President Polk sent American troops into territory claimed by Mexico, thus provoking the Mexican American War. A young congressman named Abraham Lincoln vigorously protested Polk's unilateral assertion of power, but when he came to office and faced the secession of the South, he went much further than Polk in the assertion of power, jailing people without trial, enlarging the size of the army and navy, withdrawing money from the Treasury, and blockading Southern ports without authorization from Congress. In more recent times, President Truman committed America to fight in Korea without a congressional declaration, and President Kennedy ordered a naval blockade of Cuba in 1962 without even consulting Congress.

The mid-1960s marked the high-water period of unchallenged presidential war making. Between 1961 and 1963, Kennedy sent 16,000 armed "advisers" to Vietnam, and between 1964 and 1968, President Johnson escalated American involvement to 500,000 troops—all without a formal declaration of war. But that period of congressional indulgence was soon to end. By the early 1970s, Congress was starting on a course that would culminate in the cut-off of funds for Vietnam and legislative efforts to head off any more undeclared wars. In 1973, over President Nixon's veto, Congress passed the War Powers Resolution, which required the president to notify Congress within 48 hours after putting troops in harm's way, withdraw them within 60 to 90 days absent a congressional authorization, and submit periodic progress reports to Congress during that period. In practice, the War Powers Resolution has been largely ignored by Ronald Reagan when he sent troops into Grenada, by George H. W. Bush when he sent them to Panama, and by Bill Clinton when he sent them into Somalia, Haiti, and Bosnia.

Perhaps ironically, the War Powers Resolution may even have been useful to President George W. Bush in obtaining congressional authorization for the invasion of Iraq. In October 2002, Congress passed a joint resolution giving the president the authority to use the armed forces "as he determines to be necessary and appropriate" to defend national security and enforce all U.N. resolutions against Iraq. The resolution added that this constituted "specific statutory authorization" for war within the meaning of the War Powers Resolution. Such broadly worded language has come back to haunt many members of Congress who voted for it but now wish they hadn't. The new Democratic Congress elected in 2006 considered various options for challenging President Bush's war-making ability as it related to Iraq, including the repeal or modification of the 2002 authorization for going to war.

For President Barack Obama, the question of unilateral war powers surfaced most significantly when determining whether to attack Bashar al-Assad (Syrian dictator) after strong evidence emerged showing that he had used chemical weapons against his own people. In 2012, Obama had issued an ultimatum to Assad: if he used chemical weapons, the United States would have no choice but to respond. Yet with over half of Americans polled favoring an intervention (and less than 10 percent actually supporting such action), Obama had to decide whether Syria was worth going against the wishes of Americans in a way similar to his predecessor. The key is that Obama was stuck wondering whether he should or should not proceed, not whether he could or could not. Much like with Libya in 2011, there was never a question on whether Obama possessed the ability to launch attacks against a foreign enemy without a formal declaration from Congress.

Ultimately, Obama opted to move forward with diplomacy and not launch attacks despite his earlier warning. After the Bush administration's battles in Iraq and Afghanistan, many Americans began labeling the Republican Party as the one most tied to superseding Congress when deciding whether to attack foreign countries. But Obama's recent internal deliberations have reminded us that all presidents—regardless of partisanship—are forced to weight these options. Only a president with no interest in power would blindly hand off the ability to launch unilateral military action, but a wise one would find a way to work in concert with Congress to assure backing and support. Wag the Dog, after all, does not exist in reality. We cannot simply fabricate conflicts to bump polling numbers. In today's America, such actions would likely harm a leader in the polls. Instead, a majority of Americans are still looking for the branches of government to come together in an effort to solve potential problems.

In the selections that follow, John C. Yoo, a Law Professor at the University of California, Berkeley, argues that the language of the Constitution, long-accepted precedents, and the practical need for speedy action in emergencies all support broad executive power during war. Opposing that view is President Barack Obama, who points to a strong need to consult with Congress in order to assure maximum effectiveness and efficiency in dealing with foreign policy and threats to homeland security.

# YES

John C. Yoo

## The President's Constitutional Authority to Conduct Military Operations Against Terrorists and Nations Supporting Them: Memorandum Opinion for the Deputy Counsel to the President

Our review establishes that all three branches of the Federal Government—Congress, the Executive, and the Judiciary—agree that the President has broad authority to use military force abroad, including the ability to deter future attacks.

### I.

The President's constitutional power to defend the United States and the lives of its people must be understood in light of the Founders' express intention to create a federal government "cloathed with all the powers requisite to [the] complete execution of its trust." *The Federalist* No. 23 (Alexander Hamilton). Foremost among the objectives committed to that trust by the Constitution is the security of the Nation. As Hamilton explained in arguing for the Constitution's adoption, because "the circumstances which may affect the public safety are [not] reducible within certain determinate limits, . . . it must be admitted, as a necessary consequence that there can be no limitation of that authority which is to provide for the defense and protection of the community in any matter essential to its efficiency."

"It is 'obvious and unarguable' that no governmental interest is more compelling than the security of the Nation." (1981). Within the limits that the Constitution itself imposes, the scope and distribution of the powers to protect national security must be construed to authorize the most efficacious defense of the Nation and its interests in accordance "with the realistic purposes of the entire instrument." (1948) Nor is the authority to protect national security limited to actions necessary for "victories in the field." (1946) The authority over national security "carries with it the inherent power to guard against the immediate renewal of the conflict."

We now turn to the more precise question of the President's inherent constitutional powers to use military force.

## Constitutional Text

The text, structure and history of the Constitution establish that the Founders entrusted the President with the primary responsibility, and therefore the power, to use military force in situations of emergency. Article II, Section 2 states that the "President shall be Commander in Chief of the Army and Navy of the United States, and of the Militia of the several States, when called into the actual Service of the United States." He is further vested with all of "the executive Power" and the duty to execute the laws. These powers give the President broad constitutional authority to use military force in response to threats to the national security and foreign policy of the United States. During the period leading up to the Constitution's ratification, the power to initiate hostilities and to control the escalation of conflict had been long understood to rest in the hands of the executive branch.

By their terms, these provisions vest full control of the military forces of the United States in the President. The power of the President is at its zenith under the Constitution when the President is directing military operations of the armed forces, because the power of Commander in Chief is assigned solely to the President. It has long been the view of this Office that the Commander-in-Chief Clause is a substantive grant of authority to the President and that the scope of the President's authority to commit the armed forces to combat is very broad. The President's complete discretion in exercising the Commander-in-Chief power has also been recognized by the courts. In the *Prize Cases,* (1862), for example, the Court explained that, whether the President "in fulfilling his duties as Commander in Chief" had met with a situation justifying treating the southern States as belligerents and instituting a blockade, was a question "to be *decided by him*" and which the Court could not question, but must leave to "the political department of the Government to which this power was entrusted."

Some commentators have read the constitutional text differently. They argue that the vesting of the power to declare war gives Congress the sole authority to decide whether to make war. This view misreads the constitutional text and misunderstands the nature of a declaration of war. Declaring war is not tantamount to making war—indeed, the Constitutional Convention specifically amended the working draft of the Constitution that had given Congress the power to make war. An earlier draft of the Constitution had given to Congress the power to "make" war. When it took up this clause on August 17, 1787, the Convention voted to change the clause from "make" to "declare." A supporter of the change argued that it would "leav[e] to the Executive the power to repel sudden attacks." Further, other elements of the Constitution describe "engaging" in war, which demonstrates that the Framers understood making and engaging in war to be broader than simply "declaring" war. . . . If the Framers had wanted to require congressional consent before the initiation of military hostilities, they knew how to write such provisions.

Finally, the Framing generation well understood that declarations of war were obsolete. Not all forms of hostilities rose to the level of a declared war: during the seventeenth and eighteenth centuries, Great Britain and colonial America waged numerous conflicts against other states without an official declaration of war. . . . Instead of serving as an authorization to begin hostilities, a declaration of war was only necessary to "perfect" a conflict under international law. A declaration served to fully transform the international legal relationship between two states from one of peace to one of war. Given this context, it is clear that Congress's power to declare war does not constrain the President's independent and plenary constitutional authority over the use of military force.

## Constitutional Structure

Our reading of the text is reinforced by analysis of the constitutional structure. First, it is clear that the Constitution secures all federal executive power in the President to ensure a unity in purpose and energy in action. "Decision, activity, secrecy, and dispatch will generally characterize the proceedings of one man in a much more eminent degree than the proceedings of any greater number." *The Federalist* No. 70 (Alexander Hamilton). The centralization of authority in the President alone is particularly crucial in matters of national defense, war, and foreign policy, where a unitary executive can evaluate threats, consider policy choices, and mobilize national resources with a speed and energy that is far superior to any other branch. As Hamilton noted, "Energy in the executive is a leading character in the definition of good government. It is essential to the protection of the community against foreign attacks." This is no less true in war. "Of all the cares or concerns of government, the direction of war most peculiarly demands those qualities which distinguish the exercise of power by a single hand." *The Federalist* No. 74.

Second, the Constitution makes clear that the process used for conducting military hostilities is different from other government decisionmaking. In the area of domestic legislation, the Constitution creates a detailed, finely wrought procedure in which Congress plays the central role. In foreign affairs, however, the Constitution does not establish a mandatory, detailed, Congress-driven procedure for taking action. Rather, the Constitution vests the two branches with different powers—the President as Commander in Chief, Congress with control over funding and declaring war—without requiring that they follow a specific process in making war. By establishing this framework, the Framers expected that the process for warmaking would be far more flexible, and capable of quicker, more decisive action, than the legislative process. Thus, the President may use his Commander-in-Chief and executive powers to use military force to protect the Nation, subject to congressional appropriations and control over domestic legislation.

Third, the constitutional structure requires that any ambiguities in the allocation of a power that is executive in nature—such as the power to conduct military hostilities—must be resolved in favor of the executive branch. Article II, section 1 provides that "[t]he executive Power shall be vested in a President of the United States." By contrast, Article I's Vesting Clause gives Congress only the powers "herein granted." This difference in language indicates that Congress's legislative powers are limited to the list enumerated in Article I, section 8, while the President's powers include inherent executive powers that are unenumerated in the Constitution. To be sure, Article II lists specifically enumerated powers in addition to the Vesting Clause, and some have argued that this limits the "executive Power" granted in the Vesting Clause to the powers on that list. But the purpose of the enumeration of executive powers in Article II was not to define and cabin the grant in the Vesting Clause. Rather, the Framers unbundled some plenary powers that had traditionally been regarded as "executive," assigning elements of those powers to Congress in Article I, while expressly reserving other elements as enumerated executive powers in Article II. So, for example, the King's traditional power to declare war was given to Congress under Article I, while the Commander-in-Chief authority was expressly reserved to the President in Article II. Further, the Framers altered other plenary powers of the King, such as treaties and appointments, assigning the Senate a share in them in Article II itself. Thus, the enumeration in Article II marks the points at which several traditional executive powers were diluted or reallocated. Any *other,* unenumerated executive powers, however, were conveyed to the President by the Vesting Clause.

There can be little doubt that the decision to deploy military force is "executive" in nature, and was traditionally so regarded. It calls for action and energy in execution, rather than the deliberate formulation of rules to govern the conduct of private individuals. Moreover, the Framers understood it to be an attribute of the executive. "The direction of war implies the direction of the common strength," wrote Alexander Hamilton, "and the power of directing and employing the common strength forms a usual and essential part in the definition of the executive authority." *The Federalist* No. 74 (Alexander Hamilton). As a result, to the extent that the constitutional text does not explicitly allocate the power to initiate military hostilities to a particular branch, the Vesting Clause provides that it remain among the President's unenumerated powers.

Fourth, depriving the President of the power to decide when to use military force would disrupt the basic constitutional framework of foreign relations. From the very beginnings of the Republic, the vesting of the executive, Commander-in-Chief, and treaty powers in the executive branch has been understood to grant the President plenary control over the conduct of foreign relations. As Secretary of State Thomas Jefferson observed during the first Washington Administration: "the constitution has divided the powers of government into three branches [and] has declared that the executive powers shall be vested in the president, submitting only special articles of it to a negative by the senate." Due to this structure, Jefferson continued, "the transaction of business with foreign nations is executive altogether; it belongs, then, to the head of that department, except as to such portions of it as are specially submitted to the senate. Exceptions are to be construed strictly." In defending President Washington's authority to issue the Neutrality Proclamation, Alexander Hamilton came to the same interpretation of the President's foreign affairs powers. According to Hamilton, Article II "ought . . . to be considered as intended . . . to specify and regulate the principal articles implied in the definition of Executive Power; leaving the rest to flow from the general grant of that power." As future Chief Justice John Marshall famously declared a few years later, "The President is the sole organ of the nation in its external relations, and its sole representative with foreign nations. . . . The [executive] department . . . is entrusted with the whole foreign intercourse of the nation. . . ." Given the agreement of Jefferson, Hamilton, and Marshall, it has not been difficult for the executive branch consistently to assert the President's plenary authority in foreign affairs ever since. . . .

## II.

### Executive Branch Construction and Practice

The position we take here has long represented the view of the executive branch and of the Department of Justice. Attorney General (later Justice) Robert Jackson formulated the classic statement of the executive branch's understanding of the President's military powers in 1941:

> "Article II, section 2, of the Constitution provides that the President "shall be Commander in Chief of the Army and Navy of the United States." By

virtue of this constitutional office he has supreme command over the land and naval forces of the country and may order them to perform such military duties as, in his opinion, are necessary or appropriate for the defense of the United States. These powers exist in time of peace as well as in time of war. . . .

"Thus the President's responsibility as Commander in Chief embraces the authority to command and direct the armed forces in their immediate movements and operations designed to protect the security and effectuate the defense of the United States. . . . [T]his authority undoubtedly includes the power to dispose of troops and equipment in such manner and on such duties as best to promote the safety of the country." . . .

Attorney General (later Justice) Frank Murphy, though declining to define precisely the scope of the President's independent authority to act in emergencies or states of war, stated that: "the Executive has powers not enumerated in the statutes—powers derived not from statutory grants but from the Constitution. It is universally recognized that the constitutional duties of the Executive carry with them the constitutional powers necessary for their proper performance. These constitutional powers have never been specifically defined, and in fact cannot be, since their extent and limitations are largely dependent upon conditions and circumstances. . . . The right to take specific action might not exist under one state of facts, while under another it might be the absolute duty of the Executive to take such action." . . .

## Judicial Construction

Judicial decisions since the beginning of the Republic confirm the President's constitutional power and duty to repel military action against the United States through the use of force, and to take measures to deter the recurrence of an attack. As Justice Joseph Story said long ago, "[i]t may be fit and proper for the government, in the exercise of the high discretion confided to the executive, for great public purposes, to act on a sudden emergency, or to prevent an irreparable mischief, by summary measures, which are not found in the text of the laws." (1824). The Constitution entrusts the "power [to] the executive branch of the government to preserve order and insure the public safety in times of emergency, when other branches of the government are unable to function, or their functioning would itself threaten the public safety." (1946, Stone, C.J., concurring).

If the President is confronted with an unforeseen attack on the territory and people of the United States, or other immediate, dangerous threat to American interests and security, the courts have affirmed that it is his constitutional responsibility to respond to that threat with whatever means are necessary, including the use of military force abroad. . . .

## III.

The historical practice of all three branches confirms the lessons of the constitutional text and structure. The normative role of historical practice in constitutional law, and especially with regard to separation of powers, is well settled. . . . Indeed, as the Court has observed, the role of practice in fixing the meaning of the separation of powers is implicit in the Constitution itself: "'the Constitution . . . contemplates that practice will integrate the dispersed powers into a workable government.'" (1989). In addition, governmental practice enjoys significant weight in constitutional analysis for practical reasons, on "the basis of a wise and quieting rule that, in determining . . . the existence of a power, weight shall be given to the usage itself—even when the validity of the practice is the subject of investigation." (1915). . . .

The historical record demonstrates that the power to initiate military hostilities, particularly in response to the threat of an armed attack, rests exclusively with the President. As the Supreme Court has observed, "[t]he United States frequently employs Armed Forces outside this country—over 200 times in our history—for the protection of American citizens or national security." (1990). On at least 125 such occasions, the President acted without prior express authorization from Congress. Such deployments, based on the President's constitutional authority alone, have occurred since the Administration of George Washington. . . . Perhaps the most significant deployment without specific statutory authorization took place at the time of the Korean War, when President Truman, without prior authorization from Congress, deployed United States troops in a war that lasted for over three years and caused over 142,000 American casualties.

Recent deployments ordered solely on the basis of the President's constitutional authority have also been extremely large, representing a substantial commitment of the Nation's military personnel, diplomatic prestige, and financial resources. On at least one occasion, such a unilateral deployment has constituted full-scale war. On March 24, 1999, without any prior statutory authorization and in the absence of an attack on the United States, President Clinton ordered hostilities to be initiated against the Republic of Yugoslavia. The President informed Congress that, in the initial wave of air strikes, "United States and NATO forces have targeted the [Yugoslavian] government's integrated air defense system, military and security police command and control elements, and military and security police facilities and infrastructure. . . . I have taken these actions pursuant to my constitutional authority to conduct U.S. foreign relations and as Commander in Chief and Chief Executive." Bombing attacks against targets in both Kosovo and Serbia ended on June 10, 1999, seventy-nine days after the war began. More than 30,000 United States military personnel participated in the operations; some 800 U.S. aircraft flew more than 20,000 sorties; more than 23,000 bombs and missiles were used. As part of the peace settlement, NATO deployed some 50,000 troops into Kosovo, 7,000 of them American. . . .

## Conclusion

In light of the text, plan, and history of the Constitution, its interpretation by both past Administrations and the courts, the longstanding practice of the executive branch, and the express affirmation of the President's constitutional authorities by Congress, we think it beyond question that the President has the plenary constitutional power to take such military actions as he deems necessary and appropriate to respond to the terrorist attacks upon the United States on September 11, 2001. Force can be used both to retaliate for those attacks, and to prevent and deter future assaults on the Nation. Military actions need not be limited to those individuals, groups, or states that participated in the attacks on the World Trade Center and the Pentagon: the Constitution vests the President with the power to strike terrorist groups or organizations that cannot be demonstrably linked to the September 11 incidents, but that, nonetheless, pose a similar threat to the security of the United States and the lives of its people, whether at home or overseas. In both the War Powers Resolution and the Joint Resolution, Congress has recognized the President's authority to use force in circumstances such as those created by the September 11 incidents. Neither statute, however, can place any limits on the President's determinations as to any terrorist threat, the amount of military force to be used in response, or the method, timing, and nature of the response. These decisions, under our Constitution, are for the President alone to make.

---

**John C. Yoo,** a Professor of Law at Boalt Hall, University of California, Berkeley, served as Deputy Assistant Attorney General in the Office of Legal Counsel in the U.S. Department of Justice from 2001 to 2003. He is the author of *The Powers of War and Peace* (University of Chicago, 2005) and *War by Other Means: An Insider's Account of the War on Terrorism* (Grove/Atlantic, 2006).

**Barack Obama**

 **NO**

# The Future of Our Fight Against Terrorism

It's an honor to return to the National Defense University. Here, at Fort McNair, Americans have served in uniform since 1791—standing guard in the early days of the Republic, and contemplating the future of warfare here in the 21st century.

For over two centuries, the United States has been bound together by founding documents that defined who we are as Americans, and served as our compass through every type of change. Matters of war and peace are no different. Americans are deeply ambivalent about war, but having fought for our independence, we know that a price must be paid for freedom. From the Civil War, to our struggle against fascism, and through the long, twilight struggle of the Cold War, battlefields have changed, and technology has evolved. But our commitment to Constitutional principles has weathered every war, and every war has come to an end.

With the collapse of the Berlin Wall, a new dawn of democracy took hold abroad, and a decade of peace and prosperity arrived at home. For a moment, it seemed the 21st century would be a tranquil time. Then, on September 11th 2001, we were shaken out of complacency. Thousands were taken from us, as clouds of fire, metal and ash descended upon a sun-filled morning. This was a different kind of war. No armies came to our shores, and our military was not the principal target. Instead, a group of terrorists came to kill as many civilians as they could.

And so our nation went to war. We have now been at war for well over a decade. I won't review the full history. What's clear is that we quickly drove al Qaeda out of Afghanistan, but then shifted our focus and began a new war in Iraq. This carried grave consequences for our fight against al Qaeda, our standing in the world, and—to this day—our interests in a vital region.

Meanwhile, we strengthened our defenses—hardening targets, tightening transportation security, and giving law enforcement new tools to prevent terror. Most of these changes were sound. Some caused inconvenience. But some, like expanded surveillance, raised difficult questions about the balance we strike between our interests in security and our values of privacy. And in some cases, I believe we compromised our basic values—by using torture to interrogate our enemies, and detaining individuals in a way that ran counter to the rule of law.

After I took office, we stepped up the war against al Qaeda, but also sought to change its course. We relentlessly targeted al Qaeda's leadership. We ended the war in Iraq, and brought nearly 150,000 troops home. We pursued a new strategy in Afghanistan, and increased our training of Afghan forces. We unequivocally banned torture, affirmed our commitment to civilian courts, worked to align our policies with the rule of law, and expanded our consultations with Congress.

Today, Osama bin Laden is dead, and so are most of his top lieutenants. There have been no large-scale attacks on the United States, and our homeland is more secure. Fewer of our troops are in harm's way, and over the next 19 months they will continue to come home. Our alliances are strong, and so is our standing in the world. In sum, we are safer because of our efforts.

Now make no mistake: our nation is still threatened by terrorists. From Benghazi to Boston, we have been tragically reminded of that truth. We must recognize, however, that the threat has shifted and evolved from the one that came to our shores on 9/11. With a decade of experience to draw from, now is the time to ask ourselves hard questions—about the nature of today's threats, and how we should confront them.

These questions matter to every American. For over the last decade, our nation has spent well over a trillion dollars on war, exploding our deficits and constraining our ability to nation build here at home. Our service-members and their families have sacrificed far more on our behalf. Nearly 7,000 Americans have made the ultimate sacrifice. Many more have left a part of themselves on the battlefield, or brought the shadows of battle back home. From our use of drones to the detention of terrorist suspects, the decisions we are making will define the type of nation—and world—that we leave to our children.

So America is at a crossroads. We must define the nature and scope of this struggle, or else it will define us, mindful of James Madison's warning that "No nation could preserve its freedom in the midst of continual warfare." Neither I, nor any President, can promise the total defeat of terror. We will never erase the evil that lies in the hearts of some human beings, nor stamp out every danger to our open society. What we can do—what we must do—is dismantle networks that pose a direct danger, and make it less likely for new groups to gain a foothold, all while maintaining the freedoms and ideals that we defend. To define that strategy, we must make decisions based not on fear, but hard-earned wisdom. And that begins with understanding the threat we face.

Obama, Barack. From speech delivered at National Defense University, May 23, 2013.

Today, the core of al Qaeda in Afghanistan and Pakistan is on a path to defeat. Their remaining operatives spend more time thinking about their own safety than plotting against us. They did not direct the attacks in Benghazi or Boston. They have not carried out a successful attack on our homeland since 9/11. Instead, what we've seen is the emergence of various al Qaeda affiliates. From Yemen to Iraq, from Somalia to North Africa, the threat today is more diffuse, with al Qaeda's affiliate in the Arabian Peninsula—AQAP—the most active in plotting against our homeland. While none of AQAP's efforts approach the scale of 9/11 they have continued to plot acts of terror, like the attempt to blow up an airplane on Christmas Day in 2009.

Unrest in the Arab World has also allowed extremists to gain a foothold in countries like Libya and Syria. Here, too, there are differences from 9/11. In some cases, we confront state-sponsored networks like Hizbollah that engage in acts of terror to achieve political goals. Others are simply collections of local militias or extremists interested in seizing territory. While we are vigilant for signs that these groups may pose a transnational threat, most are focused on operating in the countries and regions where they are based. That means we will face more localized threats like those we saw in Benghazi, or at the BP oil facility in Algeria, in which local operatives—in loose affiliation with regional networks—launch periodic attacks against Western diplomats, companies, and other soft targets, or resort to kidnapping and other criminal enterprises to fund their operations.

Finally, we face a real threat from radicalized individuals here in the United States. Whether it's a shooter at a Sikh Temple in Wisconsin; a plane flying into a building in Texas; or the extremists who killed 168 people at the Federal Building in Oklahoma City—America has confronted many forms of violent extremism in our time. Deranged or alienated individuals—often U.S. citizens or legal residents—can do enormous damage, particularly when inspired by larger notions of violent jihad. That pull towards extremism appears to have led to the shooting at Fort Hood, and the bombing of the Boston Marathon.

Lethal yet less capable al Qaeda affiliates. Threats to diplomatic facilities and businesses abroad. Homegrown extremists. This is the future of terrorism. We must take these threats seriously, and do all that we can to confront them. But as we shape our response, we have to recognize that the scale of this threat closely resembles the types of attacks we faced before 9/11. In the 1980s, we lost Americans to terrorism at our Embassy in Beirut; at our Marine Barracks in Lebanon; on a cruise ship at sea; at a disco in Berlin; and on Pan Am Flight 103 over Lockerbie. In the 1990s, we lost Americans to terrorism at the World Trade Center; at our military facilities in Saudi Arabia; and at our Embassy in Kenya. These attacks were all deadly, and we learned that left unchecked, these threats can grow. But if dealt with smartly and proportionally, these threats need not rise to the level that we saw on the eve of 9/11.

Moreover, we must recognize that these threats don't arise in a vacuum. Most, though not all, of the terrorism we face is fueled by a common ideology—a belief by some extremists that Islam is in conflict with the United States and the West, and that violence against Western targets, including civilians, is justified in pursuit of a larger cause. Of course, this ideology is based on a lie, for the United States is not at war with Islam; and this ideology is rejected by the vast majority of Muslims, who are the most frequent victims of terrorist acts.

Nevertheless, this ideology persists, and in an age in which ideas and images can travel the globe in an instant, our response to terrorism cannot depend on military or law enforcement alone. We need all elements of national power to win a battle of wills and ideas. So let me discuss the components of such a comprehensive counter-terrorism strategy.

First, we must finish the work of defeating al Qaeda and its associated forces.

In Afghanistan, we will complete our transition to Afghan responsibility for security. Our troops will come home. Our combat mission will come to an end. And we will work with the Afghan government to train security forces, and sustain a counter-terrorism force which ensures that al Qaeda can never again establish a safe-haven to launch attacks against us or our allies.

Beyond Afghanistan, we must define our effort not as a boundless 'global war on terror'—but rather as a series of persistent, targeted efforts to dismantle specific networks of violent extremists that threaten America. In many cases, this will involve partnerships with other countries. Thousands of Pakistani soldiers have lost their lives fighting extremists. In Yemen, we are supporting security forces that have reclaimed territory from AQAP. In Somalia, we helped a coalition of African nations push al Shabaab out of its strongholds. In Mali, we are providing military aid to a French-led intervention to push back al Qaeda in the Maghreb, and help the people of Mali reclaim their future.

Much of our best counter-terrorism cooperation results in the gathering and sharing of intelligence; the arrest and prosecution of terrorists. That's how a Somali terrorist apprehended off the coast of Yemen is now in prison in New York. That's how we worked with European allies to disrupt plots from Denmark to Germany to the United Kingdom. That's how intelligence collected with Saudi Arabia helped us stop a cargo plane from being blown up over the Atlantic.

But despite our strong preference for the detention and prosecution of terrorists, sometimes this approach is foreclosed. Al Qaeda and its affiliates try to gain a foothold in some of the most distant and unforgiving places on Earth. They take refuge in remote tribal regions. They hide in caves and walled compounds. They train in empty deserts and rugged mountains.

In some of these places—such as parts of Somalia and Yemen—the state has only the most tenuous reach into the territory. In other cases, the state lacks the capacity or will to take action. It is also not possible for America to simply deploy a team of Special Forces to capture every terrorist. And even when such an approach may be possible, there are places where it would pose profound risks to our troops and local civilians—where a terrorist compound cannot be breached without triggering a firefight with surrounding tribal communities that pose no threat to us, or when putting U.S. boots on the ground may trigger a major international crisis.

To put it another way, our operation in Pakistan against Osama bin Laden cannot be the norm. The risks in that case were immense; the likelihood of capture, although our preference, was remote given the certainty of resistance; the fact that we did not find ourselves confronted with civilian casualties, or embroiled in an extended firefight, was a testament to the meticulous planning and professionalism of our Special Forces—but also depended on some luck. And even then, the cost to our relationship with Pakistan—and the backlash among the Pakistani public over encroachment on their territory—was so severe that we are just now beginning to rebuild this important partnership.

It is in this context that the United States has taken lethal, targeted action against al Qaeda and its associated forces, including with remotely piloted aircraft commonly referred to as drones. As was true in previous armed conflicts, this new technology raises profound questions—about who is targeted, and why; about civilian casualties, and the risk of creating new enemies; about the legality of such strikes under U.S. and international law; about accountability and morality.

Let me address these questions. To begin with, our actions are effective. Don't take my word for it. In the intelligence gathered at bin Laden's compound, we found that he wrote, "we could lose the reserves to the enemy's air strikes. We cannot fight air strikes with explosives." Other communications from al Qaeda operatives confirm this as well. Dozens of highly skilled al Qaeda commanders, trainers, bomb makers, and operatives have been taken off the battlefield. Plots have been disrupted that would have targeted international aviation, U.S. transit systems, European cities and our troops in Afghanistan. Simply put, these strikes have saved lives.

Moreover, America's actions are legal. We were attacked on 9/11. Within a week, Congress overwhelmingly authorized the use of force. Under domestic law, and international law, the United States is at war with al Qaeda, the Taliban, and their associated forces. We are at war with an organization that right now would kill as many Americans as they could if we did not stop them first. So this is a just war—a war waged proportionally, in last resort, and in self-defense.

And yet as our fight enters a new phase, America's legitimate claim of self-defense cannot be the end of the discussion. To say a military tactic is legal, or even effective, is not to say it is wise or moral in every instance. For the same human progress that gives us the technology to strike half a world away also demands the discipline to constrain that power—or risk abusing it. That's why, over the last four years, my Administration has worked vigorously to establish a framework that governs our use of force against terrorists—insisting upon clear guidelines, oversight and accountability that is now codified in Presidential Policy Guidance that I signed yesterday.

In the Afghan war theater, we must support our troops until the transition is complete at the end of 2014. That means we will continue to take strikes against high value al Qaeda targets, but also against forces that are massing to support attacks on coalition forces. However, by the end of 2014, we will no longer have the same need for force protection, and the progress we have made against core al Qaeda will reduce the need for unmanned strikes.

Beyond the Afghan theater, we only target al Qaeda and its associated forces. Even then, the use of drones is heavily constrained. America does not take strikes when we have the ability to capture individual terrorists—our preference is always to detain, interrogate, and prosecute them. America cannot take strikes wherever we choose—our actions are bound by consultations with partners, and respect for state sovereignty. America does not take strikes to punish individuals—we act against terrorists who pose a continuing and imminent threat to the American people, and when there are no other governments capable of effectively addressing the threat. And before any strike is taken, there must be near-certainty that no civilians will be killed or injured—the highest standard we can set.

This last point is critical, because much of the criticism about drone strikes—at home and abroad—understandably centers on reports of civilian casualties. There is a wide gap between U.S. assessments of such casualties, and non-governmental reports. Nevertheless, it is a hard fact that U.S. strikes have resulted in civilian casualties, a risk that exists in all wars. For the families of those civilians, no words or legal construct can justify their loss. For me, and those in my chain of command, these deaths will haunt us as long as we live, just as we are haunted by the civilian casualties that have occurred through conventional fighting in Afghanistan and Iraq.

But as Commander-in-Chief, I must weigh these heartbreaking tragedies against the alternatives. To do nothing in the face of terrorist networks would invite far more civilian casualties—not just in our cities at home and facilities abroad, but also in the very places—like Sana'a and Kabul and Mogadishu—where terrorists seek a foothold. Let us remember that the terrorists we are after target civilians, and the death toll from their acts of terrorism against Muslims dwarfs any estimate of civilian casualties from drone strikes.

Where foreign governments cannot or will not effectively stop terrorism in their territory, the primary alternative to targeted, lethal action is the use of conventional military options. As I've said, even small Special Operations carry enormous risks. Conventional airpower or missiles are far less precise than drones, and likely to cause more civilian casualties and local outrage. And invasions of these territories lead us to be viewed as occupying armies; unleash a torrent of unintended consequences; are difficult to contain; and ultimately empower those who thrive on violent conflict. So it is false to assert that putting boots on the ground is less likely to result in civilian deaths, or to create enemies in the Muslim world. The result would be more U.S. deaths, more Blackhawks down, more confrontations with local populations, and an inevitable mission creep in support of such raids that could easily escalate into new wars.

So yes, the conflict with al Qaeda, like all armed conflict, invites tragedy. But by narrowly targeting our action against those who want to kill us, and not the people they hide among, we are choosing the course of action least likely to result in the loss of innocent life. Indeed, our efforts must also be measured against the history of putting American troops in distant lands among hostile populations. In Vietnam, hundreds of thousands of civilians died in a war where the boundaries of battle were blurred. In Iraq and Afghanistan, despite the courage and discipline of our troops, thousands of civilians have been killed. So neither conventional military action, nor waiting for attacks to occur, offers moral safe-harbor. Neither does a sole reliance on law enforcement in territories that have no functioning police or security services—and indeed, have no functioning law.

This is not to say that the risks are not real. Any U.S. military action in foreign lands risks creating more enemies, and impacts public opinion overseas. Our laws constrain the power of the President, even during wartime, and I have taken an oath to defend the Constitution of the United States. The very precision of drone strikes, and the necessary secrecy involved in such actions can end up shielding our government from the public scrutiny that a troop deployment invites. It can also lead a President and his team to view drone strikes as a cure-all for terrorism.

For this reason, I've insisted on strong oversight of all lethal action. After I took office, my Administration began briefing all strikes outside of Iraq and Afghanistan to the appropriate committees of Congress. Let me repeat that—not only did Congress authorize the use of force, it is briefed on every strike that America takes. That includes the one instance when we targeted an American citizen: Anwar Awlaki, the chief of external operations for AQAP.

This week, I authorized the declassification of this action, and the deaths of three other Americans in drone strikes, to facilitate transparency and debate on this issue, and to dismiss some of the more outlandish claims. For the record, I do not believe it would be constitutional for the government to target and kill any U.S. citizen—with a drone, or a shotgun—without due process. Nor should any President deploy armed drones over U.S. soil.

But when a U.S. citizen goes abroad to wage war against America—and is actively plotting to kill U.S. citizens; and when neither the United States, nor our partners are in a position to capture him before he carries out a plot—his citizenship should no more serve as a shield than a sniper shooting down on an innocent crowd should be protected from a swat team.

That's who Anwar Awlaki was—he was continuously trying to kill people. He helped oversee the 2010 plot to detonate explosive devices on two U.S. bound cargo planes. He was involved in planning to blow up an airliner in 2009. When Farouk Abdulmutallab—the Christmas Day bomber—went to Yemen in 2009, Awlaki hosted him, approved his suicide operation, and helped him tape a martyrdom video to be shown after the attack. His last instructions were to blow up the airplane when it was over American soil. I would have detained and prosecuted Awlaki if we captured him before he carried out a plot. But we couldn't. And as President, I would have been derelict in my duty had I not authorized the strike that took out Awlaki.

Of course, the targeting of any Americans raises constitutional issues that are not present in other strikes—which is why my Administration submitted information about Awlaki to the Department of Justice months before Awlaki was killed, and briefed the Congress before this strike as well. But the high threshold that we have set for taking lethal action applies to all potential terrorist targets, regardless of whether or not they are American citizens. This threshold respects the inherent dignity of every human life. Alongside the decision to put our men and women in uniform in harm's way, the decision to use force against individuals or groups—even against a sworn enemy of the United States—is the hardest thing I do as President. But these decisions must be made, given my responsibility to protect the American people.

Going forward, I have asked my Administration to review proposals to extend oversight of lethal actions outside of warzones that go beyond our reporting to Congress. Each option has virtues in theory, but poses difficulties in practice. For example, the establishment of a special court to evaluate and authorize lethal action has the benefit of bringing a third branch of government into the process, but raises serious constitutional issues about presidential and judicial authority. Another idea that's been suggested—the establishment of an independent oversight board in the executive branch—avoids those problems, but may introduce a layer of bureaucracy into national-security decision-making, without inspiring additional public confidence in the process. Despite these challenges, I look forward to actively engaging Congress to explore these—and other—options for increased oversight.

I believe, however, that the use of force must be seen as part of a larger discussion about a comprehensive counter-terrorism strategy. Because for all the focus on the use of force, force alone cannot make us safe. We cannot use force everywhere that a radical ideology takes root; and in the absence of a strategy that reduces the well-spring of extremism, a perpetual war—through drones or Special Forces or troop deployments—will prove self-defeating, and alter our country in troubling ways.

So the next element of our strategy involves addressing the underlying grievances and conflicts that feed extremism, from North Africa to South Asia. As we've learned this past decade, this is a vast and complex undertaking. We must be humble in our expectation that we can quickly resolve deep rooted problems like poverty and sectarian hatred. Moreover, no two countries are alike, and some will undergo chaotic change before things get better. But our security and values demand that we make the effort.

This means patiently supporting transitions to democracy in places like Egypt, Tunisia and Libya—because the peaceful realization of individual aspirations will serve as a rebuke to violent extremists. We must strengthen the opposition in Syria, while isolating extremist elements—because the end of a tyrant must not give way to the tyranny of terrorism. We are working to promote peace between Israelis and Palestinians—because it is right, and because such a peace could help reshape attitudes in the region. And we must help countries modernize economies, upgrade education, and encourage entrepreneurship—because American leadership has always been elevated by our ability to connect with peoples' hopes, and not simply their fears.

Success on these fronts requires sustained engagement, but it will also require resources. I know that foreign aid is one of the least popular expenditures—even though it amounts to less than one percent of the federal budget. But foreign assistance cannot be viewed as charity. It is fundamental to our national security, and any sensible long-term strategy to battle extremism. Moreover, foreign assistance is a tiny fraction of what we spend fighting wars that our assistance might ultimately prevent. For what we spent in a month in Iraq at the height of the war, we could be training security forces in Libya, maintaining peace agreements between Israel and its neighbors, feeding the hungry in Yemen, building schools in Pakistan, and creating reservoirs of goodwill that marginalize extremists.

America cannot carry out this work if we do not have diplomats serving in dangerous places. Over the past decade, we have strengthened security at our Embassies, and I am implementing every recommendation of the Accountability Review Board which found unacceptable failures in Benghazi. I have called on Congress to fully fund these efforts to bolster security, harden facilities, improve intelligence, and facilitate a quicker response time from our military if a crisis emerges.

But even after we take these steps, some irreducible risks to our diplomats will remain. This is the price of being the world's most powerful nation, particularly as a wave of change washes over the Arab World. And in balancing the trade-offs between security and active diplomacy, I firmly believe that any retreat from challenging regions will only increase the dangers we face in the long run.

Targeted action against terrorists. Effective partnerships. Diplomatic engagement and assistance. Through such a comprehensive strategy we can significantly reduce the chances of large scale attacks on the homeland and mitigate threats to Americans overseas. As we guard against dangers from abroad, however, we cannot neglect the daunting challenge of terrorism from within our borders.

As I said earlier, this threat is not new. But technology and the Internet increase its frequency and lethality. Today, a person can consume hateful propaganda, commit themselves to a violent agenda, and learn how to kill without leaving their home. To address this threat, two years ago my Administration did a comprehensive review, and engaged with law enforcement. The best way to prevent violent extremism is to work with the Muslim American community—which has consistently rejected terrorism—to identify signs of radicalization, and partner with law enforcement when an individual is drifting towards violence. And these partnerships can only work when we recognize that Muslims are a fundamental part of the American family. Indeed, the success of American Muslims, and our determination to guard against any encroachments on their civil liberties, is the ultimate rebuke to those who say we are at war with Islam.

Indeed, thwarting homegrown plots presents particular challenges in part because of our proud commitment to civil liberties for all who call America home. That's why, in the years to come, we will have to keep working hard to strike the appropriate balance between our need for security and preserving those freedoms that make us who we are. That means reviewing the authorities of law enforcement, so we can intercept new types of communication, and build in privacy protections to prevent abuse. That means that—even after Boston—we do not deport someone or throw someone in prison in the absence of evidence. That means putting careful constraints on the tools the government uses to protect sensitive information, such as the State Secrets doctrine. And that means finally having a strong Privacy and Civil Liberties Board to review those issues where our counter-terrorism efforts and our values may come into tension.

The Justice Department's investigation of national security leaks offers a recent example of the challenges involved in striking the right balance between our security and our open society. As Commander-in-Chief, I believe we must keep information secret that protects our operations and our people in the field. To do so, we must enforce consequences for those who break the law and breach their commitment to protect classified information. But a free press is also essential for our democracy. I am troubled by the possibility that leak investigations may chill the investigative journalism that holds government accountable.

Journalists should not be at legal risk for doing their jobs. Our focus must be on those who break the law. That is why I have called on Congress to pass a media shield law to guard against government over-reach. I have raised these issues with the Attorney General, who shares my concern. So he has agreed to review existing Department of Justice guidelines governing investigations that involve reporters, and will convene a group of media organizations to hear their concerns as part of that review. And I have directed the Attorney General to report back to me by July 12th.

All these issues remind us that the choices we make about war can impact—in sometimes unintended ways—the openness and freedom on which our way of life depends. And that is why I intend to engage Congress about the existing Authorization to Use Military Force, or AUMF, to determine how we can continue to fight terrorists without keeping America on a perpetual war-time footing.

The AUMF is now nearly twelve years old. The Afghan War is coming to an end. Core al Qaeda is a shell of its former self. Groups like AQAP must be dealt with, but in the years to come, not every collection of thugs that labels themselves al Qaeda will pose a credible threat to the United States. Unless we discipline our thinking and our actions, we may be drawn into more wars we don't need to fight, or continue to grant Presidents unbound powers more suited for traditional armed conflicts between nation states. So I look forward to engaging Congress and the American people in efforts to refine, and ultimately repeal, the AUMF's mandate. And I will not sign laws designed to expand this mandate further. Our systematic effort to dismantle terrorist organizations must continue. But this war, like all wars, must end. That's what history advises. That's what our democracy demands.

And that brings me to my final topic: the detention of terrorist suspects.

To repeat, as a matter of policy, the preference of the United States is to capture terrorist suspects. When we do detain a suspect, we interrogate them. And if the suspect can be prosecuted, we decide whether to try him in a civilian court or a Military Commission. During the past decade, the vast majority of those detained by our military were captured on the battlefield. In Iraq, we turned over thousands of prisoners as we ended the war. In Afghanistan, we have transitioned detention facilities to the Afghans, as part of the process of restoring Afghan sovereignty. So we bring law of war detention to an end, and we are committed to prosecuting terrorists whenever we can.

The glaring exception to this time-tested approach is the detention center at Guantanamo Bay. The original premise for opening GTMO—that detainees would not be able to challenge their detention—was found unconstitutional five years ago. In the meantime, GTMO has become a symbol around the world for an America that flouts the rule of law. Our allies won't cooperate with us if they think a terrorist will end up at GTMO. During a time of budget cuts, we spend $150 million each year to imprison 166 people –almost $1 million per prisoner. And the Department of Defense estimates that we must spend another $200 million to keep GTMO open at a time when we are cutting investments in education and research here at home.

As President, I have tried to close GTMO. I transferred 67 detainees to other countries before Congress imposed restrictions to effectively prevent us from either transferring detainees to other countries, or imprisoning them in the United States. These restrictions make no sense. After all, under President Bush, some 530 detainees were transferred from GTMO with Congress's support. When I ran for President the first time, John McCain supported closing GTMO. No person has ever escaped from one of our super-max or military prisons in the United States. Our courts have convicted hundreds of people for terrorism-related offenses, including some who are more dangerous than most GTMO detainees. Given my Administration's relentless pursuit of al Qaeda's leadership, there is no justification beyond politics for Congress to prevent us from closing a facility that should never have been opened.

Today, I once again call on Congress to lift the restrictions on detainee transfers from GTMO. I have asked the Department of Defense to designate a site in the United States where we can hold military commissions. I am appointing a new, senior envoy at the State Department and Defense Department whose sole responsibility will be to achieve the transfer of detainees to third countries. I am lifting the moratorium on detainee transfers to Yemen, so we can review them on a case by case basis. To the greatest extent possible, we will transfer detainees who have been cleared to go to other countries. Where appropriate, we will bring terrorists to justice in our courts and military justice system. And we will insist that judicial review be available for every detainee.

Even after we take these steps, one issue will remain: how to deal with those GTMO detainees who we know have participated in dangerous plots or attacks, but who cannot be prosecuted—for example because the evidence against them has been compromised or is inadmissible in a court of law. But once we commit to a process of closing GTMO, I am confident that this legacy problem can be resolved, consistent with our commitment to the rule of law.

I know the politics are hard. But history will cast a harsh judgment on this aspect of our fight against terrorism, and those of us who fail to end it. Imagine a future—ten years from now, or twenty years from now—when the United States of America is still holding people who have been charged with no crime on a piece of land that is not a part of our country. Look at the current situation, where we are force-feeding detainees who are holding a hunger strike. Is that who we are? Is that something that our Founders foresaw? Is that the America we want to leave to our children?

Our sense of justice is stronger than that. We have prosecuted scores of terrorists in our courts. That includes Umar Farouk Abdulmutallab, who tried to blow up an airplane over Detroit; and Faisal Shahzad, who put a car bomb in Times Square. It is in a court of law that we will try Dzhokhar Tsarnaev, who is accused of bombing the Boston Marathon. Richard Reid, the shoe bomber, is as we speak serving a life sentence in a maximum security prison here, in the United States. In sentencing Reid, Judge William Young told him, "the way we treat you . . . is the measure of our own liberties." He went on to point to the American flag that flew in the courtroom—"That flag," he said, "will fly there long after this is all forgotten. That flag still stands for freedom."

America, we have faced down dangers far greater than al Qaeda. By staying true to the values of our founding, and by using our constitutional compass, we have overcome slavery and Civil War; fascism and communism. In just these last few years as President, I have watched the American people bounce back from painful recession, mass shootings, and natural disasters like the recent tornados that devastated Oklahoma. These events were heartbreaking; they shook our communities to the core. But because of the resilience of the American people, these events could not come close to breaking us.

I think of Lauren Manning, the 9/11 survivor who had severe burns over 80 percent of her body, who said, "That's my reality. I put a Band-Aid on it, literally, and I move on."

I think of the New Yorkers who filled Times Square the day after an attempted car bomb as if nothing had happened.

I think of the proud Pakistani parents who, after their daughter was invited to the White House, wrote to us, "we have raised an American Muslim daughter to dream big and never give up because it does pay off."

I think of the wounded warriors rebuilding their lives, and helping other vets to find jobs.

I think of the runner planning to do the 2014 Boston Marathon, who said, "Next year, you are going to have more people than ever. Determination is not something to be messed with."

That's who the American people are. Determined, and not to be messed with.

Now, we need a strategy—and a politics—that reflects this resilient spirit. Our victory against terrorism won't be measured in a surrender ceremony on a battleship, or a statue being pulled to the ground. Victory will be measured in parents taking their kids to school; immigrants coming to our shores; fans taking in a ballgame; a veteran starting a business; a bustling city street. The quiet determination; that strength of character and bond of fellowship; that refutation of fear—that is both our sword and our shield. And long after the current messengers of hate have faded from the world's memory, alongside the brutal despots, deranged madmen, and ruthless demagogues who litter history—the flag of the United States will still wave from small-town cemeteries, to national monuments, to distant outposts abroad. And that flag will still stand for freedom.

Thank you. God Bless you. And may God bless the United States of America.

---

**BARACK OBAMA** served as U.S. Senator for Illinois prior to defeating John McCain in the 2008 presidential election to become the 44th President of the United States. He is the first African American to hold the position. In 2012, President Obama defeated Republican challenger Mitt Romney to win a second term.

# EXPLORING THE ISSUE

## Does the President Have Unilateral War Powers?

## Critical Thinking and Reflection

1. What legal precedents does John Yoo cite to bolster his case that the president has unilateral war powers?
2. Do you believe President Obama has done enough to consult with Congress on issues related to terrorism? Why or why not?
3. The Congress has the sole power to "declare" war, but does that leave the president the sole power to "make" war? Or is there a real difference between the two?
4. Do you believe Yoo would back President Obama's utilization of drone strikes against suspected terrorists in Pakistan and Yemen? Why or why not?
5. Should the president or Congress have ultimate war-making powers? Why?

## Is There Common Ground?

The only thing in common between the two sides is their tendency to occupy each other's position with a change of administration. When a Republican president faced a Democratic Congress in 2007–2009, there was much complaining from the latter about the president's unilateral war-making. But a few years later, with a Democratic president, many of the same practices—targeting terrorists, holding them indefinitely, wiretapping, rendition—continued, this time with tacit approval from many Democrats in Congress. Now it was time for the Republicans to make a show of indignation.

The battle over unilateral war-making is not a partisan one. Historically, we have seen both of today's major parties exercising this power at different times they deem appropriate. From a citizen's perspective, this makes any efforts at remedying the situation quite difficult. It will never be as simple as removing a president or a party. Instead, the rules of the game will need to change if citizens are that unhappy with a president's decision to act without Congress's consent. If Congress takes it upon itself to prevent a president from acting, it does little but divide the country from the elites to the masses. And as history has shown, a divided house is the most likely to fall.

## Create Central

www.mhhe.com/createcentral

## Additional Resources

Mark Brandon, *The Constitution in Wartime: Beyond Alarmism and Complacency* (Duke University Press, 2005)

Louis Fisher, *Presidential War Power* (University Press of Kansas, 2004)

Richard Neustadt, *Presidential Power and the Modern Presidents: The Politics of Leadership from Roosevelt to Reagan* (Free Press, 1991)

Richard Posner, *Not a Suicide Pact: The Constitution in a Time of National Emergency* (Oxford University Press, 2006)

John C. Yoo, *The Powers of War and Peace: The Constitution and Foreign Affairs After 9/11* (University of Chicago Press, 2006)

# Internet References . . .

Congressional Research Service: The War Powers Resolution: After Thirty Years

www.au.af.mil/au/awc/awcgate/crs/rl32267.htm

Department of Justice on War Powers

www.justice.gov/olc/warpowers925.htm

Liberty Classroom

www.libertyclassroom.com/warpowers/

Reclaiming the War Power

http://object.cato.org/sites/cato.org/files/serials/files/cato-handbook-policymakers/2009/9/hb111-10.pdf

War Powers: Law Library of Congress

http://loc.gov/law/help/usconlaw/war-powers.php

Selected, Edited, and with Issue Framing Material by:
**William J. Miller,** *Flagler College*
**George McKenna,** *City College, City University of New York*
**and**
**Stanley Feingold,** *City College, City University of New York*

# ISSUE

# Should the Courts Seek the "Original Meaning" of the Constitution?

YES: **Antonin Scalia**, from "Constitutional Interpretation," Remarks at Woodrow Wilson International Center for Scholars (March 14, 2005)

NO: **Stephen Breyer**, from Active *Liberty: Interpreting Our Democratic Constitution* (Knopf/Vintage, 2005)

---

## Learning Outcomes

**After reading this issue, you will be able to:**

- Describe what is meant by original meaning.
- Assess whether anyone can fully determine the original meaning of the Constitution.
- Explain how stare decisis works in the legal system.
- Discuss how the Supreme Court operates in decision-making.
- Identify matters where original meaning may be more easily ascertained.

---

### ISSUE SUMMARY

YES: Supreme Court Justice Antonin Scalia rejects the notion of a "living Constitution," arguing that the judges must try to understand what the Framers meant at the time.

NO: Supreme Court Justice Stephen Breyer contends that in finding the meaning of the Constitution, judges cannot neglect to consider the probable consequences of different interpretations.

On many matters the U.S. Constitution speaks with crystal clarity. In Article II, it says that "the Senate of the United States shall be composed of two Senators from each State." Even if it were desirable to have more than two Senators, or less, per state, there is no room for interpretation; "two" can only mean "two," and the only way of making it "one" or "three" is by constitutional amendment (this process is itself clearly spelled out in Article V of the Constitution). Other clauses, too, are defined in such a way as to put them beyond interpretative argument. Presidents Reagan and Clinton very much wanted to run again after their two terms, but there was no way either of them could get around the unambiguous words of the twenty-second amendment: "No person shall be elected to the office of President more than twice." The same clarity is found in many other provisions in the Constitution, such as the age requirements for Senators, Representatives, and Presidents (Articles I and II); direct election of Senators (Amendment XVII); and both Prohibition and its repeal (Amendments XVIII and XXI).

But other clauses in the Constitution are not so clear-cut. The first amendment states that "Congress shall make no law respecting an establishment of religion. . . ." What is an "establishment of religion?" The Constitution itself does not say. Some constitutional scholars take it to mean that the state may not single out any particular religion for state sponsorship or support; others interpret it to mean that the state may not aid any religions. Which interpretation is correct? And what method do we use to determine which is correct? The same questions have to be asked about other fuzzy-sounding phrases, such as "due process of law" (Article V and Amendment XIV), "cruel and unusual punishment" (Amendment VIII), and "commerce among the several states" (Article I). Down through the years, jurists and legal commentators have tried to devise guiding principles for interpreting these and other phrases that have been subjects of dispute in the courts.

One set of principles made headlines in the 1980s when federal Appeals Court judge Robert Bork was nominated to the Supreme Court by President Ronald Reagan. Bork was a champion of "originalism," interpreting the Constitution according to what he called the "original intent" of its Framers. What the courts should do, Bork argued, is to go back to what the Framers meant at the time they wrote the particular clauses in dispute. Since the effect of Bork's approach was to call into question some of the more recent decisions by the Court, such as those upholding affirmative action and abortion, his nomination provoked a tumultuous national debate, and in the end he failed to win Senate confirmation. As Justice Antonin Scalia explains,

> The theory of originalism treats a constitution like a statute, and gives it the meaning that its words were understood to bear at the time they were promulgated. You will sometimes hear it described as the theory of original intent. You will never hear me refer to original intent, because as I say I am first of all a textualist, and then an originalist. If you are a textualist, you don't care about the intent, and I don't care if the framers of the Constitution had some secret meaning in mind when they adopted its words. I take the words as they were promulgated to the people of the United States, and what is the fairly understood meaning of those words.

On its face, originalism seems to comport with common sense. In making a will, to take an analogy, people rightly expect that their will should be interpreted according to their intent, not what their heirs might want it to mean. The analogy, however, comes under serious strain when we consider that the Constitution is not, like a will, the product of one person, or even one generation. Its various clauses have been crafted over 220 years; they are the work of many people in various Congresses, and many, many more who ratified them in state conventions or legislatures. Each one of those people may have had a different idea of what those clauses meant. When we come to clauses like "establishment of religion" or "equal protection of the laws," how can we possibly determine what the "original intent" of these clauses was—or even if there was any single intent? The reply of the originalists is that the goal of determining the Framers' intent must be striven for even when it is not perfectly attained. Moreover, what are we going to put in its place? Surely we can't have judges simply making things up, slipping in their own personal policy preferences in place of the Constitution and statutes of the United States.

Beyond the inherent difficulty in assuming that the Founders spoke with one voice and we can successfully interpret it, what happens when technologies entirely unknown to the Founders find their way before the court? Consider sexting and drones. The concept that a court of law would need to one day determine how to punish a teenage girl for passing photographs across airwaves from cell phone to cell phone or determine the appropriateness of using joystick guided unmanned air vehicles to fire on suspected terrorists is unheard of. Consequently, could we not assume any alleged original intent on these issues is largely constructed post facto by a party looking for a particular result? And does this occurrence not defy what Americans claim to want out of their justice system? If we intend for the Constitution to endure over time, should its interpretation not be flexible and responsive to circumstantial changes? It is intentionally difficult to amend the Constitution, especially in a timely fashion, so would it not be easier to permit for interpretations to change as necessary?

This is one of the arguments—what he calls the "killer argument"— advanced by Justice Antonin Scalia in the selections that follow. As if replying to him, Justice Stephen Breyer rises to Scalia's challenge by suggesting that in interpreting the Constitution judges should weigh the probable consequences of varying interpretations of disputed clauses in the Constitution.

# YES ↵

**Antonin Scalia**

## Constitutional Interpretation

I am one of a small number of judges, small number of anybody: judges, professors, lawyers; who are known as originalists. Our manner of interpreting the Constitution is to begin with the text, and to give that text the meaning that it bore when it was adopted by the people. I'm not a strict constructionist, despite the introduction. I don't like the term "strict construction." I do not think the Constitution, or any text should be interpreted either strictly or sloppily; it should be interpreted reasonably. Many of my interpretations do not deserve the description "strict." I do believe, however, that you give the text the meaning it had when it was adopted.

This is such a minority position in modern academia and in modern legal circles that on occasion I'm asked when I've given a talk like this a question from the back of the room—"Justice Scalia, when did you first become an originalist?"—as though it is some kind of weird affliction that seizes some people—"When did you first start eating human flesh?"

Although it is a minority view now, the reality is that, not very long ago, originalism was orthodoxy. Everybody, at least purported to be an originalist. If you go back and read the commentaries on the Constitution by Joseph Story, he didn't think the Constitution evolved or changed. He said it means and will always mean what it meant when it was adopted.

Or consider the opinions of John Marshall in the Federal Bank case,* where he says, we must not, we must always remember it is a constitution we are expounding. And since it's a constitution, he says, you have to give its provisions expansive meaning so that they will accommodate events that you do not know of which will happen in the future.

Well, if it is a constitution that changes, you wouldn't have to give it an expansive meaning. You can give it whatever meaning you want and when future necessity arises, you simply change the meaning. But anyway, that is no longer the orthodoxy.

Oh, one other example about how not just the judges and scholars believed in originalism, but even the American people. Consider the Nineteenth Amendment, which is the amendment that gave women the vote. It was adopted by the American people in 1920. Why did we adopt a constitutional amendment for that purpose? The Equal Protection Clause existed in 1920; it was adopted right after the Civil War. And you know that if that issue of the franchise for women came up today, we would not have to have a constitutional amendment. Someone would come to the Supreme Court and say, "Your Honors, in a democracy, what could be a greater denial of equal protection than denial of the franchise?" And the Court would say, "Yes! Even though it never meant it before, the Equal Protection Clause means that women have to have the vote." But that's not how the American people thought in 1920. In 1920, they looked at the Equal Protection Clause and said, "What does it mean?" Well, it clearly doesn't mean that you can't discriminate in the franchise—not only on the basis of sex, but on the basis of property ownership, on the basis of literacy. None of that is unconstitutional. And therefore, since it wasn't unconstitutional, and we wanted it to be, we did things the good old fashioned way and adopted an amendment.

Now, in asserting that originalism used to be orthodoxy, I do not mean to imply that judges did not distort the Constitution now and then, of course they did. We had willful judges then, and we will have willful judges until the end of time. But the difference is that prior to the last fifty years or so, prior to the advent of the "Living Constitution," judges did their distortions the good old fashioned way, the honest way—they lied about it. They said the Constitution means such and such, when it never meant such and such.

It's a big difference that you now no longer have to lie about it, because we are in the era of the evolving Constitution. And the judge can simply say, "Oh yes, the Constitution didn't used to mean that, but it does now." We are in the age in which not only judges, not only lawyers, but even school children have come to learn the Constitution changes. I have grammar school students come into the court now and then, and they recite very proudly what they have been taught: "The Constitution is a living document." You know, it morphs.

Well, let me first tell you how we got to the "Living Constitution." You don't have to be a lawyer to understand it. The road is not that complicated. Initially, the Court began giving terms in the text of the Constitution a meaning they didn't have when they were adopted. For example, the First Amendment, which forbids Congress to abridge the freedom of speech. What does the freedom of speech mean? Well, it clearly did not mean that Congress, or government could not impose any restrictions upon speech. Libel laws for example, were clearly Constitutional. Nobody thought the First Amendment was *carte blanche* to

---

*McCulloch v. Maryland,* 4 Wheat, 316 (1819). [*Eds.*]

From a speech delivered at the Woodrow Wilson International Center for Scholars, March 14, 2005.

libel someone. But in the famous case of *New York Times v. Sullivan*, the Supreme Court said, "But the First Amendment does prevent you from suing for libel if you are a public figure and if the libel was not malicious." That is, the person, a member of the press or otherwise, thought that what the person said was true. Well, that had never been the law. I mean, it might be a good law. And some states could amend their libel law.

It's one thing for a state to amend its libel law and say, "We think that public figures shouldn't be able to sue." That's fine. But the courts have said that the First Amendment, which never meant this before, now means that if you are a public figure, that you can't sue for libel unless it's intentional, malicious. So that's one way to do it.

Another example is: the Constitution guarantees the right to be represented by counsel; that never meant the State had to pay for your counsel. But you can reinterpret it to mean that.

That was step one. Step two, I mean, that will only get you so far. There is no text in the Constitution that you could reinterpret to create a right to abortion, for example. So you need something else. The something else is called the doctrine of "Substantive Due Process." Only lawyers can walk around talking about substantive process, inasmuch as it's a contradiction in terms. If you referred to substantive process or procedural substance at a cocktail party, people would look at you funny. But lawyers talk this way all the time.

What substantive due process is, is quite simple, the Constitution has a Due Process Clause, which says that no person shall be deprived of life, liberty or property without due process of law. Now, what does this guarantee? Does it guarantee life, liberty or property? No, indeed! All three can be taken away. You can be fined, you can be incarcerated, you can even be executed, but not without due process of law. It's a procedural guarantee. But the Court said, and this goes way back, in the 1920s at least, in fact the first case to do it was Dred Scott. But it became more popular in the 1920s. The Court said there are some liberties that are so important, that no process will suffice to take them away. Hence, substantive due process.

Now, what liberties are they? The Court will tell you. Be patient. When the doctrine of substantive due process was initially announced, it was limited in this way, the Court said it embraces only those liberties that are fundamental to a democratic society and rooted in the traditions of the American people.

Then we come to step three. Step three: that limitation is eliminated. Within the last twenty years, we have found to be covered by Due Process the right to abortion, which was so little rooted in the traditions of the American people that it was criminal for two hundred years; the right to homosexual sodomy, which was so little rooted in the traditions of the American people that it was criminal for two hundred years.

So it is literally true, and I don't think this is an exaggeration, that the Court has essentially liberated itself from the text of the Constitution, from the text, and even from the traditions of the American people. It is up to the Court to say what is covered by substantive due process. What are the arguments usually made in favor of the Living Constitution? As the name of it suggests, it is a very attractive philosophy, and it's hard to talk people out of it: the notion that the Constitution grows. The major argument is the Constitution is a living organism, it has to grow with the society that it governs or it will become brittle and snap.

This is the equivalent of, an anthropomorphism equivalent to what you hear from your stock broker, when he tells you that the stock market is resting for an assault on the eleven-thousand level. The stock market panting at some base camp. The stock market is not a mountain climber and the Constitution is not a living organism for Pete's sake; it's a legal document, and like all legal documents, it says some things, and it doesn't say other things.

And if you think that the aficionados of the Living Constitution want to bring you flexibility, think again. My Constitution is a very flexible Constitution. You think the death penalty is a good idea: persuade your fellow citizens and adopt it. You think it's a bad idea: persuade them the other way and eliminate it. You want a right to abortion: create it the way most rights are created in a democratic society. Persuade your fellow citizens it's a good idea, and enact it. You want the opposite, persuade them the other way. That's flexibility. But to read either result into the Constitution is not to produce flexibility, it is to produce what a constitution is designed to produce: rigidity.

Abortion, for example, is offstage, it is off the democratic stage, it is no use debating it, it is unconstitutional. I mean prohibiting it is unconstitutional. I mean it's no use debating it anymore. Now and forever, coast to coast, I guess until we amend the constitution, which is a difficult thing. So, for whatever reason you might like the Living Constitution, don't like it because it provides flexibility. That's not the name of the game.

Some people also seem to like it because they think it's a good liberal thing. That somehow this is a conservative/liberal battle. And conservatives like the old-fashioned originalist Constitution and liberals ought to like the Living Constitution. That's not true either. The dividing line between those who believe in the Living Constitution and those who don't is not the dividing line between conservatives and liberals.

Conservatives are willing to grow the Constitution to cover their favorite causes just as liberals are. And the best example of that is two cases we announced some years ago on the same day, the same morning. One case was *Romer v. Evans*, in which the people of Colorado had enacted an amendment to the State Constitution by plebiscite, which said that neither the State, nor any subdivision of the State would add to the protected statuses against which private individuals cannot discriminate. The usual ones are: race, religion, age, sex, disability and so forth. Would not add sexual preference. Somebody thought that was a terrible idea, and since it was a terrible idea, it must be unconstitutional. Brought a lawsuit, it came to the Supreme Court. And the Supreme Court said, "Yes, it is unconstitutional." On the basis of . . . I don't know. The Sexual Preference Clause of the Bill of Rights, presumably. And the liberals loved it; and the conservatives gnashed their teeth.

The very next case we announced is a case called *BMW v. [Gore]*. Not the [Gore] you think; this is another [Gore]. Mr. Gore had bought a BMW, which is a car supposedly advertised at least as having a superb finish, baked seven times in ovens deep in the Alps, by dwarfs. And his BMW apparently had gotten scratched on the way over. They did not send it back to the Alps, they took a can of spray-paint and fixed it. And he found out about this and was furious, and he brought a lawsuit. He got his compensatory damages, a couple of hundred dollars, the difference between a car with a better paint job and a worse paint job. Plus, $2 million against BMW for punitive damages for being a bad actor, which is absurd of course, so it must be unconstitutional. BMW appealed to my court, and my court said, "Yes, it's unconstitutional." In violation of, I assume, the Excessive Damages Clause of the Bill of Rights. And if excessive punitive damages are unconstitutional, why aren't excessive compensatory damages unconstitutional? So you have a federal question whenever you get a judgment in a civil case. Well, that one the conservatives liked, because conservatives don't like punitive damages, and the liberals gnashed their teeth.

I dissented in both cases because I say, "A pox on both their houses." It has nothing to do with what your policy preferences are; it has to do with what you think the Constitution is.

Some people are in favor of the Living Constitution because they think it always leads to greater freedom. There's just nothing to lose. The evolving Constitution will always provide greater and greater freedom, more and more rights. Why would you think that? It's a two-way street. And indeed, under the aegis of the Living Constitution, some freedoms have been taken away. . . .

Well, I've talked about some of the false virtues of the Living Constitution, let me tell you what I consider its, principal, vices are. Surely the greatest, you should always begin with principal, its greatest vice is its illegitimacy. The only reason federal courts sit in judgment of the constitutionality of federal legislation is not because they are explicitly authorized to do so in the Constitution. Some modern constitutions give the constitutional court explicit authority to review German legislation or French legislation for its constitutionality. Our Constitution doesn't say anything like that. But John Marshall says in *Marbury v. Madison*: look, this is lawyers' work. What you have here is an apparent conflict between the Constitution and the statute. And, all the time, lawyers and judges have to reconcile these conflicts; they try to read the two to comport with each other. If they can't, it's judges' work to decide which ones prevail. When there are two statutes, the more recent one prevails. It implicitly repeals the older

one. But when the Constitution is at issue, the Constitution prevails because it is a "superstatute." I mean, that's what Marshall says: it's judges' work.

If you believe, however, that the Constitution is not a legal text, like the texts involved when judges reconcile or decide which of two statutes prevail; if you think the Constitution is some exhortation to give effect to the most fundamental values of the society as those values change from year to year; if you think that it is meant to reflect, as some of the Supreme Court cases say, particularly those involving the Eighth Amendment, if you think it is simply meant to reflect the evolving standards of decency that mark the progress of a maturing society, if that is what you think it is, then why in the world would you have it interpreted by nine lawyers? What do I know about the evolving standards of decency of American society? I'm afraid to ask.

If that is what you think the Constitution is, then *Marbury v. Madison* is wrong. It shouldn't be up to the judges, it should be up to the legislature. We should have a system like the English. Whatever the legislature thinks is constitutional is constitutional. They know the evolving standards of American society, I don't. So in principle, it's incompatible with the legal regime that America has established.

Secondly, and this is the killer argument, I mean, it's the best debater's argument. They say in politics, you can't beat somebody with nobody, it's the same thing with principles of legal interpretation. If you don't believe in originalism, then you need some other principle of interpretation. Being a non-originalist is not enough. You see, I have my rules that confine me. I know what I'm looking for. When I find it, the original meaning of the Constitution, I am handcuffed. If I believe that the First Amendment meant when it was adopted that you are entitled to burn the American flag, I have to come out that way, even though I don't like to come out that way. When I find that the original meaning of the jury trial guarantee is that any additional time you spend in prison which depends upon a fact, must depend upon a fact found by a jury, once I find that's what the jury trial guarantee means, I am handcuffed. Though I'm a law-and-order type, I cannot do all the mean conservative things I would like to do to this society. You got me.

Now, if you're not going to control your judges that way, what other criterion are you going to place before them? What is the criterion that governs the living constitutional judge? What can you possibly use, besides original meaning? Think about that. Natural law? We all agree on that, don't we? The philosophy of John Rawls? That's easy. There really is nothing else. You either tell your judges, "Look, this is a law, like all laws, give it the meaning it had when it was adopted." Or, you tell your judges, "Govern us. You tell us whether people under eighteen, who committed their crimes when they were under eighteen, should be executed. You tell us whether there ought to be an unlimited right to abortion or a partial right to abortion. You make these decisions for us."

I have put this question, you know I speak at law schools with some frequency just to make trouble, and I put this question to the faculty all the time, or incite the students to ask their living constitutional professors. "OK professor, you are not an originalist, what is your criterion?" There is none other.

And finally, this is what I will conclude with, although it is not on a happy note, the worst thing about the Living Constitution is that it will destroy the Constitution. I was confirmed, close to nineteen years ago now, by a vote of ninety-eight to nothing. The two missing were Barry Goldwater and Jake Garn, so make it a hundred. I was known at that time to be, in my political and social views, fairly conservative. But still, I was known to be a good lawyer, an honest man, somebody who could read a text and give it its fair meaning, had judicial impartiality and so forth. And so I was unanimously confirmed.

Today, barely twenty years later, it is difficult to get someone confirmed to the Court of Appeals. What has happened? The American people have figured out what is going on. If we are selecting lawyers, if we are selecting people to read a text and give it the fair meaning it had when it was adopted, yes, the most important thing to do is to get a good lawyer. If on the other hand, we're picking people to draw out of their own conscience and experience, a new constitution, with all sorts of new values to govern our society, then we should not look principally for good lawyers. We should look principally for people who agree with us, the majority, as to whether there ought to be this right, that right, and the other right. We want to pick people that would write the new constitution that we would want.

And that is why you hear in the discourse on this subject, people talking about moderate, we want moderate judges. What is a moderate interpretation of the text? Halfway between what it really means and what you'd like it to mean? There is no such thing as a moderate interpretation of the text. Would you ask a lawyer, "Draw me a moderate contract?" The only way the word has any meaning is if you are looking for someone to write a law, to write a constitution, rather than to interpret one. The moderate judge is the one who will devise the new constitution that most people would approve of. So for example, we had a suicide case some terms ago, and the Court refused to hold that there is a constitutional right to assisted suicide. We said, "We're not yet ready to say that. Stay tuned, in a few years, the time may come, but we're not yet ready." And that was a moderate decision, because I think most people would not want—if we had gone, looked into that and created a national right to assisted suicide that would have been an immoderate and extremist decision.

I think the very terminology suggests where we have arrived: at the point of selecting people to write a constitution, rather than people to give us the fair meaning of one that has been democratically adopted. And when that happens, when the Senate interrogates nominees to the Supreme Court, or to the lower courts you know, "Judge so and so, do you think there is a right to this in the Constitution? You don't? Well, my constituents think there ought to be, and I'm not going to appoint to the court someone who is not going to find that." When we are in that mode, you realize, we have rendered the Constitution useless, because the Constitution will mean what the majority wants it to mean. The senators are representing the majority. And they will be selecting justices who will devise a constitution that the majority wants.

And that of course, deprives the Constitution of its principle utility. The Bill of Rights is devised to protect you and me against, who do you think? The majority. My most important function on the Supreme Court is to tell the majority to take a walk. And the notion that the justices ought to be selected because of the positions that they will take that are favored by the majority is a recipe for destruction of what we have had for two hundred years.

---

**Antonin Scalia** is an Associate Justice of the U.S. Supreme Court. He was appointed in 1986 by President Ronald Reagan.

**Stephen Breyer**

# Active Liberty: Interpreting Our Democratic Constitution

**M**y discussion sees individual constitutional provisions as embodying certain basic purposes, often expressed in highly general terms. It sees the Constitution itself as a single document designed to further certain basic general purposes as a whole. It argues that an understanding of, and a focus upon, those general purposes will help a judge better to understand and to apply specific provisions. And it identifies consequences as an important yardstick to measure a given interpretation's faithfulness to these democratic purposes. In short, focus on purpose seeks to promote active liberty by insisting on interpretations, statutory as well as constitutional, that are consistent with the people's will. Focus on consequences, in turn, allows us to gauge whether and to what extent we have succeeded in facilitating workable outcomes which reflect that will.

Some lawyers, judges, and scholars, however, would caution strongly against the reliance upon purposes (particularly abstractly stated purposes) and assessment of consequences. They ask judges to focus primarily upon text, upon the Framers' original expectations, narrowly conceived, and upon historical tradition. They do not deny the occasional relevance of consequences or purposes (including such general purposes as democracy), but they believe that judges should use them sparingly in the interpretive endeavor. They ask judges who tend to find interpretive answers in those decision-making elements to rethink the problem to see whether language, history, tradition, and precedent by themselves will not yield an answer. They fear that, once judges become accustomed to justifying legal conclusions through appeal to real-world consequences, they will too often act subjectively and undemocratically, substituting an elite's views of good policy for sound law. They hope that language, history, tradition, and precedent will provide important safeguards against a judge's confusing his or her personal, undemocratic notion of what is good for that which the Constitution or statute demands. They tend also to emphasize the need for judicial opinions that set forth their legal conclusions in terms of rules that will guide other institutions, including lower courts.

This view, which I shall call "textualist" (in respect to statutes) or "originalist" (in respect to the Constitution) or "literalist" (shorthand for both), while logically consistent with emphasizing the Constitution's democratic objectives, is not hospitable to the kinds of arguments I have advanced. Nor is it easily reconciled with my illustrations. Why, then, does it not undercut my entire argument?

The answer, in my view, lies in the unsatisfactory nature of that interpretive approach. First, the more "originalist" judges cannot appeal to the Framers themselves in support of their interpretive views. The Framers did not say specifically what factors judges should take into account when they interpret statutes or the Constitution. This is obvious in the case of statutes. Why would the Framers have preferred (1) a system of interpretation that relies heavily on linguistic canons to (2) a system that seeks more directly to find the intent of the legislators who enacted the statute? It is close to obvious in respect to the Constitution. Why would the Framers, who disagreed even about the necessity of *including* a Bill of Rights in the Constitution, who disagreed about the *content* of that Bill of Rights, nonetheless have agreed about *what school of interpretive thought* should prove dominant in interpreting that Bill of Rights in the centuries to come?

In respect to content, the Constitution itself says that the "enumeration" in the Constitution of some rights "shall not be construed to deny or disparage others retained by the people." Professor Bernard Bailyn concludes that the Framers added this language to make clear that "rights, like law itself, should never be fixed, frozen, that new dangers and needs will emerge, and that to respond to these dangers and needs, rights must be newly specified to protect the individual's integrity and inherent dignity." Given the open-ended nature of *content*, why should one expect to find fixed views about the nature of interpretive practice?

If, however, justification for the literalist's interpretive practices cannot be found in the Framers intentions, where can it be found—other than in an appeal to *consequences*, that is, in an appeal to the presumed beneficial consequences for the law or for the nation that will flow from adopting those practices? And that is just what we find argued. That is to say, literalist arguments often try to show that that approach will have favorable *results*, for example, that it will deter judges from substituting their own views about what is good for the public for those of Congress or for those embodied in the Constitution. They argue, in other words, that a more literal approach to interpretation will better control judicial subjectivity. Thus, while literalists eschew consideration of consequences case by case, their interpretive rationale is consequentialist in this important sense.

Second, I would ask whether it is true that judges who reject literalism necessarily open the door to subjectivity. They do not endorse subjectivity. And under their approach important safeguards of objectivity remain. For one thing, a judge who emphasizes consequences, no less than any other, is aware of the legal precedents, rules, standards, practices, and institutional understanding that a decision will affect. He or she also takes account of the way in which this system of legally related rules, institutions, and practices affects the world.

To be sure, a court focused on consequences may decide a case in a way that radically changes the law. But this is not always a bad thing. For example, after the late-nineteenth-century Court decided *Plessy v. Ferguson*, the case which permitted racial segregation that was, in principle, "separate but equal," it became apparent that segregation did not mean equality but meant disrespect for members of a minority race and led to a segregated society that was totally unequal, a consequence directly contrary to the purpose and demands of the Fourteenth Amendment. The Court, in *Brown v. Board of Education* and later decisions, overruled *Plessy*, and the law changed in a way that profoundly affected the lives of many.

In any event, to focus upon consequences does not automatically invite frequent dramatic legal change. Judges, including those who look to consequences, understand the human need to plan in reliance upon law, the need for predictability, the need for stability. And they understand that too radical, too frequent legal change has, as a consequence, a tendency to undercut those important law-related human needs. Similarly, each judge's individual need to be consistent over time constrains subjectivity. As Justice O'Connor has explained, a constitutional judge's initial decisions leave "footprints" that the judge, in later decisions, will almost inevitably follow.

Moreover, to consider consequences is not to consider simply whether the consequences of a proposed decision are good or bad, in a particular judge's opinion. Rather, to emphasize consequences is to emphasize consequences related to the particular textual provision at issue. The judge must examine the consequences through the lens of the relevant constitutional value or purpose. The relevant values limit interpretive possibilities. If they are democratic values, they may well counsel modesty or restraint as well. And I believe that when a judge candidly acknowledges that, in addition to text, history, and precedent, consequences also guide his decision-making, he is more likely to be disciplined in emphasizing, for example, constitutionally relevant consequences rather than allowing his own subjectively held values to be outcome determinative. In all these ways, a focus on consequences will itself constrain subjectivity.

Here are examples of how these principles apply. The First Amendment says that "Congress shall make no law respecting an establishment of religion." I recently wrote (in dissent) that this clause prohibits government from providing vouchers to parents to help pay for the education of their children in parochial schools. The basic reason, in my view, is that the clause seeks to avoid among other things the "social conflict, potentially created when government becomes involved in religious education." Nineteenth- and twentieth-century immigration has produced a nation with fifty or more different religions. And that fact made the risk of "social conflict" far more serious after the Civil War and in twentieth-century America than the Framers, with their eighteenth-century experience, might have anticipated. The twentieth-century Supreme Court had held in applicable precedent that, given the changing nature of our society, in order to implement the basic value that the Framers wrote the clause to protect, it was necessary to interpret the clause more broadly than the Framers might have thought likely.

My opinion then turned to consequences. It said that voucher programs, if widely adopted, could provide billions of dollars to religious schools. At first blush, that may seem a fine idea. But will different religious groups become concerned about which groups are getting the money and how? What are the criteria? How are programs being implemented? Is a particular program biased against particular sects, say, because it forbids certain kinds of teaching? Are rival sects failing to live up to the relevant criteria, say, by teaching "civil disobedience" to "unjust laws"? How will claims for money, say, of one religious group against another, be adjudicated? In a society as religiously diverse as ours, I saw in the administration of huge grant programs for religious education the potential for religious strife. And that, it seemed to me, was the kind of problem the First Amendment's religion clauses seek to avoid.

The same constitutional concern—the need to avoid a "divisiveness based upon religion that promotes social conflict"—helped me determine whether the Establishment Clause forbade two public displays of the tables of the Ten Commandments, one inside a Kentucky state courthouse, the other on the grounds of the Texas State Capitol. It is well recognized that the Establishment Clause does not allow the government to compel religious practices, to show favoritism among sects or between religion and non-religion, or to promote religion. Yet, at the same time, given the religious beliefs of most Americans, an absolutist approach that would purge all religious references from the public sphere could well promote the very kind of social conflict that the Establishment Clause seeks to avoid. Thus, I thought, the Establishment Clause cannot *automatically* forbid every public display of the Ten Commandments, despite the religious nature of its text. Rather, one must examine the context of the *particular* display to see whether, in that context, the tablets convey the kind of government-endorsed religious message that the Establishment Clause forbids.

The history of the Kentucky courthouse display convinced me and the other members of the Court's majority that the display sought to serve its sponsors' primarily religious objectives and that many of its viewers would understand it as reflecting that motivation. But the context of the Texas display differed significantly. A private civic (and primarily secular) organization had placed the tablets on the Capitol grounds as part of the organization's efforts to combat juvenile delinquency. Those grounds contained seventeen other monuments and twenty-one historical markers, none of which conveyed any religious message and all of which sought to illustrate the historical "ideals" of Texans. And the monument had stood for forty years without legal challenge. These circumstances strongly suggested that the public visiting the Capitol grounds had long considered the tablets' religious message as a secondary part of a broader moral and historical message reflecting a cultural heritage—a view of the display consistent with its promoters' basic objective.

It was particularly important that the Texas display stood uncontested for forty years. That fact indicated, as a practical matter of degree, that (unlike the Kentucky display) the Texas display was unlikely to prove socially divisive. Indeed, to require the display's removal itself would encourage disputes over the the removal of long-standing depictions of the Ten Commandments from public buildings across the nation, thereby creating the very kind of religiously based divisiveness that the Establishment Clause was designed to prevent. By way of contrast, the short and stormy history of the more contemporary Kentucky display revealed both religious motivation and consequent social controversy. Thus, in the two cases, which I called borderline cases, consideration of likely consequences—evaluated in light of the purposes or values embodied within the Establishment Clause—helped produce a legal result: The Clause allowed the Texas display, while it forbade the display in Kentucky.

I am not arguing here that I was right in any of these cases. I am arguing that my opinions sought to identify a critical value underlying the Religion Clauses. They considered how that value applied in modern-day America; they looked for consequences relevant to that value. And they sought to evaluate likely consequences in terms of that value. That is what I mean by an *interpretive approach* that emphasizes consequences. Under that approach language, precedent, constitutional values, and factual circumstances all constrain judicial subjectivity.

Third, "subjectivity" is a two-edged criticism, which the literalist himself cannot escape. The literalist's tools—language and structure, history and tradition—often fail to provide objective guidance in those truly difficult cases about which I have spoken. Will canons of interpretation provide objective answers? One canon tells the court to choose an interpretation that gives every statutory word

a meaning. Another permits the court to ignore a word, treating it as surplus, if otherwise the construction is repugnant to the statute's purpose. Shall the court read the statute narrowly as in keeping with the common law or broadly as remedial in purpose? Canons to the left to them, canons to the right of them, which canons shall the judges choose to follow?

. . . Fourth, I do not believe that textualist or originalist methods of interpretation are more likely to produce clear, workable legal rules. But even were they to do so, the advantages of legal rules can be overstated. Rules must be interpreted and applied. Every law student whose class grade is borderline knows that the benefits that rules produce for cases that fall within the heartland are often lost in cases that arise at the boundaries.

. . . Fifth, textualist and originalist doctrines may themselves produce seriously harmful consequences—outweighing whatever risks of subjectivity or uncertainty are inherent in other approaches.

. . . Literalism has a tendency to undermine the Constitution's efforts to create a framework for democratic government—a government that, while protecting basic individual liberties, permits citizens to govern themselves, and to govern themselves effectively. Insofar as a more literal interpretive approach undermines this basic objective, it is inconsistent with the most fundamental original intention of the Framers themselves.

For any or all of these reasons, I hope that those strongly committed to textualist or literalist views—those whom I am almost bound not to convince—are fairly small in number. I hope to have convinced some of the rest that active liberty has an important role to play in constitutional (and statutory) interpretation.

That role, I repeat, does not involve radical change in current professional interpretive methods nor does it involve ignoring the protection the Constitution grants fundamental (negative) liberties. It takes Thomas Jefferson's statement as a statement of goals that the Constitution now seeks to fulfill: "[A]ll men are created equal." They are endowed by their Creator with certain "unalienable Rights." "[T]o secure these Rights, Governments are instituted among Men, *deriving their just powers from the consent of the governed.*" It underscores, emphasizes, or reemphasizes the final democratic part of the famous phrase. That reemphasis, I believe, has practical value when judges seek to assure fidelity, in our modern society, to these ancient and unchanging ideals.

---

**Stephen Breyer** is an Associate Justice of the U.S. Supreme Court. He was appointed in 1994 by President Bill Clinton.

# EXPLORING THE ISSUE

## Should the Courts Seek the "Original Meaning" of the Constitution?

### Critical Thinking and Reflection

1. What does Justice Scalia mean by the "original meaning" of the Constitution?
2. Why does Justice Breyer reject the concept of an original meaning?
3. If there is no "original meaning," are Justices free to read their views into the Constitution?
4. How should the Supreme Court determine the constitutional status of actions that the authors of the Constitution could not imagine?
5. What impact do divided Supreme Court decisions have on the resolution of controversial issues?

### Is There Common Ground?

The close division on the present U.S. Supreme Court reflects a division that runs through the nation's history. The size of the two blocs varies, depending on which president fills a vacancy, but the conflict remains. Each side represents itself a truer embodiment of the spirit of the Constitution's authors. Both sides will be respecters of stare decisis (to stand by an earlier decision) when it conforms to their views, and both sides will overthrow a precedent when it does not. The only common ground they share is the U.S. Constitution, but it is the point at which they part.

Given that none of our Founding Fathers are still around today, we will never be able to know their true intent in what was written into the Constitution. More importantly, this fact means there is no neutral arbiter to actually say who is right when different parties attempt to determine what the Founders meant. It is clear that James Madison helped pen a document in which there is clarity on numerous important points. Yet slowly the Supreme Court is being asked to interpret every non-explicit phrase. And when it is nothing more than a Supreme Court ruling,

it is always open for reinterpretation when the crucial swing vote shifts. Such a situation leads to potential instability. Perhaps this is what the Founders really wanted: a country forced to continually examine what it does and why.

### Create Central

www.mhhe.com/createcentral

### Additional Resources

Ronald Dworkin, *Freedom's Law: The Moral Reading of the American Constitution* (Harvard University Press, 1996)

Mary Ann Glendon, *A Nation Under Lawyers* (Farrar, Straus & Giroux, 1994)

Leonard Levy, *Original Intent and the Framers' Constitution* (Ivan R. Dee, 2012)

Jeffrey A. Segal, *The Supreme Court in the Legal System* (Cambridge University Press, 2005)

Jeffrey Toobin, *The Nine: Inside the Secret World of the Supreme Court* (Doubleday, 2007)

## *Internet References . . .*

George Washington Law Review

www.gwlr.org/wp-content/uploads/2012/11
/Greene_80_6.pdf

Legislative Intent Service

www.legintent.com

Original Intent

www.originalintent.org

Tenth Amendment Center

http://tenthamendmentcenter.com/2012/05/21
/original-intent-original-understanding-original
-meaning/

Utah Legislative Intent and Legislative History

http://archives.utah.gov/research/guides
/legislative-history.htm

**Selected, Edited, and with Issue Framing Material by:**
William J. Miller, *Flagler College*
George McKenna, *City College, City University of New York*
**and**
Stanley Feingold, *City College, City University of New York*

# ISSUE

# Is Congress a Dysfunctional Institution?

YES: **Ezra Klein**, from "What Happens When Congress Fails to Do Its Job," *Newsweek* (March 27, 2010)

NO: **William Mo Cowan**, from "Cowan Farewell Address," remarks before U.S. Senate (June 26, 2013)

---

## Learning Outcomes

**After reading this issue, you will be able to:**

- Identify sources of institutional deadlock.
- Explain how partisan rancor impacts government.
- Describe how members of Congress view their work within the body.
- Assess whether an insider or outsider perspective is more accurate.
- Describe how Congress compares to other branches of government when it comes to power.

---

### ISSUE SUMMARY

**YES:** Columnist Ezra Klein contends that institutional deadlock and partisan rancor have paralyzed Congress, causing it to lose power to the president and the bureaucracy.

**NO:** Former Massachusetts Senator Mo Cowan describes how he has come to view the work of Congress—along with fellow members—after fulfilling the remainder of John Kerry term upon the nomination of Governor Deval Patrick.

---

Those who teach introductory American government usually look forward to the unit on the American presidency. It sets off lively class participation, especially when students talk about the actions of whoever happens to be in the White House. The same happens when the topic is the Supreme Court; students can argue about controversial decisions like school prayer, flag-burning, and abortion, and the instructor sometimes has to work hard to keep the discussion from getting too hot.

But when Congress, the third branch of the federal government, comes up for discussion, it is hard to get anything going beyond a few cynical shrugs and wisecracks. Seriously intended comments, when they finally emerge, may range from skeptical questions ("What do they do for their money?") to harsh pronouncements ("Bunch of crooks!").

Students today can hardly be blamed for these reactions. They are inheritors of a rich American tradition of Congress-bashing. At the end of the nineteenth century, the novelist Mark Twain quipped that "there is no distinctly native American criminal class except Congress." In the 1930s, the humorist Will Rogers suggested that "we

have the best Congress money can buy." In the 1940s, President Harry Truman coined the term do-nothing Congress, and Fred Allen's radio comedy show had a loud-mouth "Senator Claghorn" who did nothing but bluster. In the 1950s, the Washington Post's "Herblock" and other cartoonists liked to draw senators as potbellied old guys chewing cigars.

Needless to say, the drafters of the U.S. Constitution did not anticipate that kind of portrayal; they wanted Congress to stand tall in power and stature. Significantly, they listed it first among the three branches, and they gave it an extensive list of powers, 18 in all, rounding them off with the power to "make all laws which shall be necessary and proper" for executing its express powers. Given their fear of a tyrannical king, it makes sense that Congress was supposed to have the power. It was closest to the citizens, had one of its bodies directly elected, and would still be checked on all sides.

Throughout the first half of the nineteenth century, Congress played a very visible role in the business of the nation, and some of its most illustrious members, like Daniel Webster, Henry Clay, and John C. Calhoun, were national superstars. Men and women crowded into the visitors' gallery when Webster was about to deliver one of his powerful orations; during these performances they sometimes wept openly.

What, then, happened to Congress over the years to bring about this fall from grace? A number of factors have come into play, two of which can be cited immediately.

First, Congress has become a very complicated institution. In both houses, especially in the House of Representatives, legislation is not hammered out on the floor but in scores of committees and subcommittees, known to some journalists and political scientists but to relatively few others. Major bills can run hundreds of pages, and are written in a kind of lawyerspeak inaccessible to ordinary people. Congressional rules are so arcane that even a bill with clear majority support can fall through the cracks and disappear. The public simply doesn't understand all this, and incomprehension can easily sour into distrust and suspicion.

A second reason why Congress doesn't get much respect these days is connected with the increased visibility of its sometime rival, the presidency. Ever since Abraham Lincoln raised the possibility of what presidents can do during prolonged emergencies, charismatic presidents like Woodrow Wilson, Franklin Roosevelt, and Ronald Reagan, serving during such times, have aggrandized the office of the president, pushing Congress into the background. They have thus stolen much of the prestige and glamour that once attached to the legislative branch. The president has become a very visible "one" and Congress has faded into a shadowy "many." Everyone knows who the president is, but how many people can name the leaders of Congress? Can you?

The current Congress is currently being lambasted in the mainstream media for being unproductive in its term. As *USA Today* explains, "Congress is on track to beat its own low record of productivity, enacting fewer laws this year than at any point in the past 66 years." While there are obvious concerns about using such a simple metric to show productivity, it does demonstrate some of the issues currently at play in Congress. With political parties ideologically polarized like never before, it is hard to find compromises that are meaningful while still being agreeable. This was witnessed during the September/October 2013 government shutdown. Knowing that government would stop working if a compromise was not reached, neither Republicans nor Democrats would come to a middling solution prior to reaching the crisis point. One member of the Senate opted to read *Green Eggs and Ham* rather than attempt to reach a workable solution.

Further, the demands on members of Congress have increased. Citizens hold high expectations that their representative will be able and willing to fill their every need and desire. With these expectations, there is less time to spend focusing on national issues. And with the advent and development of social media, members of Congress need to have more time focused on what is occurring at the national level. Any decision leading to increased taxes, bureaucracy, or size of government will be broadcast to the world via Twitter and blogs and used against the offending Congressperson in their next election campaign. No matter how well-intentioned or skilled a politician, it seems that Washington, DC has the ability to change people these days. The founders were careful to make sure that Congress would need consensus to accomplish any meaningful goals, but today, legislative nuances are used to stall progress in the name of politics. It is not that there is something wrong with a policy that leads to it being killed anymore. Instead, it can be just a matter of taste.

In the following selections, *Washington Post* columnist Ezra Klein blames them on the ideological polarization of our two parties in Congress, which, he believes, has virtually paralyzed the institution. Mo Cowan, a former member of Congress, takes a different position, arguing that the noisy clash of viewpoints and interests serves the public by demonstrating passion and an acknowledgement of the seriousness of each decision reached.

# YES

**Ezra Klein**

## What Happens When Congress Fails to Do Its Job?

I. In 2008 Barack Obama almost asked Evan Bayh to be his running mate. It was "a coin toss," recalls David Plouffe, Obama's campaign manager. Bayh lost that toss, but the fact that he was a finalist—much as he'd been for John Kerry four years earlier—was proof that he was doing something right in his day job as junior senator from Indiana. His future seemed bright.

Last month he announced his retirement.

There was no scandal. Bayh wasn't plagued by poor fundraising or low poll numbers. Nor is fatigue a likely explanation: at 54, Bayh is fairly young, at least when you're grading on the curve that is the United States Senate.

What drove Bayh from office, rather, was that he'd grown to hate his job. Congress, he wrote in a *New York Times* op-ed, is "stuck in an endless cycle of recrimination and revenge. The minority seeks to frustrate the majority, and when the majority is displaced it returns the favor. Power is constantly sought through the use of means which render its effective use, once acquired, impossible."

The situation had grown so grim, Bayh said, that continued service was no longer of obvious use. Americans were left with a bizarre spectacle: a member of the most elite legislative body in the most powerful country in the world was resigning because the dysfunctions of his institution made him feel ineffectual. "I simply believe I can best contribute to society in another way," Bayh explained, "creating jobs by helping grow a business, helping guide an institution of higher learning, or helping run a worthy charitable endeavor."

This is what it's come to, then: our senators envy the influence and sway held by university presidents.

II. In the months leading up to the health-care-reform vote, there was much talk that Congress is broken and serious reform is necessary. Some would say the bill's passage is a decisive refutation of that position. They are wrong.

What we have learned instead is that even in those rare moments when bold action should be easy, little can be done. Consider the position of the Democrats over the last year: a popular new president, the largest majority either party has held in the Senate since the post-Watergate wave, a 40-seat majority in the House, and a financial crisis. Congress has managed to pass a lot of legislation,

and some of it has been historic. But our financial system is not fixed and our health-care problems are not solved. Indeed, when it comes to the toughest decisions Congress must make, our representatives have passed them off to some other body or some future generation.

The architects of the health-care-reform bill, for instance, couldn't bring themselves to propose the difficult reforms necessary to assure Medicare—and the government's—solvency. So they created an independent panel of experts who will have to propose truly difficult reforms to enable the Medicare system to survive. These recommendations would take the fast track through Congress, protected from not just the filibuster but even from revision. In fact, if Congress didn't vote on them, they'd still become law. "I believe this commission is the largest yielding of sovereignty from the Congress since the creation of the Federal Reserve," says Office of Management and Budget Director Peter Orszag, and he meant it as a compliment.

Cap-and-trade, meanwhile, is floundering in the Senate. In the event that it dies, the Environmental Protection Agency has been preparing to regulate carbon on its own. Some senators would like to block the EPA from doing so, and may yet succeed. But those in Congress who want to avert catastrophic climate change, but who don't believe they can pass legislation to help do so, are counting on the EPA to act in their stead.

The financial meltdown was, in many ways, a model of quick congressional action. TARP had its problems, and the stimulus was too small, but both passed, and quickly. After they'd passed, though, it became clear they weren't sufficient, and that Congress wasn't going to be able to muster further action. So the Federal Reserve, in consultation with congressional leaders, unleashed more than a trillion dollars into the marketplace. It was still the American people's money being invested, but it didn't need 60 votes in the Senate.

Congress was reticent to do more about the financial crisis because of concern over the deficit. But even apparent bipartisan agreement wasn't sufficient to compel action. Sens. Kent Conrad (D-N.D.) and Judd Gregg (R-N.H.) [led] the Budget Committee, and they called for their committee—and all the other committees—to be bypassed altogether in favor of a deficit commission operating outside the normal legislative structure. "Some have argued that House and Senate committees with jurisdiction over health, retirement and revenue issues should individually take up legislation to address the imbalance," they wrote in a joint op-ed. "But that path will never work. The inability of the regular legislative process to meaningfully act on this couldn't be clearer." They were right: their proposal was defeated by a filibuster and the president formed a deficit commission by executive order instead.

As for foreign policy and national security, Congress has so abdicated its role over war and diplomacy that Garry Wills, in his new book, *Bomb Power,* says that we've been left with an "American monarch," which is only slightly scarier-sounding than the "unitary executive" theory that the Bush administration advocated and implemented.

This is not a picture of a functioning legislature.

Some might throw up their hands and welcome the arrival of outside cavalries, of rule by commissions and central banks and executive agencies. But there is a cost when Congress devolves power to others. The American public knew much more about the stimulus than about the Federal Reserve's "quantitative easing" program because Congress is much more accessible and paid more attention by the media. The EPA can impose blunt regulations on polluters, but it can't put a price on carbon in order to create a real market for cleaner energy. The debt commission's recommendations will still require a congressional vote. When Congress doesn't work, the federal government doesn't work, no matter how hard it tries.

III. So why doesn't Congress work? The simplest answer is that the country has changed, and Congress has not changed alongside it. Congress used to function despite its extraordinary minority protections because the two parties were ideologically diverse. Democrats used to provide a home to the Southern conservatives known as the Dixiecrats. The GOP used to include a bloc of liberals from the Northeast. With the parties internally divided and different blocs arising in shifting coalitions, it wasn't possible for one party to pursue a strategy of perpetual obstruction. But the parties have become ideologically coherent, leaving little room for cooperation and creating new incentives for minority obstruction.

Take the apparent paradox of the filibuster. It is easier than at any other point in our history to break a filibuster. Until 1917, there was no way to shut down debate, and until 1975, it took 67 votes rather than today's 60. And yet, the United States Senate had to break more filibusters in 2009 than in the 1950s and 1960s combined.

"It's not uncommon today to have things filibustered that, once they get past the filibuster, are passed unanimously," complains Bayh. "So it's clearly for the purpose of preventing action, not because of any underlying, substantive disagreement." Even Bill Frist, the former Republican Senate majority leader, has been surprised by the Senate's embrace of the tactic. "Compared to 10 years ago, 15 years ago, 20 years ago," he said during an appearance on MSNBC, "it's being used way too much."

The problem has become sufficiently severe that senators, who normally cling to their institutional traditions like Vatican cardinals, are talking about addressing it. "Next Congress," Harry Reid said to a group of reporters in March, "we are going to take a look at the filibuster. And we're going to make some changes in it."

But the rise of the filibuster is not just a case of rules-gone-wild: it's evidence of a broader polarization in the United States Congress. As the party heretics lost or switched sides, Republicans and Democrats found themselves more often in agreement with themselves and less often in agreement with each other. According to the political scientists Nolan McCarty, Keith T. Poole, and Howard Rosenthal, Democrats and Republicans now vote against each other more regularly than at any time since Reconstruction.

As the Reconstruction watermark suggests, polarized parties are often the result of a polarized country. In this case, it's the opposite. We are no more divided than we were in the 1950s and '60s, when civil rights and the Vietnam War and the feminist revolution split the country. But where the legislative process once worked to harmonize those differences, today it accentuates them. "When the public sees all Democrats on one side of the issue and all Republicans on the other, it's a cue," explains Ron Brownstein, author of The Second Civil War. "And so people's opinions harden, which in turn hardens the politicians on both sides. Then you have the increasingly politicized media, and the activist groups launching primaries. It's all a machine where the whole system is working to amplify our differences."

Senate Republican leader Mitch McConnell said as much . . . in an interview with National Journal. "Whether it became the stimulus, the budget, Guantánamo, health care," he said, "what I tried to do and what John [Boehner] did very skillfully, as well, was to unify our members in opposition to it. Had we not done that, I don't think the public would have been as appalled as they became."

Minority obstruction works because voters and the media often blame the majority. If nothing is getting done and the two sides bicker ceaselessly, it seems sensible to blame the people who are running the place.

But the lesson that the minority could prosper if Washington failed was a bad one for the system to learn. The rules of the United States Congress made it possible for the minority to make the majority fail by simply obstructing their agenda. And so they did. Republicans won in 1994, after killing health-care reform. Democrats adopted the tactic a decade later, taking Congress back in 2006 after killing Social Security privatization. This year, Republicans' strategy was to kill health-care reform again. That's what Sen. Jim DeMint meant when he promised conservative activists that "if we're able to stop Obama on this, it will be his Waterloo. It will break him."

What's important about all those examples is that at no point did the minority party come to the table and propose a serious alternative. Republicans left the health-care system to deteriorate, and Bob Dole went so far as to vote against two bills that had his name on them in the mid-'90s. Democrats enforced a simple proposition in the Social Security fight: there would be no Democratic Social Security reform bill. This year Sen. Lamar Alexander gave the introductory remarks for the Republicans at the president's recent health-care summit. Alexander said the Republicans—the party that pushed No Child Left Behind, the Iraq War, the Medicare prescription-drug benefit, and a total restructuring of the tax code—had come to the conclusion that the United States Congress shouldn't attempt "comprehensive" reforms.

The strategy behind all this is to deny the other side an accomplishment, not put the minority's stamp of approval on a bill that would strengthen the majority's campaign for reelection. Obstruction, not input, has become the minority's credo. And that means gridlock, not action, has become Washington's usual signature.

IV. We like to think of American politics in terms of individuals. Candidates promise to bring a businessman's eye to Congress, or to be an independent voice from Massachusetts. They tell us about their families and their life trials. By the end of most campaigns, we could pick the winner's golden retriever out of a lineup if we had to.

This is a terrible error, because it leads us to change individuals when we need to change the system. And here is the system's problem: the minority wins when the majority fails, and the minority has the power to make the majority fail. Since the rules work no matter which party is in the minority, it means no one can ever govern.

We've become so accustomed to the current state of affairs that some think it core to the functioning of our democracy. "It's called the filibuster," Senator Gregg lectured Democrats from the floor of the Senate. "That's the way the Senate was structured. . . . The Founding Fathers realized when they structured this[;] they wanted checks and balances."

In fact, the filibuster was not an invention of the Founding Fathers. It was an accident: in the early 19th century, the Senate cleaned out its rule book and deleted the provision that let them call a vote to move from one issue to another. It took decades until anybody realized the filibuster had been created.

But Gregg is right to emphasize the importance of checks and balances to the system. The problem is that gridlock—which is partly the result of the filibuster—is eroding them. If the minority is always obstructing, then Congress can never govern. And when Congress can't act, the body cedes power to others. That worries long-time observers of the institution. "The Founders would be appalled at the notion of Congress delegating its fundamental lawmaking responsibilities to others," says Norm Ornstein, a congressional expert at the American Enterprise Institute.

Meanwhile, those who can act gain power at the expense of the Congress. The office of the president has grown in stature and authority. Early presidents delivered the State of the Union as a written letter because giving a big, dramatic speech to Congress would have been seen as overstepping the boundaries of the executive office. Modern presidents use the State of the Union to set the legislative agenda for Congress's next session, a development that would have shocked the Founders.

But it makes sense to us. The president is the main character in the media's retelling of our politics. His approval ratings are more important than the approval ratings of Congress even when we are voting only for congressmen. And it's getting worse: the political scientist Frances Lee has found that on average, each successive Congress spends a larger percentage of its time on the president's agenda than did its predecessor. The result is that there's the president's party in Congress, which mostly tries to help him out, and the opposition party, which tries to hinder him.

Like a parliamentary system, our politics is now defined by tightly knit teams and organized around the leader of the party or government. When Republicans controlled Congress in the early 2000s, they were so subjugated to the White House that Frist was handpicked by President Bush as the Republican Senate leader when Trent Lott, at Bush's urging, resigned over controversial comments he made.

But unlike a parliamentary system, our institutions are built to require minority cooperation. "We are operating in what amounts to a parliamentary system without majority rule," writes Brownstein in a recent National Journal column. "A formula for futility."

V. Sen. Michael Bennett, a Democrat from Colorado, is an expert at assessing and repairing failing institutions. He began in the world of corporate debt restructuring and recently ran Denver's public schools. The difficulty with saving troubled organizations, he says, is that the creditors and interests fight over the remains rather than banding together to nurse the body back to health. "Every one of those negotiations was about getting people to see their self-interest in moving the institution forward," he recalls.

Last year he was appointed to the United States Senate. After a year in the body, what he sees looks uncomfortably familiar: a culture of mistrust in an institution that requires radical transformation. Stakeholders ferociously trying to eke out every last advantage, and in doing so, destroying the very thing they all have a stake in.

Polls back him up: a recent Gallup survey found that only 18 percent of Americans approve of the job Congress is doing. Compare that with the president's approval ratings, which hover around 50 percent—despite the fact that Congress is largely just considering the president's agenda. One of the implications of these numbers: Americans are so disgusted by Congress that they don't trust it to do anything big. But our problems aren't politely waiting around until Congress gets its act together.

So how to change Congress? Well, carefully. Reform may be impossible in the day-to-day context, as the minority cannot unilaterally disarm itself. But the day-to-day context isn't the only possible context. "You have to do the John Rawls thing," says John Sides, a political scientist at George Washington University. "Go behind the veil of ignorance. Figure out the system we'd want without knowing who will be in charge or what they will be doing."

This work should start with a bipartisan group of legislators charged with reforming the rules that Congress works by, but their recommendations should only go into force in six or eight years, when no one knows who will hold the gavel. That lets everyone think of themselves as a potential majority as well as an embattled minority, and more important, it lets members of Congress focus on the health of the institution rather than their fortunes in the next election. It lets Congress be Congress again, if only in theory.

As for what the rules should say, the technical details should be hashed out by smart people from both parties. But the place to start is by ridding the Senate of the filibuster and its lesser-known friends (holds, unanimous consent to work for longer than two hours at a time, and so on), admitting that they are no longer appropriate given the polarizing realities of our politics.

That may seem like a radical change, but recall that the filibuster is an accident, and there is nothing radical or strange about majority voting: we use it for elections (Scott Brown won with 51 percent of the vote, not 60 percent), Supreme Court decisions, and the House of Representatives. As for a majority using its power unwisely, elections can remedy that. And voters can better judge Washington based on what it has done than on what it has been obstructed from doing.

The irony is that getting rid of the rules meant to ensure bipartisanship may actually discourage partisanship. Obstructionism is a good minority strategy as long as it actually works to stymie the majority's agenda and return you to power. But if it just means you sit out the work of governance while the majority legislates around you, your constituents and interest groups will eventually begin demanding that you include them in the process. And that's as it should be: we hire legislators to legislate. We need a system that encourages them to do so.

---

**Ezra Klein** is a blogger and columnist for *The Washington Post*, *Bloomberg*, *Newsweek*, and a contributor to MSNBC.

**William Mo Cowan**

 **NO**

# Cowan Farewell Address

On January 30 of this year, Governor Deval Patrick sent me to this chamber to represent the people of Massachusetts and their interests. Yesterday on June 25 those same people took to the voting booths and called me home. And in doing so, they called Senator-elect Ed Markey to the high honor of serving in this August body.

After serving in the House Senator-elect Ed Markey now has the opportunity to offer his voice, wisdom, accumulated experiences, humor and tireless devotion to justice and equality to the United States Senate. I for one believe that Massachusetts and the country will be better for it. Like the majority of Massachusetts voters who expressed themselves yesterday, I am quite confident that Senator-elect Markey will serve with distinction and act in the best interest of the citizens he's now privileged to represent. And the Senator-elect bested a strong candidate who brought a new voice and, yes, a new visage to the Massachusetts political scene. I applaud Gabriel Gomez on a well-run campaign and most importantly, his willingness to sacrifice so much in an effort to serve the people of the commonwealth. He started this journey as a relative unknown, but I suspect we have not heard the last of Mr. Gomez. I thank him and his family for their sacrifices and their willingness to engage.

Mr. President, when it comes to farewell speeches few will top the words offered by John Kerry on this floor a few months ago. After 28 years of distinguished service to the people of Massachusetts, now Secretary Kerry spent nearly an hour reflecting on his service to this body. By the same measure, Mr. President, as merely an interim Senator serving but a few short months, I probably should have ended my remarks about 45 seconds ago. But before I yield, Mr. President, I will take a few minutes to reflect on my brief time in this body and extend my gratitude to a number of folks.

First, I want to acknowledge and recognize the outstanding staff members in Boston and D.C. who have helped me serve our constituents to the best of my ability. When Governor Patrick named me as interim Senator, a few people—okay, more than a few—openly questioned whether I would be up to the task and whether I was capable of accomplishing anything other than locating the lavatory during my temporary assignment. I knew something those doubters did not know. I knew I was going to do my best for the folks back home because I came to the Senate armed with the knowledge of the issues by dint of my time in the Patrick-Murray administration

and I planned to make a few key hires and convince the bulk of the Secretary's staff to stay on and do the job the Governor sent me to do. In other words, I knew what I didn't know but I knew enough to hire the people who knew the considerable rest. Boy, have they proven me a genius. If you work in the Senate but a day—and I suspect the same is true in the House of Representatives—you will learn quickly that staff make this place hum and good staff make all the difference in the world.

I hope my team will forgive me if I do not list them all by name thereby avoiding the state of omission. But instead all of the staff will accept my heartfelt appreciation for their willingness to join my team, show me the ropes, teach a new dog some old tricks, educate me in all the rules that matter, which seem to be written nowhere, and their exhibition of the degrees of professionalism and service to our country that the public too often thinks is missing in our Congress.

To my entire staff, I have been in awe at your greatness and am forever in your debt for your immeasurable contributions to our work in the interest of Massachusetts residents. And I look forward to your many successes yet to come. To two on my team in particular, Val Young, Chief of Staff and Lauren Rich, my scheduler, who have known and worked for me for years, thank you for your continued willingness to partner with and trust in me.

And if I am being honest, Mr. President, about the people who help me look like I belonged here, I will spend a moment or two acknowledging the wonderful women and men who comprise the Senate staff. From the capitol police who protect us every day and somehow knew my name on the first day, to the subway operators who always deliver us on time and unfazed, to the elevator operators who excel in the art of cutting off reporters and annoying questions, to the cloakroom staff who field every cloying call about calling schedules, to the clerks who discreetly tell you what to say and do as presiding officer while the public and gallery silently wonders why everyone addresses you as Mr. or Madam President while sitting in that chair, to the generous food service staff who look the other way while you go back for seconds or thirds, to the others who make this engine oil and hum, to each of you who showed patience, support and grace that I know your love for this institution may trump even the members' affection for this place and will sustain the institution long after any one or all of us leave this chamber. You are tremendous resources for every new Senator, and I suspect great comfort to even the longest serving among

Cowan, Mo. From remarks before U.S. Senate, June 26, 2013.

us. The public may not know you by name or know the importance of your work, but now I do. And I have been honored to serve with you.

The next folks I recognize are the youngest and most silent among us. Of course I speak of the pages, the young women and men who spent part of a high school year dressing and acting in the formal traditions of this body. I have yet to speak with an uninteresting page or a page uninterested in the Senate and our government. These are dynamic young people who could be doing so many different things with their time, but they give their time and service to the Senate and its members. And they are indispensable to both. I look forward to the day when my young boys will be of age to follow in the footsteps of these outstanding young people.

Last and by no means least I want to thank the many family and friends who supported my family and me during my short tenure. We often say that it takes a village to raise a child, but I can attest that it also takes a village to help an interim Senator meet his duties in Congress and at home. Whether offering me a spare bedroom in Silver Spring or agreeing to last-minute baby sitting duties so my wife and I both could celebrate Black History Month at the White House, our village is vast and generous. And of course, every village needs a queen and the queen of my village is my wife, Stacy. I was able to serve because she was willing to be mom and dad and sacrifice in ways known and unknown while I have been in D.C. Over the past few months I've missed many homework assignments, some birthday dinners, pediatric appointments, school performances and parent-teacher meetings. But our sons never felt that their dad was absent and unaccounted for because their mom, a supermom, more than made up for my absence. Stacy has been my rock and salvation for nearly 20 years now, and I am better every day for it. And let the Senate record show for now and all time my love and dedication to Stacy.

Mr. President, in January of this year I planned to leave Deval Patrick's administration and transition back into private life. I was looking forward to more conventional hours, a reprieve from working under the public scrutiny of the press and spending more time with my wife and our young sons. So, I came to the United States Senate. Go figure. I was surprised but deeply honored when Governor Patrick sent me here to represent the folks back home and I'm eternally grateful for the Governor's faith and trust in my ability to serve. This floor on which I stand today and with which I have become so closely acquainted over the past five months has been occupied by some of the most dynamic and greatest political figures of our nation's history. From my own state of Massachusetts alone, names like Adams, Webster, Sumner, Kennedy, all who have come before me are enough to make anyone feel daunted when assuming a desk on this floor.

I was appointed to fill the seat of John Kerry and work alongside another great Senator, Elizabeth Warren. Thank you for being here, Elizabeth. With my work here,

although my time was short, I sought to uphold not only Secretary Kerry's legacy in this body, but the work of all the esteemed Senators who have dedicated their service to the commonwealth of Massachusetts, and I pledge to be the—pledged to be the best partner I could to Senator Warren. I entered the Senate at a vexing time in this body's history. As we all know, congressional approval levels are dismally low. People across the nation and political pundits everywhere believe that partisanship is a bridge too wide—a divide too wide to bridge and a wall too high to overcome. Yet despite the overwhelming public pessimism, I came to Washington with two achievable objectives. To serve the people of Massachusetts to the best of my ability, and to work with any Senator willing to implement smart, sensible and productive policy to advance the ideals of our nation. From the outside, the prospects for bipartisanship may seem slim. Party-line votes are the norm. The threat of the filibuster demands a supermajority of the past leading to the legislation. And the American people have come to believe Congress is more committed to obstruction than compromise.

To the everyday observer, we have reached a standstill where partisanship outweighs progress, and neither side is willing to reach across the aisle for the good of the American people. But what I have encountered in the Senate is not a body defined by vitriol but one more defined by congeniality and common respect. And that began before I even started here, Mr. President. On the day the Governor announced my appointment, I was pleasantly surprised to receive calls on my personal cell phone— I still don't know how they got those numbers—from Senators King, Hagan and Cardin, and I had the pleasure of receiving warm welcomes from majority leader Reid and Republican leader McConnell, among so many others, my first day. One of the first persons to congratulate me after Senator Warren and Secretary Kerry escorted me for my swearing in was my colleague from across the aisle, Senator Tim Scott.

Since then, Senator Rand Paul and I have recounted our days at Duke and our affection for college basketball. On a bipartisan congressional delegation to the Middle East, I traded life stories and perspectives with Senators Klobuchar and Hoeven and discussed the comedic genius of Will Ferrell with Senators Gillibrand and Graham. Senator Portman stopped by my commonwealth coffee last week to wish me well as I leave the Senate and encourage me every day during my time here. Senator Burr, my next-door neighbor in the Russell building, has always been good to remind me that I came from North Carolina before I had the privilege to serve in Massachusetts. Senator McCain invited me to cosponsor my first Senate resolution. And Senator Manchin has shown me more kindness than I can count.

The freshman Senators on both sides welcomed me to their class and offered never-ending encouragement, and indeed one of them, Heidi Heitkamp, has become the North Dakota sister I never knew I had. I wish I had time to recount every kindness each of the other 99, including the late Senator Lautenberg, gifted me while here, but I don't, but each has been recorded indelibly in my memory and is returned with gratitude.

In April, I experienced the very best of this body's character in the wake of the Boston marathon bombings when members from every corner of this nation extended their sympathies, their prayers and pledged their assistance and support to the city of Boston and to all those affected by that tragedy. In the aftermath, we all came together as Americans to honor those killed and to support the wounded during their time of recovery. And we saw the same in the wake of the terrible tornadoes that swept through Oklahoma. Upon closer inspection, it is clear that all of us here have common bonds and share similar goals. If only we are willing to seek out those bonds and focus on the goals that are in the best interests of our nation. While we may not agree on every policy, every line item or every vote, we have each embraced the role of republic servants, committed to serving the country we have pledged to support and defend. And as I have discovered in my time here, there is more opportunity for cooperation than the American public might believe.

And this cooperation has led to some noted successes. Thanks to the bipartisan work in the agriculture committee and on the Senate floor, we were able to send the farm bill to the house. Through the joint leadership of the so-called Gang of Eight, we are debating right now a workable approach to comprehensive immigration reform. We have confirmed five cabinet secretaries. And in what will remain the most memorable all-nighter of my Senate career, through a marathon session and more votes in one night than most interim Senators have in a career, the Senate passed the budget, and now we anxiously await the urgent opportunity to conference with the House.

I have seen progress, and I remain a true believer in the democratic process. The core functionality of our government endowed to us by our Founding Fathers so many decades ago. And I remain a true believer in our system of government and the Senate's role in that system. If I have been asked any question more frequently than what are you going to do next, Mo, it has been is our system of government broken? Is Congress broken? And I have answered truthfully each time—no. Our system of government is the greatest ever known, and the best example of democracy in human history. The Genius of our founding fathers is on display every day on capitol hill, in every state capital, in every city or town hall across this nation. And part of the Founders' genius was the birth of a government designed to function as the people need it to but function only as effectively as the privileged few empowered to work within it want it to work. Or as Secretary Kerry himself said when he said it best a few months ago right on this floor, and I quote—"I do not believe the Senate is broken. There is nothing wrong with the Senate that can't be fixed by what's right with the Senate. The predominant and weighty notion that 100 American citizens, chosen by their neighbors—[or their governor, in my case]—to serve from states as different from Massachusetts to Montana can always choose to put parochial or personal interests aside and find the national interest." What an awesome responsibility and privilege. And in my scant five months, I have seen the promise of those words realized in more ways and in more interactions than the public, unfortunately, has had occasion to witness. So I believe in that unlimited promise still.

I have also been part of history while I was here. With my appointment and coincident with the appointment of Senator Scott, two African-Americans are serving in this body concurrently for the first time in our nation's history. Senator Scott and I are respectively the seventh and eighth black Senators to serve in this body. While I believe this number to be far too few, I am also hopeful that it is a sign that these United States will soon be represented by a more diverse population that more closely reflects the diverse country that we are and the diversity of opinions that exist across and within our diverse nation. With different perspectives, different backgrounds, different races, religions and creeds, we are better equipped to confront the issues that face our vast and changing nation.

America has been and always will be a nation of immigrants where religious freedom is in our DNA. Where more and more we are chipping away at the barriers preventing us from achieving true marriage equality and where people worldwide still yearn to reach our shores to enjoy our freedoms. And a Congress that is more reflective of this America as this Congress is becoming will be good for America.

Finally, Mr. President, I offer my heartfelt gratitude to the people of Massachusetts. Not one person was given the chance to vote for or against me, but I have gone about my work every day as if they had. I came to this body beholden to Massachusetts, her residents and the country only and leave confident that I have stayed true to that honor. And ladies and gentlemen of the commonwealth, it has been a true honor and privilege to represent you as your junior Senator in the United States Senate. With that, Mr. President, and for what will likely be the final time, I yield the floor.

---

**WILLIAM MO COWAN** is an American politician and lawyer who served as the junior U.S. Senator from Massachusetts in 2013. He previously served as legal counsel and Chief of Staff to Massachusetts Governor Deval Patrick. He is now a Fellow at the Institute of Politics in the Harvard Kennedy School.

# EXPLORING THE ISSUE

## Is Congress a Dysfunctional Institution?

### Critical Thinking and Reflection

1. Do we really want a speedy system in which laws would be pushed through before a consensus develops?
2. Do we really want a system in which the viewpoint of the minority gets trampled by a rush to action by the majority?
3. How does the public tend to view the work of Congress? Do you agree or disagree? Why?
4. Why is Congress viewed as dysfunctional by some Americans?
5. How could Congress make itself appear less dysfunctional?

### Is There Common Ground?

In theory, at least, there is common ground between the assertion that bills should not be hastily run through Congress and the assertion that the passage of laws should not be hamstrung indefinitely by a minority. The problem comes in trying to craft a synthesis of those two assertions in today's polarized Congress. Some hope that a temporary solution—there is never a permanent one—will come when a new election gives one of the parties decisive control of both houses of Congress. Yet that happened in 2008, and, while it did result in the passage of at least three important pieces of legislation, it also set off a powerful backlash against the majority party in the political arena.

In 2013, with a divided Congress, we have seen the smallest amount of legislative output in over a half century. Some will argue that this is a positive fact since it means that unnecessary legislation was not created. Critics, on the other hand, will point to the fact that we elect members of Congress into office to pass legislation. Instead of seeing new laws, recently we have seen little except partisan bickering and utilization of loopholes for political reasons. As a nation, we seem to be missing opportunities to take concentrated efforts to fix the problems ailing our fellow citizens.

### Create Central

www.mhhe.com/createcentral

### Additional Resources

Charles B. Cushman, *An Introduction to the U.S. Congress* (Shape, 2006)

Lawrence C. Dodd and Bruce Oppenheimer, *Congress Reconsidered* (CQ Press, 2004)

Diana Evans, *Greasing the Wheels: Using Pork Barrel Projects to Build Majority Coalitions in Congress* (Cambridge University Press, 2004)

Richard Fenno, *Home Style: House Members in Their Districts* (Longman, 2002)

Sally Friedman, *Dilemmas of Representation: Local Politics, National Factors, and the Home Styles of Modern U.S. Congress Members* (State University of New York, 2007)

# *Internet References . . .*

**No Labels**

www.nolabels.org/gridlock

**Reclamation of the U.S. Congress**

http://repositories.lib.utexas.edu/bitstream/handle/
2152/20957/FinalReclamationoftheUSCongress_
9-27.pdf?sequence=6

**Steven Kull on Congressional Gridlock**

www.c-spanvideo.org/program/Kul

**The Gridlock Illusion**

www.wilsonquarterly.com/essays/gridlock-illusion

**U.S. Electoral System and Congressional Gridlock**

www.c-spanvideo.org/program/316150-4

**Selected, Edited, and with Issue Framing Material by:**
**William J. Miller,** *Flagler College*
**George McKenna,** *City College, City University of New York*
**and**
**Stanley Feingold,** *City College, City University of New York*

# ISSUE

## Do Whistleblowers Help Government?

**YES: Maggie Severns,** from "What Really Drives a Whistleblower Like Edward Snowden?" *Mother Jones* (June 13, 2013)

**NO: Frederick A. Elliston,** from "Anonymity and Whistleblowing," *Journal of Business Ethics* (August 1982)

---

### Learning Outcomes

**After reading this issue, you will be able to:**

- Describe what whistleblowing is.
- Assess whether enough is done to protect the whistleblowers.
- Explain when whistleblowing is good for government.
- Identify times when whistleblowing could hurt government.
- Explain why whistleblowers may be less willing to come forward today.

---

### ISSUE SUMMARY

**YES:** Columnist Maggie Severns uses an interview with University of Maryland's Political Psychology Professor C. Frederick Alford to show how whistleblowers aim to make government more effective and efficient through their actions.

**NO:** Academic Frederick A. Elliston points out that due to the anonymous nature of whistleblowing many individuals can file false claims out of their own self-interest as opposed to those of society at large.

Whistleblowers only need to exist because individuals within agencies do not always act in a prescribed, ethical, or legal manner. A whistleblower is an individual who exposes any type of misconduct or illegal activity occurring within an organization. There are numerous ways to classify the types of activities that could push a whistleblower to come forward. The activity may be a violation of a rule, regulation, or law. More severely, perhaps, it could be a threat to the general public interest, such as corruption, fraud, or a health and safety violation. The whistleblower may only internally report what is witnessed or they could go public and talk to external regulators or the media. Such activities are not confined to either public or private organizations. But public organizations tend to merit more concern from citizens given the expectation of government working to benefit all members of society.

Whistleblowing is not a new concept. In 1778, the Continental Congress passed the first law designed to protect whistleblowers. The group was moved to act unanimously after a 1777 incident, in which Richard Marven and Samuel Shaw blew the whistle on a government matter and faced extreme retaliation by Esek Hopkins who was commander-in-chief of the Navy. Hopkins, unhappy with the information released by his two inferiors, chose to file a libel suit in federal court. The U.S. government—through the Continental Congress—chose to represent the whistleblowers against Hopkins and further declared that it was the duty of "all persons in the service of the United States, as well as all other the inhabitants thereof "to inform the Continental Congress of "misconduct, frauds or misdemeanors committed by any officers in the service of these states, which may come to their knowledge." From this initial beginning, the United States has a history of protecting those individuals who risk their own well-being to bring forth questionable activities that could otherwise go unnoticed.

Since the initial legal decisions, however, protections have varied according to numerous factors: namely, the subject matter involved and the state in which the case arises. In 2002, Congress passed Sarbanes-Oxley, which quite correctly noted that protections for potential whistleblowers were dependent on the "patchwork and vagaries" of state statutes. Despite the volume of laws passed pertaining to whistleblowing, there is still no nationally clear standard letting public workers know for sure that they will be protected and safe.

Given the "patchwork and vagaries," it is essential for individuals who face negative consequences due to blowing the whistle to know what laws exist so they are sure to follow legal protocols. In some states, there may only be a 10-day window in which to file a complaint. In certain areas there may be a similar window of opportunity (environmental issues get 30 days, civil rights get 45, corporate fraud has 90, and nuclear issues have 180 days.) Miss the window and lose the opportunity to be guaranteed protection. Other areas, such as union organizing, equal employment, minimum wages, and overtime all have far longer periods of time in which to file a complaint with the proper body. With these varying deadlines, it becomes clear why whistleblowers need to do their research before filing any information. The whistleblowing process is unfortunately not as clear and direct as it could be.

The major piece of guiding legislation for federal whistleblowers in the United States today is the Whistleblower Protection Act (WPA) of 1989. While not doing much in terms of simplifying the maze of reporting wrongdoings, it does provide potential whistleblowers at the federal level of assurances that they will be protected if they opt to put the interests of society ahead of those of a few individuals within government. Congress—through this bill—guaranteed that if any agency either threatened to take, or actually took, retaliatory action against a whistleblower, they will be punished.

After almost a quarter century in action, the Act was updated in 2012 through the Whistleblower Protection Enhancement Act. The updated policy states: "federal whistleblowers have seen their protections diminish in recent years, largely as a result of a series of decisions by the United States Court of Appeals for the Federal Circuit, which has exclusive jurisdiction over many cases brought under the Whistleblower Protection Act (WPA). Specifically, the Federal Circuit has wrongly accorded a narrow definition to the type of disclosure that qualifies for whistleblower protection. Additionally, the lack of remedies under current law for most whistleblowers in the intelligence community and for whistleblowers who face retaliation in the form of withdrawal of the employee's security clearance leaves unprotected those who are in a position to disclose wrongdoing that directly affects our national security."

Whistleblowing, most argue, presents a net positive for government since it brings to light information that could otherwise very well slip through the cracks and cause long-term problems. It is not, necessarily, always good, however. H.L. Luframboise states that whistleblowers can be categorized into one of two categories: "'Vile wretches' are those whose acts of whistleblowing are more offensive to the community or to their peer groups than the acts on which they have blown the whistle. A hillbilly who told the revenuers that his neighbor was making moonshine would be a 'vile wretch.' 'Public heroes,' in contrast, are those who blow the whistle on events and conditions deemed by the community or peer group to be so abhorrent as to justify their being reported . . . peer group repugnance against 'vile wretches' runs very deep."

Perhaps there is no greater debate between public hero and vile wretch with regards to public whistleblowing in global history than the one currently surrounding Edward Snowden. An American computer specialist, Snowden is a former CIA and NSA employee/contractor who willingly (and knowingly) disclosed nearly 200,000 classified documents to the mainstream media. Nearly all of the information has centered on the NSA mass surveillance program operating in the United States and international peers in Israel, Britain, Canada, Australia, and Norway. In short, Snowden told the world about America's spy operations and potentially national security secrets.

Snowden's actions were the most direct and significant leak of classified material since Daniel Ellsberg released the Pentagon Papers in 1971. Out of Snowden's documents came public knowledge of Internet surveillance (including Tempora, PRISM, and XKeyscore) along with the capturing of both American and European phone metadata. At the time Snowden accessed the classified information, he was employed at defense contractor Booz Allen Hamilton. He chose *The Guardian* and *The Washington Post* to share the information with and by the end of November 2013, only approximately one percent had been released.

To some, Snowden is a hero and a patriot who was attempting to curb the American government from their unprecedented and potentially illegal tracking of information. To others, he is a dissident traitor who willingly sacrificed American security interest through the release of this data. When asked to explain his actions, Snowden stated that his "sole motive" for leaking the documents was "to inform the public as to that which is done in their name and that which is done against them." At present, Snowden is a fugitive of the United States and has been charged with espionage and theft of government property. He has received temporary asylum from Russia, where he resides.

In the following articles, Maggie Severns argues that whistleblowers are well-intentioned and strive to improve the performance of the government and public trust in elected institutions. On the opposite side, Frederick Elliston makes the point that the anonymous nature of whistleblowing in government today leads to the process being misused by employees with a grudge—causing government to become patently less effective.

**Maggie Severns**

# What Really Drives a Whistleblower Like Edward Snowden?

After Edward Snowden went public as the man who leaked the NSA's secret surveillance system to the country via a 12-minute video interview with the *Guardian*, questions immediately sprang up around his motivation for whistleblowing, his personal life, and whether his background is what he claims it to be.

Why is suspicion and distrust the natural reaction? Because a lot rests on whether Snowden is telling the truth, yes, but also because most of us (perhaps nearly everyone but whistleblowers themselves) have trouble understanding exactly what motivates a whistleblower. As University of Maryland political psychology professor C. Frederick Alford notes, humans are tribal beings, and even though society considers whistleblowers brave in theory, in practice there tends to be a sense of discomfort with those who break from the tribe.

Alford has spent more than a decade asking why some people reveal government secrets in the name of public good while most don't, asking what makes Edward Snowden Edward Snowden, and not one of the many other Booz Allen analysts who presumably saw the same information that Snowden did but kept quiet about it. Alford's 2001 book, *Whistleblowers: Broken Lives and Organizational Power*, examines the psychology of whistleblowing based on the extensive time he spent with people who've done it—some to much fanfare, others to very little. He says he's received a phone call or an email from a whistleblower about every month since the book came out 12 years ago, and in many cases has kept up for years with those who reach out. He spoke with *Mother Jones* about the Edward Snowden-Daniel Ellsberg parallel, why whistleblowers tend to have big egos, and what Snowden might face in the coming weeks and months.

**Mother Jones:** Based on what we know about Edward Snowden so far, does he remind you of other whistleblowers you've spent time with or studied over the years?

**C. Frederick Alford:** Daniel Ellsberg, overwhelmingly. I don't think Bradley Manning: Bradley Manning committed a data dump. He just released tons of information, and I don't think he understood all the information he was releasing. I don't think anyone could have understood it all.

Ellsberg, who worked at the RAND Corporation at the time and had this contract to analyze the Vietnam War, but realized at a point long before the war had ended that [the government] knew they were never going to win it, and realized that this information should be part of the public debate, and decided *in a very self-conscious way* to make this information part of the public debate. Snowden reminded me so much of Ellsberg. Not in his personality, but in the reflective way he decided to be.

If we take the *Guardian* at its word, and we take Snowden at his word, he released information that would not endanger active agents or reveal the location of CIA stations. So I think Ellsberg is an obvious comparison. And I think the significance of all this is going to end up being comparable to the significance of the Pentagon papers.

**MJ:** Are there personality traits that make someone prone to becoming a whistleblower?

**FA:** I thought there were when I started to write my book. I thought that's what I was setting out to do. I decided there may be but I don't think I'm going to find it, and I don't think anybody's going to find it. I do think there are certain moral descriptions we can make about whistleblowers, that they tend to be conservative in some ways.

The best way I can describe it: A whistleblower I spoke with whose name will never make the newspaper, he said something like, "I wasn't against the system, I *was* the system! I just didn't realize that there were two systems."

Most of us grow up to realize that what people say and what people do are two things. We learn a certain cynicism about life, like that everything a politician promises isn't necessarily going to be what he does. I think whistleblowers somehow come late to this realization. They're naive in a certain sense, and then when they come to realize that people are lying, cheating, stealing, whatever, they're shocked. It's kind of like, what's that line from *Casablanca*? They're "shocked that gambling's going on in this place"!

Whistleblowers are shocked in a way that the rest of us aren't, and that leads them to act. In a sense, they hardly have a choice. This is what most of them said to me; I don't know what Snowden will say in 5 or 10 years. But the ones I spoke with who had blown the whistle maybe 5, 10 years ago, many of them said they wouldn't do it again, and many of them said they would. All of them said they didn't have a choice. They couldn't live with themselves anymore without doing something.

**MJ:** So Edward Snowden seems authentic to you?

**FA:** I mean, how can you know for sure? But as I listen to him, as I look at the *Guardian*'s account, and I look at the background—they paid a lot of time and attention checking out this guy.

What makes him an unusual whistleblower is that he's not just putting his job and his personal happiness on the line, he's putting the rest of his life in jail on the line. I don't think that's likely, but it's certainly possible. Ellsberg was prosecuted, and had Nixon's gang not bungled the burglary at Lewis Fielding's office, Ellsberg could have gone to jail for 20 years.

**MJ:** Do you think most whistleblowers understand what the long-term consequences of their actions will be? Do you think Edward Snowden did?

**FA:** Most don't. Most have no idea. Let me put it this way: What you reveal when you talk about immorality or another ethical behavior as organizational policy is that you're somebody who remembers the outside even when you're on the inside. You've given yourself away, and many whistleblowers think they'll be rewarded or they'll be thanked. And if they think, "Well, I'll get fired," they certainly don't understand how their friends at work—many of whom they've spent more time with than their families—will be so scared they won't even look at them. Many of them have no understanding of their years in exile, and the stress it takes on their families.

I get calls and emails from whistleblowers. I tell them, check your finances, check the state of your marriage, to try to give them some idea of what's going to be involved. Usually, they've just become a whistleblower and things have started to go bad. And I try to tell them, "Well, that's normal." They're in for a long, tough road. And unfortunately, what it takes to become a whistleblower—that certain naivete—isn't what it takes to survive as a whistleblower, which is a hard-hearted cynicism.

I think Snowden is different. I think he understands very well.

**MJ:** I wonder if those sacrifices are as painful for someone with a whistleblower's personality, or if he's more comfortable being alone in the first place.

**FA:** It hurts. They're all wounded. They really are. Even people who are used to it, it's just like anyone else. Maybe people like this are a little more used to being alone.

**MJ:** Whistleblowers have a reputation for being egotistical. Why is that?

**FA:** I think it's more a survival strategy than anything else. I don't think whistleblowers have more ego invested in what they do, or maybe they need it.

They tend to be a little more obsessive than other people. They're not necessarily the person I'd like to have a drink with. You start to go talk to whistleblowers in their homes—now people's old records are more electronic, but even just a few years ago—and their basements or their attics would be filled with troves of file after file after file.

**MJ:** Do you think it would be possible for an agency or organization to screen out whistleblower-types? There's certainly an incentive to try.

**FA:** I don't think so. Because if you think about it, they're awfully close to the all-American boy or girl. They're not the zealot, the deviant, the crusader—they may become some of these things later on but they don't enter the organization this way.

**MJ:** Often whistleblowers are cast as having ulterior motives for doing what they did, like Bradley Manning being driven by gender confusion. What do you think when you see that happening?

**FA:** The whistleblowers have a name for it: "nuts and sluts." That the response of the organization will be to pathologize the whistleblower: Take the focus off the issue and put the focus on the whistleblower. I think with Bradley Manning, one has to ask the question I've already asked: Whether a large data dump is really the way to go about whistleblowing and what other alternatives where there to him.

**MJ:** What does Edward Snowden have in store for him in the coming days and months?

**FA:** People are already talking about his age. I read a column by David Brooks that wasn't entirely damning, but it was already about his social alienation. That this is the consequence of social alienation, where half of him may have some good qualities, but he's socially alienated and doesn't understand his obligation to his fellow citizens as a consequence.

To be a whistleblower, to be a moral human being in this society, probably requires some level of—well, he can call it alienation, I call it not having completely bought into the system. It sounds like Edward Snowden had a pretty good life in Hawaii, he had a girlfriend. He's not like some hermit that crawled out of the woods after 27 years.

It's going to be hard to make [the socially alienated idea] stick if Snowden can keep his presence out there a little bit. Because he doesn't seem like a crazed, alienated zealot.

**MJ:** When he talked about the government in the *Guardian* video, he seemed suspicious of it, and like he has a very hardline view on privacy issues.

**FA:** He does. But these are policies that are able to be discussed publicly without compromising the security of the nation. I see the ACLU is already suing to stop some of these data-gathering practices and that's the way they ought to be, and if people don't know about them then they can't stop them. That's the point: They ought to be subject to debate.

What he is absolutely right about, and he said it right out front: Whistleblowing has to be connected to a name and a face to really make a difference, and doing this anonymously is far less effective.

**MJ:** Why do these stories need a face attached to them?

**FA:** I don't know. Why do we like to go to the movies? This is a personal story, and we like to tell narratives, and he makes it interesting. Because how many people are going to sit down and read these documents and make

sense of them? If attaching his name to it somehow keeps the story alive, it's too bad, but that's the way it is.

---

**Maggie Severns** is a former Senior Online Editorial Fellow at *Mother Jones*. Previously, she worked as an analyst at a DC think tank. She has written for the *Washington Post*, *The Washington Monthly*, *Slate*, and others.

**Frederick A. Elliston**

 **NO**

# Anonymity and Whistleblowing

. . .

## Whistleblowing and Anonymity

Should people who blow the whistle do so publicly? Are they obliged to make their identity known or may they remain anonymous? The prohibition on anonymity is pervasive and strong. My purpose is to sound out and assess alternative rationales for it.

Before turning to an appraisal of anonymous whistle-blowing, we need to distinguish it from related phenomena. In general, someone acts anonymously when his (or her) identity is not publicly known. For example, a bomb threat is anonymous when no one knows who wrote the letter or made the telephone call. Yet clearly to say literally that *no one at all* knows is mistaken: the writer himself knows he sent the letter, and therefore at least one person knows.

Is an action done anonymously when no one but the agent knows? This notion comes close to the extreme form of secrecy: the greatest secret concerns information I share with no one else. But secrecy in this sense is too extreme, for how did I come by this information? If someone told me, at least one other person knows. Paradigmatically information is secret when shared among few people, with two as the limiting case. But it does not suffice that only these two people know and merely by chance no one else. Such 'accidental secrets' are not secrets in the strict sense. To qualify as a secret, there must be a conspiracy of silence. It is the exclusion of others, the denial of access by them to information, that marks a secret.

Yet something more is built into the notion of secrecy that becomes clearer if we consider a related concept—privacy. Information is private when I justifiably deny the right of others to share it. The facts about my sex life or income tax return are private in that others (ordinarily) cannot demand access to them. The domain of privacy is one in which I claim a *right* to exclude others, unless they can invoke a higher right to override mine.

In the case of privacy, the burden of proof rests with those who would secure access to what is protected under this rubric. In the case of secrecy, the burden of proof is reversed: those who would withhold information must provide the justification. In the case of privacy, the presumption is that others should not intrude. In the case of secrecy, the presumption is that something be shared. This presumption is countered by 'Top Secret' documents with

an appeal to national security. In the case of secret acts of espionage, the presumption is not met: information not shared should be, but is wrongfully and deliberately kept from others.

Is anonymity more like privacy or secrecy? First one needs to note that the information kept from others is of a particular sort—namely about a person's identity. Moreover the sharing of this information may be limited or extensive. For one to be anonymous, the public must be precluded from knowledge of the individual's identity, but their exclusion does not entail no one else knows. Anonymity is neutral, lying in the middle ground between secrecy and privacy: it entails that the public does not know or have access to the identity of an individual, but does not locate the burden of proof in withholding this information.

Accordingly, one can ask: Does the public have a right to know the whistleblower's identity, or does he (or she) have a right to withhold it? Withholding such information strikes many as wrong. But why is it wrong, and in what sense?

A refusal to let one's identity be known could be construed as bad manners. Blowing the whistle anonymously is like snitching on someone behind his back. As kids we were all taught that such tattle-tailing is wrong. It is a paradigm of bad manners to say nasty things about people not present to defend themselves. Anonymity in whistleblowers is a breach of manners—faulty etiquette in people who should know better as they act in the more consequential professional world. But why are such breaches of etiquette condemned so harshly, and is this harshness justified?

Typically, the answer is couched in terms of loyalty. To be a faithful member of a group is to protect the interests of that group as a whole and of its members individually. Saying nasty things about people behind their backs disrupts the cohesion of the group, undermining trust in each other and threatening the group solidarity. As a threat to the welfare of the group, individually or collectively, as well as to the very basis of its existence, tattle-tailing is severely condemned.

Yet clearly a blanket prohibition on tattle-tailing is unwarranted, as three analogies can serve to demonstrate.

(1) Suppose my older sister is about to swallow some pills I think may be dangerous. To tell mother may not be wrong, but right and indeed obligatory. Though I have 'blown the whistle' on my sister, if I am doing so for her own good in a situation that is serious and urgent, it is

not objectionable—even if I ask mother not to tell on me. Clearly, it is preferable to saying or doing nothing at all. My sister's ignorance may help us to live together, to get along in situations where her anger might be disruptive and counter-productive for each of us. Since my sister does not know what I did, I have acted anonymously—at least as far as she is concerned. Even though mother knows, her knowledge, like that of the closed Congressional Committee to which a whistleblower testifies in *camera*, does not totally dispel anonymity.

Typically the boyhood scenario is less serious: my sister takes a cookie from the cookie jar without asking, and I squeal on her. My action may be condemned because the incident is trivial. But as the *seriousness* of the incident increases, the condemnation of anonymous whistleblowing weakens. The extent of the harm threatened is one factor to be weighed in making a moral judgment. The seriousness of the harm the whistleblower seeks to disclose and thereby curtail may be measured in several ways: the number of people affected; the extent to which they are hurt, physically or psychologically. Alternatively one might appraise this seriousness in less consequentialist terms by invoking deontological principles: perhaps someone's rights are denied—such as the right to privacy—even though no physical or psychological harm ensues. Whichever approach one takes, the more serious the offense, the less stringent the prohibition on anonymity.

One might respond that my analogy confuses two different concepts: whistleblowing and anonymity. Conceding that one is more obliged to blow the whistle the greater the harm threatened, one could nevertheless insist that one should always do so publicly and never anonymously. Consider three possibilities: $P_1$ blowing the whistle publicly; $P_2$ blowing the whistle anonymously; and $P_3$ not blowing the whistle at all. *Prima facie* $P_1$ is morally preferable to $P_2$, and $P_2$ is morally preferable to $P_3$. Though this ranking holds at the *individual* level, one can adopt a rule-utilitarian perspective on the effects on the *practice* of whistleblowing from acting anonymously: anonymity is justified if it increases the number who with good reason blow the whistle, that is, if anonymity promotes the practice of effective warranted whistleblowing. Accordingly, the first analogy asserts that blowing the whistle anonymously is preferable to not blowing it at all—especially when the particular harm threatened is serious; and it hypothesizes that if a veil of ignorance increases the number of effective and legitimate whistleblowers, the principle of anonymity has a rule-utilitarian defense. But the analogy does not show that anonymously blowing the whistle is always preferable to blowing the whistle publicly. Consider now a second case to elicit a second factor in addition to seriousness.

(2) The school bully is about to beat up a new kid who looks very frail and helpless. Since I am unable to stop him, I run to the teacher to report the incident. After the teacher has intervened, I ask him not to say I reported the incident: to protect myself from retaliation, I want to remain anonymous. If the bully is very strong and I am very weak, my request is justified: there is no moral reason why I too should suffer unfairly at his hands. By the same token, corporations bully employees who cannot easily defend themselves. Because of their vulnerability, anonymity is warranted. As a second thesis I propose that the greater the *probability of unfair retaliation*, the weaker the prohibition on anonymity should be.

The literature to date suggests that most whistleblowers—even those who act for good moral reasons—pay a very high price for dissenting. In many cases they are fired or demoted, transferred to unattractive assignments or locales, ostracized by their peers and cast into psychological and professional isolation. Should they try to obtain another job in the same field, they often find they are 'blacklisted': many employers do not want to hire someone who 'caused trouble' on his (or her) last job. Moreover under the prevailing legal doctrine of 'employment at will', fired whistleblowers have only limited legal recourse: in most jurisdictions the courts uphold an employer's right to fire someone for almost any reason. In the absence of such legal protection, the burden of defending himself falls very heavily on the shoulders of the whistleblower alone.

In asserting that the probability of unfair retaliation decreases the strength of the prohibition on anonymity, I do want to distinguish two concepts: permissible and obligatory. My point, to put it briefly, is that moral heroism is not and should not be mandated. Though we praise the courage of a professional engineer who speaks out regarding dangerous practices when he (or she) risks his job, to require extraordinary self-sacrifices demands too much. His unwillingness to risk his career, his personal livelihood and the means whereby he supports his family are perfectly understandable reasons for remaining silent. Indeed, they may justify silence. When such individual self-sacrifice is the only way to protect the public, one must look instead to the development of other mechanisms—the law, the courts, unions, the press, professional associations or watchdog agencies.

To return to the earlier threefold distinction, blowing the whistle publicly may be ideal but one cannot demand it. One cannot condemn the persons who act anonymously to protect themselves, those who depend on them, love them and care for them. There is a limit to what we can ask a person to give up in order to do the right thing. Insofar as anonymity reduces what may be an unfair burden to begin with, it reduces an evil promoting a good.

So far I have identified two factors that enter into an appraisal of anonymous whistleblowing: the seriousness of the harm threatened, and the probability of unfair retaliation.

(3) A third moral factor can be elicited with the following modification in the second analogy: Suppose the bully is my friend. This social relationship places an obligation on me to go to my friend. Even if I am frail and

helpless, given that he is my friend, I am duty bound by friendship to ask him to stop. Even if he is not my friend but only is a member of my gang, I should not blow the whistle straight away but go to our leader first—ask him to intervene. If that is not possible or fails, recourse to an outside group may be warranted. My third thesis is that the strength of the prohibition on anonymity is a function of the *social relationship*: the closer the whistleblower stands to the accused, the stronger the prohibition on anonymity. Most whistleblowers feel an 'I vs. them' or 'us vs. them'. Within polarized groups whistleblowers discuss problems with other members of their group, but hesitate—legitimately I contend—to go outside it without the protection anonymity brings.

This third factor is related to the second: social distance affects the probability of retaliation. If an intermediary can ensure that justice is done within the group, anonymity is less warranted—if not unwarranted. If the Federal Office of Professional Responsibility can guarantee that whistleblowers protesting unfair, illegal or corrupt practices will not suffer for their efforts to correct them, anonymity is less warranted. It is also less needed. But until employees' rights are secure, a veil of ignorance is one of their few safeguards.

Anonymity may be condemned because it impedes the pursuit of truth. The person who levels accusations against another while withholding his own identity makes it difficult to determine whether what he charges is true or false: we cannot question him, ask for his sources of information, verify his accusations—or so it may be argued.

But to assert that we cannot verify anonymous charges at all, is too strong and unfounded. Verification, if it is to count as a proof, must be public and repeatable. Consequently the means whereby the whistleblower verified *to himself* that what he suspected was true must be available *to others* . . . if indeed he knows the truth. Those who would learn the truth can discover it by the same means the whistleblower used—even though they do not know his identity.

In the movie and book *All the President's Men,* the character called 'Deep Throat' played this role. Without revealing his own identity, he led the two reporters Bernstein and Woodward along a path that provided the evidence they needed to implicate the President in the Watergate break-ins. He did not need to reveal his own identity. It was enough that from the darkness he provided clues that would trace out a path, perhaps the one he followed but perhaps not, to the truth.

Admittedly in some cases it may be difficult if not impossible for the whistleblower to provide any conclusive evidence that will not reveal his own identity. In such cases, the choice is not between blowing the whistle anonymously and blowing it publicly. Rather, the choice is between blowing it publicly and not blowing it at all. Accordingly, I do not assert that anonymity is always possible. But I do assert that where it is possible we can-

not always fault it as a breach of professional etiquette or because it conceals the truth.

Therefore, I conclude that the blanket condemnation on anonymity is not warranted. Rather, its justification depends on three factors: the seriousness of the offense, the probability of unfair retaliation, and the social relationships. Let me now turn to some practical considerations.

Perhaps anonymity is not a breach of professional etiquette or an obstacle to the truth but an act of foolishness. The individual who tries to shield himself may find anonymity makes his action *self-defeating*: to be effective one must act publicly—or so one argument may run. What can be said for or against it?

First, one must concede a paradox. The whistleblower attempts to draw public attention to an action he regards as wrong, yet is not willing to make his own identity public. His means and ends conflict: he uses ignorance to promote knowledge, identifies others while hiding himself. What he is trying to do is refuted by the way he does it. This paradoxical juxtaposition of means and ends raises our suspicions. It reminds us of those who make war to end war, who deceive to get at the truth, who use force to protect freedom.

Though our suspicions are justifiably aroused, they may turn out to be unjustified. Society may need an institution like the police, based on the legal use of physical force, to protect the freedom of its members. It may indeed be necessary to reveal less than the whole truth to determine if others are telling the truth. We are right to be suspicious when the means contradict the ends, but may find the contradiction only apparent: the whistleblower may succeed at uncovering abusive practices without blowing his cover.

Alternatively, our suspicions may be aroused not by the logical paradox but by the questions of motives: Why does the whistleblower conceal his identity—what does *he* have to hide? To show his intentions are pure, we demand that he stand up and be counted, that he accept responsibility for his actions and not hide from public view. Hiding makes us uneasy that he seeks some private gain rather than the public good, that he himself may be implicated and protecting himself by pointing at others.

A sharp distinction can be drawn between reasons and causes, the justification and the motivation, the evidence that proves a statement true or false and the personal considerations that lead a person to utter it. Anonymity calls the latter into question but need not affect the former. Whether the charges are true or false does not depend on the motivation of the individual who levies them. One can appraise the truth of accusations knowing nothing of motives. Whether the whistleblower draws attention to corruption out of spite or altruism makes no difference in one respect: if corruption exists, it should be ended.

Naturally our attitude towards the whistleblower depends very much on his motives. If he genuinely seeks the public good, he should be held in high esteem. If he does not benefit in any way, his altruism is commendable. In appraising his character, his motives are of the utmost importance. But in appraising his *charges*, his motives are logically irrelevant. Anonymity helps guard against a fallacious counter-attack—an *argumentum ad hominem*. Individuals called to account by the whistleblower may try to protect themselves by diverting attention to him, by shifting the issue from what he says to why he says it. They may seek to redirect attention from the truth of his claims to the truthfulness of the claimant. But logicians have long recognized this strategy as fallacious: whether or not what someone says is true does not depend on his personal motive for saying it.

Anonymity may be treated as self-defeating because it calls into question the motives of the whistleblower, but I contend it is wrong to insist it must. However, one genuine issue is raised by this attack on anonymity: How do we distinguish the accusations that should be investigated from those that need not be? A filtering process is needed to make this determination. Anonymity is not and should not be the main factor in the filter: one should not decide to investigate a charge only if the person who makes it identifies himself publicly. One is less inclined to investigate anonymous charges because of difficulties anonymity creates—the problems of gathering data, identifying the relevant participants, fixing the time, location, and extent of the act or practice. But then it should be for these reasons, and not because of anonymity *per se*, that no further action is taken.

From what I have said already several factors emerge in the determination of the point at which the whistleblower's charges should be investigated. The main factor is the seriousness of the harm to others if the charges are true. Clearly if the risk to their lives and health is very great, steps must be taken to protect them. The first step is to determine whether the risk is real or imaginary—and this requires investigating the whistleblower's accusations. If he claims that money has been misspent, stolen or siphoned off for illegal purposes, then the greater the amount involved the more serious the charge and the greater the need to verify it.

In judging the harm to be done, one must also weigh the costs of determining this harm. If an investigation is likely to destroy the morale of an otherwise socially useful and productive organization, an investigation is probably not warranted. If it is likely to cost more money than might be saved, then it is likewise unwarranted. It is the *net harm*, after the costs of an investigation have been subtracted, that must be given moral weight in fixing the threshold.

Should the likelihood that the charges are true be considered? The objection to giving this probability estimate any weight is that the whistleblower's dilemma arises precisely because people do not know. An estimate based on ignorance is unreliable, and acting on it irrational. But at the other extreme, to investigate charges that are preposterous, about events logically impossible or astronomically remote, will be wasteful if not harmful. Accordingly,

the probability that the charges will prove unfounded should serve as a factor only to eliminate extreme cases of the preposterous, impossible, or improbable.

So far I have offered three interpretations of the thesis that whistleblowers should not remain anonymous. On the first, anonymity is in bad taste—it offends our sense of etiquette in saying nasty things about someone behind their back. On the second, it is a barrier to the truth. And on the third it is self-defeating. I want now to consider several moral objections.

*Fair Play*: It may be argued that everyone has a right to confront their accusers. If someone claims I have done something wrong, I should be allowed to question him face to face. It violates our sense of fairness to have accusations levelled against someone with no opportunity to defend themselves. Does this sense of fair play preclude anonymity among whistleblowers?

In fact we do not always regard concealing one's identity as morally bad. Quite the contrary, we sometimes regard it as good and proper. For example, within academia blind reviewing is a widespread practice: members of an editorial board passing judgment on an article submitted for publication may find the author's name removed. Conversely, the reviewers of manuscripts for publication may not reveal their name. In the first case the practice is justified on the grounds that it equalizes the competition: established authors can less readily exploit their reputation, and the decision to accept or reject an article is made on the basis of quality alone. The second practice supposedly allows more candor: reviewers can offer an honest evaluation without fear of reprisals or alienating a colleague with whom they may need to cooperate in the future. Note that in the first case anonymity serves as an equalizer to factor out extraneous and unwarranted influences like reputation. And in the second case it produces harmony. Insofar as it promotes fairness, equality or harmony, the practice of concealing one's identity has a moral justification.

The objection to anonymity can likewise be rebutted on the grounds that it promotes other values, or that the rights of the accused can be protected in other ways. It allows individuals to come forward who would otherwise remain silent for fear of reprisals. In so doing it promotes the *public welfare* which may be subverted by abuses of power by government officials, or the *public safety*, which may be threatened by dangerous practices of private industry. It may also promote *honesty* and *accountability* among managers who know they will find it difficult to conceal their indulgences. Admittedly individuals have a right to protect themselves against false accusations that can ruin their careers and compromise their good name. But to guarantee this right, the identity of whistleblowers need not be known: it is only necessary that accusations be properly investigated, proven true or false, and the results widely disseminated.

If the whistleblower and the accused confronted each other as equals, anonymity would be unnecessary.

But typically the power differentials are enormous, and most whistleblowers pay dearly for the action: they lose their jobs, get transferred to a less attractive if not unattractive locale and assignment, find their family life disrupted and their friends and colleagues less amiable. The taunt of the accused that the whistleblower come forward and 'face him like a man' is a bully's challenge when issued by the powerful. In a court, where the judge, lawyers and legal process serve as an equalizer, anonymity is less warranted. The prohibition on anonymity denies employees one of their few safeguards from retaliation of powerful, aroused enemies. Until positive steps have been taken to protect employees' rights to dissent, the condemnation of anonymity discourages one of the few checks on the abuse of power by corporate or government officials.

*The Slippery Slope*: Behind the prohibition on anonymity lurks the fear: What if everyone does that? The need to come forward and be identified acts as a check on a practice that threatens the day to day operation of bureaucracies, corporations and institutions. People have jobs to do, and precious time is wasted in unproductive activities if they go about secretly complaining of others—or so the argument may run. Furthermore, to continue this attack, damage is done to the moral fabric of an organization by anonymous whistleblowers who destroy the peace and harmony on which a smooth operation is based. To keep this practice within reasonable bounds and limit its corrosive impact, we must insist that whistleblowers publicly identify themselves. Without this restriction we slide down a slippery slope into corporate chaos and institutional anarchy.

What can be said against this slippery slope argument? First it is important to maintain a realistic perspective: How many more employees are likely to blow the whistle if anonymity protected them? The simple answer is: We do not know. Clearly to argue rationally against a practice, our argument should be based on information—not misinformation, suspicions and fears. Logically the slippery slope contention is an *argumentum ad ignoratiam*, a fallacious inference from our ignorance.

Second, it is important to locate clearly the burden of proof: Does it lie with the defenders of anonymity or its critics? As a form of dissent, whistleblowing is an exercise of a highly valued right—freedom of speech.

Admittedly the context is not political but bureaucratic, not dissent against one's government but against one's employer, (though for some whistleblowers the two are the same). Insofar as whistleblowers are speaking out, the burden of proof rests with those who would restrict them from exercising their freedom of speech. Until they can demonstrate clear and present danger to society—and not just themselves, their fears or hysteria will not serve as an adequate moral basis for restricting the rights of others to dissent.

Third, it is important to be clear that this burden will be difficult to sustain for the right to dissent is not easily overriden. For example, though an organization might be destroyed by the actions of an anonymous whistleblower, proving this would not necessarily establish the moral right of the institution's executives to silence the whistleblower. For suppose the institution is a chemical company, polluting the water the public drinks with toxic substances. Given that they have no moral right to endanger the health of others to begin with, they have no right to silence a whistleblower from disclosing this danger—even if his actions threaten their corporate existence.

To establish a right of corporations to silence whistleblowers, one would have to show that *society* would be better off if corporations had such a right. The very claim that they do or should have it sounds dangerously close to the rhetorical flourish: What's good for General Motors is good for the country. Today we recognize the dangers of air polution from automobiles, and the harm of gas-guzzlers to the nation's economy. Such claims can now more readily be seen for what they are: self-deluded or hypocritical attempts to equate corporate profits with the social good. For a utilitarian the burden of proof can be sustained only by demonstrating that restricting the whistleblower's right of dissent will work to the long-term advantage of society, rather than the corporation. I for one do not think that the empirical evidence can be marshalled to establish this claim.

---

**FREDERICK A. ELLISTON** was an academic researcher at the Criminal Justice Research Center in Albany, New York.

# EXPLORING THE ISSUE

## Do Whistleblowers Help Government?

## Critical Thinking and Reflection

1. What is whistleblowing?
2. Should whistleblowing be encouraged in government agencies? Why or why not?
3. In what ways do whistleblowers help government? Hurt?
4. Do you believe Edward Snowden was right to leak NSA secrets? Why or why not?
5. Should whistleblowing not be anonymous? Why or why not?

## Is There Common Ground?

One man's hero is another man's traitor. As a result, it is difficult to believe that any meaningful middle ground could be found regarding the benefit of whistleblowing to government. There is little question that society as a whole benefits when individuals feel safe in deciding to tell someone about wrongdoing that is occurring in their agencies. Further, few would disagree that genuine whistleblowers should not be able to be punished for taking the step to correct wrongs.

But what happens when government employees realize the protections they have been afforded and choose to use the power for impure purposes. After all, with no fear of retribution, there are limited concerns on potentially filing blatantly false reports. Once this occurs and eventually becomes public information, citizens begin questioning the legitimacy of the very policy in process to assure government legitimacy. It is possible to find common ground on this issue (after all, whistleblowing does present some framework to understand what is right and wrong,) but much more work must be done to assure whistleblowing works to improve government.

## Create Central

www.mhhe.com/createcentral

## Additional Resources

Ronald J. Burke and Cary L. Cooper, *Voice and Whistleblowing in Organizations* (Edward Elgar, 2013)

Glenn Greenwald, *No Place to Hide: Edward Snowden, the NSA, and the U.S. Surveillance State* (Metropolitan Books, 2014)

Joel Hersch, *Whistleblowing: Rewards for Reporting Fraud Against the Government* (Goshen Press, 2013)

Roberta A. Johnson, *Whistleblowing: When It Works—and Why* (Lynne Rienner, 2002)

Marcia P. Miceli, Janet Pollex Near, and Terry M. Dworkin, *Whistle-Blowing in Organizations* (Psychology Press, 2008)

# Internet References . . .

**Government Accountability Project**

www.whistleblower.org

**National Whistleblowers Center**

www.whistleblowers.org/

**SEC office of the Whistleblower**

www.sec.gov/whistleblower

**Transparency International**

www.transparency.org

**Whistleblower Protection Program**

www.whistleblowers.gov/

# Unit 3

# UNIT

# Social Change and Public Policy

*E*conomic and moral issues divide Americans along an ideological spectrum from "left" to "right." The issues are exceedingly diverse; they include economic equality, social welfare, gay rights, abortion, race relations, religious freedom, drug legalization, and whether there should be limits on speech activities. Disagreements break out on the floor of Congress, in state legislatures, in the nation's courtrooms, and sometimes in the streets. These controversial issues generate intense emotions because they force us to defend our most deeply held values and explain how they can be worked out in public policy.

In some cases, debate and deliberation can lead to individuals altering their views or opinions. Yet for other issues, there is no budging; this is especially true for morally centered issues. While institutions and culture may have an impact on the functioning of American government and its relationship to the citizenry, it is through policy issues where we see citizens becoming most active and involved. Look at just the past three years as the international community has experienced the power of protest. From the Tea Party movement to Occupy to the Arab Spring, citizens react when policy decisions do not reflect their perceived interests, hence the importance of the following debates.

**Selected, Edited, and with Issue Framing Material by:**
**William J. Miller,** *Flagler College*
**George McKenna,** *City College, City University of New York*
**and**
**Stanley Feingold,** *City College, City University of New York*

# ISSUE

# Does Affirmative Action Advance Racial Equality?

**YES: Anthony P. Carnevale and Jeff Strohl,** from "Separate & Unequal: How Higher Education Reinforces the Intergenerational Reproduction of White Racial Privilege," *Georgetown University Public Policy Institute Center on Education and the Workforce* (July 2013)

**NO: Dan Slater,** from "Does Affirmative Action Do What It Should?" *The New York Times* (March 16, 2013)

---

## Learning Outcomes

**After reading this issue, you will be able to:**

- Describe affirmative action.
- Assess whether affirmative actions has worked in America.
- Explain the unintended consequences of affirmative action.
- Assess whether America still needs affirmative action.
- Identify the successes and failures of affirmative action.

---

### ISSUE SUMMARY

**YES:** Policy researchers Anthony P. Carnevale and Jeff Strohl show there are still wide racial and ethnic discrepancies present in education in the United States and how more direct efforts by government to achieve equality will be needed to level the playing field.

**NO:** Commentator Dan Slater presents information related to the mismatch theory which suggests that affirmative action can harm those it's supposed to help by placing them at schools in which they fall below the median level of ability.

"**W**e didn't land on Plymouth Rock, my brothers and sisters—Plymouth Rock landed on us!" Malcolm X's observation is borne out by the facts of American history. Snatched from their native land, transported thousands of miles—in a nightmare of disease and death—and sold into slavery, blacks were reduced to the legal status of farm animals. Even after emancipation, blacks were segregated from whites—in some states by law, and by social practice almost everywhere. American apartheid continued for another century.

In 1954 the Supreme Court declared state-compelled segregation in schools unconstitutional, and it followed up that decision with others that struck down many forms of official segregation. Still, discrimination survived, and in most southern states blacks were either discouraged or prohibited from exercising their right to vote. Not until the 1960s was compulsory segregation finally and effectively challenged. Between 1964 and 1968 Congress passed the most sweeping civil rights legislation since the end of the Civil War.

But is that enough? Equality of condition between blacks and whites seems as elusive as ever. The black unemployment rate is double that of whites, and the percentage of black families living in poverty is nearly four times that of whites. Only a small percentage of blacks ever make it into medical school or law school.

Advocates of affirmative action have focused upon these de facto differences to bolster their argument that it is no longer enough just to stop discrimination. The damage done by three centuries of racism now has to be remedied, they argue, and effective remediation requires a policy of "affirmative action." At the heart of affirmative action is the use of "numerical goals." Opponents call them "racial quotas." Whatever the name, what they imply is the setting aside of a certain number of jobs or positions for blacks or other historically oppressed groups. Opponents charge that affirmative action penalizes innocent people simply because they are white, that it often results in unqualified appointments, and that it ends up harming instead of helping blacks.

Affirmative action has had an uneven history in U.S. federal courts. In *Regents of the University of California v. Allan Bakke* (1978), which marked the first time the Supreme Court directly dealt with the merits of affirmative action, a 5–4 majority ruled that a white applicant to a medical school had been wrongly excluded due to the school's affirmative action policy; yet the majority also agreed that "race-conscious" policies may be used in admitting candidates—as long as they do not amount to fixed quotas. Since *Bakke,* other Supreme Court decisions have tipped toward one side or the other, depending on the circumstances of the case and the shifting line-up of Justices. Notable among these were two cases decided by the Court on the same day in 2003, *Gratz v. Bollinger* and *Grutter v. Bollinger.* Both involved affirmative action programs at the University of Michigan, *Gratz* pertaining to undergraduate admissions and *Grutter* to the law school. The court struck down the undergraduate program in *Gratz* on grounds that it was not "narrowly tailored" enough; it awarded every black and other protected minority an extra 20 points out of a 100 point scale—which, the Court said, amounted to a "quota." But the law school admissions criteria in *Grutter* were more flexible, using race as only one criterion among others, and so the Court refused to strike them down.

The most radical popular challenge to affirmative action was the ballot initiative endorsed by California voters in 1996. Proposition 209 banned any state program based upon racial or gender "preferences." Among the effects of this ban was a sharp decline in the numbers of non-Asian minorities admitted to the elite campuses of the state's university system, especially Berkeley and UCLA. (Asian admissions to the elite campuses either stayed the same or increased, and non-Asian minority admissions to some of the less-prestigious branches increased.)

A survey from Pew Research in May 2013 shows that a majority of white and black Americans believe there is a least some discrimination against African Americans. Eighty-eight percent of black Americans saw discrimination against African Americans, with 46 percent saying that there is "a lot" of it. The percentage of white Americans who see discrimination against African Americans is smaller, but still a majority, 57 percent, says there is discrimination against African Americans, with 16 percent saying that there is a lot. A 2008 Gallup poll found that 56 percent of adults nationally believe that there is "widespread" racism against black Americans. That includes 78 percent of black Americans who held that belief. And it's not just that Americans hold a vague sense of discrimination. Nearly 70 percent of black Americans believe that the U.S. justice system is biased against them, according to recent Gallup polling. A quarter of white Americans, and a third of all adults nationally, agree.

If this many Americans believe there are still signs of racism within society—despite the marked success of minorities in recent years—it begs the question of how we can better assure equality for all members of society. For a nation founded as a group of self-exiled individuals seeking acceptance and the ability to express individual ideals, it is essential that we offer the same for those presently in our borders. Rather than passing state laws requiring particular minorities to be ready, able, and willing to show proof of citizenship for any reason, perhaps our efforts would be better spent assuring that legal means of immigration functioned effectively and efficiently.

Today, members of the Tea Party are largely assumed to be racists due to their strong opposition to President Barack Obama. Yet, as Mark Joseph writes in *USA Today*, there is no evidence of this being true. In fact, Joseph explains how he asks white conservative friends, "If your daughter were thinking of marrying a man like Clarence Thomas or one like Chris Matthews, which would you choose?" He further explains, "The answer is quick and unanimous: They'd choose to spend their holidays with a son-in-law who looks nothing like them but shares their values rather than one who merely shares their skin color."

Affirmative action will always be a debated topic in American politics, especially with an increasing number of examples where reverse discrimination is occurring. Yet without remembering the historical context of why it came into existence, it is nearly impossible to fairly assess the success of the program and its potential moving forward.

In the following selections, Anthony Carnevale and Jeff Strohl discuss in detail disparities in education in the United States today and explain how government involvement is necessary if we hope to create a meaningful dent in current numbers and trends. On the other side, Dan Slater discusses mismatch theory and mentions how in some cases affirmative action in schools can lead to students being less likely to succeed in the long run.

# YES

**Anthony P. Carnevale and Jeff Strohl**

## Separate & Unequal: How Higher Education Reinforces the Intergenerational Reproduction of White Racial Privilege

### Introduction

White flight from the center city to better neighborhood schools in the leafy green suburbs has finally arrived on the nation's ivy-covered college campuses. The racial and ethnic stratification in educational opportunity entrenched in the nation's K-12 education system has faithfully reproduced itself across the full range of American colleges and universities. Racial stratification permeates the two- and four-year college and university system among the more than 4,400 institutions analyzed in this study.

Even more striking is the growing polarization of the most selective institutions and the least selective open-access schools. White students are increasingly concentrated today, relative to population share, in the nation's 468 most well-funded, selective four-year colleges and universities while African-American and Hispanic students are more and more concentrated in the 3,250 least well-funded, open-access, two- and four-year colleges.

*The American postsecondary system is a dual system of racially separate and unequal institutions despite the growing access of minorities to the postsecondary system.* Polarization by race and ethnicity in the nation's postsecondary system has become the capstone for K-12 inequality and the complex economic and social mechanisms that create it. The postsecondary system mimics and magnifies the racial and ethnic inequality in educational preparation it inherits from the K-12 system and then projects this inequality into the labor market.

*The education system is colorblind in theory. In fact, it operates, at least in part, as a systematic barrier to college for many minorities who finish high school unprepared for college. It also limits college and career opportunities for many African Americans and Hispanics who are well prepared for higher education but tracked into crowded and underfunded colleges where they are less likely to develop fully or to graduate.* Increasing racial and ethnic polarization appears to be inseparable from the expansion of access to American educational opportunity first in K-12 education and now in the postsecondary system.

*The polarization of the postsecondary system matters because resources matter.* The 468 most selective colleges spend anywhere from two to almost five times as much per student. Higher spending in the most selective colleges leads to higher graduation rates, greater access to graduate and professional schools, and better economic outcomes in the labor market, when comparing with white, African-American, and Hispanic students who are equally qualified but attend less competitive schools. Greater postsecondary resources and completion rates for white students concentrated in the 468 most selective colleges confer substantial labor market advantages, including more than $2 million dollars per student in higher lifetime earnings, and access to professional and managerial elite jobs, as well as careers that bring personal and social empowerment.

*Affluent white students as well as prestige seeking four-year colleges are flowing to the top tiers of selectivity while lower income minority students are flooding low tuition, open-access, two- and four-year institutions.* In addition, while the number of institutions classified in the selective tiers is growing, the number of open-access, four-year colleges is declining as institutions move up the selectivity tiers. The result of this dynamic is increased spending per student at the most selective colleges and overcrowding and reduced resources per student in the open-access sector.

*The postsecondary system is more and more complicit as a passive agent in the systematic reproduction of white racial privilege across generations.* More college completion among white parents brings higher earnings that fuel the intergenerational reproduction of privilege by providing more highly educated parents the means to pass their educational advantages on to their children. Higher earnings buy more expensive housing in the suburbs with the best schools and peer support for educational attainment. The synergy between the growing economic value of education and the increased sorting by housing values makes parental education the strongest predictor of a child's educational attainment and future earnings. As a result, the country also has the least intergenerational educational and income mobility among advanced nations.

*Preparation for higher education matters in allocating access and success at the 468 most selective colleges, but it's not the whole story.* Differences in access,

---

Carnevale, Anthony P. and Strohl, Jeff. From a report: *Separate & Unequal: How Higher Education Reinforces the Intergenerational Reproduction of White Racial Privilege,* July 2013, pp. 7–14. Copyright © 2013 by Georgetown Center on Education and the Workforce/Public Policy Institute. Used with permission.

completion, and earnings persist even among equally qualified whites, African Americans, and Hispanics. The relative lack of K-12 preparation among African Americans and Hispanics does not explain fully the growing racial and ethnic stratification in postsecondary completion and subsequent economic outcomes.

The postsecondary system does not treat similarly qualified white and African-American or Hispanic students equally and thereby blunts individual opportunity and wastes valuable talent. Many African Americans and Hispanics are unprepared for college, but whites who are equally unprepared still get more postsecondary opportunities. Moreover, African-American and Hispanic students who are prepared for college are disproportionately tracked into crowded and underfunded two-year colleges and open-access four-year colleges. The postsecondary system leaves a substantial number of qualified minorities on educational pathways that don't allow them to fulfill their educational and career potential.

- More than 30 percent of African Americans and Hispanics with a high school grade point average (GPA) higher than 3.5 go to community colleges compared with 22 percent of whites with the same GPA.
- Among African-American and Hispanic college students who score more than 1200 out of a possible 1600 points on the SAT/ACT, 57 percent eventually get a certificate, an Associate's degree, or a Bachelor's degree or better; for white students the percentage rises to 77 percent.
- Among African-American and Hispanic college students who score between 1000 and 1200 points on the SAT/ACT, 47 percent of African Americans and 48 percent of Hispanics earn a certificate, an Associate's degree, or a Bachelor's degree or better compared with 68 percent of whites.
- Among African-American and Hispanic college students who score above 1200 points on the SAT/ACT, 57 percent of African Americans and 56 percent of Hispanics graduate with a certificate, an Associate's degree, or a Bachelor's degree or better compared with 77 percent of whites.

***African American and Hispanics' access to postsecondary education over the past 15 years is a good news/bad news story.*** The good news is that African Americans and Hispanics scored big gains in access to postsecondary education. The bad news is that both groups are losing ground in their move up to the most selective colleges relative to their growing population shares.

The absolute numbers of African Americans and Hispanics going on to postsecondary institutions have increased markedly and their share of enrollment in the top 468 colleges has increased slightly since the 1990s. But between 1995 and 2009, more than eight in 10 of net new white students have gone to the 468 most selective colleges and more than seven in 10 of net new African-American and Hispanic students have gone to the 3,250 open-access, two- and four-year colleges.

Similarly, the larger growth in college seats has been in the most selective tiers as compared with open-access colleges. Enrollments at the most selective and better resourced colleges grew significantly (78%), reflecting increased demand for high-quality postsecondary education; the vast majority of the new seats went to white students. Among open-access, four-year colleges, growth has been significantly slower (21%), but the net increases in minority enrollments were concentrated at those schools, leading to more crowding and fewer resources per student.

Since 1995, 82 percent of new white enrollments have gone to the 468 most selective colleges, while 72 percent of new Hispanic enrollment and 68 percent of new African-American enrollment have gone to the two-year and four-year open-access schools.

As a result of these uneven flows, the white share of seats at the top 468 colleges has increased, and the white share of seats at open-access colleges has declined relative to the white share of the college-age population (ages 18–24). Conversely, the relative share of new seats going to African Americans and Hispanics at the 468 most selective colleges has declined while the African-American and Hispanic share of seats at the 3,250 open-access colleges has increased relative to their share of the college-age population.

The most telling metrics of racial polarization in postsecondary education are comparisons of white, African-American, and Hispanic enrollments to their respective shares of the college-age population. Whites have increased their enrollment share in the top 468 colleges relative to their share of the college-age population.

- In 1995, the white share of the college-age population was 68 percent, and the white share of enrollments at the top 468 colleges was 77 percent, a 9 percentage point advantage of enrollment share over population share.
- By 2009, the white share of the college-age population was 62 percent and the white share of enrollments at the top 468 colleges was 75 percent, a 13 percentage point advantage of enrollment over population share and an increase of 4 percentage points within the college-age population.

The white share of enrollment in the 3,250 open-access, two- and four-year colleges has declined relative to the white share of the college-age population.

- In 1995, the white share of the college-age population was 68 percent and the white share of enrollment at the 3,250 open-access, two- and four-year colleges was 69 percent, reflecting a balance between enrollment and population shares.
- By 2009, the white share of the college-age population was 62 percent and the white share of enrollment at the 3,250 open-access, two- and four-year colleges was 57 percent, a 5 percentage point deficit of enrollment relative to population share and a decline of 6 percentage points within the college-age population.

The enrollment shares of African Americans and Hispanics in the top 468 colleges declined relative to their shares of the college-age population.

- In 1995, the African-American and Hispanic share of the college-age population was 27 percent, and their share of enrollments at the top 468 colleges was 12 percent, a 15 percentage point deficit of enrollment compared with population share.
- By 2009, the African-American and Hispanic share of the college-age population was 33 percent, and their share of enrollment at the top 468 colleges was 15 percent, an 18 percentage point deficit of enrollment versus population share and a decline of 3 percentage points within the college-age population.

The African-American and Hispanic share of enrollment in the 3,250 open-access, two- and four-year colleges increased relative to their share of the college-age population.

- In 1995, the African-American and Hispanic share of the college-age population was 27 percent, and their share of enrollment at the 3,250 open-access, two- and four-year colleges was 24 percent, a 3 percentage point deficit of enrollment relative to population share.
- By 2009, the African-American and Hispanic share of the college-age population was 33 percent, and their share of enrollment at the 3,250 open-access, two- and four-year colleges was 37 percent, a 4 percentage point average of enrollment relative to population share.

*College readiness is important in explaining low completion rates, but the polarization of resources in the higher education system is one of the root causes of increasing college dropout rates and increasing time required to complete degrees.* For every 300 college graduates, postsecondary education now produces 200 college dropouts. The completion rate for the 468 most selective four-year colleges is 82 percent, compared with 49 percent for open-access, two-and four-year colleges. Virtually all of the increase in dropout rates and the slowdown in completions are concentrated in open-access colleges; in substantial part because they are too crowded and underfunded. African Americans and Hispanics are more likely to go to open-access, two- and four-year colleges and less likely to achieve a Bachelor's degree or better because of it. Ultimately this leads to powerful earnings differences and reduced capacity for intergenerational investments in children's education.

*This dynamic leads to significant loss of talent among minorities and lower-income students.* This study also found that more than 240,000 high school students every year, who graduate in the top half of their high school class and come from the bottom half of the income distribution, do not get a two- or four-year degree within eight years of graduation from high school. The data show

that roughly one in four (62,000) of these high-scoring, low-income students are African American or Hispanic.

More than 111,000 African Americans and Hispanics who graduate from high school each year in the top half of their class do not achieve a two- or four-year degree within eight years. If these students had attended one of the top 468 colleges and graduated at similar rates, 73 percent could have graduated. *Whites, African Americans, and Hispanics who score in the top half of the SAT/ACT test score distribution go to college at the same rate (90%). Yet whites have higher graduation rates and graduate school attendance because they attend more selective colleges.*

Among students who score in the top half of the test-score distribution in the nation's high schools and attend college:

- Thirty percent of white students compared with more than 48 percent of African-American students and 51 percent of Hispanic students either don't go or don't complete college; and
- Fifty-seven percent of white students get a Bachelor's degree or better compared with roughly 37 percent of African-American and 36 percent of Hispanic students.

Among those who graduate from college:

- More than 81 percent of whites get a Bachelor's degree or better compared with a little more than 72 percent of African Americans and Hispanics; and
- Less than 19 percent of whites stop with a certificate or an Associate's degree compared with roughly 27 percent of African Americans and Hispanics.

*Access to the 468 most selective four-year colleges and their greater completion rates are especially important to African Americans and Hispanics.*

- African Americans and Hispanics gain 21 percent in earnings advantages when they attend the more selective schools compared with 15 percent for whites who attend the same colleges.
- Among African Americans and Hispanics who score in the upper half of the SAT/ACT test-score distribution, those who attend one of the top 468 colleges graduate at a rate of 73 percent compared with a rate of 40 percent for equally qualified minorities who attend open-access colleges.
- One-third of high-scoring African Americans and Hispanics who get Bachelor's degrees at the top 468 colleges attain graduate degrees compared with 23 percent of minorities who attend open-access colleges.
- African Americans and Hispanics benefit from access to selective colleges even when their test scores are several hundred points below the averages at those colleges.

*Moreover, this study's data support the axiom that the Bachelor's degree is the crucial postsecondary threshold for racial and ethnic equality.* White, African-American, and Hispanic students who graduate with a Bachelor's degree from the 468 most selective colleges go on to graduate school at the same rate. African Americans and Hispanics who graduate with Bachelor's degrees from the open-access colleges go on to graduate school at slightly higher rates (23%) than their white counterparts (20%).

*Stratification by income is strong.* Earlier research demonstrates underrepresentation by income is quite stark. High-income students were 45 percentage points overrepresented compared to population share in the most selective colleges while white students were "only" 15 points overrepresented. African-American and Hispanic students were underrepresented in the most selective colleges, relative to population share by 9 percentage points; low-income students were underrepresented by 20 percentage points. While income stratification is strong, this fact does not take away from or mitigate strong and persistent racial stratification.

*Race- and class-based inequalities in education overlap considerably, but race has a unique negative effect on college and career opportunities.* African Americans and Hispanics are especially vulnerable to class-based economic disadvantages because they are more concentrated in low-income groups and because they are more isolated both spatially and socially from the general society.

African Americans and Hispanics usually remain concentrated in poorer neighborhoods, even as individual family income increases. As a result, race gives additional power to the negative efects of low-income status and limits the positive effects of income gains, better schools, and other educational improvements. Hence, minorities are disproportionately harmed by increasing income inequality and don't benefit as much as whites from generational improvements in educational attainment or income growth.

The traditional channel of intergenerational mobility, parental education, is particularly muted for African Americans and Hispanics. In comparison to white students whose parents did not go beyond high school, African-American and Hispanic students drop out of college at higher rates (34% vs. 27%), obtain certificates or Associate's degrees more often (21% vs. 18%), and do not attain Bachelor's degree as often (8% vs. 14%).

At the other end of the parental education spectrum the problem is even worse. African Americans and Hispanics benefit less than whites from their parents' educational attainment. Among students whose parents have attained at least a Bachelor's degree, African-American and Hispanic students do not attend college at twice the rate of similarly situated white students (15% vs. 7%), drop out of college much more often (37% vs. 25%), and graduate with a Bachelor's degree or better less often (35% vs. 58%).

Exacerbating this problem is the fact that low-income status appears to further dampen African-American and Hispanic educational attainment more than similarly situated whites. Compared with white students whose families are in the bottom half of the income distribution,

African Americans (55%) and Hispanics (59%) drop out of college much more often than whites (45%) while African Americans stop out with a certificate at very significant rates (24% vs. 17%). Low-income whites are more likely to graduate with a Bachelor's degree (23%) than low-income African Americans (12%) and Hispanics (13%).

It is difficult to clearly mark the point where racial discrimination ends and economic deprivation begins, but the evidence is clear that both negatively affect educational and economic opportunity and are most powerful in combination. The interaction of race and class disadvantages result in the spatial, social, and economic isolation that signify persistent hardship. This is why some class-based metrics that reflect class-based disadvantages in their most extreme form, like differences in wealth, family structure, parental education, and occupational status, can translate into proxies for race in college admissions.

Conversely, racial isolation can be an effective metric of class disadvantage. An example would be the use of class rank as an effective proxy for race in the ongoing brawl over race-based affirmative action: The current legal standard in affirmative action, established in *Grutter v. Bollinger* and affirmed in *Fisher v. University of Texas,* is that racial diversity is a legitimate goal for college admissions but race alone cannot be used as a standard for admission. Because of the spatial isolation of minorities, targeting specific geographic areas or high schools can produce racial diversity without using race alone as an admissions criterion. Spatial isolation of low-income minorities is what accounts for the relative success of the Texas affirmative action system, which guarantees admission for any student in the top 10 percent of his or her high school class. The Texas 10-percent solution does not use race alone but still allows substantial racial diversity in the Texas postsecondary system because it is predicated on continued racial and economic segregation in particular areas and high schools.

---

**Anthony P. Carnevale** is the Director and Research Professor of the Georgetown University Center on Education and the Workforce. Between 1996 and 2006, Dr. Carnevale served as Vice-President for Public Leadership at the Educational Testing Service (ETS). While at ETS, Dr. Carnevale was appointed by President George Bush to serve on the White House Commission on Technology and Adult Education.

**Jeff Strohl** is the Director of Research at the Georgetown University Center on Education and the Workforce where he continues his long involvement in the analysis of education and labor market outcomes and policy. He leads the Center's research, investigating the supply and demand of education and how education enhances career opportunities for today's workforce. Dr. Strohl also focuses on how to quantify skills and how to better understand competencies given the evolving nature of the U.S. workplace.

**Dan Slater**

 **NO**

# Does Affirmative Action Do What It Should?

What's more important to how your life turns out: the prestige of the school you attend or how much you learn while you're there? Does the answer to this question change if you are the recipient of affirmative action?

From school admissions to hiring, affirmative action policies attempt to compensate for this country's brutal history of racial discrimination by giving some minority applicants a leg up. This spring the Supreme Court will decide the latest affirmative action case, weighing in on the issue for the first time in 10 years.

The last time around, in 2003, the court upheld the University of Michigan Law School's affirmative action plan. A divided court ruled, 5 to 4, that "student body diversity is a compelling state interest that can justify the use of race in university admissions." Writing for the majority, Justice Sandra Day O'Connor said, "We expect that 25 years from now, the use of racial preferences will no longer be necessary to further the interest approved today."

In the intervening period, scholars have been looking more closely at how affirmative action works in practice. Based on how they interpret the data that have been collected, some of these scholars have come to believe that affirmative action doesn't always help the students it's supposed to. Why? Because some minority students who get into a top school with the help of affirmative action might actually be better served by attending a less elite institution to which they could gain admission with less of a boost or no boost at all.

The idea that affirmative action might harm its intended beneficiaries was suggested as early as the 1960s, when affirmative action, a phrase introduced by the Kennedy administration, began to take hold as government and corporate policy. One long-simmering objection to affirmative action was articulated publicly by Clarence Thomas years before he joined the Supreme Court in 1991. Mr. Thomas, who has opposed affirmative action even while conceding that he benefited from it, told a reporter for The New York Times in 1982 that affirmative action placed students in programs above their abilities. Mr. Thomas, who was then the 34-year-old chairman of the Equal Employment Opportunity Commission, didn't deny the crisis in minority employment. But he blamed

a failed education system rather than discrimination in admissions. "I watched the operation of such affirmative action policies when I was in college," he said, "and I watched the destruction of many kids as a result."

Scholars began referring to this theory as "mismatch." It's the idea that affirmative action can harm those it's supposed to help by placing them at schools in which they fall below the median level of ability and therefore have a tough time. As a consequence, the argument goes, these students suffer learningwise and, later, careerwise. To be clear, mismatch theory does not allege that minority students should not attend elite universities. Far from it. But it does say that students—minority or otherwise—do not automatically benefit from attending a school that they enter with academic qualifications well below the median level of their classmates.

The mismatch theory, if true, would affect many kids. According to a 2009 book, "No Longer Separate, Not Yet Equal: Race and Class in Elite College Admission and Campus Life," by Thomas J. Espenshade and Alexandria Walton Radford, a black student with an otherwise similar application to a white student receives the equivalent of a 310-point bump in SAT scores.

Mismatch theory attracted little attention until 2005, when a law professor at U.C.L.A., Richard H. Sander, published a provocative article in the Stanford Law Review, which focused on how affirmative action affected law students. Mr. Sander claimed that "a student who gains special admission to a more elite school on partly nonacademic grounds is likely to struggle more" and contended that "if the struggling leads to lower grades and less learning, then a variety of bad outcomes may result: higher attrition rates, lower pass rates on the bar, problems in the job market. The question is how large these effects are, and whether their consequences outweigh the benefits of greater prestige."

In other words, do the benefits of the connections made at, say, U.C.L.A. School of Law, and the weight U.C.L.A. carries in the job market, outweigh the cost of struggling academically there? Based on his reading of the data, Mr. Sander concluded that they did not.

Law school, as it turns out, is a somewhat natural, though imperfect, environment for studying mismatch effects. Law students have their knowledge tested in a fairly uniform way, first on the LSAT and then again, after graduation, on a state licensing exam, the bar.

Much of the squabble over mismatch centers on differing interpretations of the Bar Passage Study. The B.P.S. was commissioned by the Law School Admission Council in 1989 to determine whether blacks and Hispanics had disproportionately poor bar-passage rates. In 1991, more than 27,000 incoming law students—about 2,000 of them black—completed questionnaires for the B.P.S. and gave permission to track their performance in law school and later on the bar.

Among other things, the questionnaire asked students (a) whether they got into their first-choice law school, (b) if so, whether they enrolled at their first choice, and (c) if not, why not.

Data showed that 689 of the approximately 2,000 black applicants got into their first-choice law school. About three-quarters of those 689 matriculated at their first choice. The remaining quarter opted instead for their second-choice school, often for financial or geographic reasons. So, of the 689 black applicants who got into their first choice, 512 went, and the rest, 177, attended their second choice, presumably a less prestigious institution.

This data presented a plausible opportunity to gauge mismatch. The fact that 689 black students got into their first-choice law school meant that all 689 were similar in at least that one regard (though possibly dissimilar in many other ways). If mismatch theory held any water, then the 177 students who voluntarily opted for their second-choice school—and were therefore theoretically better "matched"—could be expected, on average, to have better outcomes on the bar exam than their peers who chose the more elite school. Mr. Sander's analysis of the B.P.S. data found that 21 percent of the black students who went to their second-choice schools failed the bar on their first attempt, compared with 34 percent of those who went to their first choice.

The experiment is far from ideal. Mismatch opponents argue that there are many unobservable differences between second-choice and first-choice students and that those differences, because they're unknown, cannot be accounted for in a formula. In the case of the B.P.S. data, maybe the second-choice students tended to have undergraduate majors that made them particularly well suited to flourish in the classroom and on the bar, regardless of which law school they attended. "All this work on mismatch assumes you know enough to write an algebraic expression that captures what's really going on," says Richard A. Berk, a professor of criminology and statistics at the University of Pennsylvania. "Here, there's so much we don't know. Besides, the LSAT is a very imperfect measure of performance in law school and thereafter, as is the bar exam."

Daniel E. Ho, a law professor at Stanford, also disputes the mismatch hypothesis. In a response to Mr. Sander's 2005 law review article, Mr. Ho wrote in the Yale Law Journal that "black law students who are similarly qualified when applying to law school perform equally well on the bar irrespective of what tier school they attend."

Political changes in the '90s created another opportunity to study mismatch. In 1996, California voters passed Prop 209, a ban on affirmative action. Critics of Prop 209 expected black and Hispanic enrollment at top University of California schools, like U.C.L.A. and Berkeley, to plummet—and it did, for a while. But these schools eventually saw increases in minority enrollment, particularly among Hispanics, as sophisticated new outreach programs kicked in. Enrollment has not, however, gotten back to pre-Prop 209 levels.

Recently, economists from Duke studied the effects of Prop 209, comparing undergraduate graduation rates for blacks, Hispanics and American Indians before and after the ban. In a paper being considered for publication by *The Quarterly Journal of Economics,* the Duke economists conclude that mismatch effects are strongest for students in so-called STEM majors—science, technology, engineering and math. These subjects proceed in a more regimented way than the humanities, with each topic and class building on what came before. If you don't properly learn one concept, it's easier to get knocked off track.

The Duke economists say that lower-ranked schools in the University of California system are better at graduating minority students in STEM majors. For example, they conclude that had the bottom third of minority students at Berkeley who hoped to graduate with a STEM major gone to Santa Cruz instead, they would have been almost twice as likely to earn such a degree.

"Prior to California's ban on affirmative action," Peter Arcidiacono, one of the study's authors, told me, "what Berkeley did well was switch relatively ill-prepared minority students out of the sciences and into majors where credentials are relatively less important."

Soon the Supreme Court will decide *Fisher v. University of Texas.* The case is complex, but essentially boils down to a young woman's claim that U.T. violated the Constitution's equal protection clause by denying her admission because she is white. The justices, save perhaps Clarence Thomas, are unlikely to address mismatch in their opinions. But the court could force schools to be more transparent about the racial preferences they use in admissions, and even to track the consequences for their students. For now, social scientists debate what can be gleaned from flawed data sets. They continue to argue over whether mismatch even exists and the extent of the harm it causes if it does. This raises another question: Do some of the more concrete if intangible benefits of affirmative action, like prestige and the superior connections one makes attending a fancier school, outweigh the potential cost? If affirmative-action admits are less likely to pass the bar after going to a certain type of school, or less likely to follow through with their field of choice, then the cost is potentially considerable. But are we really going to tell a kid embarking on adult life that he's better off attending a less prestigious school?

"The real question is what we want affirmative action to achieve," says Richard Brooks, a law professor at Yale. "Are we trying to maximize diversity? Engagement in the classroom? Whatever it is, I don't think the purpose of affirmative action is for everyone to have average grades." Mr. Brooks believes that mismatch exists. But he rejects the idea that it's as insidious as others claim and says that some mismatch might even be a good thing. Striving alongside people more capable than we are is a key ingredient for growth of all kinds.

In the *Fisher* case, Messrs. Brooks, Berk and Ho signed a friend-of-the-court brief disputing a brief on mismatch that was co-written by Mr. Sander and the legal journalist Stuart Taylor Jr. Messrs. Sander and Taylor also wrote a book together that was published last fall, "Mismatch: How Affirmative Action Hurts Students It's Intended to Help, and Why Universities Won't Admit It."

"Mismatch angers affirmative-action supporters because it quantifies a downside without weighing it against potential upsides," says Theodore Eisenberg, a law professor at Cornell, "such as the benefit of a diverse classroom, and the reality that some people who do attend better schools because of affirmative action are more successful in life as a result and help other minorities thrive." Mr. Eisenberg is on the board of *The Journal of Empirical Legal Studies,* which in June is publishing a paper by E. Douglass Williams, an economist at Sewanee: The University of the South, that appears to corroborate Mr. Sander's "first-choice/second-choice" analysis of the B.P.S. data.

In essence, affirmative action is about how to fairly distribute opportunity after our long history of racial discrimination. Whether it "works" is as much an issue for school administrators as for policy makers. That is, before we tell a student to choose School B over School A, it's worth asking what schools can do to improve the experiences of students, particularly those pursuing STEM majors, who arrive less well prepared.

The upside of affirmative action might be harder to quantify. But part of the problem with the current affirmative action regime is how its supporters define the goal, what the Supreme Court calls the "compelling state interest": classroom diversity. Meanwhile, little regard is given to the actual forms of adversity that disadvantaged students of all races must overcome. If affirmative action continues—either until Justice O'Connor's 2028 horizon or beyond—then the results from California and the Bar Passage Study suggest it's worth a closer, numbers-based look at the consequences, for everyone.

**DAN SLATER** is a widely published author of journalism and creative nonfiction. A former legal affairs reporter for *The Wall Street Journal,* he is currently a contributor to *Fast Company* and has written for *The New York Times, The Washington Post, The Boston Globe, New York Magazine, Men's Health,* and *GQ.*

# EXPLORING THE ISSUE

## Does Affirmative Action Advance Racial Equality?

## Critical Thinking and Reflection

1. What is the mismatch theory? Do you believe it is true? Why or why not?
2. What statistics surprised you most regarding minority performance in education?
3. Why was affirmative action initially created in the 1960s? Is that why it still exists today?
4. What is meant by "color blindness"? To what extent can our laws be color blind?
5. Is there a danger that temporary color-consciousness can turn into a permanent policy? What safeguards are there?

## Is There Common Ground?

In reacting against California's Proposition 209 banning the use of racial quotas in the admission policies of the state's colleges and universities, some of those on the losing side said, in effect, "OK, we won't use strict quotas, all we're saying is that admission officers can simply note the race of the applicants." But that, too, is unlikely to survive when measured against the sweeping ban in Prop 209. The best sort of common ground is to make available to all applicants some sort of pretesting tutoring program, and that has already begun in California. Police and fire departments in many cities have also initiated these programs.

It is difficult to bring together both sides of the affirmative action debate and find common ground. This particular issue brings together two difficult policies: race and employment. Racial differences—as the United States has shown historically—are difficult to smooth over, especially when being encouraged from the outside. And individuals tend to get very upset when it comes to matters of employment and the ability to support oneself and one's family. The infamous Jesse Helms ad involving the concept of a white citizen not getting a job due to a company's need to make an affirmative action hire still resonates today. Yet, oddly enough, the most recent renditions have

aired on behalf of Vernon Robinson—an African American Republican who has turned the tide on illegal immigrants. As long as affirmative action is viewed through the lens of politics rather than as a civil rights (or even human rights concern), there is little hope of middle ground being reached.

## Create Central

www.mhhe.com/createcentral

## Additional Resources

Barbara Bergmann, *In Defense of Affirmative Action* (Basic Books, 1996)

George E. Curry, *The Affirmative Action Debate* (Perseus, 1996)

Hugh D. Graham, *Collision Course: The Strange Convergence of Affirmative Action and Immigration Policy in America* (Oxford University Press, 2002

Peter Schmidt, *Color and Money: How Rich White Kids Are Winning the War over College Affirmative Action* (Palgrave Macmillan, 2007)

Jim Sleeper, *Liberal Racism* (Viking, 1997)

# *Internet References . . .*

**American Civil Liberties Union**

www.aclu.org

**Center for Equal Opportunity**

www.ceousa.org/

**Equal Employment Opportunity Commission**

www.eeoc.gov/

**Institute for Justice**

www.ij.org

**U.S. Department of Labor**

www.dol.gov/dol/topic/hiring/affirmativeact.htm

**Selected, Edited, and with Issue Framing Material by:**
**William J. Miller,** *Flagler College*
**George McKenna,** *City College, City University of New York*
**and**
**Stanley Feingold,** *City College, City University of New York*

# ISSUE

# Should Abortion Be Restricted?

YES: **Marco Rubio,** from "Why Abortion Is Bad for America," *The Human Life Review* (Winter 2012)

NO: **Wendy Davis,** from "Filibuster of the Texas State Senate," speech delivered at the Texas State Senate (June 25, 2013)

| Learning Outcomes |
| --- |
| **After reading this issue, you will be able to:** <br><br> • Identify arguments in support of abortion. <br> • Identify arguments in support of banning abortion. <br> • Assess the impact abortions have on American society. <br> • Discuss whether it's possible to legislate moral policy. <br> • Explain why Americans regularly debate the issue of abortion. |

## ISSUE SUMMARY

YES: U.S. Senator Marco Rubio discusses why abortion harms American society from multiple angles, including moral, economic, and political, during a speech at the Susan B. Anthony List Campaign for Life Gala.

NO: Texas Representative Wendy Davis presents her case for why Texas Governor Rick Perry should not sign a new abortion measure that has been deemed the most restrictive state-level effort anywhere in the United States.

**U**ntil 1973 the laws governing abortion were set by the states, most of which barred legal abortion except where pregnancy imperiled the life of the pregnant woman. In that year, the U.S. Supreme Court decided the controversial case *Roe v. Wade.* The *Roe* decision acknowledged both a woman's "fundamental right" to terminate a pregnancy before fetal viability and the state's legitimate interest in protecting both the woman's health and the "potential life" of the fetus. It prohibited states from banning abortion to protect the fetus before the third trimester of a pregnancy, and it ruled that even during that final trimester, a woman could obtain an abortion if she could prove that her life or health would be endangered by carrying to term. (In a companion case to *Roe,* decided on the same day, the Court defined health broadly enough to include "all factors—physical, emotional, psychological, familial, and the woman's age—relevant to the well-being of the patient.") These holdings, together with the requirement that state regulation of abortion had to survive "strict scrutiny" and demonstrate a "compelling state interest," resulted in later decisions striking down mandatory 24-hour waiting periods, requirements that abortions

be performed in hospitals, and so-called informed consent laws.

The Supreme Court did uphold state laws requiring parental notification and consent for minors (though it provided that minors could seek permission from a judge if they feared notifying their parents). And federal courts have affirmed the right of Congress not to pay for abortions. Proabortion groups, proclaiming the "right to choose," have charged that this and similar action at the state level discriminates against poor women because it does not inhibit the ability of women who are able to pay for abortions to obtain them. Efforts to adopt a constitutional amendment or federal law barring abortion have failed, but antiabortion forces have influenced legislation in many states.

Can legislatures and courts establish the existence of a scientific fact? Opponents of abortion believe that it is a fact that life begins at conception and that the law must therefore uphold and enforce this concept. They argue that the human fetus is a live human being, and they note all the familiar signs of life displayed by the fetus: a beating heart, brain waves, thumb sucking, and so on. Those who defend abortion maintain that human life does not begin before the development of specifically human characteristics and possibly not until the birth of a child. As Justice Harry A. Blackmun put it in 1973, "There has always been strong support for the view that life does not begin until live birth."

Antiabortion forces sought a court case that might lead to the overturning of *Roe v. Wade*. Proabortion forces rallied to oppose new state laws limiting or prohibiting abortion. In *Webster v. Reproductive Health Services* (1989), with four new justices, the Supreme Court upheld a Missouri law that banned abortions in public hospitals and abortions that were performed by public employees (except to save a woman's life). The law also required that tests be performed on any fetus more than 20 weeks old to determine its viability. In the later decision of *Planned Parenthood v. Casey* (1992), however, the Court affirmed what it called the "essence" of the constitutional right to abortion while permitting some state restrictions, such as a 24-hour waiting period and parental notification in the case of minors.

In 2000, a five-to-four decision of the Supreme Court in *Stenberg v. Carhart* overturned a Nebraska law that outlawed "partial birth" abortions. The law defined "partial birth abortion" as a procedure in which the doctor "partially delivers vaginally a living child before killing" the child, further defining the process as "intentionally delivering into the vagina a living unborn child, or a substantial portion thereof, for the purpose of performing a procedure that the [abortionist] knows will kill the child." The Court's stated reason for striking down the law was that it lacked a "health" exception. Critics complained that the Court has defined "health" so broadly that it includes not only physical health but also "emotional, psychological," and "familial" health, and that the person the Court has authorized to make these judgments is the attendant physician, that is, the abortionist himself.

In the past year, the United States has witnessed a rebirth of restrictive abortion measures that have yet to fully play their way through the federal court system. Perhaps the most prominent example has been the Texas abortion debate, which drew national attention thanks to the filibustering of Texas state senator Wendy Davis. Texas HB 2 criminalizes abortions after 20 weeks and imposes harsh regulations on abortion providers that will force the vast majority of them to close their doors. HB 2 combines several pieces of anti-abortion legislation that were unable to advance during Texas' regular legislative session. Perry called two special sessions specifically to give lawmakers more time to push them through. During the first session, thousands of protesters helped delay the abortion restrictions until the last minute, giving Davis a chance to block the bill with a dramatic filibuster that lasted for more than 11 hours. But those tactics weren't enough to prevent the bill's advancement during a second special session. In November, the Supreme Court voted 5-4 to leave in effect a provision requiring doctors who perform abortions in clinics to have admitting privileges at a nearby hospital. Challenges to the bill still exist in federal appellate court, meaning the Texas law could find itself back in the court sooner rather than later.

Ohio, on the other hand, has spent the past decade enacting more restrictive controls on the availability of abortion without drawing as much negative attention at Texas. The state has become a laboratory of sorts for what anti-abortion leaders call the incremental strategy. Under this plan, the state, under the leadership of Republican Governor John Kasich, has passed a series of rules aimed at pushing the limits set by the Supreme Court without directly violating them. The provisions put in place attempt to both discourage women from choosing to have an abortion and hampering clinic operations. There have been two recently passed provisions that will unquestionably make abortions more difficult to receive. First, Ohio has passed a heartbeat bill, which requires women about to have an abortion to both view an ultrasound and watch its beating heart. Through guilt the hope is the woman will have a change of heart. The second provision will perhaps be even more effective. Ohio has required abortion clinics to have formal transfer agreements with nearby hospitals for emergency care for some time despite this being largely unnecessary as hospitals must treat emergency patients. But now public hospitals are barred from signing these agreements, meaning a few clinics will likely have to shut down unless they find a suitable private hospital partner. In short, it is clear that states are still working to find ways to restrict abortion within their borders and the Supreme Court sits in waiting to consider appeals.

In the following selections, Marco Rubio discusses the moral, economic, and political arguments against abortion. He claims that each of us was a human being from conception and as a result abortion should be banned. Wendy Davis, on the other hand, asserts that the fetus removed in most abortions may not be considered a person and that women must retain the right to make decisions regarding their sexual lives.

# YES

**Marco Rubio**

# Why Abortion Is Bad for America

Thank you for having me. This is such an important issue for me that I had written out a speech—some of the things I wanted to say to you tonight—and then I lost it.

So I brought my—I re-wrote it in a note here, so you'll forgive me, I'm a little disjointed. And the teleprompter was broken. We weren't able to—we sent it to the teleprompter shop but someone else in Washington was apparently in the shop ahead of us [*laughter*]. So, anyway, we're going to have to wait to get that one back. So I'll just kind of go off my notes here.

Let me just start by saying how honored I am to be a part of this event tonight, I am really blown away to see so many of you who are involved, who give not just money but time to this extraordinarily important cause. I was really inspired to see the young women who stood on the stage moments ago. Because I understand that in the culture we live in today, it's difficult to be pro-life. When I was running for office, throughout my career, I've been consistently pro-life—throughout my life—and I always laugh that some characterize that as "radical," even though all the polls show that at least, at a minimum, half of the people in this country agree with me. Other polling indicates that in fact, when you dig deeper, between 70 and 75 percent of Americans really agree with us at the end of the day in terms of seeing significant restrictions on abortions. So that alone indicates the mindset that exists among those who cover politics and make commentary on politics, that somehow being pro-life is a radical position. Being a young person who's pro-life makes those comments happen even more often, and being a young woman who is pro-life is perhaps the most—you get perhaps more pressure there, and more scorn, than any other demographic in our country when it comes to that issue. So as we look at these young women who came here tonight, not just pro-life, but working on behalf of life as a fundamental tenet of our society, I'm inspired by that, and I really want to thank them, and everyone else who wasn't recognized, but who is also part of that movement, and all of you for making it possible for them to do that.

Being in politics, being in the Senate, I give a lot of speeches about a lot of things. Tax policy, the national debt—these are all very important issues. These are important political issues, and policy decisions that confront our country. The issue of life is not a political issue, nor is it a policy issue. It's a definitional issue. It is a basic, core issue that every society needs to answer, and the answer that it gives on this issue ends up defining what kind of society you have. That's how important the issue is. And what I wanted to do briefly tonight for a few moments is just encourage all of you who are involved in this cause, because I know that sometimes it's easy to get discouraged, especially for those who enter the public arena—you take a beating for being pro-life from those who cover politics too often. And I think sometimes it has a tendency to wear people down. Sometimes—listen, when I criticize people, I always include myself—sometimes you feel like, maybe let's just not touch that issue today, because it divides people, let's just focus on the 80 percent issues, and the stuff people want you to talk about. And I know I have, and many of you have as well, had people ask: "Why do you have to talk about that? It makes us uncomfortable. Why do you have to speak about this issue, it divides people. Just focus on the economic issues. Focus on the economy, focus on jobs, focus on the national debt. That's what people want to hear about." Well, we can't do that. Because the national debt is important, the economy is important, and it is the central political issue of our time. But this is not a political issue. In fact, this is an issue that, especially for those who enter the public arena and refuse to leave our faith behind, speaks to more than just our politics. It speaks to what we want to do with the opportunity we've been given in our life, to serve, and to glorify our Creator. And so that's what this issue is about, as well.

Let me just say at the outset that there are multiple reasons to be pro-life, not the least of which is that *Roe v. Wade* is bad Constitutional law, irrespective of how you feel about the issue. It is bad law. It is perhaps the most egregious and devastating example of a court deciding that because the political branch will not deal with an issue it believes is important, it will step in and make a policy decision. The Supreme Court literally created a Constitutional right out of nothing for the purpose of advocating a specific political position. So just on the legal grounds alone there is enough reason to be against *Roe v. Wade*.

There's one reason I won't go into in depth tonight because a) I don't have to, and b) it's not why you wanted me to speak. There's a spiritual aspect to this, which is very real. I think virtually every religion condemns the practice of abortion, recognizes that life is a gift from the Creator, and compels followers to believe that as well, as a basic tenet of faith. So, in the spiritual realm, there are multiple ways to defend this. But what I want to focus on tonight are the pure, logical, public-policy reasons why abortion is bad for America, bad for our society, and bad for our people, and why it—why *Roe v. Wade* should be overturned.

Now, the argument is that there is a fundamental right to abortion in America. That is the argument that those in the pro-abortion, so-called pro-choice community would make, that there is a fundamental right to abortion. Women in this country have a right to have an abortion. So what's the source of this right? As you engage people in this conversation—by the way, I've never met anyone who's admitted to me that they're pro-abortion. They'll say they're pro-choice, but almost everyone I've ever met has told me they personally disagree with abortion, they just think it should be legal.

But, where does this fundamental right to abortion come from? You engage people that believe in what they call abortion rights, and sometimes here's what they'll do: They'll point to the circumstances of the pregnancy. They'll say, well it's an unwanted child. This is a child who's going to enter life and not be wanted, not be cared for. There are parents who don't want children, perhaps, but you know there are a lot of unwanted children in the world. There are a lot of unwanted children in the world who are born. We know that they exist in this country, but especially all over the world. That cannot be the justification for this. Because if it were, then that would justify by logic that somehow all those unwanted children as well should be dealt with in a similar manner, and that's a horrific conclusion. It's an indefensible position. And so that cannot be the source of this right. And quickly they move on from the argument because it's absurd and they don't want to think about it. When they say that to you, that this is an unwanted child, and you say to them, listen, there are a lot of unwanted children born all over this planet—they're orphaned, they're born disabled, they're born to families who can't afford them—you can't possibly be saying that those children should also be eliminated. And so they move quickly away from that argument because it makes no sense and it's indefensible.

The most common argument I hear next, what they quickly pivot to, is the argument of, well, it's a woman's body, and a woman has a right to do anything she wants with her body. And let's recognize right now, there is a fundamental right—there is a right to control your body, you do have a right to your body, there's no doubt about it. You do have a right to decide what to do with your body and what others can do to it, there's no doubt about it. But there is another right. And that's a right to live. And so, when you analyze this issue of pro-life vs. pro-choice in America, what we basically have are two rights which are in conflict with one another: a woman's right to choose—whatever they mean by that—is directly in conflict with an unborn child's right to live. And the question for our society is, how do you resolve a conflict like that when two fundamental rights that everyone recognizes exist are in conflict with one another?

And so immediately the other side will say, well our right to choose is more important than the right to live. And they'll say the reason why—the first argument they almost always relate—is because it's not a person, an embryo is not a person, a fetus is not a person. It's not a person yet. Well, if it's not a person, then what is it? Because if you left it alone, that's the only thing it can become. It can't develop into a cat! [*laughter*] It has the DNA of a person and it was certainly created by people. And left to nature, it will become a person, naturally. So it is a person. Then they'll argue, well, okay, maybe it is a person, but it's not a *life*. What do you mean, it's not a life? Well, it's not a life, because the first argument—the one they love to talk about—is viability. It's not a life because it cannot sustain itself without the person who has a right to choose—it cannot live outside the womb. That argument first and foremost is already a slippery slope because viability's a moving target. Viability in 1973 meant something very different than what it means today, medically. Children who were not viable back then are very viable now, and we have no idea what other advances are going to occur over the next few years, so if you build it on that, you're already on slippery sand.

Then they go on and say, well, they're not viable without the support of the mother. But that also can't be a good argument. Because a newborn isn't viable without the mother either! A one-year-old child, a two-year-old child—leave a two-year-old child by himself. [*laughter*] Leave a six-month-old child by herself; she's not viable either! Even the day you were born, and for years thereafter—some of you are chuckling because, leave a 19-year-old by him or herself! [*laughter, applause*]. My point is, this viability thing is not a good argument. Because the truth is that a child who has been born isn't viable by herself either. Just because they're not receiving nutrition through an umbilical cord doesn't mean that they can sustain themselves. And by the way, the third reason the viability thing doesn't work is because you apply it to the other spectrum of life, and you start to get scary. It starts to get scary. If in fact what we are saying is that human beings are only worthy of protection if they are able to sustain themselves independently of other people, that covers a lot of people in our society. It covers people who are disabled, it covers people who are temporarily incapacitated—it covers a lot of people. And so, there is no compelling argument for why a woman's right to choose trumps a child's right to live. There isn't any.

The fact of the matter is that we as a society, as a nation, from a political realm, have always understood that my rights, as important as they may be, . . . end where other people's rights begin. Yes, a woman should have a right to choose the kinds of things that happen to her body. But that right is not unlimited. It ends when it begins to interfere with the right of another human being to pursue life, to have a life. And that's at the core of this issue. That's really what this issue is about at its heart. And an increasing number of people are understanding that. I think the public polling shows it. And I hope that it will continue to be reflected in our political debate, because this is an essential issue. Well, let's ask ourselves, then why, if that's the case, if this is such a clear-cut argument, if it's so simple the way I've laid it out, and it's not more complex than this, then why is the law of the land what it is? Why are 50 percent of the people in this country, maybe a little less now, pro-choice? Why do they disagree with the things I've just said?

And the answer is, because in this equation, in this battle between the right to choose and the right to live, the only ones who can vote are the ones with the right to choose. The only ones who can participate in the political process are the ones with the right to choose. Unborn children can't vote; unborn children can't speak. Actually, they can. You speak for them. That's what you are. In this competition between two competing sets of rights, you are the voice of children who cannot speak for themselves. Of lives that may never have a chance to contribute to our society and make a difference. Of the unknown names of millions of children whose contributions to our world will never happen because the right to life was not respected. You vote for them when you vote. You participate in the political process for them when you participate. This is who you work for. Real people, no longer with us, who never had the chance to do what you or I did. And just as importantly, you are the voice and the vote of countless other children who have yet to be created, but whose lives will soon be challenged as well.

The truth is, I believe in all my heart that future generations will look back at this era in American history and condemn us. They'll look at what's happened here since 1973, and they will characterize this nation as barbaric. At some point, hopefully in our lifetime, but certainly at some point, people will look back at this practice and say, how could that be possible? In the way that we look back at the atrocities of the past, at things that occurred 100, 200, 300 years ago, at institutions that we as a nation have banned and now look at and say, how could people have supported this stuff? How could people have turned a blind eye to these things? How could people have ignored that these things were happening? The way we look at those things in history and condemn them, this era will be condemned for this. I have no doubt about it. Our job is to accelerate the process of getting there, to ensure that sooner rather than later, and God willing, in our lifetime, we can arrive at a consciousness in this nation that this is wrong. That the right to life is a fundamental one that trumps virtually any other right I can imagine. Because without it, none of the other rights matter. There can be no liberty without life. There can't be a Constitution without life. There can't be a nation without life. And there can't be other *lives* without life. I can't imagine any other right that we have more fundamental and more important than this one. And so the reason I'm so excited about the young people who are involved in this is because sometimes in contemporary life in America, we come to believe

that all the great causes are something lost to history, that past generations fought all the great battles: abolition, the civil rights movement, women's suffrage. That all the great causes have already been fought and won. It's not true. In fact, maybe one of the most important battles that has ever been fought is the one you're engaged in now. And so I encourage you to remain involved. Because at the end of the day, our nation can never truly become what it fully was intended to be unless it deals with this issue squarely. America cannot truly fulfill its destiny unless this issue is resolved. It's that important.

And I know that it's tough, I know. Especially for young people, I know that it's tough. When you take this position in public office or public policy, people look at you as an intolerant person. Oh, he's intolerant. Oh, they're radicals. Oh, you're trying to impose your religion on us. I understand the challenges to taking a position on this. But this issue's so important that it's different from the others. And this is where my faith comes in, and I hope most of yours as well. You see, I think our life here is important and everything we do here matters. This is now at the personal level, I'm no longer even speaking as a Senator, nor trying to impose what I believe on anybody else, I'm just sharing with you why this issue's important to me. And I'll tell you why. Because I've felt the same pressures. I've had people tell me, gosh, we love your tax policy, we love your fiscal policy, just don't do the social stuff on us, I don't want to hear about it. Turns people off, I've heard that too. And it gets to you sometimes. And I think, from now and then—probably not the people in this room—people are guilty of saying, let's just tone that one down. This is not the time for that. And then you realize that, you know, the office that we have is important, but this stuff's all fleeting. Comes and goes, you're a Senator today, you won't be tomorrow; you're in office today, you lose your next election. But at least my faith teaches that this life will end. You live—you're lucky, you live 80 years . . . you'll still be a Senator [*laughter*], and then you'll be held to account. Whatever your faith teaches you, they almost all teach the same thing: You will be held to account. At least in my case, I'm going to be asked very squarely, I know this. Look at what I gave you, God will say. I brought your family out of extraordinarily bad circumstances, and gave them opportunities. I gave you the opportunity to do things that your family never had a chance to do. I blessed you with children, who are healthy and vibrant and make a lot of noise. I blessed you with parents who encouraged you to dream, and a wife who supported you in pursuit of those dreams. I opened doors for you that you never thought were possible. When you polled below the margin of error in the first polls they took in your Senate race. When the only people who thought you could win your election all lived in your house. And when most of them were under the age of ten! I gave you the ability to speak to people and influence people. What did you do with it? And what am I going to say? Oh I had really good poll numbers? I got re-elected three times? I raised more money than anybody ever had? I was popular, people loved me; they patted me on the back, they gave me nice introductions? That's what I'm going to say I did with that? The more you are given, the more that is expected of you.

And that's not just true for us as people, that's true for us as a nation. America's not great because we're smarter than other people or we work harder than anybody else. There are smart and hardworking people all over the world. America is great because God has blessed America, and America has always honored those blessings by being an example to the world. For 230-some-odd years, there has been nothing more powerful on this planet than the American example. And the way we live our lives, and the principles we have stood for. Others don't always agree with the things we do, they disagree with our foreign policy, they get frustrated at America. But they admire us. Because when we get involved around the world, almost always it's behind principles and ideals. And so we are a blessed nation. And we're not just blessed so we can have. We're also blessed so we can give. And there's nothing that America can give this world right now more important than to show that all life, irrespective of the circumstances of its creation, irrespective of the circumstances of its birth, irrespective of the conditions it finds itself in, all life, on a planet where life is increasingly not valued, on a planet where people

are summarily discarded, all life is worthy of protection, and all life enjoys God's love.

We are called to different tasks, whatever they may be. If we stand for these things, if we honor God in these things, He'll honor us. He'll bless us. He won't always give us what we want, but He'll always give us what we need. And you will know that you lived your life with purpose, and that in all the things you did, you honored the blessings that you had. And if we as a nation do this, well, God will continue to do what He has done for 230-some-odd years, bless us like no other people in all of human history. This is the great cause before us. And I encourage you to stay engaged and involved. If I falter at some point, remind me of the speech tonight. I hope not to. I don't expect to. And with your help, I won't. So thank you so much, I appreciate it. Thank you very much.

---

**MARCO RUBIO** served in the Florida House of Representatives from 2000 to 2008 and was elected to the U.S. Senate in 2010. His committee assignments currently include Commerce, Science, and Transportation; Foreign Relations; Intelligence; and Small Business and Entrepreneurship. He and his wife, Jeanette, have four young children and live in West Miami.

**Wendy Davis**                                           **NO**

# Filibuster of the Texas State Senate

Yes, Mr. President. I intend to speak for an extended period of time on the bill. Thank you very much.

Thank you, Mr. President and thank you members. As we began to debate this bill on the senate floor last week, we talked about the fact that we were here on this particular motion because we had taken extraordinary measures to be here, and I want to talk about that for a moment, how we wound up at this moment, on this day, on the senate floor, debating this bill. And we wound up here because extraordinary measures were taken in order to assure that we would land here. We all know that the bills that are before us today, that have been folded into this one bill, Senate Bill 5, are bills that were filed during the regular called session of the Texas Legislature, and we all know, as a body, why we did not hear this bill during the regular session. And that is because, of course, under our rules, our traditions, it takes two-thirds of the members of this body in order to suspend the regular order of business, because it is typical for a blocker bill to be filed, in order for a bill to be taken up. And we know that there were eleven members of this body who refused to allow the suspension of that particular rule. We know that there were no real courses of action on the house fight on this bill during the regular session as well. And when the session ended, and within the hour, Governor Perry called us back, he initially called us back for another matter that also could not be heard on this senate floor during the regular session because of that two-thirds rule, and of course that was our redistricting bills. And now something extraordinary has happened; we were called to a special session, our presiding officer has decided against tradition of the Texas Senate to have us convene in order to talk about bills that could not be taken up in the regular session and to not follow the tradition of the two-thirds rule in order to accommodate that occurring.

This bill, of course, is one that impacts many, many people. And it's one that took extraordinary measures in order for us to be here and to converse on it today. Members, I'm rising on the floor today to humbly give voice to thousands of Texans who have been ignored. These are Texans who relied on the minority members of this senate in order for their voices to be heard. These voices have been silenced by a governor who made blind partisanship and personal political ambition the official business of our great state. And sadly he's being abetted by legislative leaders who either share this blind partisanship, or simply do not have the strength to oppose it. Partisanship and ambition are not unusual in the state capital, but here in Texas, right now, it has risen to a level of profound irresponsibility and the raw abuse of power. The actions intended by our state leaders on this particular bill hurt Texans. There is no doubt about that. They hurt women; they hurt their families. The actions in this bill undermine the hard work and commitment of fair-minded, mainstream, Texas families, who want nothing more than to work hard, raise their children, stay healthy and be a productive part of the greatest state in our country. These mainstream Texas families embrace the challenge to create the greatest possible Texas. Yet, they are pushed back and they're held down by narrow and divisive interests that are driving our state, and this bill is an example of that narrow partisanship.

Today I'm going to talk about the paths these leaders have chosen under this bill and the dark place that the bill will take us. I will try to explain the history of the failed legislation before us, the impact of that legislation, and most importantly what history tells us about these policies and the motivations behind them. They do real damage to our state and to the families whose rights are violated, and whose personal relationship with their doctor and their creator, which should belong to them and them alone, are being violated. Most importantly today I will share with you what thousands of families have had to say about this legislation and those bringing this legislation to the floor, when the majority of Texans want us working to press upon genuine business of the state of Texas.

The legislation before you has a history, as we talked about a moment ago and I'm going to go specifically through the history of this particular bill. There was ample opportunity during the special sessions to move theses pieces of legislation and some did move, but the will of the legislature did not propel them timely through the process. And here are the basics about what happened to each of those. SB 25 by Senator Hegar was the 20 week abortion bill, filed on March the 5th. It was referred to state affairs on March the 12th; it never received a senate hearing. The house companion, House Bill 2364, by Representative Laubenberg, was filed on March the 5th, referred to state affairs on March the 11th. A hearing was held on April 10th. It was reported out of house state affairs on May the 2nd. The bill was sent to house calendars on May 7th, and it was never placed on the calendar. SB 97, by Senator Patrick, regarding abortion inducing drugs and regulations on the administration of those drugs, was filed

Davis, Wendy. From speech delivered at the Texas State Senate, June 25, 2013.

on November the twelfth, it was referred to health and human services on January 28th and the senate hearing was held on February 26th. It was reported out of the senate health and human service committee on March 28th but it died on the senate intent's calendar, and it died for the reason that I mentioned a moment ago, because a third of the members of this senate, who represented voices who deserve to be heard, prevented the bill from coming forward. There was no house companion to that bill. SB 537, by Senator Deuell, related to the regulation of abortion facilities requiring that they all have a standard met for ambulatory surgical centers. That bill was filed on February 13th. It was referred to health and human services on March 19th, excuse me, February 20th. There was a senate hearing on the bill March 19th. It was reported out of committee on March 26th and it died on the senate intent calendar. Again, it died because a third of the members of this body made it so. There was no house companion filed to that bill. SB 1198, by Senator Taylor, relating to hospital admitting privileges and the requirement that doctors who perform abortions have admitting privileges at a hospital within a certain distance. It was filed on March the sixth; it was referred to health and human services committee on March the twelfth. The senate hearing was held on April the 16th. It was reported out of committee on April 22nd and it died on the senate intent calendar for the reasons that I mentioned a moment ago, because the minority group of senators, who represent voices across the state of Texas, made it so. There was a house companion to that bill. HB 2816, by Representative Burkett. It was filed on March the seventh. It was referred to house state affairs on March 18th, the house hearing was held on March 27th. It was reported out of committee on April 24th, and sent to house calendars on April 26th, where it died.

And how did we get here? Well, of course we were called to a special session, and as I said, that session did not begin with the addition of this bill, it began with redistricting. On June the 10th, Governor Perry added transportation funding to the call, and of course, the Democrats in this chamber had indicated our intention that we would vote to advance that bill were it placed before this one today. We understand that transportation is a priority. On June the eleventh, these bills were filed, several bills were filed, um, including also a bill by Senator Huffman, SB 23, a bill again that the Democrats have indicated were it taken up today, before this bill, we would have joined our colleagues in passing it because we believe it's important. Governor Perry, of course, on that day also expanded the special session to include legislation relating to the regulation of abortion procedures, providers and facilities. He also spoke, in support of that call, about the horrors of The National Late Term Abortion Industry. He said that sadly some of those atrocities happen in our own state. And in Texas we value all life and we've worked to cultivate a culture that supports the birth of every child. He said that we have an obligation to protect unborn children and to hold those who peddle abortions to standards that would minimize the death, disease, and pain that they cause. What he did not do was place on the call anything that would help to prevent unplanned pregnancy. What he did not do is place anything on the call that would aid women in making sure they never find themselves in need of the occasion that we meet here today to discuss. On that same day the call was broadened again. The bills were referred and put on a fast track for a hearing the following day, living—leaving little to no advance notice for a public hearing. But fortunately a procedural action forced the committee to wait an extra day; a tagging of the bill, allowing more Texans the opportunity to have their voices heard on these issues. Ultimately, the Republican leadership agreed to move only one bill on the senate floor and that was SB 5 that is before us today. Before bringing the bill up there was discussion amongst the majority and the 20 week fetal pain portion of the bill was removed by Republicans before the bill was presented to us for our consideration on the floor. As you probably remember from that night, Democratic senators offered seventeen amendments to the bill on the senate floor to address concerns from stakeholders, primarily to address concerns, again, that prevention of abortion is the surest way . . .? excuse me, that prevention of pregnancy is the surest way to decrease the demand for abortion. Included in those amendments were a request that we accept Medicaid funding from the federal level, which we knew would bring down a tremendous amount of money and assistance for women's health. Included in that was a full funding of the Women's Health Program which provides a ninety to ten match for uses of helping women who are in need of family planning services. But all of those amendments were rejected. The bill was voted out on party lines and then moved over to the house. The bill was received by the house on June 20th and was set for a public hearing the following day. The hearing also included HB 16 which was the 20-week stand-alone bill and HB 60, the omnibus bill. Hundreds of Texans from all over the state appeared to testify at the hearing, but unfortunately the hearing, which lasted sometime until the wee hours of the morning, 3:30 to 4 o'clock, was halted before all of the testimony was given by those who had waited, many of them from the prior morning, to voice their feelings on the bill. And it is my intention today to give them a voice by reading all of their testimonies on the senate floor. In committee SB 5 was changed to include the section of the bill, the 20-week ban, that was removed in the senate: also, HB 60 and HB 61. On the house floor there was minimal engagement and participation by the house author on the legislation. House D's offered thirteen amendments targeted at addressing concerns raised by stakeholders. All were rejected. And now, we find ourselves here.

This is the omnibus piece of legislation that contains these elements of bills that were filed in the 83rd session: the 20-week ban, the abortion inducing drugs provision, the ambulatory surgical center standards, and the hospital admitting privileges. The alleged reason for the bill is to enhance patient safety. But what they really do is create provisions that treat women as though they are not capable of making their own medical decisions. They weaken standards of care because as we all know, every member on this floor knows that the provisions of the ambulatory surgical center standards will immediately place 37 of the 42 abortion clinics in Texas out of compliance. And though the arguments on the senate floor were made that the reason for those standards was for patient safety, not a single instance, not a single instance, could be demonstrated to illustrate why those ambulatory surgical standards were important in assuring women's safety. Not a single example was provided where women had been provided a less safe atmosphere in the existing clinical setting today than they would receive in that setting. What this bill really does is to threaten the doctor-patient relationship, and we know that we received a great deal of information from doctors' groups which I'll read into the record in a little while about the intrusion on that relationship and we know that in no other instance has this legislature chosen to place itself between a woman and her doctor, or any patient and their doctor. We know that these additional standards are unnecessary. They're unsupported by scientific evidence, including unnecessary requirements that may be extremely difficult and in some cases impossible to meet without a basis in public health or safety.

As we've been debating this issue, we have been reminded that there was a time in our country when only the wealthy could afford to access abortion services because they had the ability to travel to places that it was legal, and that women who didn't have that access to care were relegated either to carrying a pregnancy to term or, and very sadly, to some unsafe methods that they turned to, to try to address that need. And we know that women lost their lives over that. We also know, in written testimony from the group, The National Obstetrics and Gynecologic Group, that their fear is the same thing is going to happen. In the state of Texas, through this bill, we are asking that women be forced to step back in history, back to a time when once again wealthy women who have the ability and the flexibility in their lives and their schedules to travel for these services will be accommodated, and women who will not will suffer a different and unfortunately, probably in some instances, a life-threatening consequence.

The 20-week ban on abortion, we've heard a great deal of testimony about that particular provision and I want to hit a few highlights of what has been shared with us. Number one, and most importantly, from our medical community we've heard the concern that this interferes with the practice of medicine. As important, we know that concerns have been raised that this ban interferes with a woman's healthcare decision before she and her doctor may have important health information about her own health and the health of the pregnancy. The ban will have devastating consequences when a woman is experiencing medical complications, and unfortunately it bans abortion before a woman may receive important information about her own health and the health of her pregnancy. Fewer than two percent of abortions occur after 20 weeks and while they are uncommon, it is important that a woman and her doctor have every medical option available. On the abortion inducing drugs restrictions, some of the key concerns that we have had—heard about that: one, that it requires that the physician preferred course of treatment be replaced with a treatment that is potentially more physically harmful to the patient, and again, though asked, no one on this senate floor was able to provide information to us that demonstrated any other incidents where the legislature had taken it upon itself to interfere in such a dramatic way in a physician's decision-making as it pertains to the administration of treatment. The bill would require physicians to follow an outdated protocol, limiting women's access to safe, effective, medication abortion. It directly contradicts a physician's ability to provide the highest level of care for their patients by requiring a government prescribed course of treatment. It prohibits—prohibits physicians in Texas from providing the standard of care to their patients, subjecting physicians to disciplinary action for providing the nationally recognized standard of care endorsed by the leading medical professional association of obstetrician and gynecologists, ACOG. On the ambulatory surgical center standards, additional state government regulation on an already heavily regulated practice of medicine was one of the primary concerns raised there. Healthcare providers comply with all federal, state, and local laws and regulations, and they strongly opposed regulations that failed to make healthcare more cost effective, safer, efficient, or accessible. Texas already requires abortions performed after 16 weeks to be performed in ambulatory surgical centers. And we know, and I'll read some information in a little while about the fact, that there is a reason for that, because the incidents of problems that arise prior to that period of time at existing clinical settings is extremely low. Much lower, in fact, than any complications that arise from the live births, of which we are not subjecting to the same standards. When these facilities close, and they will, women will lose access to their trusted provider. These closed facilities cannot offer any other services that they may have been providing. And we know that in Texas sometimes these facilities are shared facilities where family planning services are also provided.

What is required of reproductive healthcare centers today? Today in the United States, reproductive healthcare services are among the safest and most commonly sought forms of care in the United States. Placing unreasonable requirements on healthcare centers that provide safe, legal abortions today is uncalled for, and again, not a hint of evidence has been offered as to why it's needed. And we know why. Governor Dewhurst's Tweet told us why. It is because the real aim of this bill is not to make women safer but it is to force the closure of multiple facilities across the state of Texas without a single care or concern for the women whose lives will be impacted by that decision. Not a single care or concern. Because our leadership has demonstrated that it is prioritizing its own political possibilities over potential and devastating consequences for individual women.

Let's talk about the parts of the bill that are medically unnecessary. First of all, I think each of us would agree that as patients we trust our doctors, not the government, to determine what medical equipment and what sized room is necessary to provide us with good care. It is medically unnecessary to require health centers to build a hospital-grade operating room for an abortion procedure when one is not required for this type of procedure. And in fact, we know there are many outpatient clinical procedures that are more invasive, have higher incidences of problems, that today are allowed to take place in clinical settings such as a doctor's office without the standards that are being required in this bill. Texas, of course, as I said a moment ago, already requires that abortions performed after 16 weeks be performed at ambulatory surgical centers. This provision, the provision in these bills, goes further by requiring that all health centers that provide abortions comply with regulations that are equivalent to the governing places where surgery takes place. The vast majority of abortions, however, are outpatient procedures that can be performed in a health center, making those requirements inappropriate, unnecessary, and not at all about the health of women.

---

**WENDY DAVIS** is an American lawyer and Democratic politician from Fort Worth, Texas who represents District 10 of the Texas Senate. She previously served on the Fort Worth city council.

# EXPLORING THE ISSUE

## Should Abortion Be Restricted?

### Critical Thinking and Reflection

1. What arguments are made for restricting abortion in the United States?
2. What arguments are made for not restricting abortion in the United States?
3. Do you believe the government should be involved in abortion policy? Why or why not?
4. Is being a "person" different from being a "human being"? Why does this question matter?
5. When does human life begin? Is an 8-month fetus essentially different from a 2-minute old baby? If so, how? If not, what does that mean for policy moving forward?

### Is There Common Ground?

There are some areas where common ground can be found. They include help for women who decide not to abort, such as medical assistance during pregnancy and after birth, care for their babies, assistance in housing, and job searches for the mothers. Pro-lifers would also like greater information about child development in the womb, so that women can make a more informed decision about whether to abort. Pro-choicers would like more information to be given to young people about methods of birth control, to which pro-lifers would rejoin that information about the advantages of "waiting until marriage" would be better. If *Roe v. Wade* is ever overturned, still other areas of common ground might be found in various states, such as banning late-term abortions, favored by large majorities of Americans.

Yet there are other areas where there can simply be no common ground. When it comes to abortions that are not medically necessary, for example, it will be difficult to convince the two sides to come to any meaningful middle point. The main issue is the absence of firm data or agreement on when life begins and at what stage a fetus is viable. If such information could be universally proven, it may be easier to convince the two sides of the argument to find neutral ground. But as the political environment

stands today, it is hard to imagine circumstances in which an individual who sees an action as murder and another who views the same action as free choice will be able to agree on much of anything.

### Create Central

www.mhhe.com/createcentral

### Additional Resources

Jack M. Balkin, *What Roe v. Wade Should Have Said* (New York University Press, 2005)

Francis J. Beckwith, *Defending Life: A Moral and Legal Case Against Abortion Choice* (Cambridge University Press, 2007)

Barbara H. Craig and David M. O'Brien, *Abortion and American Politics* (Chatham House, 1993)

Peter C. Hoffer, *The Abortion Rights Controversy in America: A Legal Reader* (University of North Carolina Press, 2004)

William Saletan, *Bearing Right: How Conservatives Won the Abortion War* (University of California Press, 2000)

## *Internet References . . .*

**Americans United for Life**

www.aul.org

**Center for Disease Control Abortion Surveillance**

www.cdc.gov/mmwr/preview/mmwrhtml/ss6208a1 .htm?s_cid=ss6208a1_w

**National Abortion Federation**

www.prochoice.org

**National Right to Life**

www.nrlc.org

**Planned Parenthood**

www.plannedparenthood.org

**Selected, Edited, and with Issue Framing Material by:**
**William J. Miller,** *Flagler College*
George McKenna, *City College, City University of New York*
**and**
Stanley Feingold, *City College, City University of New York*

# ISSUE

# Should the United States Be More Restrictive of Gun Ownership?

**YES: Barack Obama and Joe Biden**, from "Gun Control," remarks delivered at South Court Auditorium, The White House, Washington, DC (January 16, 2013)

**NO: Jeffrey Goldberg**, from "The Case for More Guns (and More Gun Control)," *The Atlantic Magazine* (December 2012)

| Learning Outcomes |
| --- |
| **After reading this issue, you will be able to:**<br><br>• Discuss current gun ownership restrictions in the United States.<br>• Assess the threats gun pose to society.<br>• Describe efforts by the Obama administration to limit gun ownership.<br>• Explain why some argue that society would be safer with more guns.<br>• Identify key political players in the battle over gun control. |

## ISSUE SUMMARY

**YES:** President Barack Obama and Vice President Joe Biden, speaking in the wake of the Newtown shooting, discuss why America needs to take a more proactive stance in limiting control to guns to prevent further mass shootings.

**NO:** Columnist Jeffrey Goldberg presents an argument that Americans own plenty of guns to protect themselves but will only be able to prevent mass shootings if they are more readily able to carry them at all times.

**S**hould Americans have the right to self-defense? Does the Second Amendment not give all Americans a fundamental right to bear arms in order to protect themselves and their property in the pursuit of life and liberty? Without guns, rebellion against a tyrannical government would not have been possible and the American Revolution would not mark the beginning of America's independence from England. In fact, search and seizure of firearms and ammunition were a major catalyst for events leading to the American Revolution. While the Second Amendment laid the foundation for gun rights in America, it was not until recently that courts began to clarify exactly who the Second Amendment impacts. Without such clarification, state and local governments have been slowly stripping away access to firearms and therefore a citizen's right to self-defense with false claims of more guns equals more violence.

The Second Amendment, ratified in 1791, states, "A well-regulated militia, being necessary to the security

of a free State, the right of the people to keep and bear Arms, shall not be infringed." Proponents of gun control believe the word "militia" was specifically used to guarantee the right of states to have an armed militia, like our current National Guard. Of course, opponents of gun control believe it to be an individual right to bear arms and a denial of access to guns is unconstitutional. Prior to *District of Columbia v. Heller* in 2008, the Supreme Court had not reviewed a Second Amendment case since *United States v. Miller* in 1939, which did not answer if the Second Amendment was an individual right or one specifically held by the state militia. Without a Supreme Court standing on the issue, states and local governments spent nearly 70 years with little authoritative guidance and have been able to push gun restrictions to the edge, including all out handgun bans in places like the District of Columbia and the city of Chicago.

In 2008, *District of Columbia v. Heller* finally answered the question as to individual rights granted by the Second Amendment. In 1976 the District of Columbia banned all handguns within the district, and all long guns had to be disassembled and a trigger lock used at all times, ultimately defeating the usefulness of a firearm for self-defense in one's home. In siding with *Heller*, the Supreme Court showed that such stringent controls are unconstitutional and obstruct a person's right of self-defense. The *Heller* case was a monumental movement to solidifying the individual right to bear arms, at least at the federal level, but did not express whether the case was enforceable against the states. In 2010, the Supreme Court heard the case of *McDonald v. Chicago*, in which the Supreme Court ruled that the Second Amendment was enforceable against the state under the Privileges and Immunities Clause of the Fourteenth Amendment. *District of Columbia v. Heller* and *McDonald v. Chicago* have been two of the most influential cases in decades to address the right to bear arms, but as is often the result with major court decisions, the rulings have raised many new questions.

The problem with imposing excessive gun bans like those in Chicago and the District of Columbia is that they may not do much to actually reduce crime. Instead, they hinder the law-abiding citizen's right to self-defense, and at best create unreasonable barriers to access firearms. According to a Harvard study by Don Kates and Gary Mauser, Russia's gun controls are so stringent that very few civilians have access to firearms, yet as of 2002 Russia had the highest murder rate of any developed country. Russia is not alone, ownership of any gun in Luxembourg is minimal and handguns are banned, yet they have a murder rate nine times that of countries with high gun ownership such as Germany, Norway, Switzerland, and Austria. In 1996, Australia banned most guns and made the defensive use of a firearm illegal, which resulted in armed robberies rising 51 percent, unarmed robberies by 37 percent, assaults by 24 percent, and kidnappings by 43 percent in the four years following the ban. England has fared no better, during the late 1990s handguns were banned resulting in a 40 percent increase in firearm-related crimes, yet hundreds of thousands of guns were confiscated from law-abiding citizens. Countries like Australia and England are proving when stringent gun restrictions are imposed, and the right to self-defense is taken away, there are only two people with access to guns: the government and criminals.

The idiom "guns don't kill people, people kill people" is being tested in public opinion in the United States every time a mass shooting occurs within the nation's borders. In recent months, we have experienced two such incidents that returned gun control to the federal agenda. First, on July 20, 2012, James Eagan Holmes killed 12 people and injured 70 others during a mass shooting at a Century theater in Aurora, Colorado during a late screening of *The Dark Knight Rises*. Less than five months later, Adam Lanza shot and killed twenty school children and six adults at Sandy Hook Elementary School in Newtown, Connecticut. He also killed his mother. By the time Lanza took his own life with police closing in, it had become the second deadliest mass shooting by an individual gunman in the history of the United States. In both Aurora and Newtown, there were concerns raised about gun control: how did these men gain access to weapons despite displaying signs of mental illness? Why do we have semiautomatic weapons available? Is there any way to prevent possible criminals from getting access to guns without preventing Americans from protecting themselves?

Speaking after a mass shooting in the Navy Yard, President Obama explained: "By now . . . it should be clear that the change we need will not come from Washington. . . . Change will come the only way it ever has come, and that's from the American people. . . . Part of what wears on . . . is the sense that this has happened before," the president said. "What wears on us, what troubles us so deeply, as we gather here today is this senseless violence that took place in the Navy Yard echoes other recent tragedies. . . . I do not accept that we cannot find a common sense way to preserve our traditions, including our basic Second Amendment freedoms and the rights of law-abiding gun owners while at the same time reducing the gun violence that unleashed so much mayhem on a regular basis." Yet the National Rifle Association remains a significant obstacle to any gun control in the United States. With strong membership numbers, funds, and a knack for lobbying, even after a string of massacres, the NRA has successfully prevented any new restrictions to gun ownership.

In the following selections, we hear from President Barack Obama and Vice President Joe Biden who in the aftermath of the Sandy Hook shooting took to a microphone to ask Americans to be more proactive in trying to limit access to guns in order to prevent future death. Opposing our chief executives is Jeffrey Goldberg, who claims Americans have plenty of guns but need better capabilities for carrying them on their person if they plan to prevent massacres.

# YES

**Barack Obama and Joe Biden**

## Gun Control

THE VICE PRESIDENT: Before I begin today, let me say to the families of the innocents who were murdered 33 days ago, our heart goes out to you. And you show incredible courage—incredible courage—being here. And the President and I are going to do everything in our power to honor the memory of your children and your wives with the work we take up here today.

It's been 33 days since the nation's heart was broken by the horrific, senseless violence that took place at Sandy Hook Elementary School—20—20 beautiful first-graders gunned down in a place that's supposed to be their second sanctuary. Six members of the staff killed trying to save those children. It's literally been hard for the nation to comprehend, hard for the nation to fathom.

And I know for the families who are here that time is not measured in days, but it's measured in minutes, in seconds, since you received that news. Another minute without your daughter. Another minute without your son. Another minute without your wife. Another minute without your mom.

I want to personally thank Chris and Lynn McDonald, who lost their beautiful daughter, Grace, and the other parents who I had a chance to speak to, for their suggestions and for—again, just for the courage of all of you to be here today. I admire the grace and the resolve that you all are showing. And I must say I've been deeply affected by your faith, as well. And the President and I are going to do everything to try to match the resolve you've demonstrated.

No one can know for certain if this senseless act could have been prevented, but we all know we have a moral obligation—a moral obligation—to do everything in our power to diminish the prospect that something like this could happen again.

As the President knows, I've worked in this field a long time—in the United States Senate, having chaired a committee that had jurisdiction over these issues of guns and crime, and having drafted the first gun violence legislation—the last gun violence legislation, I should say. And I have no illusions about what we're up against or how hard the task is in front of us. But I also have never seen the nation's conscience so shaken by what happened at Sandy Hook. The world has changed, and it's demanding action.

It's in this context that the President asked me to put together, along with Cabinet members, a set of recommendations about how we should proceed to meet that moral obligation we have. And toward that end, the Cabinet members and I sat down with 229 groups—not just individuals, representing groups—229 groups from law enforcement agencies to public health officials, to gun officials, to gun advocacy groups, to sportsmen and hunters and religious leaders. And I've spoken with members of Congress on both sides of the aisle, had extensive conversations with mayors and governors and county officials.

And the recommendations we provided to the President on Monday call for executive actions he could sign, legislation he could call for, and long-term research that should be undertaken. They're based on the emerging consensus we heard from all the groups with whom we spoke, including some of you who are victims of this godawful occurrence—ways to keep guns out of the wrong hands, as well as ways to take comprehensive action to prevent violence in the first place.

We should do as much as we can, as quickly as we can. And we cannot let the perfect be the enemy of the good. So some of what you will hear from the President will happen immediately; some will take some time. But we have begun. And we are starting here today and we're going to resolve to continue this fight.

During the meetings that we held, we met with a young man who's here today—I think Colin Goddard is here. Where are you, Colin? Colin was one of the survivors of the Virginia Tech massacre. He was in the classroom. He calls himself one of the "lucky seven." And he'll tell you he was shot four times on that day and he has three bullets that are still inside him.

And when I asked Colin about what he thought we should be doing, he said, "I'm not here because of what happened to me. I'm here because of what happened to me keeps happening to other people and we have to do something about it."

Colin, we will. Colin, I promise you, we will. This is our intention. We must do what we can now. And there's no person who is more committed to acting on this moral obligation we have than the President of the United States of America.

Ladies and gentlemen, President Barack Obama. (Applause.)

THE PRESIDENT: Thank you, everybody. Please have a seat. Good afternoon, everybody.

Let me begin by thanking our Vice President, Joe Biden, for your dedication, Joe, to this issue, for bringing

Obama, Barack and Biden, Joe. Remarks delivered at South Court Auditorium, The White House, Washington, DC, on January 16, 2013.

so many different voices to the table. Because while reducing gun violence is a complicated challenge, protecting our children from harm shouldn't be a divisive one.

Over the month since the tragedy in Newtown, we've heard from so many, and, obviously, none have affected us more than the families of those gorgeous children and their teachers and guardians who were lost. And so we're grateful to all of you for taking the time to be here, and recognizing that we honor their memories in part by doing everything we can to prevent this from happening again.

But we also heard from some unexpected people. In particular, I started getting a lot of letters from kids. Four of them are here today—Grant Fritz, Julia Stokes, Hinna Zeejah, and Teja Goode. They're pretty representative of some of the messages that I got. These are some pretty smart letters from some pretty smart young people.

Hinna, a third-grader—you can go ahead and wave, Hinna. That's you—(laughter.) Hinna wrote, "I feel terrible for the parents who lost their children . . . I love my country and [I] want everybody to be happy and safe."

And then, Grant—go ahead and wave, Grant. (Laughter.) Grant said, "I think there should be some changes. We should learn from what happened at Sandy Hook . . . I feel really bad."

And then, Julia said—Julia, where are you? There you go—"I'm not scared for my safety, I'm scared for others. I have four brothers and sisters and I know I would not be able to bear the thought of losing any of them."

These are our kids. This is what they're thinking about. And so what we should be thinking about is our responsibility to care for them, and shield them from harm, and give them the tools they need to grow up and do everything that they're capable of doing—not just to pursue their own dreams, but to help build this country. This is our first task as a society, keeping our children safe. This is how we will be judged. And their voices should compel us to change.

And that's why, last month, I asked Joe to lead an effort, along with members of my Cabinet, to come up with some concrete steps we can take right now to keep our children safe, to help prevent mass shootings, to reduce the broader epidemic of gun violence in this country.

And we can't put this off any longer. Just last Thursday, as TV networks were covering one of Joe's meetings on this topic, news broke of another school shooting, this one in California. In the month since 20 precious children and six brave adults were violently taken from us at Sandy Hook Elementary, more than 900 of our fellow Americans have reportedly died at the end of a gun—900 in the past month. And every day we wait, that number will keep growing.

So I'm putting forward a specific set of proposals based on the work of Joe's task force. And in the days ahead, I intend to use whatever weight this office holds to make them a reality. Because while there is no law or set of laws that can prevent every senseless act of violence completely, no piece of legislation that will prevent every tragedy, every act of evil, if there is even one thing we can

do to reduce this violence, if there is even one life that can be saved, then we've got an obligation to try.

And I'm going to do my part. As soon as I'm finished speaking here, I will sit at that desk and I will sign a directive giving law enforcement, schools, mental health professionals and the public health community some of the tools they need to help reduce gun violence.

We will make it easier to keep guns out of the hands of criminals by strengthening the background check system. We will help schools hire more resource officers if they want them and develop emergency preparedness plans. We will make sure mental health professionals know their options for reporting threats of violence—even as we acknowledge that someone with a mental illness is far more likely to be a victim of violent crime than the perpetrator.

And while year after year, those who oppose even modest gun safety measures have threatened to defund scientific or medical research into the causes of gun violence, I will direct the Centers for Disease Control to go ahead and study the best ways to reduce it—and Congress should fund research into the effects that violent video games have on young minds. We don't benefit from ignorance. We don't benefit from not knowing the science of this epidemic of violence.

These are a few of the 23 executive actions that I'm announcing today. But as important as these steps are, they are in no way a substitute for action from members of Congress. To make a real and lasting difference, Congress, too, must act—and Congress must act soon. And I'm calling on Congress to pass some very specific proposals right away.

First: It's time for Congress to require a universal background check for anyone trying to buy a gun. (Applause.) The law already requires licensed gun dealers to run background checks, and over the last 14 years that's kept 1.5 million of the wrong people from getting their hands on a gun. But it's hard to enforce that law when as many as 40 percent of all gun purchases are conducted without a background check. That's not safe. That's not smart. It's not fair to responsible gun buyers or sellers.

If you want to buy a gun—whether it's from a licensed dealer or a private seller—you should at least have to show you are not a felon or somebody legally prohibited from buying one. This is common sense. And an overwhelming majority of Americans agree with us on the need for universal background checks—including more than 70 percent of the National Rifle Association's members, according to one survey. So there's no reason we can't do this.

Second: Congress should restore a ban on military-style assault weapons, and a 10-round limit for magazines. (Applause.) The type of assault rifle used in Aurora, for example, when paired with high-capacity magazines, has one purpose—to pump out as many bullets as possible, as quickly as possible; to do as much damage, using bullets often designed to inflict maximum damage.

And that's what allowed the gunman in Aurora to shoot 70 people—70 people—killing 12 in a matter of minutes. Weapons designed for the theater of war have no place in a movie theater. A majority of Americans agree with us on this.

And, by the way, so did Ronald Reagan, one of the staunchest defenders of the Second Amendment, who wrote to Congress in 1994, urging them—this is Ronald Reagan speaking—urging them to "listen to the American public and to the law enforcement community and support a ban on the further manufacture of [military-style assault] weapons." (Applause.)

And finally, Congress needs to help, rather than hinder, law enforcement as it does its job. We should get tougher on people who buy guns with the express purpose of turning around and selling them to criminals. And we should severely punish anybody who helps them do this. Since Congress hasn't confirmed a director of the Bureau of Alcohol, Tobacco and Firearms in six years, they should confirm Todd Jones, who will be—who has been Acting, and I will be nominating for the post. (Applause.)

And at a time when budget cuts are forcing many communities to reduce their police force, we should put more cops back on the job and back on our streets.

Let me be absolutely clear. Like most Americans, I believe the Second Amendment guarantees an individual right to bear arms. I respect our strong tradition of gun ownership and the rights of hunters and sportsmen. There are millions of responsible, law-abiding gun owners in America who cherish their right to bear arms for hunting, or sport, or protection, or collection.

I also believe most gun owners agree that we can respect the Second Amendment while keeping an irresponsible, law-breaking few from inflicting harm on a massive scale. I believe most of them agree that if America worked harder to keep guns out of the hands of dangerous people, there would be fewer atrocities like the one that occurred in Newtown. That's what these reforms are designed to do. They're common-sense measures. They have the support of the majority of the American people.

And yet, that doesn't mean any of this is going to be easy to enact or implement. If it were, we'd already have universal background checks. The ban on assault weapons and high-capacity magazines never would have been allowed to expire. More of our fellow Americans might still be alive, celebrating birthdays and anniversaries and graduations.

This will be difficult. There will be pundits and politicians and special interest lobbyists publicly warning of a tyrannical, all-out assault on liberty—not because that's true, but because they want to gin up fear or higher ratings or revenue for themselves. And behind the scenes, they'll do everything they can to block any common-sense reform and make sure nothing changes whatsoever.

The only way we will be able to change is if their audience, their constituents, their membership says this time must be different—that this time, we must do something to protect our communities and our kids.

I will put everything I've got into this, and so will Joe. But I tell you, the only way we can change is if the American people demand it. And by the way, that doesn't just mean from certain parts of the country. We're going to need voices in those areas, in those congressional districts, where the tradition of gun ownership is strong to speak up and to say this is important. It can't just be the usual suspects. We have to examine ourselves and our hearts, and ask ourselves what is important.

This will not happen unless the American people demand it. If parents and teachers, police officers and pastors, if hunters and sportsmen, if responsible gun owners, if Americans of every background stand up and say, enough; we've suffered too much pain and care too much about our children to allow this to continue—then change will come. That's what it's going to take.

In the letter that Julia wrote me, she said, "I know that laws have to be passed by Congress, but I beg you to try very hard." (Laughter.) Julia, I will try very hard. But she's right. The most important changes we can make depend on congressional action. They need to bring these proposals up for a vote, and the American people need to make sure that they do.

Get them on record. Ask your member of Congress if they support universal background checks to keep guns out of the wrong hands. Ask them if they support renewing a ban on military-style assault weapons and high-capacity magazines. And if they say no, ask them why not. Ask them what's more important—doing whatever it takes to get a A grade from the gun lobby that funds their campaigns, or giving parents some peace of mind when they drop their child off for first grade? (Applause.)

This is the land of the free, and it always will be. As Americans, we are endowed by our Creator with certain inalienable rights that no man or government can take away from us. But we've also long recognized, as our Founders recognized, that with rights come responsibilities. Along with our freedom to live our lives as we will comes an obligation to allow others to do the same. We don't live in isolation. We live in a society, a government of, and by, and for the people. We are responsible for each other.

The right to worship freely and safely, that right was denied to Sikhs in Oak Creek, Wisconsin. The right to assemble peaceably, that right was denied [to] shoppers in Clackamas, Oregon, and moviegoers in Aurora, Colorado. That most fundamental set of rights to life and liberty and the pursuit of happiness—fundamental rights that were denied to college students at Virginia Tech, and high school students at Columbine, and elementary school students in Newtown, and kids on street corners in Chicago on too frequent a basis to tolerate, and all the families who've never imagined that they'd lose a loved one to a bullet—those rights are at stake. We're responsible.

When I visited Newtown last month, I spent some private time with many of the families who lost their children that day. And one was the family of Grace McDonald.

Grace's parents are here. Grace was seven years old when she was struck down—just a gorgeous, caring, joyful little girl. I'm told she loved pink. She loved the beach. She dreamed of becoming a painter.

And so just before I left, Chris, her father, gave me one of her paintings, and I hung it in my private study just off the Oval Office. And every time I look at that painting, I think about Grace. And I think about the life that she lived and the life that lay ahead of her, and most of all, I think about how, when it comes to protecting the most vulnerable among us, we must act now—for Grace. For the 25 other innocent children and devoted educators who had so much left to give. For the men and women in big cities and small towns who fall victim to senseless violence each and every day. For all the Americans who are counting on us to keep them safe from harm. Let's do the right thing. Let's do the right thing for them, and for this country that we love so much.

---

**BARACK OBAMA** served as U.S. Senator for Illinois prior to defeating John McCain in the 2008 presidential election to become the 44th President of the United States. He is the first African American to hold the position. In 2012, President Obama defeated Republican challenger Mitt Romney to win a second term.

**JOE BIDEN** is Vice President of the United States. He is a member of the Democratic Party and was a United States Senator from Delaware from January 3, 1973, until his resignation on January 15, 2009, following his election to the Vice Presidency. In 2012, Biden was elected to a second term alongside Obama.

**Jeffrey Goldberg**

 **NO**

# The Case for More Guns (and More Gun Control)

### How Do We Reduce Gun Crime and Aurora-Style Mass Shootings When Americans Already Own Nearly 300 Million Firearms? Maybe by Allowing More People to Carry Them

The Century 16 Cineplex in Aurora, Colorado, stands desolate behind a temporary green fence, which was raised to protect the theater from prying eyes and mischief-makers. The parking lots that surround the multiplex are empty—weeds are pushing through the asphalt—and the only person at the theater when I visited a few weeks ago was an enervated Aurora police officer assigned to guard the site.

I asked the officer whether the building, which has stood empty since the night of July 20, when a former graduate student named James E. Holmes is alleged to have killed 12 people and wounded 58 others at a midnight showing of *The Dark Knight Rises,* still drew the curious. "People drive by to look," he said, but "not too many." The Aurora massacre is noteworthy, even in the crowded field of mass shootings, as one of the more wretched and demoralizing in the recent history of American violence, and I was surprised that the scene of the crime did not attract more attention. "I guess people move on," he said.

I walked up a slight rise that provided an imperfect view of the back of Theater 9, where the massacre took place, and tried to imagine the precise emotions the victims felt as the gunfire erupted.

"The shooting started at a quiet moment in the movie," Stephen Barton told me. He was shot in the opening fusillade. "I saw this canister-type thing, a smoking object, streak across the screen. I thought it was a kid with fireworks playing a prank."

Barton is 22 years old. He had been preparing to leave for Russia this fall on a Fulbright scholarship. "The first feeling I remember was bewilderment. I don't remember having a single thought before I was shot, because I was shot early on. I was sitting in the middle of the row, toward the back. I got blasted in my head, neck, and face—my whole upper body—by shotgun pellets."

As he lay wounded on the floor by his seat, he said, his bafflement gave way to panic. "I had this unwillingness to accept that this was actually happening. I wanted to believe that there was no way that someone in the same room as me was shooting at people," he said. "So it was disbelief and also this really strong feeling that I'm not ready to die. I'm at someone else's mercy. I've never felt more helpless."

In the chaos of smoke and gunshots, Barton saw the emergency exit door open, and managed to escape into the parking lot. "If I hadn't seen that door, I might not have made it," he said.

I left the theater and drove into Denver, to meet a man named Tom Mauser, who lost a son in the 1999 massacre at Columbine High School, 19 miles from the Aurora theater.

Daniel Mauser, who was 15 years old when he died, tried to hide from the Columbine killers, Eric Harris and Dylan Klebold. Harris found the boy under a table in the school library. A classmate told *The Denver Post* shortly after the massacre, "Eric shot him once, and Daniel pushed chairs at him to try to make him stop, and Eric shot him again."

After the murder of his son, Tom Mauser became a gun-control activist. In the days after Columbine, advocates of more-stringent controls of firearms thought they could feel a shift in the culture. People were disgusted that Harris and Klebold, neither of whom was of the legal age to buy firearms, had found a way to acquire guns: an 18-year-old woman, a friend of the two shooters, bought three weapons legally at a gun show, where federal background checks were not required.

After Columbine, Colorado closed its "gun-show loophole," but efforts to close the loophole on the national level failed. The National Rifle Association and other anti-gun-control groups worked diligently to defend the loophole—misnamed, because while *loophole* suggests a small opening not easily negotiated, about 40 percent of all legal gun sales take place at gun shows, on the Internet, or through more-informal sales between private sellers and buyers, where buyers are not subject to federal background checks. Though anti-loophole legislation passed the U.S. Senate, it was defeated in the House of Representatives. On top of that, the 1994 ban on sales of certain types of semiautomatic weapons, known as the assault-weapons ban, expired in 2004 and was not reauthorized.

After the Aurora shooting, gun-control activists who expected politicians to rise up in outrage were quickly disappointed. Shortly after the massacre, John Hickenlooper, the Democratic governor of Colorado, suggested that stricter gun laws would not have stopped the shooter. "If there were no assault weapons available and no this or no that, this guy is going to find something, right?," Hickenlooper said. "He's going to know how to create a bomb."

Hickenlooper's statement helped Mauser realize that his side was losing the fight. "I had deep anger when I heard that," he told me. "I heard the same kinds of statements from some people after Columbine: 'Well, you know, they had bombs, too.' The fact is that the deaths were from guns."

Mauser believes the public has grown numb to mass violence. "People say 'How tragic' and then move on," he said. "They're told by their governor, their political leaders, that there's no solution. So they don't see a solution out there."

According to a 2011 Gallup poll, 47 percent of American adults keep at least one gun at home or on their property, and many of these gun owners are absolutists opposed to any government regulation of firearms. According to the same poll, only 26 percent of Americans support a ban on handguns.

To that 26 percent, American gun culture can seem utterly inexplicable, its very existence dispiriting. Guns are responsible for roughly 30,000 deaths a year in America; more than half of those deaths are suicides. In 2010, 606 people, 62 of them children younger than 15, died in accidental shootings.

Mauser expresses disbelief that the number of gun deaths fails to shock. He blames the American attachment to guns on ignorance, and on immaturity. "We're a pretty new nation," he told me. "We're still at the stage of rebellious teenager, and we don't like it when the government tells us what to do. People don't trust government to do what's right. They are very attracted to the idea of a nation of individuals, so they don't think about what's good for the collective."

Mauser said that if the United States were as mature as the countries of Europe, where strict gun control is the norm, the federal government would have a much easier time curtailing the average citizen's access to weapons. "The people themselves would understand that having guns around puts them in more danger."

There are ways, of course, to make it at least marginally more difficult for the criminally minded, for the dangerously mentally ill, and for the suicidal to buy guns and ammunition. The gun-show loophole could be closed. Longer waiting periods might stop some suicides. Mental-health professionals could be encouraged—or mandated—to report patients they suspect shouldn't own guns to the FBI-supervised National Instant Criminal Background Check System, although this would generate fierce opposi-

tion from doctors and patients. Background checks, which are conducted by licensed gun shops, have stopped almost 1 million people from buying guns at these stores since 1998. (No one knows, of course, how many of these people gave up their search for a gun, and how many simply went to a gun show or found another way to acquire a weapon.)

Other measures could be taken as well. Drum-style magazines like the kind James Holmes had that night in Aurora, which can hold up to 100 rounds of ammunition and which make continuous firing easy, have no reasonable civilian purpose, and their sale could be restricted without violating the Second Amendment rights of individual gun owners.

But these gun-control efforts, while noble, would only have a modest impact on the rate of gun violence in America.

Why?

Because it's too late.

There are an estimated 280 million to 300 million guns in private hands in America—many legally owned, many not. Each year, more than 4 million new guns enter the market. This level of gun saturation has occurred not because the anti-gun lobby has been consistently outflanked by its adversaries in the National Rifle Association, though it has been. The NRA is quite obviously a powerful organization, but like many effective pressure groups, it is powerful in good part because so many Americans are predisposed to agree with its basic message.

America's level of gun ownership means that even if the Supreme Court—which ruled in 2008 that the Second Amendment gives citizens the individual right to own firearms, as gun advocates have long insisted—suddenly reversed itself and ruled that the individual ownership of handguns was illegal, there would be no practical way for a democratic country to locate and seize those guns.

Many gun-control advocates, and particularly advocates of a total gun ban, would like to see the United States become more like Canada, where there are far fewer guns per capita and where most guns must be registered with the federal government. The Canadian approach to firearms ownership has many attractions—the country's firearm homicide rate is one-sixth that of the U.S. But barring a decision by the American people and their legislators to remove the right to bear arms from the Constitution, arguing for applying the Canadian approach in the U.S. is useless.

Even the leading advocacy group for stricter gun laws, the Brady Campaign to Prevent Gun Violence, has given up the struggle to convince the courts, and the public, that the Constitution grants only members of a militia the right to bear arms. "I'm happy to consider the debate on the Second Amendment closed," Dan Gross, the Brady Campaign's president, told me recently. "Reopening that debate is not what we should be doing. We have to respect the fact that a lot of decent, law-abiding people believe in gun ownership."

Which raises a question: When even anti-gun activists believe that the debate over private gun ownership is closed; when it is too late to reduce the number of guns in private hands—and since only the naive think that legislation will prevent more than a modest number of the criminally minded, and the mentally deranged, from acquiring a gun in a country absolutely inundated with weapons— could it be that an effective way to combat guns is with more guns?

Today, more than 8 million vetted and (depending on the state) trained law-abiding citizens possess state-issued "concealed carry" handgun permits, which allow them to carry a concealed handgun or other weapon in public. Anti-gun activists believe the expansion of concealed-carry permits represents a serious threat to public order. But what if, in fact, the reverse is true? Mightn't allowing more law-abiding private citizens to carry concealed weapons—when combined with other forms of stringent gun regulation—actually reduce gun violence?

This thought has been with me for nearly two decades. On December 7, 1993, a bitter and unstable man named Colin Ferguson boarded an eastbound Long Island Rail Road train at the Jamaica, Queens, station. As the train pulled into the Merillon Avenue station in Nassau County, Ferguson pulled out a Ruger 9 mm pistol he had bought legally in California (which had a 15-day waiting period) and began walking down the aisle, calmly shooting passengers as he went. He killed six people and wounded 19 others before three passengers tackled him while he was reloading.

I had been an LIRR commuter not long before this happened, and I remember clearly my reaction to the slaughter, and I remember as well the reaction of many New York politicians. Much of the political class, and many editorialists, were of the view that the LIRR massacre proved the need for stricter gun control, and even for the banning of handguns. I shared—and continue to share—the view that muscular gun-control regulations, ones that put stumbling blocks in front of criminals seeking firearms, are necessary. But I was also seized by the thought that, had I been on the train, I would much rather have been armed than unarmed. I was not, and am not, under the illusion that a handgun would have necessarily provided a definitive solution to the problem posed by Colin Ferguson. But my instinct was that if someone is shooting at you, it is generally better to shoot back than to cower and pray.

Would a civilian firing back at Ferguson have wounded or killed innocent people? Quite possibly yes. Is that a risk potential victims quaking under train seats or classroom desks might accept? Quite possibly yes. Especially when you consider the massacres that have been prevented or interrupted by armed civilians before the police arrived.

Many of the worst American massacres end not in the capture of the gunman but in his suicide. In the 2007 mass shooting at Virginia Tech, for instance, the gunman,

Seung-Hui Cho, killed himself as the police were set to capture him. But in other cases, massacres were stopped early by the intervention of armed civilians, or off-duty or retired police officers who happened to be nearby.

In 1997, a disturbed high-school student named Luke Woodham stabbed his mother and then shot and killed two people at Pearl High School in Pearl, Mississippi. He then began driving toward a nearby junior high to continue his shooting spree, but the assistant principal of the high school, Joel Myrick, aimed a pistol he kept in his truck at Woodham, causing him to veer off the road. Myrick then put his pistol to Woodham's neck and disarmed him. On January 16, 2002, a disgruntled former student at the Appalachian School of Law in Grundy, Virginia, had killed three people, including the school's dean, when two students, both off-duty law-enforcement officers, retrieved their weapons and pointed them at the shooter, who ended his killing spree and surrendered. In December 2007, a man armed with a semiautomatic rifle and two pistols entered the New Life Church in Colorado Springs and killed two teenage girls before a church member, Jeanne Assam—a former Minneapolis police officer and a volunteer church security guard—shot and wounded the gunman, who then killed himself.

And so I put a question to Stephen Barton, who described feeling helpless in the Aurora theater: Would he rather have been armed, or at least been in the theater with armed patrons, when the massacre started?

"Intuitively it makes sense for people to have that reaction, to want to defend themselves," he said. "It's easy to say that if more people had guns to defend themselves, they could take criminals down, but I don't think concealed-carry weapons are the answer." In a dark and crowded theater, he said, facing someone wearing bullet-resistant armor on much of his body, a gun, even in trained hands, would have been unlikely to do much good.

I put to Tom Mauser a variation of the question I had asked Barton. What if a teacher or an administrator inside Columbine High School had been armed on the day of the massacre? Unlike the theater in Aurora, the school was brightly lit, and not as densely packed. If someone with a gun had confronted Harris and Klebold in the library, he or she would have been able, at the very least, to distract the killers—perhaps even long enough for them to be tackled or disarmed.

"That kind of speculation doesn't solve anything," Mauser said. "I don't know if that person might have shot my son accidentally."

But the worst thing that could have happened to Daniel Mauser did, in fact, happen. The presence in the Columbine library of a well-trained, armed civilian attempting to stop the killers could hardly have made the situation worse. Indeed, the local police—who waited 45 minutes to enter the school, while a SWAT team assembled—were severely criticized for the delay.

But Mauser remained implacable. "We know that if the country adopts this vision that everyone should be armed—that administrators and janitors in school are armed, that people are walking around armed—we won't be safe," Mauser told me. "In Aurora, if five people in that theater had guns, they could have just ended up shooting each other or innocent people in the crossfire. It just makes sense that if people are walking around armed, you're going to have a high rate of people shooting each other."

Earlier this year, a man who was upset with the anti-gay-rights position of the Family Research Council entered the group's Washington, D.C., headquarters and allegedly shot and wounded the building manager (who subsequently tackled the gunman). At the time, Washington's mayor, Vincent Gray, said: "We don't need to make more guns available to people. . . . The more access they have, the more they threaten people."

The District of Columbia does not allow for concealed carry, though its residents can now apply for a license allowing them to keep handguns at home, thanks to the 2008 Supreme Court ruling in a case brought on behalf of a D.C. man who wanted a gun for self-protection.

I called Gray to ask him about his assertion that more guns mean more violence, noting that he himself travels the city with armed police bodyguards, a service not afforded the typical Washington resident. "Well, first of all, I've never even seen the guns that the security people have. When I travel outside the city, I don't have security. I would be fine without security," he said. "But we have 3,800 police officers to protect people. They may not be at someone's side at every moment, but they're around."

I asked him whether he could envision a scenario in which an armed civilian might be able to stop a crime from occurring. "There are those who believe that if they have a weapon, they can combat crime, but I don't think that way," he said.

The police, of course, have guns to stop crime. So why couldn't a well-trained civilian also stop crime? "If you have a gun on you, that's just another opportunity to use it," Gray said. "It's the temptation of the moment. I just think the opportunity is there to create more violence."

In 2004, the Ohio legislature passed a law allowing private citizens to apply for permits to carry firearms outside the home. The decision to allow concealed carry was, of course, a controversial one. Law-enforcement organizations, among others, argued that an armed population would create chaos in the streets. In 2003, John Gilchrist, the legislative counsel for the Ohio Association of Chiefs of Police, testified, "If 200,000 to 300,000 citizens begin carrying a concealed weapon, common sense tells us that accidents will become a daily event."

When I called Gilchrist recently, he told me that events since the state's concealed-carry law took effect have proved his point. "Talking to the chiefs, I know that there is more gun violence and accidents involving guns," he said. "I think there's more gun violence now because there are more guns. People are using guns in the heat of arguments, and there wouldn't be as much gun violence

if we didn't have people carrying weapons. If you've got people walking around in a bad mood—or in a divorce, they've lost their job—and they get into a confrontation, this could result in the use of a gun. If you talk to emergency-room physicians in the state, [they] see more and more people with gunshot wounds."

Gilchrist said he did not know the exact statistics on gun-related incidents (or on incidents concerning concealed-carry permit holders specifically, because the state keeps the names of permit holders confidential). He says, however, that he tracks gun usage anecdotally. "You can look in the newspaper. I consciously look for stories that deal with guns. There are more and more articles in *The Columbus Dispatch* about people using guns inappropriately."

Gilchrist's argument would be convincing but for one thing: the firearm crime rate in Ohio remained steady after the concealed-carry law passed in 2004.

It is an unexamined assumption on the part of gun-control activists that the possession of a firearm by a law-abiding person will almost axiomatically cause that person to fire it at another human being in a moment of stress. Dave Kopel, the research director of the libertarian-leaning Independence Institute, in Denver, posits that opposition to gun ownership is ideological, not rational. "I use gay marriage as an analogue," he said. "Some people say they are against gay marriage because they think it leads to worse outcomes for kids. Now, let's say in 2020 all the social-science evidence has it that the kids of gay families turn out fine. Some people will still say they're against it, not for reasons of social science, but for reasons of faith. That's what you have here in the gun issue."

There is no proof to support the idea that concealed-carry permit holders create more violence in society than would otherwise occur; they may, in fact, reduce it. According to Adam Winkler, a law professor at UCLA and the author of *Gunfight: The Battle Over the Right to Bear Arms in America*, permit holders in the U.S. commit crimes at a rate lower than that of the general population. "We don't see much bloodshed from concealed-carry permit holders, because they are law-abiding people," Winkler said. "That's not to say that permit holders don't commit crimes, but they do so at a lower rate than the general population. People who seek to obtain permits are likely to be people who respect the law." According to John Lott, an economist and a gun-rights advocate who maintains that gun ownership by law-abiding citizens helps curtail crime, the crime rate among concealed-carry permit holders is lower than the crime rate among police officers.

Today, the number of concealed-carry permits is the highest it's ever been, at 8 million, and the homicide rate is the lowest it's been in four decades—less than half what it was 20 years ago. (The number of people allowed to carry concealed weapons is actually considerably higher than 8 million, because residents of Vermont, Wyoming, Arizona, Alaska, and parts of Montana do not need government permission to carry their personal firearms. These states have what Second Amendment absolutists refer to as "constitutional carry," meaning, in essence, that the Second Amendment is their permit.)

Many gun-rights advocates see a link between an increasingly armed public and a decreasing crime rate. "I think effective law enforcement has had the biggest impact on crime rates, but I think concealed carry has something to do with it. We've seen an explosion in the number of people licensed to carry," Lott told me. "You can deter criminality through longer sentencing, and you deter criminality by making it riskier for people to commit crimes. And one way to make it riskier is to create the impression among the criminal population that the law-abiding citizen they want to target may have a gun."

Crime statistics in Britain, where guns are much scarcer, bear this out. Gary Kleck, a criminologist at Florida State University, wrote in his 1991 book, *Point Blank: Guns and Violence in America,* that only 13 percent of burglaries in America occur when the occupant is home. In Britain, so-called hot burglaries account for about 45 percent of all break-ins. Kleck and others attribute America's low rate of occupied-home burglaries to fear among criminals that homeowners might be armed. (A survey of almost 2,000 convicted U.S. felons, conducted by the criminologists Peter Rossi and James D. Wright in the late '80s, concluded that burglars are more afraid of armed homeowners than they are of arrest by the police.)

Others contend that proving causality between crime rates and the number of concealed-carry permits is impossible. "It's difficult to make the case that more concealed-carry guns have led to the drop in the national crime rate, because cities like Los Angeles, where we have very restrictive gun-control laws, have seen the same remarkable drop in crime," Winkler told me. (Many criminologists tend to attribute America's dramatic decrease in violent crime to a combination of demographic changes, longer criminal sentencing, innovative policing techniques, and the waning of the crack wars.)

But it is, in fact, possible to assess with some degree of accuracy how many crimes have been stopped because the intended victim, or a witness, was armed. In the 1990s, Gary Kleck and a fellow criminologist, Marc Gertz, began studying the issue and came to the conclusion that guns were used defensively between 830,000 and 2.45 million times each year.

In only a minority of these cases was a gun fired; the brandishing of a gun in front of a would-be mugger or burglar is usually enough to abort a crime in progress. Another study, the federal government's National Crime Victimization Survey, asked victims of crimes whether they, or someone else, had used a gun in their defense. This study came up with a more modest number than Kleck and Gertz, finding 108,000 defensive uses of firearms a year.

All of these studies, of course, have been contested by gun-control advocates. So I asked Winkler what he thought. He said that while he is skeptical of the 2.45 million figure, even the smaller number is compelling: 108,000 "would represent a significant reduction in criminal activity."

Universities, more than most other institutions, are nearly unified in their prohibition of licensed concealed-carry weapons. Some even post notices stating that their campuses are gun-free zones. At the same time, universities also acknowledge that they are unable to protect their students from lethal assault. How do they do this? By recommending measures that students and faculty members can take if confronted by an "active shooter," as in the massacre at Virginia Tech.

These recommendations make for depressing reading, and not only because they reflect a world in which random killing in tranquil settings is a genuine, if rare, possibility. They are also depressing because they reflect a denial of reality.

Here are some of the recommendations:

- Wichita State University counsels students in the following manner: "If the person(s) is causing death or serious physical injury to others and you are unable to run or hide you may choose to be compliant, play dead, or fight for your life."
- The University of Miami guidelines suggest that when all else fails, students should act "as aggressively as possible" against a shooter. The guidelines, taken from a Department of Homeland Security directive, also recommend "throwing items and improvising weapons," as well as "yelling."
- Otterbein University, in Ohio, tells students to "breathe to manage your fear" and informs them, "You may have to take the offensive if the shooter(s) enter your area. Gather weapons (pens, pencils, books, chairs, etc.) and mentally prepare your attack."
- West Virginia University advises students that if the situation is dire, they should "act with physical aggression and throw items at the active shooter." These items could include "student desks, keys, shoes, belts, books, cell phones, iPods, book bags, laptops, pens, pencils, etc."
- The University of Colorado at Boulder's guidelines state, "You and classmates or friends may find yourselves in a situation where the shooter will accost you. If such an event occurs, quickly develop a plan to attack the shooter. . . . Consider a plan to tackle the shooter, take away his weapon, and hold him until police arrive."

It is, of course, possible to distract a heavily armed psychotic on a suicide mission by throwing an iPod at him, or a pencil. But it is more likely that the psychotic would respond by shooting the pencil thrower.

The existence of these policies suggests that universities know they cannot protect their students during an armed attack. (At Virginia Tech, the gunman killed 30 students and faculty members in the 10 minutes it took the police to arrive and penetrate the building he had blockaded.) And yet, these schools will not allow adults with state-issued concealed-carry permits to bring their weapons onto campus, as they would be able to almost anywhere else. "Possession or storage of a deadly weapon, destructive device, or fireworks in any form . . . is prohibited," West Virginia University's policy states.

To gun-rights advocates, these policies are absurd. "The fact that universities are providing their faculties and students with this sort of information is, of course, an admission that they can't protect them," Dave Kopel told me. "The universities are unable to protect people, but then they disable people from protecting themselves."

It is also illogical for campuses to advertise themselves as "gun-free." Someone bent on murder is not usually dissuaded by posted anti-gun regulations. Quite the opposite—publicly describing your property as gun-free is analogous to posting a notice on your front door saying your home has no burglar alarm. As it happens, the company that owns the Century 16 Cineplex in Aurora had declared the property a gun-free zone.

"As a security measure, it doesn't seem like advertising that fact is a good idea," Adam Winkler says of avowedly gun-free campuses, though he adds that "advertising a school's gun-free status does provide notice to potentially immature youth that they're not allowed to have guns."

In Colorado, the epicenter of the American gun argument, the state supreme court recently ruled that the University of Colorado must lift its ban on the carrying of concealed handguns by owners who have been licensed by local sheriffs. (The university has responded by requiring students who own guns to move to a specified housing complex.) The ruling has caused anxiety among some faculty. The chairman of the faculty assembly, a physics professor named Jerry Peterson, told the Boulder *Daily Camera*, "My own personal policy in my classes is if I am aware that there is a firearm in the class—registered or unregistered, concealed or unconcealed—the class session is immediately canceled. I want my students to feel unconstrained in their discussions."

Peterson makes two assumptions: The first is that he will know whether someone is carrying a concealed weapon in class. The second is that students will feel frightened about sharing their opinions if a gun is present. (I could find no evidence that any American educational institution has ever seen fatalities or serious gun-related injuries result from a heated classroom discussion.)

Claire Levy, a Colorado state legislator, says she intends to introduce a bill that would ban guns once again. "If discussions in class escalated," she argues, "the mere fact that someone is potentially armed could have an inhibiting effect on the classroom, This is genuinely scary to faculty members." The push to open up campuses to concealed-carry permit holders, Levy says, is motivated by ideological gun-rights advocacy, rather than an actual concern for campus safety. Guns, even those owned by licensed and trained individuals, she insists, would simply make a campus more dangerous. "American campuses are the safest places to be in the whole world," she said. "The homicide rate on campuses is a small fraction of the rate in the rest of the country. So there's no actual rational public-safety reason that anyone would need to bring a gun on campus."

However, the University of Colorado's own active-shooter recommendations state:

> Active harming incidents have occurred at a number of locations in recent years, and the University of Colorado is not immune to this potential. While the odds of this occurring at CU are small, the consequences are so potentially catastrophic it makes sense for all students, staff, faculty and visitors to CU to consider the possibility of such an incident occurring here.

In making her argument against concealed-carry weapons to me, Levy painted a bit of a contradictory picture: On the one hand, campuses are the safest places in the country. On the other hand, campus life is so inherently dangerous that the introduction of even licensed guns could mean mayhem. "You're in this milieu of drugs and alcohol and impulsive behavior and mental illness; you've got a population that has a high propensity for suicide," she told me. "Theft is a big concern, and what if you had a concealed-carry gun and you're drinking and become violent?"

For much of the population of a typical campus, concealed-carry permitting is not an issue. Most states that issue permits will grant them only to people who are at least 21 years old. But the crime-rate statistics at universities that do allow permit holders on campus with their weapons are instructive. An hour north of Boulder, in Fort Collins, sits Colorado State University. Concealed carry has been allowed at CSU since 2003, and according to James Alderden, the former sheriff of Larimer County, which encompasses Fort Collins, violent crime at Colorado State has dropped since then.

Despite the fact that CSU experienced no violent incidents involving concealed-carry permit holders, the university governing board voted two years ago to ban concealed carry. The ban never went into effect, however, because the state appeals court soon ruled against a similar ban at the University of Colorado, and because Sheriff Alderden announced that he would undermine the ban by refusing to process any violator in the county jail, which serves the university's police department.

Alderden, who recently retired, told me that opponents of concealed carry "make an emotional argument rather than a logical one. No one could show me any study that concealed carry leads to more crime and more violence. My idea of self-defense is not those red rape phones on campus, where you get to the phone and tell someone you're getting raped. I have a daughter, and I'd rather have her have the ability to defend herself. I'm not going to violate a citizen's right to self-defense because someone else has an emotional feeling about guns."

Though Colorado is slowly shading blue, Alderden said he believes most of its residents "still don't rely on the government to protect them." He added: "Maybe in Boulder they do, but most people believe they have a right to self-defense."

Boulder may be the locus of left-wing politics in Colorado, but it is also home to the oversubscribed Boulder Rifle Club, which I visited on a bright early-fall morning with Dave Kopel, of the Independence Institute. The existence of the rifle club surprised me, given Boulder's reputation. But Kopel argued that gun ownership and sport shooting are not partisan phenomena, and he made the plausible assertion that Boulder is home to "the largest population of armed vegans in America."

I wanted to understand from Kopel the best arguments against government intervention in gun ownership, and Kopel wanted to fire some of the many handguns he owns, so we alternately talked and shot. Kopel brought with him a bag of guns: a Ruger Mark II .22 LR pistol; a Springfield Armory XD-9 9 mm; a Glock 9 mm; a Springfield Armory 1911 tactical-response pistol (similar to a Colt .45); and a Ruger Alaskan .45 revolver, powerful enough to drop a bear. The Ruger Alaskan is the most powerful weapon we used, but the act of firing even a .22 underscores for most thinking people the notion that firing a gun is a serious business. Kopel argued that a law-abiding citizen is less likely to get into a confrontation after a traffic accident or an exchange of insults if he or she is carrying a weapon: "You're aware of the power you have, and you naturally want to use that power very carefully."

I expressed to Kopel my concern that the overly lax standards some states set for concealed-carry permitting means that the occasional cowboy gets passed through the system. Florida—which has among the most relaxed standards for gun permitting, and granted a license to George Zimmerman, who famously killed Trayvon Martin, apparently during an exercise in freelance vigilantism—is a case in point. (Zimmerman has pled not guilty, claiming he shot Martin in self-defense.) Applicants in Florida must submit to a background check, take a brief class, and pay $112 to obtain a license.

In Colorado, the standards are slightly more stringent. Permit seekers must submit to criminal checks, fingerprinting, and safety classes, but in addition, they must pass what James Alderden referred to as the "naked man" rule: if a local sheriff learns that a person has no criminal record, and has not been deemed mentally ill, but nevertheless was, say, found naked one night in a field howling at the moon, the sheriff is granted the discretion to deny that person a permit.

Kopel argued, correctly, that Florida, like Colorado, has seen a drop in crime since 1987, when it started granting concealed-carry permits—which suggests to him that permit holders are not, in the main, engaging in crime sprees or taking the law into their own hands. But for Kopel, the rigor, or laxity, of the permitting process from state to state is not his principal concern, because

he believes that in most cases, the government has no right to interfere with an adult's decision to buy or carry a weapon. Those who seek to curtail gun rights, he insists, are promoting the infantilization of Americans.

"If they get their way," he said of the anti-gun forces, "people who are the victims of violent crimes wouldn't be able to fight back; women who are abused couldn't protect themselves; criminals will know that their intended victims, who have no access to the black market, will be unable to defend themselves.

"It's more than that," he went on. "Telling the population that they are incapable of owning a tool that can be dangerous means you are creating a population that loses its self-reliance and increasingly sees itself as wards of the state."

James Alderden put it another way: "Your position on concealed-carry permits has a lot to do with your position on the reliability and sanity of your fellow man."

The ideology of gun-ownership absolutism doesn't appeal to me. Unlike hard-line gun-rights advocates, I do not believe that unregulated gun ownership is a defense against the rise of totalitarianism in America, because I do not think that America is ripe for totalitarianism. (Fear of a tyrannical, gun-seizing president is the reason many gun owners oppose firearms registration.)

But I am sympathetic to the idea of armed self-defense, because it does often work, because encouraging learned helplessness is morally corrupt, and because, however much I might wish it, the United States is not going to become Canada. Guns are with us, whether we like it or not. Maybe this is tragic, but it is also reality. So Americans who are qualified to possess firearms shouldn't be denied the right to participate in their own defense. And it is empirically true that the great majority of America's tens of millions of law-abiding gun owners have not created chaos in society.

A balanced approach to gun control in the United States would require the warring sides to agree on several contentious issues. Conservative gun-rights advocates should acknowledge that if more states had stringent universal background checks—or if a federal law put these in place—more guns would be kept out of the hands of criminals and the dangerously mentally unstable. They should also acknowledge that requiring background checks on buyers at gun shows would not represent a threat to the Constitution. "The NRA position on this is a fiction," says Dan Gross, the head of the Brady Campaign. "Universal background checks are not an infringement on our Second Amendment rights. This is black-helicopter stuff." Gross believes that closing the gun-show loophole would be both extremely effective and a politically moderate and achievable goal. The gun lobby must also agree that concealed-carry permits should be granted only to people who pass rigorous criminal checks, as well as thorough training-and-safety courses.

Anti-gun advocates, meanwhile, should acknowledge that gun-control legislation is not the only answer to gun violence. Responsible gun ownership is also an answer. An enormous number of Americans believe this to be the case, and gun-control advocates do themselves no favors when they demonize gun owners, and advocates of armed self-defense, as backwoods barbarians. Liberals sometimes make the mistake of anthropomorphizing guns, ascribing to them moral characteristics they do not possess. Guns can be used to do evil, but guns can also be used to do good. Twelve years ago, in the aftermath of Matthew Shepard's murder, Jonathan Rauch launched a national movement when he wrote an article for *Salon* arguing that gay people should arm themselves against violent bigots. Pink Pistol clubs sprang up across America, in which gays and lesbians learn to use firearms in self-defense. Other vulnerable groups have also taken to the idea of concealed carry: in Texas, African American women represent the largest percentage increase of concealed-carry permit seekers since 2000.

But even some moderate gun-control activists, such as Dan Gross, have trouble accepting that guns in private hands can work effectively to counteract violence. When I asked him the question I posed to Stephen Barton and Tom Mauser—would you, at a moment when a stranger is shooting at you, prefer to have a gun, or not?—he answered by saying, "This is the conversation the gun lobby wants you to be having." He pointed out some of the obvious flaws in concealed-carry laws, such as too-lax training standards and too much discretionary power on the part of local law-enforcement officials. He did say that if concealed-carry laws required background checks and training similar to what police recruits undergo, he would be slower to raise objections. But then he added: "In a fundamental way, isn't this a question about the kind of society we want to live in?" Do we want to live in one "in which the answer to violence is more violence, where the answer to guns is more guns?"

What Gross won't acknowledge is that in a nation of nearly 300 million guns, his question is irrelevant.

---

**JEFFREY GOLDBERG** is a national correspondent for *The Atlantic* Magazine and a recipient of the National Magazine Award for Reporting. Author of the book *Prisoners: A Story of Friendship and Terror*, Goldberg also writes the magazine's advice column.

# EXPLORING THE ISSUE

## Should the United States Be More Restrictive of Gun Ownership?

## Critical Thinking and Reflection

1. What are the arguments for placing greater restrictions on gun ownership in the United States? Which argument do you believe is most persuasive, why?
2. What are the arguments for loosening present restrictions on gun ownership in the United States? Which argument do you believe is most persuasive, why?
3. Do you believe mass tragedies like those in Aurora and Newtown can ever be prevented? Why or why not?
4. Cities like Chicago, which have some of the strictest gun control laws in the country, have the highest rates of gun violence in the United States. How does this happen? How can it be prevented?
5. Do you believe the Second Amendment is properly applied and understood in the United States? Why or why not?

## Is There Common Ground?

While it may seem that lines are clearly drawn in the sand when it comes to gun control in the United States, in reality there is great potential for middle ground to be discovered. Throughout the history of guns in America, compromises have been reached. There are certain restrictions and purchasing protocols in place currently trying to assure that malintenioned individuals struggle to gain access to a firearm. In another vein, across the country concealed carry laws are becoming prominent, permitting skilled individuals to keep their piece on their person at all times. What these examples show is that both sides of the argument have made certain sacrifices already.

But there are concerns that are perhaps more difficult to bridge the gap on. Those opposed to gun control, for example, routinely point to the fact that criminals are not likely to obey any form of law passed related to access to weapons. In this scenario, law abiding citizens could find themselves vulnerable as only lawbreakers maintain firearms. At the same time, those in favor of curbing access will seemingly always have a fresh mass shooting to use when driving home key arguments. Few Americans are on the fence with regards to gun control and consequently the sharpness of opinions leads one to believe that middle ground may be more difficult to realize than we originally expected.

## Create Central

www.mhhe.com/createcentral

## Additional Resources

Gregg L. Carter, *Gun Control in the United States: A Reference Handbook* (ABC-CLIO, 2006)

Saul Cornell, *A Well-Regulated Militia: The Founding Fathers and the Origins of Gun Control in America* (Oxford University Press, 2008)

John R. Lott Jr., *More Guns, Less Crime: Understanding Crime and Gun Control Laws* (University of Chicago Press, 2010)

Robert Spitzer, *The Politics of Gun Control* (Paradigm, 2011)

Craig Whitney, *Living with Guns: A Liberal's Case for the Second Amendment* (PublicAffairs, 2012)

# Internet References . . .

**Brady Campaign to Prevent Gun Violence (BCPGV)**

www.handguncontrol.org

**Coalition to Stop Gun Violence (CSGV)**

www.gunfree.org

**National Criminal Justice Reference Service**

www.ncjrs.gov/App/Topics/Topic.aspx?topicid=87

**National Rifle Association**

www.nra.org

**Revolution PAC**

www.revolutionpac.com

Selected, Edited, and with Issue Framing Material by:
**William J. Miller,** *Flagler College*
**George McKenna,** *City College, City University of New York*
**and**
**Stanley Feingold,** *City College, City University of New York*

# ISSUE

# Will the Affordable Care Act Successfully Transform the American Health Care System?

**YES: Kathleen Sebelius,** from "Address to the National Conference of State Legislatures Health Summit" (August 12, 2013)

**NO: Jason Fodeman,** from "The New Health Law: Bad for Doctors, Awful for Patients," *Galen Institute* (April 7, 2011)

---

### Learning Outcomes

**After reading this issue, you will be able to:**

- Describe the Affordable Care Act.
- Assess the current state of health care in America.
- Determine what positives the Affordable Care Act will bring to American health care.
- Determine what negatives the Affordable Care Act will bring to American health care.
- Explain the view of medical professionals regarding the Affordable Care Act.

---

### ISSUE SUMMARY

**YES:** Secretary of Health and Human Services Kathleen Sebelius, speaking to the National Conference of State Legislatures, discusses current problems with health care in the United States and how the Affordable Care Act will succeed in curbing these concerns once implemented.

**NO:** Jason Fodeman, a doctor, writes from the perspective of a medical professional on how the Affordable Care Act will lead to negative impacts for medical professionals and how ultimately patients will suffer within the new system.

Its critics call it "ObamaCare," but its short official name is the "Affordable Care Act" (ACA) of 2010. Its stated purposes are to ensure health care coverage for virtually all Americans while reducing costs. To accomplish these aims, the ACA requires individual Americans to purchase health insurance and requires insurance companies to abide by a variety of new regulations, including coverage for those with preexisting conditions.

During the 8-month battle over passage of the ACA, critics launched a variety of complaints about both the substance of the legislation and the methods used to pass it. One challenge to the bill, however, formally began only after its passage, and that was the claim that the new law, or a part of it anyway, violates the U.S. Constitution. Specifically, the charge was that it exceeds the powers granted to the Congress under Article I of the Constitution.

Article I grants many powers to Congress, including the power to "regulate Commerce with foreign Nations, and among the several States, and with the Indian Tribes." Particularly since the time of President Franklin Roosevelt's "New Deal" in the 1930s, the federal government has relied on this clause to justify the expansion of its powers. In 1940, an Ohio farmer named Roscoe Filburn was fined by a federal court for growing 11.9 more acres of wheat than he was allowed under the Agricultural Adjustment Act (AAA) of 1938. The AAA, a Depression-era law, limited the acreage on which farmers could grow crops on the theory that fewer bushels of farm products would mean higher prices for farmers, thus helping to stimulate the economy. Filburn appealed the ruling to the Supreme Court, charging that the federal government had exceeded its authority under the Commerce Clause. Much of those 11.9 acres, Filburn insisted, grew wheat never brought to market but consumed entirely on his farm. But in

*Wickard v. Filburn* (1942), the Court rejected that argument, noting that even if the wheat is never marketed, "it supplies a need of a man who grew it which would otherwise be reflected by purchases in the open market." Multiply farmer Filburn by all the other farmers doing the same and in the aggregate it "would have a substantial effect in defeating and obstructing" the government's authority to stimulate commerce.

*Wickard v. Filburn* has never been overturned, but in recent years it has been qualified by the Court. In the 1995 case of *United States v. Lopez*, the Court struck down a federal law prohibiting the possession of guns in a public school zone. Congress, it held, exceeded its authority under the Commerce Clause. "The possession of a gun in a local school zone is in no sense an economic activity that must, through repetition elsewhere, substantially affect any sort of interstate commerce." And in *United States v. Morrison* (2000), which involved allegations of sexual assault and rape of a female student at Virginia Tech by members of the football team, the Court held unconstitutional a part of the Violence Against Women Act of 1994. Its reason: Congress lacks the power under the Commerce Clause to authorize civil suits for such cases. "Gender-motivated crimes of violence are not, in any sense of the phrase, economic activity."

One thread tying together Wickard, Lopez, and Morrison is the question of whether the activities alleged, growing wheat for home consumption, carrying a firearm in a school zone, committing rape and sexual assault, are properly called "commercial." Purchasing health insurance is certainly a commercial activity. But the focus here is not on the purchase but the non-purchase of health insurance. The question is whether Congress has the power under the Commerce Clause to penalize an individual for not doing something. Of course, many non-activities, such as not paying federal taxes or not showing up for a federal trial, can be penalized by the federal government. But the question here is whether the federal government may penalize someone for not purchasing a certain product. By the spring of 2011, four U.S. District Court judges had rendered decisions on the constitutionality of the ACA, two ruling in the affirmative and two in the negative. Coincidentally or not, the former were appointed by Democratic presidents and the latter by Republicans. And in June 2012, the Supreme Court handed down its decision in *National Federation of Independent Business v.*

*Sebelius*, ruling that the individual mandate provision of ObamaCare was constitutional. The news sent a shockwave through the political world, and for many on the right, that shockwave was apocalyptic.

With questions of basic legality settled, questions immediately turned to whether the Affordable Care Act would actually succeed in relieving the United States' growing health disparities—especially for the roughly 50 million uninsured Americans. The new system is fundamentally from a single payer system and as a result it is difficult to determine its potential for long-term success. At present, President Obama is being forced to apologize for two key errors in the rollout of the ACA: first, the exchange website failed to function properly on October 1 when it went live and second, the president had to apologize and change measures to assure that individuals who were happy with their current coverage could keep it after earlier making that promise to all Americans. From a health angle, there is no doubt that those who previously had no access will have a greater opportunity than ever before. But at what cost? Will America become a healthier country? Or will the Affordable Care Act function as a new moral hazard, permitting individuals to not worry about their health now that everyone will carry some minimal level of coverage?

The court battle is not necessarily over, however, on all accounts. In enacting the ACA, Congress required large employers who offer health care services to provide a range of preventive care, including no-copay contraceptive services. Religious nonprofits (such as the Catholic Church) were exempted from this requirement, but not for-profit corporations. As a result, Hobby Lobby will be arguing before the Supreme Court that this provision should be struck down. Oral arguments will be heard this spring. Given the Court's ruling in *Citizens United*, which gave corporations the same freedom of speech rights as individuals, it would not be surprising to see corporations given the right to exercise freedom of religion as well.

In the following selections, Secretary of Health and Human Services Kathleen Sebelius discussed the current issues with the American health care system and how the ACA will succeed in helping all Americans receive better health care once it is fully implemented. Arguing on the other side is Jason Fodeman, a medical doctor, who maintains that patient care—on the whole—will decrease once the new system is in place for myriad of reasons.

# YES

Kathleen Sebelius

## Address to the National Conference of State Legislatures Health Summit

Thank you, Speaker Norelli, for that introduction. It's great to be with you and the other NCSL leaders again after our meeting in Washington earlier this year. And I want to thank you all for being here and for your service to your states and to our country.

As a recovering state legislator myself, getting the opportunity to come to NCSL feels a lot like home. I've seen firsthand the incredible work you do—from strengthening local economies to helping families gain the opportunity to live safer, healthier, more productive lives.

And today I'd like to talk about some of the ways our Department is working with states to meet the challenges and seize the opportunities your states have ahead.

For starters, we know that quality early education is critical to the emotional, social, health and wellbeing of our children, families, and communities. These might be the best investments we can make in the future, and President Obama has proposed an historic federal-state partnership aimed at getting all of our children ready for school success and lifelong learning.

Focused on supporting our children from birth to age 5, it starts with increased investments in home-visiting programs to support parents and caregivers in their role as a child's first and foremost educator. We're then building on the great work states are doing with Early Head Start and Head Start to improve early learning quality and curriculum in the places where many of our children spend their early days.

And these improvements for infants and toddlers lead to partnering with states to provide every child in America with access to affordable preschool. It's a plan that helps them perform better in school and saves working families hard-earned dollars in daycare costs. It also strengthens our communities by savings on public assistance and criminal justice programs.

These kinds of investments have bipartisan political support. Business and military leaders, teachers and child advocates have called for these investments. And I look forward to continue working with you to make sure that more of our children have access to early learning experiences that can make a lifetime of difference for their health and wellbeing.

But we also know their future—and our country's future—depends on the overall health of all of our families and their communities. As some of you will hear later from Dr. Frieden, our Director of Centers for Disease and Control and Prevention, ensuring people have access to affordable, quality care is a pressing public health need.

And that's the need the Affordable Care Act is designed to meet.

I know you've already heard from Chiquita Brooks-LaSure and Cindy Mann, who represent the great team from our Department, about our ongoing work implementing the law.

But just as a reminder, the first thing to know is that for the 85% of Americans who already have insurance—the law has already improved that coverage.

First—being a woman is no longer considered a pre-existing condition. And soon no one will be denied insurance because of a pre-existing condition, like diabetes, cancer, asthma, or anything else.

More than three million young people now have insurance under their parents' health plans through the age of 26—giving them the freedom to pursue their dreams without worrying about their health coverage.

Seventy-one million adults with private insurance can now get many types of preventive care, like cancer and cholesterol screenings, at no out-of-pocket costs.

Last year alone, nearly 3.5 million seniors on Medicare saved an average of more than $706 each on their prescriptions—enough to cover 2 or 3 months worth of groceries.

In 2012, 8.5 million Americans received more than half a billion dollars in refunds because insurance companies didn't spend at least 80 percent of their premium dollar on medical care and quality improvements.

But a critical part of the law is still to come. So the second thing to know is that for the 15% percent of Americans who don't have coverage, or for Americans who buy their own insurance right now but aren't happy with it, they'll have better options coming this fall.

First, a new online Health Insurance Marketplace will open for individuals and small business owners in every state through HealthCare.gov.

When open enrollment begins on October 1st, the Marketplace will give families a whole new way to find coverage that fits their budget—and the benefits start in January.

Sebelius, Kathleen. Address to the National Conference of State Legislatures Health Summit, Atlanta GA, August 12, 2013.

All plans in the Marketplace must cover a set of essential benefits, including doctor visits, prescription drugs, and mental health services. Discrimination based on gender or pre-existing conditions, like diabetes or cancer, will be outlawed. And since these consumers don't have affordable employer coverage, many individuals, families, and small businesses will qualify for a break on the costs of their monthly premiums.

Because of the Marketplace, insurers will now have to compete for business the way that all companies do—by offering the best products at the lowest price. We're moving past the days where insurers could just lock out, dump out, or price out anyone who might get sick.

And here's what we know about the new rates in the Marketplace. While it's unfortunate that some states have inaccurately speculated what the final rates will be, we've heard some great news from many of your states about rates that have been finalized.

New York announced that premiums could be 50 percent less costly in their Marketplace than they generally are today. States from California and Oregon to Maryland and Vermont have all announced rates for plans offered through the Marketplace that will also be significantly more affordable than the current market. All the state rates will be available by the end of September—but so far, there is plenty of competition and positive news for consumers.

Another way the health care law is covering more people is by building on the Administration's efforts to strengthen Medicaid.

From day one, we've known that states are the laboratories for innovation—and it's why we've worked to provide the flexibility and support to test strategies to improve care and bring down costs in the Medicaid program.

Right now, more than 20 states are working to better coordinate care for their Medicare-Medicaid enrollees, and share in the savings. Other states are implementing or receiving planning grants for Medicaid medical health homes to reduce unnecessary hospital costs.

More than $300 million has been awarded in performance bonuses to 23 states making innovative, sustainable improvements to their children's health coverage. And earlier this year we announced another $300 million in innovation grants to help states test statewide models for improving care and lowering costs.

And despite some of the rhetoric in Washington, the cost outlook for Medicaid is as strong as it's been in a long time. In 2012, Medicaid spending per beneficiary actually fell 1.9%, the first time it had fallen in 47 years, except for the year when prescription drug costs shifted to Medicare Part D. As a result, our independent actuary has estimated that Medicaid spending will actually be 14% lower than previously projected in 2020.

It's clear that state reforms aided by HHS support are working. And going forward, we will continue to work with each of your states to give you the flexibility you need.

But there's perhaps no greater opportunity to strengthen Medicaid than by expanding the program in your states—and providing millions of previously uninsured parents and adults with health coverage.

Medicaid expansion would reduce the burden of uncompensated care by billions of dollars across the nation. It would create local jobs and inject significant resources into local economies and hospitals. It would free up state dollars that can be invested in other priority areas.

And that's in addition to the many families you represent who would finally be able to enjoy the daily security of reliable health coverage.

As a former governor and state legislator, I know the best part for states is the deal we're offering: The federal government will cover 100% of the costs of Medicaid expansion for three years and never less than 90% after that. And the program is fully paid for; not a dime is added to the federal deficit.

I know some of you have concerns that this deal could be changed. But if you look at Medicaid's history, you'll see that there's no precedent for the federal government cutting its matching rate. Furthermore, states are free to take up the coverage expansion at any point and they are free to drop that coverage, without financial penalty, at any point.

So we've been pleased to see governors and legislatures from across the country and the political spectrum seize this opportunity. And the door will remain open for others to walk through.

But if states don't expand their Medicaid programs, a lot of people in your district could fall through the cracks, with no support and no source of affordable health coverage at all. We can't let that happen.

There's money left on the table and lives left at risk. And no one's health should depend on their zip code.

But here's the key point: just because new coverage options may be available doesn't guarantee that people will even know about them, let alone take advantage of them. And getting them covered shouldn't be about politics or ideology or winners and losers.

Remember, the debate in Washington is over. The President signed the law. The Supreme Court affirmed it. The people have spoken and President Obama was re-elected. Now it's about making sure that people know about the choices and opportunities that are about to become available to them—in many cases for the first time in their lives.

Over the last three years, I've traveled to more than 100 cities across nearly all 50 states meeting those families, small business owners, and people of all ages who are excited about what's ahead and hungry for information.

They simply want to cut through the clutter and hear the real facts. And when it comes to something as serious as their health and the health of their family, they deserve that chance.

That's why HealthCare.gov will make the process easier and more transparent for millions of Americans.

For many people, enrolling will be a quick process they can complete on their own. For others who may want more assistance, we have great resources available. For those who prefer the phone to the computer, there's a 24/7 customer call center ready to answer questions in 150 languages. We will have trained volunteers, at health centers and working in communities across the country, to provide one-on-one assistance.

But we also know that we can't do this alone—and that was never the plan. And even if you're not the biggest supporter of the law, your constituents who stand to benefit from the law will be coming to you with questions—and we want to help you with the answers.

That's why we have a toolkit specifically for elected officials—copies are available in the back of the room today, so you can get started right away. I also want to thank NCSL for including the toolkit on their website, so you can download a copy once you get back to your home district.

And we also have dedicated, knowledgeable staff in our 10 regional offices around the country, who can serve as your go-to resources. Our Regional Directors are leading the education and outreach efforts on the ground and can ensure you're connected to efforts underway in your area.

On October 1st, we'll be ready to finally offer millions of Americans the health security and peace of mind they need and deserve.

Getting your constituents signed up for health coverage is the smart thing to do for individuals, for families, and for your states.

And it's the right thing to do so that health care is available to everyone—and so we can build a healthier, more prosperous country together.

---

**KATHLEEN SEBELIUS** was sworn in as the 21st Secretary of the Department of Health and Human Services (HHS) on April 28, 2009. *Forbes* has named Secretary Sebelius one of the 100 most powerful women in the world. Before her Cabinet appointment in April, 2009, she served as Governor of Kansas beginning in 2003, where she was named one of America's Top Five Governors by *Time Magazine*. From 1995 to 2003 she served as Kansas Insurance Commissioner. She was a member of the Kansas House of Representatives from 1987 to 1995.

Jason Fodeman

 **NO**

# The New Health Law: Bad for Doctors, Awful for Patients

Despite multiple speeches, town hall meetings, radio addresses, and Democratic majorities in both the House and Senate, President Obama's radical health care agenda has failed to garner widespread support. The president often claims this is because the public does not understand the contents of the package. Yet the problem for the administration is that people understand it all too well.

The president was unmoved by public opposition and a historic Republican Senate victory in Massachusetts; ultimately, he and the Democratic leadership in Congress passed the Patient Protection and Affordable Care Act (PPACA) via reconciliation along party lines without even a single Republican vote. To accomplish this, they employed a myriad of budgetary gimmicks, smoke and mirrors, and sweetheart deals—definitely not the type of political showmanship reserved for C-SPAN, as President Obama had previously promised.

The health care overhaul rolls the dice with the world's premier health care system and approximately one-sixth of the economy. Of course there is room for improvement, but why start from scratch? A better approach would have been to build off current strengths and target the shortcomings.

While the 2,800 pages of mandates, red tape, spending, and regulations will not control spiraling costs, it will change health care as we know it. Approximately 90% of Americans have health insurance in this country, and of those, 84% rate their coverage as good or excellent.

The deleterious effects of this legislation will be felt the most by physicians and their patients. It is brutal for physicians, and the detriment transcends dollars and cents. New regulations will place unaccountable regulators in Washington, D.C., between physicians and patients and will grant these bureaucrats unprecedented control in the medical decision-making process. It will strip away physician autonomy, drown doctors in bureaucracy, and drain job satisfaction. As physicians are required to do more, they will likely be paid less.

As medicine deteriorates as a profession, older doctors will retire while younger doctors will try to switch careers. The composition of those still practicing will be a stark contrast from those currently in the field: the best educated, the brightest, the best trained, and the most dedicated.

The supply of providers will decrease at a time when the demand for services will be at an all-time high.

Ultimately, the consequences of the health overhaul law will be passed along to patients through restricted access, long waits for appointments, and compromised quality of care. PPACA is indeed bad for physicians; however, it will always be the patient that suffers the most.

## Less Time with Patients

Medicare's physician reimbursement regimen is characterized by underpayments and perverse incentives. The brunt of Medicare's declining reimbursements is shifted to patients in the form of decreased access to physicians and inferior care. Rather than trying to reform this flawed reimbursement system, which jeopardizes patient safety, PPACA expands its scope to more people.

During the health care debate, supporters of reform sought the expansion of government in health care, in part, based on their praise of Medicare's ability to control costs by exploiting its mammoth size to obtain lower fees with providers. Despite a lengthy and thorough debate, this faulty argument went largely unchallenged.

Ignoring the fact Medicare has trillions of dollars in unfunded liabilities, and Medicare's own nonpartisan Office of the Actuary concluded that health care reform will increase health care costs, not decrease them, the idea that the government can or will be the trendsetter in curbing rising health care costs lacks credence. It is true that the government can bludgeon down provider fees in certain areas with the inevitable corollary being reduced doctor-patient face time and shorter hospital stays. However, this is no panacea and has significant ramifications on the patient-doctor relationship and quality of care.

This "bargaining" ability is not Medicare's greatest strength, but actually one of its greatest weaknesses. Medicare, with its sheer size, can indeed "negotiate" reimbursements in a take it or leave it manner, but this does not benefit patients.

## Underpayments

Medicare reimburses hospitals and doctors, on average, 71% and 81%, respectively, of private rates. Medicaid reimburses doctors even less, on average 56% of private rates. The federal government's payments to health care professionals are so low that on average, overall, hospitals lose money caring for Medicare and Medicaid patients. In

2008, hospitals received only 91 cents from the government for every dollar spent on a Medicare patient. That same year hospitals received only 89 cents for every dollar spent on Medicaid patients. According to data compiled by the American Hospital Association, on average, Centers for Medicare and Medicaid Services (CMS) payments are less than hospital costs and the amount of underpayment has increased over time. In 2000, Medicare and Medicaid's underpayments amounted to $3.8 billion. By 2008 they had increased to $32 billion. At first glimpse, this is the doctor's problem and not that of the patient. Unfortunately for the nation's infirmed, this is not the case. Ultimately, these consequences are passed along to the patient.

From an economics point of view, Medicare's below-market reimbursements create cost-shifting onto private payers where hospitals raise private payer fees to compensate for lower payments from government programs. In a 2006 *Health Affairs* study, researchers focused on this phenomenon by studying data from California private hospitals. The authors discovered a statistically significant inverse relationship between Medicare fee changes and private payer fee changes. The research revealed that a 1% decrease in average Medicare price correlated with a .17% increase in private payer price, and that a 1% decrease in the Medicaid rate was associated with a .04% increase. From 1997 to 2001, Medicare and Medicaid cost-shifting accounted for 12.3% of increases in private payer prices.

From a clinical perspective, Medicare's underpayments result in diminished access and compromised quality care. The most widely cited effect is the difficulty that Medicare and Medicaid patients encounter trying to find a physician. This problem is increasing. The American Academy of Family Physicians discovered 13% of doctors surveyed did not partake in Medicare in 2009, up significantly from 6% in 2004. According to the American Osteopathic Association, 15% of members don't take Medicare and 19% don't take new patients with Medicare. In New York state, approximately 1,100 physicians have stopped participating in Medicare. According to a 2009 *New York Times* article, at New York Presbyterian Hospital, only 37 of the 93 affiliated internists accept Medicare. Even fewer doctors are taking Medicaid, with its lower reimbursements and administrative burden. A Center for Health System Change survey discovered that in 2004–2005, 35.3% of solo practitioners and two doctor practices were not accepting new Medicaid patients compared to 29% in 1996–1997. The survey also showed that over this same period, small group practices accepting no new Medicaid patients had increased from 16.2% to 24%. This translates into access problems for patients. According to a 2008 Medicare Payment Advisory Commission report, 30% of beneficiaries seeking a new primary care physician had problems obtaining one.

Finding a physician is a serious problem for patients with government health care plans, however, Medicare's harmful influence on access to physicians is more broad and complicated. In the outpatient setting, low reimbursements force doctors to see more and more patients to stay in business. The nonpartisan Congressional Budget Office (CBO) agrees. It wrote in 2006 that, "Considerable evidence suggests that a reduction in payment rates leads physicians to increase the volume and intensity of services they perform." This leads to shorter visits and less doctor-patient face time. It forces doctors to race through medical appointments so they can fit as many into the daily schedule as possible. It compels doctors to frantically bounce from exam room to exam room like a wayward pinball, practically having one foot out the door even before stepping into the exam room.

The time constraints of the medical appointment are frustrating for both clinicians and patients. Patients get upset when they don't get to spend the time that they would like with their physician. They are less likely to get questions answered and be educated appropriately. They can often be left feeling that their physician just doesn't care. While this is usually not the case, it is an inevitable consequence of the rationing Medicare already places on the health care system.

These shorter visits are not only frustrating, but both common sense and the published literature suggest they are dangerous. University of California at Davis researchers examined the effect of visit length by recording 294 primary care appointments and discovered that patient satisfaction increased with visit length. Multiple studies have confirmed this, and other research has indicated that patient satisfaction can improve outcomes. *British Medical Journal* research studied consultation length and linked shorter medical visits with the inability of patients to understand and cope with illness. Research from the New England Medical Center has also associated shorter office visits with decreased patient participation in the decision-making process, which could be detrimental to quality.

For doctors, this is equally troubling. Doctors enter medicine to heal the sick, establish rapport, and advocate for their patients. Perhaps this used to be possible, but sadly it's becoming less and less common under Medicare's reimbursement regimen. It's demoralizing for physicians who want to be there for their patients, who want to give their patients all the time they want, who want to make sure patients have all their questions answered, and want to make sure patients know how to best care for themselves. However, working in a reimbursement system that rewards quantity at the expense of quality, it is difficult to make a living doing so. The situation can become even more upsetting for physicians when patients publicly display their discontent or take it out on the physician. This is especially difficult since many physicians would echo their patients' concerns about time constraints, but unfortunately no one asked them. Physicians have little control over the situation, other than, of course, to move on to the next patient.

In the inpatient setting, Medicare's reimbursement system similarly hinders the practice of good medicine.

It indeed decreases patient-doctor face time, but its main impact is pushing toward early and quick hospital discharges. Medicare pays hospitals based on diagnosis related groups (DRGs), a fixed payment depending on disease. Thus, in general, the longer patients stay in the hospital, the more money hospitals lose. This puts tremendous pressure on hospitals to discharge patients. Physicians responsible for writing discharge orders feel this pressure from social workers, case coordinators, nurses, department chiefs, and even hospital administrators. The planning for discharges in some hospitals begins as early as the day of admission. This places unnecessary stress on physicians and can serve as a point of contention with patients who know their bodies the best and may not believe they are ready to go home. It also puts physicians in a particularly tough spot when they themselves are not convinced that the patient is stable enough to leave, but superiors want the patient discharged.

Just as in the outpatient environment, the quality of inpatient medicine suffers because of Medicare's underpayments. Inevitably, some patients get pushed out prematurely and some of these patients come right back. It's not good care. Readmissions are dissatisfying for physicians. These premature discharges also unnecessarily expose doctors to malpractice risks. And of course Medicare administrators want it both ways. Their reimbursement rates force hospitals to rush patients out the door, but if that patient comes back, Medicare looks to punish the hospital.

In hospitals, Medicare's underpayments also translate into less ancillary staff, such as transporters and nurses. Thus, critical tests necessary to guide life-saving medical intervention decisions can take longer. In teaching hospitals, this also means there is a greater reliance on medical residents.

Ultimately, the excess work hospitals must do merely to survive in a climate dominated by Medicare and its underpayments puts significant unnecessary strain on the system and promotes medical errors. Medicare's ability to get itself a good "deal," is anything but for patients. . . .

## Harm the Doctor-Patient Relationship

The Patient Protection and Affordable Care Act certainly does not protect the doctor-patient relationship. This relationship is about to change drastically.

New regulations and red tape will force physicians to spend more time in back rooms doing paperwork and less time at the bedside with patients. Reductions in reimbursements will compel doctors to see more patients in less time. Doctors' daily schedules are already full and patient visits are already very short. It remains to be seen how these encounters can be made any shorter, but no doubt they will. Inevitably, worsening time constraints of medical practice will significantly strain patients' relationships with their physicians. Time pressures will further push patient-doctor interactions away from a patient participatory discussion with emphasis on patient comprehension and compliance, to a more paternalistic physician-dominated approach. Physicians will also have less time to educate, counsel, answer questions, and offer explanations to their patients. As a result, patients will be less likely to understand their diseases and how best to treat them. This will understandably be frustrating for patients and even more so when they feel rushed and don't get their questions answered.

While worsening time constraints will harm the patient-doctor relationship, the mountain of new regulatory requirements in the health overhaul law could kill this relationship. Supporters of PPACA contend a more centralized approach to medicine could better coordinate care and better serve patients. This theory is based on the faulty premise that federal regulators know better than doctors.

Regulations such as the Patient-Centered Outcomes Research Institute and the Value-Based Payment Modifier will impinge on physician autonomy and could prevent patients from getting the care they need. Medical decisions and treatment courses will become standardized. Bureaucrats in Washington will be put between patients and their doctor. These regulators, with little medical background and most likely no knowledge or compassion for the individual situation, will have unprecedented control over health care decisions.

This will be frustrating for both patients and doctors. Patients could encounter difficulty obtaining the care they have been accustomed to and want. Patients will feel helpless. This will be very upsetting for them. They will likely blame the doctors and could possibly take this anger out on physicians as well.

Physicians will not be able to practice medicine as they have for years and as they would like. They will be unable to order the tests, consults, and medicine that patients need. This will be very frustrating for physicians who will want to give patients the care they desperately are pleading for, but will have little alternatives or flexibility against rigid regulators in an increasingly more powerful Washington. Physicians will feel hapless. Their ability to help and advocate for their patients will be limited. Job satisfaction will decrease significantly.

## Exacerbate the Physician Shortage

A severe physician shortage exists in this country. There simply are not enough doctors or doctors in training. In 2005, the Council on Graduate Medical Education issued a report on the status of the physician work force. It concluded that even though the absolute number of doctors will expand between 2000 and 2020, the demand for physicians will grow at a relatively faster rate than the supply of physicians. Thus, the number of physicians per 100,000 Americans will decrease. In November 2008, the Association of American Medical Colleges (AAMC) also examined this issue and predicted a national shortage of 124,000 full-time equivalent physicians by 2025.

While these deficiencies may be most significant in both number and newsworthiness in the field of primary care, the dearth of doctors actually encompasses most medical and surgical subspecialties.

Unfortunately, the Patient Protection and Affordable Care Act will only exacerbate this harmful trend. After the passage of the legislation, the AAMC readdressed the supply of physicians and reached a similar conclusion.

PPACA will affect the physician shortage in two ways. It offers insurance to the uninsured without significantly increasing the number of providers. The 1997 Balanced Budget Act (BBA) capped funding for medical residencies. This has limited the number of new physicians, since all physicians must complete a residency to practice medicine. By increasing demand for care without a comparable increase in the supply of doctors to treat the additional infusion of patients, this will add to the current physician shortage. Although the magnitude of this effect could be less than anticipated, as the Emergency Medical Treatment and Active Labor Act already guarantees emergency medical care to all regardless of ability to pay.

The federal government's decision to cap residency funding in the 1997 BBA deserves at least part of the blame for the current physician shortage. It was a short-sighted decision based primarily on lowering costs as opposed to the best interest of patients. It is likely that PPACA's National Health Care Workforce Commission designed to study the health care workforce and make recommendations to Congress and the executive branch will exhibit similar faulty priorities.

## Decrease Physician Supply

The health care overhaul law will mainly worsen the physician shortage by inevitably decreasing physician supply. The onslaught of increased bureaucracy, additional paperwork, more oversight, and less autonomy will likely drain job satisfaction and could push some doctors to retire or switch careers. Some might postulate that the time doctors must invest before they can actually practice medicine would make their supply quite inelastic. The published literature, although limited in this area, suggests otherwise. Doctors, like any other employee, can and will, only tolerate so much.

A study in the *Journal of Law & Economics* reinforced this by showing that practice climate does indeed influence the physician work force. Helland et al. studied doctor work schedules in relation to malpractice risk. They determined that doctors work 1.7 hours less per week when the risk of medical liability increases a mere ten percent. This effect was most pronounced for older physicians and those physicians who own their practice. Malpractice and regulations are certainly different issues per se. Yet just as the fear of malpractice drains job satisfaction and lowers take home pay, so too do costly, time-consuming regulations. Thus it seems reasonable to conclude they would similarly deter physicians from working.

Physicians agree. In September 2009, an *Investor's Business Daily*/TIPP poll of 1,376 practicing doctors randomly chosen throughout the country revealed that 65% of doctors opposed the Obama administration's health care agenda, and that 45% of practicing physicians would consider leaving their practice or retiring early if it passed. Applied to the entire physician population, this translates to 360,000 doctors who might stop practicing medicine. A more recent survey of 1,195 doctors conducted by Medicus, a national physician search firm, reached a similar conclusion. This poll showed that almost one third of physicians and 46% of primary care physicians would want to leave medicine if health care reform passed. Obviously, not every doctor who said they would quit will, but when faced with more hassle and red tape, many will seriously entertain this option.

Older doctors will retire early. This most likely won't be a feasible option for younger physicians with families to support and loans to repay but many could pursue opportunities outside of clinical medicine, such as jobs with consulting firms, corporate America, finance, or even in politics. Those who continue to practice might opt out of the third party system (although if enough doctors did this, it would be tempting for federal regulators to outlaw this). In all fairness, many doctors will stick with medicine. Some will want to continue practicing while others will find it easiest to continue working, just with less effort and lower morale. The upfront investment to practice medicine and subsequent barriers to exit the profession could keep the number of physicians practicing artificially high, but this certainly won't serve patients' best interests. Obviously this would result in poor patient care.

## Deter Young People from Pursuing Medicine

PPACA will also dissuade young people interested in medicine from pursuing it. This will likely comprise health care reform's main influence on the physician shortage. A career in medicine requires a tremendous investment in both time and money. After four years of undergraduate studies, future doctors must complete four years of medical school. Upon graduation from medical school, young doctors must then complete an intense residency training program before they can practice independently. Depending on the specialty, residencies range from three to six years. After residency, most doctors also then complete a fellowship. Fellowships are typically an additional two to three years of training. By the time doctors start their career, most are in their mid-30s and have accumulated an average of $150,000 in education-related debt. Some physicians accrue even more.

Residency is not only mentally challenging, but physically and psychologically demanding as well. It's rigorous training consisting of regular 30 hour shifts and 80 hour plus work weeks. When residents work these lengthy shifts on a floor block, they typically only get four days off per month. Throughout this training marathon, residents receive an hourly compensation, which hovers just above minimum wage. This salary lacks any correlation with responsibility, skill set, or education.

Medical training is not just a job for young physicians. It's their lives. It requires major sacrifices to become a physician. Doctors should be rewarded for giving up so much for this noble calling. They certainly should not be discouraged or punished, which is exactly what the health care reform law will do.

PPACA will deter bright young minds from entering medicine altogether. The composition of those who do decide to pursue medicine will probably deteriorate. It will likely be a stark deviation from the status quo of the brightest, best educated, best trained, and most dedicated.

Fewer new physicians coupled with an exodus of those already in practice will create an access nightmare for patients desperately seeking care. While it will be a nuisance for doctors having to change practice style or switch careers, ultimately the patient always suffers the most. New patients will not be able to find a physician and with time, despite President Obama's "if you like your doctor" promise, many patients content with their health care and content with their doctor will encounter a similar fate. This will inevitably lead to restricted access, long waits for appointments, and rationed care.

. . .

# Conclusion

PPACA's detriment to physicians is extensive. It will drown doctors in red tape and bureaucracy. It will limit physician autonomy and their ability to help and advocate for their patients. Job satisfaction will be drained and the patient-doctor relationship ruined. As federal regulators require physicians to do more, they will actually get paid less. As the situation worsens, older doctors will retire and younger doctors will look to switch careers. This will come at a time when the demand for physician services will be higher than ever. Ultimately the consequences of the Patient Protection and Affordable Care Act will translate into restricted access and inferior quality of care. No matter how you look at it, this legislation is terrible for physicians; however, it is always the patient that suffers the most.

---

**Jason Fodeman,** MD, is an Internal Medicine Resident at UCONN and a former Graduate Health Policy Fellow at the Heritage Foundation where he studied the etiology of rising health care costs. His research was featured online in the *Wall Street Journal*. He also studied the impact of health care reform on physicians at the Galen Institute as a Visiting Fellow. His health care commentary pieces have been published in *National Review Online, Washington Times, Hartford Courant*, and the *DailyCaller* and he has appeared on *Fox and Friends* to discuss health care policy matters. Recently he was appointed to serve on the State of Connecticut's Medical Inefficiency Committee.

# EXPLORING THE ISSUE

## Will the Affordable Care Act Successfully Transform the American Health Care System?

### Critical Thinking and Reflection

1. What are the potential benefits of the Affordable Care Act for Americans?
2. What are the potential costs of the Affordable Care Act for Americans?
3. Do you believe the government should be permitted to mandate that individuals purchase insurance? Why or why not?
4. Why may doctors be opposed to the Affordable Care Act? Should their concerns carry any extra weight?
5. Do you believe the Affordable Care Act will still be in place in ten years or in fifty years? Why or why not?

### Is There Common Ground?

It is the nature of judicial proceedings that there isn't any common ground. One side wins the case and the other loses. When the so-called "individual mandate" was upheld, there was for some exemptions. (The Obama administration had already granted some.) But opinion is still strongly divided on whether ObamaCare will ultimately work. Many Republicans still hope to repeal it—as was evidenced by the Ted Cruz filibuster during the lead-up to the government shutdown in October. Still others believe the legislation will implode on its own. They point to the failure of the website to function properly and the corny efforts Organizing for America is taking to convince the uninsured to sign up.

Perhaps even more importantly, it will be difficult to reach a common ground until all of the court battles are heard. Once the question of for-profit corporations and birth control is cleared up, nearly all of the most objectionable elements of the Affordable Care Act will be in place and ready to roll out. At that time, it will do no good to continue fighting the health care reforms. Perhaps then we will be able to accept that the Affordable Care Act was passed, signed into law, and affirmed by the Supreme Court as being constitutional. From there, we can determine ways to make the program as effective and efficient as possible in helping to raise the health care expectations and outcomes for individuals who are currently unable to do so.

### Create Central

www.mhhe.com/createcentral

### Additional Resources

Mario K. Castillo, *The Business Owner's Guide to the Employer Mandate* (Antaeus Books, 2013)

Stephen Davidson, *A New Era in U.S. Health Care* (Stanford University Press, 2013)

Guy Faguet, *The Affordable Care Act* (Algora, 2013)

Chinyere Ogbonna, *A Different Perspective on the Patient Protection and Affordable Care Act* (University Press of America, 2013)

Writers of the Washington Post, *Landmark* (Public-Affairs, 2010)

# *Internet References . . .*

**Department of Labor**

www.dol.gov/ebsa/healthreform/

**HealthCare.gov**

www.healthcare.gov

**Medicaid**

www.medicaid.gov/affordablecareact/affordable-care
-act.html

**U.S. Department of Health and Human Services**

www.hhs.gov/healthcare/rights/

**White House**

www.whitehouse.gov/healthreform

Selected, Edited, and with Issue Framing Material by:
William J. Miller, *Flagler College*
George McKenna, *City College, City University of New York*
**and**
Stanley Feingold, *City College, City University of New York*

# ISSUE

# Is Same-Sex Marriage Close to Being Legalized Across the United States?

**YES: Theodore B. Olson**, from "The Conservative Case for Gay Marriage: Why Same-Sex Marriage Is an American Value," *The Daily Beast* ( January 8, 2010)

**NO: Antonin Scalia**, from "Dissenting Opinion in *United States v. Windsor*," Supreme Court of the United States, 570 U.S. (June 26, 2013)

| Learning Outcomes |
| --- |
| **After reading this issue, you will be able to:** |
| • Discuss the current status of same-sex marriage in the United States. |
| • Assess arguments for and against same-sex marriage. |
| • Explain public opinion toward same-sex marriage today. |
| • Describe recent rulings of the Supreme Court related to same-sex marriage. |
| • Identify states that currently allow same-sex marriage. |

## ISSUE SUMMARY

**YES:** Attorney Theodore B. Olson argues that the right of homosexual people to marry, is the logical extension of the equality proclaimed in the Declaration of Independence and guaranteed by the Fourteenth Amendment.

**NO:** Supreme Court Justice Antonin Scalia argues that same-sex marriage should remain a state issue and that the Court's ruling in *United States v. Windsor* would wrongly invalidate state efforts to limit lawful marriage to opposite-sex couples.

Fifty years ago, talk of "gay marriage" would have likely been found in a comedy sketch than in a courtroom or a legislative chamber. Until 1961 all 50 states outlawed homosexual behavior. It was condemned by the clergy of all denominations, barely hinted at in Hollywood movies, and could hardly be spoken of in middle-class homes. The image of an official ceremony legitimizing and celebrating the sexual union of two men or two women would have been beyond shocking; it would have been farcical.

But times change, sometimes very quickly. In 2003, the Supreme Court, overturning its own ruling from two years earlier, struck down as unconstitutional the sodomy laws that still remained in 24 states. In dissent, Justice Antonin Scalia posed a rhetorical question intended as a kind of reductio ad absurdum: With this case as a precedent, Scalia wrote, "[W]hat [remaining] justification could there possibly be for denying the benefits of marriage to homosexual couples . . . .?" Some of the members of the Court's majority went to pains to show that the decision

could not possibly become a precedent for gay marriage, but within a decade Scalia's words had become prophetic.

Hawaii had blazed the trail in 1996 when its highest court ruled that the state must present a compelling public reason for prohibiting gay marriage. The ruling set off widespread alarms, because Article IV, Section 1 of the Constitution stipulates that "Full Faith and Credit shall be given in each state to the public Acts, Records, and judicial Proceedings of every other State." Thus, if a gay couple got married in Hawaii, they could go back to their home state or to any other state and force it to recognize the validity of their marriage, permitting them to enjoy all the same benefits and rights accorded to other married couples in that state—effectively nationalizing gay marriage.

To prevent that from happening, Congress passed the Defense of Marriage Act (DOMA) in 1996. It stipulated that "the word 'marriage' means only a legal union between one man and one woman" and protects states against having to grant legal recognition to out-of-state unions between people of the same sex. That seemed at least to be a kind of fail-safe. If a state actually were to legitimize gay marriage (Hawaii's 1998 court ruling was reversed by an amendment to the state's constitution), DOMA would keep it limited to that one state.

But events were now moving quickly in various states. In 1999, the Vermont Supreme Court held that denying same-sex couples the rights that come with civil marriage violates the state's equality guarantee, and the Vermont legislature followed it up in 2000 with a "civil union" statute for gays, the first in the nation. Later that year, San Francisco became the first city to compel private businesses to extend the benefits accorded to married couples to cohabiting couples regardless of sex. Still, full-fledged gay marriage had not yet arrived. That changed in 2004, when the Massachusetts Supreme Court ruled unconstitutional the state's ban on gay marriage.

As of this writing, 16 of the 50 states and the District of Columbia now allow same-sex marriage: California, Connecticut, Iowa, Massachusetts, New Jersey, Delaware, Hawaii, Illinois, Minnesota, New Hampshire, New York, Rhode Island, Vermont, Maine, Maryland, and Washington. But gay marriage is banned in 33 states, and popular votes have consistently opposed it. A case in point is California, where in 2000 the voters overturned a decision by the California Supreme Court legitimating gay marriage. In February 2012, the Ninth Circuit Court of Appeals affirmed that California's anti-gay marriage initiative known as Proposition 8 was unconstitutional. That case was appealed to the U.S. Supreme Court, and on June 26, 2013, in a 5-4 decision, the Supreme Court ruled that defenders of Proposition 8 lacked "standing" to represent the case. As a result, the Ninth Circuit Court of Appeals lifted its stay blocking same-sex marriages. Further, the tide seems to be changing in regards to public opinion, with three states (Maine, Maryland, and Washington) all legalizing gay marriage through public opinion during the past two years.

The 1996 DOMA was also challenged in the courts recently, and when the Supreme Court struck it down, every state in the Union had to give "full faith and credit" to a gay marriage ceremony conducted in any single state.

Although DOMA is a federal law, in February 2010, the Obama administration's Attorney General refused to defend it in the federal court. Justice Kennedy, writing for the Court, explains, "By seeking to displace this protection and treating those persons as living in marriages less respected than others, the federal statute" violates the Constitution. It is not a complete victory, however, since the present decision leaves in place another provision in the law that says no state is required to recognize gay marriages performed in any other state. The case involved Edith Windsor, a New York widow who was sent a $363,000 estate tax bill by the Internal Revenue Service after her wife died in 2009.

Opponents of gay marriage often emphasize the novelty of it. The practice has never existed in recorded history of any people on earth. Its supporters argue that time-honored practices or taboos is a shaky way to make a case.

Yet change has its own problems. Once we start down its road, how do we know when to get off? Once we allow marriage between two people of the same sex, how can we object to a threesome or beyond? And what about Polygamy or marriage between brother and sister? Many opponents point to the slippery slope that legalizing gay marriage could lead to. At some point, the Court will need to draw a line on what is a recognized marriage and what is not.

Can we draw limits meaningfully when we're on a slippery slope? Yet drawing limits is a task any lawmaker has to face, especially when breaking new ground, and the difficulty in doing so is not a good argument for stifling needed reforms. Whether gay marriage is a needed reform, or a reform at all, is a question that divides the two discussants in this section. Ted Olson writes that the right of homosexuals to marry is a logical extension of the ideals of equality espoused in the Declaration of Independence and promised to Americans via the Fourteenth Amendment. On the opposite side, Antonin Scalia argues that individual voters within states are best suited to make these decisions and the federal courts would be wise to not be seen as attempting to trump the popular will of residents.

# YES ↵

Theodore B. Olson

## The Conservative Case for Gay Marriage: Why Same-Sex Marriage Is an American Value

Together with my good friend and occasional courtroom adversary David Boies, I am attempting to persuade a federal court to invalidate California's Proposition 8—the voter-approved measure that overturned California's constitutional right to marry a person of the same sex.

My involvement in this case has generated a certain degree of consternation among conservatives. How could a politically active, lifelong Republican, a veteran of the Ronald Reagan and George W. Bush administrations, challenge the "traditional" definition of marriage and press for an "activist" interpretation of the Constitution to create another "new" constitutional right?

My answer to this seeming conundrum rests on a lifetime of exposure to persons of different backgrounds, histories, viewpoints, and intrinsic characteristics, and on my rejection of what I see as superficially appealing but ultimately false perceptions about our Constitution and its protection of equality and fundamental rights.

Many of my fellow conservatives have an almost knee-jerk hostility toward gay marriage. This does not make sense, because same-sex unions promote the values conservatives prize. Marriage is one of the basic building blocks of our neighborhoods and our nation. At its best, it is a stable bond between two individuals who work to create a loving household and a social and economic partnership. We encourage couples to marry because the commitments they make to one another provide benefits not only to themselves but also to their families and communities. Marriage requires thinking beyond one's own needs. It transforms two individuals into a union based on shared aspirations, and in doing so establishes a formal investment in the well-being of society. The fact that individuals who happen to be gay want to share in this vital social institution is evidence that conservative ideals enjoy widespread acceptance. Conservatives should celebrate this, rather than lament it.

Legalizing same-sex marriage would also be a recognition of basic American principles, and would represent the culmination of our nation's commitment to equal rights. It is, some have said, the last major civil-rights milestone yet to be surpassed in our two-century struggle to attain the goals we set for this nation at its formation.

This bedrock American principle of equality is central to the political and legal convictions of Republicans, Democrats, liberals, and conservatives alike. The dream that became America began with the revolutionary concept expressed in the Declaration of Independence in words that are among the most noble and elegant ever written: "We hold these truths to be self-evident, that all men are created equal, that they are endowed by their Creator with certain unalienable Rights, that among these are Life, Liberty and the pursuit of Happiness."

Sadly, our nation has taken a long time to live up to the promise of equality. In 1857, the Supreme Court held that an African-American could not be a citizen. During the ensuing Civil War, Abraham Lincoln eloquently reminded the nation of its founding principle: "our fathers brought forth on this continent, a new nation, conceived in liberty and dedicated to the proposition that all men are created equal."

At the end of the Civil War, to make the elusive promise of equality a reality, the 14th Amendment to the Constitution added the command that "no State shall deprive any person of life, liberty or property, without due process of law; nor deny to any person the equal protection of the laws."

Subsequent laws and court decisions have made clear that equality under the law extends to persons of all races, religions, and places of origin. What better way to make this national aspiration complete than to apply the same protection to men and women who differ from others only on the basis of their sexual orientation? I cannot think of a single reason—and have not heard one since I undertook this venture—for continued discrimination against decent, hardworking members of our society on that basis.

Various federal and state laws have accorded certain rights and privileges to gay and lesbian couples, but these protections vary dramatically at the state level, and nearly universally deny true equality to gays and lesbians who wish to marry. The very idea of marriage is basic to recognition as equals in our society; any status short of that is inferior, unjust, and unconstitutional.

The United States Supreme Court has repeatedly held that marriage is one of the most fundamental rights that we have as Americans under our Constitution. It is an expression of our desire to create a social partnership, to live and share life's joys and burdens with the person we love, and to form a lasting bond and a social identity. The Supreme Court has said that marriage is a part of the Constitution's protections of liberty, privacy, freedom of association, and spiritual identification. In short, the right to marry helps us to define ourselves and our place in a community. Without it, there can be no true equality under the law.

It is true that marriage in this nation traditionally has been regarded as a relationship exclusively between a man and a woman, and many of our nation's multiple religions define marriage in precisely those terms. But while the Supreme Court has always previously considered marriage in that context, the underlying rights and liberties that marriage embodies are not in any way confined to heterosexuals.

Marriage is a civil bond in this country as well as, in some (but hardly all) cases, a religious sacrament. It is a relationship recognized by governments as providing a privileged and respected status, entitled to the state's support and benefits. The California Supreme Court described marriage as a "union unreservedly approved and favored by the community." Where the state has accorded official sanction to a relationship and provided special benefits to those who enter into that relationship, our courts have insisted that withholding that status requires powerful justifications and may not be arbitrarily denied.

What, then, are the justifications for California's decision in Proposition 8 to withdraw access to the institution of marriage for some of its citizens on the basis of their sexual orientation? The reasons I have heard are not very persuasive.

The explanation mentioned most often is tradition. But simply because something has always been done a certain way does not mean that it must always remain that way. Otherwise we would still have segregated schools and debtors' prisons. Gays and lesbians have always been among us, forming a part of our society, and they have lived as couples in our neighborhoods and communities. For a long time, they have experienced discrimination and even persecution; but we, as a society, are starting to become more tolerant, accepting, and understanding. California and many other states have allowed gays and lesbians to form domestic partnerships (or civil unions) with most of the rights of married heterosexuals. Thus, gay and lesbian individuals are now permitted to live together in state-sanctioned relationships. It therefore seems anomalous to cite "tradition" as a justification for withholding the status of marriage and thus to continue to label those relationships as less worthy, less sanctioned, or less legitimate.

The second argument I often hear is that traditional marriage furthers the state's interest in procreation—and that opening marriage to same-sex couples would dilute, diminish, and devalue this goal. But that is plainly not the case. Preventing lesbians and gays from marrying does not cause more heterosexuals to marry and conceive more children. Likewise, allowing gays and lesbians to marry someone of the same sex will not discourage heterosexuals from marrying a person of the opposite sex. How, then, would allowing same-sex marriages reduce the number of children that heterosexual couples conceive?

This procreation argument cannot be taken seriously. We do not inquire whether heterosexual couples intend to bear children, or have the capacity to have children, before we allow them to marry. We permit marriage by the elderly, by prison inmates, and by persons who have no intention of having children. What's more, it is pernicious to think marriage should be limited to heterosexuals because of the state's desire to promote procreation. We would surely not accept as constitutional a ban on marriage if a state were to decide, as China has done, to discourage procreation.

Another argument, vaguer and even less persuasive, is that gay marriage somehow does harm to heterosexual marriage. I have yet to meet anyone who can explain to me what this means. In what way would allowing same-sex partners to marry diminish the marriages of heterosexual couples? Tellingly, when the judge in our case asked our opponent to identify the ways in which same-sex marriage would harm heterosexual marriage, to his credit he answered honestly: he could not think of any.

The simple fact is that there is no good reason why we should deny marriage to same-sex partners. On the other hand, there are many reasons why we should formally recognize these relationships and embrace the rights of gays and lesbians to marry and become full and equal members of our society.

No matter what you think of homosexuality, it is a fact that gays and lesbians are members of our families, clubs, and workplaces. They are our doctors, our teachers, our soldiers (whether we admit it or not), and our friends. They yearn for acceptance, stable relationships, and success in their lives, just like the rest of us.

Conservatives and liberals alike need to come together on principles that surely unite us. Certainly, we can agree on the value of strong families, lasting domestic relationships, and communities populated by persons with recognized and sanctioned bonds to one another. Confining some of our neighbors and friends who share these same values to an outlaw or second-class status undermines their sense of belonging and weakens their ties with the rest of us and what should be our common aspirations. Even those whose religious convictions preclude endorsement of what they may perceive as an unacceptable "lifestyle" should recognize that disapproval should not warrant stigmatization and unequal treatment.

When we refuse to accord this status to gays and lesbians, we discourage them from forming the same relationships we encourage for others. And we are also telling them, those who love them, and society as a whole that their relationships are less worthy, less legitimate, less permanent, and less valued. We demean their relationships and we demean them as individuals. I cannot imagine how we benefit as a society by doing so.

I understand, but reject, certain religious teachings that denounce homosexuality as morally wrong, illegitimate, or unnatural; and I take strong exception to those who argue that same-sex relationships should be discouraged by society and law. Science has taught us, even if history has not, that gays and lesbians do not choose to be homosexual any more than the rest of us choose to be heterosexual. To a very large extent, these characteristics are immutable, like being left-handed. And, while our Constitution guarantees the freedom to exercise our individual religious convictions, it equally prohibits us from forcing our beliefs on others. I do not believe that our society can ever live up to the promise of equality, and the fundamental rights to life, liberty, and the pursuit of happiness, until we stop invidious discrimination on the basis of sexual orientation.

If we are born heterosexual, it is not unusual for us to perceive those who are born homosexual as aberrational and threatening. Many religions and much of our social culture have reinforced those impulses. Too often, that has led to prejudice, hostility, and discrimination. The antidote is understanding, and reason. We once tolerated laws throughout this nation that prohibited marriage between persons of different races. California's Supreme Court was the first to find that discrimination unconstitutional. The U.S. Supreme Court unanimously agreed 20 years later, in 1967, in a case called *Loving v. Virginia*. It seems inconceivable today that only 40 years ago there were places in this country where a black woman could not legally marry a white man. And it was only 50 years ago that 17 states mandated segregated public education—until the Supreme Court unanimously struck down that practice in *Brown v. Board of Education*. Most Americans are proud of these decisions and the fact that the discriminatory state laws that spawned them have been discredited. I am convinced that Americans will be equally proud when we no longer discriminate against gays and lesbians and welcome them into our society.

Reactions to our lawsuit have reinforced for me these essential truths. I have certainly heard anger, resentment, and hostility, and words like "betrayal" and other pointedly graphic criticism. But mostly I have been overwhelmed by expressions of gratitude and goodwill from persons in all walks of life, including, I might add, from many conservatives and libertarians whose names might surprise. I have been particularly moved by many personal renditions of how lonely and personally destructive it is to be treated as an outcast and how meaningful it will be to be respected by our laws and civil institutions as an American, entitled to equality and dignity. I have no doubt that we are on the right side of this battle, the right side of the law, and the right side of history.

Some have suggested that we have brought this case too soon, and that neither the country nor the courts are "ready" to tackle this issue and remove this stigma. We disagree. We represent real clients—two wonderful couples in California who have longtime relationships. Our lesbian clients are raising four fine children who could not ask for better parents. Our clients wish to be married. They believe that they have that constitutional right.

They wish to be represented in court to seek vindication of that right by mounting a challenge under the United States Constitution to the validity of Proposition 8 under the equal-protection and due-process clauses of the 14th Amendment. In fact, the California attorney general has conceded the unconstitutionality of Proposition 8, and the city of San Francisco has joined our case to defend the rights of gays and lesbians to be married. We do not tell persons who have a legitimate claim to wait until the time is "right" and the populace is "ready" to recognize their equality and equal dignity under the law.

Citizens who have been denied equality are invariably told to "wait their turn" and to "be patient." Yet veterans of past civil-rights battles found that it was the act of insisting on equal rights that ultimately sped acceptance of those rights. As to whether the courts are "ready" for this case, just a few years ago, in *Romer v. Evans,* the United States Supreme Court struck down a popularly adopted Colorado constitutional amendment that withdrew the rights of gays and lesbians in that state to the protection of anti-discrimination laws. And seven years ago, in *Lawrence v. Texas,* the Supreme Court struck down, as lacking any rational basis, Texas laws prohibiting private, intimate sexual practices between persons of the same sex, overruling a contrary decision just 20 years earlier.

These decisions have generated controversy, of course, but they are decisions of the nation's highest court on which our clients are entitled to rely. If all citizens have a constitutional right to marry, if state laws that withdraw legal protections of gays and lesbians as a class are unconstitutional, and if private, intimate sexual conduct between persons of the same sex is protected by the Constitution, there is very little left on which opponents of same-sex marriage can rely. As Justice Antonin Scalia, who dissented in the Lawrence case, pointed out, "[W]hat [remaining] justification could there possibly be for denying the benefits of marriage to homosexual couples exercising '[t]he liberty protected by the Constitution'?" He is right, of course. One might agree or not with these decisions, but even Justice Scalia has acknowledged that they lead in only one direction.

California's Proposition 8 is particularly vulnerable to constitutional challenge, because that state has now enacted a crazy-quilt of marriage regulation that makes no sense to anyone. California recognizes marriage between men and women, including persons on death row, child abusers, and wife beaters. At the same time, California prohibits marriage by loving, caring, stable partners of the same sex, but tries to make up for it by giving them the alternative of "domestic partnerships" with virtually all of the rights of married persons except the official, state-approved status of marriage. Finally, California recognizes 18,000 same-sex marriages that took place in the months between the state Supreme Court's ruling that upheld gay-marriage rights and the decision of California's citizens to withdraw those rights by enacting Proposition 8.

So there are now three classes of Californians: heterosexual couples who can get married, divorced, and remarried, if they wish; same-sex couples who cannot get married but can live together in domestic partnerships; and same-sex couples who are now married but who, if they divorce, cannot remarry. This is an irrational system, it is discriminatory, and it cannot stand.

Americans who believe in the words of the Declaration of Independence, in Lincoln's Gettysburg Address, in the 14th Amendment, and in the Constitution's guarantees of equal protection and equal dignity before the law cannot sit by while this wrong continues. This is not a conservative or liberal issue; it is an American one, and it is time that we, as Americans, embraced it.

---

**Theodore B. Olson** served as an Assistant Attorney General in the Reagan administration (1981–1984). In private legal practice, Olson later successfully represented presidential candidate George W. Bush in the Supreme Court case *Bush v. Gore* (2000).

**Antonin Scalia**

 **NO**

# Dissenting Opinion in *United States v. Windsor*

Justice Scalia, with whom Justice Thomas joins, and with whom The Chief Justice joins as to Part I, dissenting.

This case is about power in several respects. It is about the power of our people to govern themselves, and the power of this Court to pronounce the law. Today's opinion aggrandizes the latter, with the predictable consequence of diminishing the former. We have no power to decide this case. And even if we did, we have no power under the Constitution to invalidate this democratically adopted legislation. The Court's errors on both points spring forth from the same diseased root: an exalted conception of the role of this institution in America.

## I

### A

The Court is eager—*hungry*—to tell everyone its view of the legal question at the heart of this case. Standing in the way is an obstacle, a technicality of little interest to anyone but the people of We the People, who created it as a barrier against judges' intrusion into their lives. They gave judges, in Article III, only the "judicial Power," a power to decide not abstract questions but real, concrete "Cases" and "Controversies." Yet the plaintiff and the Government agree entirely on what should happen in this lawsuit. They agree that the court below got it right; and they agreed in the court below that the court below that one got it right as well. What, then, are we *doing* here?

The answer lies at the heart of the jurisdictional portion of today's opinion, where a single sentence lays bare the majority's vision of our role. The Court says that we have the power to decide this case because if we did not, then our "primary role in determining the constitutionality of a law" (at least one that "has inflicted real injury on a plaintiff") would "become only secondary to the President's." *Ante,* at 12. But wait, the reader wonders—Windsor won below, and so *cured* her injury, and the President was glad to see it. True, says the majority, but judicial review must march on regardless, lest we "undermine the clear dictate of the separation-of-powers principle that when an Act of Congress is alleged to conflict with the Constitution, it is emphatically the province and duty of the judicial department to say what the law is." *Ibid.* (internal quotation marks and brackets omitted).

That is jaw-dropping. It is an assertion of judicial supremacy over the people's Representatives in Congress and the Executive. It envisions a Supreme Court standing (or rather enthroned) at the apex of government, empowered to decide all constitutional questions, always and everywhere "primary" in its role.

This image of the Court would have been unrecognizable to those who wrote and ratified our national charter. They knew well the dangers of "primary" power, and so created branches of government that would be "perfectly coordinate by the terms of their common commission," none of which branches could "pretend to an exclusive or superior right of settling the boundaries between their respective powers." The Federalist, No. 49, p. 314 (C. Rossiter ed. 1961) (J. Madison). The people did this to protect themselves. They did it to guard their right to self-rule against the black-robed supremacy that today's majority finds so attractive. So it was that Madison could confidently state, with no fear of contradiction, that there was nothing of "greater intrinsic value" or "stamped with the authority of more enlightened patrons of liberty" than a government of separate and coordinate powers. *Id.,* No. 47, at 301.

For this reason we are quite forbidden to say what the law is whenever (as today's opinion asserts) "'an Act of Congress is alleged to conflict with the Constitution.'" *Ante,* at 12. We can do so only when that allegation will determine the outcome of a lawsuit, and is contradicted by the other party. The "judicial Power" is not, as the majority believes, the power "'to say what the law is,'" *ibid.,* giving the Supreme Court the "primary role in determining the constitutionality of laws." The majority must have in mind one of the foreign constitutions that pronounces such primacy for its constitutional court and allows that primacy to be exercised in contexts other than a lawsuit. See, *e.g.,* Basic Law for the Federal Republic of Germany, Art. 93. The judicial power as Americans have understood it (and their English ancestors before them) is the power to adjudicate, with conclusive effect, disputed government claims (civil or criminal) against private persons, and disputed claims by private persons against the government or other private persons. Sometimes (though not always) the parties before the court disagree not with regard to the facts of their case (or not *only* with regard to the facts) but with regard to the applicable law—in which event (and *only* in which event) it becomes the "'province and duty

Scalia, Antonin. Supreme Court of the United States, 570 U.S., no. 12–307, June 2013, excerpts.

of the judicial department to say what the law is.'" *Ante*, at 12.

In other words, declaring the compatibility of state or federal laws with the Constitution is not only not the "primary role" of this Court, it is not a separate, free-standing role *at all*. We perform that role incidentally—by accident, as it were—when that is necessary to resolve the dispute before us. Then, and only then, does it become "'the province and duty of the judicial department to say what the law is.'" That is why, in 1793, we politely declined the Washington Administration's request to "say what the law is" on a particular treaty matter that was not the subject of a concrete legal controversy. 3 Correspondence and Public Papers of John Jay 486–489 (H. Johnston ed. 1893). And that is why, as our opinions have said, some questions of law will *never* be presented to this Court, because there will never be anyone with standing to bring a lawsuit. See *Schlesinger v. Reservists Comm. to Stop the War,* 418 U.S. 208, 227 (1974); *United States v. Richardson,* 418 U.S. 166, 179 (1974). As Justice Brandeis put it, we cannot "pass upon the constitutionality of legislation in a friendly, non-adversary, proceeding"; absent a "'real, earnest and vital controversy between individuals,'" we have neither any work to do nor any power to do it. *Ashwander v. TVA,* 297 U.S. 288, 346 (1936) (concurring opinion) (quoting *Chicago & Grand Trunk R. Co. v. Wellman,* 143 U.S. 339, 345 (1892)). Our authority begins and ends with the need to adjudge the rights of an injured party who stands before us seeking redress. *Lujan v. Defenders of Wildlife,* 504 U.S. 555, 560 (1992).

That is completely absent here. Windsor's injury was cured by the judgment in her favor. And while, in ordinary circumstances, the United States is injured by a directive to pay a tax refund, this suit is far from ordinary. Whatever injury the United States has suffered will surely not be redressed by the action that it, as a litigant, asks us to take. The final sentence of the Solicitor General's brief on the merits reads: "For the foregoing reasons, the judgment of the court of appeals *should be affirmed*." Brief for United States (merits) 54 (emphasis added). That will not cure the Government's injury, but carve it into stone. One could spend many fruitless afternoons ransacking our library for any other petitioner's brief seeking an affirmance of the judgment against it. What the petitioner United States asks us to do in the case before us is exactly what the respondent Windsor asks us to do: not to provide relief from the judgment below but to say that that judgment was correct. And the same was true in the Court of Appeals: Neither party sought to undo the judgment for Windsor, and so that court should have dismissed the appeal (just as we should dismiss) for lack of jurisdiction. Since both parties agreed with the judgment of the District Court for the Southern District of New York, the suit should have ended there. The further proceedings have been a contrivance, having no object in mind except to elevate a District Court judgment that has no precedential effect in other courts, to one that has precedential effect throughout the Second Circuit, and then (in this Court) precedential effect throughout the United States.

We have never before agreed to speak—to "say what the law is"—where there is no controversy before us. In the more than two centuries that this Court has existed as an institution, we have never suggested that we have the power to decide a question when every party agrees with both its nominal opponent *and the court below* on that question's answer. The United States reluctantly conceded that at oral argument. See Tr. of Oral Arg. 19–20.

The closest we have ever come to what the Court blesses today was our opinion in *INS v. Chadha,* 462 U.S. 919 (1983). But in that case, two parties to the litigation disagreed with the position of the United States and with the court below: the House and Senate, which had intervened in the case. Because *Chadha* concerned the validity of a mode of congressional action—the one-house legislative veto—the House and Senate were threatened with destruction of what they claimed to be one of their institutional powers. The Executive choosing not to defend that power, we permitted the House and Senate to intervene. Nothing like that is present here.

To be sure, the Court in *Chadha* said that statutory aggrieved-party status was "not altered by the fact that the Executive may agree with the holding that the statute in question is unconstitutional." *Id.,* at 930–931. But in a footnote to that statement, the Court acknowledged Article III's separate requirement of a "justiciable case or controversy," and stated that *this* requirement was satisfied "because of the presence of the two Houses of Congress as adverse parties." *Id.,* at 931, n. 6. Later in its opinion, the *Chadha* Court remarked that the United States' announced intention to enforce the statute also sufficed to permit judicial review, even absent congressional participation. *Id.,* at 939. That remark is true, as a description of the judicial review conducted in the Court of Appeals, where the Houses of Congress had not intervened. (The case originated in the Court of Appeals, since it sought review of agency action under 8 U.S.C. §1105a(a) (1976 ed.).) There, absent a judgment setting aside the INS order, Chadha faced deportation. This passage of our opinion seems to be addressing that initial standing in the Court of Appeals, as indicated by its quotation from the lower court's opinion, 462 U.S., at 939–940. But if it was addressing standing to pursue the appeal, the remark was both the purest dictum (as congressional intervention at that point made the required adverseness "beyond doubt," *id.,* at 939), and quite incorrect. When a private party has a judicial decree safely in hand to prevent his injury, additional judicial action requires that a party injured by the decree *seek to undo it*. In *Chadha,* the intervening House and Senate fulfilled that requirement. Here no one does.

The majority's discussion of the requirements of Article III bears no resemblance to our jurisprudence. It accuses the *amicus* (appointed to argue against our jurisdiction) of "elid[ing] the distinction between . . . the jurisdictional requirements of Article III and the prudential limits on its exercise." *Ante,* at 6. It then proceeds to call the requirement of adverseness a "prudential" aspect of standing. *Of standing.* That is incomprehensible. A plaintiff (or appellant) can have all the standing in the world—satisfying all three standing requirements of *Lujan* that the majority so carefully quotes, *ante,* at 7—and yet no Article III controversy may be before the court. Article III requires not just a plaintiff (or appellant) who has standing to complain but *an opposing party* who denies the validity of the complaint. It is not the *amicus* that has done the eliding of distinctions, but the majority, calling the quite separate Article III requirement of adverseness between the parties an element (which it then pronounces a "prudential" element) of standing. The question here is not whether, as the majority puts it, "the United States retains a stake sufficient to support Article III jurisdiction," *ibid.* the question is whether there is any controversy (which requires *contradiction*) between the United States and Ms. Windsor. There is not.

I find it wryly amusing that the majority seeks to dismiss the requirement of party-adverseness as nothing more than a "prudential" aspect of the sole Article III requirement of standing. (Relegating a jurisdictional requirement to "prudential" status is a wondrous device, enabling courts to ignore the requirement whenever they believe it "prudent"—which is to say, a good idea.) Half a century ago, a Court similarly bent upon announcing its view regarding the constitutionality of a federal statute achieved that goal by effecting a remarkably similar *but completely opposite* distortion of the principles limiting our jurisdiction. The Court's notorious opinion in *Flast v. Cohen,* 392 U.S. 83, 98–101 (1968), held that *standing* was merely an element (which it pronounced to be a "prudential" element) of the sole Article III requirement of *adverseness.* We have been living with the chaos created by that power-grabbing decision ever since, see *Hein v. Freedom From Religion Foundation, Inc.,* 551 U.S. 587 (2007), as we will have to live with the chaos created by this one.

The authorities the majority cites fall miles short of supporting the counterintuitive notion that an Article III "controversy" can exist without disagreement between the parties. In *Deposit Guaranty Nat. Bank v. Roper,* 445 U.S. 326 (1980), the District Court had entered judgment in the individual plaintiff's favor based on the defendant bank's offer to pay the full amount claimed. The plaintiff, however, sought to appeal the District Court's denial of class certification under Federal Rule of Civil Procedure 23. There was a continuing dispute between the parties concerning the issue raised on appeal. The same is true of the other case cited by the majority, *Camreta v. Greene,* 563 U.S. ___ (2011). There the District Court found that the defendant state officers had violated the Fourth Amendment, but rendered judgment in their favor because they were entitled to official immunity, application of the Fourth Amendment to their conduct not having been clear at the time of violation. The officers sought to appeal the holding of Fourth Amendment violation, which would

circumscribe their future conduct; the plaintiff continued to insist that a Fourth Amendment violation had occurred. The "prudential" discretion to which both those cases refer was the discretion to *deny* an appeal even when a live controversy exists—not the discretion to *grant* one when it does not. The majority can cite no case in which this Court entertained an appeal in which both parties urged us to affirm the judgment below. And that is because the existence of a controversy is not a "prudential" requirement that we have invented, but an essential element of an Article III case or controversy. The majority's notion that a case between friendly parties can be entertained so long as "adversarial presentation of the issues is assured by the participation of *amici curiae* prepared to defend with vigor" the other side of the issue, *ante,* at 10, effects a breathtaking revolution in our Article III jurisprudence.

It may be argued that if what we say is true some Presidential determinations that statutes are unconstitutional will not be subject to our review. That is as it should be, when both the President and the plaintiff agree that the statute is unconstitutional. Where the Executive is enforcing an unconstitutional law, suit will of course lie; but if, in that suit, the Executive admits the unconstitutionality of the law, the litigation should end in an order or a consent decree enjoining enforcement. This suit saw the light of day only because the President enforced the Act (and thus gave Windsor standing to sue) even though he believed it unconstitutional. He could have equally chosen (more appropriately, some would say) neither to enforce nor to defend the statute he believed to be unconstitutional, see Presidential Authority to Decline to Execute Unconstitutional Statutes, 18 Op. Off. Legal Counsel 199 (Nov. 2, 1994)—in which event Windsor would not have been injured, the District Court could not have refereed this friendly scrimmage, and the Executive's determination of unconstitutionality would have escaped this Court's desire to blurt out its view of the law. The matter would have been left, as so many matters ought to be left, to a tug of war between the President and the Congress, which has innumerable means (up to and including impeachment) of compelling the President to enforce the laws it has written. Or the President could have evaded presentation of the constitutional issue to this Court simply by declining to appeal the District Court and Court of Appeals dispositions he agreed with. Be sure of this much: If a President wants to insulate his judgment of unconstitutionality from our review, he can. What the views urged in this dissent produce is not insulation from judicial review but insulation from Executive contrivance.

The majority brandishes the famous sentence from *Marbury v. Madison,* 1 Cranch 137, 177 (1803) that "[i]t is emphatically the province and duty of the judicial department to say what the law is." *Ante,* at 12 (internal quotation marks omitted). But that sentence neither says nor implies that it is *always* the province and duty of the Court to say what the law is—much less that its responsibility in that regard is a "primary" one. The very next sentence of

Chief Justice Marshall's opinion makes the crucial quali-fication that today's majority ignores: *"Those who apply the rule to particular cases, must of necessity expound and interpret that rule."* 1 Cranch, at 177 (emphasis added). Only when a "particular case" is before us—that is, a controversy that it is our business to resolve under Article III—do we have the province and duty to pronounce the law. For the views of our early Court more precisely addressing the question before us here, the majority ought instead to have consulted the opinion of Chief Justice Taney in *Lord v. Veazie,* 8 How. 251 (1850):

> "The objection in the case before us is . . . that the plaintiff and defendant have the same inter-est, and that interest adverse and in conflict with the interest of third persons, whose rights would be seriously affected if the question of law was decided in the manner that both of the parties to this suit desire it to be.
>
> "A judgment entered under such circum-stances, and for such purposes, is a mere form. The whole proceeding was in contempt of the court, and highly reprehensible. . . . A judgment in form, thus procured, in the eye of the law is no judgment of the court. It is a nullity, and no writ of error will lie upon it. This writ is, therefore, dis-missed." *Id.,* at 255–256.

There is, in the words of *Marbury,* no "necessity [to] expound and interpret" the law in this case; just a desire to place this Court at the center of the Nation's life. 1 Cranch, at 177.

There are many remarkable things about the major-ity's merits holding. The first is how rootless and shifting its justifications are. For example, the opinion starts with seven full pages about the traditional power of States to define domestic relations—initially fooling many readers, I am sure, into thinking that this is a federalism opinion. But we are eventually told that "it is unnecessary to decide whether this federal intrusion on state power is a viola-tion of the Constitution," and that "[t]he State's power in defining the marital relation is of central relevance in this case quite apart from principles of federalism" be-cause "the State's decision to give this class of persons the right to marry conferred upon them a dignity and status of immense import." *Ante,* at 18. But no one questions the power of the States to define marriage (with the con-comitant conferral of dignity and status), so what is the point of devoting seven pages to describing how long and well established that power is? Even after the opinion has formally disclaimed reliance upon principles of federal-ism, mentions of "the usual tradition of recognizing and accepting state definitions of marriage" continue. See, *e.g., ante,* at 20. What to make of this? The opinion never explains. My guess is that the majority, while reluctant to suggest that defining the meaning of "marriage" in fed-eral statutes is unsupported by any of the Federal Gov-ernment's enumerated powers, nonetheless needs some

rhetorical basis to support its pretense that today's pro-hibition of laws excluding same-sex marriage is confined to the Federal Government (leaving the second, state-law shoe to be dropped later, maybe next Term). But I am only guessing.

Equally perplexing are the opinion's references to "the Constitution's guarantee of equality." *Ibid.* Near the end of the opinion, we are told that although the "equal protec-tion guarantee of the Fourteenth Amendment makes [the] Fifth Amendment [due process] right all the more specific and all the better understood and preserved"—what can *that* mean?—"the Fifth Amendment itself withdraws from Government the power to degrade or demean in the way this law does." *Ante,* at 25. The only possible interpreta-tion of this statement is that the Equal Protection Clause, even the Equal Protection Clause as incorporated in the Due Process Clause, is not the basis for today's holding. But the portion of the majority opinion that explains why DOMA is unconstitutional (Part IV) begins by citing *Bol-ling v. Sharpe,* 347 U.S. 497 (1954), *Department of Agriculture v. Moreno,* 413 U.S. 528 (1973), and *Romer v. Evans,* 517 U.S. 620 (1996)—*all* of which are equal-protection cases. And those three cases are the *only* authorities that the Court cites in Part IV about the Constitution's meaning, except for its citation of *Lawrence v. Texas,* 539 U.S. 558 (2003) (not an equal-protection case) to support its passing asser-tion that the Constitution protects the "moral and sexual choices" of same-sex couples, *ante,* at 23.

Moreover, if this is meant to be an equal-protection opinion, it is a confusing one. The opinion does not resolve and indeed does not even mention what had been the central question in this litigation: whether, under the Equal Protection Clause, laws restricting marriage to a man and a woman are reviewed for more than mere rational-ity. That is the issue that divided the parties and the court below, compare Brief for Respondent Bipartisan Legal Advisory Group of U.S. House of Representatives (merits) 24–28 (no), with Brief for Respondent Windsor (merits) 17–31 and Brief for United States (merits) 18–36 (yes); and compare 699 F. 3d 169, 180–185 (CA2 2012) (yes), with *id.,* at 208–211 (Straub, J., dissenting in part and concur-ring in part) (no). In accord with my previously expressed skepticism about the Court's "tiers of scrutiny" approach, I would review this classification only for its rationality. See *United States v. Virginia,* 518 U.S. 515, 567–570 (1996) (SCALIA, J., dissenting). As nearly as I can tell, the Court agrees with that; its opinion does not apply strict scru-tiny, and its central propositions are taken from rational-basis cases like *Moreno.* But the Court certainly does not *apply* anything that resembles that deferential framework. See *Heller v. Doe,* 509 U.S. 312, 320 (1993) (a classification "'must be upheld . . . if there is any reasonably conceiv-able state of facts'" that could justify it).

The majority opinion need not get into the strict-vs.-rational-basis scrutiny question, and need not justify its holding under either, because it says that DOMA is uncon-stitutional as "a deprivation of the liberty of the person protected by the Fifth Amendment of the Constitution," *ante,* at 25; that it violates "basic due process" principles, *ante,* at 20; and that it inflicts an "injury and indignity" of a kind that denies "an essential part of the liberty protected by the Fifth Amendment," *ante,* at 19. The majority never utters the dread words "substantive due process," perhaps sensing the disrepute into which that doctrine has fallen, but that is what those statements mean. Yet the opinion does not argue that same-sex marriage is "deeply rooted in this Nation's history and tradition," *Washington v. Glucksberg,* 521 U.S. 702, 720–721 (1997), a claim that would of course be quite absurd. So would the further suggestion (also necessary, under our substantive-due-process precedents) that a world in which DOMA exists is one bereft of " 'ordered liberty.' " *Id.,* at 721 (quoting *Palko v. Connecticut,* 302 U.S. 319, 325 (1937)).

Some might conclude that this loaf could have used a while longer in the oven. But that would be wrong; it is already overcooked. The most expert care in preparation cannot redeem a bad recipe. The sum of all the Court's nonspecific hand-waving is that this law is invalid (maybe on equal-protection grounds, maybe on substantive-due-process grounds, and perhaps with some amorphous federalism component playing a role) because it is motivated by a " 'bare . . . desire to harm' " couples in same-sex marriages. *Ante,* at 20. It is this proposition with which I will therefore engage.

In my opinion, however, the view that *this* Court will take of state prohibition of same-sex marriage is indicated beyond mistaking by today's opinion. As I have said, the real rationale of today's opinion, whatever disappearing trail of its legalistic argle-bargle one chooses to follow, is that DOMA is motivated by " 'bare . . . desire to harm' " couples in same-sex marriages. *Supra,* at 18. How easy it is, indeed how inevitable, to reach the same conclusion with regard to state laws denying same-sex couples marital status. . .

By formally declaring anyone opposed to same-sex marriage an enemy of human decency, the majority arms well every challenger to a state law restricting marriage to its traditional definition. Henceforth those challengers will lead with this Court's declaration that there is "no legitimate purpose" served by such a law, and will claim that the traditional definition has "the purpose and effect to disparage and to injure" the "personhood and dignity" of same-sex couples, see *ante,* at 25, 26. The majority's limiting assurance will be meaningless in the face of language like that, as the majority well knows. That is why the language is there. The result will be a judicial distortion of our society's debate over marriage—a debate that can seem in need of our clumsy "help" only to a member of this institution.

As to that debate: Few public controversies touch an institution so central to the lives of so many, and few inspire such attendant passion by good people on all sides. Few public controversies will ever demonstrate so vividly the beauty of what our Framers gave us, a gift the Court pawns today to buy its stolen moment in the spotlight: a system of government that permits us to rule *ourselves.* Since DOMA's passage, citizens on all sides of the question have seen victories and they have seen defeats. There have been plebiscites, legislation, persuasion, and loud voices—in other words, democracy. Victories in one place for some, see North Carolina Const., Amdt. 1 (providing that "[m]arriage between one man and one woman is the only domestic legal union that shall be valid or recognized in this State") (approved by a popular vote, 61% to 39% on May 8, 2012), are offset by victories in other places for others, see Maryland Question 6 (establishing "that Maryland's civil marriage laws allow gay and lesbian couples to obtain a civil marriage license") (approved by a popular vote, 52% to 48%, on November 6, 2012). Even in a *single State,* the question has come out differently on different occasions. Compare Maine Question 1 (permitting "the State of Maine to issue marriage licenses to same-sex couples") (approved by a popular vote, 53% to 47%, on November 6, 2012) with Maine Question 1 (rejecting "the new law that lets same-sex couples marry") (approved by a popular vote, 53% to 47%, on November 3, 2009).

In the majority's telling, this story is black-and-white: Hate your neighbor or come along with us. The truth is more complicated. It is hard to admit that one's political opponents are not monsters, especially in a struggle like this one, and the challenge in the end proves more than today's Court can handle. Too bad. A reminder that disagreement over something so fundamental as marriage can still be politically legitimate would have been a fit task for what in earlier times was called the judicial temperament. We might have covered ourselves with honor today, by promising all sides of this debate that it was theirs to settle and that we would respect their resolution. We might have let the People decide.

But that the majority will not do. Some will rejoice in today's decision, and some will despair at it; that is the nature of a controversy that matters so much to so many. But the Court has cheated both sides, robbing the winners of an honest victory, and the losers of the peace that comes from a fair defeat. We owed both of them better. I dissent.

---

**Antonin Scalia** is an Associate Justice of the U.S. Supreme Court. He was appointed in 1986 by President Ronald Reagan.

# EXPLORING THE ISSUE

## Is Same-Sex Marriage Close to Being Legalized Across the United States?

## Critical Thinking and Reflection

1. What role should tradition and precedent play in the argument over same sex marriage?
2. Can the radical novelty of same-sex marriage in human history be a valid argument for not beginning the practice today?
3. Do you agree with Olson's argument that Thomas Jefferson would be in favor of same-sex marriage? Why or why not?
4. What do you think about the slippery slope argument that once we start legitimizing gay marriage, what is to stop us from doing the same with polygamy and incest?
5. Do you think same-sex marriage will be legalized across the country in the next decade? Why or why not?

## Is There Common Ground?

The common ground that might once have appealed to both sides in this controversy no longer does so. The common ground was the "civil union" compromise, once favored by moderates and many liberals. Enacted in a number of states, civil unions provide virtually all the benefits granted to married couples, but without the full title of marriage. The gay rights movement rejects this as an anemic halfway measure, insisting that it fails to achieve real equality between gays and straights. The fight over gay marriage, then, can no longer be compromised: one side will win and the other side will lose.

Gay marriage advocates, convinced that they are on the winning side, tend to the view that the losers will eventually come to terms with defeat, much as racial segregationists have come to accept the end of Jim Crow. But, just as the parallel to the civil rights struggle may not be as obvious to others as it is to them, so the outcome of the struggle may not emerge in quite the same way.

Recent trends show signs of hope for gay marriage advocates. Public support for gay marriage has never been higher. In 1996, Gallup first asked Americans how they felt and found only 27 percent support. In July 2013, support had swelled to 54 percent. While there are unquestionably pockets of the country where there is little chance of gay marriage being legalized in the near future, it appears a more meaningful discourse is both possible and likely as we move forward. Through such discourse, perhaps a new middle ground can be found.

## Create Central

www.mhhe.com/createcentral

## Additional Resources

Adam Liptak, *To Have and Uphold: The Supreme Court and the Battle for Same-Sex Marriage* (Byliner, 2013)

Jonathan Rauch, *Gay Marriage: Why It Is Good for Gays, Good for Straights, and Good for America* (Time Book, 2004)

Peter Sprigg, *Outrage: How Gay Activists and Liberal Judges Are Trashing Democracy to Redefine Marriage* (Regnery, 2004)

Mark Strasser, *The Challenge of Same-Sex Marriages: Federalist Principles and Constitutional Protections* (Praeger, 1999)

Andrew Sullivan, *Virtually Normal: An Argument about Homosexuality* (Alfred A. Knopf, 1995)

# *Internet References . . .*

**American Family Association**

www.afa.net/

**Freedom to Marry Coalition**

www.freedomtomarry.org/

**Human Rights Campaign**

www.hrc.org/campaigns/marriage-center

**Pew Forum**

www.pewforum.org/topics/gay-marriage-and
-homosexuality/

**Traditional Values Coalition**

www.traditionalvalues.org/

**Selected, Edited, and with Issue Framing Material by:**
**William J. Miller,** *Flagler College*
George McKenna, *City College, City University of New York*
**and**
*Stanley Feingold, City College, City University of New York*

# ISSUE

# Do Corporations Have the Same Free Speech Rights as Persons?

**YES: Anthony Kennedy,** from Opinion of the Court in *Citizens United v. Federal Election Commission* (2010)

**NO: John Paul Stevens,** from Dissenting Opinion in *Citizens United v. Federal Election Commission* (2010)

---

## Learning Outcomes

**After reading this issue, you will be able to:**

- Explain what is meant by free speech rights.
- Discuss how corporations and individuals are similar and different.
- Assess the pros and cons of corporations having free speech rights.
- Identify how corporations having free speech rights could impact campaigns.
- Explain the arguments made by the Court in rendering their decisions.

---

### ISSUE SUMMARY

**YES:** Supreme Court Justice Anthony Kennedy, for the majority, hold the view that corporations have all the rights and privileges of citizens under the Constitution, so their free speech rights are not to be violated.

**NO:** Supreme Court Justice John Paul Stevens insists that corporations are not citizens under the Constitution, so Congress may restrict their political speech prior to an election.

---

Citizens United is an independent conservative political organization founded in 1988. Early in 2008, when it appeared likely that Senator Hillary Clinton would be the Democratic presidential nominee, it produced "Hillary: The Movie," a motion picture that was highly critical of her candidacy. When the Federal Election Commission, in accord with existing law, sought to bar the telecast of that film during the 60 days prior to the presidential election, the United States Supreme Court, in a 5-4 decision, denied the right of the federal government to restrict the free speech rights of an independent organization.

When the Supreme Court several months later, with the same 5-4 division, rejected the imposition of contribution limits to an independent political organization, the nonpartisan Congressional Research Service concluded that these judicial opinions "arguably represent the most fundamental changes to campaign finance law in decades." Most conservatives and some liberals who favor unrestrained free speech were delighted; most liberals and some conservatives who deplore unlimited campaign spending were dismayed.

For four decades, Congress has sought, with limited success, to constrain the role of unlimited financial expenditures in federal elections. After the Watergate affair in which President Richard Nixon and members of his administration were accused of illegal efforts to influence the outcome of a presidential election, Congress adopted the Federal Election Campaign Act to limit contributions to and spending on federal elections. In 1976, after further revisions of the law, the Supreme Court upheld both limits on individual contributions and public financing for candidates who chose to accept it instead of raising private campaign funds. At the same time, the Court held that limits on campaign expenditures are unconstitutional restrictions on protected expression and association, whether they are by individuals or groups or by a candidate from personal funds.

Congress continued to adopt laws to reduce campaign expenses. In 2003, the Supreme Court upheld major campaign law revisions on radio and television advertisements that mentioned a candidate's name within 30 days of a primary election or 60 days of a general election, and restrictions on "soft money" donations to political parties. "Soft money" refers to contributions to a political party or other organization, as distinct from "hard money" contributions that go directly to a candidate. Since then,

Congress had debated but not adopted proposals to prohibit foreign influence in federal elections and bar businesses that receive government contracts from making political contributions.

What made *Citizens United v. Federal Election Commission* different from the earlier decisions on campaign contributions was Congress's effort to impose and the Supreme Court's decision to bar any limits on expenditures by corporations. Even before considering the question of campaign limits, the majority had to assume that corporations possessed the right of freedom of speech and the minority had to deny the existence of that right. The constitutional question is whether corporations enjoy First Amendment rights and other rights of persons. If that question is answered affirmatively, corporations possess the same right of political participation as persons, and any restriction on showing a political film shortly before an election would have to be answered as it would be for an individual person. The answer would clearly be no. But if corporations do not enjoy the constitutional rights of persons, Congress may exercise its legislative discretion to impose narrow limits on the corporation's speech. The issue has been defined as "corporate personhood."

Do corporations have the same free speech and other constitutional rights of persons? It did not seem so when the United States was formed. Corporations are not mentioned in the Constitution; the American Revolution was prompted by colonial opposition to the tax on tea imposed by Britain's East India Company, and the charters of early corporations contained precise restrictions on their operation and duration. Despite these inhibitions, the wealth and power of corporations grew in the nation's first century, and so did their judicial influence. A corporation chartered under the laws of one state is able to do business in all states. Lawyers began to refer to corporations as "artificial persons." In business transactions, corporations were treated as if they were individual entities.

In the late nineteenth century, the Supreme Court assumed that corporations have the constitutional rights of persons, applying this not only to the First Amendment's grant of freedom of speech, but in later cases to the Fourth Amendment right of unreasonable searches, the Fifth Amendment right against being tried twice for the same offense, and the Seventh Amendment right to a jury trial in a civil case. The Supreme Court saw no difference between the constitutional rights accorded to persons and those given to corporations.

Critics resist the Court's conclusion because they claim that corporations are impersonal organizations whose sole purpose is the financial profit of its investors and management. They argue that the corporation has no intrinsic altruistic motive. It has no need to do good; it needs only to make money. Against this moral distinction, defenders of corporate personhood point out that,

without the unique attributes of corporations, Andrew Carnegie could not have created the American free library system, Bill Gates could not have organized vast resources to combat preventable diseases, and countless good works would have gone undone by nonprofit foundations created in the name of—and with the wealth created by—Rockefeller, Ford, Pew, and other individuals who derived their wealth from corporations.

As a consequence of the *Citizens United* decision, Super PACs (political action committees) permitted to receive unlimited political contributions have been created. At least nominally independent of the political parties, but often close to nonprofit organizations that do not have to disclose their donors, they are typically closely aligned with individual candidates. Experience will demonstrate their impact on American elections and politics.

In 2011, the Supreme Court once again returned to examine the constitutional status of campaign finance law. A 5-4 majority (the same five as in *Citizens United*) struck down an Arizona law that provided escalating matching funds to candidates who accepted public financing, and agreed to limit their personal spending to $500. The Supreme Court majority objected to Arizona's providing additional support for the publicly funded candidate in response to increasing expenditures by privately financed candidates and the independent groups that are supporting them. Chief Justice John Roberts wrote that such laws "inhibit robust and wide-open debate." Justice Elena Kagan, writing for the four dissenters, argued that "what the law does—all the law does—is fund more speech."

At the conclusion of the 2012 presidential election between Barack Obama and Mitt Romney, Americans finally have an opportunity to examine the impact of the *Citizens United* ruling. According to the Federal Election Commission, $933 million came directly into the campaign from companies, unions, and individuals who use Citizens United to funnel funding to super PACs. Overwhelmingly, this money went to pay for attack ads that filled television screens for the entire campaign. Roughly two-thirds of the money went to ten super PACs or political nonprofits, nine of which were solely dedicated to purchasing media spots for candidates. Of all the ads purchased using this funding, just below 90 percent were found to be negative in tone regarding a political opponent. While it is only evidence from one election cycle, it is clear that Citizens United is having an impact on the political process. It will take more time, however, to determine how strong the impact actually proves to be.

Justice Anthony Kennedy and Justice John Paul Stevens provide opposing eloquent arguments on the constitutional status and free speech rights of corporations in their majority and dissenting opinions in *Citizens United v. Federal Election Commission*.

# YES ⤺

**Anthony Kennedy**

## Opinion of the Court

Federal law prohibits corporations and unions from using their general treasury funds to make independent expenditures for speech defined as an "electioneering communication" or for speech expressly advocating the election or defeat of a candidate. . . . The Government may regulate corporate political speech through disclaimer and disclosure requirements, but it may not suppress that speech altogether. . . .

In January 2008, Citizens United released a film entitled *Hillary: The Movie.* We refer to the film as *Hillary.* It is a 90-minute documentary about then-Senator Hillary Clinton, who was a candidate in the Democratic Party's 2008 Presidential primary elections. *Hillary* mentions Senator Clinton by name and depicts interviews with political commentators and other persons, most of them quite critical of Senator Clinton. *Hillary* was released in theaters and on DVD, but Citizens United wanted to increase distribution by making it available through video-on-demand. . . .

Before the Bipartisan Campaign Reform Act of 2002 (BCRA), federal law prohibited—and still does prohibit—corporations and unions from using general treasury funds to make direct contributions to candidates or independent expenditures that expressly advocate the election or defeat of a candidate, through any form of media, in connection with certain qualified federal elections. . . .

The movie, in essence, is a feature-length negative advertisement that urges viewers to vote against Senator Clinton for President. In light of historical footage, interviews with persons critical of her, and voiceover narration, the film would be understood by most viewers as an extended criticism of Senator Clinton's character and her fitness for the office of the Presidency. The narrative may contain more suggestions and arguments than facts, but there is little doubt that the thesis of the film is that she is unfit for the Presidency. The movie concentrates on alleged wrongdoing during the Clinton administration, Senator Clinton's qualifications and fitness for office, and policies the commentators predict she would pursue if elected President. . . .

Courts, too, are bound by the First Amendment. We must decline to draw, and then redraw, constitutional lines based on the particular media or technology used to disseminate political speech from a particular speaker. It must be noted, moreover, that this undertaking would require substantial litigation over an extended time, all to interpret a law that beyond doubt discloses serious First Amendment flaws. The interpretive process itself would create an inevitable, pervasive, and serious risk of chilling protected speech pending the drawing of fine distinctions that, in the end, would themselves be questionable. . . .

Throughout the litigation, Citizens United has asserted a claim that the FEC has violated its First Amendment right to free speech. All concede that this claim is properly before us. And "'[o]nce a federal claim is properly presented, a party can make any argument in support of that claim; parties are not limited to the precise arguments they made below.' ". . .

It is well known that the public begins to concentrate on elections only in the weeks immediately before they are held. There are short timeframes in which speech can have influence. The need or relevance of the speech will often first be apparent at this stage in the campaign. The decision to speak is made in the heat of political campaigns, when speakers react to messages conveyed by others. A speaker's ability to engage in political speech that could have a chance of persuading voters is stifled if the speaker must first commence a protracted lawsuit. By the time the lawsuit concludes, the election will be over and the litigants in most cases will have neither the incentive nor, perhaps, the resources to carry on, even if they could establish that the case is not moot because the issue is "capable of repetition, yet evading review.". . . Here, Citizens United decided to litigate its case to the end. Today, Citizens United finally learns, two years after the fact, whether it could have spoken during the 2008 Presidential primary—long after the opportunity to persuade primary voters has passed. . . .

When the FEC issues advisory opinions that prohibit speech, "[m]any persons, rather than undertake the considerable burden (and sometimes risk) of vindicating their rights through case-by-case litigation, will choose simply to abstain from protected speech—harming not only themselves but society as a whole, which is deprived of an uninhibited marketplace of ideas.". . .

The FEC has created a regime that allows it to select what political speech is safe for public consumption by applying ambiguous tests. If parties want to avoid litigation and the possibility of civil and criminal penalties, they must either refrain from speaking or ask the FEC to issue an advisory opinion approving of the political speech in question. Government officials pore over each word of a text to see if, in their judgment, it accords with the 11-factor test they have promulgated. This is an unprecedented governmental intervention into the realm of speech. The ongoing chill upon speech that is beyond all doubt protected makes it necessary in this case to invoke the earlier precedents that a statute which chills speech can and must be invalidated where its facial invalidity has been demonstrated. . . .

The law before us is an outright ban, backed by criminal sanctions. [It] makes it a felony for all corporations—including nonprofit advocacy corporations—either to expressly advocate the election or defeat of candidates or to broadcast electioneering communications within 30 days of a primary election and 60 days of a general election. Thus, the following acts would all be felonies under §441b: The Sierra Club runs an ad, within the crucial phase of 60 days before the general election, that exhorts the public to disapprove of a Congressman who favors logging in national forests; the National Rifle Association publishes a book urging the public to vote for the challenger because the incumbent U.S. Senator supports a handgun ban; and the American Civil Liberties Union creates a Web site telling the public to vote for a Presidential candidate in light of that candidate's defense of free speech. These prohibitions are classic examples of censorship. [It] is a ban on corporate speech notwithstanding the fact that a PAC created by a corporation can still speak. . . .

Section 441b's prohibition on corporate independent expenditures is thus a ban on speech. As a "restriction on the amount of money a person or group can spend on political communication during a campaign," that statute "necessarily reduces the quantity of expression by restricting the number of issues discussed, the depth of their exploration, and the size of the audience reached." Were the Court to uphold these restrictions, the Government could repress speech by silencing certain voices at any of the various points in the speech process. . . .

The right of citizens to inquire, to hear, to speak, and to use information to reach consensus is a precondition to enlightened self-government and a necessary means to protect it. The First Amendment "'has its fullest and most urgent application' to speech uttered during a campaign for political office." . . . For these reasons, political speech must prevail against laws that would suppress it, whether by design or inadvertence. Laws that burden political speech are "subject to strict scrutiny," which requires the Government to prove that the restriction "furthers a compelling interest and is narrowly tailored to achieve that interest." . . . By taking the right to speak from some and giving it to others, the Government deprives the disadvantaged person or class of the right to use speech to strive to establish worth, standing, and respect for the speaker's voice. The Government may not by these means deprive the public of the right and privilege to determine for itself what speech and speakers are worthy of consideration. . . .

The Court has upheld a narrow class of speech restrictions that operate to the disadvantage of certain persons, but these rulings were based on an interest in allowing governmental entities to perform their functions: . . . protect-

ing the "function of public school education"; furthering "the legitimate penological objectives of the corrections system," . . . ensuring "the capacity of the Government to discharge its [military] responsibilities." . . . The corporate independent expenditures at issue in this case, however, would not interfere with governmental functions, so these cases are inapposite. These precedents stand only for the proposition that there are certain governmental functions that cannot operate without some restrictions on particular kinds of speech. By contrast, it is inherent in the nature of the political process that voters must be free to obtain information from diverse sources in order to determine how to cast their votes. . . . We find no basis for the proposition that, in the context of political speech, the Government may impose restrictions on certain disfavored speakers. Both history and logic lead to this conclusion.

The Court has recognized that First Amendment protection extends to corporations. . . . This protection has been extended by explicit holdings to the context of political speech. . . . Corporations and other associations, like individuals, contribute to the discussion, debate, and the dissemination of information and ideas "that the First Amendment seeks to foster." . . . The Court has thus rejected the argument that political speech of corporations or other associations should be treated differently under the First Amendment simply because such associations are not "natural persons." . . .

At least since the latter part of the 19th century, the laws of some States and of the United States imposed a ban on corporate direct contributions to candidates. . . . Yet not until 1947 did Congress first prohibit independent expenditures by corporations and prohibit independent expenditures by corporations and labor unions. . . . In passing this Act Congress overrode the veto of President Truman, who warned that the expenditure ban was a "dangerous intrusion on free speech." . . .

If the First Amendment has any force, it prohibits Congress from fining or jailing citizens, or associations of citizens, for simply engaging in political speech. . . . Political speech is "indispensable to decisionmaking in a democracy, and this is no less true because the speech comes from a corporation rather than an individual."

It is irrelevant for purposes of the First Amendment that corporate funds may "have little or no correlation to the public's support for the corporation's political ideas." All speakers, including individuals and the media, use money amassed from the economic marketplace to fund their speech. The First Amendment protects the resulting speech, even if it was enabled by economic transactions with persons or entities who disagree with the speaker's ideas. . . .

There is no precedent supporting laws that attempt to distinguish between corporations which are deemed to be exempt as media corporations and those which are not. "We have consistently rejected the proposition that the institutional press has any constitutional privilege beyond that of other speakers." . . . Even assuming the most doubtful proposition that a news organization has a right to speak when others do not, the exemption would allow a conglomerate that owns both a media business and an unrelated business to influence or control the media in order to advance its overall business interest. At the same time, some other corporation, with an identical business interest but no media outlet in its ownership structure, would be forbidden to speak or inform the public about the same issue. This differential treatment cannot be squared with the First Amendment.

There is simply no support for the view that the First Amendment, as originally understood, would permit the suppression of political speech by media corporations. The Framers may not have anticipated modern business and media corporations. . . . Yet television networks and major newspapers owned by media corporations have become the most important means of mass communication in modern times. The First Amendment was certainly not understood to condone the suppression of political speech in society's most salient media. It was understood as a response to the repression of speech and the press that had existed in England and the heavy taxes on the press that were imposed in the colonies. . . . The great debates between the Federalists and the Anti-Federalists over our founding document were published and expressed in the most important means of mass communication of that era—newspapers owned by individuals. . . . At the founding, speech was open, comprehensive, and vital to society's definition of itself; there were no limits on the sources of speech and knowledge. . . .

Corporations, like individuals, do not have monolithic views. On certain topics corporations may possess valuable expertise, leaving them the best equipped to point out errors or fallacies in speech of all sorts, including the speech of candidates and elected officials. . . . The Government may not suppress political speech on the basis of the speaker's corporate identity. No sufficient governmental interest justifies limits on the political speech of nonprofit or for-profit corporations. . . .

The Framers may have been unaware of certain types of speakers or forms of communication, but that does not mean that those speakers and media are entitled to less First Amendment protection than those types of speakers and media that provided the means of communicating political ideas when the Bill of Rights was adopted. . . .

The purpose and effect of this law is to prevent corporations, including small and nonprofit corporations, from presenting both facts and opinions to the public. . . . When Government seeks to use its full power, including the criminal law, to command where a person may get his or her information or what distrusted source he or she may not hear, it uses censorship to control thought. This is unlawful. The First Amendment confirms the freedom to think for ourselves. . . .

The appearance of influence or access, furthermore, will not cause the electorate to lose faith in our democracy. By definition, an independent expenditure is political speech presented to the electorate that is not coordinated with a candidate. . . . The fact that a corporation, or any other speaker, is willing to spend money to try to persuade voters presupposes that the people have the ultimate influence over elected officials. . . . This is inconsistent with any suggestion that the electorate will refuse "'to take part in democratic governance'" because of additional political speech made by a corporation or any other speaker. . . .

When Congress finds that a problem exists, we must give that finding due deference; but Congress may not choose an unconstitutional remedy. If elected officials succumb to improper influences from independent expenditures; if they surrender their best judgment; and if they put expediency before principle, then surely there is cause for concern. We must give weight to attempts by Congress to seek to dispel either the appearance or the reality of these influences. The remedies enacted by law, however, must comply with the First Amendment; and, it is our law and our tradition that more speech, not less, is the governing rule. An outright ban on corporate political speech during the critical pre-election period is not a permissible remedy. . . .

Corporations, like individuals, do not have monolithic views. On certain topics corporations may possess valuable expertise, leaving them the best equipped to point out errors or fallacies in speech of all sorts, including the speech of candidates and elected officials. . . . The Government may not suppress political speech on the basis of the speaker's corporate identity. No sufficient governmental interest justifies limits on the political speech of nonprofit or for-profit corporations. . . .

When word concerning the plot of the movie *Mr. Smith Goes to Washington* reached the circles of Government, some officials sought, by persuasion, to discourage its distribution. . . . After all, it, like *Hillary*, was speech funded by a corporation that was critical of Members of Congress. *Mr. Smith Goes to Washington* may be fiction and caricature; but fiction and caricature can be a powerful force.

Modern day movies, television comedies, or skits on Youtube.com might portray public officials or public policies in unflattering ways. Yet if a covered transmission during the blackout period creates the background for candidate endorsement or opposition, a felony occurs solely because a corporation, other than an exempt media corporation, has made the "purchase, payment, distribution, loan, advance, deposit, or gift of money or anything of value" in order to engage in political speech. . . . Speech would be suppressed in the realm where its necessity is most evident: in the public dialogue preceding a real election. Governments are often hostile to speech, but under our law and our tradition it seems stranger than fiction for our Government to make this political speech a crime. Yet this is the statute's purpose and design.

Some members of the public might consider *Hillary* to be insightful and instructive; some might find it to be neither high art nor a fair discussion on how to set the Nation's course; still others simply might suspend judgment on these points but decide to think more about issues and candidates. Those choices and assessments, however, are not for the Government to make. "The First Amendment underwrites the freedom to experiment and to create in the realm of thought and speech. Citizens must be free to use new forms, and new forums, for the expression of ideas. The civic discourse belongs to the people, and the Government may not prescribe the means used to conduct it."

---

**ANTHONY KENNEDY** is an Associate Justice of the United States Supreme Court. He was appointed in 1988 by President Ronald Reagan.

John Paul Stevens

 **NO**

# Dissenting Opinion

The real issue in this case concerns how, not if, the appellant may finance its electioneering. Citizens United is a wealthy nonprofit corporation that runs a political action committee (PAC) with millions of dollars in assets. Under the Bipartisan Campaign Reform Act of 2002 (BCRA), it could have used those assets to televise and promote *Hillary: The Movie* wherever and whenever it wanted to. It also could have spent unrestricted sums to broadcast *Hillary* at any time other than the 30 days before the last primary election. Neither Citizens United's nor any other corporation's speech has been "banned." . . . All that the parties dispute is whether Citizens United had a right to use the funds in its general treasury to pay for broadcasts during the 30-day period. The notion that the First Amendment dictates an affirmative answer to that question is, in my judgment, profoundly misguided. Even more misguided is the notion that the Court must rewrite the law relating to campaign expenditures by for-profit corporations and unions to decide this case.

The basic premise underlying the Court's ruling is its iteration, and constant reiteration, of the proposition that the First Amendment bars regulatory distinctions based on a speaker's identity, including its "identity" as a corporation. While that glittering generality has rhetorical appeal, it is not a correct statement of the law. Nor does it tell us when a corporation may engage in electioneering that some of its shareholders oppose. It does not even resolve the specific question whether Citizens United may be required to finance some of its messages with the money in its PAC. The conceit that corporations must be treated identically to natural persons in the political sphere is not only inaccurate but also inadequate to justify the Court's disposition of this case.

In the context of election to public office, the distinction between corporate and human speakers is significant. Although they make enormous contributions to our society, corporations are not actually members of it. They cannot vote or run for office. Because they may be managed and controlled by nonresidents, their interests may conflict in fundamental respects with the interests of eligible voters. The financial resources, legal structure, and instrumental orientation of corporations raise legitimate concerns about their role in the electoral process. Our lawmakers have a compelling constitutional basis, if not also a democratic duty, to take measures designed to guard against the potentially deleterious effects of corporate

spending in local and national races. The majority's approach to corporate electioneering marks a dramatic break from our past. Congress has placed special limitations on campaign spending by corporations ever since the passage of the Tillman Act in 1907. . . .

S203's prohibition on certain uses of general treasury funds . . . applies in a viewpoint-neutral fashion to a narrow subset of advocacy messages about clearly identified candidates for federal office, made during discrete time periods through discrete channels. In the case at hand, all Citizens United needed to do to broadcast *Hillary* right before the primary was to abjure business contributions or use the funds in its PAC, which by its own account is "one of the most active PACs in America." . . .

The election context is distinctive in many ways, and the Court, of course, is right that the First Amendment closely guards political speech. But in this context, too, the authority of legislatures to enact viewpoint-neutral regulations based on content and identity is well settled. We have, for example, allowed state-run broadcasters to exclude independent candidates from televised debates. . . . We have upheld statutes that prohibit the distribution or display of campaign materials near a polling place. . . . Although we have not reviewed them directly, we have never cast doubt on laws that place special restrictions on campaign spending by foreign nationals. And we have consistently approved laws that bar Government employees, but not others, from contributing to or participating in political activities. These statutes burden the political expression of one class of speakers, namely, civil servants. Yet we have sustained them on the basis of longstanding practice and Congress' reasoned judgment that certain regulations which leave "untouched full participation . . . in political decisions at the ballot box," help ensure that public officials are "sufficiently free from improper influences," id., at 564, and that "confidence in the system of representative Government is not . . . eroded to a disastrous extent." . . .

The same logic applies to this case with additional force because it is the identity of corporations, rather than individuals, that the Legislature has taken into account. As we have unanimously observed, legislatures are entitled to decide "that the special characteristics of the corporate structure require particularly careful regulation" in an electoral context. NRWC, 459 U.S., at 209–210.50 Not only has the distinctive potential of corporations to corrupt the electoral process long been recognized, but within the area of campaign finance, corporate spending is also "furthest from the core of political expression, since corporations' First Amendment speech and association interests are derived largely from those of their members and of the public in receiving information." . . . Campaign finance distinctions based on corporate identity tend to be less worrisome, in other words, because the "speakers" are not natural persons, much less members of our political community, and the governmental interests are of the highest order. Furthermore, when corporations, as a class, are distinguished from noncorporations, as a class, there is a lesser risk that regulatory distinctions will reflect invidious discrimination or political favoritism.

If taken seriously, our colleagues' assumption that the identity of a speaker has no relevance to the Government's ability to regulate political speech would lead to some remarkable conclusions. Such an assumption would have accorded the propaganda broadcasts to our troops by "Tokyo Rose" during World War II the same protection as speech by Allied commanders. More pertinently, it would appear to afford the same protection to multinational corporations controlled by foreigners as to individual Americans. Under the majority's view, I suppose it may be a First Amendment problem that corporations are not permitted to vote, given that voting is, among other things, a form of speech. . . .

The Court invokes "ancient First Amendment principles," and original understandings . . . to defend today's ruling, yet it makes only a perfunctory attempt to ground its analysis in the principles or understandings of those who drafted and ratified the Amendment. Perhaps this is because there is not a scintilla of evidence to support the notion that anyone believed it would preclude regulatory distinctions based on the corporate form. To the extent that the Framers' views are discernible and relevant to the disposition of this case, they would appear to cut strongly against the majority's position.

This is not only because the Framers and their contemporaries conceived of speech more narrowly than we now think of it, . . . but also because they held very different views about the nature of the First Amendment right and the role of corporations in society. Those few corporations that existed at the founding were authorized by grant of a special legislative charter. . . .

The individualized charter mode of incorporation reflected the "cloud of disfavor under which corporations labored" in the early years of this Nation. . . . Thomas Jefferson famously fretted that corporations would subvert the Republic. General incorporation statutes, and widespread acceptance of business corporations as socially useful actors, did not emerge until the 1800's. . . .

The Framers thus took it as a given that corporations could be comprehensively regulated in the service of the public welfare. Unlike our colleagues, they had little trouble distinguishing corporations from human beings, and when they constitutionalized the right to free speech in the First Amendment, it was the free speech of individual

Americans that they had in mind. While individuals might join together to exercise their speech rights, business corporations, at least, were plainly not seen as facilitating such associational or expressive ends. Even "the notion that business corporations could invoke the First Amendment would probably have been quite a novelty," given that "at the time, the legitimacy of every corporate activity was thought to rest entirely in a concession of the sovereign.". . .

A century of more recent history puts to rest any notion that today's ruling is faithful to our First Amendment tradition. At the federal level, the express distinction between corporate and individual political spending on elections stretches back to 1907, when Congress passed the Tillman Act, . . . banning all corporate contributions to candidates. The Senate Report on the legislation observed that "[t]he evils of the use of [corporate] money in connection with political elections are so generally recognized that the committee deems it unnecessary to make any argument in favor of the general purpose of this measure. It is in the interest of good government and calculated to promote purity in the selection of public officials." . . . President Roosevelt, in his 1905 annual message to Congress, declared: "'All contributions by corporations to any political committee or for any political purpose should be forbidden by law; directors should not be permitted to use stockholders' money for such purposes; and, moreover, a prohibition of this kind would be, as far as it went, an effective method of stopping the evils aimed at in corrupt practices acts.'" . . .

[The Tillman Act] was primarily driven by two pressing concerns: first, the enormous power corporations had come to wield in federal elections, with the accompanying threat of both actual corruption and a public perception of corruption; and second, a respect for the interest of shareholders and members in preventing the use of their money to support candidates they opposed. . . .

Over the course of the past century Congress has demonstrated a recurrent need to regulate corporate participation in candidate elections to "'[p]reserv[e] the integrity of the electoral process, preven[t] corruption, . . . sustai[n] the active, alert responsibility of the individual citizen,'" government.'" . . . Time and again, we have recognized these realities in approving measures that Congress and the States have taken. . . .

On numerous occasions we have recognized Congress' legitimate interest in preventing the money that is spent on elections from exerting an "'undue influence on an officeholder's judgment'" and from creating "'the appearance of such influence,'" beyond the sphere of quid pro quo relationships. . . . Corruption can take many forms. Bribery may be the paradigm case. But the difference between selling a vote and selling access is a matter of degree, not kind. And selling access is not qualitatively different from giving special preference to those who spent money on one's behalf. Corruption operates along a spectrum, and the majority's apparent belief that quid pro quo arrangements can be neatly demarcated from other improper influences does not accord with the theory or reality of politics. . . .

Corporations, as a class, tend to be more attuned to the complexities of the legislative process and more directly affected by tax and appropriations measures that receive little public scrutiny; they also have vastly more money with which to try to buy access and votes. . . . Business corporations must engage the political process in instrumental terms if they are to maximize shareholder value. The unparalleled resources, professional lobbyists, and single-minded focus they bring to this effort, I believe, make quid pro quo corruption and its appearance inherently more likely when they (or their conduits or trade groups) spend unrestricted sums on elections.

It is with regret rather than satisfaction that I can now say that time has borne out my concerns. The legislative and judicial proceedings relating to BCRA generated a substantial body of evidence suggesting that, as corporations grew more and more adept at crafting "issue ads" to help or harm a particular candidate, these nominally independent expenditures began to corrupt the political process in a very direct sense. The sponsors of these ads were routinely granted special access after the campaign was over; "candidates and officials knew who their friends were." . . . Many corporate independent expenditures, it seemed, had become essentially interchangeable with direct contributions in their capacity to generate quid pro quo arrangements. In an age in which money and television ads are the coin of the campaign realm, it is hardly surprising that corporations deployed these ads to curry favor with, and to gain influence over, public officials.

The majority appears to think it decisive that the BCRA record does not contain "direct examples of votes being exchanged for . . . expenditures." It would have been quite remarkable if Congress had created a record detailing such behavior by its own Members. Proving that a specific vote was exchanged for a specific expenditure has always been next to impossible. . . .

Starting today, corporations with large war chests to deploy on electioneering may find democratically elected bodies becoming much more attuned to their interests. The majority both misreads the facts and draws the wrong conclusions when it suggests that the BCRA record provides "only scant evidence that independent expenditures . . . ingratiate," and that, "in any event," none of it matters. . . .

In America, incumbent legislators pass the laws that govern campaign finance, just like all other laws. To apply a level of scrutiny that effectively bars them from regulating electioneering whenever there is the faintest whiff of self-interest, is to deprive them of the ability to regulate electioneering. . . .

The fact that corporations are different from human beings might seem to need no elaboration, except that the majority opinion almost completely elides it. . . . Unlike natural persons, corporations have "limited liability" for their owners and managers, "perpetual life," separation of ownership and control, "and favorable treatment of the accumulation and distribution of assets . . . that enhance their ability to attract capital and to deploy their resources in ways that maximize the return on their shareholders' investments." . . . Unlike voters in U.S. elections, corporations may be foreign controlled. Unlike other interest groups, business corporations have been "effectively delegated responsibility for ensuring society's economic welfare"; they inescapably structure the life of every citizen. "'[T]he resources in the treasury of a business corporation,'" furthermore, "'are not an indication of popular support for the corporation's political ideas.'" . . . "'They reflect instead the economically motivated decisions of investors and customers. The availability of these resources may make a corporation a formidable political presence, even though the power of the corporation may be no reflection of the power of its ideas.'" . . .

It might also be added that corporations have no consciences, no beliefs, no feelings, no thoughts, no desires. Corporations help structure and facilitate the activities of human beings, to be sure, and their "personhood" often serves as a useful legal fiction. But they are not themselves members of "We the People" by whom and for whom our Constitution was established. . . .

It is an interesting question "who" is even speaking when a business corporation places an advertisement that endorses or attacks a particular candidate. Presumably it is not the customers or employees, who typically have no say in such matters. It cannot realistically be said to be the shareholders, who tend to be far removed from the day-to-day decisions of the firm and whose political preferences may be opaque to management. Perhaps the officers or directors of the corporation have the best claim to be the ones speaking, except their fiduciary duties generally prohibit them from using corporate funds for personal ends. Some individuals associated with the corporation must make the decision to place the ad, but the idea that these individuals are thereby fostering their self-expression or cultivating their critical faculties is fanciful. It is entirely possible that the corporation's electoral message will conflict with their personal convictions. Take away the ability to use general treasury funds for some of those ads, and no one's autonomy, dignity, or political equality has been impinged upon in the least. . . .

The marketplace of ideas is not actually a place where items—or laws— are meant to be bought and sold, and when we move from the realm of economics to the realm of corporate electioneering, there may be no "reason to think the market ordering is intrinsically good at all." . . .

The Court's blinkered and aphoristic approach to the First Amendment may well promote corporate power at the cost of the individual and collective self-expression the Amendment was meant to serve. It will undoubtedly cripple the ability of ordinary citizens, Congress, and the States to adopt even limited measures to protect against corporate domination of the electoral process. Americans may be forgiven if they do not feel the Court has advanced the cause of self-government today. . . .

When corporations use general treasury funds to praise or attack a particular candidate for office, it is the shareholders, as the residual claimants, who are effectively footing the bill. Those shareholders who disagree with the corporation's electoral message may find their financial investments being used to undermine their political convictions. The PAC mechanism, by contrast, helps assure that those who pay for an electioneering communication actually support its content and that managers do not use general treasuries to advance personal agendas. . . .

Today's decision is backwards in many senses. It elevates the majority's agenda over the litigants' submissions, facial attacks over as-applied claims, broad constitutional theories over narrow statutory grounds, individual dissenting opinions over precedential holdings, assertion over tradition, absolutism over empiricism, rhetoric over reality. . . . Their conclusion that the societal interest in avoiding corruption and the appearance of corruption does not provide an adequate justification for regulating corporate expenditures on candidate elections relies on an incorrect description of that interest, along with a failure to acknowledge the relevance of established facts and the considered judgments of state and federal legislatures over many decades.

In a democratic society, the longstanding consensus on the need to limit corporate campaign spending should outweigh the wooden application of judge-made rules. The majority's rejection of this principle "elevate[s] corporations to a level of deference which has not been seen at least since the days when substantive due process was regularly used to invalidate regulatory legislation thought to unfairly impinge upon established economic interests." . . . At bottom, the Court's opinion is thus a rejection of the common sense of the American people, who have recognized a need to prevent corporations from undermining self-government since the founding, and who have fought against the distinctive corrupting potential of corporate electioneering since the days of Theodore Roosevelt. It is a strange time to repudiate that common sense. While American democracy is imperfect, few outside the majority of this Court would have thought its flaws included a dearth of corporate money in politics.

---

**JOHN PAUL STEVENS** was an Associate Justice of the United States Supreme Court. He was appointed in 1975 by President Gerald Ford and served until his retirement in 2010.

# EXPLORING THE ISSUE

## Do Corporations Have the Same Free Speech Rights as Persons?

## Critical Thinking and Reflection

1. How does the Supreme Court distinguish between campaign contributions and campaign expenditures?
2. What would be the likely constitutional and political consequences of public financing of national elections?
3. Should corporations possess the constitutional rights of persons? Why or why not?
4. Should all contributions to candidates and office-holders be made public? Why or why not?
5. How does the Supreme Court distinguish between public and private financing of election campaigns?

## Is There Common Ground?

If the long-standing division on the U.S. Supreme Court is a guide, the answer must be that there is little or no common ground on the question of the constitutional rights of corporations, and specifically on the question of whether they enjoy an uninhibited First Amendment right to free speech in American elections. The five jurists who have rendered the decisions discussed here are Chief Justice John Roberts and Justices Antonin Scalia, Anthony Kennedy, Clarence Thomas, and Samuel Alito. The four Justices who have dissented in the most recent cases are Justices Ruth Bader Ginsburg, Stephen Breyer, Sonia Soto-mayor, and Elena Kagan (who succeeded Justice John Paul Stevens, who retired in 2010). Similarly, sharp and seemingly irreconcilable divisions have existed on the Supreme Court in the past, sometimes broken by a shift in sentiment by a member of the Court, but more often by a change in the Court's composition.

The conduct of elections since *Citizens United* is likely to provoke more congressional consideration of election reform, and it may be influenced by public reaction to what is likely to be greater amounts of money being spent on behalf of candidates by the new Super PACs. Public reaction to the anticipated increase in political advertising is likely to influence future congressional action on the length and financing of national election campaigns.

As a case, *Citizens United* will be back under the microscope when the Supreme Court sits to determine whether corporations should have the ability to express religious freedom in the same way an individual does. Based on the outcome of that case—which pits Hobby Lobby against provisions of the Affordable Care Act—the public may begin to more directly question the long-term legal and societal impacts of allowing corporations the same rights and responsibilities of individuals. What would be next on the slippery slope? Corporations having the right to vote?

## Create Central

www.mhhe.com/createcentral

## Additional Resources

Jeffrey D. Clements, *Corporations Are Not People: Why They Have More Rights Than You Do and What You Can Do About It* (Berrett-Koehler, 2012)

Thomas Hartmann, *Unequal Protection: The Rise of Corporate Dominance and the Theft of Human Rights* (Rodale Books, 2004)

David C. Korten, *When Corporations Rule the World* (Berrett-Koehler, 2001)

Monica Youn, *Money, Politics, and the Constitution* (The Century Foundation, 2011)

David A. Westbrook, *Between Citizen and State: An Introduction to the Corporation* (Paradigm Publishers, 2008)

# *Internet References . . .*

**Citizens United**

www.citizensunited.org/

**Federal Election Commission**

www.fec.gov/disclosure.shtml

**OpenSecrets**

www.opensecrets.org

**The Campaign Finance Institute**

www.cfinst.org/

**Top All-Time Donors, 1989–2012**

www.opensecrets.org/orgs/list.php

Selected, Edited, and with Issue Framing Material by:
William J. Miller, *Flagler College*
George McKenna, *City College, City University of New York*
**and**
Stanley Feingold, *City College, City University of New York*

# ISSUE

# Should "Recreational" Drugs Be Legalized?

YES: **Bryan Stevenson**, from "Drug Policy, Criminal Justice, and Mass Imprisonment," paper presented to the Global Commission on Drug Policies (January 2011)

NO: **Charles D. Stimson**, from "Legalizing Marijuana: Why Citizens Should Just Say No," *Heritage Foundation Legal Memorandum* (September 13, 2010)

---

## Learning Outcomes

**After reading this issue, you will be able to:**

- Identify different interpretations of what should be classified as recreational drugs.
- Explain how individual choices can impact public well-being.
- Discuss the potential long-term health effects of drug usage.
- Explain why some argue that using certain drugs is not risky behavior.
- Identify the possible impacts to law enforcement of legalizing or not legalizing recreational drugs.

---

### ISSUE SUMMARY

**YES:** Law professor Bryan Stevenson focuses on how the criminalization of drugs has led to mass imprisonment with negative consequences for law enforcement.

**NO:** Charles D. Stimson, former Deputy Assistant Secretary of Defense, explains that marijuana is not safe and makes more sense than the prohibition of alcohol did in the early 1900s. Further, he demonstrates that the economic benefits would not outweigh the societal costs.

**P**rohibition is a word Americans associate with the prohibition of liquor, which was adopted as a national policy with the ratification of the Eighteenth Amendment to the U.S. Constitution in 1920 and repealed with the adoption of the Twenty-first Amendment in 1933. Many states had earlier banned whiskey and other intoxicating beverages, and some states have had various restrictions since repeal.

Similarly, certain categories of illicit drugs were banned in some states prior to the passage of the Controlled Substance Act in 1970, which made the prohibition a national policy. Unlike the Prohibition Amendment, this was achieved by an Act of Congress. Many claimed then, and many still do today, that to do this in the absence of a constitutional amendment exceeds the power of the national government. Nevertheless, it has been upheld by the federal courts and has continued to function for more than four decades.

The principal substances that are banned include opium, heroin, cocaine, and marijuana. Marijuana is also known as cannabis (the plant from which it is obtained) and by a variety of informal names, most familiarly "pot." Its use dates back several thousand years, sometimes for religious or medical purposes. However, it is a so-called recreational drug that a United Nations committee characterized as "the most widely used illicit substance in the world." Because opium, heroin, and cocaine are more powerful, more addictive, and less prevalent, advocates of legalization often restrict their appeal to removing the ban on marijuana.

In the 50 years following an international convention in 1912 that urged the restriction of dangerous drugs, the use in the United States of illicit drugs other than marijuana was consistently below 1/2 of 1 percent of the population, with cocaine rising somewhat in the counter culture climate that began in the late 1950s. Illicit drug use was widely promoted as mind-expanding and relatively harmless. It is estimated that its use peaked in the 1970s. Present estimates for drugs other than marijuana suggest that between 5 and 10 percent of the population at least occasionally engages in the use of some illicit drugs.

In 2006, there were approximately 1.9 million drug arrests in the United States. Of these, 829,625 (44 percent of the total) were marijuana arrests. During the past two decades, the price of marijuana has gone down, its potency has increased, and it has become more readily available. Further, it has begun being mixed with other substances, increasing the potential for unintended side effects.

Studies, principally conducted in Sweden, Holland, and other nations with more tolerant drug policies, conclude that social factors influence drug use. Apart from peer pressure, particularly in the use of marijuana, hard drugs generally become more common in times of higher unemployment and lower income. Apart from cannabis, which is easily grown, the illicit character of hard drugs makes them expensive, but the profit motive induces growers, distributors, and "pushers" to risk arrest and punishment. It has been estimated that as many as one-sixth of all persons in federal prisons have been convicted of selling, possessing, or using marijuana.

The movement to legalize these drugs, often with a focus on marijuana, has existed as long as their prohibition, but in recent years has won recruits from both liberal and conservative ranks. As with the prohibition of alcohol, experience with the unintended consequences of prohibition of drugs led some to wonder whether this has not only failed to eliminate their use but has increased public health problems. Under the Prohibition Amendment, people drank unlicensed alcohol, often adulterated by the addition of poisonous substances. Illicit drug prohibition has led to the sale of toxic ingredients added to the drugs resulting in more impure and more dangerous products. Drug users injecting the drugs employ dirty reused needles that spread HIV and hepatitis B and C. While illicit drug use has never rivaled the widespread public acceptance of alcohol, their use has been extensive enough to spawn new networks of organized crime, violence related to the drug market, and the corruption of law enforcement and governments. We have recently witnessed this in the drug gang wars in Mexico that have slipped over into the American southwest.

Milton Friedman, who was America's most influential conservative economist, reached the interesting conclusion that drug prohibition has led to the rise of drug cartels. His reasoning was that only major retailers can handle massive shipments, own aircraft fleets, have armed troops, and employ lawyers and methods of eluding and bribing the police. Consequently, law enforcement as well as competition drives out smaller, less ruthless, and less efficient drug dealers.

The economic cost of legislating and attempting to enforce drug prohibition is very high. When the national policy went to effect, the federal cost was $350 million in 1971. Thirty-five years later in 2006, the cost was $30 billion. To this should be added the revenue that could be obtained if marijuana were subject to taxation. If it were taxed at the same rate as alcohol or tobacco, it has been estimated that it would yield as much as $7.7 billion. It may be, as advocates of legalization suggest, that the financial costs exceed the damages that the drugs themselves cause.

Against these arguments for repeal, those who support the war on drugs claim that prohibitive drug laws suppress drug use. Compare the large majority of Americans who consume legal alcohol with the very much smaller proportion who use illicit drugs. The Drug Enforcement Administration (DEA) has demonstrated that people under the influence of drugs are more than six times more likely to commit homicides than people looking for money to buy drugs. Drug use changes behavior and causes criminal activity. Cocaine-related paranoia frequently results in assaults, drugged driving, and domestic violence. These crimes are likely to increase when drugs are more readily available.

The point that liberalization advocates miss is that the illicit drugs are inherently harmful. In the short term, illicit drugs cause memory loss, distorted perception, a decline of motor skills, and an increased heart rate and anxiety. Particularly for young people, drug use produces a decline in mental development and motivation, as well as a reduced ability to concentrate in school.

The United States Centers for Disease Control and Prevention has concluded that although there are more than seven times more Americans who use alcohol than drugs, during a single year alone (2000), there were almost as many drug-induced deaths (15,8520) as alcohol-induced (18, 539). The DEA concludes that drugs are "far more deadly than alcohol." This is true even for marijuana, which is deemed more potent than it was a generation ago. It contains more than 400 chemicals (the toxicity of some is clear and of many others is unknown) and one marijuana cigarette deposits four times more tar than a filtered tobacco cigarette.

The widespread support for medicinal marijuana seems to be changing public attitudes toward potential legalization. Colorado and Washington voters have sent a message that their respective states will exercise their rights under the Constitution legalizing the recreational use of marijuana. This process began with the legalization of medical marijuana in over a dozen states, opening the doors of debate with regards to the benefits of marijuana and dispelling some misconceptions. Party support has increased across the board. Republican support increased from 33 percent to 35 percent between November 2012 and October 2013, with Democratic changes increases from 61 percent to 65 percent and Independents from 50 percent to 62 percent within the same time period respectively. While marijuana is still illegal at the federal level, the Obama administration has made it clear that they will not go after users in states that choose to legalize. A memo sent from Attorney General Eric Holder to all U.S. attorneys informs them the federal government will not intervene with state laws as long as the states follow certain protocols and guidelines in regulating product. Perhaps the tides are actually changing.

In the following selections, Bryan Stevenson, Executive Director of the Equal Justice Initiative, focuses on how the criminalization of drugs has led to mass imprisonment with negative consequences for law enforcement. Charles D. Stimson argues, on the other hand, that marijuana is by no means the safe drug some make it out to be and that the economic benefits of legalization will not be able to surmount the societal costs.

# YES ⤶

**Bryan Stevenson**

# Drug Policy, Criminal Justice, and Mass Imprisonment

The last three decades have witnessed a global increase in the criminalization of improper drug use. Criminalization has resulted in increased use of harsh punitive sanctions imposed on drug offenders and dramatic increases in rates of incarceration. These policies have had limited impact on eliminating or reducing illegal drug use and may have resulted in adverse consequences for social and community health. The criminal justice system has proved to be an ineffective forum for managing or controlling many aspects of the drug trade or the problem of illegal drug usage. In recent years, some progress has been reported when governing bodies have managed drug use and addiction as a public health problem which requires treatment, counseling and medical interventions rather than incarceration. Primarily as a result of drug policy, the number of people currently incarcerated worldwide is at an all time high of ten million.

In the United States, the prison population has increased from 300,000 in 1972 to 2.3 million people today. One in 31 adults in the United States is in jail, prison, on probation or parole. The American government currently spends over 68 billion dollars a year on incarceration. Drug Policy and the incarceration of low-level drug offenders is the primary cause of mass incarceration in the United States. [Forty percent] of drug arrests are for simple possession of marijuana. There is also evidence that drug enforcement has diverted resources from law enforcement of violent crimes and other threats to public safety.

Incarceration of low-level drug offenders has criminogenic effects that increase the likelihood of recidivism and additional criminal behavior. Enforcement of drug policy against low-level users and small scale trafficking has been racially biased and fueled social and political antagonisms that have undermined support of drug policy.

Growing evidence indicates that drug treatment and counseling programs are far more effective in reducing drug addiction and abuse than is incarceration. Needle exchange, compulsory treatment, education, counseling, drug substitutes like Methadone or Naxolene have proved highly effective in reducing addiction, overdose and the spread of HIV and Hepatitis C.

The last three decades have witnessed a global increase in the criminalization of improper drug use. Criminalization has resulted in increased use of harsh punitive sanctions imposed on drug offenders and dramatic increases in rates of incarceration. These policies have had limited impact on eliminating or reducing illegal drug use and may have resulted in adverse consequences for social and community health. The criminal justice system has proved to be an ineffective forum for managing or controlling many aspects of the drug trade or the problem of illegal drug usage. In recent years, some progress has been reported when governing bodies have managed drug use and addiction as a public health problem which requires treatment, counseling and medical interventions rather than incarceration. Most experts agree that drug-related HIV infection, the spread of infectious diseases like Hepatitis C and related public health concerns cannot be meaningfully addressed through jail and imprisonment and are often aggravated by policies which are primarily punitive. This paper briefly reviews this issue and identifies some of the costs of over-reliance on incarceration and outlines new strategies.

## Criminal Justice Policy and Increased Use of Sanctions and Incarceration for Low-Level Drug Offenders

### The Criminalization of Drugs and the Legacy of Mass Imprisonment

Criminalization of possession and illegal use of drugs compounded by mandatory sentencing and lengthy prison sanctions for low-level drug use has become the primary cause of mass incarceration. The global prison population has skyrocketed in the last three decades with ten million people worldwide now in jails and prisons. The extraordinary increase in the number of people now incarcerated has had tremendous implications for state and national governments dealing with global recession and a range of economic, social and political challenges. Research indicates that resources that would otherwise be spent on development, infrastructure, education and health care have been redirected over the last two decades to incarcerating drug offenders, many of whom are low-level users. The trend toward mass incarceration has been especially troubling in the United States. In the last thirty-five years, the number of U.S. residents in prison has increased from 330,000 people in jails and prisons in 1972 to almost 2.3 million imprisoned people today. The United States now has the highest rate of incarceration in the world.

Over five million people are on probation and parole in America. Currently, one out of 100 adults is in jail or prison and one out of 31 adults is in jail, prison on probation or parole. The consequences of increased incarceration and penal control strategies have been dramatic and costly. Many states spend in excess of $50,000 a year to incarcerate each prisoner in a state prison or facility, including non-violent, low-level drug offenders. Corrections spending by state and federal governments has risen from $6.9 billion in 1980 to $68 billion in 2006 in America. During the ten year period between 1985 and 1995, prisons were constructed at a pace of one new prison opening each week.

The economic toll of expansive imprisonment policies has been accompanied by socio-political consequences as well. Mass incarceration has had discernible impacts in poor and minority communities which have been disproportionately impacted by drug enforcement strategies. Collateral consequences of drug prosecutions of low-level offenders have included felon disenfranchisement laws, where in some states drug offenders permanently lose the right to vote. Sociologists have also recently observed that the widespread incarceration of men in low-income communities has had a profound negative impact on social and cultural norms relating to family and opportunity. Increases in the imprisonment of poor and minority women with children have now been linked with rising numbers of displaced children and dependents. Drug policy and the over-reliance on incarceration is seen by many experts as contributing to increased rates of chronic unemployment, destabilization of families and increased risk of reincarceration for the formerly incarcerated.

There are unquestionably serious consequences for community and public health when illegal use of drugs is widespread. Addiction and other behavioral issues triggered by drug abuse have well known consequences for individuals, families, communities and governing bodies trying to protect public safety. Governing bodies are clearly justified in pursuing policies and strategies that disrupt the drug trade and the violence frequently associated with high-level drug trafficking. Similarly, drug abuse is a serious problem within communities that threatens public health and merits serious attention. However, some interventions to address drug abuse are now emerging as clearly more effective than others. Consequently, interventions that reduce drug dependence and improve the prospects for eliminating drug addiction and abuse are essential if measurable improvements on this issue are to be achieved in the coming years.

## Drug Policy and the Criminal Justice System

Many countries have employed the rhetoric of war to combat the drug trade. While there are countries where violent drug kingpens have created large militias that have necessitated more militarized responses from law enforcement, most drug arrests are directed at low-level users who have been the primary targets in the "war on drugs." States have criminalized simple possession of drugs like marijuana and imposed harsh and lengthy sentences on people arrested. Small amounts of narcotics, unauthorized prescription medicines and other drugs have triggered trafficking charges that impose even lengthier prison sentences. The introduction of habitual felony offender laws has exacerbated drug policy as it is not uncommon for illegal drug users to accumulate multiple charges in a very short period of time. Under the notorious "three strikes laws" that have become popular in America, drug offenders with no history of violence may face mandatory minimum sentences in excess of 25 years in prison. Thousands of low-level drug offenders have been sentenced to life imprisonment with no chance of parole as a result of these sentencing laws.

In the United States, drug arrests have tripled in the last 25 years, however most of these arrests have been for simple possession of low-level drugs. In 2005, nearly 43% of all drug arrests were for marijuana offenses. Marijuana possession arrests accounted for 79% of the growth in drug arrests in the 1990s. Nearly a half million people are in state or federal prisons or a local jail for a drug offense, compared to 41,000 in 1980. Most of these people have no history of violence or high-level drug selling activity.

The "war on drugs" has also generated indirect costs that many researchers contend have undermined public safety. The federal government has prioritized spending and grants for drug task forces and widespread drug interdiction efforts that often target low-level drug dealing. These highly organized and coordinated efforts have been very labor intensive for local law enforcement agencies with some unanticipated consequences for investigation of other crimes. The focus on drugs is believed to have redirected law enforcement resources that have resulted in more drunk driving, and decreased investigation and enforcement of violent crime laws. In Illinois, a 47% increase in drug arrests corresponded with a 22% decrease in arrests for drunk driving. Florida researchers have similarly linked the focus on low level drug arrests with an increase in the serious crime index.

In prison, as a result of the increased costs of incarceration, most drug addicts are less likely to receive drug treatment and therapy. The increasing costs of mass imprisonment have eliminated funds for treatment and counseling services even though some of these services have proved to be very effective. In 1991, one in three prison inmates was receiving treatment while incarcerated, today the rate is down to one in seven. The decline of treatment and counseling services makes re-offending once released much more likely. This is one of the ways in which incarceration and criminal justice intervention has proved costly and less effective than other models of managing illegal drug use.

## Racially Discriminatory Enforcement of Drug Laws

In the United States, considerable evidence demonstrates that enforcement of drug policy has proved to be racially discriminatory and very biased against the poor. America's criminal justice system is very wealth sensitive which makes it difficult for low-income residents to obtain equally favorable outcomes as more wealthy residents when they are charged with drug crimes. Targeting communities of color for enforcement of drug laws has added to the problems of racial bias in American society and generated some of the fiercest debates about the continuing legacy of racial discrimination. Illegal use of drugs is not unique to communities of color and rates of offending are not higher in these communities than they are in non-minority communities. African Americans comprise 14% of regular drug users in the United States, yet are 37% of those arrested for drug offenses and 56% of those incarcerated for drug crimes. Black people in the United States serve almost as much time in federal prison for a drug offense (58.7 months) as whites serve for a violent crime (61.7 months), primarily as a result of the racially disparate sentencing laws such as the 100-1 crack powder cocaine disparity. For years, the sentences for illegal possession or use of crack cocaine, which is more prevalent in communities of color, were 100 times greater than possession or use of equivalent amounts of powder cocaine, leading to dramatically longer prison sentences for African Americans. In 2010, Congress amended this law and reduced the disparity from 100-1 to 12-1. However, the failure to make the law retroactive has left the costly and troubling racial disparities uncorrected. Hispanic people are also disproportionately at much greater risk of arrest and prosecution for drug crimes than are whites in the United States.

Discriminatory enforcement of drug laws against communities of color has seriously undermined the integrity of drug policy initiatives and frequently these policies are perceived as unfair, unjust and targeted at racial minorities. Enforcement of drug laws tends to be directed at low-income communities or residential and social centers where residents have less political power to resist aggressive policing and engagement. Even some reforms aimed at shielding low-level drug offenders from incarceration have been skewed against the poor and people of color. Some data show that people of color are more likely to be redirected back to the criminal courts if drug court personnel have discretion. Similarly, many community-based programs that permit drug offenders to avoid jail or prison have significant admission fees and costs that many poor people simply cannot afford. Discriminatory enforcement of drug policy has undermined its effectiveness and

legitimacy and contributed to continuing dysfunction in the administration of criminal justice.

## There Is Growing Evidence that Drug Treatment Is More Cost Effective than Incarceration and Incapacitation Strategies

One of the clear consequences of mass incarceration directed at low level drug offenders has been to acculturate and socialize illegal drug users into criminality through extended incarceration. This criminogenic effect has been seen in studies that examined rates of recidivism among drug offenders who are given probation and not sent to jail or prison and drug offenders who are incarcerated for the same offenses. In purely human terms, these findings reveal that incarceration may be dramatically more costly than other approaches.

However, the economic analysis of approaches to low level drug offending that avoid incarceration are even more compelling. Whatever the measure, data indicates that drug treatment is more cost effective than incarceration. In California, a study has recently shown that spending on drug treatment is eight times more likely to reduce drug consumption than spending on incarceration. Corresponding decreases in drug-related crime were also documented when comparing drug treatment programs with incarceration. In a RAND analysis study, treatment was estimated to reduce crime associated with drug use and the drug trade up to 15 times as much as incarceration. These findings have been reflected in other studies that have also found that drug treatment is more cost effective in controlling drug abuse and crime than continued expansion of the prison system when looking at low level drug offenders.

Consequently, many states have now started to shift their management of drug offenders to drug courts that have discretion to redirect people who illegally use drugs away from jail or prison and into community-based treatment, counseling and therapeutic interventions. The early signs suggest that these innovations are saving states millions of dollars and accomplishing improved public safety. For the first time in 38 years, 2010 saw a slight decrease in the national state prison population in the United States. Significant reductions will need to continue to deal with a global recession and decreasing resources available for incarceration.

## New and More Effective Strategies for Managing Low-Level Drug Offenders Are Emerging

Proponents of "Harm Reduction" have long argued that a more effective way to combat illegal drug use is to spend more on public education, treatment and interventions that view illegal drug use as a public health problem rather than continued spending on incarceration and harsh sanctions. Supporters of harm reduction acknowledge that the use of incarceration and sanctions will be necessary when illegal drug trafficking or distribution threatens public safety, however, they contend that most drug arrests don't directly implicate public safety. States are beginning to recognize the benefits associated with harm reduction and in recent years have begun to reallocate resources with surprisingly good outcomes.

## Sentencing Reform

In recent years, states have begun to retreat from mandatory sentences and other harsh strategies for enforcing drug laws and moved to alternative models that involve probation, treatment, counseling and education. Between 2004 and 2006, at least 13 states expanded drug treatment or programs which divert drug offenders away from jail or prison into community-based programs. States like Michigan have recently amended statutes that required a mandatory sentence of life imprisonment without parole for distribution of cocaine or heroin. With over 5 million people on probation or parole in the United States, drug use on parole or probation has become the primary basis by which thousands of people are returned to prison. These technical violations of parole or probation account for as many as 40% of new prison admissions in some jurisdictions. In recent years, states have restricted the length of incarceration imposed when formerly incarcerated people test positive for recent drug use. These new statues . . . incarcerated drug users into drug therapy and counseling programs.

The federal government has amended mandatory sentencing laws for drug offenders and seen a dramatic reduction in the number of people facing long-term incarceration for low-level drug use. These sentencing reforms are considered critical to containing the costs of mass imprisonment in the United States and for generating resources necessary to approach drug addiction and abuse as a public health problem.

Drug courts have also emerged in the last decade to play a critical role in redirecting low-level drug offenders away from traditional, punitive models of intervention for illegal drug use. Drug courts have been set up in hundreds of communities. Court personnel have discretion to order drug treatment and community-based programs where offenders must receive counseling and treatment and receive education concerning drug addiction and abuse. By shielding thousands of drug offenders from incarceration and transfer to overcrowded prisons, drug courts have reduced the collateral consequences of illegal drug use, saved millions of dollars and had more favorable outcomes for people who have been identified as illegally using drugs. Drug court participants can avoid a criminal record and all the disabling collateral consequences associated with a criminal record.

Reducing the penalties for some low-level drug crimes, giving judges more discretion to avoid unwarranted

and lengthy mandatory sentences and retreating from the rhetoric of war and unscientific policy analysis could substantially reduce incarceration rates and provide additional resources for treatment options that are more effective at eliminating drug abuse.

## Medical and Public Health Models for Drug Abuse Intervention

The risk of criminal prosecution has had many unintended consequences, especially for people with addiction problems who also have critical medical issues that require treatment and intervention. HIV infection and AIDS continue to threaten many countries with tragic and devastating effect. Intravenous drug users are primary targets for infection and have extremely elevated risks of illness from sharing needles. Rather than facilitating less hazardous practices for this community, criminal justice interventions have forced people with addiction underground and infection rates have spiraled. Providing clean needles and other strategies associated with needle exchange have had a significant impact on reducing the rate of HIV infection and offering people with addiction issues an opportunity for treatment. Creating safe zones where people struggling with drug addiction can safely come has also greatly increased the ability of public health officials to provide education, counseling and treatment opportunities that are scientifically proven to be effective to the population with the greatest needs. For example, where needle-exchange has been implemented, the results have been extremely promising for controlling illegal drug use and reducing public health threats.

Policies that make it permissible for people to safely admit to drug addiction problems are well established to be more effective at managing drug addiction. In 2006, there were 26,000 deaths in the United States from accidental drug overdose, the highest level ever recorded by the Centers for Disease Control. Accidental death through overdose is currently the leading cause of injury-related death for people between the ages of 35–54. This extraordinarily high level of death through overdose can only be meaningfully confronted with public education efforts and improving treatment options for people who are abusing drugs.

Criminalization has created huge and complex obstacles for people motivated to eliminate their drug dependence to seek or obtain necessary health care and support. When public health options are made available, studies have reported dramatic declines in drug dependence, mortality and overdose. Medical developments have proved extremely effective in reducing drug dependence and addiction. A range of maintenance therapies are available for people with addiction problems. Methadone maintenance has been cited as the primary intervention strategy for people with heroin addiction. Drugs like Naloxone have been utilized in an extremely effective manner to save lives when people ingest too many opiates. However, these very cost effective treatments are not possible without providing safe opportunities to report drug and overdose issues to health care providers who are free to treat rather than arrest people with addiction and drug dependence.

Mass imprisonment, the high economic and social costs of incarcerating low-level drug offenders and the ineffectiveness of criminalization and punitive approaches to drug addiction have had poor outcomes in many countries. Governing bodies have available dozens of new, scientifically tested interventions which have been proved to lower rates of drug abuse and addiction without incar-ceration. Reducing illegal drug use and disrupting the sometimes violent drug trade will require new and more effective strategies in the 21st century. The politics of fear and anger that have generated many of these policies must be resisted and adoption of scientifically established treatment protocols that have been found effective and successful should be pursued vigorously.

**BRYAN STEVENSON** is a faculty member of the New York University School of Law and executive director of the Equal Justice Initiative, an organization that focuses on criminal justice reform.

**Charles D. Stimson**

 **NO**

# Legalizing Marijuana: Why Citizens Should Just Say No

The scientific literature is clear that marijuana is addictive and that its use significantly impairs bodily and mental functions. Marijuana use is associated with memory loss, cancer, immune system deficiencies, heart disease, and birth defects, among other conditions. Even where decriminalized, marijuana trafficking remains a source of violence, crime, and social disintegration.

Nonetheless, this November, California voters will consider a ballot initiative, the Regulate, Control and Tax Cannabis Act of 2010 (RCTCA), that would legalize most marijuana distribution and use under state law. (These activities would remain federal crimes.) This vote is the culmination of an organized campaign by pro-marijuana activists stretching back decades.

The current campaign, like previous efforts, downplays the well-documented harms of marijuana trafficking and use while promising benefits ranging from reduced crime to additional tax revenue. In particular, supporters of the initiative make five bold claims:

1. "Marijuana is safe and non-addictive."
2. "Marijuana prohibition makes no more sense than alcohol prohibition did in the early 1900s."
3. "The government's efforts to combat illegal drugs have been a total failure."
4. "The money spent on government efforts to combat the illegal drug trade can be better spent on substance abuse and treatment for the allegedly few marijuana users who abuse the drug."
5. "Tax revenue collected from marijuana sales would substantially outweigh the social costs of legalization."

As this paper details, all five claims are demonstrably false or, based on the best evidence, highly dubious.

Further, supporters of the initiative simply ignore the mechanics of decriminalization—that is, how it would directly affect law enforcement, crime, and communities. Among the important questions left unanswered are:

- How would the state law fit into a federal regime that prohibits marijuana production, distribution, and possession?
- Would decriminalization, especially if combined with taxation, expand market opportunities for

the gangs and cartels that currently dominate drug distribution?
- Would existing zoning laws prohibit marijuana cultivation in residential neighborhoods, and if not, what measures would growers have to undertake to keep children from the plants?
- Would transportation providers be prohibited from firing bus drivers because they smoke marijuana?

No one knows the specifics of how marijuana decriminalization would work in practice or what measures would be necessary to prevent children, teenagers, criminals, and addicts from obtaining the drug.

The federal government shares these concerns. Gil Kerlikowske, Director of the White House Office of National Drug Control Policy (ONDCP), recently stated, "Marijuana legalization, for any purpose, is a non-starter in the Obama Administration." The Administration— widely viewed as more liberal than any other in recent memory and, for a time, as embodying the hopes of pro-legalization activists—has weighed the costs and benefits and concluded that marijuana legalization would compromise public health and safety.

California's voters, if they take a fair-minded look at the evidence and the practical problems of legalization, should reach the same conclusion: Marijuana is a dangerous substance that should remain illegal under state law.

## The Initiative

The RCTCA's purpose, as defined by advocates of legalization, is to regulate marijuana just as the government regulates alcohol. The law would allow anyone 21 years of age or older to possess, process, share, or transport up to one full ounce of marijuana "for personal consumption." Individuals could possess an unlimited number of living and harvested marijuana plants on the premises where they were grown. Individual landowners or lawful occupants of private property could cultivate marijuana plants "for personal consumption" in an area of not more than 25 square feet per private residence or parcel.

The RCTCA would legalize drug-related paraphernalia and tools and would license establishments for on-site smoking and other consumption of marijuana. Supporters have included some alcohol-like restrictions against, for example, smoking marijuana while operating a vehicle. Finally, the act authorizes the imposition and collection of taxes and fees associated with legalization of marijuana.

## Unsafe in Any Amount: How Marijuana Is Not Like Alcohol

Marijuana advocates have had some success peddling the notion that marijuana is a "soft" drug, similar to alcohol, and fundamentally different from "hard" drugs like cocaine or heroin. It is true that marijuana is not the most dangerous of the commonly abused drugs, but that is not to say that it is safe. Indeed, marijuana shares more in common with the "hard" drugs than it does with alcohol.

A common argument for legalization is that smoking marijuana is no more dangerous than drinking alcohol and that prohibiting the use of marijuana is therefore no more justified than the prohibition of alcohol. As Jacob Sullum, author of *Saying Yes: In Defense of Drug Use*, writes:

> Americans understood the problems associated with alcohol abuse, but they also understood the problems associated with Prohibition, which included violence, organized crime, official corruption, the erosion of civil liberties, disrespect for the law, and injuries and deaths caused by tainted black-market booze. They decided that these unintended side effects far outweighed whatever harms Prohibition prevented by discouraging drinking. The same sort of analysis today would show that the harm caused by drug prohibition far outweighs the harm it prevents, even without taking into account the value to each individual of being sovereign over his own body and mind.

At first blush, this argument is appealing, especially to those wary of over-regulation by government. But it overlooks the enormous difference between alcohol and marijuana.

Legalization advocates claim that marijuana and alcohol are mild intoxicants and so should be regulated similarly; but as the experience of nearly every culture, over the thousands of years of human history, demonstrates, alcohol is different. Nearly every culture has its own alcoholic preparations, and nearly all have successfully regulated alcohol consumption through cultural norms. The same cannot be said of marijuana. There are several possible explanations for alcohol's unique status: For most people, it is not addictive; it is rarely consumed to the point of intoxication; low-level consumption is consistent with most manual and intellectual tasks; it has several positive health benefits; and it is formed by the fermentation of many common substances and easily metabolized by the body.

To be sure, there are costs associated with alcohol abuse, such as drunk driving and disease associated with excessive consumption. A few cultures—and this nation

for a short while during Prohibition—have concluded that the benefits of alcohol consumption are not worth the costs. But they are the exception; most cultures have concluded that it is acceptable in moderation. No other intoxicant shares that status.

Alcohol differs from marijuana in several crucial respects. First, marijuana is far more likely to cause addiction. Second, it is usually consumed to the point of intoxication. Third, it has no known general healthful properties, though it may have some palliative effects. Fourth, it is toxic and deleterious to health. Thus, while it is true that both alcohol and marijuana are less intoxicating than other mood-altering drugs, that is not to say that marijuana is especially similar to alcohol or that its use is healthy or even safe.

In fact, compared to alcohol, marijuana is not safe. Long-term, moderate consumption of alcohol carries few health risks and even offers some significant benefits. For example, a glass of wine (or other alcoholic drink) with dinner actually improves health. Dozens of peer-reviewed medical studies suggest that drinking moderate amounts of alcohol reduces the risk of heart disease, strokes, gallstones, diabetes, and death from a heart attack. According to the Mayo Clinic, among many others, moderate use of alcohol (defined as two drinks a day) "seems to offer some health benefits, particularly for the heart." Countless articles in medical journals and other scientific literature confirm the positive health effects of moderate alcohol consumption.

The effects of regular marijuana consumption are quite different. For example, the National Institute on Drug Abuse (a division of the National Institutes of Health) has released studies showing that use of marijuana has wide-ranging negative health effects. Long-term marijuana consumption "impairs the ability of T-cells in the lungs' immune system to fight off some infections." These studies have also found that marijuana consumption impairs short-term memory, making it difficult to learn and retain information or perform complex tasks; slows reaction time and impairs motor coordination; increases heart rate by 20 percent to 100 percent, thus elevating the risk of heart attack; and alters moods, resulting in artificial euphoria, calmness, or (in high doses) anxiety or paranoia. And it gets worse: Marijuana has toxic properties that can result in birth defects, pain, respiratory system damage, brain damage, and stroke.

Further, prolonged use of marijuana may cause cognitive degradation and is "associated with lower test scores and lower educational attainment because during periods of intoxication the drug affects the ability to learn and process information, thus influencing attention, concentration, and short-term memory." Unlike alcohol, marijuana has been shown to have a residual effect on cognitive ability that persists beyond the period of intoxication. According to the National Institute on Drug Abuse, whereas alcohol is broken down relatively quickly in the human body, THC (tetrahydrocannabinol, the main active chemical in marijuana) is stored in organs and fatty tissues, allowing it to remain in a user's body for days or even weeks after consumption. Research has shown that marijuana consumption may also cause "psychotic symptoms."

Marijuana's effects on the body are profound. According to the British Lung Foundation, "smoking three or four marijuana joints is as bad for your lungs as smoking twenty tobacco cigarettes." Researchers in Canada found that marijuana smoke contains significantly higher levels of numerous toxic compounds, like ammonia and hydrogen cyanide, than regular tobacco smoke. In fact, the study determined that ammonia was found in marijuana smoke at levels of up to 20 times the levels found in tobacco. Similarly, hydrogen cyanide was found in marijuana smoke at concentrations three to five times greater than those found in tobacco smoke.

Marijuana, like tobacco, is addictive. One study found that more than 30 percent of adults who used marijuana in the course of a year were dependent on the drug. These individuals often show signs of withdrawal and compulsive behavior. Marijuana dependence is also responsible for a large proportion of calls to drug abuse help lines and treatment centers.

To equate marijuana use with alcohol consumption is, at best, uninformed and, at worst, actively misleading. Only in the most superficial ways are the two substances alike, and they differ in every way that counts: addictiveness, toxicity, health effects, and risk of intoxication.

## Unintended Consequences

Today, marijuana trafficking is linked to a variety of crimes, from assault and murder to money laundering and smuggling. Legalization of marijuana would increase demand for the drug and almost certainly exacerbate drug-related crime, as well as cause a myriad of unintended but predictable consequences.

To begin with, an astonishingly high percentage of criminals are marijuana users. According to a study by the RAND Corporation, approximately 60 percent of arrestees test positive for marijuana use in the United States, England, and Australia. Further, marijuana metabolites are found in arrestees' urine more frequently than those of any other drug.

Although some studies have shown marijuana to inhibit aggressive behavior and violence, the National Research Council concluded that the "long-term use of marijuana may alter the nervous system in ways that do promote violence." No place serves as a better example than Amsterdam.

Marijuana advocates often point to the Netherlands as a well-functioning society with a relaxed attitude toward drugs, but they rarely mention that Amsterdam is one of Europe's most violent cities. In Amsterdam, officials are in the process of closing marijuana dispensaries, or "coffee shops," because of the crime associated with their operation. Furthermore, the Dutch Ministry of Health, Welfare and Sport has expressed "concern about drug and alcohol use among young people and the social consequences, which range from poor school performance and truancy to serious impairment, including brain damage."

Amsterdam's experience is already being duplicated in California under the current medical marijuana statute. In Los Angeles, police report that areas surrounding cannabis clubs have experienced a 200 percent increase in robberies, a 52.2 percent increase in burglaries, a 57.1 percent increase in aggravated assault, and a 130.8 percent increase in burglaries from automobiles. Current law requires a doctor's prescription to procure marijuana; full legalization would likely spark an even more acute increase in crime.

Legalization of marijuana would also inflict a series of negative consequences on neighborhoods and communities. The nuisance caused by the powerful odor of mature marijuana plants is already striking California municipalities. The City Council of Chico, California, has released a report detailing the situation and describing how citizens living near marijuana cultivators are disturbed by the incredible stink emanating from the plants.

Perhaps worse than the smell, crime near growers is increasing, associated with "the theft of marijuana from yards where it is being grown." As a result, housing prices near growers are sinking.

Theoretical arguments in favor of marijuana legalization usually overlook the practical matter of how the drug would be regulated and sold. It is the details of implementation, of course, that will determine the effect of legalization on families, schools, and communities. Most basically, how and where would marijuana be sold?

- Would neighborhoods become neon red-light districts like Amsterdam's, accompanied by the same crime and social disorder?
- If so, who decides what neighborhoods will be so afflicted—residents and landowners or far-off government officials?
- Or would marijuana sales be so widespread that users could add it to their grocery lists?
- If so, how would stores sell it, how would they store it, and how would they prevent it from being diverted into the gray market?
- Would stores dealing in marijuana have to fortify their facilities to reduce the risk of theft and assault?

The most likely result is that the drug will not be sold in legitimate stores at all, because while the federal government is currently tolerating medical marijuana dispensaries, it will not tolerate wide-scale sales under general legalizational statutes. So marijuana will continue to be sold on the gray or black market.

The act does not answer these or other practical questions regarding implementation. Rather, it leaves those issues to localities. No doubt, those entities will pass a variety of laws in an attempt to deal with the many problems caused by legalization, unless the local laws are struck down by California courts as inconsistent with the underlying initiative, which would be even worse. At best, that patchwork of laws, differing from one locality to another, will be yet another unintended and predictable problem arising from legalization as envisioned under this act.

Citizens also should not overlook what may be the greatest harms of marijuana legalization: increased addiction to and use of harder drugs. In addition to marijuana's harmful effects on the body and relationship to criminal conduct, it is a gateway drug that can lead users to more dangerous drugs. Prosecutors, judges, police officers, detectives, parole or probation officers, and even defense attorneys know that the vast majority of defendants arrested for violent crimes test positive for illegal drugs, including marijuana. They also know that marijuana is the starter drug of choice for most criminals. Whereas millions of Americans consume moderate amounts of alcohol without ever "moving on" to dangerous drugs, marijuana use and cocaine use are strongly correlated.

While correlation does not necessarily reflect causation, and while the science is admittedly mixed as to whether it is the drug itself or the people the new user associates with who cause the move on to cocaine, heroin, LSD, or other drugs, the RAND Corporation reports that marijuana prices and cocaine use are directly linked, suggesting a substitution effect between the two drugs. Moreover, according to RAND, legalization will cause marijuana prices to fall as much as 80 percent. That can lead to significant consequences because "a 10-percent decrease in the price of marijuana would increase the prevalence of cocaine use by 4.4 to 4.9 percent." As cheap marijuana floods the market both in and outside of California, use of many different types of drugs will increase, as will marijuana use.

It is impossible to predict the precise consequences of legalization, but the experiences of places that have eased restrictions on marijuana are not positive. Already, California is suffering crime, dislocation, and increased drug use under its current regulatory scheme. Further liberalizing the law will only make matters worse.

## Flouting Federal Law

Another area of great uncertainty is how a state law legalizing marijuana would fit in with federal law to the contrary. Congress has enacted a comprehensive regulatory scheme for restricting access to illicit drugs and other controlled substances. The Controlled Substances Act of 1970 prohibits the manufacture, distribution, and possession of all substances deemed to be Schedule I drugs—drugs like heroin, PCP, and cocaine. Because marijuana has no "currently accepted medical use in treatment in the United States," it is a Schedule I drug that cannot be bought, sold, possessed, or used without violating federal law.

Under the Supremacy Clause of the Constitution of the United States, the Controlled Substances Act is the supreme law of the land and cannot be superseded by state laws that purport to contradict or abrogate its terms. The RCTCA proposes to "reform California's cannabis laws in a way that will benefit our state" and "[r]egulate cannabis like we do alcohol." But the act does not even purport to address the fundamental constitutional infirmity that it would be in direct conflict with federal law. If enacted and unchallenged by the federal government, it would call into question the government's ability to regulate all controlled substances, including drugs such as Oxycontin, methamphetamine, heroin, and powder and crack cocaine. More likely, however, the feds would challenge the law in court, and the courts would have no choice but to strike it down.

Congress has the power to change the Controlled Substances Act and remove marijuana from Schedule I. Yet after decades of lobbying, it has not, largely because of the paucity of scientific evidence in support of a delisting.

California, in fact, is already in direct violation of federal law. Today, its laws allow the use of marijuana as a treatment for a range of vaguely defined conditions, including chronic pain, nausea, and lack of appetite, depression, anxiety, and glaucoma. "Marijuana doctors" are listed in the classified advertising sections of newspapers, and many are conveniently located adjacent to "dispensaries." At least one "doctor" writes prescriptions from a tiny hut beside the Venice Beach Boardwalk.

This "medical marijuana" law and similar ones in other states are premised on circumvention of the Food and Drug Administration (FDA) approval process. "FDA's drug approval process requires well-controlled clinical trials that provide the necessary scientific data upon which FDA makes its approval and labeling decisions." Marijuana, even that supposedly used for medicinal purposes, has been rejected by the FDA because, among other reasons, it "has no currently accepted or proven medical use."

The lack of FDA approval means that marijuana may come from unknown sources, may be adulterated with foreign substances, or may not even be marijuana at all. Pot buyers have no way to know what they are getting, and there is no regulatory authority with the ability to go after bogus manufacturers and dealers. Even if one overlooks its inherently harmful properties, marijuana that is commonly sold is likely to be far less safe than that studied in the lab or elsewhere.

Marijuana advocates claim that federal enforcement of drug laws, particularly in jurisdictions that allow the use of medical marijuana, violates states' rights. The Supreme Court, however, has held otherwise. In 2002, California resident Angel Raich produced and consumed marijuana, purportedly for medical purposes. Her actions, while in accordance with California's "medical marijuana" law, clearly violated the Controlled Substances Act, and the local sheriff's department destroyed Raich's plants. Raich claimed that she needed to use marijuana, prescribed by her doctor, for medical purposes. She sued the federal government, asking the court to stop the government from interfering with her right to produce and use marijuana.

In 2006, the Supreme Court held in *Gonzales vs. Raich* that the Commerce Clause confers on Congress the authority to ban the use of marijuana, even when a state approves it for "medical purposes" and it is produced in small quantities for personal consumption. Many legal scholars criticize the Court's extremely broad reading of the Commerce Clause as inconsistent with its original meaning, but the Court's decision nonetheless stands.

If the RCTCA were enacted, it would conflict with the provisions of the Controlled Substances Act and invite extensive litigation that would almost certainly result in its being struck down. Until that happened, state law enforcement officers would be forced into a position of uncertainty regarding their conflicting obligations under federal and state law and cooperation with federal authorities.

## Bogus Economics

An innovation of the campaign in support of RCTCA is its touting of the potential benefit of legalization to the government, in terms of additional revenues from taxing marijuana and savings from backing down in the "war on drugs." The National Organization for the Reform of Marijuana Laws (NORML), for example, claims that legalization "could yield California taxpayers over $1.2 billion per year" in tax benefits. According to a California NORML Report updated in October 2009, an excise tax of $50 per ounce would raise about $770 million to $900 million per year and save over $200 million in law enforcement costs per year. It is worth noting that $900 million equates to 18 million ounces—enough marijuana for Californians to smoke one billion marijuana cigarettes each year.

But these projections are highly speculative and riddled with unfounded assumptions. Dr. Rosalie Liccardo Pacula, an expert with the RAND Corporation who has studied the economics of drug policy for over 15 years, has explained that the California "Board of Equalization's estimate of $1.4 billion [in] potential revenue for the state is based on a series of assumptions that are in some instances subject to tremendous uncertainty and in other cases not validated." She urged the California Committee on Public Safety to conduct an honest and thorough cost-benefit analysis of the potential revenues and costs associated with legalizing marijuana. To date, no such realistic cost-benefit analysis has been done.

In her testimony before the committee, Dr. Pacula stated that prohibition raises the cost of production by at least 400 percent and that legalizing marijuana would cause the price of marijuana to fall considerably—much more than the 50 percent price reduction incorporated into the state's revenue model. Furthermore, she noted that a $50-per-ounce marijuana tax was not realistic, because it would represent a 100 percent tax on the cost of the product.

Under the state scheme, she testified, there would be "tremendous profit motive for the existing black market providers to stay in the market." The only way California could effectively eliminate the black market for marijuana, according to Dr. Pacula, "is to take away the substantial profits in the market and allow the price of marijuana to fall to an amount close to the cost of production. Doing so, however, will mean substantially smaller tax revenue than currently anticipated from this change in policy."

The RCTCA, in fact, allows for so much individual production of marijuana that even the Board of Equalization's $1.4 billion per year revenue estimate seems unlikely. Under the law, any resident could grow marijuana for "personal use" in a plot at home up to 25 square feet in size. One ounce of marijuana is enough for 60 to 120 marijuana cigarettes. One plant produces one to five pounds, or 16 to 80 ounces, of marijuana each year, and 25 square feet of land can sustain about 25 plants. Therefore, an individual will be able to produce 24,000 to 240,000 joints legally each year.

Not only is this more than any individual could possibly consume; it is also enough to encourage individuals to grow and sell pot under the individual allowance. Who would buy marijuana from a state-regulated store and pay the $50 tax per ounce in addition to the sale price when they can either grow it themselves or buy it at a much lower price from a friend or neighbor? In this way, the RCTCA undermines its supporters' lavish revenue claims.

## Other Negative Social Costs

In addition to its direct effects on individual health, even moderate marijuana use imposes significant long-term costs through the ways that it affects individual users. Marijuana use is associated with cognitive difficulties and influences attention, concentration, and short-term memory. This damage affects drug users' ability to work and can put others at risk. Even if critical workers—for example, police officers, airline pilots, and machine operators—used marijuana recreationally but remained sober on the job, the long-term cognitive deficiency that remained from regular drug use would sap productivity and place countless people in danger. Increased use would also send health care costs skyrocketing—costs borne not just by individual users, but also by the entire society.

For that reason, among others, the Obama Administration also rejects supporters' economic arguments. In his speech, Kerlikowske explained that tax revenue from cigarettes is far outweighed by their social costs: "Tobacco also does not carry its economic weight when we tax it; each year we spend more than $200 billion and collect only about $25 billion in taxes." If the heavy taxation of cigarettes is unable even to come close to making up for the health and other costs associated with their use, it seems doubtful at best that marijuana taxes would be sufficient to cover the costs of legalized marijuana—especially considering that, in addition to the other dangers of smoking marijuana, the physical health effects of just three to four joints are equivalent to those of an entire pack of cigarettes.

Other claims also do not measure up. One of the express purposes of the California initiative is to "put dangerous, underground street dealers out of business, so their influence in our communities will fade." But as explained above, many black-market dealers would rationally choose to remain in the black market to avoid taxation and regulation. Vibrant gray markets have developed throughout the world for many products that are legal, regulated, and heavily taxed. Cigarettes in Eastern Europe, alcohol in Scandinavia, luxury automobiles in Russia, and DVDs in the Middle East are all legal goods traded in gray markets that are wracked with violence. In Canada, an attempt at a $3 per pack tax on cigarettes was greeted with the creation of a black market that "accounted for perhaps 30 percent of sales."

Further, even if the RCTCA were to pass, marijuana would remain illegal in the entire United States under federal law while taxed only in California, a situation that would strengthen both California's gray market and the nationwide black market in illegal drugs. Fueled by generous growing allowances and an enormous supply in California, criminal sales operations would flourish as excess California marijuana was sold outside the state and, at the same time, out-of-state growers attempted to access the more permissive market inside the state.

In sum, legalization would put additional strain on an already faltering economy. In 2008, marijuana alone was involved in 375,000 emergency room visits. Drug overdoses already outnumber gunshot deaths in America and are approaching motor vehicle crashes as the nation's leading cause of accidental death. It is true that taxing marijuana sales would generate some tax revenue, but the cost of handling the influx of problems resulting from increased use would far outweigh any gain made by marijuana's taxation. Legalizing marijuana would serve only to compound the problems already associated with drug use.

## Social Dislocation and Organized Crime

The final two arguments of those favoring legalization are intertwined. According to advocates of legalization, the government's efforts to combat the illegal drug trade have been an expensive failure. Consequently, they argue, focusing on substance abuse and treatment would be a more effective means of combating drug abuse while reducing the violence and social ills stemming from anti-drug enforcement efforts.

There is no doubt that if marijuana were legalized, more people, including juveniles, would consume it. Consider cigarettes: While their purchase by people under 18 is illegal, 20 percent of high school students admit to having smoked cigarettes in the past 30 days. Marijuana's illegal status "keeps potential drug users from using" marijuana in a way that no legalization scheme can replicate

"by virtue of the fear of arrest and the embarrassment of being caught." With increased use comes increased abuse, as the fear of arrest and embarrassment will decrease.

Legalization advocates attempt to create in the minds of the public an image of a typical "responsible" user of marijuana: a person who is reasonable and accountable even when under the influence of marijuana. And for those few that don't fit that image? Society will treat them and restore them to full health. The facts, however, are much uglier.

The RAND Corporation projects a 50 percent increase in marijuana-related traffic fatalities under the RCTCA. That alone should weigh heavily on California voters this fall. In a 2008 national survey, approximately 3 million Americans 12 years old or older started using illicit drugs in the past year—almost 8,000 new users per day. The most commonly used illicit drug is marijuana, especially among the 20 million Americans over 12 who were users in 2008. In California, 62 percent of all marijuana treatment cases are already individuals under 21. Legalization will increase the number of underage users.

Keeping marijuana illegal will undoubtedly keep many young people from using it. Eliminate that criminal sanction (and moral disapprobation), and more youth will use the drug, harming their potential and ratcheting up treatment costs.

Educators know that students using marijuana underperform when compared to their non-using peers. Teachers, coaches, guidance counselors, and school principals have seen the negative effect of marijuana on their students. The Rev. Dr. D. Stuart Dunnan, Headmaster of Saint James School in St. James, Maryland, says of marijuana use by students:

> The chemical effect of marijuana is to take away ambition. The social effect is to provide an escape from challenges and responsibilities with a like-minded group of teenagers who are doing the same thing. Using marijuana creates losers. At a time when we're concerned about our lack of academic achievement relative to other countries, legalizing marijuana will be disastrous.

Additionally, making marijuana legal in California will fuel drug cartels and violence, particularly because the drug will still be illegal at the national level. The local demand will increase in California, but reputable growers, manufacturers, and retailers will still be unwilling—as they should be—to produce and distribute marijuana. Even without the federal prohibition, most reputable producers would not survive the tort liability from such a dangerous product. Thus, the vacuum will be filled by illegal drug cartels.

According to the Department of Justice's National Drug Threat Assessment for 2010, Mexican drug trafficking organizations (DTOs) "have expanded their cultivation operations in the United States, an ongoing trend for the past decade. . . . Well-organized criminal groups and

DTOs that produce domestic marijuana do so because of the high profitability of and demand for marijuana in the United States."

Legalize marijuana, and the demand for marijuana goes up substantially as the deterrence effect of law enforcement disappears. Yet not many suppliers will operate legally, refusing to subject themselves to the established state regulatory scheme—not to mention taxation—while still risking federal prosecution, conviction, and prison time. So who will fill the void?

Violent, brutal, and ruthless, Mexican DTOs will work to maintain their black-market profits at the expense of American citizens' safety. Every week, there are news articles cataloguing the murders, kidnappings, robberies, and other thuggish brutality employed by Mexican drug gangs along the border. It is nonsensical to argue that these gangs will simply give up producing marijuana when it is legalized; indeed, their profits might soar, depending on the actual tax in California and the economics of the interstate trade. While such profits might not be possible if marijuana was legalized at the national level and these gangs were undercut by mass production, that is unlikely ever to happen. Nor does anyone really believe that the gangs will subject themselves to state and local regulation, including taxation. And since the California ballot does nothing to eliminate the black market for marijuana— quite the opposite, in fact—legalizing marijuana will only incentivize Mexican DTOs to grow more marijuana to feed the demand and exploit the black market.

Furthermore, should California legalize marijuana, other entrepreneurs will inevitably attempt to enter the marketplace and game the system. In doing so, they will compete with Mexican DTOs and other criminal organizations. Inevitably, violence will follow, and unlike now, that violence will not be confined to the border as large-scale growers seek to protect their turf—turf that will necessarily include anywhere they grow, harvest, process, or sell marijuana. While this may sound far-fetched, Californians in Alameda County are already experiencing the reality of cartel-run marijuana farms on sometimes stolen land, protected by "guys [who] are pretty heavily armed and willing to protect their merchandise."

It is not uncommon for drugs with large illegal markets to be controlled by cartels despite attempts to roll them into the normal medical control scheme. For instance, cocaine has a medical purpose and can be prescribed by doctors as *Erythroxylum coca*, yet its true production and distribution are controlled by drug cartels and organized crime. As competition from growers and dispensaries authorized by the RCTCA cuts further into the Mexican DTOs' business, Californians will face a real possibility of bloodshed on their own soil as the cartels' profit-protection measures turn from defensive to offensive.

Thus, marijuana legalization will increase crime, drug use, and social dislocation across the state of California— the exact opposite of what pro-legalization advocates promise.

## Conclusion

Pro-marijuana advocates promoting the Regulate, Control and Tax Cannabis Act of 2010 invite Californians to imagine a hypothetical and idyllic "pot market," but America's national approach to drug use, addiction, and crime must be serious, based on sound policy and solid evidence.

In 1982, President Ronald Reagan adopted a national drug strategy that took a comprehensive approach consisting of five components: international cooperation, research, strengthened law enforcement, treatment and rehabilitation, and prevention and education. It was remarkably successful: Illegal drug use by young adults dropped more than 50 percent.

Reagan was right to make drug control a major issue of his presidency. Illegal drugs such as marijuana are responsible for a disproportionate share of violence and social decline in America. Accordingly, federal law, representing the considered judgment of medical science and the nation's two political branches of government, takes the unequivocal position that marijuana is dangerous and has no significant beneficial uses.

California cannot repeal that law or somehow allow its citizens to contravene it. Thus, it has two options. By far the best option is to commit itself seriously to the federal approach and pursue a strategy that attempts to prevent illegal drug use in the first place and reduce the number of drug users. This may require changes in drug policy, and perhaps in sentencing guidelines for marijuana users charged with simple possession, but simply legalizing a harmful drug—that is, giving up—is not a responsible option.

The other option is to follow the above path in the short term while conducting further research and possibly working with other states in Congress to consider changes in federal law. Although those who oppose the legalization of marijuana have every reason to believe that further, legitimate scientific research will confirm the dangers of its use, no side should try to thwart the sober judgment of the national legislature and sister states.

In short, no state will likely be allowed to legalize marijuana on its own, with such serious, negative cross-state spillover effects. Yet even if California could act as if it were an island, the legalization route would still end very badly for the Golden State. There is strong evidence to suggest that legalizing marijuana would serve little purpose other than to worsen the state's drug problems— addiction, violence, disorder, and death. While long on rhetoric, the legalization movement, by contrast, is short on facts.

**CHARLES D. STIMSON** is a senior legal fellow in the Center for Legal & Judicial Studies at The Heritage Foundation. Before joining The Heritage Foundation, he served as deputy assistant secretary of defense, as a local, state, federal, and military prosecutor, and as a defense attorney and law professor.

# EXPLORING THE ISSUE

## Should Recreational Drugs Be Legalized?

## Critical Thinking and Reflection

1. How harmful are illegal drugs? Are they more dangerous than alcohol? Can we distinguish among them?
2. Is the history of prohibition of alcohol relevant in revealing the consequences of prohibition? Are the indicted substances sufficiently different so that comparisons are not useful?
3. In view of crowded prisons, should we consider alternative means of punishment for some categories of drug offenders? Does prohibition inspire its violation?
4. Why shouldn't we have a civil right to do what may be harmful to ourselves?
5. Do you believe there would be a larger societal impact if recreational drugs were to be legalized? If so, what could it be? If not, why not?

## Is There Common Ground?

Advocates of legalization mostly believe that it must be accompanied by restraints on drug usage. Just as alcohol is subject to restrictions regarding its manufacturing and sale, and states vary in their requirements regarding the sale of alcohol, so legal drugs may be subject to strict controls. Absolute libertarians will dissent, arguing that there should be no regulation, but a vast majority of Americans would disagree. It would be likely that legalization would involve laws on purity of contents and other requirements that apply to alcohol and other legal drugs.

It is possible that supporters of prohibition may distinguish among the illicit drugs based on present awareness of their different effects. Defenders of drug prohibition might consent to the sale of medical marijuana, due to the claim that its use can reduce the pain of certain diseases. However, the experience in California and elsewhere is that licensing medical marijuana is likely to lead to the easy medical dispensing of medical marijuana to persons who are not legally entitled to it.

Perhaps the true common ground has already begun to emerge. States are able to legalize within their boundaries and not fear federal crackdowns so long as they regulate the drug within federal guidelines. While such a measure works well for the time being, questions will arise in 2016 when a new president takes office. After all, the current set-up keeps recreational drugs illegal at the federal level and relies on policy memos from a political appointee. For the states to feel safe in their status, it will be necessary for a clearer relationship to develop between federal and state authorities on these issues so enforcement does not ultimately become a political whim of the sitting president.

## Create Central

www.mhhe.com/createcentral

## Additional Resources

Jonathan P. Caulkins, Angela Hawken, Beau Kilmer, and Mark A.R. Kleiman, *Marijuana Legalization: What Everyone Needs to Know* (Oxford University Press, 2012)

Larry Gaines, *Drug, Crimes, & Justice* (Waveland Press, 2002)

James A. Inciardi, *The Drug Legalization Debate* (Greenhaven Press, 2013)

Robert J. MacCoun and Peter Reuter, *Drug War Heresies* (Cambridge University Press, 2001)

U.S. Department of Justice and Drug Enforcement Administration, *Speaking Out Against Drug Legalization* (CreateSpace, 2012)

# *Internet References . . .*

**Citizens Against Legalizing Marijuana**

www.calmca.org/about/

**Gallup**

www.gallup.com/poll/165539/first-time-americans
-favor-legalizing-marijuana.aspx

**Marijuana Policy Project**

www.mpp.org/

**National Organization for the Reform of Marijuana Laws**

http://norml.org/

**Public Broadcasting Service**

www.pbs.org/wnet/need-to-know/ask-the-experts
/ask-the-experts-legalizing-marijuana/15474/

# Unit 4

# UNIT

# America and the World

*A*t one time the United States could isolate itself from much of the world, and it did. But today's America affects and is affected—for good or ill—by what happens anywhere on the planet. Whether the topic is ecology, finance, war, or terrorism, America is integrally tied to the rest of the world. With a globalized economy and instant communication, no nation lives in a bubble, regardless of its intent or desire to. What happens in one country will impact societies across the globe.

The United States, then, simply has no choice but to act and react in relation to a constantly shifting series of events; the arguments turn on whether it acts morally or immorally, wisely or foolishly, what methods are morally justified in protecting the American homeland from attack? Do they include warrantless wiretapping and indefinite detention of suspected terrorists? Does global warming caused by humans threaten the future of the planet, and, if so, what responsibility does the United States have in the international effort to curb it?

Selected, Edited, and with Issue Framing Material by:
**William J. Miller,** *Flagler College*
**George McKenna,** *City College, City University of New York*
**and**
**Stanley Feingold,** *City College, City University of New York*

# ISSUE

# Do We Need to Curb Global Warming?

**YES: Gregg Easterbrook,** from "Case Closed: The Debate About Global Warming Is Over," *Issues in Governance Studies* (June 2006)

**NO: Larry Bell,** from *Climate of Corruption: Politics and Power Behind the Global Warming Hoax* (Greenleaf Book Group, 2011)

## Learning Outcomes

**After reading this issue, you will be able to:**

- Describe the science of global warming.
- Explain the arguments for and against global warming.
- Assess how severe a problem of global warming is today.
- Identify potential ways to begin curbing global warming.
- Indicate potential difficulties in curbing global warming.

## ISSUE SUMMARY

**YES:** Editor Gregg Easterbrook argues that global warming, causing deleterious changes in the human condition, is a near certainty for the next few generations.

**NO:** Professor Larry Bell insists that the climate models predicting global warming are speculative at best, and in some cases based upon manipulated data.

**W**hether or not he actually said it, Mark Twain has often been quoted as saying, "Everyone talks about the weather, but no one does anything about it." Today, many scientists and others think that we are doing something about it—something bad. Their contention is that, for roughly the last century, human activities have been generating increasing amounts of carbon dioxide and other "greenhouse gases," that these gases have been heating the planet, that these temperature increases are already having a deleterious effect on human and animal life, and, unless they are checked, may soon produce catastrophic and irreversible consequences for the planet.

The scientists who have reached these alarming conclusions have justified them in many densely argued presentations, papers, and published works. Other scientists, although apparently fewer in number, have dissented from some or all of those conclusions, and they, too, have marshaled the typical array of graphs, charts, and equations that scientists commonly use to illustrate their findings.

What is not in dispute between the two sides is that humans are producing increasing amounts of carbon dioxide from a wide variety of fuels, that the carbon content of the global atmosphere has been slowly increasing since early in the last century (although much of it was produced before 1940, when modern industry really started taking off), that carbon dioxide warms the lower troposphere, and that the globally averaged surface temperature of the Earth is at least 1 degree Fahrenheit warmer than it was about a century ago. What they disagree upon is whether the increase in average temperature is due to the increase in the production of carbon dioxide by humans.

Scientists, of course, disagree about many things, and their debates play a vital role in scientific progress. The natural inclination of nonscientists is to let them fight it out among themselves, in the expectation that the truth will eventually emerge. Why, then, include the topic of global warming in a book of political issues? Isn't that a little presumptuous?

It would be, if the topic concerned only the scientific community. If the argument were about the expansion of the universe or the speed of neutrinos, it would be better for students of politics to stand back and let the scientists sort it out. But the global warming debate is inescapably tied to politics because it involves the future of the human race. If man-made global warming is a fact, within a generation coastal cities like New York could be wiped out, gigantic farming regions could be destroyed by drought, tropical diseases like malaria could migrate north, and hurricanes the size of Katrina could become endemic; the only way to head off these consequences would be for the world's political leaders to take immediate steps to curtail the use of fossil fuels; they must take the lead in moving us toward electric cars, banning coal-fired power plants, and discouraging the burning of oil and its derivatives. But if the global warming alarm is bogus, the future of the planet faces a different but no less serious threat. In head-long pursuit of "green energy," governments would have to force major industries to either shut down or change over to largely untested energy sources like wind and solar. Unemployment, already at crisis levels, would quickly rise, and hard-pressed consumers would pay more for energy. So would nations as a whole in the industrialized world, as they spent hundreds of billions subsidizing developing countries to persuade them to follow the green path. The result could be stagnation in much of the developing world and economic ruin of the industrialized countries.

Either way, the stakes are much too high to leave the debate entirely up to the scientists. Not surprisingly, then, global warming has become a major political issue in domestic and international politics. On the world stage, green politics made its first major appearance in 1997, in Kyoto, Japan, where the heads of state of 191 nations met to negotiate what came to be known as the Kyoto Protocol. Its goal was to reduce worldwide greenhouse gases to 5.2 percent below 1990 levels between 2008 and 2012. To achieve that end, it set specific emission reductions targets for each industrialized nation, but excluded developing countries, even rapidly developing ones like India and China.

President Bill Clinton was one of the main authors of the Kyoto Protocol, but it never got much traction in the United States. Even before it was drafted, the U.S. Senate passed a resolution by 95-0 saying the United States should not sign any carbon-emission cuts that failed to apply to developing countries or that would "result in serious harm to the economy of the United States." Clinton's successor, George W. Bush, declined even to submit Kyoto to the Senate for ratification.

Despite Congress's bipartisan wariness, Democrats have been more receptive than Republicans to Kyoto's spirit and intent. After the 2008 election of a Democratic president and a large Democratic majority in Congress, the green movement hoped to revive Kyoto by pushing for legislation that Democrats called "cap and trade." (Republicans called it "cap and tax.") This proposed law would set limits ("cap") on the total amount of greenhouse gases that could be emitted nationally. Those companies

coming in under the allowable limits because of efficient emission controls could then sell ("trade") their leftover allowances to others lacking such controls.

Despite a 256-175 Democratic majority in the House, cap and trade passed by a slim 219-212 margin in June of 2009. Supporters were disappointed not only by the narrow margin but also by the tardiness of the whole process. The previous December, President Obama attended the United Nations Climate Change Conference in Copenhagen, Denmark, and he had hoped to be able to bring with him a copy of the United States' first cap-and-trade law. Arriving instead empty-handed, he tried to assure the other delegates that the legislation was in the pipeline, but the general mood of the meeting was gloomy; without guaranteed U.S. cooperation, the chances of meaningful international action against global warming were slim at best. The final blow to cap-and-trade law came in July 2009, when the bill arrived in the Senate. Majority Leader Harry Reid decided not to bring it to the floor, saying that Republican opposition doomed any chances of passage. But some Democratic Senators, especially from coal-mining states, were also opposed to it.

In September 2013, a United Nations panel presented firm scientific evidence that the environmental changes witnessed in recent years were caused predominantly by human action. The chair of the Intergovernmental Panel on Climate Change explained that "our assessment of the science finds that the atmosphere and ocean have warmed, the amount of snow and ice has diminished, the global mean sea level has risen and the concentrations of greenhouse gases have increased." The new report will play an important role in shaping any new U.N. climate deal. The new agreement is supposed to be in place by 2015, but nations such as China and the United States would need to agree to emissions cuts to keep temperatures below a limit at which the worst effects of climate change can be avoided. Like most things, the idea of curbing global warming sounds good in theory until one is asked to make individual sacrifices. We have yet to determine whether citizens of the world are willing to alter their own behavior to assure a better environment for future generations.

Whatever the eventual fate of cap-and-trade and other measures aimed at curbing carbon emissions, the larger debate over global warming will continue until one side or the other prevails. That, however, is unlikely to happen soon, for both sides seem equally vigorous and confident in presenting their cases—as we see in the following selections. *New Republic* Editor Gregg Easterbrook argues that global warming, causing deleterious changes in the human condition, is a near certainty for the next few generations; architecture Professor Larry Bell insists that the climate models predicting global warming are speculative at best, and in some cases based upon manipulated data.

# YES ↵

**Gregg Easterbrook**

## Case Closed: The Debate About Global Warming Is Over

. . .

### The Scientific Verdict Is In

When global-warming concerns became widespread, many argued that more scientific research was needed before any policy decisions. This was hardly just the contention of oil-company executives. "There is no evidence yet" of dangerous climate change, the National Academy of Sciences declared in 1991. A 1992 survey of members of the American Geophysical Union and American Meteorological Society, two professional groups of climatologists, found only 17 percent believed there was a sufficient ground to declare an artificial greenhouse effect in progress. In 1993 Thomas Karl, director of the National Climatic Data Center, said there exists "a great range of uncertainty" regarding whether the world is warming. My own contrarian 1995 book about environmental issues, *A Moment on the Earth,* spent 39 pages reviewing the nascent state of climate science and concluded that rising temperatures "might be an omen or might mean nothing." Like others, I called for more research.

That research is now in, and the scientific uncertainty that once justified skepticism has been replaced by near-unanimity among credentialed researchers that an artificially warming world is a real phenomenon posing real danger. The American Geophysical Union and American Meteorological Society, skeptical in 1992, in 2003 both issued statements calling signs of global warming compelling. In 2004 the American Association for the Advancement of Science declared in its technical journal *Science* that there is no longer any "substantive disagreement in the scientific community" that artificial global warming is happening and could become dangerous. In 2005, the National Academy of Sciences joined the science academies of the United Kingdom, Japan, Germany, China and other nations in a joint statement saying, "There is now strong evidence" that Data Center said research now supports "a substantial human impact on global temperature increases." And this month the Climate Change Science Program, the George W. Bush Administration's coordinating agency for global-warming research, declared it had found "clear evidence of human influences on the climate system."

Case closed.

In roughly the last decade, the evidence of artificial global warming has gone from sketchy to overpowering.

That does not mean that substantial uncertainties don't remain. All researchers agree that knowledge of Earth's climate is rudimentary. (For instance, would a warming world be wetter or drier? Your guess is as good as the next Ph.D. climatologist's.) And considering that the most sophisticated meteorological computer models cannot predict the weather next week, computer predictions of future temperatures are expensive guesswork at best. But incomplete knowledge does not diminish the seriousness of climate change. Some continue to argue, "Because there are significant uncertainties, science cannot issue meaningful warnings about the greenhouse effect." This reasoning is akin to putting a live round in a revolver, spinning the chamber and saying, "Because there are significant uncertainties regarding the location of the bullet, firearms experts cannot issue meaningful warnings about whether to place the gun to your head." Warnings can be imperative even when much remains unknown.

Emissions of artificial greenhouse gases continue to rise at a brisk pace worldwide. Even if reforms are enacted, it seems cast in stone that sometime during the 21st century, atmospheric concentrations of carbon dioxide—the primary greenhouse gas emitted by human activity—will reach double their preindustrial level. This makes a warming world a near certainty for the next few generations.

### Would Artificial Global Warming Be Bad?

Bearing in mind that projections are speculation, the current scientific consensus estimate is that if carbon dioxide in the atmosphere doubles, global temperatures will increase by 4–6 degrees Fahrenheit during this century. Everything from pop-culture presentations of global warming to political and pundit commentary has assumed that such a warming world would be a place of horrors. The big-studio 2004 movie *The Day After Tomorrow* depicted an artificial greenhouse effect wiping out much of Western society in mere days. No effects remotely resembling what happened in *The Day After Tomorrow* have ever been observed in nature, and scientists viewed the movie as little more than two hours of pretentious drivel. While the sort of "instant doomsday" scenarios favored by global warming alarmists cannot be ruled out, they are highly unlikely.

Nor should it be assumed that a warming world would, in itself, be cause for concern. Consensus science shows the world has warmed about 1 degree Fahrenheit during the last century: that warming moderated global energy demand and lengthened growing seasons, both of which are positives. Some researchers think the warming of the 20th century extended the range of equatorial diseases. But even if this was so, the initial phase of artificial global warming appears to have had a net benefit.

Further warming would likely confer some additional benefits. A vast area of the former Soviet Union might open to agricultural production, while large permafrost regions in Russia and Canada might open to petroleum exploration or even residential development. (For the purposes of this briefing, we are contemplating only impacts on human society, skipping whether such possibilities as melting the permafrost may be good or bad in the abstract ecological sense.) Extended global warming might make Antarctica habitable again—before ice ages began, it was lush—thus adding an entire continent to the part of the world useful to people. And global warming might make my hometown of Buffalo, New York, a vacation paradise where Hollywood celebrities compete to snatch up prime lakefront real estate.

But though there could be benefits to a warming world, the bad is likely to outweigh the good. Here are the main dangers:

- **Significant extension of the range of equatorial diseases.** The equator is the world's most disease-prone region. If global temperatures rise by several degrees Fahrenheit, the equatorial disease zone may extend much farther north and south, further afflicting impoverished nations and increasing the odds that air travelers bring equatorial diseases with them to the northern and southern nations that today have low rates of most communicable illnesses.
- **Sea-level rise.** The 2005 statement by the National Academy of Sciences endorsed an estimate that artificial global warming will cause sea levels to rise from 4 to 35 inches in the coming century. The low end of that range would flood parts of Micronesia; the midpoint would inundate much of Bangladesh, and make the survival of New Orleans in any future hurricane problematic; the high end would flood coastal cities worldwide. Coastal cities could be abandoned and new cities built inland, but the cost would be breathtaking—and almost surely exceed the cost of reforms to slow greenhouse emissions in the first place.
- **Melting ice.** Melting glaciers and ice sheets may alter the primary Atlantic Ocean current that warms Europe, causing European Union nations to become significantly colder even as global average temperatures rise. Studies suggest that some Atlantic Ocean currents are already changing.
- **Altering the biology of the sea.** Major shifts of ocean currents have occurred in the past, and in the geologic record, are associated with mass extinctions of marine organisms. This suggests that greenhouse-induced changes in the oceans might harm fish stocks. While it is also possible that greenhouse-induced ocean current changes would be beneficial to fish stocks, the gamble is a major one, as much of the seas are already overfished and much of the developing world relies on fish for dietary protein.
- **Misery in poor nations.** Developing nations might be impacted by global warming much more than wealthy nations. Setting aside Antarctica, the largest chunks of the world's cold land mass are in Alaska, Canada, Greenland and Russia. Extended global warming might make these areas significantly more valuable, while rendering low-latitude poor nations close to uninhabitable. Summer temperatures of 110 degrees Fahrenheit are already common in Pakistan, where most of the population has no access to air conditioning and only sporadic electric power for fans. Imagine the human suffering if 115 degree days became common.

Beyond these concerns is the great danger of artificial global warming—namely, climate change. Global warming and climate change sound like the same thing, but are different. If the world became warmer while climate remained the same, the change would be manageable. In that scenario, the benefits might outweigh the harm. Significant climate change, by contrast, could cause awful problems.

The first danger of climate change involves storms and wind. Tropical storm activity is currently in an up cycle. Whether this is caused by artificial global warming or by natural variability is not known, but the weight of evidence points toward artificial greenhouse gases. Continued global warming may cause more and stronger hurricanes in the Atlantic and typhoons in the Pacific. More frequent or powerful tropical storms might not just wreak havoc with America's Gulf Coast cities; they could bring regular misery to coastal areas of Central America, Indonesia, Malaysia, Bangladesh and other nations. North and south of the tropical-storm band, tornadoes, strong thunderstorms and torrential rains might increase. (There are already indications that rainfall in much of North America is becoming less frequent but more intense.) If jet streams or other major winds increase, air travel and air cargo could be impacted or even become impractical during some parts of the year, and the globalized economy increasingly depends on air travel and air cargo.

The second danger of climate change lies in activating the unknown. We live in an "interglacial," a warm period between ice ages; our interglacial is called the Holocene. Ice-core readings from the interglacial period that preceded ours, called the Eemian, suggest that it was common then for global temperatures to shift from warm to cool and back again, with climate havoc ensuing. Why these shifts occurred is unknown. But during our era, Earth's climate has been magnificently stable—almost strangely so. For roughly the last 8,000 years, coinciding with the advent of the controlled agriculture on which civilization is based, global temperatures, ocean currents, rainfall patterns and the timing of the seasons have varied by only small amounts. Scientists don't know why the climate has been so stable during the last 8,000 years. We do know that stable climate is associated with civilization, while climate change is associated with mass extinctions. We would be fools to tempt that equation.

The third and gravest danger of climate change is disruption of global agriculture. The predicted Malthusian calamities of the postwar era have not occurred. For instance, none of the mass starvations predicted by Paul Ehrlich have happened, though the world population has doubled since Ehrlich said mass famines were just around the corner. The reason Malthusian calamities have not occurred is that global agricultural yields have increased faster than population growth. But the world's agricultural system is perilously poised, barely covering global needs. Suppose climate change shifted precipitation away from the breadbasket regions of the six food-producing continents, sending rain clouds instead to the world's deserts. Over the generations, society will adjust. But years or decades of global food shortages might stand between significant climate shifts and agricultural adjustment. Huge numbers of people might die of malnourishment, while chaos rendered impossible social progress in many developing nations and armies of desperate refugees came to the borders of the wealthy nations.

In 2005, the United Nations Food and Agriculture Organization reported that "chronic hunger is on the decline." Despite rising global population, malnourishment is now believed to be at the lowest level in human history. Because food is in oversupply in the West and malnutrition is declining generally, commentators have begun to take food supply for granted. Climate change that disrupts the agricultural system on which the global economy is based—and almost all successful nations are agricultural nations—could spark a worldwide calamity. Do we really want to stick a bullet into a revolver, spin the chamber and see what happens with global food production?

## Are There Cheap Solutions?

If you think the Kyoto Protocol on greenhouse gas emissions can save the world from artificial global warming, think again. The United States has withdrawn from the Kyoto mechanism—and advocating a reversal of that decision seems a waste of everyone's time, since there is no chance the Senate will ever ratify a treaty that grants the United Nations authority over U.S. domestic policymaking. The United States would ignore any attempt by the United Nations to exercise such authority, of course—but then why bother with an empty treaty? Most nations that have ratified the Kyoto treaty are merrily ignoring it. Canada, for example, frequently hectors the United States

about being an environmental offender, yet its greenhouse gas emissions are currently 24 percent above the level mandated by Kyoto—and Ottawa has no meaningful program to change that. Canada's greenhouse gas emissions are also rising faster than greenhouse gas emissions in the United States. Even Japan, which staked much of its international prestige on an agreement signed in its glorious ancient capital city, is turning a blind eye to the treaty's requirements: Japan's emissions of greenhouse gases are 9 percent above the promised level.

At current rates only Russia, Germany and the United Kingdom are close to complying with the Kyoto mandates, and most of the compliance by Russia and Germany is the result of backdated credits for the closing of Warsaw Pact-era power plants and factories that had already been shuttered before the Kyoto agreement was initialed in 1997. Meanwhile, developing nations especially India and China are increasing their greenhouse gas emissions at prodigious rates—so much so that in the short term developing nations will swamp any reductions achieved by the West. Since 1990, India has increased its emissions of greenhouse gases by 70 percent and China by 49 percent, versus an 18 percent increase by the United States. China is on track to pass the United States as the leading emitter of artificial greenhouse gases. If current trends continue, the developing world will emit more greenhouse gases than the West by around 2025. And here's the real kicker: even if all the provisions of the Kyoto Protocol were enforced to perfection, atmospheric concentrations of greenhouse gases in the year 2050 would be only about 1 percent less than without the treaty.

These can sound like reasons to despair about combating artificial global warming, but they are not. Rather, they are reasons to shifts gears from the overly ponderous Kyoto approach to a market-driven, innovation-based approach. The latter approach may not only work much better than Kyoto but be relatively cheap. This is the Big Thought that's missing from the global warming debate: there may be an optimistic path that involves affordable reforms that do not stifle prosperity. Greenhouse gases are an air pollution problem[1] and *all* previous air pollution problems have been addressed much faster than expected, at much lower cost than projected.

True, previous air pollution problems have been national or regional in character; greenhouse gases are a global issue whose resolution must involve all nations. But this does not mean greenhouse gases cannot be overcome using the same tools that have worked against other air pollution problems. In the last 30 years, the United States has substantially reduced air pollution—during the same period the United States population and economy have both boomed. If air pollution can be reduced even as a national economy grows, there is good reason to hope that greenhouse gases can be reduced even as the global economy grows.

Nor do developing nations need an "era of pollution" in order to industrialize. In the 19th century, it was true that air pollution and industrialization were inexorably linked: then, the unregulated smokestack was essential to manufacturing advancement. Today power plants and factories are being built that emit only a fraction of the air pollution of their predecessors—and efficient, low-polluting facilities tend to have the highest rates of return. Already China to a great extent and India to a lesser extent are switching to low-pollution approaches to power production and manufacturing, observing that low-polluting industry not only is good for the environment but for the bottom line. Fifteen years ago, smog was rising at dangerous rates in Mexico City. Mexico adopted anti-pollution technology and now Mexico City smog is in decline, even as the city booms economically and its population grows. Such examples suggest that the air pollution controls that have worked so well in the United States can be expanded to the world. And if the whole world can act against air pollution, maybe the whole world can act against greenhouse gas.

Consider that a little more than three decades ago in the United States rising urban smog from automobiles was widely viewed as an unsolvable problem, just as artificial global warming is widely described as unsolvable today. During the early 1970s, Los Angeles averaged more than 100 Stage One smog alerts annually, while automakers declared that building low-emission cars would raise the price of an automobile by $10,000 or more (in current dollars), if not be technically impossible. In 1970, Congress created an ambitious national smog-reduction goal and gave automakers a strong incentive to comply—devise anti-smog technology if you want to keep selling cars. Engineers turned their attention to the task and in less than a decade a cheap and effective anti-smog device—the catalytic converter—was perfected.

Today, any make or model new car purchased in the United States emits about 1 percent of the amount of smog-forming compounds per mile as a car of 1970, and the cost of the anti-smog technology is less than $100 per vehicle. Air pollution in Los Angeles, as in most other American cities, has declined spectacularly fast, at unexpectedly low cost. Nationally, smog-forming emissions have declined by almost half since 1970, even though Americans now drive their vehicles more than twice as many miles annually. In the last five years combined, Los Angeles has experienced just one Stage One smog alert.

Now consider acid rain, which is caused mainly by the emission of sulfur compounds by coal-fired power plants. In the 1980s, it was said that acid rain would cause a "new silent spring" for the Appalachians, which are downwind from the coal-fired generating stations of the Midwest. Supposedly, by now, the Appalachians would be a dead zone. In 1991, Congress enacted a program that allowed power plants to trade acid-rain emissions permits, without government involvement. The permits annually decline in value, forcing reductions. Any power plant that cut its emissions below a legal maximum could sell its extra credits on the open market. Given a profit incentive,

power-plant engineers and managers rapidly found ways to "overcontrol," cutting emissions more than the law required. Since 1990, acid rain emissions have declined by 36 percent, even as the amount of coal burned for power has risen. When the permit-trading program was enacted, reducing acid rain was expected to cost about $2,000 a ton (in current dollars). Instead most permits of the 1990s sold for about $200 a ton, meaning acid rain control cost only about 10 percent as much as predicted. The reason the phrase "acid rain" has largely vanished from American politics is that acid rain is no longer a problem in the United States—and the Appalachian forests are currently in their best health since Europeans first laid eyes on them. Big cuts in acid rain, considered impossible just two decades ago, happened faster and at a much lower price than anyone would have guessed, and without any harm at all to the economy. . . .

What world leaders most urgently need to know today about global warming is not what computer models say the temperature will be, say, in Paraguay in 2063 or any similar conjecture. Rather, they need to know if a program of mandatory greenhouse gas reduction via market-based trading will work without harming the global economy. If the answer is "yes," then an artificial greenhouse effect is not destiny. The only way to find out if the answer is yes is to start greenhouse trading programs that include mandatory reductions.

A significant fraction of corporate America already assumes that mandatory greenhouse reductions are inevitable and is simply waiting for Washington to say a single word: "Go." Leader companies such as DuPont, General Electric, 3M and others have already instituted corporate-wide greenhouse gas reduction programs and are running them without loss of profits—and cutting greenhouse emissions even as their manufacturing output increases.

The Kyoto Protocol might not have been right for the United States, but a mandatory program of greenhouse gas reduction is. For decades, the United States has led the world in technology development, economic vision and pollution control. Right now the catalytic converter and "reformulated" gasoline, anti-smog technology invented here, are beginning to spread broadly throughout developing nations. If America were to impose greenhouse gas reductions on a solely domestic basis—keep the United Nations out of this—it is likely that the United States would soon develop the technology that would light the way for the rest of the world on reducing global warming. The United States was the first country to overcome smog (ahead of the European Union by years), the first to overcome acid rain, and we should be first to overcome global warming. Once we have shown the world that greenhouse gas emissions can be reduced without economic harm, other nations will follow our lead voluntarily. The United States needs to start now with mandatory greenhouse gas reductions not out of guilt or shame, but because it is a fight we can win.

## Note

1. It can be argued that carbon dioxide is not a pollutant because plants, rain and rocks participate in a natural carbon dioxide cycle much greater in scope than artificial emissions of this gas. The point is not merely theoretical: that carbon dioxide is emitted naturally in large quantities probably means carbon dioxide does not fall under the aegis of the Clean Air Act, which regulates only "pollutants." Probably any binding federal program of greenhouse gas reduction will require new legislation from Congress, not merely an interpretation of the Clean Air Act. But for the sake of shorthand, carbon dioxide can be called "air pollution" because artificial greenhouse gases act like pollution, by causing environmental problems.

---

**GREGG EASTERBROOK** is a writer, lecturer, and a senior editor of *The New Republic*. He was a fellow at the Brookings Institution and is the author of *The Progressive Paradox* and *Sonic Boom*.

**Larry Bell**

 **NO**

# Climate of Corruption: Politics and Power Behind the Global Warming Hoax

## . . . The Big Climate Crisis Lie

Spaceship Earth reporting . . . all systems functioning . . . thermal controls optimum. Thank you, God.

Larry Bell

Conscientious environmentalism does not require or benefit from subscription to hysterical guilt over man-made climate crisis claims. Perhaps some may argue that unfounded alarmism is justifiable, even necessary, to get our attention to do what we should be doing anyway: for example, conserve energy and not pollute the planet. Hey, who wants to challenge those important purposes?

But what about examining motives? For example, when those who are twanging our guilt strings falsely portray polar bears as endangered climate victims to block drilling in Alaska's Arctic Natural Wildlife Reserve (ANWR), and when alarmists classify $CO_2$ as an endangering pollutant to promote lucrative cap-and-trade legislation and otherwise unwarranted alternative energy subsidies. What if these representations lack any sound scientific basis? Is that okay?

## The Hot Spin Cycle

Cyclical, abrupt, and dramatic global and regional temperature fluctuations have occurred over millions of years, long before humans invented agriculture, industries, automobiles, and carbon-trading schemes. Many natural fac-

tors are known to contribute to these changes, although even our most sophisticated climate models have failed to predict the timing, scale (either up or down), impacts, or human influences. While theories abound, there is no consensus, as claimed, that "science is settled" on any of those theories—much less is there consensus about the human influences upon or threat implications of climate change.

Among these hypotheses, man-made global warming caused by burning fossils has been trumpeted as an epic crisis. $CO_2$, a "greenhouse gas," has been identified as a primary culprit and branded as an endangering "pollutant." This, despite the fact that throughout Earth's history the increases in the atmospheric $CO_2$ level have tended to follow, not lead, rising temperatures. It should also be understood that $CO_2$ accounts for only 0.04 of 1 percent of the atmosphere, and about 97 percent of that tiny trace amount comes from naturally occurring sources that humans haven't influenced.

The big lie is that we are living in a known climate change crisis. Climate warming and cooling have occurred throughout the ages. Is the Earth warming right now? Probably not, but what if it is? It might be cooling next year. The models that predict a crisis are speculative at best, and two recent events have cast even more doubt on their accuracy. One relates to undisputable evidence that influential members of the climate science community have cooked the books to advance their theories and marginalize contrary findings. The other problem is evidence provided directly by Mother Nature herself that the global climate appears to have entered a new cooling cycle.

Public exposure of hacked e-mail files retrieved from the Climate Research Unit (CRU) at Britain's University of East Anglia revealed scandalous communications among researchers who have fomented global warming hysteria. Their exchanges confirm long-standing and broadly suspected manipulations of climate data. Included are conspiracies to falsify and withhold information, to suppress contrary findings in scholarly publications, and to exaggerate the existence and threats of man-made global warming. Many of these individuals have had major influence over summary report findings issued by the United Nations' IPCC. This organization has been recognized as the world authority on such matters, and it shares a Nobel Prize with Al Gore for advancing climate change awareness.

Among the more than three thousand purloined CRU documents is an e-mail from its director, Philip Jones, regarding a way to fudge the data to hide evidence of temperature declines: "I've just completed Mike's *Nature* [journal] trick of adding the real temperatures to each series for the past 20 years [i.e., from 1981 onward] and from 1961 for Keith's *to hide the decline* [emphasis mine]." "Mike," in this instance, refers to climatologist Michael Mann, who created the now infamous "hockey stick" chart that has repeatedly appeared in IPCC reports, as well as in Al Gore promotions, to portray accelerated global warming beginning with the Industrial Revolution—hence, caused by humans. The chart has been thoroughly debunked thanks to careful analyses by two Canadian researchers who uncovered a variety of serious problems. Included are calculation errors, data used twice, and a computer program that produced a hockey stick out of whatever data was fed into it.

Some of the e-mails reveal less than full public candor about what scientists don't know about past temperatures. For example, one from Edward Cook, director of tree ring research at the Lamont-Doherty Earth Laboratory, to CRU's deputy director Keith Briffa on September 3, 2003, admitted that little could be deduced regarding past Northern Hemisphere temperatures from the tree ring proxy data Mann used: "We can probably say a fair bit about [less than] 100-year extra-tropical NH temperature variability . . . but honestly know f\*\*k-all [expletive deleted] about what the [more than] 100-year variability was like with any certainty."

Correspondence leaves no doubt that the members of the network were concerned the cooling since 1998 they had observed would be publicly exposed. In an October 26, 2008, note from CRU's Mick Kelly to Jones, he comments, "Yeah, it wasn't so much 1998 and all that I was concerned about, used to dealing with that, but the possibility that we might be going through a longer 10-year period of relatively stable temperatures . . ." He added, "Speculation but if I see this possibility, then others might also. Anyway, I'll maybe cut the last few points off the filtered curve before I give the talk again as that's trending down as a result of the effects and the recent cold-ish years."

Another e-mail to Michael Mann (which James Hansen at NASA was copied on), sent by Kevin Trenberth, head of the Climate Analysis Section of the US National Center for Atmospheric Research, reflected exasperation concerning a lack of global warming evidence: "Well, I have my own article on where the heck is global warming. We are asking here in Boulder where we have broken records the past two days for the coldest days on record. We had four inches of snow." He continued, "The fact is that we can't account for the lack of warming at the moment, and it is a travesty that we can't . . . the data is surely wrong. Our observing system is inadequate."

Trenberth, an advisory IPCC high priest and manmade global warming spokesperson, didn't waste a publicity opportunity to link a devastating 2005 US hurricane

season to this cause. After ignoring admonitions from top expert Christopher Landsea that this assumption was not supported by known research, Trenberth proceeded with the unfounded claim that dominated world headlines.

Clearly, members of the CRU e-mail network used their considerable influence to block the publication of research by climate crisis skeptics, thus preventing inclusion of contrary findings in IPCC reports. In one e-mail, Tom Wigley, a senior scientist and Trenberth associate at the National Center for Atmospheric Research, shared his disdain for global warming challengers, common among global warming proponents: "If you think that [Yale professor James] Saiers is in the greenhouse skeptics camp, then, if we can find documentary evidence of this, we could go through official [American Geophysical Union] channels to get him ousted."

Possibly one of the most serious and legally hazardous breaches of professional accountability is seen in an e-mail from Jones to Mann concerning withholding of taxpayer-supported scientific data: "If they ever hear there is a Freedom of Information Act now in the UK, I think I'll delete the file rather than send it to anyone." He then asks Mann to join him in deleting official IPCC-related files: "Can you delete any e-mails you may have had with Keith re: AR4 [the IPCC's Fourth Assessment Report]?" A different e-mail from Jones assures Mann of the way some troublesome contrarian research will be handled: "I can't see either of these papers being in the next IPCC report. Kevin and I will keep them out somehow, even if we have to redefine what the peer-reviewed process is!"

A Jones letter to his colleagues instructed them, "Don't any of you three tell anyone that the UK has a Freedom of Information Act." Still another stated, "We also have a data platform act, which I will hide behind."

The CRU fallout is spreading: It now includes broader allegations by a Russian scientific group that climate-change data obtained from that country has been cherry-picked to overstate a rise in temperatures. Russia accounts for a large portion of the world's landmass, and incorrect data there would affect overall global temperature analyses.

Two things are clear from the CRU emails: (1) Perpetrators of climate science fraud have routinely conspired to exaggerate temperature increases since the Industrial Revolution, and (2) these same perpetrators virtually ignored comparable and even warmer times that preceded this period, as well as prolonged temperature declines since this period, that contradict greenhouse theory and model predictions. Other explanations that conform much more closely to observed fluctuations have been dismissed or aggressively attacked. These practices have produced unsupportable alarmist statements trumpeted in the world press that continue to influence multitrillion-dollar US and international policy decisions—decisions based upon a contrived crisis of hysteria . . . a climate of corruption.

# Chilling News for "Warm-Mongers"

The climate is always changing, in long and short cycles, and mankind has survived and thrived in conditions that have varied greatly from what they are right now.

It is apparent that our planet is once again experiencing a global cooling trend, just as it did quite recently between 1940 and 1975, when warnings of a coming new ice age received front-page coverage in the *New York Times* and other major publications. NASA satellite measurements of the lower atmosphere, where warming greenhouse models predicted effects would be greatest, stopped rising as a decadal trend after 1998 *despite increased levels of $CO_2$*. Measurements recorded by four major temperature-tracking outlets showed that world temperatures plummeted by more than 1 degree Fahrenheit (1°F) during 2007. This cooling approached the total of all the warming that had occurred over that past 100 years. In other words, temperatures worldwide and collectively never rose more than 1°F in a century. 2008 was significantly colder than 2007 had been. Although models predicted that the year 2008 would be one of the warmest on record, it actually ranked fourteenth coldest since satellite records commenced in 1979, and the coldest since 2000.

If ordinary citizens don't receive or heed scientific reports, many may legitimately question global warming assertions from direct experience. Take the year 2007, for example. North America had the most snow it's recorded in the past 50 years. A Boston storm in December dumped 10 inches of snow, more than the city typically receives in that entire month, and Madison, Wisconsin, had the highest seasonal snowfall since record keeping began. Record cold temperatures were recorded in Minnesota, Texas, Florida, and Mexico.

Those trends continued into the following 2 years. During October 2008, Oregon temperatures mid-month dipped to record lows, and Boise, Idaho, received its earliest-ever recorded snowfall. December 2008 witnessed 3.6 inches of snow in the Las Vegas Valley, the most to have fallen at that time of year since 1938, when record keeping began. Houston witnessed its earliest-ever recorded snowfall on December 4, 2009.

A blizzard on February 20, 2010, broke a Washington, DC, 110-year-old annual snowfall record of 55 inches as well as seasonal records in Baltimore and Philadelphia. Then, on February 26 and 27, another storm that pummeled New York City for 2 days broke a monthly snowfall record (37 inches) in Central Park that had stood for 114 years; the previous record for February was 28 inches in 1934, and the largest for any month was 30.5 inches in March 1896.

Most people's perceptions about warming and cooling trends depend on where they happen to reside and the time range they have experienced for reference. During July 2010, those throughout New England witnessed temperatures among the ten warmest recorded during that month in about a century, while temperatures in south-eastern US states registered below normal. Simultaneously, Los Angeles broke a coldest July day record set in 1926, Australia since 1966, and the southern cone of South America saw the coldest July in half a century. Freezing temperatures in eastern Bolivia (normally above 68°F) killed millions of fish in three major rivers, characterized there as an environmental catastrophe.

Going back to 2007, Baghdad saw its first snowfall ever recorded, and China experienced its coldest winter in 100 years. Record cold temperatures were also recorded in Argentina, Chile, and yes, even Greenland. The end of 2007 set a record for the largest Southern Hemisphere sea ice expanse since satellite altimeter monitoring began in 1979, it was about 1 million square kilometers more than the previous 28-year average. In 2008, Durban, South Africa, had its coldest September night in history, and parts of that country experienced an unusual late-winter snow. A month earlier, New Zealand officials at Mount Ruapehu reported the largest snow accumulation ever.

According to records collected by NASA, the National Oceanographic and Atmospheric Administration (NOAA), and the Hadley Centre for Climate Change, 2008 was cooler than 2007, making it the coldest year thus far of the 21st century. And this has occurred while atmospheric $CO_2$ levels have continued to rise.

This picture is far different from much of the information presented in the media. As a case in point, a 2008 Associated Press report claimed that the 10 warmest days recorded have occurred since the time of President Bill Clinton's second inaugural in January 1997. The report quoted James Hansen, who heads NASA's Godard Institute for Space Studies (GISS); Hansen is a principal adviser to Al Gore and has been a primary source of much global warming alarmism. NASA later issued corrections. In reality, the warmest recorded days—in descending order-occurred in 1934, 1998, 1921, 2006, 1931, 1934, 1953, 1990, 1938, and 1939. As Jay Lehr, a senior fellow and science director at the Heartland Institute, stated on CNN's *Lou Dobbs Tonight* program in December 2008, "If we go back in really recorded human history, in the 13th century we were probably 7 degrees Fahrenheit warmer than we are now."

Bear in mind that monthly, annual, decadal and much longer temperature fluctuations are fundamental aspects of Earth's dynamic climate history. Also remember that incredibly complex and interactive mechanisms and effects of those changes are geographically distributed in ways that confound global generalization. Most recently, NOAA's National Climatic Data Center reported that March, April, May and June of 2010 set records for the warmest year worldwide since record-keeping began in 1880. However, June was actually cooler than average across Scandinavia, southeastern China, and the northwestern US according to the same report.

NOAA ground stations reported the June average to be 1.22°F higher than normal, while NASA satellite data showed the average to be only 0.79°F above a 20-year average. This made June 2010 the second warmest in the short 32-year satellite temperature record, and the first six months of 2010 were also the second warmest. So what can we really deduce from all of this to predict a trend? Not much of anything, and certainly nothing to be alarmed about.

## Climate, Carbon, and Conspirators

So, who stands to gain from climate science corruption? There are many culprits, and they are becoming ever more powerful. Principal among these are certain agenda-driven federal government regulatory agencies, alternative energy and environmental lobbies, and yes, the UN and other organizations that seek global resource and wealth redistribution. Many of these organs of misinformation are joined at a common colon.

The IPCC has long served as the authoritative source of alarmist climate change predictions cited in media and activist warm-mongering campaigns. A richly funded example is Al Gore's Alliance for Climate Protection (ACP), which has routinely enlisted celebrities in advertising for united action against a "climate crisis." In reality, the IPCC only conducts literature reviews, although many of the publications it selectively cites are produced by the same influential people that author its reports. Moreover, illuminating CRU e-mails revealed that a small group within that organization actively worked to prevent research findings that contradicted their biases from being published in leading journals, hence blocking dissenting views from being reviewed and cited in IPCC reports.

Global warming doom-speakers and promoters of fossil energy alternatives are united behind carbon-capping politics. Climate change alarm drives the development and marketing of technologies that are otherwise uncompetitive without major government support. Unwarranted climate fear, combined with legitimate public concern about fossil-fuel depletion and dependence upon foreign oil, is promoted to justify to taxpayers and consumers the use of more costly energy options. Media campaigns portray images of dying polar bears as fossil fuel-generated carbon casualties to support arguments against drilling in ANWR and, by association, other national oil and natural gas reserves. Fossil-fuel prices rise higher, assisted by massive $CO_2$ sequestration costs and de facto cap-and-trade taxes, so consumers pay more, making alternatives seem all the more attractive.

Does it seem remarkable that the US Environmental Protection Agency (EPA) applied a global warming argument to declare that $CO_2$, the natural molecule essential for all plant life, is a "pollutant"? Might that possibly have to do with a larger agenda supported by the EPA and other organizations, such as wind and solar power lobbies and prospective carbon brokers, to limit fossil fuel use by requiring costly carbon sequestration, in turn making alternatives more price competitive, justifying subsidies, and supporting cap-and-trade schemes? But of course,

those purposes wouldn't fall within EPA responsibilities, would they? And they wouldn't make any sense at all if man-made carbon emissions didn't pose a dire climate threat.

Yet consider the implications of the suppressed EPA "Internal Study on Climate" report that was kept under wraps, its author silenced, due to pressure to support the agency's agenda to regulate $CO_2$. Alan Carlin, a senior research analyst at the EPA's National Center for Environmental Economics (NCEE), had stated in that report that after examining numerous global warming studies, his research showed the available observable data to invalidate the hypothesis that humans cause dangerous global warming. He concluded, "Given the downward trend in temperatures since 1998 (which some think will continue until at least 2030), there is no particular reason to rush into decisions based upon a scientific hypothesis that does not appear to explain most of the available data."

After serving with the EPA for 38 years, Alan Carlin was taken off climate-related work and was forbidden from speaking to anyone outside the organization on endangerment issues such as those in his then-suppressed report. A then-proposed "endangerment finding" under the Clean Air Act would enable the EPA to establish limits on $CO_2$ and other GHG concentrations as threats to public health, directly supporting cap-and-trade carbon regulations. That finding is now in force.

Bowing to pressure from global warming alarmists, the US Department of the Interior (DOI) placed polar bears on its Endangered Species Act list in 2008. Reported threats of massive melting in their habitats prompted this action. While the act's purview doesn't extend to actually regulating GHGs, there is little doubt that the classification establishes the species as poster cubs for the man-made global warming movement. It also supports environmentalist opposition to oil and gas drilling in ANWR.

But are polar bear populations really declining, as tragically depicted in Al Gore's film, *An Inconvenient Truth*? Apparently not, according to Mitchell Taylor, manager of Wildlife Research for the Government of the Canadian Territory of Nunavut, which monitors these conditions: "Of the thirteen populations of polar bears in Canada, eleven are stable or increasing in number. They are not going extinct [nor do they] even appear to be affected at present . . . [It is] silly to present the demise of polar bears based on media-assisted hysteria."

Cap-and-trade legislation, a major priority of President Barack Obama's administration, has no defensible purpose without a supporting global warming rationale. It also makes no sense from an economic standpoint. It will place onerous cost burdens upon energy consumers, continue to drive businesses overseas, and offer no real climate or environmental benefits whatsoever. Such legislation will multiply the price of electricity by dramatically increasing coal plant construction and operating costs for $CO_2$ sequestration. While intended to make such "renewables" as wind and solar more attractive, even this legislation won't make them competitive without large tax-supported subsidies. A new stock exchange would then be created that treats ("bad") carbon as a valuable ("good") commodity, providing billions of profits for operators.

Al Gore, now a very wealthy "green energy" proponent, strongly lobbies for carbon-emission trading through a London-based hedge fund called Generation Investment. He cofounded the company with David Blood, former head of investment management at Goldman Sachs, which in turn is a large shareholder in the Chicago Climate Exchange, a "voluntary pilot agency" established in 2003 to advance trading in US carbon emissions. Both organizations are working hard to persuade governments to block new power plants that use fossils. Gore exuberantly told members at a March 2007 Joint House Hearing of the Energy and Science Committee: "As soon as carbon has a price, you're going to see a wave [of investment] in it. . . . There will be unchained investment."

Perhaps the most serious public deception perpetrated by this "war against climate change" (e.g., the carbon enemy) is the notion that cleaner, sustainable options are *available* in sufficient abundance to replace dependence upon fossil resources that currently provide about 85 percent of all US energy. Regrettably, this is broadly recognized not to be the case at all. Ironically, many of the same groups that champion environmental and human causes are inhibiting progress toward vital solutions.

Extravagantly funded media campaigns continue to advertise a "climate change crisis," despite obvious evidence that the Earth began cooling once more at least a decade ago. Meanwhile, America's energy and industrial progress is being held hostage by political and legal pressures applied by groups that no one elected to represent us, and industries and other businesses that provide jobs and revenues are being driven overseas. And, as artificially manipulated energy costs continue to add unsustainable burdens to already out-of-control government borrowing and spending deficits, those impacts will fall hardest upon people who can least afford them.

## . . . Setting the Records Straight

### The Science Unanimity Myth

Widely circulated statements that scientists unanimously agree about global warming and human contributions to it or the importance and consequences of it are patently false. The apparent purpose of such claims is to discredit those with opposing viewpoints, deriding them with contempt previously reserved for those who deny the Holocaust, the dangers of tobacco, and the achievements of NASA's Apollo program. Al Gore has little tolerance for unbelievers, as evidenced in this statement: "Fifteen percent of the population believes the Moon landing was staged in a movie lot in America, and somewhat fewer believe the Earth is flat. I think they should all get together with the global warming deniers on a Saturday night and party."

"Scientific consensus" representations attached to scary climate projections have played well to legitimize highly speculative research conclusions useful to justify additional funding, sell newspapers, and enhance television audience ratings. But several petitions and surveys involving science communities present a far from unified picture.

- In 1992, a "Statement of Atmospheric Scientists on Greenhouse Warming" that opposed global controls on GHG emissions drew about 100 signatures, mostly from American Meteorological Society technical committee members.
- In 1992, a "Heidelberg Appeal," which also expressed skepticism on the urgency of restraining GHG emissions, drew more than 4,000 signatures from scientists worldwide.
- In 1996, a "Leipzig Declaration on Climate Change" that emerged from an international conference addressing the GHG controversy, was signed by more than 100 scientists in climatology and related fields.
- In 1997, a survey of American state climatologists (the official climate monitors in each of the fifty states) found 90 percent agreed that "scientific evidence indicates variations in global temperatures are likely to be naturally occurring and cyclical over very long periods of time."
- In 2001, the American Association of State Climatologists concluded that "climate prediction is complex, with many uncertainties; the AASC recognizes climate prediction is an extremely difficult undertaking. For time scales of a decade or more, understanding the empirical accuracy of such prediction—called verification—is simply impossible, since we have to wait a decade or more to assess the accuracy of the forecasts."
- In May 2007, a survey of 530 climate scientists by the Heartland Institute revealed that only about one-half agreed that "climate change is mostly the result of anthropogenic causes," and only one-third of those agreed that "climate models can accurately predict conditions in the future."
- In April 2008, the results of a survey of 489 scientists, conducted by the Statistical Assessment Service (STATS), indicated that most (74 percent) believed that some human-induced greenhouse warming has occurred, up from 41 percent reported in the 1991 Gallup survey. Only 41 percent of those polled, however, said they were directly involved in any aspect of global climate science.
- In 2008, a US Senate minority report issued by Senator James Inhofe (R-OK) presents the testimony of 650 climate-related scientists from around the world who strongly challenge global warming crisis claims. They include a Nobel laureate and former IPCC study participants.
- In March 2009, more than 600 skeptical people attended a conference organized by the Heartland Institute in New York City to protest cap-and-trade regulations favored by President Obama that

would roll GHG emissions back to 1990s levels. President Vaclav Klaus of Czech Republic delivered the keynote speech. Speaking again the next day to Columbia University faculty and students, he reaffirmed his strong opposition to a concept that global warming is man-made. "The problem is not global warming . . . by the ideology which uses or misuses it—it has gradually turned the most efficient vehicle for advocating extensive government intervention into all fields of life and for suppressing human freedom and economic prosperity."

Scientific questions and disputes will never be resolved by opinion poll tabulations. If that were the case we might now be fleeing in seal-oil fueled snowmobiles the ravages of the miles-thick glaciers predicted a few decades ago. Yet it is disingenuous to suggest that the debate is over. Or if it is, that will come as a big disappointment to those with a few remaining contrary opinions that they may be required to abandon by majority vote. In fact, some man-made warming proponents are attempting to discredit skeptical scientific opinions out of existence altogether.

For instance, in a December 2004 article titled "Beyond the Ivory Tower: The Scientific Consensus on Climate Change," published in the journal *Science*, Naomi Oreskes, a University of California–San Diego history professor, reported that her search of the Internet under the term "climate change" turned up 928 studies, based on which she cheerfully concluded that there was complete scientific agreement.

Few, if any, scientific papers claim to "refute" the theory of human-induced warming, and a search under the term "climate cycles" rather than "climate change" would have produced a different result. Hundreds of studies have been published that discuss potentially important and dominant natural forces that influence global warming and cooling over both short and very long periods, including solar climate-forcing factors (hereafter referred to at times simply as climate forcings).

Issues of debate cannot be resolved by claims that a consensus among authorities has settled the matters so long as a minority, even a small one, believes otherwise. Objective science and progress have always been advanced by those who have proven that simple lesson.

If global warming crisis skeptics and deniers are heretics, they may perhaps take some comfort in the fact that their numbers are rapidly growing. This is particularly true in the US. A 2010 Gallup poll indicates that the percentage of respondents who said they worry "a great deal" about global warming was only 28 percent, down from 33 percent in 2009 and 41 percent in 2007, when worry peaked. Global warming ranked last of eight environmental issues listed in the survey.

Gallup also conducted a 2010 poll that asked the question "Thinking about what is said in the news, in your view is the seriousness of global warming generally exag-

gerated, generally correct, or generally underestimated?" In just 4 years the percentage of Americans who believe global warming has been exaggerated has grown by 60 percent, constituting 48 percent of the respondents.

## Embracing Changes and Challenges

Two realities are quite clear: (1) that the short era of inexpensive energy resources is nearing an end; and (2) that there are no single or simple solutions. No known technology advancement or combination of advancements will satisfy the needs of uncontrolled consumption. The future we experience and introduce to those who follow will depend instead upon our human resources of vision, intellect, creativity, and discipline. We must apply all available means to expand the development and use of renewable as well as other resources, yet recognize their realistic limitations. We must strive to implement efficient processes and systems that minimize, recycle, and reuse wastes. We must apply personal and corporate lifestyles that do more with less, recognizing that this makes good economic and moral sense.

Our human ability to gain knowledge about changes we are imposing upon our planet provides opportunities to adapt our living habits, industries, and technologies to prevent avoidable surprises that lead to unfortunate events. Earth-sensing satellite observations and advancements in information technology are yielding a better understanding of nature's complexities and intricacies. This better understanding provides us with lessons we can apply to be more positive contributors. Humans are also blessed with gifts of curiosity, intelligence, and compassion, all of which enable us to recognize our responsibilities and interdependencies within a larger world community.

There is inescapable evidence that human activities are impacting Earth's environment and ecosystems, often not for the better. Air, water, and land pollution are an expanding global reality. Scientists who study these matters do us great service in pointing such things out and helping us to do better. We are not beneficially served, however, by exaggerated statements—purporting to be based upon science—that are calibrated to get maximum public attention. Alarmism, however well intentioned, is not conducive to sound judgment and reasoned responses.

Failure to rapidly develop essential energy capacities will have widespread, destructive social and economic consequences that will be particularly burdensome upon the poorest among us. A 3-decade-long blockage of US nuclear power development has already caused depletion of natural gas that could have been conserved or applied for other, more appropriate fuel and feedstock purposes. This has contributed to high natural gas prices that have forced many US energy- and chemical-intensive industries overseas, along with the jobs and tax revenues they might have otherwise provided.

Expansion of existing energy production capacity infrastructures, and creation of new ones, requires lots of time and investment in a friendly legislative environment.

This applies to nuclear plant licensing; fossil drilling; refinery construction; clean coal and coal shale development; organic and fossil synthetic liquid fuels; and yes, wind farms. While coal is our most abundant long-term fossil source, onerous and unwarranted $CO_2$ sequestration mandates, in combination with prospective carbon caps, will continue to kill incentives to build new coal-fired plants. US coal use decreased in relation to oil and gas over a 50-year [sic] period between about 1910 and 1940, and transitioning back to cleaner and liquid derivative technologies may require decades under the best circumstances. Time is very much of the essence.

Some groups and individuals advertised as "environmentalists" seem to want society to return to what they regard as the simpler, ecologically superior lifestyle of the past. This is neither possible nor desirable. Looking back, earlier tribes may have had lighter ecological footprints only because there weren't nearly as many feet then. Their lives were much harder and shorter than ours, and they used substantially more land per capita to survive and raise larger families.

We can, however, learn much from the past. From a truly "big picture" time perspective, we can readily observe that Earth's climate has changed often and dramatically over long, short, and irregular cycles, with no influence from our ancestors. From a human perspective, we can take heart that our species has adapted to rapid and severe climate shifts on numerous occasions, and the worst by far were periods of cold. We can relearn ways that indigenous peoples in all climate zones have applied logical conservation principles in dwelling construction that make resourceful use of sunlight and natural ventilation.

There should be no doubt that we humans are highly resilient creatures with remarkable abilities to survive in difficult times. In 2002, a report issued jointly by the Ocean Studies Board, the Polar Research Board, and the Board on Atmospheric Sciences and Climate of the National Research Council—titled "Abrupt Climate Change: Inevitable Surprises"—advocated preparation without panic: "The climate record for the past 100,000 years clearly indicates that the climate system has undergone periodic and extreme shifts, sometimes in as little as a decade or less. . . . Societies have faced both gradual and abrupt changes for millennia and have learned to adapt."

The report went on to advise: "It is important not to be fatalistic about the threats of abrupt climate change. . . . Nevertheless, because climate change will likely continue in the coming decades, denying the likelihood or downplaying the relevance of abrupt changes could be costly."

How do we prepare for rapid climate change? Consider that the most important impact, whether average temperatures rise or drop, will be upon energy demands. A warmer climate will increase crop yields, just as it always has, along with power consumption for air-conditioning. A cooler climate may further accelerate population shifts from US northern states to the Sun Belt, also increasing air-conditioning demands but increasing fuel consumption for winter heating in much of the country as well. Those who pay attention will have noticed that US temperatures, which had warmed until the mid-1940s, then cooled through the late 1970s, warmed until the late 1990s, and now seem to be cooling again, potentially for decades to come. All this is despite steady and "alarming" increases in human $CO_2$ releases and other activities.

Apart from climate, each of us affects the course of human events, adaptation, and technological, social, and economic progress through our choices and actions. Individually and collectively, we change the world for better or worse in a variety of important ways. We determine which businesses and products will be successful in the marketplace through our purchasing power. We decide how many resources we will consume, how much waste will be created, and whether waste will be recycled, based upon priorities that guide how we live. We influence our children and others around us through our conservation outlooks and the examples we put into practice. And we determine whom we trust to lead us and implement policies we believe in through active participation and informed votes in local, state, and national electoral processes that affect the political climate. That's the climate crisis that we urgently need to address.

---

**LARRY BELL** is a professor of architecture at the University of Houston and is the founder and director of the Sasakawa International Center for Space Architecture (SICSA).

# EXPLORING THE ISSUE

## Do We Need to Curb Global Warming?

## Critical Thinking and Reflection

1. Is global warming necessarily bad? Why or why not?
2. What is the strongest evidence that global warming is occurring? Why?
3. What is the strongest evidence that global warming is not occuring? Why?
4. Are you willing to alter aspects of your personal life (gas consumption, electric usage, etc.) in order to curb global warming? Why or why not?
5. Should international organizations be playing a larger role in the global climate change debate?

## Is There Common Ground?

There should be. No one on either side of the debate over global warming should be complacent about smoke-belching factories and generating plants. Since 1970, the United States has made significant progress toward getting rid of them. President Nixon signed the Clean Air Act that year, and since then the emission of six major pollutants, including carbon monoxide, ozone, and lead, has been cut in half. Remarkably, these reductions came during a period of rapid economic growth, when the U.S. economy grew by more than 187 percent and U.S. energy consumption by 47 percent. This is not to suggest that America can sit back on its laurels while congratulating itself. On the contrary, it should stir us to greater efforts, for it shows that a nation can clean up its act without destroying its economy.

With the international community becoming more accepting of the realities of global warming, it seems likely that the opportunity for increased dialogue will emerge. Yet there is still a large volume of global warming deniers in existence and it appears no amount of scientific data or explanation will succeed in opening their eyes to the realities of climate change. As long as there are believers and nonbelievers, common ground may be difficult to find. Yet even with such a chasm between the two sides, it seems possible to agree that pollution is not healthy for our environment or world.

## Create Central

www.mhhe.com/createcentral

## Additional Resources

David Archer, *Global Warming: Understanding the Forecast* (Wiley, 2011)

Arnold J. Bloom, *Global Climate Change* (Sinauer Associates, 2009)

Paul Epstein and Dan Ferber, *Changing Planet, Changing Health* (University of California Press, 2011)

Al Gore, *An Inconvenient Truth* (Rodale Books, 2006)

Roy W. Spencer, *Climate Confusion* (Encounter Books, 2010)

# *Internet References . . .*

**Climate Hot Map**

www.climatehotmap.org/

**Environmental Protection Agency**

www.epa.gov/climatechange/

**National Resources Defense Council**

www.nrdc.org/globalwarming/

**Union of Concerned Scientists**

www.ucsusa.org/global_warming/

**United Nations**

www.un.org/climatechange/

Selected, Edited, and with Issue Framing Material by:
William J. Miller, *Flagler College*
George McKenna, *City College, City University of New York*
and
Stanley Feingold, *City College, City University of New York*

# ISSUE

# Should Homeland Security Focus More on Cyber Crime Moving Forward?

**YES: Rick "Ozzie" Nelson and Rob Wise,** from "Homeland Security at a Crossroads: Evolving DHS to Meet the Next Generation of Threats," *Center for Strategic and International Studies Commentary* (February 1, 2013)

**NO: Stephen Flynn,** from "Recalibrating Homeland Security: Mobilizing American Society to Prepare for Disaster," *Foreign Affairs* (May/June 2011)

---

| Learning Outcomes |
|---|
| **After reading this issue, you will be able to:** |
| • Identify new threats to homeland security. |
| • Describe how homeland security must adapt to meet new threats. |
| • Explain potential consequences of failing to adapt. |
| • Assess the viability of new categories of threat. |
| • Describe why the United States is potentially vulnerable to a cyber attack. |

### ISSUE SUMMARY

**YES:** Rick Nelson, former Director of the CSIS Homeland Security and Counterterrorism Program, argues that threats have fundamentally changed over the past decade and that only by better preparing for new waves of attack can we ultimately remain protected.

**NO:** Professor Stephen Flynn believes that national security measures should be focused more on instilling the faith of the American public and being as transparent as logistically possible rather than concentrating on any given area.

In the immediate aftermath of the deadly September 11, 2001 terrorist attacks, it makes sense that the United States clearly identified defending the domestic borders from further potential acts of terrorism as the main guiding principle of domestic homeland security. On that fateful day, four domestic airliners were hijacked by 19 al-Qaeda terrorists and used as suicide weapons. AA 11 and UA175 targeted the World Trade Center in New York while AA 77 hit the Pentagon and UA93 crashed in rural Pennsylvania while heading back to the Washington, DC area. By the time all was said and done, nearly 3,000 individuals would perish. In response, the United States—under President George W. Bush—launched a global war on terrorism designed to curb al-Qaeda influence and power across the world. While the war has fundamentally changed in terms of strategy and tactics under President Barack Obama, it has successfully brought Osama bin Laden, as well as thousands of other operatives, to their deaths, potentially saving thousands of lives worldwide.

Now over 12 years removed from the attacks, there are questions regarding exactly how at risk the United States is

of another similar domestic attack. Most officials seem to be making clear opinions known that suggest traditional forms of terrorism are becoming less of a threat while other, less recognized types are gaining traction. As part of U.S. efforts to protect domestic territory, President Bush created the Department of Homeland Security to work in the civilian sphere and protect the country. Today it stands as the third largest Cabinet department in American government (falling behind only the Department of Defense and the Department of Veterans Affairs.) Yet it does not stand alone in combating potential threats domestically. The Department of Homeland Security receives only approximately 20 percent of the consolidated U.S. Homeland Security—Homeland Defense funding. Internationally, however, it is comparatively the most well-funded homeland counter-terror organization, received over 40 percent of global homeland security funding in fiscal year 2010. Its internal structures range from Immigration and Customs Enforcement to Citizenship and Immigration Services and Homeland Security Investigations.

According to the National Strategy for Homeland Security, homeland security is "a concentrated national effort to prevent terrorist attacks within the United States, reduce America's vulnerability to terrorism, and minimize the damage and recover from attacks that do occur." The broad scope includes emergency preparedness and response, domestic and international intelligence, critical infrastructure and perimeter protection, border security, transportation security, biodefense, radioactive material detection, and research on next-generation technologies. As compared to pre-September 11, 2001, the United States has taken great strides to assure the homeland is safe from traditional terrorist attacks. While there may be fewer concerns today regarding the possibility of a traditional attack, America still has vulnerabilities. There is one area that has been routinely identified as a potential problem: cyberterrorism.

At its broadest level, cyberterrorism has been defined as "the premeditated use of disruptive activities, or the threat thereof, against computers and/or networks, with the intention to cause harm or further social, ideological, religious, political or similar objectives. Or to intimidate any person in furtherance of such objectives." Other organizations have chosen to define it as "the use of information technology by terrorist groups and individuals to further their agenda. This can include use of information technology to organize and execute attacks against networks, computer systems and telecommunications infrastructures, or for exchanging information or making threats electronically. Examples are hacking into computer systems, introducing viruses to vulnerable networks, website defacing, denial-of-service attacks, or terroristic threats made via electronic communication." It is important to note that cyberterrorism is strictly limited to attacks led by individuals, non-state relate groups, or organizations. Foreign governments partaking in cyberterrorism are clearly violating international law.

According to the Industrial Control Systems Cyber Emergency Response Team (stationed within the Department of Homeland Security,) terrorist organizations do not pose a great threat due to less developed computer network capabilities. Per their interpretation: "since bombs still work better than bytes, terrorists are likely to stay focused on traditional attack methods in the near term." However, the analysis also continues to explain that more substantial threats are likely to be found as a more technically competent generation enters the various organizations. The goal of terrorist groups considering cyberterrorism—according to ICS-CERT—is to spread terror throughout the American population by causing 50,000 or more casualties, weakening the economy, or more generally detracting efforts from the war on terrorism currently being waged in Pakistan and Yemen and relying heavily on utilization of drones.

Yet with the ability of the United States to successfully curb numerous efforts and avenues for traditional terrorism, one can only assume that somewhere in the global terror network there are highly skilled computer and network hackers feverishly working to determine ways to attack Americans using their own technologies. Some elements of American homeland security have begun to recognize the threat. In 2012, FBI Director Robert Mueller and National Intelligence Director James Clapper spoke publicly about the growing concerns brought on by cyberterrorism. Mueller stated, "I do not think today it is necessarily [the] number one threat, but it will be tomorrow. . . . Counterterrorism—stopping terrorist attacks—with the FBI is the present number one priority. But down the road, the cyberthreat, which cuts across all [FBI] programs, will be the number one threat to the country." To which Clapper echoed, "The cyberthreat is one of the most challenging ones we face . . . among state actors, we're particularly concerned about entities within China and Russia conducting intrusions into U.S. computer networks and stealing U.S. data. And the growing role that nonstate actors are playing in cyberspace is a great example of the easy access to potentially disruptive and even lethal technology and know-how by such groups. . . . We foresee a cyber-environment in which emerging technologies are developed and implemented before security responses can be put in place."

Knowing American reliance on computers, networks, and technology, imagine the possibilities for attack: shutting down banks, cancelling credit cards, downloading information from computers, controlling missile defense systems, or perhaps even hijacking a drone. Any of these could be reality if (a) the United States fails to do enough to secure its networks and (b) global terrorists devote the energy and resources to this strand of attack. In the following selections, you will read from two individuals deeply involved in counterterrorism in the United States. Rick Nelson begins by arguing that America faces a new and different type of threat today than it did 12 years ago. Only by focusing energy on the emerging cyber concerns can we truly protect ourselves. On the other hand, Stephen Flynn tells us that homeland security as a whole can only hope to remain relevant and successful if it takes a concerted effort to restore faith with the American public. Given the string of controversies surrounding wiretapping and citizen concerns of spying and civil liberties, a focus on cyberterrorism would likely do little but exacerbate fears already festering within the American populous.

Rick "Ozzie" Nelson and Rob Wise

# Homeland Security at a Crossroads: Evolving DHS to Meet the Next Generation of Threats

**R**ick "Ozzie" Nelson and Rob Wise The Department of Homeland Security (DHS) finds itself at a crossroads as it enters its second decade of existence. Since its creation in 2002, DHS has worked diligently to keep the United States safe from the specter of another catastrophic terrorist attack. In doing so, the Department has wrestled with a variety of significant challenges, including coordinating across 22 pre-existing agencies, reporting to a multitude of congressional committees, and interacting with the U.S. public in a manner that constantly tests the balance between security and privacy. Some have pointed to these challenges as evidence of a dysfunctional department that is unable to effectively protect the nation. However, the Department's record is clear; there have been no major terrorist attacks on American soil in the years since DHS' creation. Furthermore, during this time DHS has achieved new levels of interagency coordination, improved cooperation with state and local agencies, and has begun integrating the private sector into a true homeland security enterprise. The Department should be congratulated for this record, as should the men and women whose hard work and constant vigilance have helped prevent another 9/11. However, after DHS spent the past 10 years focused on al Qaeda and its ideologically-inspired brand of terrorism, DHS is now confronted with a variety of new threats and challenges that will require an evolution of the Department's priorities, structures, and missions.

While the pressing need to prevent further terrorist attacks after 9/11 naturally led DHS to devote much of its energy and resources to protecting against this threat, the Department can no longer afford to focus on al Qaeda as the preeminent threat to the nation. The ability of al Qaeda and its international affiliates to launch sophisticated strikes within the United States has been degraded to a significant degree over the past several years. While terrorists are still capable of taking lives and wreaking mayhem, the potential for an attack approaching the scale of 9/11 is low. Yet even as the threat of al Qaeda recedes, new challenges are emerging. DHS must find ways to increase the nation's defenses against cyberattacks, establish enhanced systems for secure screening and credentialing, and improve intelligence and information sharing, all while operating in a constrained fiscal environment.

In some ways, the current budget climate presents a unique opportunity to transform the direction of the Department. Limited dollars will force hard decisions regarding what programs and capabilities to fund or cut, yet ultimately these decisions may be necessary to ensure DHS's future utility and health. Furthermore, these budget cuts provide an opportunity not only to increase the Department's efficiency but also to overcome and move past difficult policy issues. Fiscal realities may force resolutions to questions and problems that would have otherwise remained unaddressed, ultimately leading to a more efficient and effective Department. For instance, recent moves towards risk-based security models have been accelerated by budgetary concerns. These models hold the potential to improve not only the nation's security, but also the Department's relationship with the public. As DHS moves forward, identifying and implementing such efficiencies will be vital if the Department is to evolve to meet the demands of today's complex and dynamic threat environment.

## The Greatest Challenge: Cybersecurity

Perhaps the greatest threat the Department must defend against in the coming years will come not from a physical opponent, but from cyberspace. This threat will only grow more dire as information and communication technology continues to evolve at a rapid rate and state and non-state actors increasingly invest in cyber-capabilities. The danger posed by cyberattacks extends not only to critical infrastructure systems such as the power grid and water systems but to the nation's economy as well. Equally if not more worrying than the potential for a catastrophic "cyber Pearl Harbor," as described by Defense Secretary Leon Panetta, is the ongoing theft of intellectual property from U.S. corporations and businesses. As noted by General Keith Alexander, Commander of USCYBERCOM and director of the National Security Agency, intellectual property theft represents "the greatest transfer of wealth in history." This theft not only leeches billions of dollars from the nation's economy each year, but also grants potential adversaries access to sensitive information regarding U.S.

technologies, including those related to national security. One of DHS' greatest challenges in the coming years will be to protect against these attacks and intrusions yet in order to be effective the Department must first put in place systems and architectures designed to support its growing role in cybersecurity.

Any effort to build the nation's defenses against cyber-attacks will necessitate a robust system for the sharing of cyber-threat information and intelligence. Cyberattacks pose a challenge not just for a specific sector but span all elements of government and industry. Furthermore, an attack against a government system may well originate from the same source as an intrusion attempt directed at a private corporation, and may employ similar methods and signatures. As such, the sharing of information across and between government and industry will be vital. If various sectors can work together to ensure that information is passed to the right people at the right time and is actionable, attacks can be blunted and damage mitigated. Furthermore, the sharing of information related to adversaries' tools and tradecraft can provide early warning of emerging threats (e.g., zero hour threats), allowing those potentially affected to prevent an attack before it can inflict damage.

However, in order for this to take place a number of steps must be taken to improve the speed and breadth of sharing. Given that private industry owns 85 percent of the critical infrastructure the Department is tasked with protecting, including many of the systems most likely to be targeted for cyberattacks, methods of sharing information with and between private sector entities must be improved. Congress has made clear that it will not compel the private sector to share information. As such, DHS will need to find ways in which it can promote cooperation by lowering the costs and barriers for private industry to share cyberthreat information, both with DHS but also with one another. Informal networks for such sharing already exist between a variety of private sector entities; DHS can build upon these existing relationships by establishing a robust consortium for cyber-threat information sharing. Funded by DHS but utilized by the private sector, this consortium would serve as a forum for private industry to share information regarding cyberthreats with one another and could potentially build off the work already being conducted by the Information Technology Information Sharing and Analysis Center (IT-ISAC). However, in order to be effective this consortium would have to extend beyond the information technology sector to include members across the critical infrastructure spectrum. Furthermore, unlike the Defense Industrial Base (DIB) Cyber Pilot and the Enduring Security Framework, these efforts must focus on working to obtain and share threat information from the private sector. Simply distributing threat and intelligence briefings created by the government is insufficient; the private sector, who possesses significant and valuable insights into threat tools and tradecraft, must be an active partner.

While sharing information will do much to build cyberdefenses, DHS must also seek means by which to reduce the number of attacks being launched. The Department and its partners will always be one step behind if they focus solely on blocking or countering attacks that have already been launched, and cyberaggressors will only continue to increase the frequency, sophistication, and scope of their attacks if there are no consequences for their actions. As such, DHS must begin working, along with its partners, to develop a coordinated strategy intended to deter cyberattacks against U.S. institutions and critical infrastructure. As part of this strategy, international cooperation will be essential. Continuing to advocate for expanded multi- and bilateral arrangements between the United States and its international partners to provide for the prosecution of cybercriminals will help ensure that attackers will face legal repercussions for attacks. Further, DHS should explore assigning "cyberattaches" to a variety of nations, both to provide expertise and improve coordination. There are already precedents for these types of attaches in the customs, port, and border officers DHS already deploys to embassies. The relationships these attaches build, as well as the law enforcement and intelligence cooperation they could foster, would potentially do more to build effective bilateral and multilateral relationships than any purely diplomatic relationships. However, such a program would need to be fully supported by the State Department in order to realize its true potential. By raising the costs of launching cyberattacks, the Department has a chance to reduce their number through a strategy of aggressive deterrence.

Another measure which would be relatively easy to implement would be for DHS to establish a basic training program for federal employees across the U.S. government instructing them on how to identify, understand, and report suspicious cyberactivity. Similar standardized training could also be offered to major government contractors and industries most at risk for a cyberattack. Such training would not only reduce the risk that a given employee would become the victim of a cyberattack, but by emphasizing reporting of attempted attacks, would increase the speed at which information regarding the attack could be disseminated. However, the speed of information sharing will always be limited if it is left entirely in human hands. As such, the increased automation of information sharing, in both human and machine-readable formats, should be explored. By more rapidly sharing cyberthreat information across sectors, government and industry have the chance to limit the efficacy of cyberattacks.

In order to prepare for cyberthreats that will likely only continue to grow in frequency and sophistication, the Department must enhance long-term planning and investments. Most importantly, DHS must accelerate its efforts to build a workforce of cybersecurity experts. Without a dynamic, trained cadre of cyber practitioners and analysts, DHS is likely to fall behind when attempting to defend against rapidly-evolving cyberthreats. While DHS should be commended for recent initiatives to hire hundreds of new cyberworkers, the Department may experience limited success if it does not find ways to better appeal to these potential and current employees. Many skilled cyberexperts who might otherwise apply to these jobs lack the formal education or background expected by DHS and may not fit the mold of a traditional government employee. In order to attract and retain talented individuals, DHS must be willing to look past traditional hiring practices and requirements and instead focus on the skills and traits needed to succeed in a cyberworkforce. For example, DHS could establish a cyberworkforce rotation program with academic institutions and the private sector. DHS has an opportunity to build a workforce capable of meeting and countering tomorrow's cyber threats but only if the Department is able to attract and retain the best and brightest.

## The Core Capability: Screening and Credentialing

Beyond cybersecurity, in the coming years DHS will be faced with the growing challenge of providing vital screening and credentialing services for an increasing number of individuals even as budgets are tightened. At present, the Department is responsible not only for screening millions of airline passengers each day for security threats but for credentialing thousands of individuals seeking access to everything from the transportation system to critical infrastructure. As such, responsibility for screening and credentialing is spread across multiple agencies within DHS who employ dozens of unique systems. However, this diffuse model is inefficient and, as demand rises and budgets fall, will increasingly become untenable. For instance, with the President's National Travel and Tourism Strategy seeking to attract millions of additional foreign visitors to the United States each year, the strain on visa and customs screening is only likely to grow. Yet long wait-times at gateway airports demonstrate that these screening systems are already overtaxed. DHS must seek new efficiencies in order to continue to provide the screening and credentialing services necessary to keep the nation safe.

For the Department's screening and credentialing services, the way ahead may lie with an enterprise approach. At present, the multitude of systems being utilized contributes to significant redundancies. Collecting information that is only entered into a single system wastes time and money if that information has already been entered into another system. Furthermore, due to a lack of integration, there is the danger that vital existing information on one system will be overlooked when making a decision based on information in a second system. However, by implementing common, enterprise-wide systems, there is an opportunity not only to reduce redundancies and thereby increase efficiency but improve security as well.

A number of steps can and should be taken in order to foster an enterprise approach to screening and credentialing. While the Department has made great strides towards integration of its various databases, this process is not yet complete. Full integration of all DHS databases should be accelerated so that all elements of the Department have as much information as possible regarding those they are screening and credentialing, whether that information was originally collected by Customs and Border Protection (CBP), the Transportation Security Administration (TSA), Immigration and Customs Enforcement (ICE) or any of DHS's other component agencies. In addition to greater connectivity across DHS, the Department should also explore greater integration with other government databases. Furthermore, screening and credentialing processes could benefit substantially from greater automation. The introduction of automated processes could significantly reduce the time needed for many tasks associated with screening and credentialing, greatly improving efficiency. However, a functional and useful system will require not only advances in automation technology, but that the Department as well as the public come to accept and trust automation to a greater degree. Furthermore, the Department should examine the creation of a Department-wide targeting center for the analysis of screening data from across DHS. While various component agencies maintain their own targeting centers, no single agency has a complete picture of all the information residing in the Department's many screening and credentialing systems. A DHS targeting center could provide a more complete view, putting together pieces that other, smaller centers might miss. By focusing on greater integration of databases, increased automation, and the creation of a Department-wide targeting center, DHS has an opportunity to create a more efficient and effective screening and credentialing enterprise.

Further advances in risk-based security will also play a vital role in ensuring efficient and effective screening and credentialing systems. As budgets are reduced and demand for screening and credentialing grows, the targeted application of resources will become increasingly necessary. DHS will need to spend fewer resources screening those who represent a low risk, yet in order to realize savings, the Department must build a better picture of these low-risk individuals. Programs like TSA's Pre-Check and CBP's Global Entry represent valuable steps forward. Yet in order to fully realize the benefits, these programs should be expanded to include a greater number of trusted travelers from a variety of sources. Further, trusted travelers enrolled in one program should be provided an ID number or biometric profile that would be recognized across programs, greatly increasing interoperability while decreasing the resources wasted screening those who have already been screened by another program. By expanding risk-based security, DHS can not only increase security, but save limited budget dollars.

As DHS pursues methods for improving screening and credentialing systems, the Department must also look to improve its identity management capabilities. Establishing identity is often the first and most important step in the screening and credentialing methods employed by the Department. Biographical data, such as an applicant's name and date of birth, comprises the vast majority of information currently used to establish identity yet biographical data is relatively insecure and open to counterfeiting. Furthermore, this information is subject to a variety of potential errors that can limit its utility. For instance, while Umar Farouk Abdulmutallab, the "Christmas Day bomber" was placed on a terrorism watch list, he was not prevented from boarding a United States-bound flight because his name was spelled incorrectly when searched against a database. However, biometric information offers the potential to improve the security of the Department's identity management efforts while reducing the risk of errors. Abdulmutallab would likely have been discovered before he attempted to ignite his explosives if his fingerprints or iris scan, rather than his name, had been compared. Furthermore, such biometric identifiers are significantly more difficult to counterfeit than biographical information, greatly reducing the risk of fraud. The increased incorporation of such biometric information into the process of establishing identity will go far toward bolstering the effectiveness of DHS's screening and credentialing efforts.

## The Mission Accelerant: Intelligence and Information Sharing

Given the wide variety of rapidly-evolving threats facing the Department, intelligence, and particularly the sharing of information, is only becoming more vital to fulfilling homeland security missions. In an environment of reduced budgets, intelligence is of even greater value, allowing for the effective targeting of limited resources. Given that the Department is increasingly employing risk-based models of security, which are inherently intelligence-driven, the Department's need for timely and accurate information is only likely to grow in the immediate future. DHS and the greater homeland security enterprise have made enormous strides over the past decade in promoting the sharing of intelligence and information in order to meet these needs. New organizations and systems have been created and existing organizations have radically altered their structures and cultures to reduce stovepipes and cross boundaries that existed before 9/11. However, there exists a significant risk that as the specter of another catastrophic terrorist attack recedes from the public consciousness support for information sharing will decline, allowing organizations to retrench into their pre-9/11 positions of isolation. In order to prevent this from occurring, DHS needs to be a forceful advocate for the continued, and potentially even expanded, sharing of intelligence and information.

While the traditional core of al Qaeda has been decimated in recent years, its adherents and supporters continue to pose a worrying, if somewhat reduced, threat to the security of the nation. Al Qaeda in the Arabian Peninsula has repeatedly attempted to strike within the United States and on at least two occasions has managed to operationalize plots that would have brought down aircraft over the United States. Al Qaeda in the Islamic Maghreb has not yet sought to launch attacks against America itself, yet recent events have demonstrated their increasingly sophisticated capabilities as well as the willingness of their associates to target U.S. institutions and personnel. However, the terrorist threats that face the nation are not just external but internal as well. Homegrown terrorists, already residing in the United States and familiar with U.S. culture and customs, continue to pose a unique and troubling challenge. While the overall frequency of homegrown terrorism has declined from 2009 levels, plots continue to be uncovered, evidenced by the arrest in December, 2012 of two Florida men accused of conspiring to employ weapons of mass destruction within the United States. In such cases, a mixture of externally and internally-focused intelligence is often required to detect and disrupt the plot, necessitating robust and continued information sharing efforts.

DHS must better define its role with regards intelligence in order to be effective. However, in order to begin this process the Department will first need to define what constitutes "homeland security intelligence." Given the variety of entities from across the federal government, state and local governments, and the private sector involved in the collection and analysis of homeland security intelligence, a common definition is of immense value. DHS should provide a common definition for all those involved in the homeland security intelligence enterprise. The Department must also better establish its position within this enterprise. While a variety of agencies and organizations are capable of collecting and analyzing this intelligence, the multitude of entities involved demands that there be a single, coordinated point of control for the movement and distribution of this intelligence. In order to increase its effectiveness, DHS should firmly establish itself as this focal point, serving as the primary lead organization for the movement of information and intelligence between the federal government, state and local governments, and private industry.

At the tactical level, the network of fusion centers established since 9/11 represent a valuable means of bringing federal counterterrorism agencies together with the state and local entities who are most likely to observe suspicious terrorism-related activity. Furthermore, by allowing for outside oversight, fusion centers provide the high degree of transparency required when information regarding U.S. citizens is being shared. Such a transparent environment will be critical in the coming years, given that the amount of information available regarding U.S. citizens is only likely to increase in the future. As such, DHS must take steps to ensure that increased controversy over how these centers are employed does not threaten their continued utility. The Department and other federal agencies must accept that state and local entities will only be willing to continue to participate in fusion centers if they add value beyond counterterrorism. As such, federal and state and local agencies must work together to strike a working balance between counterterrorism and all-hazards missions. Federal agencies such as DHS must also collaborate with state and local agencies in order to gain a better understanding of what information is most useful to them, so that no agency feels that they are sacrificing more than they are gaining by participating in a fusion center. The Department should also encourage state and local partners to participate in standardized intelligence training, in order to better equip those on the ground with a better understanding of the intelligence process and equalize some of the disparities between various fusion centers. Additionally, the fusion centers need to find a means to better engage with the private sector. This includes not only finding new avenues for integrating information provided by the private sector, but keeping private companies and businesses informed of potential threats in a useful and timely manner while remaining cognizant of privacy and civil liberties concerns. Fusion centers have the potential to continue to play a vital role in protecting the nation but will be hampered in their mission unless the Department and its partners can come together to address these challenges.

As the threats facing the homeland evolve beyond terrorism, so too must the Department's employment of information sharing. Utilizing existing models, technologies, and lessons learned from counterterrorism, DHS has an opportunity to begin building information sharing capabilities dedicated to countering a variety of other pressing threats, most notably illicit activity along the border and cyber-threats. For instance, the Department employs a significant number of sensors and thousands of personnel along the nation's borders, collecting massive amounts of information each day. However, this data loses any long-term value if it is not quickly integrated, shared, and analyzed. By putting structures and systems in place to encourage this sharing and analysis, DHS has a chance to allocate its resources along the border in a more strategic fashion, so that border security is no longer purely reactive but increasingly predictive. A similar model can be applied to cyber-security. However, in order for these efforts to meet with success, DHS, working

with the Program Manager for the Information Sharing Environment (PM-ISE), must lead the establishment of institutionalized means of sharing not just within the Department, but across government agencies as well as with foreign partners and private industry. By applying information sharing lessons taken from years of counterterrorism efforts, the Department can begin to build the capabilities necessary to address the next generation of threats to the homeland.

The coming years will hold a variety of new challenges for the Department which will require an ability to quickly evolve and adapt. While DHS has succeeded in fulfilling its primary mission over the past decade—protecting the nation from terrorism—the coming years will bring with them a variety of new dangers and dynamics. DHS must begin moving to address these now, so that the nation is not left unprotected in a rapidly-changing security landscape, even in the midst of significant budget constraints. By focusing its efforts and resources on building cyber-security, screening and credentialing, and information sharing capabilities, the Department has an opportunity to counter a new generation of threats before they can inflict significant damage to the United States.

**Rick "Ozzie" Nelson** is Vice President for Business Development at Cross Match Technologies, a former Director of the CSIS Homeland Security and Counterterrorism Program, and currently a Nonresident Senior Associate at CSIS. He is a former Navy helicopter pilot with over 20 years of operational and intelligence experience, including assignments at the National Security Council (NSC) and the National Counterterrorism Center (NCTC).

**Rob Wise** is the research assistant and program coordinator for the Homeland Security and Counterterrorism Program at CSIS. He has coauthored publications on a wide variety of topics, including the future of al Qaeda, the evolving dynamics of Special Operations, and the direction of the nation's homeland security enterprise. He received a B.A. in political science from the University of Pennsylvania, where he focused on the study of conflict and international security.

Stephen Flynn

# Recalibrating Homeland Security: Mobilizing American Society to Prepare for Disaster

The United States has made a mess of homeland security. This is hardly surprising. The policymakers responsible for developing homeland security policy in the wake of September 11, 2001, did so under extraordinary conditions and with few guideposts. The Bush administration's emphasis on combating terrorism overseas meant that it devoted limited strategic attention to the top-down law enforcement and border-focused efforts of the federal departments and agencies assigned new homeland security responsibilities. President Barack Obama has largely continued his predecessor's policies, and congressional oversight has been haphazard. As a result, nearly a decade after al Qaeda struck the World Trade Center and the Pentagon, Washington still lacks a coherent strategy for harnessing the nation's best assets for managing risks to the homeland—civil society and the private sector.

For much of its history, the United States drew on the strength of its citizens in times of crisis, with volunteers joining fire brigades and civilians enlisting or being drafted to fight the nation's wars. But during the Cold War, keeping the threat of a nuclear holocaust at bay required career military and intelligence professionals operating within a large, complex, and highly secretive national security establishment. The sheer size and lethality of U.S. and Soviet nuclear arsenals rendered civil defense measures largely futile. By the time the Berlin Wall came down and the Soviet Union collapsed, two generations of Americans had grown accustomed to sitting on the sidelines and the national security community had become used to operating in a world of its own.

To an extraordinary extent, this same self-contained Cold War-era national security apparatus is what Washington is using today to confront the far different challenge presented by terrorism. U.S. federal law enforcement agencies, the border agencies, and the Transportation Security Administration (TSA) are subsumed in a world of security clearances and classified documents. Prohibited from sharing information on threats and vulnerabilities with the general public, these departments' officials have become increasingly isolated from the people that they serve.

This is the wrong approach to protecting the homeland. Even with the help of their state and local counterparts, these federal agencies cannot detect and intercept every act of terrorism. Police, firefighters, and other emergency responders will not always be immediately at hand to protect and rescue those in harm's way. Professionals are usually not the first responders to terrorist attacks and other disasters. A sidewalk T-shirt vendor, not a police patrol officer, sounded the alarm about Faisal Shahzad's SUV in his May 2010 car-bombing attempt on New York's Times Square. Courageous passengers and flight-crew members, not a federal air marshal, helped disrupt the suicide-bombing attempt by Umar Farouk Abdulmutallab aboard Northwest Airlines Flight 253 on Christmas Day 2009. It often falls to ordinary citizens—family, friends, neighbors, and bystanders—to lend a hand in times of crisis.

Coping with terrorism requires localized, open, and inclusive engagement of civil society. But the U.S. government has neither adequately informed nor empowered civilians to play a meaningful role in defending the country. To better involve civilians in homeland security, the United States must remove the inadvertent obstacles it has placed in their way. Citizens, in turn, must be willing to grapple with the risks they and their communities are likely to face and embrace a more active role in preparing for disasters.

## Developing Trust

To improve the nation's capacity to manage dangers, federal agencies must avoid alienating the very people they are responsible for protecting. Regrettably, Washington's growing homeland security bureaucracy has largely overlooked the need to garner support from the public. New security measures are advanced without spelling out the vulnerability that they are designed to address. The American public has generally tolerated this thus far, but presuming the public's submissiveness risks breeding resentment and lack of cooperation over time. Alternatively, when citizens understand the appropriateness of a given security measure, they will be more willing to collaborate to achieve its goal.

Flynn, Stephen. From *Foreign Affairs*, vol. 90, no. 3, May/June 2011, pp. 130–140. Copyright © 2011 by Council on Foreign Relations, Inc. Reprinted by permission of Foreign Affairs. www.ForeignAffairs.com

When the TSA introduced full-body x-ray scanners and enhanced pat-downs at U.S. airports last fall, it prioritized public compliance over public acceptance. Given the coercive tools at its disposal, the TSA correctly presumed that it could force civilian acquiescence to this more intrusive passenger screening process. But the marginal additional capabilities provided by the scanners and pat-downs came at a heavy cost. Public confusion and anger over the new program, expressed by the Thanksgiving holiday travel opt-out campaign, spawned a vocal minority that has sown general public skepticism and may impede future U.S. government efforts to improve homeland security.

In explaining its security measures to the public, the government should not promise more than it can deliver. U.S. officials should avoid making the kind of statements issued frequently after September 11 to the effect that terrorists have to be right only once, whereas U.S. officials have to be right 100 percent of the time. Such declarations might demonstrate firm resolve, but they set an impossible standard; no security regime is foolproof. Common drug-smuggling techniques can evade the new scanning technology at U.S. airports. Radiation portal monitors, deployed with much fanfare at U.S. seaports, are unlikely to detect shielded nuclear material, raising the possibility that a nuclear weapon or dirty bomb encased in lead could pass through undetected. Public officials should acknowledge the potential limits of these technologies and other security protocols in deterring terrorists. Creating unrealistic expectations guarantees anger, disappointment, and mistrust should a terrorist attack succeed.

U.S. policymakers should also refrain from measures that provide the optics of security rather than real security. For example, the presence of cement barriers outside a train station may reassure daily commuters. But if those barriers are not anchored to the ground, an explosive-laden truck could ram them aside and make it to the station's entrance. The ensuing tragedy would leave commuters feeling rightfully deceived and the families of victims outraged. Security protocols must survive a "morning-after test"; that is, they should be able to withstand a postmortem by the public about their adequacy, even if they failed to thwart an attack. If the post-incident assessment deems the security measures to be lacking credibility, there will be hell to pay.

## Open Up

National security officials should also resist the secrecy reflex. U.S. intelligence and federal law enforcement agencies perform too much homeland security work behind closed doors. Their proclivity to operate in a world of restricted documents and windowless rooms often leaves both the private sector and the general public out of the loop.

On the surface, it seems sensible to avoid releasing information about vulnerabilities or security measures that potential adversaries could exploit. But this insularity often undermines the defense of critical infrastructure, such as seaports, dams, and waterworks. In determining the best way to protect a suspension bridge, for example, the bridge's chief engineer is likely to have ideas that would not occur to a law enforcement or military professional working in the Department of Homeland Security. But government officials frequently fail to consult that engineer. They will share security information only with vetted company security officers, who in turn are barred from passing this information on to senior executives and managers who do not hold active security clearances. As a result, investment and operational decisions are often made with scant attention paid to the potential security stakes.

The U.S. government should increase its transparency with the broader public as well. Many policymakers believe that candor about potential dangers may generate excessive public fear. Yet the secrecy reflex often contributes to public anxiety. People are most frightened when they sense their vulnerability to threats but feel powerless to address them. U.S. officials have stated for nearly a decade that terrorism is a clear and present danger, but they have given citizens little information about how to cope with that hazard. Instead, citizens are told to proceed with their daily routines because the government is hard at work protecting them. The psychological effect of this is similar to that of a doctor telling a patient that she is suffering from a potentially life-threatening illness but providing only vague guidance about how to combat it. No one wants to receive disturbing news from his physician, but a prognosis becomes less stressful when doctors provide patients with all the details, a clear description of the available treatments, and the opportunity to make decisions that allow the patient to assert some personal control over the outcome. In the same way, the U.S. government can decrease fears of terrorism by giving the American public the information it needs to better withstand, rapidly recover from, and adapt to the next major terrorist attack.

Flight attendants routinely tell passengers that they may need to use their seat cushions to stay afloat in the event of an emergency water landing. Although escaping a plane in the water is a frightening scenario, this safety instruction does not generate panic among passengers. Similarly, there is no reason why civilians should not be told what bombs and detonators look like, on the very remote chance that someone like the "Christmas Day bomber" ends up seated next to one of them on a plane. Having better-informed airport workers, flight crews, and passengers could prove a far more effective safeguard than deploying hundreds of new body scanners at airports.

## Avoid Overreacting

Washington must also avoid overstating the threat of terrorism. Terrorist attacks are not all the same. Small-scale attacks of limited destructiveness pose the most likely terrorist danger to the United States today. Although Osama bin Laden remains on the loose, al Qaeda's senior leadership infrastructure has essentially been dismantled, undermining its ability to conduct sophisticated large-scale operations in North America. Aligned groups or other terrorist organizations may still organize catastrophic attacks, but such ambitious terrorist operations require groups of operatives with capable leaders, communications with those overseeing the planning, and time to conduct surveillance and to rehearse. Money, identity documents, and safe houses for operatives must be secured, and other logistical needs must be met. All this effort creates multiple opportunities for intelligence and law enforcement agents to disrupt plots before they come to fruition.

In the face of these challenges, terrorists have adapted their tactics. Now, attacks on U.S. soil are likely to be perpetrated by homegrown operatives who act alone or with one or two accomplices. Such operations are difficult to detect and intercept. Yet lone gunmen and suicide bombers can inflict only limited damage. Tragically, such attacks will destroy property and take innocent lives. But Mother Nature generates far more frequent and disastrous incidents. Virtually no terrorist scenario could equal the devastation caused by the March 2011 earthquake and tsunami that hit northern Japan. Similarly, it is hard to imagine that a terrorist armed with a weapon of mass destruction could produce more casualties than a global outbreak of a virulent strain of the flu virus: epidemiologists estimate that as many as 100 million people died of the Spanish flu in 1918. Even when terrorism is measured against other national security challenges, some perspective is warranted. During the height of the Cold War, a nuclear exchange with the Soviet Union would have left two-thirds of the American people dead and much of the world in ruins. That was a true existential danger, and one that the most ambitious terrorists cannot hope to match.

Similarly, U.S. policymakers must avoid overreacting to terrorist incidents when they do occur. In the aftermath of the bombing attempt aboard Northwest Airlines Flight 253, congressional leaders on both the left and the right declared it better to overreact than underreact to the risk of terrorism. This rare bipartisan consensus was unfortunately entirely wrong. Terrorism is fueled by the confidence that Americans will react to it by embracing draconian measures that damage the U.S. economy. Al Qaeda's October 2010 attempt to bomb airplanes by hiding explosives in ink cartridges shipped from Yemen was consistent with this strategy. The terrorists hoped that the midair destruction of any plane—cargo or civilian—would spur U.S. officials to respond with costly and disruptive methods that would undermine the movement of global cargo. In other words, their strategy depends on how Americans react—or, more precisely, overreact—to acts of terrorism.

Yet such smaller-scale, less destructive, and less lethal operations, even if unsuccessful, can produce this overreaction only when overwrought media coverage and political recriminations generate a rush to deploy expensive and often counterproductive new defenses. Conversely, a response of confident resilience to acts of terrorism would provide a real measure of deterrence by demonstrating that such attacks will not achieve their desired ends. Although the United States cannot prevent every act of terrorism, it can control how it responds to them.

## The Way Forward

The U.S. government can avoid hindering its own actions to protect the homeland by building trust and setting proper expectations with civilians. To develop a comprehensive homeland security strategy, however, Washington should place greater emphasis on developing adequate societal resilience. Resilience is the capacity of individuals, communities, companies, and the government to withstand, respond to, adapt to, and recover from disasters. Since disruptions can come not just from terrorism but also from natural and accidental sources as well, advancing resilience translates into building a general level of preparedness. Ideally, a program of resilience would address the most likely risks that people, cities, or enterprises may face. This would minimize the potential for complacency while assuring a level of basic skills, such as first aid and effective emergency communications, which are useful no matter the hazard.

Building societal resilience requires a bottom-up, open, and participatory process—that is, the exact inverse of the way U.S. policymakers have approached homeland security to date. A program of resilience mandates individuals, communities, and companies to take precautions within their respective areas of control. Success is measured by the continuity or rapid restoration of important systems, infrastructure, and societal values in the face of an attack or other danger.

Resilience begins on the level of individuals. A program of resilience would promote self-reliance in the face of unexpected events, encouraging civilians to remain calm when the normal rhythms of life get interrupted. It would also teach individuals to make themselves aware of the risks that may confront them and to be resourceful by learning how to react to crises. And it would make preparedness a civic virtue by instructing civilians to refrain from requesting professional assistance unless absolutely necessary, thus freeing up manpower for those in the greatest need.

Promoting individual resilience involves acknowledging that many Americans have become increasingly complacent and helpless in the face of large-scale danger. Reversing this trend demands a special emphasis on educating young people. Students should learn to embrace preparedness as both a practical necessity and an opportunity to serve others. These students, in turn, can teach their parents information-age survival skills, such as texting, which may offer the only means to communicate when cellular networks are overloaded (800 text messages consume the same bandwidth as a one-minute call). As demonstrated in the aftermath of the 2010 Haitian earthquake and the Deepwater Horizon oil spill that same year, social media are transforming the way rescuers and survivors respond to crises. These new tools have the power to turn traditional, top-down emergency management on its head.

Resilience also applies to communities. The U.S. government can promote resilience on the communal level by providing meaningful incentives for collaboration across the public, private, and nonprofit sectors before, during, and after disasters. Much like at the individual level of resilience, communities should aspire to cope with disasters without outside assistance to the greatest degree possible.

Building resilient communities requires providing community leaders with tools to measure and improve their preparedness based on a widely accepted standard. The Community and Regional Resilience Institute, a government-funded research program based at Tennessee's Oak Ridge National Laboratory, has spearheaded an attempt to define the parameters of resilience, modeled on the method by which fire and building codes were created and are maintained. It has drawn on a network of former governors and former and current mayors, emergency planners, and academics to develop detailed guidelines and comprehensive supporting resources that will allow communities to devise resilience plans tailored to their needs. Other countries, including Australia, Israel, and the United Kingdom, have instituted similar programs. Federal and state governments could provide communities that implement a comprehensive risk-awareness strategy and a broad-based engagement program with tangible financial rewards, such as reduced insurance premiums and improved bond ratings.

U.S. companies compose the third tier of resilience. Resilient companies should make business continuity a top priority in the face of a disaster. They should invest in contingency planning and employee training that allow them to serve and protect their customers under any circumstance. Corporations must also study the capabilities of and partner with their suppliers and surrounding communities. Much like individuals and communities, corporations with resilience would possess the ability to sustain essential functions and quickly resume their operations at full capacity after a disaster. Resilience may also bring financial benefits to companies able to demonstrate their dependability in the wake of a major disruption. Such companies are likely to experience an increase in market share by maintaining regular customers and attracting new ones as well.

Although most large corporations invest in measures that improve resilience, smaller companies—which are the backbone of local economies and yet are constrained by limited resources—generally do not. But small businesses can rectify this in a low-cost manner by creating a buddy system between companies located in different regions. For instance, a furniture store in Gulfport, Mississippi, that may fall victim to an August hurricane could partner with a furniture store in Nashville, Tennessee, that may suffer from spring flooding. These businesses would

agree to assist each other in providing backup support for data, personnel, customers, and suppliers in the event of a disaster.

## Instilling Resilience

To his credit, Obama explicitly identified resilience as a national security imperative in his May 2010 National Security Strategy. Homeland Security Secretary Janet Napolitano did the same in the February 2010 Quadrennial Homeland Security Review. Both have made frequent references to the importance of resilience in their speeches. But neither the federal bureaucracy nor the general public appears to be paying much attention.

The approaching tenth anniversary of September 11 will provide Obama with an opportunity to recalibrate the nation's approach to homeland security. While honoring the enormous sacrifice of the U.S. armed forces and those who have been working to protect the U.S. homeland, he should ask citizens to step forward and assume their own unique role. For individuals, families, neighbors, employers, and employees, the way to honor the lives so tragically lost in the Twin Towers, in the Pentagon, and aboard United Airlines Flight 93 is to unite in preparing for future emergencies. The president should ask citizens from every walk of life to embrace a personal commitment to making the United States more resilient.

When passengers enter the new body scanners at U.S. airports, they are directed by TSA screeners to hold their hands above their heads and stand still while their images are taken. The position closely resembles the universal stance for surrendering—undoubtedly why many find the process so uncomfortable. An emphasis on resilience, by contrast, is consistent with the U.S. tradition of grit, determination, and hope in the face of adversity. When tested, Americans have always bounced back better and stronger. It is long past time for Washington to stop treating civil society as a child to be sheltered and to acknowledge the limits and counterproductive consequences of relying so heavily on protective measures. In good times and bad, the greatest asset of the United States has always been its people.

---

**STEPHEN FLYNN** is Professor of Political Science and the founding director of the Center for Resilience Studies at Northeastern University in Boston, Massachusetts. He is also co-director of the George J. Kostas Research Institute for Homeland Security and director of Northeastern's Master of Security and Resilience Studies Program. Dr. Flynn is the author of the critically acclaimed *The Edge of Disaster: Rebuilding a Resilient Nation* (Random House, 2007), and the national bestseller, *America the Vulnerable* (HarperCollins 2004). He is a senior research fellow at the Wharton School's Risk Management and Decision Processes Center at the University of Pennsylvania. Since 9/11 he has provided testimony on 28 occasions on Capitol Hill.

# EXPLORING THE ISSUE

## Should Homeland Security Focus More on Cyber Crime Moving Forward?

### Critical Thinking and Reflection

1. What do you believe is the greatest threat to homeland security today? Why?
2. What area of homeland security do you believe is over-emphasized currently?
3. Do you believe the American people still believe in homeland security? Why or why not?
4. Do we devote too many resources to homeland security? Why or why not?
5. In what ways are the United States vulnerable to a cyber attack? Is there a way to prepare for these attacks?

### Is There Common Ground?

Common ground is actually quite easy to identify in theory for this particular debate. America should be easily capable of protecting the domestic homeland from both cyberterrorism and more traditional strands of attacks simultaneously. While both pulling from the Department of Homeland Security, the resources required come from different groups, indicating that both could be feverishly working at any point without detracting from each other. If this were to happen, we would hopefully have solid lines of communication open between the two sides assuring that efforts were not being unnecessarily duplicated.

While saying that we should be able to run a multi-faceted counterterrorism program is quite simple, maintaining funding and public support is not. There are growing concerns that counterterror efforts could become a victim of its own success. Within the liberty-security debate, some argue that when too much time passes without a clear reminder of the dangers lurking for Americans across the globe, citizens become complacent and less willing to make sacrifices in the name of protection. Tied to this is budgetary dollars. With continuing deficits and efforts to maintain a presence fighting the global war on terrorism, there are only so many homeland security dollars to be had. Without taking money from other areas,

it may be difficult to assure a multi-faceted counterterror strategy is fairly funded across the board in a way that allows for effective defense.

### Create Central

www.mhhe.com/createcentral

### Additional Resources

Jason Andress and Steve Winterfeld, *Cyber Warfare: Techniques, Tactics, and Tools for Security Practitioners* (Syngress, 2013)

Joel Brenner, *America the Vulnerable: Inside the New Threat Matrix of Digital Espionage, Crime, and Warfare* (Penguin Press, 2011)

Richard A. Clarke and Robert Knake, *Cyber War: The Next Threat to National Security* (Ecco, 2012)

Frank Hsu and Dorothy Marinucci, *Advances in Cyber Security: Technology, Operations, and Experiences* (Fordham University Press, 2013)

Franklin D. Kramer, Stuart H. Starr, and Larry Wents, *Cyberpower and National Security* (Potomac Books, 2009)

# *Internet References . . .*

**Center for Strategic and International Studies**

http://csis.org/category/topics/technology
/cybersecurity

**Cybersecurity—Department of Homeland Security**

www.dhs.gov/topic/cybersecurity

**Department of Homeland Security**

www.dhs.gov

**The White House**

www.whitehouse.gov/issues/foreign-policy
/cybersecurity

**U.S. Computer Emergency Readiness Team**

www.us-cert.gov/ncas/tips

**Selected, Edited, and with Issue Framing Material by:**
**William J. Miller,** *Flagler College*
**George McKenna,** *City College, City University of New York*
**and**
**Stanley Feingold,** *City College, City University of New York*

# ISSUE

# Is Warrantless Wiretapping Ever Justified to Protect National Security?

**YES: Andrew C. McCarthy,** from "How to 'Connect the Dots'," *National Review* (January 30, 2006)

**NO: Al Gore,** from "Restoring the Rule of Law," from a speech presented to the American Constitution Society for Law and Policy and the Liberty Coalition (January 15, 2006)

---

### Learning Outcomes

**After reading this issue, you will be able to:**

- Discuss what a warrantless wiretap is.
- Assess whether these wiretaps are ever justified.
- Identify circumstances when warrantless wiretaps may be needed.
- Explain the process for legally obtaining a wiretap.
- Describe the president's extra-constitutional powers with regards to foreign policy.

---

### ISSUE SUMMARY

**YES:** Former Federal Prosecutor Andrew C. McCarthy supports the National Security Agency program of surveillance without a warrant as an effective means of protecting national security that employs the inherent power of the president to protect the country against subversion.

**NO:** Former Vice President Al Gore views the warrantless wiretapping of American citizens as a brazen violation of the Constitution and of specific acts of Congress that have spelled out the circumstances under which a president may receive judicial permission to wiretap or otherwise invade the privacy of citizens.

**A**mericans overwhelmingly believe in the right to privacy. They subscribe to the old adage that a man's home is his castle (adding that a woman's home is hers). Yet the Constitution makes no explicit mention of a right to privacy. Controversy revolves not around the right to privacy but under what circumstances there are conflicting societal interests that would curtail it.

As it has on earlier occasions, privacy rights became a political issue when, shortly after the terrorist attack on September 11, 2001, on the World Trade Center in New York and the Pentagon in Washington, DC, President Bush issued a secret executive order authorizing the National Security Agency (NSA) to conduct warrantless electronic surveillance of telecommunications into and out of the United States of persons who might be linked to al Qaeda or other terrorist organizations. Some NSA surveillance involved persons in the United States.

The classified presidential authorization was made known to select members of the congressional leadership and intelligence committees, but was concealed from public knowledge until *The New York Times* reported it in December 2005, more than a year after it acquired information regarding it. (President Bush's administration had sought to have the newspaper not publish the article.)

The 1978 Foreign Intelligence Surveillance Act (FISA) had barred electronic surveillance of persons within the United States without the approval of a newly established FISA. Before the public revelation of warrantless wiretapping, President Bush stated, with regard to domestic surveillance, "Constitutional guarantees are in place when it comes to doing what is necessary to protect our homeland, because we value the Constitution." He later maintained that warrantless surveillance was justified in dealing with international communications that threaten nation security, and that such surveillance was implicitly authorized by the 2001 congressional Authorization for Use of Military Force adopted days after 9/11. Supporting the president, some legal authorities argued that Congress cannot interfere with the means and methods the president uses to engage an enemy.

Critics of warrantless wiretapping hold that FISA established a clear and exclusive procedure for authorizing emergency wiretaps. They charge that such wiretaps by the president, when based upon the claim of "inherent authority," risk unauthorized government recording of the communications of a wholly domestic character.

Publication by *The Times* precipitated widespread public debate regarding the right to privacy and the legality of warrantless electronic surveillance of American citizens. Despite later revelations by *The Times* and the *Washington Post*, details of the extent of wiretapping or other secret interception of messages have not been revealed. Defending this silence, White House Press Secretary Scott McClellan said, "There's a reason we don't get into discussing ongoing intelligence activities, because it could compromise our efforts to prevent attacks from happening."

As for the success of warrantless wiretapping, General Michael Hayden, Principal Deputy Director for National Intelligence, stated, "The program has been successful in detecting and preventing attacks inside the United States." Along with administration officials, General Hayden has asserted, "Had this program been in effect prior to 9/11, it is my professional judgment that we would have detected some of the 9/11 al Qaeda operatives in the United States, and we would have identified them as such."

Many members of both parties disagreed with the president's secret executive action. It is unlikely that all the facts regarding the extent of the program or what it achieved will be known for years, but the constitutional questions require answers. Yet warrantless wiretapping was not confined to just the Bush administration. Throughout 2013, President Barack Obama was questioned for activities undertaken by the NSA during his leadership. First, there have been renewed efforts to determine exactly how much information cellular service providers Verizon and AT&T are providing.

This surveillance program is designed to collect foreign intelligence in order to protect the domestic homeland from attack. Systems are only supposed to look at individuals outside of the United States, but there has been firm evidence presented that domestic citizens are also having information collected. Equipment attached to AT&T and Verizon computers allow NSA to copy, scan, and filter large volumes of information, including voice calls, text messages, and e-mails. As we learned in 2006, the NSA has set up monitoring points at key locations, including the now famous Room 641A at 611 Folsom Street in San Francisco. While the program began prior to Obama's inauguration, he is still facing criticism for not being upfront with the American public or doing more to eliminate the problem.

Perhaps more concerning, however, were recent revelations about American targets. In the past month, we have learned that the NSA has spied on Angela Merkel, chancellor of Germany, since 2002, the pope and the enclave that brought him to power in March, the secretary general of the United Nations (UN), and even hacked into servers at both Yahoo! and Google. Even if these wiretaps are meant with the best of intentions, they do little to instill faith in the U.S. government abroad. While allied leaders are likely low-level priorities, the simple act of illegally tapping the lines of friends can only lead to problems.

No one is arguing that Merkel or the UN need to be monitored in the same way as al Qaeda leaders; Russian, Chinese, or Iranian politicians; or the nuclear operations of North Korea or even Pakistan, but they are to a degree being treated the same today by American intelligence officials. Now American ambassadors across the globe are being called into meetings with foreign leaders and diplomats to attempt to mend fences and provide assurances that President Obama has stopped the monitoring. Again, Obama may not have been fully aware of what the NSA was doing overseas. In fact, most involved claim he was left out of the loop and should not be expected to be aware of every wiretap being utilized by the NSA. But when American citizens and the country's allies are being monitored, should there not be more direct oversight from somewhere outside the intelligence community?

Former Federal Prosecutor Andrew C. McCarthy defends secret surveillance as having been widely used (although sometimes abused) and wholly within the president's power. Former presidential candidate Al Gore believes that this activity is dangerous, unnecessary, and violates the rule of law.

# YES ↵

**Andrew C. McCarthy**

## How to 'Connect the Dots'

Washington's scandal *du jour* involves a wartime surveillance program President Bush directed the National Security Agency to carry out after al-Qaeda killed nearly 3,000 Americans on September 11, 2001. The idea that there is anything truly scandalous about this program is absurd. But the outcry against it is valuable, highlighting as it does the mistaken assumption that criminal-justice solutions are applicable to national-security challenges.

The intelligence community has identified thousands of al-Qaeda operatives and sympathizers throughout the world. After Congress overwhelmingly authorized the use of military force immediately following the 9/11 attacks, the president, as part of the war effort, ordered the NSA to intercept the enemy's international communications, even if those communications went into and out of the United States and thus potentially involved American citizens. According to reports from the *New York Times*, which shamefully publicized leaks of the program's existence in mid-December 2005, as many as 7,000 suspected terrorists overseas are monitored at any one time, as are up to 500 suspects inside the U.S.

As is typical of such wartime operations, the NSA program was classified at the highest level of secret information. It was, nevertheless, completely different from the kind of rogue intelligence operations of which the Nixon era is emblematic (though by no means the only case). The Bush administration internally vetted the program, including at the Justice Department, to confirm its legal footing. It reviewed (and continues to review) the program every 45 days. It briefed the bipartisan leadership of Congress (including the intelligence committees) at least a dozen times. It informed the chief judge of the federal Foreign Intelligence Surveillance Court (FISC), the tribunal that oversees domestic national-security wiretapping. And it modified the program in mid-2004 in reaction to concerns raised by the chief judge, national-security officials, and government lawyers.

Far from being a pretextual use of war powers to spy on political opponents and policy dissenters, the NSA program has been dedicated to national security. More to the point, it has saved lives, helping break up at least one al-Qaeda conspiracy to attack New York City and Washington, D.C., in connection with which a plotter named Lyman Faris was sentenced to 20 years' imprisonment.

As potential scandal fodder, so unremarkable did the NSA program seem that the *Times* sat on the story for a year—and a year, it is worth noting, during which it transparently and assiduously sought to exploit any opportunity to discredit the administration and cast it as a mortal threat to civil liberties. The leak was not sprung until the eleventh hour of congressional negotiations over renewal of the Patriot Act—at which point it provided ammunition to those who would gut Patriot's crucial post-9/11 domestic surveillance powers and simultaneously served as a marketing campaign for *Times* reporter James Risen, who just happened to be on the eve of publishing a book about, among other things, Bush's domestic "spying."

In fact, so obviously appropriate was wartime surveillance of the enemy that Rep. Jane Harman, the ranking Democrat on the House Intelligence Committee, issued a statement right after the *Times* exposed the program, saying: "I have been briefed since 2003 on a highly classified NSA foreign collection program that targeted Al-Qaeda. I believe the program is essential to US national security and that its disclosure has damaged critical intelligence capabilities." (With partisan "scandal" blowing in the wind, Harman changed her tune two weeks later, suddenly deciding that the "essential" program was probably illegal after all.)

⁂

If President Bush's reelection is any indication, what most Americans will care about is that we are monitoring the enemy. Chances are they won't be overly interested in knowing whether that monitoring is done on the president's own constitutional authority or in accordance with a statutory scheme calling for judicial imprimatur. Nevertheless, the Left is already indulging in loose talk about impeachment. Even some Republican "moderates," such as Arlen Specter, say the domestic-spying allegations are troubling enough that hearings are warranted. So it's worth asking: What is all the fuss about?

At bottom, it is about a power grab that began nearly three decades ago. Ever since it became technologically possible to intercept wire communications, presidents have done so. All of them, going back to FDR, claimed that the powers granted to the chief executive under Article II of the Constitution allowed them to conduct such wiretapping for national-security purposes. Particularly in wartime, this power might be thought indisputable. The president is the commander in chief of the armed forces, and penetrating enemy communications is as much an incident of warfighting as bombing enemy targets is.

But surveillance power has been abused—and notoriously by President Nixon, whose eavesdropping on political opponents was the basis of a draft article of impeachment. Watergate-era domestic-spying controversies dovetailed with important developments in the law of electronic surveillance. In 1967, the Supreme Court, in *Katz* v. *United States*, held that Fourth Amendment protection against unreasonable searches extended to electronic surveillance—meaning that eavesdropping without a judicial warrant was now presumptively unconstitutional. Congress followed by enacting a comprehensive scheme, known as "Title III," that required law-enforcement agents to obtain a court warrant for probable cause of a crime before conducting electronic surveillance. Yet both *Katz* and Title III recognized inherent presidential authority to conduct *national-security* monitoring without being bound by the new warrant requirement.

The Supreme Court undertook to circumscribe this inherent authority in its 1972 *Keith* decision. It held that a judicial warrant was required for national-security surveillance if the target was a purely *domestic* threat—the Vietnam-era Court giving higher priority to the free-speech interests of "those suspected of unorthodoxy in their political beliefs" than to the safety of those who might be endangered by domestic terrorists. Still, the Court took pains to exempt from its ruling the "activities of *foreign* powers or their agents" (emphasis added).

The true power grab occurred in 1978, when Congress enacted the Foreign Intelligence Surveillance Act. FISA attempted to do in the national-security realm what Title III had done in law enforcement: erect a thoroughgoing legal regime for domestic eavesdropping. And therein lies the heart of the current dispute. If the president has inherent authority to conduct national-security wiretapping, it is a function of his constitutional warrant. It is not a function of Congress's having failed until 1978 to flex its own muscles. A constitutional power cannot be altered or limited by statute. Period.

But limiting presidential authority is precisely what FISA purports to do. It ostensibly prohibits national-security eavesdropping (and, since 1994, physical searches) unless the executive branch can satisfy a federal judge—one of eleven who sit on a specially created Foreign Intelligence Surveillance Court—that there is probable cause that the subject it seeks to monitor is an "agent of a foreign power" (generally either a spy or a member of a foreign terrorist organization).

FISA does not aim to restrict the power to eavesdrop on *all* conversations. Communications that are entirely foreign—in that they involve aliens communicating overseas, for example—are exempted, as are conversations that *unintentionally* capture "U.S. persons" (generally, American citizens and permanent resident aliens), as long as these communications are intercepted outside the U.S. But where it does apply, FISA holds that the president—the constitutional officer charged with the nation's security—is powerless to eavesdrop on an operative posing a threat to the United States unless a judge—who need not possess any national-security expertise—is persuaded that the operative is a genuine threat. One suspects that such a system would astonish the Founders.

*⚬❧⚬*

Does the NSA program violate FISA? That question is difficult to answer with certainty. The program remains highly classified, and many of its details are not publicly known, nor should they be. Much has been made of the fact that FISA approval is required to intercept calls into or out of the United States if an American is intentionally being targeted. But scant attention has been given to FISA's caveat that such conversations are protected only if their participants have a *reasonable expectation of privacy*. It is difficult to imagine that Americans who make or receive calls to war zones in, say, Afghanistan or Iraq, or to al-Qaeda operatives anywhere, can reasonably expect that no one is listening in.

Nevertheless, it would not be surprising to learn that at least some of the NSA monitoring transgresses the bounds of FISA. For example, the statute mandates—without qualification about the reasonable expectation of privacy—that the government seek a judicial warrant before eavesdropping on any international call to or from the U.S., if that call is intercepted *inside* our borders. A distinction based on where a call is intercepted made sense in 1978. Back then, if a conversation was intercepted inside our borders, its participants were almost certain to include at least one U.S. person. But modern technology has since blurred the distinction between foreign and domestic telephony. Packets of digital information are now routed through switches inside countries (including, predominately, the U.S.) where neither the sender nor the recipient of the call is located. The NSA has capitalized on this evolution, and is now able, from within the U.S., to seize calls between Tikrit and Kabul, or between Peshawar and Hamburg. If done without a warrant, those intercepts present no FISA problem, because all the speakers are overseas. But it's hard to believe that the NSA is using this technology *only* to acquire all-foreign calls, while intercepting calls between, say, New York and Hamburg only from locations *outside* the U.S.

Perhaps that is why the Bush administration's defense has been light on the abstruse details of FISA and heavy on the president's inherent Article II power—although carefully couched to avoid offending Congress and the FISC with suggestions that FISA is at least partly unconstitutional. Essentially, the administration argues that FISA is beneficial in ordinary times and for long-term investigations, but that it did not and cannot repeal the president's independent constitutional obligation to protect the country: an obligation that was explicitly reserved even by President Carter, who signed FISA; that has been claimed by every president since; and that is uniquely vital in a war against thousands of stateless, stealthy terrorists, in which both a "probable cause" requirement and a sclerotic bureaucracy for processing warrant applications would be dangerously impractical.

In advancing this argument, the administration finds much support in the one and only decision ever rendered by the Foreign Intelligence Court of Review—the appellate court created by FISA to review FISC decisions. That decision came in 2002, after a quarter-century of FISA experience. Tellingly, its context was a brazen effort by the FISC to reject the Patriot Act's dismantling of the "wall" that prevented intelligence agents and criminal investigators from pooling information. In overruling the FISC, the Court of Review observed that "all the other courts to have decided the issue [have] held that the President did have inherent authority to conduct warrantless searches to obtain foreign intelligence information." Notwithstanding FISA, the Court thus pronounced: "We take for granted that the President does have that authority."

The administration has also placed great stock in Congress's post-9/11 authorization of "all necessary and appropriate force" against those behind the terrorist attacks. While this resolution did not expressly mention penetrating enemy communications, neither did it explicitly include the detention of enemy combatants, which the Supreme Court, in its 2004 *Hamdi* decision, found implicit in the use-of-force authorization because it is a "fundamental incident of waging war." Capturing intelligence, of course, is as much a component of waging war as capturing operatives. Any other conclusion would lead to the absurdity of the president's having full discretion to kill terrorists but needing a judge's permission merely to eavesdrop on them.

FISA aside, the administration stresses that the NSA program fits comfortably within the Fourth Amendment. That Amendment proscribes *unreasonable* searches, not warrantless ones—and it is thus unsurprising that the Supreme Court has recognized numerous exceptions to the warrant requirement that are of far less momentous than the imperative to protect the country from attack. Plainly, there is nothing unreasonable about intercepting potential enemy communications in wartime. Moreover, the courts have long held that searches conducted at the border are part of the sovereign right of self-protection, and thus require neither probable cause nor a warrant. Cross-border communications, which might well be triggers of terror plots, are no more deserving of constitutional protection.

❦

Critics have made much of a lengthy analysis published on January 6, 2006, by the Congressional Research Service that casts doubt on the administration's core contentions. Media have treated the report as bearing special weight because the CRS is a nonpartisan entity. But that does not mean the CRS is *objective*. "The sole mission of CRS," it explains on its website, "is to serve the United States Congress." Yet the issue at stake is precisely a separation-of-powers dispute.

While the CRS study is an impressive compilation of the relevant law, it resorts to a fairly standard tactic for marginalizing executive power: reliance on the concurring opinion by Supreme Court Justice Robert Jackson in a 1952 case involving President Truman's failed effort to seize steel mills—a move Truman justified by referring to the exigencies of the Korean War. Jackson saw executive power as waxing or waning along a three-stage scale, depending on whether a president acted with the support, the indifference, or the opposition of Congress. On this theory, a statute like FISA could curb a president's inherent constitutional authority. The fatal problem with the Jackson construct, however, has always been that it makes Congress, not the Constitution, the master of presidential authority. It disregards the reality that the executive is a coequal branch whose powers exist whether Congress acts or not. But the CRS prefers Jackson's conveniently airy formula, which failed to command a Court majority, to relevant opinions that don't go Congress's way, such as that of the Foreign Intelligence Court of Review—which, unlike the Supreme Court, was actually considering FISA.

Frustrated by its inability to move public opinion, the Left is now emphasizing the large "volume of information harvested from telecommunication data and voice networks," as the *Times* breathlessly put it, "without court-approved warrants." But this is pure legerdemain. When we refer to "information" from "telecommunication data," we are talking about something that, legally, is worlds apart from the content of telephone calls or e-mail messages.

These data do not include the substance of what people privately say to one another in conversations, but rather comprise statistical facts about the use of telecommunications services (for example, what phone number called another number, the date and time of the call, how long it lasted, etc.). Court warrants have never been required for the acquisition of such information because, as the Supreme Court explained over a quarter-century ago in *Smith* v. *Maryland*, telecommunications data do not implicate the Fourth Amendment. All phone and e-mail users know this information is conveyed to and maintained by service providers, and no one expects it to be private.

Analyzing such data is clearly different from monitoring the calls and e-mails themselves. For our own protection, we should want the government to collect as many of these data as possible (since doing so affects no one's legitimate privacy interests) in order to develop investigative leads. That's how a country manages to go four years without a domestic terror attack.

Yet the Left's rage continues, despite the public's evident disinterest in the mind-numbingly technical nature of the dispute, and despite the obvious truth that the NSA program was a bona fide effort to protect the nation from harm, not to snoop on Americans—only a tiny fraction of whom were affected, and those with apparent good reason. The controversy is a disquieting barometer of elite commitment to the War on Terror. As recently as two years ago, when "connecting the dots" was all the rage, liberals ignored eight years of Clintonian nonfeasance and portrayed the Bush administration as asleep at the switch while terrorists ran amok. Now they ignore President Clinton's insistence on the very same executive surveillance power that the current administration claims and caricature Bush as the imperial president, shredding core protections of civil liberties by exaggerating the terror threat. Either way you slice it, national security becomes a game in which necessary decisions by responsible adults become political grist, and, if they get enough traction, phony scandals. What remains real, though, is the danger to Americans implicit in any system that can't tell a war from a crime.

---

**Andrew C. McCarthy** was the U.S. attorney who led the 1995 terrorism prosecution that resulted in the conviction of Islamic militants for conducting urban terrorism, including the 1993 World Trade Center bombing. His essays have been published in *The Weekly Standard*, *Commentary*, *Middle East Quarterly*, and other publications.

## Al Gore

 **NO**

# Restoring the Rule of Law

The Executive Branch of the government has been caught eavesdropping on huge numbers of American citizens and has brazenly declared that it has the unilateral right to continue without regard to the established law enacted by Congress to prevent such abuses.

It is imperative that respect for the rule of law be restored.

So, many of us have come here to Constitution Hall to sound an alarm and call upon our fellow citizens to put aside partisan differences and join with us in demanding that our Constitution be defended and preserved.

It is appropriate that we make this appeal on the day our nation has set aside to honor the life and legacy of Dr. Martin Luther King, Jr., who challenged America to breathe new life into our oldest values by extending its promise to all our people.

On this particular Martin Luther King Day, it is especially important to recall that for the last several years of his life, Dr. King was illegally wiretapped—one of hundreds of thousands of Americans whose private communications were intercepted by the U.S. government during this period.

The FBI privately called King the "most dangerous and effective negro leader in the country" and vowed to "take him off his pedestal." The government even attempted to destroy his marriage and blackmail him into committing suicide.

This campaign continued until Dr. King's murder. The discovery that the FBI conducted a long-running and extensive campaign of secret electronic surveillance designed to infiltrate the inner workings of the Southern Christian Leadership Conference, and to learn the most intimate details of Dr. King's life, helped to convince Congress to enact restrictions on wiretapping.

The result was the Foreign Intelligence and Surveillance Act (FISA), which was enacted expressly to ensure that foreign intelligence surveillance would be presented to an impartial judge to verify that there is a sufficient cause for the surveillance. I voted for that law during my first term in Congress and for almost thirty years the system has proven a workable and valued means of according a level of protection for private citizens, while permitting foreign surveillance to continue.

Yet, just one month ago, Americans awoke to the shocking news that in spite of this long settled law, the Executive Branch has been secretly spying on large numbers of Americans for the last four years and eavesdropping on "large volumes of telephone calls, e-mail messages, and other Internet traffic inside the United States." The New York Times reported that the President decided to launch this massive eavesdropping program "without search warrants or any new laws that would permit such domestic intelligence collection."

During the period when this eavesdropping was still secret, the President went out of his way to reassure the American people on more than one occasion that, of course, judicial permission is required for any government spying on American citizens and that, of course, these constitutional safeguards were still in place.

But surprisingly, the President's soothing statements turned out to be false. Moreover, as soon as this massive domestic spying program was uncovered by the press, the President not only confirmed that the story was true, but also declared that he has no intention of bringing these wholesale invasions of privacy to an end.

At present, we still have much to learn about the NSA's domestic surveillance. What we do know about this pervasive wiretapping virtually compels the conclusion that the President of the United States has been breaking the law repeatedly and persistently.

A president who breaks the law is a threat to the very structure of our government. Our Founding Fathers were adamant that they had established a government of laws and not men. Indeed, they recognized that the structure of government they had enshrined in our Constitution—our system of checks and balances—was designed with a central purpose of ensuring that it would govern through the rule of law. As John Adams said: "The executive shall never exercise the legislative and judicial powers, or either of them, to the end that it may be a government of laws and not of men."

An executive who arrogates to himself the power to ignore the legitimate legislative directives of the Congress or to act free of the check of the judiciary becomes the central threat that the Founders sought to nullify in the Constitution—an all-powerful executive too reminiscent of the King from whom they had broken free. In the words of James Madison, "the accumulation of all powers, legislative, executive, and judiciary, in the same hands, whether of one, a few, or many, and whether hereditary, self-appointed, or elective, may justly be pronounced the very definition of tyranny."

Thomas Paine, whose pamphlet, "On Common Sense" ignited the American Revolution, succinctly

Gore, Al. From a speech delivered January 15, 2006, at an event co-sponsored by The American Constitution Society for Law and Policy and The Liberty Coalition.

described America's alternative. Here, he said, we intended to make certain that "the law is king."

Vigilant adherence to the rule of law strengthens our democracy and strengthens America. It ensures that those who govern us operate within our constitutional structure, which means that our democratic institutions play their indispensable role in shaping policy and determining the direction of our nation. It means that the people of this nation ultimately determine its course and not executive officials operating in secret without constraint.

The rule of law makes us stronger by ensuring that decisions will be tested, studied, reviewed and examined through the processes of government that are designed to improve policy. And the knowledge that they will be reviewed prevents over-reaching and checks the accretion of power.

A commitment to openness, truthfulness and accountability also helps our country avoid many serious mistakes. Recently, for example, we learned from recently classified declassified documents that the Gulf of Tonkin Resolution, which authorized the tragic Vietnam War, was actually based on false information. We now know that the decision by Congress to authorize the Iraq War, 38 years later, was also based on false information. America would have been better off knowing the truth and avoiding both of these colossal mistakes in our history. Following the rule of law makes us safer, not more vulnerable.

The President and I agree on one thing. The threat from terrorism is all too real. There is simply no question that we continue to face new challenges in the wake of the attack on September 11th and that we must be ever-vigilant in protecting our citizens from harm.

Where we disagree is that we have to break the law or sacrifice our system of government to protect Americans from terrorism. In fact, doing so makes us weaker and more vulnerable.

Once violated, the rule of law is in danger. Unless stopped, lawlessness grows. The greater the power of the executive grows, the more difficult it becomes for the other branches to perform their constitutional roles. As the executive acts outside its constitutionally prescribed role and is able to control access to information that would expose its actions, it becomes increasingly difficult for the other branches to police it. Once that ability is lost, democracy itself is threatened and we become a government of men and not laws.

The President's men have minced words about America's laws. The Attorney General openly conceded that the "kind of surveillance" we now know they have been conducting requires a court order unless authorized by statute. The Foreign Intelligence Surveillance Act self-evidently does not authorize what the NSA has been doing, and no one inside or outside the Administration claims that it does. Incredibly, the Administration claims instead that the surveillance was implicitly authorized when Congress voted to use force against those who attacked us on September 11th.

This argument just does not hold any water. Without getting into the legal intricacies, it faces a number of embarrassing facts. First, another admission by the Attorney General: he concedes that the Administration knew that the NSA project was prohibited by existing law and that they consulted with some members of Congress about changing the statute. Gonzalez says that they were told this probably would not be possible. So how can they now argue that the Authorization for the Use of Military Force somehow implicitly authorized it all along? Second, when the Authorization was being debated, the Administration did in fact seek to have language inserted in it that would have authorized them to use military force domestically—and the Congress did not agree. Senator Ted Stevens and Representative Jim McGovern, among others, made statements during the Authorization debate clearly restating that that Authorization did not operate domestically.

When President Bush failed to convince Congress to give him all the power he wanted when they passed the AUMF, he secretly assumed that power anyway, as if congressional authorization was a useless bother. But as Justice Frankfurter once wrote: "To find authority so explicitly withheld is not merely to disregard in a particular instance the clear will of Congress. It is to disrespect the whole legislative process and the constitutional division of authority between President and Congress."

This is precisely the "disrespect" for the law that the Supreme Court struck down in the steel seizure case.

It is this same disrespect for America's Constitution which has now brought our republic to the brink of a dangerous breach in the fabric of the Constitution. And the disrespect embodied in these apparent mass violations of the law is part of a larger pattern of seeming indifference to the Constitution that is deeply troubling to millions of Americans in both political parties. . . .

Whenever power is unchecked and unaccountable it almost inevitably leads to mistakes and abuses. In the absence of rigorous accountability, incompetence flourishes. Dishonesty is encouraged and rewarded.

Last week, for example, Vice President Cheney attempted to defend the Administration's eavesdropping on American citizens by saying that if it had conducted this program prior to 9/11, they would have found out the names of some of the hijackers.

Tragically, he apparently still doesn't know that the Administration did in fact have the names of at least 2 of the hijackers well before 9/11 and had available to them information that could have easily led to the identification of most of the other hijackers. And yet, because of incompetence in the handling of this information, it was never used to protect the American people.

It is often the case that an Executive Branch beguiled by the pursuit of unchecked power responds to its own mistakes by reflexively proposing that it be given still more power. Often, the request itself it used to mask accountability for mistakes in the use of power it already has.

Moreover, if the pattern of practice begun by this Administration is not challenged, it may well become a permanent part of the American system. Many conservatives have pointed out that granting unchecked power to this President means that the next President will have unchecked power as well. And the next President may be someone whose values and belief you do not trust. And this is why Republicans as well as Democrats should be concerned with what this President has done. If this President's attempt to dramatically expand executive power goes unquestioned, our Constitutional design of checks and balances will be lost. And the next President or some future President will be able, in the name of national security, to restrict our liberties in a way the framers never would have thought possible.

The same instinct to expand its power and to establish dominance characterizes the relationship between this Administration and the courts and the Congress.

In a properly functioning system, the Judicial Branch would serve as the constitutional umpire to ensure that the branches of government observed their proper spheres of authority, observed civil liberties and adhered to the rule of law. Unfortunately, the unilateral executive has tried hard to thwart the ability of the judiciary to call balls and strikes by keeping controversies out of its hands—notably those challenging its ability to detain individuals without legal process—by appointing judges who will be deferential to its exercise of power and by its support of assaults on the independence of the third branch.

The President's decision to ignore FISA was a direct assault on the power of the judges who sit on that court. Congress established the FISA court precisely to be a check on executive power to wiretap. Yet, to ensure that the court could not function as a check on executive power, the President simply did not take matters to it and did not let the court know that it was being bypassed. . . .

The Executive Branch, time and again, has co-opted Congress' role, and often Congress has been a willing accomplice in the surrender of its own power.

Look for example at the Congressional role in "overseeing" this massive four year eavesdropping campaign that on its face seemed so clearly to violate the Bill of Rights. The President says he informed Congress, but what he really means is that he talked with the chairman and ranking member of the House and Senate intelligence committees and the top leaders of the House and Senate. This small group, in turn, claimed that they were not given the full facts, though at least one of the intelligence committee leaders handwrote a letter of concern to VP Cheney and placed a copy in his own safe.

Though I sympathize with the awkward position in which these men and women were placed, I cannot disagree with the Liberty Coalition when it says that Democrats as well as Republicans in the Congress must share the blame for not taking action to protest and seek to prevent what they consider a grossly unconstitutional program. . . .

Fear drives out reason. Fear suppresses the politics of discourse and opens the door to the politics of destruction. Justice Brandeis once wrote: "Men feared witches and burnt women."

The founders of our country faced dire threats. If they failed in their endeavors, they would have been hung as traitors. The very existence of our country was at risk.

Yet, in the teeth of those dangers, they insisted on establishing the Bill of Rights.

Is our Congress today in more danger than were their predecessors when the British army was marching on the Capitol? Is the world more dangerous than when we faced an ideological enemy with tens of thousands of missiles poised to be launched against us and annihilate our country at a moment's notice? Is America in more danger now than when we faced worldwide fascism on the march—when our fathers fought and won two World Wars simultaneously?

It is simply an insult to those who came before us and sacrificed so much on our behalf to imply that we have more to be fearful of than they. Yet they faithfully protected our freedoms and now it is up to us to do the same. . . .

A special counsel should immediately be appointed by the Attorney General to remedy the obvious conflict of interest that prevents him from investigating what many believe are serious violations of law by the President. We have had a fresh demonstration of how an independent investigation by a special counsel with integrity can rebuild confidence in our system of justice. Patrick Fitzgerald has, by all accounts, shown neither fear nor favor in pursuing allegations that the Executive Branch has violated other laws.

Republican as well as Democratic members of Congress should support the bipartisan call of the Liberty Coalition for the appointment of a special counsel to pursue the criminal issues raised by warrantless wiretapping of Americans by the President.

Second, new whistleblower protections should immediately be established for members of the Executive Branch who report evidence of wrongdoing—especially where it involves the abuse of Executive Branch authority in the sensitive areas of national security.

Third, both Houses of Congress should hold comprehensive—and not just superficial—hearings into these serious allegations of criminal behavior on the part of the President. And, they should follow the evidence wherever it leads.

Fourth, the extensive new powers requested by the Executive Branch in its proposal to extend and enlarge the Patriot Act should, under no circumstances be granted, unless and until there are adequate and enforceable safeguards to protect the Constitution and the rights of the American people against the kinds of abuses that have so recently been revealed.

Fifth, any telecommunications company that has provided the government with access to private information concerning the communications of Americans without a proper warrant should immediately cease and desist their complicity in this apparently illegal invasion of the privacy of American citizens.

Freedom of communication is an essential prerequisite for the restoration of the health of our democracy.

It is particularly important that the freedom of the Internet be protected against either the encroachment of government or the efforts at control by large media conglomerates. The future of our democracy depends on it.

I mentioned that along with cause for concern, there is reason for hope. As I stand here today, I am filled with optimism that America is on the eve of a golden age in which the vitality of our democracy will be re-established and will flourish more vibrantly than ever. Indeed I can feel it in this hall.

As Dr. King once said, "Perhaps a new spirit is rising among us. If it is, let us trace its movements and pray that our own inner being may be sensitive to its guidance, for we are deeply in need of a new way beyond the darkness that seems so close around us."

---

**AL GORE** was the vice president of the United States, 1993–2001, and the Democratic candidate for president in 2000. He is the author of two books on environmental issues: *Earth in the Balance: Ecology and the Human Spirit* (Plume Books, 1992) and *An Inconvenient Truth* (Rodale Books, 2006), and the narrator of a documentary film based on the latter book.

# EXPLORING THE ISSUE

## Is Warrantless Wiretapping Ever Justified to Protect National Security?

## Critical Thinking and Reflection

1. Does the president have the authority to engage in secret surveillance?
2. Is there a constitutional conflict between constitutional liberties and national security? If so, which side do you lean toward more? Why?
3. To what extent should the government be permitted to examine private medical and other personal records?
4. How does the Foreign Intelligence Surveillance Act change government policy?
5. Should the president be exempt from lawsuits when dealing with national security?

## Is There Common Ground?

Although advocates of warrantless wiretapping have urged that it be made permanent, administration officials in the last years of President George W. Bush and the first term of President Barack Obama have maintained that there have been no instances of electronic surveillance without court-approved warrants. Similarly, there have been very few charges of excessive use of other security measures under the revised Patriot Act. Although disagreement persists as to how much valuable information for national security can be obtained by actions that may violate individual liberty, a sense of greater national security may permit a reassessment of the extent to which individual rights need to be curtailed in order to ensure the nation's safety. Negative public reaction to the very minor invasion of privacy affected by airline searches of passengers has been met by government efforts to deal more efficiently and less intrusively with the potential threat.

Wiretapping involves a debate between liberty and security. What are Americans willing to sacrifice to be assured potential terrorist plots are foiled? If one has nothing to hide, does it matter if the NSA listens in to a cell phone conversation or reads a text message? Or does allowing government this access open the door to too many other possible controlling actions? At present, doubts are being raised about exactly what the NSA is doing and where. Despite concerns being voiced over the collections of volumes of cell phone data and spying on allies for the purpose of political gain, President Obama has been able to deflect most criticism with Reaganesque

claims of not knowing. Now that he has been informed, however, it will be interesting to see how he responds.

There is middle ground on this issue, but it is difficult to pinpoint. Even the most ardent defender of civil liberties will likely state that it is acceptable to tap the phone of a suicide bomber on his way to blow up a target. But this individual will want concrete evidence of the tragedy about to occur. This information is oftentimes what we use the wiretap to determine. Hence, it is a vicious cycle between rights and security with no firm way to reconcile the two opposing sides.

## Create Central

www.mhhe.com/createcentral

## Additional Resources

James Bamford, *The Shadow Factory: The NSA from 9/11 to the Eavesdropping on America* (Anchor, 2009)

Heidi Boghosian, *Spying on Democracy: Government Surveillance, Corporate Power and Public Resistance* (City Lights Publishers, 2013)

Susan Landau, *Surveillance or Security?: The Risks Posed by New Wiretapping Technologies* (The MIT Press, 2013)

Ellen F. Paul, Fred D. Miller, Jr., and Jeffrey Paul, *The Right to Privacy* (Cambridge University Press, 2000)

Jonathan White, *Terrorism and Homeland Security* (Wadsworth, 2005)

# *Internet References . . .*

**American Civil Liberties Union**

www.aclu.org/blog/tag/warrantless-wiretapping

**Congressional Research Services Report on FISA**

www.fas.org/sgp/crs/intel/RL30465.pdf

**Electronic Frontier Foundation**

www.eff.org/nsa-spying

**Foreign Intelligence Surveillance Act**

www.fas.org/irp/agency/doj/fisa/

**National Security Agency**

www.nsa.gov

**Selected, Edited, and with Issue Framing Material by:**
**William J. Miller,** *Flagler College*
**George McKenna,** *City College, City University of New York*
**and**
**Stanley Feingold,** *City College, City University of New York*

# ISSUE

# Are Entitlement Programs Creating a Culture of Dependency?

YES: **Nicholas Eberstadt**, from "The Rise of Entitlements in Modern America, 1960–2010," in *A Nation of Takers: America's Entitlement Epidemic* (Templeton Press, October 2012)

NO: **William A. Galston**, from "Have We Become 'A Nation of Takers'?," in *A Nation of Takers: America's Entitlement Epidemic* (Templeton Press, October 2012)

---

## Learning Outcomes

**After reading this issue, you will be able to:**

- Identify current entitlement programs in the United States.
- Describe what is meant by a culture of dependency.
- Assess current spending on entitlement programs on the United States budget today.
- Explain long-term concerns about entitlement spending and dependency.
- Indicate whether government can afford to maintain current entitlement programs.

---

### ISSUE SUMMARY

**YES:** Social scientist Nicholas Eberstadt argues that the increase in entitlement programs is unprecedented in American history and has created a large dependency class that has lost the will to work.

**NO:** Political theorist William A. Galston sees the growth of American entitlement programs as an appropriate response to the needs of an aging population and rising costs of higher education and medicine; he sees them not as evidence of dependency but of "interdependence."

**I**n a conference call with fundraisers and donors after the 2012 presidential election, Governor Mitt Romney attributed his defeat to what he called "gifts" bestowed by President Obama to selected constituencies, "especially the African-American community, the Hispanic community and young people." Similar claims were often voiced in the media. Radio talk-show host Rush Limbaugh and Fox News commentator Bill O'Reilly both talked about the election as being influenced by the prospect of "free stuff" from the White House. On the Internet, the Drudge Report posted a YouTube video of a woman in Cleveland bragging about getting a free "Obamaphone."

Central to the complaint about "free stuff" is what are called "entitlements," defined as "benefits provided by government to which recipients have a legally enforceable right" (Jack Plano and Milton Greenberg, *The American Political Dictionary*). Entitlement spending, in contrast to "discretionary spending," is spending that the government must make to individuals based upon certain criteria. If a certain individual meets those criteria, he or she can demand payments from the government. Major examples

of entitlements include Social Security, Medicare, veterans' benefits, government retirement plans, food stamps, and certain welfare programs. In 2010, the Affordable Care Act, a program of national health insurance, was enacted with some entitlement features, such as subsidies for those unable to purchase health insurance.

Entitlement spending has grown steeply over the past half-century. In 1960 it amounted to less than one-third of the total federal government outlays, the same share it occupied in 1940; today it constitutes roughly two-thirds of the total. At the present rate of growth, the risk is that it may soon crowd out other vital federal programs, from defense and internal security to national health and environmental protection. Most observers today agree that the growth of entitlement spending is a serious issue, though they may disagree on the best means of addressing the issue. Some think the best approach is through spending cuts, while others place greater emphasis on increases in revenues.

But the debate on entitlements is not just about fiscal issues. The complaint about "free stuff" touches one of the deepest nerves of American public morality. Since

Puritan times, Americans have honored work as a builder of character and maturity. It follows that idleness is contemptible because it weakens character. "Idleness is the Dead Sea that swallows all virtues," wrote Ben Franklin, an appraisal repeated in various languages over the past 250 years. Idleness becomes particularly problematic in the view of most Americans when it is combined with the prospect of "free stuff." Daniel Patrick Moynihan, the 1973 U.S. Senator, addressed this issue in a discussion of "dependency." At the heart of Moynihan's thesis was a distinction between dependency and poverty. "To be poor is an objective condition; to be dependent, a subjective one as well. . . . Being poor is often combined with considerable personal qualities; being dependent rarely so." Moynihan's conclusion was that long-term dependency tends to leave a person in "an incomplete state of life: normal in a child, abnormal in an adult."

But equating entitlements with dependency is not so easy. Moynihan himself was a strong supporter of Social Security, which fits the *American Political Dictionary's* definition of an entitlement as a "legally enforceable right" to a benefit. It is hard to see how Social Security puts its recipients in "an incomplete state of life," especially since they have spent most of their life paying into it. The same is true of veterans' benefits and others considered in some sense to have been earned. Yet still other benefits such as food stamps are unearned. Entitlements, like many other government programs, are an apples-and-oranges mixture that almost defies definition.

One entitlement program that did seem to fit the category of unearned entitlements was Aid to Families with Dependent Children (AFDC) which was abolished by Congress in 1996 and replaced by Temporary Assistance for Needy Families (TANF), which left to the states much of the administration of the program but directed them to require work from recipients in order to receive benefits. Recently, the Obama administration has modified the administration of the work requirement, leaving still more discretion in the hands of individual states. Returning to Brandeis' central principles, states are again laboratories of democracy. But in the current iteration, there is the potential for states to negatively impact the economic performance of the nation as a whole.

Especially since entitlement spending takes the place of discretionary monies.

The Center on Budget and Policy Priorities examined where entitlement funds go in a February 2012 report. Their finds show, "Some conservative critics of federal social programs, including leading presidential candidates, are sounding an alarm that the United States is rapidly becoming an "entitlement society" in which social programs are undermining the work ethic and creating a large class of Americans who prefer to depend on government benefits rather than work. A new CBPP analysis of budget and Census data, however, shows that more than 90 percent of the benefit dollars that entitlement and other mandatory programs spend go to assist people who are elderly, seriously disabled, or members of working households—not to able-bodied, working-age Americans who choose not to work. This figure has changed little in the past few years." These findings directly refute much of the public perceptions—and especially conservative criticisms. Further, it complements other academic research, including a study that concluded: "The U.S. system favors groups with special needs, such as the disabled and the elderly. Groups like these which are perceived as especially deserving receive disproportionate transfers and those transfers have been increasing over time. Second, the system favors workers over non-workers and has increasingly done so over time. The rise of the EITC and the decline of AFDC/TANF is most illustrative of this trend." The study also found that "the demographic group which is most underserved by the system are non-elderly non-disabled families with no continuously-employed members." Despite these studies, public perception still seems to believe that entitlements do not always assist those in need.

In the following selections, social scientist Nicholas Eberstadt argues that the increase in entitlement programs is unprecedented in American history and has created a large dependency class that has lost the will to work. Opposing that view is political theorist William A. Galston, who sees the growth of American entitlement programs as an appropriate response to the needs of an aging population and rising costs of higher education and medicine; for him, the growth of these programs is evidence not of dependency but of "interdependence."

# YES

**Nicholas Eberstadt**

# The Rise of Entitlements in Modern America, 1960–2010

## Introduction

The American republic has endured for more than two and a quarter centuries; the United States is the world's oldest constitutional democracy. But over the past fifty years, the apparatus of American governance has undergone a fundamental and radical transformation. In some basic respects—its scale, its preoccupations, even many of its purposes—the United States government today would be scarcely recognizable to a Franklin D. Roosevelt, much less an Abraham Lincoln or a Thomas Jefferson.

What is monumentally new about the American state today is the vast and colossal empire of entitlement payments that it protects, manages, and finances. Within living memory, the government of the United States of America has become an entitlements machine. As a day-to-day operation, the U.S. government devotes more attention and resources to the public transfers of money, goods, and services to individual citizens than to any other objective; and for the federal government, more to these ends than to all other purposes combined.

Government entitlement payments are benefits to which a person holds an established right under law (i.e., to which a person is entitled). A defining feature of these payments (also sometimes officially referred to as "current transfer receipts of individuals from government," or simply "transfers") is that they "are benefits received for which no current service is performed." Entitlements are a relatively new concept in U.S. politics and policy; according to *Merriam-Webster,* the first known use of the term was not until 1942. But entitlements have become very familiar, very fast. By the reckoning of the Bureau of Economic Analysis (BEA), the research group within the Commerce Department that prepares the U.S. government's GNP estimates and related national accounts, income from entitlement programs in the year 2010 was transferred to Americans under a panoply of over fifty separate types of programs, and accounted for almost one-fifth (18 percent) of personal income in that year.

In 1960, U.S. government transfers to individuals from all programs totaled about $24 billion. By 2010, the outlay for entitlements was almost 100 times more. Over that interim, the nominal growth in entitlement payments to Americans by their government was rising by an explosive average of 9.5 percent per annum for fifty straight years. The tempo of growth, of course, is exaggerated by concurrent inflation—but after adjusting for inflation, entitlement payments soared more than twelve-fold (1248 percent), with an implied average real annual growth rate of about 5.2 percent per annum. Even after adjusting for inflation and population growth, entitlement transfers to individuals have more than septupled (727 percent) over the past half-century, rising at an overall average of about 4 percent per annum.

These long-term spending trends mask shorter-run tendencies, to be sure. Over the past two decades, for example, the nominal growth in these entitlement outlays has slowed to an average of "only" 7.1 percent a year (or a doubling every decade). Adjusted for inflation by the Consumer Price Index, real entitlement outlays rose by an average of "just" 4.4 percent over those years—and by a "mere" 3.2 percent a year on a per capita basis. But if the pace of entitlement growth has slowed in recent decades, so has the growth in per capita income. From 1960 to 2010 real per capita income in America grew by a measured 2.2 percent on average—but over the past twenty years, it has increased by 1.6 percent per annum. In other words, total entitlement payouts on a real per capita basis have been growing twice as fast as per capita income over the past twenty years; the disparity between entitlement growth on the one hand and overall income growth on the other is greater in recent times than it was in earlier decades.

The magnitude of entitlement outlays today is staggering. In 2010 alone, government at all levels oversaw a transfer of over $2.2 trillion in money, goods, and services to recipient men, women, and children in the United States. At prevailing official exchange rates, that would have been greater than the entire GDP of Italy, roughly the equivalent of Britain's and close to the total for France—advanced economies all with populations of roughly 60 million each. (The U.S. transfer numbers, incidentally, do not include the cost of administering the entitlement programs.) In 2010 the burden of entitlement transfers came to slightly more than $7,200 for every man, woman, and child in America. Scaled against a notional family of four, the average entitlements burden for that year alone would have approached $29,000. And that payout required payment from others, through taxes, borrowing, or some combination of the two.

A half-century of unfettered expansion of entitlement outlays has completely inverted the priorities, structure, and functions of federal administration, as these had been understood by all previous generations of American citizens. Until 1960 the accepted purpose of the federal government, in keeping with its constitutional charge, was governing. The federal government's spending patterns reflected that mandate. The overwhelming share of federal expenditures was allocated to defending the republic against enemies foreign and domestic (defense, justice, interest payments on the national debt) and some limited public services and infrastructural investments (the postal authority, agricultural extension, transport infrastructure, and the like). Historically, transfer payments did not figure prominently (or, sometimes, at all) in our federal ledgers. . . .

In 1960, entitlement program transfer payments accounted for well under one-third of the federal government's total outlays—about the same fraction as in 1940, when the Great Depression was still shaping American life, with unemployment running in the range of 15 percent. But then—in just a decade and a half—the share of entitlements in total federal spending suddenly spurted up from 28 percent to 51 percent. It did not surpass the 50 percent mark again until the early 1990s. But over the past two decades it rose almost relentlessly, until by 2010 it accounted for just about two-thirds of all federal spending, with all other responsibilities of the federal government—defense, justice, and all the other charges specified in the Constitution or undertaken in the intervening decades—making up barely one-third. Thus, in a very real sense, American governance has literally turned upside-down by entitlements—and within living memory. . . .

## The New American Way of Life: Our National Declaration of Dependence

From the founding of our state up to the present—or rather, until quite recently—the United States and the citizens who peopled it were regarded, at home and abroad, as "exceptional" in a number of deep and important respects. One of these was their fierce and principled independence, which informed not only the design of the political experiment that is the U.S. Constitution but also the approach to everyday affairs. The proud self-reliance that struck Alexis de Tocqueville in his visit to the United States in the early 1830s extended to personal finances. The American "individualism" about which he wrote included social cooperation, and on a grand scale—the young nation was a hotbed of civic associations and voluntary organizations. Rather, it was that American men and women viewed themselves as accountable for their own situation through their own achievements in an environment bursting with opportunity—a novel outlook

at that time, markedly different from the prevailing Old World (or at least Continental) attitudes.

The corollaries of this American ethos (which might be described as a sort of optimistic Puritanism) were, on the one hand, an affinity for personal enterprise and industry; and, on the other hand, a horror of dependency and contempt for anything that smacked of a mendicant mentality. Although many Americans in earlier times were poor—before the twentieth century, practically everyone was living on income that would be considered penurious nowadays—even people in fairly desperate circumstances were known to refuse help or handouts as an affront to their dignity and independence. People who subsisted on public resources were known as "paupers," and provision for these paupers was a local undertaking. Neither beneficiaries nor recipients held the condition of pauperism in high regard.

Overcoming America's historic cultural resistance to government entitlements has been a long and formidable endeavor. But as we know today, this resistance did not ultimately prove an insurmountable obstacle to the establishment of a mass public entitlements regime or to the normalization of the entitlement lifestyle in modern America. The United States is at the verge of a symbolic threshold: the point at which more than half of all American households receive, and accept, transfer benefits from the government. From cradle (strictly speaking, from *before* the cradle) to grave, a treasure chest of government-supplied benefits is open for the taking for every American citizen—and exercising one's legal rights to these many blandishments is now part and parcel of the American way of life. . . .

## From a Nation of Takers to a Nation of Gamers to a Nation of Chiselers

With the disappearance of the historical stigma against dependence on government largesse, and the normalization of lifestyles relying upon official resource transfers, it is not surprising that ordinary Americans should have turned their noted entrepreneurial spirit not simply to maximizing their take from the existing entitlement system, but to extracting payouts from the transfer state that were never intended under its programs. In this environment, gaming and defrauding the entitlement system have emerged as a mass phenomenon in modern America, a way of life for millions upon millions of men and women who would no doubt unhesitatingly describe themselves as law-abiding and patriotic American citizens.

Abuse of the generosity of our welfare state has, to be sure, aroused the ire of the American public in the past, and continues to arouse it from time to time today. For decades, a special spot in the rhetorical public square has been reserved for pillorying unemployed "underclass" garners who cadge undeserved social benefits. (This is the "welfare Cadillac" trope, and its many coded alternatives.) Public disapproval of this particular variant of entitlement misuse was sufficiently strong that Congress managed in the mid-1990s to overhaul the notorious AFDC program in a reform of welfare that replaced the old structure with Temporary Assistance for Needy  Families (TANF). But entitlement fiddling in modern America is by no means the exclusive preserve of a troubled underclass. Quite the contrary: it is today characteristic of working America, and even those who would identify themselves as middle class.

Exhibit A in the documentation of widespread entitlement abuse in mainstream America is the explosion over the past half-century of disability claims and awards under the disability insurance provisions of the U.S. Social Security program. In 1960 an average of 455,000 erstwhile workers were receiving monthly federal payments for disability. By 2010 that total had skyrocketed to 8.2 million (and by 2011 had risen still further, to almost 8.6 million). Thus, the number of Americans collecting government disability payments soared eighteen-fold over the fifty years from 1960 and 2010. In the early 1960s almost twice as many adults were receiving AFDC checks as disability payments; by 2010, disability payees outnumbered the average calendar-year TANF caseload by more than four to one (8.20 million vs. 1.86 million). Moreover, "workers" who were recipients of government disability payments had jumped from the equivalent of 0.65 percent of the economically active eighteen- to sixty-four-year-old population in 1960 to 5.6 percent by 2010. In 1960, there were over 150 men and women in those age groups working or seeking employment for every person on disability; by 2010, the ratio was 18 to 1 and continuing to decrease. The ratios are even starker when it comes to paid work: in 1960, roughly 134 Americans were engaged in gainful employment for every officially disabled worker; by December 2010 there were just over 16. And by some measures, the situation today looks even more unfavorable than this.

Although the Social Security Administration does not publish data on the ethnicity of its disability payees, it does publish information on a state-by-state basis. These suggest that the proclivity to rely upon government disability payments today is at least as much a "white thing" as a tendency for any other American group. As of December

2011 the state with the very highest ratio of working-age disability awardees to the resident population ages eighteen to sixty-four was West Virginia (9.0 percent—meaning that every eleventh adult in this age group was on paid government disability). According to Census Bureau estimates, 93 percent of West Virginia's population was "non-Hispanic white" in 2011. In New England, by the same token, all-but-lily-white Maine (where ethnic minorities accounted for less than 6 percent of the population in 2011) records a 7.4 percent ratio of working-age disability payees to resident working-age population: more than one out of fourteen. . . .

In "playing" the disability system, or cheating it outright, many millions of Americans are making a living by putting their hands into the pockets of their fellow citizen—be they taxpayers now alive or as yet unborn (a steadily growing phenomenon, as we shall see in a moment). And it is not simply the disability gamers themselves who are complicit in this modern scam. The army of doctors and health-care professionals who are involved in, and paid for their services in, certifying dubious workers' compensation cases are direct—indeed indispensable—collaborators in the operation. The U.S. judicial system—which rules on disability cases and sets the standards for disability qualification—is likewise compromised. More fundamentally, American voters and their elected representatives are ultimately responsible for this state of affairs, as its willing and often knowing enablers. This popular tolerance for widespread dishonesty at the demonstrable expense of fellow citizens leads to an impoverishment of the country's civic spirit and an incalculable degradation of the nation's constituting principles. . . .

**Nicholas Eberstadt** is a political economist who holds the Henry Wendt Chair in Political Economy at the American Enterprise Institute (AEI). He is also a senior adviser to the National Bureau of Asian Research (NBR), a member of the visiting committee at the Harvard School of Public Health, and a member of the Global Leadership Council at the World Economic Forum.

William A. Galston

# Have We Become "A Nation of Takers"?

Nicholas Eberstadt assembles a host of empirical trends to prove a moral conclusion: the growth of the entitlement state over the past half-century has undermined the sturdy self-reliance that has long characterized most Americans, replacing it with a culture of dependence that not only distorts our government but also threatens the American experiment. This claim raises two large questions: Do these trends represent a full and fair account of what has taken place since 1960? And do they warrant the conclusion Eberstadt urges on his readers? After some brief reflections on the former question, I devote the bulk of my remarks to the latter.

## What Has Happened in the Past Half-Century?

As far as I can tell, Eberstadt's charts and statistics accurately represent the trends on which he focuses. But they are not the whole truth. In the first place, Eberstadt's accounting does not include all of the public policies that constitute entitlements as he defines them. Tax expenditures—special deductions and exemptions from, and credits against, otherwise taxable income—now constitute more than $1.1 trillion annually and they disproportionately benefit upper-income families. . . .

But suppose we consider only the list of entitlement programs on which Eberstadt focuses. Based on his presentation, one might imagine that U.S. households have become far more dependent on public programs in recent decades. This seems not to be the case, however. A Congressional Budget Report (CBO) report released in October 2011 found that government transfers did not grow as a share of household market income between 1979 (a cyclical peak in the economy) and 2007 (another such peak) but rather oscillated between 10 and 12 percent. From the beginning to the end of that period, Social Security was unchanged at 6 percent of market income; health-care programs (primary Medicare, Medicaid, and the Children's Health Insurance Program) rose from under 2 percent to a bit less than 4 percent while all other transfer programs declined.

There was a change in the distribution of these transfers, however: the share going to the poorest households declined significantly. In 1979, households in the lowest income quintile received fully 54 percent of federal transfer payments, but by 2007 that figure had fallen to only 36 percent—a reduction of one-third. Put another way,

during that period, households with low-wage or non-working adults got less, while households in the middle and upper middle classes got more. If there is a problem of growing dependence, these figures suggest that it is located more in Middle America than in the ranks of the poor and near-poor. This possibility raises the question (to which I will return in the next section) of whether transfers going to families conducting themselves in accordance with middle-class norms of work and child-rearing represent dependence in any sense that gives rise to moral concern.

At least three other long-cycle trends need to be taken into account as well if we are to understand what is happening in our society and how we might respond. In the first place, we are an aging society. The massive investments in public schools and university expansion at the height of the baby boom have given way increasingly to the funding of hospitals and nursing homes. And while we typically regard the costs of dependence at the beginning of life as primarily the responsibility of families, this is much less true for dependence at the end of life. It is easy to see why. Aging brings expanding needs for complex and costly medical procedures that exceed the resources of average families. And no matter how hard they try, middle-aged adults often find that caring for aging parents in a family setting requires strength and skills they simply do not possess.

A second trend has exacerbated the consequences of aging: the near-disappearance of the pensions and health insurance for retirees that employers provided during the decades after the World War II. America's dominance of the global industrial economy gave employers the market power to set prices high enough to fund generous contracts with unionized employees. As the devastated nations of Europe and Asia recovered and international competition intensified, the postwar bargain in the United States broke down, and government stepped into the breach. For many Americans, Social Security became the primary (not supplemental) source of retirement income, and Medicare made up the difference between having and going without health insurance.

The third trend is macroeconomic. During the generation after World War II, the economy grew briskly, and the fruits of that growth were widely shared. Since then, growth has slowed, and the distribution of gains has become more concentrated at the top. Between 1947 and 1973, incomes of families in the bottom quintile rose by 117 percent; in the middle quintile, by 103 percent; at the top, by 88 percent. From 1973 to 2000, in contrast, the bottom quintile rose by only 12 percent, the middle by 25 percent, and the top by 66 percent. And in the seven years of the twenty-first century before the Great Recession struck, family incomes at the bottom actually fell by 6 percent and stagnated for everyone else (except for those at the very top). Since 1973, meanwhile, costs for big-ticket items such as higher education and health care have risen far faster than family incomes, increasing pressure on the public sector to step into the breach.

So there are reasons—in my view, compelling ones— why the federal government has undertaken major new responsibilities during the past half-century. Even so, we still have a problem: a huge gap between the promises we have made and the resources we have been willing to devote to fulfilling them. One way or another, we must close this gap. But the moral heart of this fiscal challenge is not dependence but rather a dangerous combination of self-interest, myopia, and denial.

## What Is "Dependence"?

To understand why I subordinate dependence to these other concerns, we must begin by clarifying the meaning of the term. One thing is clear at the outset: the dependence/independence dyad is too crude to capture the complexity of social relations. At a minimum, we must take account of a third term, "interdependence," and the norm of reciprocity that undergirds it. When I do something for you that you would be hard-pressed to do for yourself and you respond by helping me with something I find difficult, we depend on one another and are the stronger for it.

Well-functioning societies are replete with relations of this sort and use them as models for public policy. But the move from families and small groups to large-scale collective action makes a difference. Reciprocity becomes extended not only demographically and geographically but also chronologically. Political communities exist not just for the here and now but for future generations as well. Much contemporary public policy rests on temporally extended interdependence—in other terms, on an intergenerational compact. When we consent to deductions from our salary to help fund our parents' retirement, it is with the expectation that our children will do the same for us. This compact is practically sustainable and morally acceptable, but only with the proviso that the burdens we impose on our children are not disproportionate to the burdens we ourselves are willing to bear. The terms of interdependence matter, not just the fact of it. And so—to descend to cases—if we can honor promises to the current generation of working Americans only by imposing heavier sacrifices on the next generation, then something has gone awry. But—to repeat—"dependence" is the wrong characterization of the problem.

So is the concept of "entitlement." To be entitled to something is not necessarily to be dependent on it—at least not in a way that should trouble us. Consider the definition Eberstadt provides: "Government entitlement payments are benefits to which a person holds an established right under law (i.e., to which a person is entitled). A defining feature of these payments (also sometimes officially referred to as government transfers to individuals) is that they are 'benefits received for which no current service is performed.'"

Note that many nongovernmental relations have the same structure. If I use my life savings to purchase a retirement annuity, I have a legally enforceable expectation of receiving over time the stream of income specified in the contract. When I begin receiving these payments, I am performing no "current service" in exchange for them. And I certainly "depend" on these payments to fund my living expenses when I am no longer working. But surely I am not dependent in the way that so concerned Daniel Patrick Moynihan.

I do not see why transferring this case to the public sector makes a moral difference. Suppose someone pays into a government account throughout his working life, in effect purchasing an annuity to fund his retirement. If the income stream is actuarially fair, then he can expect to get back the equivalent of what he contributed. He may do better or worse, of course. If he lives until ninety-five, he will get back more; if he dies at seventy, less. Relying on these payments doesn't make him dependent in any morally troubling sense.

Social Security works this way for millions of Americans. For many others, it is more complicated: some can expect to receive more than the actuarial value of their contributions, others less. Americans in the latter category are helping to fund retirement for those in the former. In effect, some workers are relying on others for a portion of their retirement income. But again, this quantitative premise does not imply a disturbing moral conclusion. When Moynihan worried about dependence, he was not thinking about individuals who have worked hard all their lives in low-wage jobs but whose payroll taxes do not suffice to fund what society regards as a dignified retirement. . . .

## Real Problems of Dependence

Eberstadt presents no direct evidence that the growth of the federal government has changed Americans' character or weakened their moral fiber, perhaps because it is very hard to find. Indeed, in-depth examinations of public attitudes suggest the reverse. In 2009, for example, the Pew Social Mobility Project asked a representative sample of Americans what is essential or very important to getting ahead. Ninety-two percent said hard work; 89 percent, ambition; 83 percent, a good education. In contrast, factors such as race (15 percent), gender (16 percent), luck (21 percent), and family wealth (28 percent) ranked at the bottom. Asked about the role of government in fostering economic mobility, 36 percent of respondents thought it did more to help than to hurt, but many more—46 percent—endorsed the opposite view. A follow-up survey two years later revealed that the share of Americans who considered government helpful for mobility had declined to only 27 percent, while those who thought it detrimental had risen to 52 percent.

That is not to say that government has no role. Large majorities thought that public policy could do more to increase jobs in the United States and reduce college and health-care costs. But in their view, mobility-enhancing programs help individuals help themselves. If the growth of government has created a culture of dependence, it is hard to discern the evidence in these surveys, which are representative of a large body of research.

Eberstadt does offer some indirect evidence of cultural change, two instances of which warrant sustained attention. There is little doubt that the Social Security Disability Insurance program (SSDI) is subject to serious abuse. During the past decade, the number of workers receiving monthly benefits has soared from 5.3 million to 8.6 million. And because SSDI recipients qualify for Medicare after receiving benefits for two years, few working-age beneficiaries leave the program once they have entered. By 2010, annual benefits had reached $115 billion plus $75 billion in added Medicare costs. . . .

But this is not necessarily evidence of a deep cultural change. The desire to get something for nothing is a hardy perennial of human nature, not a late-twentieth-century invention. U.S. history is replete with swindles and get-rich-quick schemes. What may have changed is the willingness of taxpayers to fund programs that prefer compassion to tough love. Over the past three decades, efforts to tighten up the program have repeatedly wrecked on the shoals of public resistance. Tales of individual suffering move many voters, and a prosperous society has been willing to fund public compassion—so far. It will be interesting to see what happens when these generous instincts run up against inevitable future efforts to rein in massive budget deficits.

Far more disturbing than the abuses of a single program is the evidence Eberstadt presents of the long-term withdrawal of working-age men from the labor force. Fifty years ago, more than 85 percent of men age twenty and over were in the labor force. Ever before the Great Recession hit, that figure had declined by ten percentage points, and it has dropped more in the ensuing years. During the same period, female labor force participation rose by more than twenty points, stabilizing at around 60 percent in the late 1990s.

Why have so many men checked out? Eberstadt is sure that the "entitlement society" is responsible; without all the programs that enable men to get by without working, the flight from employment "could not have been possible." Perhaps so. Still, although men and women are equally eligible to participate in these programs, they seem to have responded quite differently, at least in the aggregate. For example, nearly as many women (4.1 million) as men (4.5 million) receive disability benefits, but that has not kept the ranks of women in the paid workforce from swelling. . . .

## Conclusion

By bringing together and concisely presenting a wealth of data, Eberstadt has performed a real service. He dramatizes the remarkable rise of the entitlement state and issues warnings about its consequences that we must consider seriously. Still, there are good reasons to question the causal link between entitlement programs and dependence—at least the kind of dependence that should concern us. To be sure, Americans want a reasonable level of security in their retirement years, and they think that government programs such as Social Security and Medicare are essential to that security. But they continue to believe that government is no substitute for hard work, ambition, and the perseverance that enables young people to complete their education and put it to work in the job market. They think that government should make reasonable provision for the poor and disabled, but they do not believe that government should enable people who could be independent to depend on the efforts of others. To the extent that current programs turn out to be inconsistent with that view, they will eventually be trimmed or abolished, as was AFDC in 1996.

Left unchecked, the programs we have created in the past half-century will make it difficult to stabilize our finances, to invest in the future, and to defend the nation. These are compelling reasons to rethink the entitlement state. But they have little to do with an alleged culture of dependence, the evidence for which is thin at best. As long as we do our part, there is no harm in benefitting from programs we help sustain. As long as we contribute our share, taking is morally unproblematic. We can be a nation of takers, as long as we are a nation of givers as well. As long as we honor the norm of reciprocity for our compatriots and for posterity, we can steer a steady course.

## Note

1. David H. Autor and Mark Duggan, "Supporting Work: A Proposal for Modernizing the U.S. Disability Insurance System," Center for American Progress and The Hamilton Project, December 2010, http://www.hamiltonproject.org/files/downloads_and_links/FINAL_AutorDugganPaper.pdf

**WILLIAM A. GALSTON** holds the Ezra Zilkha Chair in the Brookings Institution's Governance Studies Program, where he serves as a senior fellow. A former policy adviser to President Clinton and presidential candidates, Galston is an expert on domestic policy, political campaigns, and elections. His current research focuses on designing a new social contract and the implications of political polarization.

# EXPLORING THE ISSUE

## Are Entitlement Programs Creating a Culture of Dependency?

### Critical Thinking and Reflection

1. Why does Nicholas Eberstadt think that the U.S. government today "would be scarcely recognizable" to Franklin Roosevelt, Abraham Lincoln, or Thomas Jefferson?
2. Eberstadt thinks that, over the last 50 years, the government has "inverted" the historic priorities of federal administration. What does he mean by that?
3. Eberstadt contends that "the United States is at the verge of a symbolic threshold." What kind of threshold?
4. William A. Galston: "If there is a problem of growing dependence . . . it is located more in Middle America than in the ranks of the poor and near-poor." Explain.
5. Galston believes that three long-term trends are better explanations than government extravagance for why entitlement spending has risen so steeply in recent years. Pick two and discuss them.
6. Instead of "dependency," Galston contends, we have moved to an era of "interdependence." Explain.

### Is There Common Ground?

The common ground between Eberstadt and Galston lies in the fact that entitlement spending is indeed rising steeply. Eberstadt presents alarming statistics on this, which Galston acknowledges to be accurate "as far as I can tell." Galston also acknowledges that, "left unchecked, the programs we have created in the past half-century will make it difficult to stabilize our finances, to invest in the future, and to defend the nation." What he denies is that entitlement programs are making Americans lazy and immature. Instead, he believes they serve their role as a safety net. Most Americans would agree that individuals in certain circumstances deserve help from their government in a temporary manner as they get back on their feet.

A pragmatist might argue that perhaps we can put aside the ideological arguments for the moment and bring together people of all ideologies in a nuts-and-bolts campaign to trim the unnecessary costs of these and other government programs. However, such a decision would be difficult to reach. Multiple parties would need to accept such cuts and many may in fact benefit from the programs being trimmed. Perhaps most worrisome is how to handle a pro-

gram like Social Security, in which citizens have paid into the program but may not be able to draw returns later in life. For these individuals, middle ground is difficult to find.

### Create Central

www.mhhe.com/createcentral

### Additional Resources

Peter Edelman, *So Rich, So Poor: Why It's Hard to End Poverty in America* (New Press, 2012)

Barbara Ehrenreich, *Nickel and Dimed: On (Not) Getting By in America* (Picador Press, 2011)

Daniel P. Moynihan, *The Politics of a Guaranteed Family Income* (Random House, 1973)

James T. Patterson, *America's Struggle Against Poverty in the Twentieth Century* (Harvard University Press, 2000)

Leonard J. Santow and Mark E. Santow, *Social Security and the Middle-Class Squeeze: Fact and Fiction about America's Entitlement Programs* (Praeger, 2005)

# *Internet References . . .*

**Administration for Children and Families**

www.acf.hhs.gov/help

**Medicaid**

www.medicaid.gov/

**Medicare**

www.medicare.gov/

**Supplemental Nutrition Assistance Program**

www.fns.usda.gov/snap/supplemental-nutrition
-assistance-program-snap

**The United States Social Security Administration**

www.ssa.gov/

**Selected, Edited, and with Issue Framing Material by:**
**William J. Miller,** *Flagler College*
**George McKenna,** *City College, City University of New York*
**and**
**Stanley Feingold,** *City College, City University of New York*

# ISSUE

# Should the United States Launch a Preemptive Strike Against Iran?

**YES: Matthew Kroenig,** from "Time to Attack Iran," *Foreign Affairs* (January/February 2012)

**NO: Colin H. Kahl,** from "Not Time to Attack Iran," *Foreign Affairs* (March/April 2012)

| Learning Outcomes |
| --- |
| **After reading this issue, you will be able to:** |
| • Assess the current political environment in Iran. |
| • Identify the benefits and costs of a preemptive strike on Iran. |
| • Explain the procedures for launching a strike. |
| • Indicate potential outside partners to assist in any attack. |
| • Ascertain whether an attack is wise given the current political environment. |

## ISSUE SUMMARY

**YES:** Defense Department Adviser Matthew Kroenig believes that the United States should launch a preemptive attack on Iran because a policy of deterrence would allow Iran to develop powerful nuclear weapons that would endanger the United States and its allies.

**NO:** Defense Department Adviser Colin H. Kahl believes that striking Iran now would not prevent future aggression, and it is undesirable as long as economic and diplomatic means to prevent Iran's nuclear armament still hold the possibility of success.

In 2006, the United States National Security Council stated: "We may face no greater challenge from a single country than from Iran." That judgment has never been revised. The radically anti-American Shiite Islamic government of Iran is closely allied with Hamas and Hezbollah, terrorist movements that are dedicated to the creation of an anti-American Muslim Middle East. Ever since revolutionary Shiites and their followers came to power in Iran more than 30 years ago, Friday night services in Iran's capital, Tehran, have repeated the vow, "Down with the United States!"

Paramount among the threats that Iran poses to the United States is its progress toward the development of nuclear energy that can result in the development of nuclear weapons. Nine nations are believed to have the capacity to build nuclear weapons. None is believed to be a formidable threat to the United States, despite the mutual hostility of the United States and North Korea. By contrast, U.S. presidents of both parties have been in agreement that Iran should be prevented from acquiring the capability of enriching uranium and building nuclear bombs. Iran claims that its nuclear program is designed for peaceful domestic use. The United States is skeptical. In late 2012, international nuclear inspectors reported that Iran has installed three-fourths of the nuclear centrifuges it needs in order to complete a deep underground site for the production of nuclear fuel.

In addition to its potential nuclear power, Iran has the naval power to close access to the Strait of Hormuz, a narrow passage that separates Iran from the Arabian Peninsula and through which one-quarter of the world's petroleum (including that from Iran) passes by sea. This could cut off a vital source of oil for other nations. Iran also has established long-range ballistic missiles that threaten Israel and American military assets.

It is impossible to understand the deterioration of relations between Iran and the United States without considering the critical events that have shaped their policies. In 1953, the United States played a minor role in the coup that overthrew the elected government of Iranian Prime Minister Mohammad Mosaddeq and resulted in the return to power of the autocratic Shah Mohammad Reza Pahlavi. In 1979, the Shah was forced to leave Iran when the Iranian revolution drove him from power and installed a Shiite Muslim theocracy. When the Shah was permitted to enter the United States in order to receive medical treatment, enraged radical Iranian students retaliated by taking more than 50 Americans hostage and holding them for 444 days. Good relations have never been restored.

The United States sees Iran as a threat to world peace because it seeks to possess decisive influence in the Middle East, because it effectively controls access to the Straits of Hormuz through which much of the region's oil (much of it from Iran itself) must pass on its way to the rest of the world, because its population is less divided than others in the area and, most threatening to the United States, because it may soon possess the ability to develop powerful nuclear weapons, which could pose an immediate threat to Israel, America's strategic ally in the region, and a long-term threat to the United States.

American Middle East scholars who believe that war with Iran can be avoided argue that the threat of a nuclear Iran can be avoided because it once had more tolerant leadership and it still contains moderate elements, because Israel has the nuclear power to destroy Iran's nuclear weaponry (there is evidence that Iran's nuclear development was set back by several years as a result of sabotage), because American-sponsored economic sanctions already in place have weakened it, and because its rulers are rational enough to know that the United States will destroy their power in any conflict.

In an October 2013 speech during a Knesset commemoration Tuesday of the 40th anniversary of the Yom Kippur War, Israeli Prime Minister Benjamin Netanyahu offered a defense of a possible Israeli preemptive strike on Iran. In the speech, he stated, "The first lesson is to never underestimate a threat, never underestimate an enemy, never ignore the signs of danger. We can't assume the enemy will act in ways that are convenient for us. The enemy can surprise us. Israel will not fall asleep on its watch again." He adds, "A preventive war, even a preventive strike, is among the most difficult decisions a government can take, because it will never be able to prove what would have happened if it had not acted . . . in the Six Day War we launched a preventive strike that broke the chokehold our enemies had placed on us, and on Yom Kippur the government decided, despite all warnings, to

absorb the full force of an enemy attack." Yet Israel and the United States have different attitudes toward dealing with the Iranians. This difference can be largely explained by geographic location. Whereas the Iranians may in fact have capabilities of reaching Israel, they do not have the same when considering the United States.

In November 2013, the United States, Great Britain, France, Germany, Russia, and China (the P5+1 Group) reached a deal with Iran to bring a halt to their nuclear weapons program. For the first time in almost 10 years, the Iranians have agreed to back off their quest for nuclear weapons. This is made even more monumental by the fact that the United States and Iran have had no formal relationship since the Revolution in 1979. Four key provisions were agreed to.

1. No uranium will be enriched above 5 percent U-235 and all uranium presently above that level will be blended down;
2. No new centrifuges will be produced and many current ones will become inoperable;
3. Heavy reactor work will stop immediately;
4. IAEA inspectors will be given full access and daily visitation.

In return, the United States and its partners have agreed to drop some of its sanctions, amounting to about $6–7 billion in relief. While the international community welcomed the agreement, Netanyahu was less satisfied. He remarked, "I think that it would be a historic mistake to ease up on Iran without it dismantling the nuclear capabilities it is developing. . . . Iran is now on the ropes, and it is possible to employ sanctions at their fullest in order to achieve the desired result. I hope that the international community will do this, and I call upon it to do so."

Both Matthew Kroenig and Colin H. Kahl have academic credentials as well as experience as Defense Department advisers on Middle East policy, yet like other thoughtful analysts of Iran both in and out of the U.S. government, they disagree on how and when to confront the challenge that the prospect of a nuclear-armed Iran poses to American national security and world peace.

# YES ⮌

**Matthew Kroenig**

# Time to Attack Iran

## Why a Strike Is the Least Bad Option

In early October, U.S. officials accused Iranian operatives of planning to assassinate Saudi Arabia's ambassador to the United States on American soil. Iran denied the charges, but the episode has already managed to increase tensions between Washington and Tehran. Although the Obama administration has not publicly threatened to retaliate with military force, the allegations have underscored the real and growing risk that the two sides could go to war sometime soon—particularly over Iran's advancing nuclear program.

For several years now, starting long before this episode, American pundits and policymakers have been debating whether the United States should attack Iran and attempt to eliminate its nuclear facilities. Proponents of a strike have argued that the only thing worse than military action against Iran would be an Iran armed with nuclear weapons. Critics, meanwhile, have warned that such a raid would likely fail and, even if it succeeded, would spark a full-fledged war and a global economic crisis. They have urged the United States to rely on nonmilitary options, such as diplomacy, sanctions, and covert operations, to prevent Iran from acquiring a bomb. Fearing the costs of a bombing campaign, most critics maintain that if these other tactics fail to impede Tehran's progress, the United States should simply learn to live with a nuclear Iran.

But skeptics of military action fail to appreciate the true danger that a nuclear-armed Iran would pose to U.S. interests in the Middle East and beyond. And their grim forecasts assume that the cure would be worse than the disease—that is, that the consequences of a U.S. assault on Iran would be as bad as or worse than those of Iran achieving its nuclear ambitions. But that is a faulty assumption. The truth is that a military strike intended to destroy Iran's nuclear program, if managed carefully, could spare the region and the world a very real threat and dramatically improve the long-term national security of the United States.

## Dangers of Deterrence

Years of international pressure have failed to halt Iran's attempt to build a nuclear program. The Stuxnet computer worm, which attacked control systems in Iranian nuclear facilities, temporarily disrupted Tehran's enrichment effort, but a report by the International Atomic Energy Agency this past May revealed that the targeted plants have fully recovered from the assault. And the latest IAEA findings on Iran, released in November, provided the most compelling evidence yet that the Islamic Republic has weathered sanctions and sabotage, allegedly testing nuclear triggering devices and redesigning its missiles to carry nuclear payloads. The Institute for Science and International Security, a nonprofit research institution, estimates that Iran could now produce its first nuclear weapon within six months of deciding to do so. Tehran's plans to move sensitive nuclear operations into more secure facilities over the course of the coming year could reduce the window for effective military action even further. If Iran expels IAEA inspectors, begins enriching its stockpiles of uranium to weapons-grade levels of 90 percent, or installs advanced centrifuges at its uranium-enrichment facility in Qom, the United States must strike immediately or forfeit its last opportunity to prevent Iran from joining the nuclear club.

Some states in the region are doubting U.S. resolve to stop the program and are shifting their allegiances to Tehran. Others have begun to discuss launching their own nuclear initiatives to counter a possible Iranian bomb. For those nations and the United States itself, the threat will only continue to grow as Tehran moves closer to its goal. A nuclear-armed Iran would immediately limit U.S. freedom of action in the Middle East. With atomic power behind it, Iran could threaten any U.S. political or military initiative in the Middle East with nuclear war, forcing Washington to think twice before acting in the region. Iran's regional rivals, such as Saudi Arabia, would likely decide to acquire their own nuclear arsenals, sparking an arms race. To constrain its geopolitical rivals, Iran could choose to spur proliferation by transferring nuclear technology to its allies—other countries and terrorist groups alike. Having the bomb would give Iran greater cover for conventional aggression and coercive diplomacy, and the battles between its terrorist proxies and Israel, for example, could escalate. And Iran and Israel lack nearly all the safeguards that helped the United States and the Soviet Union avoid a nuclear exchange during the Cold War—secure second-strike capabilities, clear lines of communication, long flight times for ballistic missiles from one country to the other, and experience managing nuclear arsenals. To be sure, a nuclear-armed Iran would not intentionally launch a suicidal nuclear war. But the volatile nuclear balance between Iran and Israel could easily spiral out of control as a crisis unfolds, resulting in a nuclear exchange between the two countries that could draw the United States in, as well.

These security threats would require Washington to contain Tehran. Yet deterrence would come at a heavy price. To keep the Iranian threat at bay, the United States would need to deploy naval and ground units and potentially nuclear weapons across the Middle East, keeping a large force in the area for decades to come. Alongside those troops, the United States would have to permanently deploy significant intelligence assets to monitor any attempts by Iran to transfer its nuclear technology. And it would also need to devote perhaps billions of dollars to improving its allies' capability to defend themselves. This might include helping Israel construct submarine-launched ballistic missiles and hardened ballistic missile silos to ensure that it can maintain a secure second-strike capability. Most of all, to make containment credible, the United States would need to extend its nuclear umbrella to its partners in the region, pledging to defend them with military force should Iran launch an attack.

In other words, to contain a nuclear Iran, the United States would need to make a substantial investment of political and military capital to the Middle East in the midst of an economic crisis and at a time when it is attempting to shift its forces out of the region. Deterrence would come with enormous economic and geopolitical costs and would have to remain in place as long as Iran remained hostile to U.S. interests, which could mean decades or longer. Given the instability of the region, this effort might still fail, resulting in a war far more costly and destructive than the one that critics of a preemptive strike on Iran now hope to avoid.

## A Feasible Target

A nuclear Iran would impose a huge burden on the United States. But that does not necessarily mean that Washington should resort to military means. In deciding whether it should, the first question to answer is if an attack on Iran's nuclear program could even work. Doubters point out that the United States might not know the location of Iran's key facilities. Given Tehran's previous attempts to hide the construction of such stations, most notably the uranium-enrichment facilities in Natanz and Qom, it is possible that the regime already possesses nuclear assets that a bombing campaign might miss, which would leave Iran's program damaged but alive.

This scenario is possible, but not likely; indeed, such fears are probably overblown. U.S. intelligence agencies, the IAEA, and opposition groups within Iran have provided timely warning of Tehran's nuclear activities in the past—exposing, for example, Iran's secret construction at Natanz and Qom before those facilities ever became operational. Thus, although Tehran might again attempt to build clandestine facilities, Washington has a very good chance of catching it before they go online. And given the amount of time it takes to construct and activate a nuclear facility, the scarcity of Iran's resources, and its failure to hide the facilities in Natanz and Qom successfully, it is unlikely that Tehran has any significant operational nuclear facilities still unknown to Western intelligence agencies.

Even if the United States managed to identify all of Iran's nuclear plants, however, actually destroying them could prove enormously difficult. Critics of a U.S. assault argue that Iran's nuclear facilities are dispersed across the country, buried deep underground and hardened against attack, and ringed with air defenses, making a raid complex and dangerous. In addition, they claim that Iran has purposefully placed its nuclear facilities near civilian populations, which would almost certainly come under fire in a U.S. raid, potentially leading to hundreds, if not thousands, of deaths.

These obstacles, however, would not prevent the United States from disabling or demolishing Iran's known nuclear facilities. A preventive operation would need to target the uranium-conversion plant at Isfahan, the heavy-water reactor at Arak, and various centrifuge-manufacturing sites near Natanz and Tehran, all of which are located aboveground and are highly vulnerable to air strikes. It would also have to hit the Natanz facility, which, although it is buried under reinforced concrete and ringed by air defenses, would not survive an attack from the U.S. military's new bunker-busting bomb, the 30,000-pound Massive Ordnance Penetrator, capable of penetrating up to 200 feet of reinforced concrete. The plant in Qom is built into the side of a mountain and thus represents a more challenging target. But the facility is not yet operational and still contains little nuclear equipment, so if the United States acted quickly, it would not need to destroy it.

Washington would also be able to limit civilian casualties in any campaign. Iran built its most critical nuclear plants, such as the one in Natanz, away from heavily populated areas. For those less important facilities that exist near civilian centers, such as the centrifuge-manufacturing sites, U.S. precision-guided missiles could pinpoint specific buildings while leaving their surroundings unscathed. The United States could reduce the collateral damage even further by striking at night or simply leaving those less important plants off its target list at little cost to the overall success of the mission. Although Iran would undoubtedly publicize any human suffering in the wake of a military action, the majority of the victims would be the military personnel, engineers, scientists, and technicians working at the facilities.

## Setting the Right Redlines

The fact that the United States can likely set back or destroy Iran's nuclear program does not necessarily mean that it should. Such an attack could have potentially devastating consequences—for international security, the global economy, and Iranian domestic politics—all of which need to be accounted for.

To begin with, critics note, U.S. military action could easily spark a full-blown war. Iran might retaliate against U.S. troops or allies, launching missiles at military installations or civilian populations in the Gulf or perhaps even Europe. It could activate its proxies abroad, stirring sectarian tensions in Iraq, disrupting the Arab Spring, and ordering terrorist attacks against Israel and the United States. This could draw Israel or other states into the fighting and compel the United States to escalate the conflict in response. Powerful allies of Iran, including China and Russia, may attempt to economically and diplomatically isolate the United States. In the midst of such spiraling violence, neither side may see a clear path out of the battle, resulting in a long-lasting, devastating war, whose impact may critically damage the United States' standing in the Muslim world.

Those wary of a U.S. strike also point out that Iran could retaliate by attempting to close the Strait of Hormuz, the narrow access point to the Persian Gulf through which roughly 20 percent of the world's oil supply travels. And even if Iran did not threaten the strait, speculators, fearing possible supply disruptions, would bid up the price of oil, possibly triggering a wider economic crisis at an already fragile moment.

None of these outcomes is predetermined, however; indeed, the United States could do much to mitigate them. Tehran would certainly feel like it needed to respond to a U.S. attack, in order to reestablish deterrence and save face domestically. But it would also likely seek to calibrate its actions to avoid starting a conflict that could lead to the destruction of its military or the regime itself. In all likelihood, the Iranian leadership would resort to its worst forms of retaliation, such as closing the Strait of Hormuz or launching missiles at southern Europe, only if it felt that its very existence was threatened. A targeted U.S. operation need not threaten Tehran in such a fundamental way.

To make sure it doesn't and to reassure the Iranian regime, the United States could first make clear that it is interested only in destroying Iran's nuclear program, not in overthrowing the government. It could then identify certain forms of retaliation to which it would respond with devastating military action, such as attempting to close the Strait of Hormuz, conducting massive and sustained attacks on Gulf states and U.S. troops or ships, or launching terrorist attacks in the United States itself. Washington would then need to clearly articulate these "redlines" to Tehran during and after the attack to ensure that the message was not lost in battle. And it would need to accept the fact that it would have to absorb Iranian responses that fell short of these redlines without escalating the conflict. This might include accepting token missile strikes against U.S. bases and ships in the region—several salvos over the course of a few days that soon taper off—or the harassment of commercial and U.S. naval vessels. To avoid the kind of casualties that could compel the White House to

escalate the struggle, the United States would need to evacuate nonessential personnel from U.S. bases within range of Iranian missiles and ensure that its troops were safely in bunkers before Iran launched its response. Washington might also need to allow for stepped-up support to Iran's proxies in Afghanistan and Iraq and missile and terrorist attacks against Israel. In doing so, it could induce Iran to follow the path of Iraq and Syria, both of which refrained from starting a war after Israel struck their nuclear reactors in 1981 and 2007, respectively.

Even if Tehran did cross Washington's redlines, the United States could still manage the confrontation. At the outset of any such violation, it could target the Iranian weapons that it finds most threatening to prevent Tehran from deploying them. To de-escalate the situation quickly and prevent a wider regional war, the United States could also secure the agreement of its allies to avoid responding to an Iranian attack. This would keep other armies, particularly the Israel Defense Forces, out of the fray. Israel should prove willing to accept such an arrangement in exchange for a U.S. promise to eliminate the Iranian nuclear threat. Indeed, it struck a similar agreement with the United States during the Gulf War, when it refrained from responding to the launching of Scud missiles by Saddam Hussein.

Finally, the U.S. government could blunt the economic consequences of a strike. For example, it could offset any disruption of oil supplies by opening its Strategic Petroleum Reserve and quietly encouraging some Gulf states to increase their production in the run-up to the attack. Given that many oil-producing nations in the region, especially Saudi Arabia, have urged the United States to attack Iran, they would likely cooperate.

Washington could also reduce the political fallout of military action by building global support for it in advance. Many countries may still criticize the United States for using force, but some—the Arab states in particular—would privately thank Washington for eliminating the Iranian threat. By building such a consensus in the lead-up to an attack and taking the outlined steps to mitigate it once it began, the United States could avoid an international crisis and limit the scope of the conflict.

## Any Time Is Good Time

Critics have another objection: even if the United States managed to eliminate Iran's nuclear facilities and mitigate the consequences, the effects might not last long. Sure enough, there is no guarantee that an assault would deter Iran from attempting to rebuild its plants; it may even harden Iran's resolve to acquire nuclear technology as a means of retaliating or protecting itself in the future. The United States might not have the wherewithal or the political capital to launch another raid, forcing it to rely on the same ineffective tools that it now uses to restrain Iran's nuclear drive. If that happens, U.S. action will have only delayed the inevitable.

Yet according to the IAEA, Iran already appears fully committed to developing a nuclear weapons program and needs no further motivation from the United States. And it will not be able to simply resume its progress after its entire nuclear infrastructure is reduced to rubble. Indeed, such a devastating offensive could well force Iran to quit the nuclear game altogether, as Iraq did after its nuclear program was destroyed in the Gulf War and as Syria did after the 2007 Israeli strike. And even if Iran did try to reconstitute its nuclear program, it would be forced to contend with continued international pressure, greater difficulty in securing necessary nuclear materials on the international market, and the lurking possibility of subsequent attacks. Military action could, therefore, delay Iran's nuclear program by anywhere from a few years to a decade, and perhaps even indefinitely.

Skeptics might still counter that at best a strike would only buy time. But time is a valuable commodity. Countries often hope to delay worst-case scenarios as far into the future as possible in the hope that this might eliminate the threat altogether. Those countries whose nuclear facilities have been attacked—most recently Iraq and Syria— have proved unwilling or unable to restart their programs. Thus, what appears to be only a temporary setback to Iran could eventually become a game changer.

Yet another argument against military action against Iran is that it would embolden the hard-liners within Iran's government, helping them rally the population around the regime and eliminate any remaining reformists. This critique ignores the fact that the hard-liners are already firmly in control. The ruling regime has become so extreme that it has sidelined even those leaders once considered to be right-wingers, such as former President Ali Akbar Hashemi Rafsanjani, for their perceived softness. And Rafsanjani or the former presidential candidate Mir Hossein Mousavi would likely continue the nuclear program if he assumed power. An attack might actually create more openings for dissidents in the long term (after temporarily uniting Iran behind Ayatollah Ali Khamenei), giving them grounds for criticizing a government that invited disaster. Even if a strike would strengthen Iran's hard-liners, the United States must not prioritize the outcomes of Iran's domestic political tussles over its vital national security interest in preventing Tehran from developing nuclear weapons.

## Strike Now or Suffer Later

Attacking Iran is hardly an attractive prospect. But the United States can anticipate and reduce many of the feared consequences of such an attack. If it does so successfully, it can remove the incentive for other nations in the region to start their own atomic programs and, more broadly, strengthen global non-proliferation by demonstrating that it will use military force to prevent the spread of nuclear weapons. It can also head off a possible Israeli operation against Iran, which, given Israel's limited capability to mitigate a potential battle and inflict lasting damage, would likely result in far more devastating consequences and carry a far lower probability of success than a U.S. attack. Finally, a carefully managed U.S. attack would prove less risky than the prospect of containing a nuclear-armed Islamic Republic—a costly, decades-long proposition that would likely still result in grave national security threats. Indeed, attempting to manage a nuclear-armed Iran is not only a terrible option but the worst.

With the wars in Afghanistan and Iraq winding down and the United States facing economic hardship at home, Americans have little appetite for further strife. Yet Iran's rapid nuclear development will ultimately force the United States to choose between a conventional conflict and a possible nuclear war. Faced with that decision, the United States should conduct a surgical strike on Iran's nuclear facilities, absorb an inevitable round of retaliation, and then seek to quickly de-escalate the crisis. Addressing the threat now will spare the United States from confronting a far more dangerous situation in the future.

**MATTHEW KROENIG** is an assistant professor of government at Georgetown University. He is the author of *Expecting the Bomb: Technology Transfer and the Spread of Nuclear Weapons* (Cornell University Press, 2010). He is also the coauthor of *The Handbook of National Legislatures: A Global Survey* (Cambridge University Press, 2009) and coeditor of *Causes and Consequences of Nuclear Proliferation* (Routledge, 2011).

Colin H. Kahl

# Not Time to Attack Iran

## Why War Should Be a Last Resort

In "Time to Attack Iran" (January/February 2012), Matthew Kroenig takes a page out of the decade-old playbook used by advocates of the Iraq war. He portrays the threat of a nuclear-armed Iran as both grave and imminent, arguing that the United States has little choice but to attack Iran now before it is too late. Then, after offering the caveat that "attacking Iran is hardly an attractive prospect," he goes on to portray military action as preferable to other available alternatives and concludes that the United States can manage all the associated risks. Preventive war, according to Kroenig, is "the least bad option." But the lesson of Iraq, the last preventive war launched by the United States, is that Washington should not choose war when there are still other options, and it should not base its decision to attack on best-case analyses of how it hopes the conflict will turn out. A realistic assessment of Iran's nuclear progress and how a conflict would likely unfold leads one to a conclusion that is the opposite of Kroenig's: now is not the time to attack Iran.

## Bad Timing

Kroenig argues that there is an urgent need to attack Iran's nuclear infrastructure soon, since Tehran could "produce its first nuclear weapon within six months of deciding to do so." Yet that last phrase is crucial. The International Atomic Energy Agency (IAEA) has documented Iranian efforts to achieve the capacity to develop nuclear weapons at some point, but there is no hard evidence that Supreme Leader Ayatollah Ali Khamenei has yet made the final decision to develop them.

In arguing for a six-month horizon, Kroenig also misleadingly conflates hypothetical timelines to produce weapons-grade uranium with the time actually required to construct a bomb. According to 2010 Senate testimony by James Cartwright, then vice chairman of the U.S. Joint Chiefs of Staff, and recent statements by the former heads of Israel's national intelligence and defense intelligence agencies, even if Iran could produce enough weapons-grade uranium for a bomb in six months, it would take it at least a year to produce a testable nuclear device and considerably longer to make a deliverable weapon. And David Albright, president of the Institute for Science and International Security (and the source of Kroenig's

six-month estimate), recently told Agence France-Presse that there is a "low probability" that the Iranians would actually develop a bomb over the next year even if they had the capability to do so. Because there is no evidence that Iran has built additional covert enrichment plants since the Natanz and Qom sites were outed in 2002 and 2009, respectively, any near-term move by Tehran to produce weapons-grade uranium would have to rely on its declared facilities. The IAEA would thus detect such activity with sufficient time for the international community to mount a forceful response. As a result, the Iranians are unlikely to commit to building nuclear weapons until they can do so much more quickly or out of sight, which could be years off.

Kroenig is also inconsistent about the timetable for an attack. In some places, he suggests that strikes should begin now, whereas in others, he argues that the United States should attack only if Iran takes certain actions—such as expelling IAEA inspectors, beginning the enrichment of weapons-grade uranium, or installing large numbers of advanced centrifuges, any one of which would signal that it had decided to build a bomb. Kroenig is likely right that these developments—and perhaps others, such as the discovery of new covert enrichment sites—would create a decision point for the use of force. But the Iranians have not taken these steps yet, and as Kroenig acknowledges, "Washington has a very good chance" of detecting them if they do.

## Riding the Escalator

Kroenig's discussion of timing is not the only misleading part of his article; so is his contention that the United States could mitigate the "potentially devastating consequences" of a strike on Iran by carefully managing the escalation that would ensue. His picture of a clean, calibrated conflict is a mirage. Any war with Iran would be a messy and extraordinarily violent affair, with significant casualties and consequences.

According to Kroenig, Iran would not respond to a strike with its "worst forms of retaliation, such as closing the Strait of Hormuz or launching missiles at southern Europe" unless its leaders felt that the regime's "very existence was threatened." To mitigate this risk, he claims, the United States could "make clear that it is interested only in destroying Iran's nuclear program, not in overthrowing the

Kahl, Colin H. From *Foreign Affairs*, March/April 2012, pp. 166–173. Copyright © 2012 by Council on Foreign Relations, Inc. Reprinted by permission of Foreign Affairs. www.ForeignAffairs.com

government." But Iranian leaders have staked their domestic legitimacy on resisting international pressure to halt the nuclear program, and so they would inevitably view an attack on that program as an attack on the regime itself. Decades of hostility and perceived U.S. efforts to undermine the regime would reinforce this perception. And when combined with the emphasis on anti-Americanism in the ideology of the supreme leader and his hard-line advisers, as well as their general ignorance about what drives U.S. decision-making, this perception means that there is little prospect that Iranian leaders would believe that a U.S. strike had limited aims. Assuming the worst about Washington's intentions, Tehran is likely to overreact to even a surgical strike against its nuclear facilities.

Kroenig nevertheless believes that the United States could limit the prospects for escalation by warning Iran that crossing certain "redlines" would trigger a devastating U.S. counter-response. Ironically, Kroenig believes that a nuclear-armed Iran would be deeply irrational and prone to miscalculation yet somehow maintains that under the same leaders, Iran would make clear-eyed decisions in the immediate aftermath of a U.S. strike. But the two countries share no direct and reliable channels for communication, and the inevitable confusion brought on by a crisis would make signaling difficult and miscalculation likely.

To make matters worse, in the heat of battle, Iran would face powerful incentives to escalate. In the event of a conflict, both sides would come under significant pressure to stop the fighting due to the impact on international oil markets. Since this would limit the time the Iranians would have to reestablish deterrence, they might choose to launch a quick, all-out response, without care for redlines. Iranian fears that the United States could successfully disrupt its command-and-control infrastructure or preemptively destroy its ballistic missile arsenal could also tempt Iran to launch as many missiles as possible early in the war. And the decentralized nature of Iran's Islamic Revolutionary Guard Corps, especially its navy, raises the prospect of unauthorized responses that could rapidly expand the fighting in the crowded waters of the Persian Gulf.

Controlling escalation would be no easier on the U.S. side. In the face of reprisals by Iranian proxies, "token missile strikes against U.S. bases and ships," or "the harassment of commercial and U.S. naval vessels," Kroenig says that Washington should turn the other cheek and constrain its own response to Iranian counterattacks. But this is much easier said than done. Just as Iran's likely expectation of a short war might encourage it to respond disproportionately early in the crisis, so the United States would also have incentives to move swiftly to destroy Iran's conventional forces and the infrastructure of the Revolutionary Guard Corps. And if the United States failed to do so, proxy attacks against U.S. civilian personnel in Lebanon or Iraq, the transfer of lethal rocket and portable air defense systems to Taliban fighters in Afghanistan, or missile strikes against U.S. facilities in the Gulf could

cause significant U.S. casualties, creating irresistible political pressure in Washington to respond. Add to this the normal fog of war and the lack of reliable communications between the United States and Iran, and Washington would have a hard time determining whether Tehran's initial response to a strike was a one-off event or the prelude to a wider campaign. If it were the latter, a passive U.S. approach might motivate Iran to launch even more dangerous attacks—and this is a risk Washington may choose not to take. The sum total of these dynamics would make staying within Kroenig's proscribed limits exceedingly difficult.

Even if Iran did not escalate, purely defensive moves that would threaten U.S. personnel or international shipping in the Strait of Hormuz—the maritime chokepoint through which nearly 20 percent of the world's traded oil passes—would also create powerful incentives for Washington to preemptively target Iran's military. Of particular concern would be Iran's "anti-access/ area-denial" capabilities, which are designed to prevent advanced navies from operating in the shallow waters of the Persian Gulf. These systems integrate coastal air defenses, shore-based long-range artillery and anti-ship cruise missiles, Kilo-class and midget submarines, remote-controlled boats and unmanned kamikaze aerial vehicles, and more than 1,000 small attack craft equipped with machine guns, multiple-launch rockets, anti-ship missiles, torpedoes, and rapid-mine-laying capabilities. The entire 120-mile-long strait sits along the Iranian coastline, within short reach of these systems. In the midst of a conflict, the threat to U.S. forces and the global economy posed by Iran's activating its air defenses, dispersing its missiles or naval forces, or moving its mines out of storage would be too great for the United States to ignore; the logic of preemption would compel Washington to escalate.

Some analysts, including Afshin Molavi and Michael Singh, believe that the Iranians are unlikely to attempt to close the strait due to the damage it would inflict on their own economy. But Tehran's saber rattling has already intensified in response to the prospect of Western sanctions on its oil industry. In the immediate aftermath of a U.S. strike on Iran's nuclear program, Iranian leaders might perceive that holding the strait at risk would encourage international pressure on Washington to end the fighting, possibly deterring U.S. escalation. In reality, it would more likely have the opposite effect, encouraging aggressive U.S. efforts to protect commercial shipping. The U.S. Navy is capable of keeping the strait open, but the mere threat of closure could send oil prices soaring, dealing a heavy blow to the fragile global economy. The measures that Kroenig advocates to mitigate this threat, such as opening up the U.S. Strategic Petroleum Reserve and urging Saudi Arabia to boost oil production, would be unlikely to suffice, especially since most Saudi crude passes through the strait.

Ultimately, if the United States and Iran go to war, there is no doubt that Washington will win in the narrow operational sense. Indeed, with the impressive array of U.S. naval and air forces already deployed in the Gulf, the United States could probably knock Iran's military capabilities back 20 years in a matter of weeks. But a U.S.-Iranian conflict would not be the clinical, tightly controlled, limited encounter that Kroenig predicts.

## Spillover

Keeping other states in the region out of the fight would also prove more difficult than Kroenig suggests. Iran would presume Israeli complicity in a U.S. raid and would seek to drag Israel into the conflict in order to undermine potential support for the U.S. war effort among key Arab regimes. And although it is true, as Kroenig notes, that Israel remained on the sidelines during the 1990–91 Gulf War, the threat posed by Iran's missiles and proxies today is considerably greater than that posed by Iraq two decades ago. If Iranian-allied Hezbollah responded to the fighting by firing rockets at Israeli cities, Israel could launch an all-out war against Lebanon. Syrian President Bashar al-Assad might also try to use the moment to divert attention from the uprising in his country, launching his own assault on the Jewish state. Either scenario, or their combination, could lead to a wider war in the Levant.

Even in the Gulf, where U.S. partners are sometimes portrayed as passive, Iranian retaliation might draw Saudi Arabia and the United Arab Emirates into the conflict. The Saudis have taken a much more confrontational posture toward Iran in the past year, and Riyadh is unlikely to tolerate Iranian attacks against critical energy infrastructure. For its part, the UAE, the most hawkish state in the Gulf, might respond to missiles raining down on U.S. forces at its Al Dhafra Air Base by attempting to seize Abu Musa, Greater Tunb, and Lesser Tunb, three disputed Gulf islands currently occupied by Iran. A strike could also set off wider destabilizing effects. Although Kroenig is right that some Arab leaders would privately applaud a U.S. strike, many on the Arab street would reject it. Both Islamist extremists and embattled elites could use this opportunity to transform the Arab Spring's populist anti-regime narrative into a decidedly anti-American one. This would rebound to Iran's advantage just at the moment when political developments in the region, chief among them the resurgence of nationalism in the Arab world and the upheaval in Syria, are significantly undermining Iran's influence. A U.S. strike could easily shift regional sympathies back in Tehran's favor by allowing Iran to play the victim and, through its retaliation, resuscitate its status as the champion of the region's anti-Western resistance.

## The Cost of Buying Time

Even if a U.S. strike went as well as Kroenig predicts, there is little guarantee that it would produce lasting results. Senior U.S. defense officials have repeatedly stated that an attack on Iran's nuclear facilities would stall Tehran's progress for only a few years. Kroenig argues that such a delay could become permanent. "Those countries whose nuclear facilities have been attacked—most recently Iraq and Syria," he writes, "have proved unwilling or unable to restart their programs." In the case of Iraq, however, Saddam Hussein restarted his clandestine nuclear weapons program after the 1981 Israeli attack on the Osirak nuclear reactor, and it required the Gulf War and another decade of sanctions and intrusive inspections to eliminate it. Iran's program is also more advanced and dispersed than were Iraq's and Syria's, meaning it would be easier to reconstitute. A U.S. strike would damage key Iranian facilities, but it would do nothing to reverse the nuclear knowledge Iran has accumulated or its ability to eventually build new centrifuges.

A U.S. attack would also likely rally domestic Iranian support around nuclear hard-liners, increasing the odds that Iran would emerge from a strike even more committed to building a bomb. Kroenig downplays the "rally round the flag" risks by noting that hard-liners are already firmly in power and suggesting that an attack might produce increased internal criticism of the regime. But the nuclear program remains an enormous source of national pride for the majority of Iranians. To the extent that there is internal dissent over the program, it is a discussion about whether the country should acquire nuclear weapons or simply pursue civilian nuclear technology. By demonstrating the vulnerability of a non-nuclear-armed Iran, a U.S. attack would provide ammunition to hard-liners who argue for acquiring a nuclear deterrent. Kroenig suggests that the United States should essentially ignore "Iran's domestic political tussles" when pursuing "its vital national security interest in preventing Tehran from developing nuclear weapons." But influencing Iranian opinion about the strategic desirability of nuclear weapons might ultimately offer the only enduring way of keeping the Islamic Republic on a peaceful nuclear path.

Finally, if Iran did attempt to restart its nuclear program after an attack, it would be much more difficult for the United States to stop it. An assault would lead Iran to distance itself from the IAEA and perhaps to pull out of the Nuclear Non-proliferation Treaty altogether. Without inspectors on the ground, the international community would struggle to track or slow Tehran's efforts to rebuild its program.

## Contain Yourself

Kroenig argues that "a nuclear-armed Iran would not intentionally launch a suicidal nuclear war" but still concludes that it is ultimately less risky to attack the Islamic Republic now than to attempt to contain it later. He warns that containment would entail a costly forward deployment of large numbers of U.S. forces on Iran's periphery for decades.

But the United States already has a large presence encircling Iran. Forty thousand U.S. troops are stationed in the Gulf, accompanied by strike aircraft, two aircraft carrier strike groups, two Aegis ballistic missile defense ships, and multiple Patriot antimissile systems. On Iran's eastern flank, Washington has another 90,000 troops deployed in Afghanistan and thousands more supporting the Afghan war in nearby Central Asian states. Kroenig claims that it would take much more to contain a nuclear-armed Iran. But U.S. forces in the Gulf already outnumber those in South Korea that are there to deter a nuclear-armed North. It is thus perfectly conceivable that the existing U.S. presence in the region, perhaps supplemented by a limited forward deployment of nuclear weapons and additional ballistic missile defenses, would be sufficient to deter a nuclear-armed Iran from aggression and blackmail.

To be sure, such a deterrence-and-containment strategy would be an extraordinarily complex and risky enterprise, and there is no doubt that prevention is preferable. Given the possible consequences of a nuclear-armed Iran, the price of failure would be very high. But Kroenig's approach would not solve the problem. By presenting the options as either a near-term strike or long-term containment, Kroenig falls into the same trap that advocates of the Iraq war fell into a decade ago: ignoring postwar scenarios. In reality, the strike that Kroenig recommends would likely be a prelude to containment, not a substitute for it.

Since a military raid would not permanently eliminate Iran's nuclear infrastructure, the United States would still need to construct an expensive, risky post-war containment regime to prevent Iran from reconstituting the program, much as it did in regard to Iraq after the Gulf War. The end result would be strikingly similar to the one that Kroenig criticizes, requiring Washington to maintain sufficient air, naval, and ground forces in the Persian Gulf to attack again at a moment's notice.

A strike carried out in the way Kroenig advocates—a unilateral preventive attack—would also make postwar containment more difficult and costly. Many countries would view such an operation as a breach of international law, shattering the consensus required to maintain an effective post-strike containment regime. The likelihood that the United States could "reduce the political fallout of military action by building global support for it in advance," as Kroenig suggests, would be extremely low absent clear evidence that Iran is dashing for a bomb. Without such evidence, Washington would be left to bear the costs of an attack and the resulting containment regime alone.

Finally, the surgical nature of Kroenig's proposed strike, aimed solely at Iran's nuclear program, would make postwar containment much harder. It would leave Tehran wounded and aggrieved but still capable of responding. Kroenig's recommended approach, then, would likely be just enough to ensure a costly, long-term conflict without actually compelling Iran to change its behavior.

## The Options on the Table

In making the case for preventive war as the least bad option, Kroenig dismisses any prospect of finding a diplomatic solution to the U.S.-Iranian standoff. He concludes that the Obama administration's dual-track policy of engagement and pressure has failed to arrest Iran's march toward a bomb, leaving Washington with no other choice but to bomb Iran.

But this ignores the severe economic strain, isolation, and technical challenges that Iran is experiencing. After years of dismissing the economic effects of sanctions, senior Iranian officials now publicly complain about the intense pain the sanctions are producing. And facing the prospect of U.S. sanctions against Iran's central bank and European actions to halt Iranian oil imports, Tehran signaled in early January some willingness to return to the negotiating table. Washington must test this willingness and, in so doing, provide Iran with a clear strategic choice: address the concerns of the international community regarding its nuclear program and see its isolation lifted or stay on its current path and face substantially higher costs. In framing this choice, Washington must be able to assert that like-minded states are prepared to implement oil-related sanctions, and the Obama administration should continue to emphasize that all options, including military action, remain on the table.

Some will undoubtedly claim that highlighting the potential risks associated with war will lead the Iranians to conclude that the United States lacks the resolve to use force. But in authorizing the surge in Afghanistan, carrying out the raid that killed Osama bin Laden, and leading the NATO air campaign to oust Libya's Muammar al-Qaddafi, President Barack Obama has repeatedly shown that he is willing to accept risk and use force—both as part of a coalition and unilaterally—to defend U.S. interests. And as Martin Dempsey, chairman of the U.S. Joint Chiefs of Staff, told CNN late last December, the United States has a viable contingency plan for Iran if force is ultimately required. But given the high costs and inherent uncertainties of a strike, the United States should not rush to use force until all other options have been exhausted and the Iranian threat is not just growing but imminent. Until then, force is, and should remain, a last resort, not a first choice.

---

**COLIN H. KAHL** is an associate professor in the Security Studies Program in the Edmund A. Walsh School of Foreign Service at Georgetown University, where he teaches courses on international relations, international security, the geopolitics of the Middle East, American foreign policy, and civil and ethnic conflict.

# EXPLORING THE ISSUE

## Should the United States Launch a Preemptive Strike Against Iran?

## Critical Thinking and Reflection

1. Why do advocates of an American preemptive strike believe that the United States should strike soon?
2. Why do critics of such action argue that it is prudent or essential that America should wait?
3. How would an American strike affect the world's ability to extract and obtain oil?
4. Should Iran have the ability to develop nuclear weapons if its potential rivals have those weapons? Why or why not?
5. Would American intervention be likely to result in a more widespread war? Why or why not?

## Is There Common Ground?

Despite the mutual suspicion and hostility, it can be argued that a long and widespread war between the United States and Iran would not advance the long-range interests of either side. It might lead to tens of thousands of military casualties and uncounted civilian deaths. It would be likely to cost vast sums that would require great economic sacrifices. Both sides must be aware that the superior military and economic strength of the United States and its allies would be certain to prevail and that the present Iranian Shiite theocracy would be removed from power so that there is no possibility of a benefit to Iran. At the same time, the American people are reluctant to engage in another war at this time. If Iran can be persuaded to avoid aggressive action, the question remains as to whether the United States can live in peace and with security with the present Iranian regime.

The recent agreement between world superpowers and the Iranians demonstrate a potential for long-lasting common ground. The Iranians have relaxed their nuclear desires and permitted international observers to have unlimited access to all sites within the country in exchange for America lifting sanctions. The removal of sanctions will save the Iranians millions of dollars and provides a sense of good faith from the United States. Ultimately, the

sanctions were successful. They are never intended to cripple a country, only to force them back to the negotiation table. In that sense, we may be witnessing the development and recognition of a middle ground between two countries that have been fighting since 1979.

## Create Central

www.mhhe.com/createcentral

## Additional Resources

Shahram Chubin, *Iran's Nuclear Ambitions* (Carnegie Endowment for International Peace, 2006)

David Crist, *The Twilight War: The Secret History of America's Thirty-Year Conflict with Israel* (Penguin, 2012)

Trita Parsi, *A Single Roll of the Dice: Obama's Diplomacy with Iran* (Yale University Press, 2012)

Kenneth M. Pollack, *The Persian Puzzle: The Conflict Between Iran and America* (Random House, 2004)

Barbara Slavin, *Bitter Friends, Bosom Enemies: Iran, the U.S., and the Twisted Path to Confrontation* (St. Martin's Press, 2007)

## *Internet References . . .*

**CIA World FactBook**

www.cia.gov/library/publications/the-world-factbook
/geos/ir.html

**International Atomic Energy Agency**

www.iaea.org/

**Islamic Republic of Iran's President**

www.president.ir/en/

**Office of the Supreme Leader Sayyid Ali Khamenei**

www.leader.ir/langs/en/

**U.S. State Department**

http://travel.state.gov/travel/cis_pa_tw/cis/cis_1142
.html